Mergers and Acquisitions

T0340109

Mergers and Acquisitions
A Global Tax Guide

PricewaterhouseCoopers

WILEY

John Wiley & Sons, Inc.

Contents

Country-by-Country Guide

ACKNOWLEDGMENTS

I take great pleasure in introducing PricewaterhouseCoopers' *Mergers and Acquisitions: A Global Tax Guide.* The information contained in this book is drawn from the breadth and depth of expertise that exists within the PricewaterhouseCoopers global network of Mergers and Acquisitions tax professionals.

Writing this book was truly a global endeavor. I would particularly like to thank some of the PricewaterhouseCoopers Mergers and Acquisitions tax professionals who made a significant personal contribution to the overall effort that was required to produce this book:

Markus Neuhaus, Zurich, Switzerland
Jon Davies, Washington, DC, United States
Marissa Thomas, London, United Kingdom
Sarah Ryan, London, United Kingdom

Daniel Santiago, Buenos Aires, Argentina
Cath Kinstler, Sydney, Australia
Bernd Hofmann, Vienna, Austria
Jan Muyldermans, Brussels, Belgium
Peter Martin, São Paulo, Brazil
John Robinson, Vancouver, British Columbia
Roberto Carlos Rivas, Santiago, Chile
Stephen Booth, Prague, Czech Republic
Viera Kucerova, Prague, Czech Republic
Daniel Noe Harboe, Hellrup, Denmark
Xavier Etienne, Paris, France
Frank Schmidt, Frankfurt, Germany
Guy Ellis, Hong Kong, Hong Kong, SAR
Cassie Wong, Hong Kong, Hong Kong, SAR
Nicola Broggi, Milan, Italy
Geraldine Piat, Luxembourg, Luxembourg
Frances Po, Kuala Lumpur, Malaysia
Jesus Chan, Mexico City, Mexico

Machiel Visser, Amsterdam, Netherlands
David Rhodes, Auckland, New Zealand
Hans Olav Hemnes, Oslo, Norway
Iwona Smith, Warsaw, Poland
Cherie Ford Hunt, Moscow, Russia
David Toh, Singapore, Singapore
Juan Ramon Ramos, Barcelona, Spain
Hans Van Turnhout, Stockholm, Sweden
Barbara Brauchli, Zurich, Switzerland
Kadir Bas, Istanbul, Turkey
Andrew Ponting, London, United Kingdom
Andrew Ross, London, United Kingdom
Bret Balonick, San Francisco, United States
Mark Boyer, Chicago, United States
Jim Banks, Los Angeles, United States
Duane Pellervo, San Francisco, United States
Joel Slavonia, San Francisco, United States
Shannon Sparks, San Francisco, United States
Pat Grube, Washington, DC, United States

I would also like to thank Gene Zasadinski, a director and senior editor in PricewaterhouseCoopers' US Thought Leadership Group, and Executive Editor Sheck Cho and his team at John Wiley & Sons for their tireless efforts in preparing this manuscript for publication.

GENE DONNELLY
Global Managing Partner
Tax and Advisory

PricewaterhouseCoopers (*www.pwc.com*) provides industry-focused assurance, tax, and advisory services to build public trust and enhance value for its clients and their stakeholders. More than 130,000 people in 148 countries work collaboratively using Connected Thinking to develop fresh prespectives and practical advice. The Merges and Acquisitions practice in our worldwide network is able to provide a full range of services to meet the needs of our clients and their businesses.

PricewaterhouseCoopers refers to the network of member firms of PricewaterhouseCoopers International Limited, each of which is a separate and independent legal entity.

INTRODUCTION

As the world economy continues to respond to increasing globalization, the problems that individual businesses have been forced to deal with have grown in number and complexity. Virtually every one of those problems shares a common element: In a truly global economy, businesses that are unable to operate effectively in a multinational environment will not achieve the economies of scale they need in order to remain competitive.

Of course, business leaders have taken a number of steps to achieve the targeted level of multinational scale, and each of those approaches carries its own unique set of challenges. However, virtually all leaders of multinational organizations realize that if their businesses are to truly achieve the level of global scale necessary to remain competitive, they will at some point in their companies' life cycles have to undertake strategic acquisitions. Ultimately, most business leaders understand that if one competitor uses merger and acquisition (M&A) transactions effectively to achieve global scale, other competitors will do the same.

When a business engages in a multinational merger or acquisition, it soon becomes apparent that dealing with a diverse set of transaction-related tax rules will be one of the major challenges to successful implementation. The fact is that a significant portion of the income earned by a posttransaction enterprise will be used to pay various types of taxes. Therefore, it would seem obvious that dealing effectively with the tax rules would be a major objective of those involved in multinational M&A transactions.

Although the world economy is globalizing at a rapid rate, the same cannot be said about the tax systems in place in the industrialized nations of the world. In fact, the opposite is true. A careful observer might conclude that many of the industrialized nations have embraced tax systems that are designed specifically to employ differences in individual tax schemes in order to attract more commercial activity to their countries.

The diverse tax environment that confronts a business that undertakes a multinational merger or acquisition demands that those who are managing the tax aspects of the proposed transaction understand global taxation on at least two levels. First, the individuals responsible for tax planning must understand the differences between the basic systems of taxation and how those systems will affect individual transactions. And they must understand the differences between direct- and indirect-transaction tax systems, global and territorial income tax systems, and entity-level and fully integrated tax systems.

Second, multinational M&A transaction planners must quickly be able to gain an understanding of how individual tax authorities apply various tax systems. It does a planner little good to know that a particular jurisdiction applies a territorial income tax to a postmerger multinational business if the planner does not understand how the jurisdiction measures the amount of income subject to tax in each individual territory.

In this book, PricewaterhouseCoopers tax professionals provide the informational foundation that tax planners need when they are involved in a multinational M&A transaction. The 31 individual country-specific chapters each offer both an overview of the general approaches to M&A transaction taxation taken by virtually all of the industrialized countries of the world and detailed information about how the tax authorities in those countries apply the rules to various aspects of a transaction. The consistency of format within each of the chapters is designed to enable a planner both to access the available data quickly and, as much as possible, to compare the rules that apply in one jurisdiction with the rules that apply in others.

In addition to the detailed individual-country discussions, the book contains several other chapters that focus on some of the broader tax issues that arise in the context of a multinational M&A transaction, including, for example, the use of hybrid entity structures to facilitate multinational acquisitions. While not focusing on the specific aspects of the laws of any particular jurisdiction, the information contained in these chapters is nevertheless extremely important in the M&A context, must be understood, and is critical to achieving a successful deal implementation program.

By adopting this approach to a discussion of global taxation, the authors have created a unique resource for planners who are involved in multinational M&A transactions. The book is focused totally on the multinational aspects of M&A transactions, it provides detailed information concerning specific issues inherent in local tax laws, it organizes the available data in a manner that is simple to use, and it accomplishes these tasks while remaining attuned to the broader tax issues that are present in almost every multinational M&A transaction.

While there is no substitute for competent local tax advisers or for detailed issue-specific research, the following chapters offer M&A tax planners a basic foundation of multinational tax knowledge.

TAXES: DEAL MAKING'S FORGOTTEN VALUE DRIVER

The CEOs of two major financial institutions are meeting to close the deal on a major acquisition of a multinational business. Discussions thus far have been heated and passionate. Exhaustive negotiations and due diligence have taken place, particularly around economic issues believed to relate to the customer base, the receivables portfolio, and other areas where potential contingent postdeal liabilities could arise. Synergies between the businesses have been identified, and redundancies have been rationalized. In short, the deal has been analyzed, scrutinized, and agreed upon; a plan has been developed to maximize the value of the combined businesses. Of course, everyone assumed that the combined enterprise would continue to pay taxes, yet no one really thought of taxes as a major issue to be addressed in the deal. As one executive put it, "Taxes are simply 40 percent of pretax earnings."

In any acquisition, money—in some cases huge amounts of it—can be saved by paying careful attention to management of the tax burden of the combined enterprise. Most chief financial officers and tax directors recognize that fact. However, in many instances, tax planning is considered to be a postdeal activity, and tax risks are assumed to be properly quantified and recorded in the balance sheet accounts. Far too often, deal makers do not attempt to identify tax strategies and risks that could seriously affect the price at which a transaction is undertaken. Ironically, in relation to the other complexities involved in most deals, the effort required to perform a thorough tax analysis is relatively small and can be easily integrated with other tasks—for instance, legal structuring—that need to be performed anyway.

A few quick examples can demonstrate the dramatic effect that income taxes can have on a transaction:

- Assume a strategic buyer is willing to pay $500 million, or 20 times earnings, measured on an International Accounting Standards (IAS) basis, for a multinational manufacturing company. The buyer intends to finance 50 percent of the transaction with debt, issued at the level of the buyer's public holding company. If the buyer knew that interest on the $250 million of debt would produce no global tax benefit, would therefore increase the cost of the transaction, and would reduce annual IAS earnings by $9 million per year, would the buyer not consider an adjustment to the purchase price?

- Assume a financial buyer is willing to pay $350 million—or seven times earnings before interest, taxes, depreciation, and amortization—for a multinational technology company. The buyer intends to finance 70 percent of the transaction with debt issued by the target company. If the buyer knows that the target's taxable income is generated in a jurisdiction where the interest will not be deductible, should the buyer not consider an adjustment to the purchase price?

- Assume the buyer of a distressed business is willing to pay creditors $250 million in exchange for what remains of that distressed enterprise. The buyer intends to recover the purchase price by selling off some of the assets of the enterprise and then reorganize the remaining parts into a profitable business. If the buyer finds out that the assets to be sold have no tax basis and that therefore 40 percent of the assets' sale price will be paid in taxes, should the buyer not consider a substantial adjustment to the purchase price?

Of course, most reasonable analysts would look at these situations and ask whether a change in the deal structure could be introduced to avoid the adverse tax consequences. Assuming that no such structural change is possible, reasonable analysts almost certainly would conclude that price adjustments should be made in each of these situations. Yet in many transactions, such price adjustments are not even considered, and in some instances, not even an effort is made to identify the issue and a method of adjusting the transaction structure to avoid the issue. Why this lack of attention to an area that could significantly affect the value realized from a transaction? There are several possible reasons.

In deal negotiations, it's not unusual for negotiators to make two assumptions: (1) that statutory tax rates are generally in the area of 35 to 40 percent of earnings and (2) that very little can be done to significantly change the rate applicable to postdeal income. Yet transactions exist where the taxes of the combined enterprise were as high as 60 percent or as low as 5 percent of postdeal earnings. When acquisitions involve multinational companies with various pools of earnings that are subject to multiple tax regimes, the variance between the aggregate rate of tax paid to the different taxing jurisdictions and the statutory rates imposed by those jurisdictions can be quite large.

In very large deals, negotiators often don't consider unrecorded tax risks to be significant enough to cause concern. Even though an identified and recorded tax risk might be as high as several billion dollars and might be subject to significant contingencies in the context of a multibillion-dollar deal, the potential deviation in the amount of tax that ultimately will be paid is sometimes considered unimportant relative to the long list of other economic matters that must be considered.

In large transactions involving public companies, confidentiality and speed are also important issues. Typically in such deals, very little information filters down through the organization before the deal is announced. As a result, top executives often trade the deal by using imperfect information and assumptions about the tax positions of the various entities involved.

In smaller deals, availability of resources is often the key issue that determines whether sufficient attention will be paid to taxes. Negotiators of such deals have to consider in their analysis of taxes whether they will realize a return on the investment of scarce resources. Of course, certain situations would more than justify such an investment—for example, the identification of a deal killer as a result of tax diligence, the elimination of a major transaction tax through a simple change in deal structure, and so on. Unfortunately, the existence of such opportunities cannot be identified in advance, and a buyer will never know the opportunities exist unless taxes are given appropriate attention at the inception of a transaction.

Some might ask whether different types of buyers should have different perspectives with respect to the tax issues related to a transaction. At first glance, one might assume that financial buyers and distressed-business buyers, because of their interest in cash flow as a measure of future return, would be more concerned with taxes than would strategic buyers, whose financial interest most often focuses on how a potential acquisition will affect the publicly reported income statement and balance sheet. Clearly, *all* types of buyers should be equally concerned with taxes: financial buyers because of the potential impact of taxes on annual cash flow, distressed-business buyers because of the impact of taxes on the cash that can be realized from the disposition of excess assets, and strategic buyers because of overwhelming interest in minimizing the tax expense charged to financial earnings.

For all types of buyers, an awareness of both the key tax risks inherent in an acquisition and the strategies that can be used to minimize future taxes and maximize both cash flow and earnings can yield tremendous benefits. These issues should be dealt with in each of three phases of an acquisition: the diligence phase, when the tax position the buyer inherits is identified; the structuring phase, when the legal and economic shape of the deal is determined; and the postdeal integration phase, when efforts are made to minimize the cost of predeal risks that were accepted by the buyer and to maximize opportunities inherent in deal structure.

CAVEAT EMPTOR: KNOW THE RISK BEFORE YOU BUY

In the mergers and acquisitions business, horror stories abound involving the assumption of risks that had not been previously identified. A simple review of deals undertaken in the past few years would reveal several such stories related to tax matters.

In one instance, a multibillion-dollar international acquisition involved two companies with recorded tax reserves of more than $2 billion—reserves that may or may not have become actual cash liabilities subsequent to closing the transaction.

In another instance, a $16-billion acquisition involved a target company that was in a dispute with the US Internal Revenue Service concerning previously taken deductions of more than $2 billion—that is, almost $1 billion of contingent tax liabilities and interest.

Situations like these are not uncommon. In fact, according to many analysts, large contingent tax liabilities are more often than not present in companies undertaking major merger and acquisition transactions.

The level of uncertainty that exists with regard to tax benefits and risks points out the necessity of understanding in detail the tax histories of each of the legal entities involved in a transaction. When it seems inevitable that a buyer will inherit a less-than-optimal tax position, risk management dictates that efforts be made to minimize the risk. However, for any buyer involved in a pricing process, the first steps ought to involve achievement of an understanding of the target's tax position, of the extent to which that tax position will be inherited by the buyer, and of the amount of risk involved. If planning is to be used to minimize those risks, a buyer must also understand the degree of risk inherent in the implementation of any such planning strategy.

Managing Risk: The Perils of Negotiation

While megadeals between industry giants dominate the business headlines, a substantial portion of all transactions involves the purchase of subsidiaries, pools of assets, and/or orphan businesses. In these types of deals, it is possible to manage some degree of tax risk through negotiation. However, the efficacy of negotiation is affected by the structure of the deal, the availability and willingness of a counterparty with whom to negotiate, and the actual rather than perceived effectiveness of warranties in providing satisfactory levels of tax indemnification.

Subsidiaries, Assets, and Orphans   Purchasing a subsidiary often means inheriting not only the tax problems of the subsidiary but also, at least to some degree, the historical tax problems of the parent. Depending on where the entities file tax returns, the parent and subsidiary might very well be jointly and severally liable for each other's taxes. In such cases, buyers are getting more than they bargained for. Even if the parent offers some form of indemnity with respect to taxes, that indemnity must be evaluated within the context of the parent's actions. For example, how good is an indemnity offered by a parent holding company that has as its priority the use of the proceeds of the sale of the subsidiary to pay down debt?

Asset sales offer the possibility of a slightly more positive scenario. In an asset purchase, the buyer can, in most legal jurisdictions, avoid a substantial portion of any preexisting income tax problems. However, income taxes are usually only one aspect of the transaction—a fact many buyers ignore. If the assets constitute an entire business, the buyer may still assume problems associated with taxes related to employment, turnover of produces and services, and transfer taxes.

With regard to orphans (businesses sold by their owners because they are noncore or off strategy), negotiations undertaken to mitigate tax risk are not likely to be very effective. It is highly probable that such businesses have not been heavily managed and have been off the radar screen of the owner for a significant period of time prior to the sale. These companies are likely to be offered to buyers on an as-is, take-it-or-leave-it basis, and therefore, making so-called risk-based adjustments to the proposed purchase price becomes an important aspect of the negotiations.

Warranties Can Be Deceptive   In any negotiation, indemnities and warranties may seem to provide high levels of comfort with regard to tax risk management. However, such forms of risk management must be scrutinized carefully to determine exactly what is being offered.

General tax warranties usually apply only to those things that are not known by or disclosed to a potential buyer. Therefore, even if a buyer is successful in negotiating very broad warranties from a financially sound seller, the warranty will be of no use in dealing with subsequently encountered tax liabilities if the issue giving rise to the tax liability was known to the buyer. For example, a seller might disclose the fact that the target company operates in several jurisdictions but has filed tax returns in only one of those jurisdictions. In such an instance, a general warranty might be unavailable to a buyer that later incurs a failure to file penalty with respect to the acquired business. Even vague disclosures by an owner often can prevent the enforcement of a warranty.

Unfortunately, the types of disclosure that frequently mitigate the benefits of a general warranty are meaningless to buyers unless those buyers have a full understanding of the tax position of the target and of the relationship of the disclosed information to that position. For example, a disclosure of the jurisdictions in which a business files is relevant only if the buyer is aware of the jurisdictions in which the target should file. The only efficient approach to such a situation is for the buyer to make sure that items carved out by the seller as exceptions to a warranty—carve outs that are usually nonnegotiable because of the way in which the disclosure statement is structured—get subjected to a rigorous risk assessment during the diligence phase of the acquisition.

STRUCTURING THE DEAL: FOCUS ON TAX

Deal structuring can be simple, or it can be complex. A plain-vanilla structure might be the optimal choice for a transaction involving a plain-vanilla company. However, most companies are not plain vanilla, and under most circumstances, educated transaction structuring can have a dramatic impact on the tax position of the postacquisition enterprise.

The value realized with respect to transactions involving multinational companies can be substantially enhanced by incorporating educated tax planning into the deal structure. There is a broad spectrum of tax planning that can be incorporated into the acquisition of a multinational company. In the recent past, several of the often-used approaches to multinational acquisition planning have come under a great deal of public scrutiny. Offshore tax-haven strategies that create so-called inverted companies—that is, companies legally resident in a jurisdiction other than the one in which the most significant operations are conducted—in an effort to shift the tax burden to alternative jurisdictions with lower tax rates, have been the subjects of a number of bills in the US Congress,[1] and have caused statutory and regulatory changes in a number of European jurisdictions.

Not all, however, agree with moves designed to limit the benefits of corporate inversion strategies. The US Chamber of Commerce, for example, "urged the US Congress to reject legislation that would penalize American businesses locating their headquarters offshore in an effort to compete with foreign companies that have an unfair tax advantage over US companies" and suggested that Congress "revisit the U.S. tax system that drives businesses offshore in the first place."[2]

The use of tax havens and inverted companies is the basis of a politically charged debate that is expected to continue for a number of years. In fact, it will probably take years for the major industrial countries to agree on definitions for the terms *tax haven* and *inverted company,* yet those who negotiate transactions need to understand that tax havens and inversions represent only two points on the spectrum of tax-planning structuring that is needed when major acquisitions are undertaken.

Negotiators must recognize that there is no global system of business taxation. In fact, the disparities that exist between the taxing systems of major industrialized nations guarantee that a multinational corporation will be subjected to a

---

1. For summaries of a number of these bills, see *http://www.citizenworks.org/enron/offshoretaxbills.php.*
2. "U.S. Chamber Urges Congress to Reject Penalties on Offshore American Businesses," October 16, 2002, *http://www.uschamber.com/press/releases/2002/october/02-172.htm.*

multitude of local tax rules that produce something substantially different from a global tax liability. Examples include:

- The tax systems of some countries are applied differently depending on the legal form—such as corporation, limited company, or partnership, and so on—adopted by the business that is paying the tax. Other countries tax all business organizations in the same manner regardless of the legal form taken by the organization.

- Some countries tax a corporate entity on the basis of the entity's country of legal incorporation. Other countries establish the taxing jurisdiction to which a corporation is subject by identifying the jurisdiction from which the corporation is managed.

- Some countries tax a business organization on the organization's income regardless of the jurisdiction in which the income is earned—that is, worldwide taxation. Other countries tax a business organization only on the income that is generated within their borders—that is, territorial taxation.

- Some countries exempt from local-country taxation dividends received from controlled foreign businesses—that is, participation systems. Other countries allow as a credit against local tax any foreign taxes paid on the earnings that are subsequently repatriated from controlled foreign businesses—that is, credit systems.

Given all of these potential differences, it would be foolish to ignore the impact of tax structuring in the consideration of a multinational transaction. Even if the combined business is unwilling to consider aggressive tax planning as a means of achieving an effective tax rate that is below the existing statutory rate, international tax planning is needed to ensure that the combined business enterprise does not subject itself to an effective rate that is substantially above the aggregate of the existing statutory rates.

AFTER THE DEAL: CAPTURING POSTDEAL SYNERGIES

Of the three phases of tax planning applicable to a transaction, postdeal integration is the one on which corporate tax teams focus most. The additional focus could be the result of any number of factors—for example, the availability of more time and more information after the deal is closed, or the additional urgency created by a you-break-it, you-own-it approach to the acquired company, or the pressure that evolves from the need to show that the deal achieved its objectives, and so forth. However, even with the additional emphasis that is placed on realizing the tax benefits and managing the tax risks associated with a deal, tax synergies still somehow manage to fall between the cracks and value is lost.

The major roadblock encountered in postdeal integration of tax matters consists of the natural tension that often exists between running the business efficiently and running the business efficiently while minimizing taxes. Immediately after an acquisition, those responsible for managing the combined business enterprise focus almost entirely on integrating business operations and achieving operational efficiency. In many instances, effective tax planning does not automatically result from the achievement of operational efficiency.

For example, in most multinational transactions, the combined organization's intercompany transaction systems and transfer-pricing mechanisms must be redesigned to ensure both global tax efficiency and territorial tax compliance. However, from an operational point of view, intercompany transaction systems and transfer-pricing mechanisms are often viewed as obstacles to organizational efficiency. In some instances, operations management believes that such systems push the organization away from global cooperation and efficiency, and therefore operations management fights to avoid implementation of such systems.

Yet if the combined enterprise is to be successful, an effort must be made to integrate tax matters and operational matters. Success cannot be achieved if the income of the combined enterprise doubles while the global effective tax rate increases from 35 percent to 75 percent. Sometime early in the post-deal integration phase of the transaction, there must be an effort to ensure that the increased efficiencies achieved by the business combination are retained for the benefit of the shareholders rather than simply turned over to various taxing jurisdictions.

Fortunately, if the tax diligence and tax-structuring phases of the acquisition have been undertaken properly, there will already exist a platform on which two major elements of the postdeal integration process can be built. First, the diligence phase of the process will have identified risks that need to be managed in the postdeal period. Every effort should be made to ensure effective implementation of the steps necessary to control and reduce the economic risks assumed.

Second, the structuring phase of the process will have outlined an operational structure that can be used to maximize the tax benefits realized by the combined business enterprise. Unfortunately, during the structuring phase, an organizational outline will have been only mapped out; during the postdeal integration phase, it will be necessary to implement the detailed procedures that are necessary to ensure that the structures work as planned.

Once the risks identified in diligence have been controlled and the opportunities inherent in the planned structure have been captured, there are still aspects of postdeal integration to be pursued. Examples include:

- It will be necessary to develop a system of tax administration that ensures that the combined enterprise complies with all applicable laws and therefore avoids incurring any risks that are not already present.
- As the business enterprises get integrated, it will become apparent that there are other, more-isolated aspects of combined tax planning that can be implemented to achieve an economic advantage.
- Once the immediate tax integration is complete, an effort should be made to develop a long-term strategic plan designed to manage global taxes in the most efficient manner.
- As the integration process gets completed, an effort should be made to ensure that the resulting plans allow for an element of flexibility that will almost certainly be needed to deal with changes in both the nature of the business and the laws of the jurisdictions in which the business operates.

In today's mergers and acquisitions environment—an environment characterized by multinational transactions involving billions in consideration—taxes are often viewed as a minor aspect of the transaction. In most cases, a great deal more emphasis is placed on global labor agreements, customer relations, intangible property rights, and tangible fixed assets. However, most multinational businesses pay more than 35 percent of their net income to various taxing jurisdictions. Most multinational businesses incur wage-based taxes in excess of 10 percent of the cost of their workforce. And most multinational businesses collect and remit taxes on goods and services transfers of 10 percent or more of the amount of their turnover. The fact is that most taxing jurisdictions collect from their citizens more than 30 percent of gross domestic product.

Taxes represent a material component of virtually any value equation. Within the world of mergers and acquisitions, a bit more focus on tax matters could result in a substantial increase in the returns realized with respect to any particular transaction.

FINANCING AND HYBRIDS: MAXIMIZING YOUR TAX AND LEGAL STRUCTURES

Hybrids. Transparent entities. Flow-through enterprises. The words themselves conjure up the image of a mad scientist cooking up a new life form in the basement of a Gothic castle. While these are the words of deals, not of pseudoscience, the analogy is not entirely without merit. When a new entity is born out of a merger or acquisition, its creators must understand its ultimate treatment, particularly from legal and tax perspectives.

A new entity must adopt a legal structure that is recognized by the various jurisdictions in which that entity intends to operate. For example, an entity may be structured under local law as a corporation or a partnership. Based on the legal structure chosen, the local jurisdiction will subject the entity to a particular tax regime.

Because global tax rules are both flexible and rigid with regard to how entities are taxed, the legal structure selected does not subject the entity to the tax regime that was sought by those that created the entity. It may be that accomplishing certain business objectives requires that the entity be established in a particular legal jurisdiction where the desired tax regime is not available. It may be that a particular tax regime is denied to a particular entity because of the type of business conducted by that entity—regardless of the legal structure adopted for the business.

The one absolute fact is that there can be considerable latitude with regard to how a particular business enterprise is taxed. In some cases, businesses obtain access to that degree of tax latitude by selecting a particular legal form through which to conduct the enterprise. In other instances, local law provides certain types of entities with a tax election that allows the entities to choose the tax regime to which they are subject—regardless of the legal form selected by that entity. In other words, in some instances, local laws allow for certain entities to be treated as hybrids—that is, entities with one status for legal purposes and another for tax purposes.

Entity structure selection is a key component of deal planning, in that it offers the opportunity to balance the application of various tax regimes to a single multinational enterprise. Understanding the opportunities inherent within the legal and tax parameters afforded by the rules governing entity structure selection and hybrid utilization is critical to achieving the optimal tax position, particularly with respect to multinational entities.

TAX-TRANSPARENT ENTITIES

For tax purposes, some entity structures result in tax-transparent entities. Such entities, in the various jurisdictions in which they exist, are recognized as legal entities and enjoy all of the privileges that their particular legal status affords. However, from a tax perspective, the entities are ignored, and the tax authorities treat them as flow-through enterprises. A US example of a tax-transparent entity would be a general partnership. Under US tax rules, general partnerships do not exist as taxable entities, though they are required to perform some information reporting. A non-US example of a similar type of entity is a Netherlands-based *Commanditaire Vennootschap* (CV). In either case, such entities can be viewed as separate entities for purposes of the application of nontax law and at the same time, as transparent entities for tax purposes. As tax-transparent entities, a US general partnership and a Dutch CV are not subject to tax in the jurisdictions in which they are formed.

The reason? Tax authorities consider the owners of such entities to be responsible for the tax consequences of the business activities undertaken by the enterprises. So, for example, it is the owners of US-based partnerships, rather than the entities themselves, who are, for tax purposes, considered to have undertaken the activities of the partnership that they own. To the extent that the owner would have been subject to US taxes if that owner had undertaken the activities directly, the owner will become subject to US taxation. Owners of a Netherlands-based CV are assessed independently by the government with respect to the activities the CV undertakes. In many cases, those owners are not subject to Dutch tax.

Both a US partnership and a Dutch CV could represent ways of undertaking economic activity in the US and the Netherlands and never being subject to local-country taxes with respect to such activity. However, the more common case is that the US partnership and the Dutch CV are examples of tax-transparent activities that can provide a means of consolidating, for tax purposes, the activities of a separate business enterprise and its owners.

Tax transparency is a major part of tax planning and deal structuring. It is a method by which an operational or strategic objective that involves locating an entity in a certain country can be achieved while, at the same time, shifting the taxation of the business activities of that entity to another jurisdiction. In an acquisition, this strategy can provide a great deal of flexibility with respect to planning the global tax position of the acquired entity.

The importance of tax transparency becomes obvious in almost every major multinational asset acquisition. If a US corporation purchases the assets of a business that operates in a non-US jurisdiction, it is almost always important for the US corporation to make sure that the assets are acquired by a subsidiary that is properly qualified to do business in the foreign jurisdiction in which the assets are located. In most cases, this objective is best accomplished by establishing a local-country entity.

However, when the acquisition is financed with local-country debt, it is highly likely that the acquired business will generate tax losses in the early years of its operations. If the local-country entity that operates the business is treated as a separate entity for both US and local-country tax purposes, the entity will pay little or no local-country income tax in the early years of operations. However, the losses generated by the local-country operations could be of no use even though the acquiring corporation is paying substantial US income taxes.

If the local-country entity is treated as tax transparent for local-country purposes, the impact on local-country taxes will be little or nothing. However, if the local-country entity is treated as tax transparent for US purposes, the early-years losses generated by the foreign business will be considered to be part of the income of the US corporate parent and will potentially result in a significant reduction of current US income taxes.

Not an Intangible Holding Company

While in some respects tax-transparent entities resemble intangible holding companies—for example, both involve movement over jurisdictional lines—there are important differences. The purpose of an intangible holding company is to transfer income-generating intangible assets, such as trademarks, and the taxable income attributable to those intangibles from entities located in high-tax jurisdictions to entities residing in jurisdictions that impose low or no income taxes.

Tax-transparent entities, however, are far more comprehensive in what they attempt to accomplish. Rather than simply moving taxable income from one jurisdiction to another by charging a royalty or a fee for the use of a transferred intangible asset, tax-transparent entities move all of the business activities of one entity to another and combine the activities of the two. From a tax perspective, the transparent entity exists only as a local-country extension of its owners. Because there are so many aspects of tax law that are affected when the operations of two entities become blended together, tax-transparent entities often offer powerful tax advantages over even the most favorable tax position that can be achieved by two stand-alone entities.

A simple extension of the foregoing example can demonstrate the difference between the two approaches to multinational tax planning. In the case of a US corporate acquisition of a pool of foreign business assets, an attempt could be made to segregate intangible assets and to move them to a low-tax jurisdiction. However, if both the intangible holding company and the local-country operating company are treated as separate entities, no real tax advantage will be incurred in the early years of operations. If the acquired asset pool is going to generate tax losses in the early years of operations, the payment of a fee to an intangible holding company will only increase the amount of that loss. Assuming that all entities are treated as separate for tax purposes, the increase in the loss of the operating company will produce no tax benefit, and the transfer of the income stream to the intangible holding company can sometimes result in an increase in taxes—the taxes levied in the low-tax home of the intangible holding company—and almost certainly will result in an increase in the operational complexity of the overall organization structure.

Of course, some acquirers have elected to combine the two strategies—tax-transparent organizations and intangible holding companies—in an effort to pursue an efficient tax strategy. If in our example, the local-country operating company is tax transparent for US tax purposes and the local-country intangible holding company is honored as a separate entity, it might be possible to achieve the best of all worlds. The increased loss of the tax-transparent operating company would flow through to the US parent corporation and reduce the current US tax liability, while the fee paid to the intangible holding company would continue to be subject to the local-country low-tax regime. Of course, US and foreign country rules intended to limit jurisdiction shopping would almost certainly make it difficult for tax planners to implement such a structure.

USING HYBRIDS EFFECTIVELY

Although the ability to use tax-transparent entities has been available for many years, the introduction of hybrid entities has substantially reduced the levels of complexity and risk inherent in implementing tax strategies based on transparent entities. A tax hybrid is an entity that is allowed to make a simple tax election to choose its tax status: transparent or separate-company treatment. In the United States, entities other than corporations are generally considered hybrids because they are provided elections through which they can select the tax regime to which they will be subject.

Prior to the creation of hybrids by US tax authorities, deal makers were always subject to the risks inherent in selecting an entity form. If the creators of an entity selected the wrong entity form or operated a properly selected entity form in an incorrect manner, they were subject to the risk that the tax authorities would treat their entity in a manner that was different from the manner intended. It was not uncommon for tax authorities to argue that a limited partnership that had been created properly under local-country law should be subject to a corporate tax regime because of the way in which the business was operated. Briefly stated, the creation of hybrids provided for a higher level of certainty with respect to various aspects of the tax-transparency issue.

Despite different regulations that govern the use of hybrids in different areas of the world, the benefits, from a tax perspective, are generally significant. One area in which opportunities exist is in the use of the US foreign tax credit. While intended to provide tax relief on a worldwide basis, use of the foreign tax credit has been fraught with problems.

When a US corporation acquires a foreign business entity that can avail itself of the US hybrid rules, an interesting opportunity is presented with respect to foreign-tax-credit planning. Assuming that the acquired foreign entity is going to pay local-country income taxes, any dividend paid from that entity to the US corporate acquirer will carry with it a foreign tax credit. That credit may be used to offset the US tax paid by the corporate acquirer and therefore reduce the possibility of triple taxation of the income ultimately earned by shareholders of US corporations.

Unfortunately, the US foreign-tax-credit rules place significant restrictions on the ability of the US corporation to ultimately realize a credit for the taxes paid by the foreign subsidiary. These restrictions take into account many factors, including the foreign-sourced gross income of the US corporation, the amount of certain expenses incurred by the US corporation, and the relative amounts of US and foreign assets held directly and indirectly by the US corporation. In many cases, US foreign-tax-credit restrictions can virtually eliminate the ability of a US acquirer to use the foreign tax credits attributable to its acquired foreign businesses.

With the use of hybrid treatment under the check-the-box regulations, the US corporation is provided with a second approach to foreign-tax-credit planning. If an election is made to treat the acquired foreign company as a tax transparent enterprise for US tax purposes, the US foreign-tax-credit computation will be undertaken as if the two legal entities constitute a single US taxpayer. Such a consolidated calculation can produce results that are substantially different from those that would result from a separate-company calculation. Thus, the existence of the hybrid rules provides deal makers with an opportunity to achieve the best overall tax result without having to make changes in either the legal or operational structure of the acquired business.

An added advantage of the US hybrid regulations is that they are generally effective across jurisdictions for US purposes but usually not effective in non-US jurisdictions. So, for example, a UK limited company might be treated as a real and taxable entity—a corporation—in the UK and as a transparent and, therefore, nontaxable entity in the United States.

US check-the-box regulations can be most effectively exploited when they are used for taking full advantage of the play that exists between US and foreign jurisdiction tax laws. For example, a US corporation acquires a foreign holding company with 35 foreign country subsidiaries. To consolidate the operations of these entities, the US corporation establishes a Dutch or Luxembourgian holding company. For US tax purposes, the acquirer checks the box with respect to the 35 companies, electing to treat each as a transparent entity. The result is that from a US tax perspective, the US corporation owns one foreign entity—the holding company—thereby avoiding all of the potentially costly issues raised by US tax law with regard to crossing jurisdictional lines. The true benefit is that this US tax result has been accomplished without changing the structure of local operating companies and while maintaining the most favorable foreign-holding-company structure.

Other jurisdictions around the world offer other types of hybrids resulting in other options and benefits. In Europe, for example, an entity's location for tax purposes is often based on a concept referred to as mind and management. Basically, the concept asserts that for tax purposes, the legal jurisdiction in which an entity is deemed to be based is determined by the location at which the directors and officers control and manage the company and at which the day-to-day operations of the company take place. So, for example, a Delaware corporation whose mind and management reside in the United Kingdom would be treated as a UK corporation for UK purposes and receive the benefits and detriments of that designation. In the United States, the same entity would be treated as a US corporation. Since the entity is subject to dual incorporation, it has many of the basic tax attributes of a hybrid.

Regardless of type, tax relief results from careful understanding and selection of hybrids and jurisdictions, with an eye toward reaping the benefits of certain consolidations. For example, the Delaware corporation headquartered in the United Kingdom that was mentioned previously, can consolidate with both its UK and US affiliates. However, it is also possible to achieve the same result with a hybrid, even though the entity does not have US legal residence.

It should be noted that in certain jurisdictions—Canada and the United Kingdom, for example—there are legal liability issues associated with the use of hybrids because from a legal perspective the entities eligible for hybrid status (transparent entities) are slightly different from the normally designated corporation. However, these issues are often not substantive and with the application of some focus to ensure that proper steps have been taken to mitigate the issues, are very easily managed.

Elective Classifications: Making All of It Work

While the options available with respect to transparency and hybrids are generally elective, they are not totally so, particularly in a multinational context. For example, the rules governing hybrids particularly and, to a certain extent, those governing transparency apply only to certain legal entities. And of these, some might automatically be transparent in certain jurisdictions, while others might need to be run in particular ways in order to achieve transparent status. Therefore, focus is important in the decision about the right combination of legal form, management, and tax status while goals with regard to this strategy are being set.

Let's consider a hypothetical case. A US business entity is involved in an acquisition and wishes to structure the deal in a way that results in a dual-status entity. For strategic or legal reasons, the acquired entity is legally organized in the Cayman Islands and is structured so that mind and management is located in Dublin. The actual directors and operational managers of the acquired company are resident in many countries, including the United States, the Cayman Islands, Ireland, and the United Kingdom.

As events unfold, nonresident directors and managers are reluctant to travel to Dublin for board meetings, preferring instead to conduct meetings telephonically. This approach to operations raises an issue for tax purposes. If, for example, several of the managers and directors are resident in the United Kingdom, the mind-and-management argument underlying and justifying the entity's dual status will come under intense scrutiny by tax authorities in the United Kingdom and possibly be in serious jeopardy for UK tax purposes. In this case, management has fallen prey to a common mistake: They have made an election but failed to act in a manner that supports its consequences. Believing that the election itself is all that matters, they have ignored the other two components necessary to make all of it work: legal necessity and management activity.

Money is another factor necessary to make all of it work. As one might imagine, the complex planning and analysis required, particularly on a multinational basis, to decide, for example, where to use a hybrid, where to use a transparent entity, or where to dual incorporate on a division-by-division and country-by-country basis is expensive, particularly because the rules concerning types of organizations, tax rates, and tax regimes change constantly around the world. Depending on the size and scope of the entity, the analysis phase alone could cost several million dollars.

Do the benefits justify the cost? Many multinationals believe they do. For example, the US Congress recently reduced by as much as three percentage points—almost 10 percent—the tax rate imposed on the US income of US manufacturers. Given that change in law, nearly every multinational manufacturer will be going through the process of determining whether, through the use of hybrids and transparency, more income can be moved into the lower-tax jurisdiction that might apply to US entities. Why? As the US rate moves below the global average, the US could effectively become a tax haven for manufacturers. In short, however expensive hybrid planning might be, that planning and analysis, if properly executed, could—and frequently will—result in payoffs that far exceed costs.

ARGENTINA

INTRODUCTION

This chapter details the principal tax issues that are relevant to purchasers and sellers engaged in the transfer of ownership of an Argentine trade or business. Unless otherwise stated, it is generally assumed that all sellers and purchasers are Argentine companies with limited liability.

The transfer of ownership of an Argentine trade or company takes the form of a disposal of shares or assets. While there are significant differences in the tax implications of an asset sale or share sale, nontax issues must also be considered.

The relevant taxes to be considered are:

- **Income tax.** This is a 35 percent tax on net profits earned by a company. Argentine companies are taxed on a stand-alone basis even if they are members of a tax group. Provisions exist, however, that allow members of a tax group to perform tax-free reorganizations—such as mergers, spin-offs, or transfers of assets—among themselves.

- **Value-added tax (VAT).** This is a sales tax whereby 21 percent is added to the sales price charged for goods or services—except for certain categories of sale that are exempt from or outside the scope of VAT. A purchaser or recipient of goods or services can generally recover VAT paid if the purchase was incurred in the course of a commercial activity. However, the level of recoverability varies from case to case.

- **Stamp duty.** This is a transfer tax levied on the value of the consideration paid for certain items such as assets, shares, and real estate. The rates vary among the provinces—for example, 1 percent and 4 percent for assets and real estate, respectively, in the province of Buenos Aires. Buyers and sellers customarily share these costs per purchase-and-sale contract.

1. ACQUISITIONS

1.1   Asset Acquisitions

As a general rule, the purchaser is severally liable with the seller for taxes due at the transfer date that are attributable to the business sold in an asset acquisition.

However, the Law on Fiscal Procedure provides a mechanism to limit the purchaser's responsibility for taxes, not already established, corresponding to the transferred business. The procedure consists of notifying the tax authorities of the transfer at least 15 days in advance of the date on which the sale will take place. If this requirement is complied with, the tax authorities have the right, but only for three months after the transfer, to claim from the purchaser any tax liability not previously assessed.

An important nontax consideration is that on a sale of assets, contracts between the seller and third parties are not automatically assigned to the purchaser. Therefore, it is necessary for the purchaser either to enter into new contracts with the third parties or to agree with the third parties that the existing contracts can be assigned from seller to purchaser. This may cause practical difficulties, particularly when there are numerous contracts or when a third party is unwilling to permit assignment.

Note also that certain regulations protect employees on the sale of a business. The regulations generally provide that the purchaser must hire the employees on the employees' current terms and conditions of employment.

An asset acquisition generally enables a step-up in the tax basis of assets. (See Section 3.1 for the basis of taxation following an asset acquisition.) The consideration paid is allocated among various assets in the sale documentation.

No tax deduction is available for goodwill acquired.

1.2   Stock Acquisitions

A stock acquisition results in the purchaser's effectively bearing all historical and future ongoing tax and nontax liabilities of the target company. There is no step-up permitted in the tax base cost of the company's assets. (See Section 3.2 for the basis of taxation following a share acquisition.)

A commercial advantage of a stock acquisition, as noted earlier, is that contracts between the target company and third parties usually remain in force and do not need to be assigned or renegotiated with the third party. However, some contracts may contain change-of-control provisions that might result in the termination of or amendment to the contract in the event of a change in ownership of the target company.

There could be a potential conflict between the preferences of purchaser and seller because a disposal of stock may be exempt from tax on capital gains under certain circumstances. (See Section 8.1 for details of the exemption.) There is no such exemption on a disposal of assets. Therefore, if the conditions are met, a purchaser may want to acquire assets, and a seller may prefer to sell stock.

2.   TRANSACTION COSTS FOR PURCHASERS

2.1   Transfer Taxes

(a) *Stock purchases*   Stamp duty is levied by the provinces, and rates depend on each jurisdiction, such as 1 percent for Buenos Aires. The buyer and seller usually share joint and several liability for the payment of the tax, depending on the province. It is customary that the parties share stamp duty costs per agreement written into the purchase/sale documentation.

(b) *Asset purchases*   Stamp duty is levied by the provinces, and rates depend on each jurisdiction, such as 1 percent and 4 percent, respectively, of the value of consideration for assets and real estate in the province of Buenos Aires. The buyer and seller usually share joint and several liability for the payment of the tax, depending on the province. It is customary that the parties share stamp duty costs per agreement written into the purchase/sale documentation.

2.2   Value-Added Tax

(a) *Stock purchases*   VAT is not levied on stock transfers.

(b) *Asset purchases*   Transfers of assets are subject to VAT at a rate of 21 percent that must be paid in addition to the purchase consideration. There are no so-called bulk sale or going-concern exemptions. However, certain assets such as intangibles not involving the concession of a commercial exploitation may be exempt from VAT. The type of agreement to be entered into should be analyzed to determine the treatment.

When the buyer is subject to the VAT rules and is obliged to charge VAT on its sales, called outputs, it may recover VAT paid on its own purchases, called inputs. A purchase of assets on which VAT has been charged by the seller is regarded as an input for the buyer. Therefore, VAT charged may be recovered by the buyer. Note that in some situations, VAT paid on inputs may not necessarily be recoverable in full, depending on the VAT characteristics of the buyer. As such, VAT paid in excess of that which is recoverable would be a real cost to the buyer.

2.3   Tax Deductibility of Transaction Costs

In general, all losses and expenses incurred in obtaining and preserving taxable profits are deductible. Based on this general rule, each kind of expense incurred should be analyzed on a case-by-case basis to determine the applicable treatment.

2.4   Tax on Financial Transactions

Any amount debited or credited in bank accounts is subject to a national tax on financial transactions at a general rate of 0.6 percent.

3. BASIS OF TAXATION FOLLOWING ASSET OR STOCK ACQUISITIONS

3.1 Asset Acquisitions

The purchase price forms the base cost of the purchased assets. With the exception of land, all fixed assets may be depreciated for tax purposes over the period of their useful lives. The following are the usual methods of computing depreciation. When it is considered technically appropriate, other methods of computation may be adopted with the express approval of the tax authorities:

- Buildings, in equal annual installments of 2 percent
- Other fixed assets, in equal annual installments over the estimated useful life

When fixed assets are sold, the loss or gain realized enters into the income tax assessment. The result is determined by applying the proceeds received against the residual historical cost value adjusted to current price levels up to March 1992 by the application of the updating wholesale-price-index coefficients. In the case of sale and replacement of movable assets within a one-year term, the taxpayer has the option to impute the profit deriving from the sale to the tax basis of the new assets—a rollover. If the option is exercised, depreciation must be taken on the resulting net amount. The same option exists for buildings in use by the owner, provided the buildings have been utilized for at least two years.

No amortization deductions are allowed for goodwill, trademarks, or any other intangible assets with a life not legally limited to a specific term. However, annual registration fees for trademarks and the like are deductible. The purchasing cost of a patent, copyright, or any other intangible asset with a life that is legally limited to a specific term may be amortized over such a term.

Typically, trade receivables are acquired at net book value. When the amount subsequently received is equal to the net book value, no taxable profit or loss arises. If one of the receivables proves irrecoverable whether in full or in part, it should be possible to obtain a tax deduction, as long as certain conditions are met.

3.2 Stock Acquisitions

(a) *Purchase price* The purchase price forms the base cost of the purchaser's stock in the acquired company. The underlying base cost in the acquired company's assets is not changed, and there is no election available to step up the tax basis of assets. Accounting goodwill arising on the consolidation of the company in the financial statements of an Argentine parent is not tax deductible.

(b) Tax grouping Argentine law has a separate entity basis of taxation, and as such, tax consolidation/grouping is not permitted.

4. FINANCING OF ACQUISITIONS

4.1 Debt

Specific tax issues related to the overall level of borrowings and the interest charged on this debt are:

- Withholding tax
- Deductibility of interest
- Thin capitaliztion
- Transfer pricing
- Key nontax issues

(a) Withholding tax Interest payments to overseas lenders are subject to withholding tax at 35 percent. The rate can be reduced to 15.05 percent in the case of payments to foreign banks located in countries not qualified as tax havens or in countries with which Argentina has signed treaties for information exchange purposes.

There are certain debt instruments that are not subject to withholding tax, such as negotiable bonds that meet specific conditions.

In general, the tax treaties signed by Argentina grant opportunities to reduce the applicable withholding rates.

(b) Deductibility of interest Interest expense related to taxable income is generally deductible on an accrual basis. However, interest paid to foreign related parties is deductible when actually paid or if the accrued liability is paid prior to the due date for filing the income tax return.

(c) Thin capitalization A recent tax reform submitted to the congress by the national executive branch introduced important changes to thin capitalization issues.

Thin-capitalization rules apply only in the case of interest on debt incurred by local companies—excluding financial entities—with nonresident persons controlling them, unless interest is subject to withholding at the rate of 35 percent. (See Section 4.1(a).)

In this case, interest is not deductible in the year to which it is allocable in the proportion corresponding to the liability generating the interest exceeding two times the amount of the net worth for that fiscal year.

(d) Transfer pricing All transactions between local companies and foreign related entities should be carried out on an arm's-length basis. Those transactions

would be subject to local transfer pricing rules that in general terms are in line with the principles of the Organization for Economic Co-operation and Development (OECD).

(e) Key nontax issues   In recent years, several measures were established in relation to the foreign exchange rules. It is advisable to verify the regulations before carrying out transactions. In many cases, prior to making interest payments abroad, the banks involved must verify that the debtor has met certain requirements.

4.2   Equity

Dividends paid on stock are not deductible by the company paying the dividend regardless of whether such stock is ordinary or preferred. However, shareholders receiving such dividends will not be taxed on them.

Corporations, limited liability partnerships, branches, and other permanent establishments of foreign entities are required to make a flat and final income tax withholding of 35 percent from dividend payments or profit distributions to resident or nonresident payees. The 35 percent rate is measured against the extent that dividends or profit distributions exceed the accumulated net income assessed through applying the general tax rules—that is, without considering any exemptions, abatements, and other adjustments arising from special promotional laws—included in their retained earnings at the end of the fiscal year immediately preceding the date of payment or distribution. To determine the possible excess that is subject to the 35 percent tax, the retained earnings determined in accordance with the tax rules must first be adjusted by adding the dividends collected in the corresponding fiscal years and subtracting the income tax determined for those fiscal years.

4.3   Key Nontax Issues

(a) Government consents   There are generally no government consents that are required in relation to the making of an acquisition or the raising of finance.

Under the Foreign Investment Law, no prior approval is required for foreign investments—other than that established by specific legislation—to carry out economic or productive activities in Argentina.

Foreign capital investments may consist of (1) freely convertible foreign currency, capital assets (fixed assets), related spare parts and accessories, local currency profits, or capital belonging to foreign investors that may be transferred abroad legally and (2) capitalization of foreign currency credits, intangible assets, and other forms of contribution. Patented and unpatented technology may constitute capital contributions to the extent allowed under the Company Law, but in such cases, their valuation is set by the National Industrial Property Institute.

(b) Antitrust regulations   Antitrust laws exist in Argentina and are generally codified in rules established by the Law for the Defense of Competition Number 25.156. Although outside the scope of this chapter, it should be noted that certain acquisitions require advance authorization. Legal counsel should be consulted regarding such requirements.

5.   MERGERS

5.1   General

A merger occurs when two or more companies are combined (in order to create a new one) without being liquidated or when an existing company acquires another or others that are combined without being liquidated. The new company or the purchaser acquires title to the rights and obligations of the companies that have been dissolved and whose respective equities are totally transferred once the definitive agreement to merge has been registered in the Public Commercial Register.

5.2   Tax Consequences

From a tax perspective, a merger entails the transfer of certain assets, potentially resulting in capital gains tax. However, there are tax-free-reorganization rules in force in Argentina. The merger is one of the three types of reorganizations covered by the law. (See Section 6.) In the event of a tax-free merger, no current taxes arise, and the entity continuing the business is considered to assume the tax rights and obligations of the predecessor entity. The business is also entitled to the tax benefits and advantages accruing to such entity or entities, provided the following requirements are met:

- Maintenance of interest for two years after the reorganization date
- Continuity of the activities of the predecessor for at least two years after the reorganization date
- Proper notification of the tax authorities
- Previous authorization for partial reorganizations
- Fulfillment of corporate law requirements

Specific obligations and benefits to which the continuing entity thus succeeds are:

- Accumulated tax losses, provided 80 percent of the interest was maintained by the owners for two years before the reorganization

- Balances of tax concessions and of other special deductions and allowances not used by the predecessor or entity by reason of limitations as to their application in any financial year
- Income and expense deferred for any purposes
- Tax concessions accorded under industrial and other business promotional legislation
- Tax basis of fixed assets, inventory, and intangible assets regardless of the value assigned thereto for purposes of the reorganization
- Basis for amortization of fixed and intangible assets
- Procedures for the allocation of income and expenses remain the same

6. OTHER TYPES OF TAX-FREE REORGANIZATIONS

According to the tax-free reorganization system in force in Argentina, there are three types of reorganizations covered by the law. These are mergers (covered in Section 5..), demergers/spin-offs, and transfer of going concern within the same economic group.

6.1 Demergers/Spin-Offs

Escisión—which includes spin-off, split-off, and split-up—exists under the following situations:

- A company, while remaining in existence, deploys part of its net worth, which is amalgamated with existing companies, or participates with existing companies in the setting up of a new company.
- A company, while remaining in existence, deploys part of its net worth to set up one company or several new companies.
- A company, while remaining in existence, deploys its entire net worth to set up new companies. The new companies either totally or partially acquire the title to the rights and obligations of the legacy company.

Generally, to maintain tax-free status, the proprietors of the predecessor companies must maintain their interests for a minimum of two years after either a tax-free merger or a demerger. The form of surviving interest that is mandated for retaining tax-free status varies according to the type of transaction—for example, either a merger or a demerger.

(a) Tax consequences From a tax perspective, a spin-off would mean the transfer of the assets involved, that is, in general, assets owned by the reorganized company and shares or participation in the company that is combined. However, in the event of a tax-free spin-off, no taxes are applicable; the reorganized entity continuing the business is considered to assume the tax rights and obligations of

the predecessor entity; and the reorganized entity is entitled to the tax benefits and advantages accruing to such an entity or entities, provided the requirements described in Section 5.1 and the mandatory holding periods are satisfied.

6.2   Transfer of a Going Concern within the Same Economic Group

(a) *Tax consequences*   In the event of a tax-free transfer of a going concern within the same economic group, no taxes are applicable; the reorganized entity continuing the business is considered to assume the tax obligations of the predecessor entity; and the reorganized entity is entitled to the tax benefits and advantages accruing to such an entity, provided the requirements described in Section 5.2 are satisfied.

According to the income tax law, there is a tax-free transfer of a going concern within the same economic group when at least 80 percent of the equity in the continuing entity is held by the owners of the reorganized company. In addition, each owner must maintain at least 80 percent of the interest held at the reorganization date.

7.   OTHER STRUCTURING AND POSTDEAL ISSUES

7.1   Proper Location of the Holding Company

From the point of view of a foreign purchaser, the jurisdiction in which the holding company of the target will be located should be carefully evaluated because this may affect, among others, the following areas:

- Tax on personal assets
- Repatriation of profits
- Requirements for foreign companies

(a) *Tax on personal assets*   The tax on personal assets is levied on the assets of individuals on December 31 each year. In 2002 an important amendment was introduced under which it is assumed, without admitting proof to the contrary, that the shares and/or participations in the equity of a local company whose owners are foreign companies belong indirectly to foreign individuals.

In this case the tax is assessed and paid by the local issuing company. The local company has the right to recover the tax paid from the shareholder. The applicable rate is 0.5 percent on the value of the shares calculated according to the equity method based on the last financial statements on December 31 each year.

There are some tax treaties signed by Argentina that would allow shareholders in those countries—for example, Spain and Switzerland—to avoid the tax.

(b) *Repatriation of profits*   As covered in Section 4.2, dividend payments are subject to a flat and final income tax withholding rate of 35 percent to the extent that the amount of such dividends or profit distributions exceeds the accumulated tax profits of the paying company at the end of the fiscal year immediately preceding the date of payment or distribution.

The provisions of the different tax treaties signed by Argentina regarding reduced tax withholdings applicable on dividend payments need to be taken into account.

(c) Requirements for foreign companies To minimize opportunities to avoid the local commercial law for businesses operating in Argentina but incorporated abroad, the Public Registry of Commerce of the City of Buenos Aires recently issued Resolution Number 7/2003, which requires foreign companies to prove that these foreign-organized entities comply outside Argentina with at least one of the following conditions:

- Proof of the existence of one or more agencies, branches, or permanent representations, with accompanying certifications of their current legal validity issued by a competent administrative or legal authority in the country in which they are located
- Holding of participation in other companies in the form of noncurrent assets according to definitions arising from the regulations or according to generally accepted accounting principles (GAAP)
- Ownership of fixed assets in their place of origin, the existence and equity value of which should be evidenced with the elements indicated in the first bulleted item

Lack of compliance with any of these requirements implies that the foreign company will be treated as a local company by the local authorities. This resolution applies not only to the foreign companies to be registered after the law's effective date but also to those already registered. Any merger or split-up procedure in which a local company owned by a foreign company participates will not be registered until the foreign company complies with the requirements of this new resolution.

7.2 Minimum Notional Income Tax

The tax on minimum notional income is a tax payable by companies and their branches organized or established in Argentina. The tax rate is 1 percent, and the tax basis is the assessed valuation of the assets for tax purposes at the end of each fiscal year, when such assessed valuation exceeds $200,000. The income tax corresponding to the same fiscal year may be recognized as a payment on account of the minimum notional income tax up to an amount that matches the latter. If a minimum notional income tax balance remains and has to be paid after subtracting the income tax, this excess may be carried forward and counted as a payment on account of the income tax established for any of the next ten fiscal years.

Shares and other equity interests in companies or partnerships subject to minimum notional income tax are not included among the taxable assets. Neither is the value corresponding to new depreciable movable assets other than motorcars during their first two years or building constructions or improvements.

8.   DISPOSALS

8.1   Stock Disposals

(a) Companies   Resident companies are subject to income tax for any capital gain obtained through the sale of shares. Losses from the sale of shares and other equity interests can be offset only against the same type of income. The statute of limitations for such losses is five years. There is no loss carryback.

Generally, Argentina does not impose a capital gains tax on foreign shareholders' dispositions of shares in Argentine companies.

(b) Individuals   Resident individuals disposing of an interest in stock are not subject to income tax unless they habitually engage in such transactions.

Resident individuals subject to capital gains due to habitual trading activity are subject to tax at the individual's respective marginal tax rate. In practice, that rate is likely to be 35 percent. The calculation of the chargeable gain is, broadly, sales proceeds minus original cost and other related sales expenses.

Capital gains from the sale of shares obtained by foreign shareholders are exempt from tax.

(c) Tax-exempt entities   Some Argentine entities are not subject to capital gains tax on the disposal of stock. This includes *administradoras de fondos de jubilaciones y pensiones,* or pension and retirement fund administrators, in the case of transactions with pension and retirement funds.

8.2   Asset Disposals (Companies Only)

Asset sales are subject to income tax on the difference between the sale price and the tax cost base of the assets sold.

If the proceeds of sale of certain types of capital assets are reinvested in the acquisition of certain types of new assets for the same or similar use within 12 months before or after disposal, the gain accruing on the sale of the old asset may instead be deferred. Rather than the gain's crystallizing, the tax basis of the new asset is reduced by the amount of the gain.

8.3   Deferred Consideration

Generally, in the case of selling companies, if an amount of deferred consideration is ascertainable at the time of the disposal, the full amount is included in the tax calculation of the disposal proceeds at the time of the sale. Individuals are taxed at the time the deferred consideration is paid.

8.4 Payments under Warranties or Indemnities

When the sales/purchase documentation contains a clause saying any warranty or indemnity payment is to be treated as an adjustment to the consideration offered and received for the transaction, the payment would be treated for tax purposes as deducted from the purchase consideration received.

9. TRANSACTION COSTS FOR SELLERS

9.1 Transfer Taxes

(a) Stock purchases Stamp duty is levied by the provinces, and rates depend on each jurisdiction—for example, 1 percent for the province of Buenos Aires.

(b) Asset purchases Stamp duty is levied by the provinces, and rates depend on each jurisdiction—for example, 4 percent and 1 percent, respectively, for real and personal property items for the province of Buenos Aires.

9.2 VAT

(a) Stock purchases VAT is not levied on stock transfers.

(b) Asset purchases Transfers of assets are subject to VAT at a rate of 21 percent that must be paid in addition to the purchase consideration. There are no bulk sale or going-concern exemptions. However, certain assets—for example, intangibles not involving the concession of a commercial exploitation—may be exempt from VAT. The type of agreement to be entered into should be analyzed to determine the treatment.

In the case of a sale of real estate, it should be noted that the VAT previously charged on buildings or other works in relation to the real estate sold and taken as fiscal credit by the seller should be added as fiscal debit if the sale takes place within the following 10 years—from the date of deduction of the VAT as tax credit.

9.3 Tax Deductibility of Transaction Costs

In general, all losses and expenses incurred in obtaining and preserving taxable profits are deductible. Case-by-case analysis of expenses incurred should be made to determine the applicable treatment.

9.4 Gross Revenue Tax

This tax is levied by the provinces and the city of Buenos Aires on the gross receipts from activities carried out within their respective jurisdictions. Sample rate is about 3 percent on the gross receipts. In many jurisdictions, the proceeds from the sale of fixed assets are excluded from taxation.

9.5 Tax on Financial Transactions

Any amount debited or credited in bank accounts is subject to a national tax on financial transactions at a general rate of 0.6 percent.

10.   PREPARING A TARGET COMPANY FOR SALE

Presale planning is important, and there are some useful tools for minimizing the tax burden of the transaction. However, in any case, it should be taken into account that Argentine fiscal law observes the substance-over-form criterion. According to that principle, the tax authority may disregard legal structures that appear inappropriate to reflect the real purpose of the parties involved.

11.   DEMERGERS

The more usual method of divesting a trade is to hive down the trade and assets of a business into a newly incorporated or an existing company. (See Section 6.1.)

12.   LISTINGS AND INITIAL PUBLIC OFFERINGS

12.1   Impact on Tax Status of Listing a Company and Its Subsidiaries

The tax status of a company generally is unaffected by listing or initial public offering (IPO).

12.2   Complete Group Listing or IPO

There are no specific rules for the case of a listing of an entire group.

12.3   Listing or IPO of Subsidiary

The immediate implications for the existing parent of the listing of a subsidiary are:

- If a parent sells in the market—that is, lists—some of its existing stock in a subsidiary, the parent is subject to income tax on chargeable gains on the disposal of stock unless it is a foreign entity, in which case the disposal would be exempt from tax. (See Section 8.1.)
- If a subsidiary issues new stock, the parent has not itself sold any stock, and consequently, no tax charge will arise.

12.4   Issuance of New Stock by a Listed Company

The issuance of new stock by a listed company should not have any tax consequences for the company.

The consideration paid becomes the investors' base cost in the stock.

12.5   Disposal of Stock by Existing Shareholders

When the listing or IPO involves a disposal of stock by existing shareholders, the tax position for those shareholders is as outlined in Section 8.1.

AUSTRALIA

INTRODUCTION

This chapter details the principal tax issues that are relevant to purchasers and sellers engaged in the transfer of ownership of an Australian trade or business. Unless otherwise stated, it is generally assumed that all sellers and purchasers are Australian companies with limited liability.

The Australian taxation system is going through a period of significant change. The government has launched various taxation initiatives in recent years, including:

- Complex tax reform measures that follow a review of business taxation
- Rewriting of the Income Tax Assessment Act into plain English
- A goods-and-services tax (GST) effective from July 1, 2000
- The new debt/equity and thin-capitalization rules effective from July 1, 2001
- Tax relief in relation to demergers effective from July 1, 2002
- The new consolidation rules effective from July 1, 2002

Legislation addressing the taxation of foreign currency gains and losses in relation to financial arrangements has also been recently passed and generally applies to foreign exchange realization gains or losses arising on or after July 1, 2003. A number of other reform proposals related to the taxation of financial arrangements are also being considered by the government. However, no further legislation has been introduced to date.

In addition, the government currently is undertaking a review of Australia's international tax arrangements. The review includes consideration of:

- Foreign-source-income rules—principally those that apply to controlled foreign companies and foreign investment funds—and foreign tax credit and exemption rules
- Overall treatment of conduit income
- Treatment of branch dividends and losses

The first two waves of legislation resulting from the review of international tax arrangements have now been passed. However, further changes are expected.

These initiatives have created a complicated tax landscape for the structuring of merger and acquisition transactions. However, there are still many opportunities to structure a merger and acquisition transaction in a manner that delivers significant value both to the vendor and to the purchaser, particularly in terms of capital gains tax planning and in terms of optimizing funding and repatriation arrangements.

The relevant taxes to be considered are:

- **Corporate income tax.** The corporate tax rate currently is 30 percent.
- **Goods-and-services tax (GST).** A broad-based GST was introduced on July 1, 2000, replacing former sales tax rules. The GST rate is currently 10 percent.
- **Other taxes.** Other taxes include state taxes, such as stamp duty on the conveyance of property: up to 6.75 percent of the fair market value of the property, fringe benefits tax (a tax on the employer) of 48.5 percent applicable to noncash benefits provided for employees, payroll tax paid by employers, and land tax.

Common Forms of Business Entities

The following are four common forms of Australian business entities:

- **Corporation.** The corporation is the most common form of business enterprise in Australia. Corporations are flexible investment vehicles that are regulated by legislation that applies to federal corporations. They are legal entities distinct from shareholders and are taxed as separate entities.
- **Partnership and trust.** Currently, both partnerships and trusts are flow-through entities for tax purposes. One exception to this rule is the Australian limited partnership, which is generally treated as a company that is taxed as a separate legal entity for Australian income tax purposes. Note that so-called foreign-hybrid rules have recently been enacted that aim to treat certain foreign partnerships and certain foreign companies as flow-through entities for Australian income tax purposes.
- **Unincorporated joint venture.** Unincorporated joint ventures are simply contractual associations between two or more parties and are sometimes used when parties wish to share in the output of a venture rather than to receive income jointly.
- **Branch.** An Australian branch of a foreign corporation is sometimes used if an investment is likely to incur losses in the early years. It is currently not regarded as a separate entity for tax purposes. However, recent changes have been enacted that go some way toward aligning the tax treatment of branches with the tax treatment of companies.

Foreign Ownership Restrictions

Australia has very few sectors in which foreign investment is restricted. Foreign investment in media, in the big four Australian banks, and in domestic airlines are examples of sectors in which restrictions apply.

The government administers its foreign investment policy through the Foreign Investment Review Board. In general terms, unless they are exempt, all foreign investment proposals must be submitted to the Board for approval. Exempt proposals include a portfolio (less than 15 percent) investment in a public or private company or a situation in which the consideration paid or asset value of the target Australian business is less than AUD50 million. The rules apply if an Australian company is acquired directly or indirectly through the acquisition of an offshore holding company. However, foreign investors may, in most instances, expect approval within 30 days. Ultimately, only approximately 2 percent of proposals are rejected by the Foreign Investment Review Board.

Withholding Taxes

Interest, dividends, and royalties paid to nonresidents are subject to Australian withholding tax, which is a final Australian tax for these nonresidents. The rates of tax vary depending on whether Australia has a double-tax agreement with the recipient jurisdiction. In summary, the rates are usually:

Type	Nontreaty Country	Treaty Country (non-US or UK)	US or UK
Interest	10%	10%	10% 0% for unrelated financial institutions
Royalties	30%	10% to 15%	5%
Unfranked dividends (paid out of untaxed profits)	30%	15%	15%, but 5% if the shareholder is a company and directly holds 10% or more of the paying company; 0% if the shareholder is a company in a listed group and has owned 80% or more of the paying company for the previous 12 months
Franked dividends (paid out of taxed profits)	0%	0%	0%
Fees for services	0%[a]	0%	0%

a. Fees for service are not currently subject to withholding tax, provided they are not considered royalties. One tax reform initiative that has been announced is the introduction of a new, broader withholding tax for all Australian-sourced income paid offshore. Final details of this mechanism have not yet been determined.

Branch Profits Tax

There are currently no taxes on the remittance of branch profits to a foreign parent. However, Australia has a peculiar law that seeks to levy tax on dividends paid by nonresidents that are sourced from Australian profits. This means that if a foreign company remits the Australian branch profits to its foreign shareholders as a dividend, the shareholders are technically liable for Australian tax (limited to any double-tax-agreement rate that may be applicable). However, the Australian Taxation Office (ATO) has jurisdictional difficulties in collecting this liability.

1.   ACQUISITIONS

A buyer should consider a sensible international structure that takes into account future exit and repatriation issues and strategies to push down debt into Australia as part of the acquisition. Interest double-dip structures may also be available depending on the home jurisdiction.

Similar structuring issues apply to the acquisition of assets and of shares. Funding issues, thin capitalization, and other structuring issues are generally the same for both assets and shares. Further, capital gains tax and other exit issues can also be similar. As such, care should be taken in establishing offshore acquisition vehicles for both Australian assets and Australian shares.

1.1   Asset Acquisitions

Traditionally, in Australia, purchasers have preferred to acquire assets rather than shares. Generally, the acquisition of assets has had several advantages, including:

- Freedom from any exposure to undisclosed tax liabilities
- Tax-effective allocation of purchase price, which may enable a step-up in basis for depreciable assets and deductions for trading stock
- Ability to acquire and locate valuable trademarks or other intangibles outside Australia, thereby enabling the licensing of the intangible to the Australian company and generating allowable deductions to reduce overall Australian tax
- Opportunity for tax-effective employee termination payment

Note: As a result of the new tax consolidation rules, share purchasers are potentially able to acquire a target that is free from certain historical tax liabilities. Further, share purchasers may be able to effectively obtain an inside-basis step-up for the underlying assets under certain circumstances. Therefore, the tax differences between share deals and asset deals are potentially diminishing under the rules.

Disadvantages of an asset purchase include the loss of historical tax attributes such as carryforward losses and franking credits. Further, stamp duty charges on asset transfers can be as high as 6.75 percent compared with approximately 0.6 percent for shares of certain private companies.

1.2 Share Acquisitions

If the target is a stand alone entity or the head entity of a consolidated group, the purchaser effectively inherits that entity's historical tax liabilities. However, if the target entity is part of an Australian consolidated tax group, generally the target—if it is not the group's head entity—exits the group with a fresh income tax identity under which only preconsolidation tax liabilities are relevant.

Note: The purchaser should consider any tax-sharing arrangements of the target's consolidated tax group because they could potentially give rise to tax liabilities.

A nonresident buyer may be concerned with structuring a share acquisition to avoid a capital gain on future disposals. This frequently involves setting up an intermediate subsidiary in a favorable jurisdiction. Selling the nonresident holding company or accessing double-tax-agreement relief on the sale of the Australian company may then mitigate capital gains tax. These strategies are now subject to potential change under tax reform proposals, as well as to general antiavoidance considerations.

2. TRANSACTION COSTS

2.1 Acquisition Expenses

While acquisition expenses are typically nondeductible, they form part of the capital cost base for calculating profit on future disposals and for calculating depreciation on depreciable assets. This includes acquisition stamp duty.

Costs related to unsuccessful takeover attempts may be deductible.

Costs of borrowing other than interest or principal payments, such as merchant bank fees, are deductible over five years or over the life of the loan if the loan term is shorter than five years.

2.2 Stamp Duty

Stamp duty is a state-based tax that varies from jurisdiction to jurisdiction within Australia. The duty is applicable to the transfer of assets and shares and is payable by the purchaser. Stamp duty on a private company share purchase is 0.6 percent of the fair market value of the shares purchased, assuming the company is not land rich. Stamp duty on the acquisition of business assets can be as high as 6.75 percent of the fair value.

2.3   Goods-and-Services Tax

The acquisition of a going concern is exempt from GST. Other asset purchases may be subject to GST. To the extent GST is payable, the GST should be allowed as an input tax credit against any GST collected by the entity. The ATO fully refunds excess GST credits to a qualifying entity.

3.   BASIS OF TAXATION FOLLOWING ASSET OR STOCK ACQUISITIONS

3.1   Asset Acquisition

When parties are acting at arm's length, the cost base of an asset is the market price negotiated between them. A buyer typically tries to allocate purchase price to depreciable assets rather than to goodwill in order to step up the cost base and maximize postacquisition deductions.

Nondeductible expenses of acquisition or sale transactions can be included in the cost base of an asset.

New capital allowance provisions provide for amortization deductions for certain types of intangible property—for example, licenses. There are no deductions available for the amortization of goodwill under current law.

3.2   Share Acquisitions

Generally, the purchase of an Australian company's shares does not affect the underlying basis of its assets. However, under the new tax consolidation regime, when a consolidated group acquires 100 percent of another entity, the purchase price paid for the shares in the target entity is pushed down into the assets of that entity to reset them for income tax purposes, including depreciation and capital gains tax. Effectively, the purchaser is treated as acquiring the assets of the target entity, and this includes any goodwill that has been reflected as a premium in the share price over the net assets of the target entity. It may mean that the tax basis in the depreciable assets of the target entity will increase, and, as a result, future tax deductions will also increase.

4.   FINANCING OF ACQUISITIONS

4.1   Debt

(a) *Withholding tax*   Interest paid offshore is subject to 10 percent Australian withholding tax except for interest paid to unrelated US or UK financial institutions, which is not subject to withholding tax. A withholding tax exemption is available for interest paid on certain qualifying, widely issued debentures.

(b) Deductibility of interest Funding costs (interest) are typically deductible, subject to thin capitalization constraints. The ATO has currently given only limited guidance with respect to the deductibility of interest in a tax-consolidated environment. Therefore, care must be taken with respect to any debt-funded post-consolidation restructuring transactions.

Other expenses of borrowing, such as bank fees, are generally deductible over five years or over the life of the loan if the loan period is less than five years.

(c) Thin capitalization and debt/equity rules

(i) Thin capitalization A key component of the government's business tax reform package was the introduction of completely new thin-capitalization rules. The new thin-capitalization rules apply from the taxpayer's first income year beginning after June 30, 2001. The rules—as they apply to nonbanks—apply to the Australian operations of both inbound (foreign entities investing in Australia) and outbound (Australian entities with controlled foreign investments) investors. Previously, the rules applied only to inbound investors.

The rules limit tax deductions related to the total debt of the Australian operations. Previously, the rules applied only to related-party foreign debt.

A safe-harbor level of total debt of 75 percent of Australian assets is available. An alternative arm's-length test requires the taxpayer to demonstrate that the gearing level could have been borne by an independent entity. A further test only for outward investing entities is based on 120 percent of their worldwide debt.

Modified rules apply to nonbank financial institutions, Australian banks, and Australian branches of foreign banks.

The thin-capitalization position of a consolidated group is determined with respect to the position of the group as a whole.

(ii) Debt/equity rules The tax law that distinguishes between debt and equity is based on a substance-over-form approach. This means that legal form debt may be treated as equity, and legal form equity may be debt for Australian tax purposes.

An instrument is classified as debt rather than equity if there is an effectively noncontingent obligation for the issuer to return the initial outlay—that is, the original investment—to an investor. In general terms, returns on interest classified as debt are deductible and cannot have dividend franking credits attached.

An equity interest will generally be characterized by returns that are contingent on the economic performance of the issuer. Returns on equity are nondeductible but generally can have dividend franking credits attached.

Under these rules, hybrid—meaning, part-debt/part-equity—instruments are classified as either all debt or all equity.

Following the introduction of these new rules, particular care will need to be taken in consideration of how the acquisition of Australian assets will be funded.

For example, if the acquisition is to be funded partly by shareholder loans, there is a risk that the related arrangement provisions may apply to deem the shareholder loans to be nonshare equity. Therefore, in the absence of proper planning, unforeseen tax consequences may result.

5.   MERGERS

There is no legal concept of a merger in Australia the way there is in other countries. An effective merger can be executed by acquiring the target company and then liquidating that company and transferring its assets to the acquisition vehicle. This can generally be achieved without any income tax or capital gains tax if the target is 100 percent owned by the acquisition company. The new consolidation rules also provide additional flexibility.

It should be noted that the transfer of property from the target company to the acquisition company may be subject to stamp duty at rates of up to 6.75 percent. Various exemptions from such stamp duty exist in some states, and therefore the ultimate stamp duty liability depends on the location of the assets.

From a legal perspective, cross-border mergers can also be achieved in a manner similar to that described earlier. However, relief from income tax, capital gains tax, and stamp duty would not likely be available. Therefore, tax costs may arise depending on the circumstances.

6.   OTHER STRUCTURING AND POSTDEAL ISSUES

6.1   Maximizing Debt-Financing Efficiency

Purchasers typically use a mixture of debt and equity to fund an acquisition. For nonresidents, maximization of debt has several advantages. Interest paid offshore is subject to only 10 percent withholding tax—or no withholding tax if paid to an unrelated US or UK financial institution or if subject to exemption—but is deductible in Australia at 30 percent subject to thin-capitalization constraints. Repayment of debt principal is also an effective method of repatriating surplus cash without a withholding tax or capital-gains-tax cost.

Under the new consolidation regime, the consolidated group is treated as a single entity, and losses and assets of individual group members are pooled. This allows a nonresident to use an Australian holding vehicle if desired. Interest deductions incurred in that entity can be used to offset the profits of the target.

Prior to the tax consolidation regime, if an Australian holding company was used to fund the acquisition, consideration needed to be given to how the debt would be serviced. Dividends paid by a newly acquired company to the holding company did not qualify for the dividend rebate unless the companies were group companies for the whole of the income year. This effectively meant that the target company was unable to pay dividends to the holding company until the next fiscal year. In addition, dividends from the target would absorb tax losses in the holding company, and the dividend rebate otherwise available would be lost. The consolidation regime has removed both of those impediments to funding the interest expense through the operating profits of the target. Under consolidation, the purchaser can use the profits of the target to immediately commence servicing of the holding company's obligations, subject to constraints imposed by corporation.

Note: Special care must be taken in these regards in the event that affiliate Australian companies are not consolidated.

6.2   Creation of a Local Company Tax Group

A consolidated group is taxed as a single entity for income tax purposes. Intra group transactions are generally ignored. However, other costs, such as stamp duty and GST, may still apply. All pre- and postconsolidation losses, franking credits, and foreign tax credits of the individual group members are pooled. Special rules apply to the formation of a consolidated group and to the entry and exit of individual members of the consolidated group.

If two or more Australian members of a wholly owned group elect to consolidate, then all other members of the wholly owned group (present and future) must also consolidate. A decision to use the Australian consolidation rules is irrevocable. Although consolidation is technically optional, the following two elements of the regime mean it is effectively mandatory:

1. Removal of the ability to transfer tax losses within wholly owned group companies unless consolidated
2. Removal of the intercorporate dividend rebate, which results in all dividends paid between wholly owned group companies being taxable unless the companies are consolidated

6.3   Repatriation of Profits

(a) Dividends paid to Australian companies   Dividends paid to Australian resident companies are fully taxable at the corporate rate, subject to the following concessions:

- Franked dividends—that is, dividends paid out of previously taxed profits—between Australian companies are effectively tax free due to the availability of tax credits for any underlying tax paid with respect to the dividend.
- Dividends franked or unfranked that are paid between members of a consolidated group are ignored for income tax purposes.
- Nonportfolio dividends received from foreign investments are typically exempt from tax. The recipient must be entitled to more than 10 percent of the vote in the foreign corporation to obtain this exemption.

(b) Dividends paid to offshore companies   Dividends paid offshore are generally subject to a 30 percent withholding tax—reduced by relevant double-tax agreements—unless they are franked. No further Australian tax is payable by the nonresident.

Australia has a conduit regime for dividends flowing through Australia to a foreign parent. Qualifying foreign dividend income received from foreign investments is credited to a foreign dividend account. Dividends paid to foreign shareholders out of this account are free of withholding tax.

If assets are acquired directly by the foreign entity—for instance, through an Australian branch—no branch profits tax is currently payable on cash paid offshore.

(c) Interest and royalties   Interest and royalties are common and efficient methods of repatriating profits because these items are typically deductible in Australia. The withholding tax cost is usually lower than the corporate tax saved.

Strategies to repatriate profits by using interest or royalties need to take into account thin capitalization constraints for interest and transfer pricing provisions generally. Australia's transfer pricing rules are broadly consistent with the guidelines of the Organization for Economic Co-operation and Development (OECD) but comparatively strict and effectively policed by the ATO.

(d) Capital returns   A capital return is not assessable to a nonresident if the shares in question do not cease to exist. However, the distribution of capital causes the shares in the Australian entity to be rebased downward for capital-gains-tax purposes. To the extent that the distribution exceeds the cost base, a capital gain occurs.

Share buybacks also represent an effective method of returning capital. However, deemed-dividend issues should be considered.

(e) Government approval requirements   Australia requires each currency transaction of more than AUD10,000, including international telegraphic and electronic transfers, to be reported to the Australian Transaction Reports and Analysis Centre. This, however, is not an approval requirement; it is merely a notification issue.

6.4   Noncore Disposals

Historically, purchasers who sold off unwanted assets postacquisition were likely to face taxable capital gains. However, because of the step-up mechanism for shares purchased by Australian consolidated tax groups, selling off surplus assets can potentially now be achieved in a more tax-efficient manner.

6.5   Preservation of Existing Tax Attributes

Generally, an unlimited carryforward applies to tax losses incurred in 1989–90 and subsequent income years. (Note that losses cannot be carried back.) Once there has been a change in the ownership of the target by more than 50 percent, carryforward losses can be utilized only if the target carries on the same business after the change of ownership. The ATO is reasonably strict on what constitutes *the same business.*

Even if the same-business test is satisfied, losses in the target cannot be transferred to new group companies unless they are consolidated. If the purchaser is part of a consolidated group, the target's losses generally can be transferred to the consolidated group. Specific rules apply to determine the rate of utilization of such preconsolidation losses. Any losses not transferred are forfeited upon entrance to the group. The head entity of the consolidated group is subject to the same continuity-of-ownership test and to the same-business test in relation to the carryforward of losses as described earlier. However, the ATO has yet to provide guidance on application of the same-business test with regard to consolidated groups. Losses incurred by the group postconsolidation must be utilized prior to losses transferred into the consolidated group.

A selling group retains a target's tax history if the target is not a head entity of a consolidated tax group. As such, the purchaser will not be able to access the target's share of the group's losses.

It should be noted that:

- Capital losses are available for offset only against future capital gains.
- Foreign losses have historically been quarantined against foreign income arising in specific classes. However, this restriction was lifted as of July 1, 2001, with respect to debt deductions incurred in deriving certain foreign income.

6.6   Receipts under Warranties or Indemnities

It is typical for a sale-and-purchase agreement to include a provision stipulating that any warranty/indemnity payments made by the vendor to the purchaser constitute adjustments to purchase price. Therefore, no immediate cash tax liability usually arises to the purchaser. However, such an adjustment would affect the capital gains tax basis of the assets in question and would need to be taken into account on any future disposals. From the vendor's perspective, these payments are typically seen as reductions to the proceeds received by them upon sale.

If no purchase price adjustment clauses have been included in the sale and purchase agreement, the receipt of a warranty/indemnity payment may have immediate cash tax implications for the purchaser and the vendor. Therefore, care must be taken in drafting such agreements.

6.7   Shareholder Loans

Care also must be taken when the target company has debt due to overseas related parties that are not likely to be repaid prior to completion of the sale.

If the debt is simply forgiven, Australian debt forgiveness rules may operate to deny future utilization of certain tax attributes of the target company, such as carried-forward tax losses, both revenue and capital, and the tax base of certain depreciable and capital assets. Similar issues may arise if the outstanding debt is capitalized.

A commonly adopted alternative is to adjust the final purchase price by the amount of the outstanding debt.

6.8   Tax Incentives

There are few tax incentives for purchasers of Australian shares. However, recent changes have been made to promote investment in innovative Australian firms (1) by providing for an extension of the previously announced exemption for capital gains realized by certain investors in venture capital investments and (2) by granting flow-through tax treatment to venture capital limited partnerships. These changes apply as of July 1, 2002.

Other significant tax incentives/grants provided in Australia include the following.

- Outright deduction for capital expenditure incurred in the Australian film industry
- Outright deduction for certain relocation costs incurred in establishing a regional headquarters
- The Export Market Development Grant program, which provides funding for up to AUD200,000 for expenditure in the development of eligible export markets
- A 125 percent deduction—increased to 175 percent for certain qualifying companies—for eligible research and development expenditure

7.   DISPOSALS

To minimize or defer tax on the sale, a seller should consider selling shares in exchange for scrip under rollover or selling shares in order to access double-tax-agreement relief when possible. Cost base step-up strategies could also be considered, but these should have due regard to general antiavoidance provisions.

7.1   Stock Disposals

(a) Companies   The selling entity's main concern is capital gains tax upon the disposal of its shares. Capital gains tax generally applies to the disposal of shares acquired on or after September 20, 1985. There is no stamp duty applicable to a seller.

Note that new capital-gains-tax concessions may apply in certain circumstances in relation to the sale of shares in foreign active companies by Australian companies.

Commercially, a seller may prefer to sell shares so as not to be left with a structure requiring liquidation or ongoing maintenance.

(i) Scrip for scrip   Scrip-for-scrip provisions provide rollover relief from capital gains tax, thereby allowing a seller to defer any capital-gains-tax liability when consideration for the sale consists of shares in the acquiring entity. This allows takeovers or mergers to occur without an immediate tax liability to the vendor.

To obtain scrip-for-scrip relief, the acquiring entity must acquire at least 80 percent of the voting shares in the target entity and issue scrip in return. The provisions are complex and in a cross-border context, are limited in scope—broadly applicable only to widely held entities.

(ii) Treaty protection   There are good arguments that suggest that the disposal of shares by companies resident in certain countries are protected from Australian capital gains tax under that country's double-tax agreement with Australia. That said, the ATO has released a tax ruling confirming its view that no protection is available under Australia's tax treaty network. Indeed, changes have recently been announced to US and UK double-tax agreements, with Australia confirming its taxing rights with respect to capital gains tax.

Australian tax law has now been enacted that empowers the Australian government to pass regulations that would impose a withholding obligation upon purchasers of shares in an Australian company to withhold tax at a prescribed rate of the gross proceeds of sale. To date, no regulations have been passed to cause the legislation to become operative.

(b) Individuals   An individual seller's main concern is also capital gains tax due upon the disposal of the seller's shares. Individuals who have held shares for more than 12 months may be entitled to a 50 percent capital gains tax discount when calculating their taxable income.

7.2   Asset Disposals

As with regard to shares, a seller's main concern is capital gains tax upon the disposal of the seller's assets. Special rules apply to the disposal by a consolidated group of shares in one of its members. In addition, the sale of depreciable assets could result in a clawback of depreciation to the extent the asset is sold above its written-down tax value.

7.3   Repatriation of Profits

Dividends paid offshore are generally subject to withholding tax unless they are franked. No further tax is payable on repatriated franked or unfranked dividends.

8.   TREATMENT OF TRANSACTION COSTS

See Section 2.

9.   PREPARING A TARGET COMPANY FOR SALE

9.1   Hive-Down of Assets/Intragroup Transfer of Assets Being Retained

Assets held by the target company that are not to be included in the sale may be transferred to other members of the vendor's wholly owned group without giving rise to an immediate tax liability, whether the members are consolidated or not. However, subject to certain exceptions, a tax liability may crystallize if the transferred asset subsequently leaves the vendor's group. This is, therefore, a factor to consider on any future reorganization of the vendor's group.

The group entity acquiring the assets will be subject to stamp duty, although exemptions may be available depending on the state in which the assets are located.

9.2   Presale Dividends

It is possible for a target to pay dividends to the vendor prior to sale in order to reduce the resulting taxable profit derived from the sale. However, the general antiavoidance rules must be addressed prior to implementation of such a strategy.

9.3   Presale Basis Step-Ups

Techniques are available to step up the cost base of an asset to market value prior to an asset sale. However, the general antiavoidance rules must be addressed prior to implementation of such a strategy.

10.   DEMERGERS

New rules have been introduced that provide tax relief in relation to demergers that take place on or after July 1, 2002. The rules are aimed at demerger transactions that involve restructuring a corporate or trust group by splitting it into two or more entities or groups, with the underlying owners thereafter holding the separate entities or groups directly.

The new rules apply to companies and trusts except discretionary trusts and superannuation funds, whether widely held or not, and allow groups a broad scope within which to structure eligible transactions.

Broadly, the new rules provide for a capital gains tax rollover and a dividend exemption for shareholders in the head entity of a demerger group—together with a capital gains tax exemption for the entities of a demerger group—if the demerger group divests itself of at least 80 percent of its ownership interests in a demerger subsidiary to the interest owners of the head entity.

The demerging entities must have the majority of their assets engaged in an active business. There are also strict conditions related to the maintenance of proportional ownership interests in the original entity and in the demerging entity(ies) before and immediately after the demerger.

Provisions concerning the treatment of tax attributes, such as losses and franking credits, are still applicable and must be given consideration in any demerger transaction. In addition, demerger transactions may still result in significant stamp duty costs.

Demerger tax relief is available to resident and nonresident entities and to the owners of such entities if ownership interests remain subject to the Australian capital gains tax rules.

However, if the demerged entity is a foreign company, a demerger will not qualify for any relief unless the head company is majority owned by Australian resident shareholders or foreign shareholders with ownership interests that have a "necessary connection with Australia."

Interaction of the demerger rules with the new consolidation rules is currently being considered by the government.

11. LISTINGS AND INITIAL PUBLIC OFFERINGS

The preferred listing or initial public offering (IPO) structure for an Australian group depends primarily on the commercial objectives and tax history of the group. It is not uncommon, however, for a newly incorporated Australian holding company to be used as the float vehicle.

AUSTRIA

INTRODUCTION

This chapter details the principal tax issues that are relevant to purchasers and sellers engaged in the transfer of ownership of an Austrian trade or business. Unless otherwise stated, it is generally assumed that all sellers and purchasers are Austrian companies with limited liability.

The following focuses on the tax implications triggered by the transfer of a company or business. Unless otherwise indicated, it is assumed that the target is Austrian resident. Note, however, that there are also a variety of nontax issues that need to be considered in the course of any such transaction. Some of these issues are also briefly covered.

Typically, an existing business is acquired either by purchasing its shares (share transfers) or by purchasing its assets (asset transfers). Austrian law also allows for a demerger of companies and, therefore, for a transfer of only a part of a business. Further, it is also possible to carry out an acquisition by a merger of companies, whereby typically one company—the transferring company—is merged into another company: the surviving company. The specific structuring of an acquisition depends on the legal form of the target business and on various tax and other issues.

The main taxes to be considered in the course of a transaction are:

- **Corporate tax.** Generally, profits of an Austrian company are subject to corporate tax at a flat rate of 25 percent (34 percent for periods up to and including December 31, 2004). Austrian companies are taxed on a stand-alone basis unless they form part of a tax group (*Unternehmens-gruppe*). In this case, the top company within the tax group is subject to corporate tax on the basis of the group's combined taxable profit.
- **Value-added tax (VAT).** The supply of goods and services is subject to 20 percent VAT, which is added to the sales price for the respective goods or services. Certain categories of supplies are exempt from VAT or are subject to a reduced tax rate of ten percent. A purchaser or recipient of services can typically recover VAT if the purchase has been made within the course of the business. However, certain VAT charges cannot be recovered, depending on the tax status of the purchaser or on the kind of business activity conducted by the purchaser.

- **Real estate transfer tax.** A tax of 3.5 percent plus a 1 percent registration duty is generally payable upon the transfer of land or real estate. Further, real estate transfer tax might also be triggered if land or real estate is effectively transferred by a share deal or a merger or demerger. Structuring alternatives often are available to avoid or minimize the occurrence of real estate transfer tax.
- **Capital tax.** When acquisitions are financed by equity, a 1 percent capital tax may be levied at the level of the purchaser. Very often, proper tax structuring will help the purchaser avoid capital tax.
- **Stamp duty on debt financing.** When acquisitions are financed by a loan or credit arrangement, stamp duty of up to 1.5 percent may arise depending on the structuring of the financing.
- **Other stamp duties.** The transfer of certain assets may trigger stamp duties of 0.8 to 1 percent on the basis of the respective purchase price.

1.   ACQUISITIONS

1.1   Asset Transfers

In an asset deal, every asset of the respective business is transferred separately by the seller to the purchaser. With respect to liabilities related to the business, the purchaser generally also becomes liable for payment—in addition to the seller—even if the liabilities are not specifically transferred from the seller to the purchaser. However, the purchaser's liability is limited by a number of legal provisions. As an alternative, it is possible for the parties to agree with the creditor that the liability is fully assumed by the purchaser, and the creditor in return releases the seller from any further responsibility for that debt.

It is important to note that contracts between the seller and third parties are not automatically assigned to the purchaser. It is therefore necessary for the purchaser either to enter into new contracts with the third party or to agree with the third party to assign the existing contract from the seller to the purchaser. Both options may attract significant stamp duties. (See Section 2.1.) Further, both options may cause a number of practical difficulties, particularly if a large number of contracts such as contracts with small businesses or private individuals are to be transferred. From a business perspective, such transfers may also lead to undesired effects with respect to the visibility of the change in ownership in the business. In practice, therefore, on the basis of these issues rather than of tax considerations, share deals very often are preferable to asset deals.

It should further be noted that there are regulations that protect employees on the sale of a business: the Adaptation of Employment Contracts Act regulations.

The regulations generally provide that the purchaser must keep existing employees on the employees' current terms and conditions of employment.

From a tax perspective, an asset deal typically allows for a step-up in the tax basis of the assets purchased. (See Section 3.1.) As a result, even though an asset deal is typically advantageous for the purchaser because of the step-up achieved, for the seller and its shareholders, this deal structure is very often disadvantageous. (See Section 7.)

1.2   Share Transfers

In a share deal, the shares in the company conducting the target business—rather than the assets themselves—are transferred by the shareholders of the company to the purchaser. As a result, the legal identity of the target company remains unchanged—except for the ownership structure. While there is no direct legal transfer of historical or future liabilities, in effect, any such liabilities are shifted from the seller to the purchaser because the purchaser becomes the shareholder in the target company following the deal.

An important advantage of a share deal is that contracts between the target company and third parties are not affected by the share deal and do not need to be assigned or renegotiated, unless such contracts contain a change-of-control provision that provides for termination or amendment of the contract in the event of a change in ownership of the target company.

From a tax perspective, there is no step-up permitted in the basis of the assets owned by the target company unless a tax group between the purchaser and the target is formed. (See Section 3.2.)

2.   TRANSACTION COSTS FOR PURCHASERS

2.1   Transfer Taxes

(a) *Asset purchases*   Austrian land or real estate that is transferred is subject to a real estate transfer tax of 3.5 percent plus a 1 percent registration duty of the consideration paid.

The transfer of accounts receivable and certain rights triggers a stamp duty of 0.8 percent of the consideration paid. Further, the assignment of contracts may also be subject to this stamp duty if a portion of the total purchase price can be allocated to the contracts assigned. In specific cases, additional stamp duties may arise. In general, there may be ways to reduce or fully avoid the incidence of stamp duty by properly structuring the transaction.

According to law, both parties are, in general, liable for payment of real estate transfer tax and stamp duties. In practice, the parties typically agree that such taxes and duties are borne by the purchaser.

(b) Stock purchases Typically, no transfer tax or stamp duty should occur when shares in the target company are transferred. There is, however, an exception. Real estate transfer tax of 3.5 percent is triggered if 100 percent of the shares in a company owning Austrian land/real estate are transferred. In this case, tax is based on a specific tax value assessed by the tax authorities. Tax can often be avoided by proper structuring, such as by transferring a nominal shareholding to a trustee.

2.2   Value-Added Tax

(a) Asset purchases From a VAT perspective, an asset deal is treated as a sale of separate assets rather than as the transfer of a business as a whole. As a general rule, the transfer triggers VAT at 20 percent on the purchase price allocated to the various assets. The transfer of certain assets—such as accounts receivable—is exempted from VAT. Liabilities transferred to the purchaser in the course of an asset deal do not reduce the VAT basis for the assets purchased.

The selling entity is required to issue an invoice charging VAT to the acquirer, who is then generally entitled to recover VAT by way of its monthly VAT return.

(b) Stock purchases Stock transfers are exempt from VAT.

2.3   Tax Deductibility of Transaction Costs

In an asset purchase, transaction costs such as due diligence costs and advisory fees are generally tax deductible for corporate tax at the level of the purchaser. In certain cases, the costs may have to be capitalized and amortized over the useful life of the underlying assets purchased.

In a share purchase, those costs normally are not tax deductible. However, they can typically be treated as incidental acquisition costs, which, therefore, increase the tax basis in the shares purchased.

With respect to finance costs, see Section 4.

3.   BASIS OF TAXATION FOLLOWING ASSET OR STOCK ACQUISITIONS

3.1   Asset Acquisitions

For tax purposes, the total consideration paid has to be allocated to the different tangible or intangible assets purchased. As a result, an asset deal allows for a step-up in tax basis of the assets purchased. Any portion of the total consideration not allocable to specific assets is typically treated as goodwill. In most cases, the tax authorities accept allocations made in the sale documentation.

As a general rule, the assets purchased, including goodwill, are eligible for straight-line tax depreciation based on the remaining useful life of the assets as determined by the purchaser upon acquisition. In general, the accounting treatment is also applicable for tax purposes unless specific tax rules provide otherwise. For example, goodwill can be amortized only over a period of 15 years regardless of the accounting treatment. Further exceptions exist for certain other assets such as real estate.

3.2   Stock Acquisitions

As a general rule, the purchase price for the shares, including incidental acquisition costs such as transaction costs (see Section 2.3), forms the purchaser's tax basis in the shares acquired. There is no tax depreciation available with respect to the stock basis except, under certain circumstances, for a write-off in connection with a loss in value of the shares; write-off is spread over seven years. The underlying base cost in the acquired company's assets remains unchanged, and there is no election available to step up the tax basis of assets.

As an exception to the aforementioned rules, new legislation provides for an amortization of goodwill over a period of 15 years if an Austrian target is acquired in an unrelated-party transaction—that is, no intragroup transfer—and if the target company is included in the tax group of the Austrian acquisition company postacquisition. (See Section 5.1.) Further, the acquired company must be engaged in an operating business. Goodwill must be calculated as the difference between acquisition cost and the statutory equity plus hidden reserves contained in unlimited-life fixed assets. Moreover, amortization is limited to the goodwill portion not exceeding 50 percent of the acquisition cost of the stock. Correspondingly, any negative goodwill has to be recognized under the same rules.

4.   FINANCING OF ACQUISITIONS

4.1   Debt Financing

(a) *Withholding tax*   In general, interest payments to Austrian resident lenders are not subject to withholding tax. Similarly, payments to nonresidents do not attract withholding tax unless the debt is secured by certain Austrian property or rights.

(b) *Deductibility of interest: General treatment*   In the case of an asset or stock acquisition, interest on acquisition debt is generally deductible for corporate tax subject to thin-capitalization and transfer-pricing rules.

In the case of a stock acquisition, further structuring is necessary to offset the interest expense against the profits of the target company: a debt push-down.

Currently, the most-common structures to be implemented to achieve a debt push-down following an acquisition of stock in an Austrian company are:

- Conversion of the target into a tax-transparent partnership, called partnership route
- Merger of the target company into the acquiring company (see Section 5).
- Formation of a tax group between the target company and the acquiring company (see Section 5.1).

(c) Deductibility of interest: Thin capitalization   Generally, in third-party borrowings, no limitations exist for tax purposes. When the financing is obtained from related parties, thin-capitalization issues should be considered. While there is no specific legislation in Austria providing a safe harbor for a debt/equity ratio, the practice of the tax authorities is to allow debt/equity ratios of up to 4:1 depending on the relevant facts and circumstances. To the extent that related-party debt is not accepted by the tax authorities, the respective amount is treated as hidden equity. In this event, the related interest expense is recharacterized as a dividend to the direct shareholder of the borrower and as such is nondeductible for corporate tax purposes. The respective interest expense may further attract 25 percent withholding tax on dividends—to be reduced or eliminated when a double-tax treaty or the European Union (EU) parent/subsidiary directive is applicable.

(d) Deductibility of interest: Transfer pricing   For related-party borrowings, the terms and conditions of the loan or other debt instrument—in particular, the interest rate—must be on an arm's-length basis. Otherwise, the debt may be partially or completely recharacterized as hidden equity for tax purposes.

4.2   Equity Financing

There is a 1 percent capital duty on the issuance of new stock. Capital tax can typically be avoided if informal equity is injected into the company by an indirect shareholder—that is, a company that is neither the direct shareholder nor a direct subsidiary of the direct shareholder. To avoid capital duty, no new stock may be issued to the indirect shareholder.

Dividends paid to the shareholders are not tax deductible by the company paying the dividend. For information on tax treatment of the shareholders receiving the dividend, see Section 5.2.

5.   MERGERS

Both Austrian company law as well as the Austrian Restructuring Tax Act provide a beneficial legal framework for several types of restructurings of companies, including mergers.

5.1   Typical Scenarios

Historically, the share deal/merger model involving a debt push-down used to be the straightforward way to obtain a tax deduction for the acquisition debt. Under this model, an Austrian acquisition vehicle was established that secured the loan for acquisition of the shares in the target company. After acquisition of the shares in the target, the two companies were merged. As a consequence, interest on the acquisition debt was—with a possible retroactive effect of up to nine months—deemed tax deductible because it was no longer deemed to be related to tax-exempt dividend income.

However, since a November 11, 1999, decision by the Austrian Supreme Court, the downstream merger of an acquisition vehicle is no longer possible if the capital preservation test—liabilities not exceeding the assets, disregarding the newly acquired shares—is not passed. In such a case, an upstream merger or, preferably, a merging conversion—both of them have the same economic effect as a downstream merger—might still be acceptable, even though according to the prevailing opinion, the rules for downstream mergers should apply.

Therefore, when there is doubt, alternative structures should be considered.

Austrian law also provides for a so-called merging conversion that currently is the only possible legal way to effectively achieve a cross-border merger of companies. It also allows for a squeeze-out of minority shareholders.

5.2   Tax Consequences

(a) Corporate tax   Under the Austrian Restructuring Tax Act, a merger may be carried out with a nine-month retroactive effect, and all assets and liabilities would be deemed to be transferred to the surviving company at book values without realization of capital gains.

In the course of a merger, any tax loss carryforwards of the transferring company are transferred to the surviving company if:

- The business of the transferring company that has given rise to the losses still exists on the merger date and has not been substantially reduced since the time the losses were incurred.
- There is no change of the tax identity. A change of identity would be assumed if there is a change of the shareholder in either the merged or the surviving company together with a change in the business and management structure of one of the companies.

(b) Transfer taxes   A merger is exempt from transfer taxes and capital duties if the transferring entity has legally existed for more than two years.

If the transferring entity owns Austrian real estate or a 100 percent participation in another company owning Austrian real estate, a 3.5 percent real estate transfer tax is due based on generally twice—or in some cases three times—the assessed tax value of the real estate, which is, in general, significantly lower than the fair market value. In the case of a change in the legal owner of the real estate, a 1 percent registration duty is due as well.

Mergers under the Restructuring Tax Act are not taxable for VAT purposes. However, the retroactive effect is not applicable for VAT purposes. That is, supplies made or received are allocated to the transferring entity until the end of the month in which the merger has been applied for registration with the companies' register.

6. OTHER STRUCTURING AND POSTDEAL ISSUES

6.1 Creation of Local-Country Tax Groups

For tax relief purposes, it is often desirable to form a tax group (*Unternehmensgruppe*) between the acquiring company and the target company postacquisition. Under a tax group, all future profits and losses of the target company are subject to corporate tax at the level of the acquiring company. As a result, the losses of one group company may be used to offset the profits of another. In particular, a tax group may be desired to offset the purchasing company's acquisition interest expense against the profits of the target company. (See Section 4.1.)

The following conditions must be met in order to qualify as a tax group:

- Participation of more than 50 percent—with exceptions—from the beginning of the tax year of the acquired company
- Agreement between the parent company and the subsidiary on the allocation of tax costs
- A written application signed by the legal representatives of both the parent company and the subsidiary that must be filed with the appropriate tax office

Note that in the case of a tax group, the parent company is not allowed a tax deduction for any write-off of the investment in the subsidiary due to a loss in value.

6.2 Repatriation of Profits

Dividends paid by an Austrian company to an Austrian corporate shareholder are, in effect, not subject to withholding tax. In the case of shareholdings of less than 25 percent, withholding tax is deducted by the company paying the dividend but is either credited against the corporate tax of the shareholder or refunded.

Dividends paid to a foreign shareholder are subject to withholding tax of 25 percent. Tax is reduced or fully eliminated if a double-tax treaty between Austria and the foreign shareholder's country has been concluded or if the EU parent/subsidiary directive is applicable.

At the resident corporate shareholder level, dividend income received from an Austrian company is exempt from corporate tax. Generally, dividend income received from a foreign company is subject to corporate tax of 25 percent unless requirements for the international participation exemption are met. (See Section 7.1(a)(i).)

6.3   Noncore Disposals

The sale of assets or stock by an Austrian company is subject to corporate tax under the general rules. Under these rules, while the sale of an Austrian subsidiary attracts corporate tax at 25 percent, the sale of a foreign subsidiary is exempt if certain requirements are met. (See Section 7.1.) In general, the sale of assets by an Austrian company is also subject to capital gains taxation at 25 percent. In certain cases, however, taxation may be deferred. (See Section 7.2.)

6.4   Preservation of Existing Tax Attributes: Tax Losses

In the transfer of a business (asset deal), tax losses related to the business cannot be transferred to the purchaser. Rather, they remain with the seller company.

In a share deal, the tax losses of the target company are generally not affected. However, the tax losses of the target company are lost in a share deal if, following the transfer of more than 75 percent of the shares in the target, the management as well as the business structure of the company is significantly changed within a certain period of time. In the absence of fixed rules, a period of at least one year should be observed before any such changes are made.

As a safe-harbor rule, the losses are not forfeited if changes have been made to secure the existence of the company with a view toward preventing the loss of jobs.

6.5   Receipts under Warranties or Indemnities

Generally, payments made by the seller to the purchasing company for breach of warranty or under an indemnity are viewed as a reduction in purchase price. As a result, the payments received are not immediately taxable in the hands of the purchaser. Rather, the purchaser accordingly reduces the tax basis in the stock or assets purchased.

If, in case of a share deal, the payments are based on an agreement between seller and purchaser but are made directly to the target company, these are typically viewed as payments to the purchaser followed by a cash contribution by the purchaser to the target company. As such, the payments should be treated as tax neutral at the levels of both the purchaser and the target company.

6.6   Key Nontax Issues of an Acquisition

There are a variety of nontax issues in relation to an acquisition, some of which are illustrated here. Lawyers and other competent professionals should always be consulted on these matters.

(a) Governmental or other consents   There are normally no governmental consents required in relation to the making of an acquisition or the raising of finance. However, acquisitions exceeding certain thresholds require approval by the Austrian cartel authorities. In certain cases, EU merger control regulations may also apply.

(b) Takeover provisions   Under Austrian law, a purchaser acquiring a controlling interest in an Austrian stock corporation listed on an Austrian stock exchange is in general required to make a public bid for all shares and other equity securities of that company. Otherwise, legal and/or administrative fines are imposed on the acquirer, including, among other things, the suspension of voting rights related to the shares held by the acquirer in the target company.

(c) Rental agreements   In the case of the transfer of a business—including a share transfer if a significant change of ownership in the target company occurs—the lease contracts generally remain with the business. The lessor, however, is entitled to increase the rent to the market value.

(d) Financial assistance   There are a number of general legal provisions as well as case law against financial assistance. The intention is to maintain share capital for the protection of creditors. These rules must be considered as part of any acquisition transaction—particularly when debt push-down or other financing transactions are contemplated.

7.   DISPOSALS

7.1   Stock Disposals

(a) Companies

(i) Disposal for cash consideration   Corporate resident entities are subject to 25 percent corporate tax on gains derived from the disposal of stock unless the requirements for the international participation exemption are met. The international participation exemption rules were amended effective January 1, 2004—with grandfathering provisions for companies registered with the Austrian companies' register until December 31, 2000—in order to

adjust the international participation exemption to the requirements set forth by the EU Code of Conduct.

As a general rule, capital gains and capital losses as well as reversal of write-offs are tax neutral if the following conditions are met:

- Participation of at least 10 percent in a foreign company
- Participations held indirectly—via a partnership—which qualify for the international participation exemption
- One-year-minimum holding period

However, the Austrian parent company has the option to treat capital gains, capital losses, and reversal of write-offs as tax effective.

Antiabuse provisions exist for low-taxed, passive foreign subsidiaries under which the tax exemption provided by the international holding privilege is replaced by a tax credit system—full taxation of dividends and capital gains at the ordinary tax rate of 25 percent with a tax credit for any underlying foreign taxes paid.

If the international participation exemption is not available, the company may be able to utilize any available tax loss (carryforwards) to offset the gain. However, under general Austrian tax law, tax loss carryforwards may be utilized to offset only 75 percent of the taxable income of a given year; that is, 25 percent of the annual taxable income is subject to corporate tax anyway. An exemption to that restriction exists for capital gains derived from the sale of a business (see Section 7.2) but not from the sale of a participation.

Nonresident sellers of Austrian shares are potentially subject to Austrian capital gains tax. However, the capital gain is typically sheltered from taxation by double tax treaties, and as such, the tax consequences depend on the residency of the seller.

(ii) Share-for-share exchange   The sale of all of the stock in a company in exchange for the stock of another company outside the scope of the Austrian Restructuring Tax Act is basically viewed as a taxable barter transaction. Any related capital gain would be calculated based on the fair market value of the stock sold in exchange for the newly acquired stock. Tax relief could again be possible under either the international participation exemption or the Austrian Restructuring Tax Act.

(b) Individuals   Capital gains realized from the sale of shares by Austrian resident individuals are subject to tax at marginal tax rates of up to 50 percent if the one-year holding period is not met. After the holding period expires, sales of qualifying shares—that is, the shareholder has owned a share of at least 1 percent at any time within five years prior to the sale—and sales of shares in Austrian companies representing part of a domestic business are subject to tax at half of the average tax rate. Generally, the calculation of an individual's capital gain is sales proceeds minus incidental sales cost minus original base cost. The comments on the tax impact of a share-for-share exchange apply to individuals as well.

Capital gains realized from the sale of shares by nonresident individuals are subject to tax at marginal tax rates of up to 50 percent only for shares in Austrian companies if the one-year holding period is not met and if no treaty protection is available.

(c) Tax-exempt entities Some Austrian entities are not subject to capital gains tax on the disposal of stock. This includes pension funds and nonprofit entities.

7.2 Asset Disposals (Companies Only)

Any capital gain derived from the sale of assets is subject to corporate tax at 25 percent and can generally be sheltered from taxation by any tax loss (carryforwards) and/or group relief surrendered from other group companies.

Tax loss carryforwards can offset gains arising from an asset disposal— subject to the 75 percent restriction discussed earlier. However, this restriction does not apply to capital gains derived from the sale or liquidation of all or part of a business. To qualify as part of a business, a separate business unit must exist that possesses identifiable assets, liabilities, and staff and that could operate on a stand-alone basis.

Gain on the sale of certain types of assets used in an Austrian business for a period of more than 7 years—or 15 years with respect to land and buildings— may be deferred if the proceeds from the sale are reinvested in the acquisition of certain types of new assets for use in the Austrian business within 12 months after disposal. The tax basis of the new asset is reduced by the amount of the gain. However, the deferral of income is not possible for any capital gain resulting from the sale of a business or part of a business.

For the shareholders of the seller company, the disadvantages of an asset deal are that the proceeds of an asset sale occur at the seller company and that the proceeds can be distributed only by way of a dividend. Upon distribution, withholding taxes might be triggered depending on the legal form of the shareholder and the stake held. (See Section 5.2.)

7.3 Deferred Consideration and Earn-Outs

Generally, if an estimate of the amount of a deferred consideration is possible, the deferred consideration is also deemed to be realized at the time of sale of the business. For example, this may be relevant in the case of an agreement for an earn-out under which the seller of a business is entitled to certain additional sales proceeds in case the net turnover or the profit of the business reaches a predetermined target within a certain period of time. The beneficial provisions of the international participation exemption are also applicable to such deferred consideration elements.

If the conditions for the deferred compensation turn out not to be fulfilled, the initial capital gain is not adjusted retroactively, but the related receivable against the acquirer would be written down, except when the international participation exemption was applicable.

If the deferred compensation is not quantifiable at the time of the sales transaction—that is, in the case of an agreement on participation in the future profits of the business sold for an unlimited period of time—then any related subsequent increase in the sales price should be treated as business income subject to corporate tax under the general rules at time the claim arises.

7.4   Payments under Warranties or Indemnities

When the sale-and-purchase documentation contains a clause that any warranty or indemnity payment is to be treated as an adjustment to the consideration offered and received for the transaction, the payment would be treated for tax purposes as a reduction of the sales price received.

8.   TRANSACTION COSTS FOR SELLERS

8.1   Transfer Taxes

The transfer of accounts receivable and certain other rights might trigger a stamp duty at a rate of 0.8 percent of the related purchase price if there is a written transfer agreement. In specific cases, additional stamp duties may be attracted. In general, there may be ways to reduce or to fully avoid the stamp duty by proper structuring of the transaction.

Real estate transfer tax at 3.5 percent plus 1 percent registration duty is due on any transfer of ownership of Austrian real estate or on similar rights based on the related portion of the sales price.

In general, according to law, both parties are liable for payment of real estate transfer tax and stamp duties. In practice, the parties typically agree that these taxes and duties are borne by the purchaser.

8.2   VAT

(a) *Asset disposals*   From a VAT perspective, an asset deal is treated as the sale of separate assets rather than as the transfer of a business as a whole. As a general rule, the transfer triggers VAT at 20 percent on the purchase price allocated to the various assets. The transfer of certain assets such as accounts receivable is exempt from VAT. Liabilities transferred to the purchaser in the course of an asset deal do not reduce the VAT basis for the assets purchased.

The seller is required to issue an invoice charging VAT to the acquirer, which is then generally entitled to recover VAT by way of its monthly VAT return.

(b) Stock disposals   The disposal of stock is exempt from VAT.

8.3   Tax Deductibility of Transaction Costs

(a) Corporate tax treatment of expenses   In general, transaction costs are tax deductible if they do not relate to a tax-exempt sale of shares in a foreign company under the international participation exemption.

(b) VAT treatment of expenses   VAT charged by third parties to the seller on transaction costs—for example, with respect to consultancy services rendered—should be recoverable for asset disposals but not for stock disposals.

9.   PREPARING A TARGET COMPANY FOR SALE

Presale planning is important if a substantial capital gain is to be expected that is not sheltered from taxation under the international participation exemption or by existing tax loss carryforwards.

9.1   Presale Dividends

If a disposal of stock is not covered by the international participation exemption, then the distribution of the excess cash of the target company by way of a tax-exempt presale dividend can be a useful planning tool in minimizing tax on capital gains.

Certain antiavoidance legislation can counteract the use of presale dividends as a planning tool. Notably, if the payment of a dividend is, from a tax perspective, to qualify as a repayment of equity—for example, in the case of repayment of an equity contribution by way of a dividend—a capital gain would be derived by the shareholder if the repayment of capital exceeds the tax book value of the participation. Therefore, a detailed analysis of the antiavoidance rules is always recommended prior to engaging in any such pretransfer transactions.

9.2   Hive-Down of Assets

If the seller is selling only a division or part of a trading business, a hive-down method of purchase may be considered. However, under Austrian tax law, no specific provisions exist for a hive-down method of purchase that involves the transfer of a specific trade and of the assets of one company to another group company.

Nevertheless, a combined business contribution/spin-off and share deal is common practice in Austria if only part of the business of the seller company is to be disposed of. In the first step, a business is tax-neutrally contributed or spun off under the Austrian Restructuring Tax Act to a newly established subsidiary of the seller company, and, subsequently, the shares in the subsidiary are sold to the acquirer. This might, in particular, be recommended if universal legal succession—as is the case under a spin-off—should be achieved for the contracts related to the business. That is, all contracts would automatically be passed on to the subsidiary without third-party consents being required. For the tax implications of the contribution/spin-off, see Section 10. Subsequent sale of the shares in Newco would, however, constitute a taxable transaction.

9.3   Cash-Box Spin-Off

To mitigate a tax on capital gains, the cash-box spin-off model might be considered. It involves a number of complex legal steps and requires careful structuring in order to be sustainable against challenge by the Austrian tax authorities under substance-over-form principles.

10.   DEMERGERS

10.1   Legal Forms

Based on Austrian company law and the Austrian Restructuring Tax Act, a company could spin off certain qualifying assets such as a business—in the sense of the Austrian tax law—or certain shareholdings either to a company newly established in course of the spin-off or to an already existing company. Under the spin-off, prior shareholders receive shares in the successor company in line with the respective shares held in the transferring company. Exchange of the shares in the transferring company and the successor company between the prior shareholders is possible within certain limits.

As a consequence of the spin-off, the successor company assumes by law all of the assets, liabilities, rights, and obligations allocated to the business transferred. The spin-off could be carried out up to nine months retroactively.

Instead of a spin-off, it is possible for qualifying assets to be transferred into an already existing company followed by disposition of that company. This contribution would have the same tax impact but may reduce legal and administrative obligations.

10.2   Tax Consequences

For tax purposes, the spin-off would be carried out at book value without realization of capital gains or losses. Any tax losses generated by the business would, under certain conditions (see Section 5.2) be passed on to the successor company.

Any exchange of the shares in the transferring and successor companies between the prior shareholders is also tax neutral within certain limits.

The spin-off of the business would not be subject to the 1 percent capital tax and would not be subject to VAT. Further, it would be exempt from assignment fees related to the transfer of receivables and to any other rights if the transferred business were held by the transferring company for at least two years.

So long as no Austrian real estate is moved in the course of the demerger, no real estate transfer tax is triggered. Otherwise, a 3.5 percent real estate transfer tax plus 1 percent registration duty of the assessed tax value would fall due for each transfer.

10.3   Spin-Offs of Trades (Assets)

Another, simpler method of divesting a trade is to hive down the trade and assets of a business into a newly incorporated company in the group. The new company is subsequently sold to a third party. This is discussed in more detail in Section 9.2.

11.   LISTINGS AND INITIAL PUBLIC OFFERINGS

11.1   Impact on the Company Being Listed

The tax status of a company generally is unaffected by a listing or an initial public offering (IPO).

The issuance of new stock by the listed company should not have any adverse tax consequences for the company, but capital tax at 1 percent will be due.

11.2   Impact on the New Shareholders

The consideration paid for the new stock either to the company—in the case of an issue of new shares—or to the existing shareholders constitutes the new shareholders' base cost.

11.3   Disposal of Stock by Existing Shareholders

When the listing or IPO involves a disposal of stock by existing shareholders, the tax position for those shareholders is as outlined in Section 7.1.

BELGIUM

INTRODUCTION

This chapter details the principal tax issues that are relevant to purchasers and sellers engaged in the transfer of ownership of a Belgian trade or business. Unless otherwise stated, it is generally assumed that all sellers and purchasers are Belgian companies with limited liability.

Belgium is dominated by entrepreneurial family-owned private companies of medium size. Private equity funds represent a growing source of finance for acquiring even large private companies. Financial buyers—in the form of private equity firms and other venture capital firms—are becoming increasingly active, providing valuable alternatives for the financing of private companies. The private equity market provides financing both in the context of large-scale buyout operations such as secondary sales and take-private acquisitions and for developmental phase operations and growth.

In practice, a target company is taken over in most cases either by means of the acquisition of assets—possibly together with liabilities—or via the acquisition of shares. However, there are other methods of obtaining control of a target business—for example, a contribution, a demerger, or a spin-off. These methods are briefly described later in this chapter.

Typically, the taxes most relevant to merger and acquisition activity in Belgium are corporate income tax, value-added tax (VAT), and registration duties.

1. ACQUISITIONS •

In the acquisition of a target business, the purchaser's objectives are key drivers—for example, whether to acquire all or part of the target business or whether to acquire target assets or shares. As discussed later, from legal, tax, accounting, and financing perspectives, the acquisition of target assets is significantly different from the acquisition of target shares.

1.1 Asset Acquisitions

The major advantage to the purchaser in an asset acquisition is that the acquiring company can choose the assets and liabilities it will acquire from the selling company. As a result, the risk that the purchaser will assume unrecorded or unknown liabilities is reduced because the historical liabilities associated with the business being purchased remain the responsibility of the purchaser unless otherwise agreed to by the parties. Conversely, the major disadvantage of an asset acquisition is the existence of specific legal rules applicable to transferring each asset from the selling to the purchasing company that may have to be complied with in order to guarantee that transferred rights or assets are enforceable against third parties—for instance, leasehold interests or royalty agreements.

1.2   Stock Acquisitions

The purchase of shares involves investment in an existing company or the purchase of shares from existing shareholders. The acquiring company buys all or part of the shares of the company from the shareholders of the target company, and the company as such continues to exist with all of its assets and liabilities, unless some activities, assets, or divisions are removed from the company before the share acquisition. As a result, the purchaser acquires the company with all of the company's historical preacquisition assets and liabilities. Therefore, it is important that purchasers undertake a thorough analysis of all of the assets and liabilities of the target company prior to acquisition and that they obtain protection against possible future unrecorded or unknown liabilities.

From a purely legal point of view, a share transaction is generally less complicated than an asset acquisition. The transfer of assets and related liabilities consists of many different transactions, while a share acquisition can be achieved via a single transfer deed. Moreover, there are fewer formalities involved in the execution of a share deal than there are in an asset deal—in order that it be enforceable against third parties.

2.   TRANSACTION COSTS

2.1   Transfer Taxes

(a) Stock purchases   No transfer tax is due with respect to the sale of shares of a company.

(b) Asset purchases   Transfer taxes may be imposed on an asset purchase depending on the nature of the assets transferred. A rate of 10 percent for the Flanders region and 12.5 percent for the Walloon and Brussels regions is due on the fair market value of real estate, 0.5 percent or 1 percent on mortgages, and 0.2 percent on long lease contracts related to real estate properties.

2.2   Value-Added Tax

(a) Stock purchases   The transfer of shares is generally exempt from VAT.

(b) Asset purchases   Generally, VAT at a rate of 21 percent is due on the sale of inventories and assets other than land, old buildings, and new buildings for which the seller has not opted for VAT. However, the transfer is not subject to

VAT to the extent that under the form of a sale or a contribution, it (1) is made between VAT payers having a right to deduct input VAT and (2) relates to a line of business or universality of goods.

Additionally, in the purchase of assets including real estate, the registration duties and VAT consequences (adjustments) have to be carefully analyzed and managed.

2.3   Capital Taxes

(a) Stock purchases

(i) Companies   Any capital gains realized by a Belgian company upon disposal of the shares of a company are tax-exempt up to 100 percent, provided the participation meets the taxation requirement for dividends under the dividend-received deduction regime and to the extent that the capital gain exceeds (old) tax-deductible capital reductions, if any, recorded on the shares in the past. This taxation condition is rather complex. In summary, it implies that taxation of the dividends at the level of either the distributing company or its subsidiaries has occurred.

Belgian domestic tax law does not provide for any other exemption conditions. Accordingly, no minimum participation requirement is applicable to capital gains on shares, and no waiting period applies in this respect.

If the shares do not meet the taxation requirement, the capital gains on shares are taxed at the general corporate income tax rate of 33.99 percent.

(ii) Individuals   As a general rule, Belgian resident individuals who hold shares as part of their private estate are exempt from any taxation on the capital gains realized upon the sale of their holding. There are important exceptions to this principle:

- Belgian resident individuals are subject to a 16.5 percent tax charge plus municipal surcharges ranging from 0 to 9 percent on capital gains realized from the sale of shares to a foreign company or foreign entity when such shares are part of a major shareholding in a Belgian company. A shareholding is deemed to be major if the individual shareholder, and the shareholder's family own or at any time during the five years preceding the share transfer have owned more than 25 percent of the shares in the Belgian company whose shares are being sold. The sale of the major shareholding is not subject to any capital gains tax if the shares are sold to a Belgian company or individual unless the shares are subsequently transferred to a foreign company or legal entity within 12 months of the initial sale.
- Belgian resident individuals are subject to tax at a rate of 33 percent plus municipal surcharges if capital gains realized from the sale of a

holding are deemed to be speculative or exceed the normal management of private assets. The tax authorities accept that the trading of shares on a stock exchange is not a speculative transaction if it can be considered as the ordinary management of the property. However, the buying and selling of shares in the short term with loaned money could qualify as a speculative transaction.

(b) *Asset purchases*   When the price paid for the acquired assets exceeds the assets' net carrying value, the selling company realizes a capital gain on the sale of the assets equal to such excess. The capital gain is taxable as profit at the general corporate income tax rate of 33.99 percent. This capital gain may be set off by tax-recoverable losses or deduction for investment, provided the purchase price has not been overvalued. Capital losses on the sale of assets are tax deductible.

The selling company can opt for a spread taxation policy for capital gains realized on tangible and intangible fixed assets older than five years—called rollover relief—provided the entire sales price and not only the capital gains are reinvested in new, depreciable fixed assets within three or five years and provided that certain formalities are complied with. Taxation of the capital gains is deferred proportionally over the depreciation period of the new asset.

2.4   Tax Deductibility of Transaction Costs

As a general rule, under Belgian tax law, costs incurred are tax deductible by the Belgian company incurring such costs, provided that the following conditions are met:

- The costs are business related.
- The costs are borne during the financial year at hand.
- The costs are incurred in order to acquire or maintain taxable income.
- Underlying documentation is available to support the existence and amount of the costs.

The wording of the invoice is an important element in illustrating to the tax authorities that a specific fee relates to a service rendered for a specific company. These general rules are also applicable to transaction costs incurred in the context of acquisitions. Accordingly, transaction costs such as advisory fees and financing fees incurred by the target company are generally tax deductible only if the fees relate to services rendered specifically for the benefit of this Belgian company.

In general terms, the position can be summarized as follows:

- Financing costs
- Investigation and due diligence costs
- Other deal costs
- VAT deduction

(a) Financing costs   These fees can generally be allocated to the various subsidiaries of the acquiring entity based on assumptions of acquisition debt by such subsidiaries. Such costs assumed by the subsidiaries of the acquiring entity are tax deductible by the assuming entity.

(b) Investigation and due diligence costs   Costs incurred that are related to the acquisition itself—for example, advisory fees for due diligence and structuring costs made on behalf of the acquirer—are generally tax deductible by the company incurring such costs regardless of whether the acquisition is one of assets or one of shares of a company. However, in circumstances when the acquiring company is a special purchase, passive holding company, such costs are not tax deductible in the hands of the underlying Belgian group subsidiaries if allocated.

(c) Other deal costs   Costs related to the acquisition but incurred subsequent to the acquisition—such as postacquisition structuring, financial forecasts, optimization of future cash flows, and financing—can generally be allocated to the acquired target and its subsidiaries. If such costs are properly allocable to the acquired subsidiaries, those costs generally will be tax deductible.

(d) VAT deduction   The possibility of deducting input VAT on costs incurred in the context of a transaction should be investigated. Indeed, although certain costs incurred in the framework of a transaction—such as certain financial services—are exempt from VAT, the majority of costs are subject to VAT. Depending on the nature of the underlying transaction and/or the capacity of the buyer or seller, respectively, limitations on the right to deduct input VAT may exist. Accordingly, VAT can prove to be a cost in the framework of the transaction.

3.   BASIS OF TAXATION FOLLOWING ASSET OR STOCK ACQUISITIONS

3.1   Asset Acquisitions

The acquiring company records the acquired assets at their respective acquisition values and may generally depreciate such costs based on those acquisition values, unless the assets are not depreciable under Belgian tax law, for example, land. In Belgium, no specific residual allocation method exists to allocate aggregate costs to individual assets acquired. In practice, the parties involved in the transaction agree upon such an allocation. Under normal circumstances, such an agreement is made between independent parties and is, therefore, generally accepted by the tax authorities absent demonstration that such an allocation is a sham. The acquisition of a target business generally results in the recognition of goodwill that can be amortized on the basis of its estimated life—for example, based on rotation of the customer list and the terms of the client contracts. For tax purposes, goodwill cannot be depreciated over less than five years.

In general, the Belgian tax authorities accept a 10- to 12-year depreciation period for goodwill. Consequently, if a shorter period of depreciation is desired, the acquiring company must be able to demonstrate to the Belgian tax authorities the appropriateness of that shorter period. With respect to other identifiable intangible assets, the acquirer is expressly precluded from using a double-declining method of amortization.

3.2   Stock Acquisitions

(a) *Purchase price*   The acquiring company records the acquisition of target shares at the shares' acquisition cost value. No depreciation is allowed on the acquired shares. The underlying base cost in the acquired company's assets is not changed, and no election to increase the basis of the assets to their respective fair value is available. Accordingly, no goodwill is recognized in connection with the acquisition of shares, and therefore no amortization of the excess of cost over the fair market value of tangible assets is allowed.

(b) *Tax grouping*   Belgium does not provide for any tax consolidation or tax groupings to permit the losses of one affiliated entity to offset income in another affiliated entity.

4.   FINANCING OF ACQUISITIONS

4.1   Debt Financing

(a) *Withholding tax*   Interest paid is generally subject to a 15 percent Belgian withholding tax, which is due either by the Belgian debtor or by a Belgian intermediary in the case of foreign debtors. Withholding tax is imposed when the interest is attributed or made payable—meaning, the moment when interest becomes a legal obligation.

Several exemptions are available with respect to interest withholding tax in the cases of both cross-border interest payments and domestic payments. For example, no withholding tax subject to specific conditions is imposed on:

- Income from Belgian-registered bonds owned by nonresident investors
- Interest paid to a Belgian bank or to a Belgian branch of a non-Belgian bank
- Interest paid to beneficiaries identified as professional investors, such as a Belgian resident company that is not a financial institution or equivalent

These exemptions do not apply in the case of a loan whose interest is capitalized or discounted—that is, a zero coupon.

The 15 percent Belgian withholding tax can be reduced or eliminated pursuant to the provisions of a relevant double taxation treaty.

(b) Deductibility of interest   Interest in connection with debt incurred for the acquisition of a company or its assets is generally tax deductible on an accrual basis, provided that the interest does not exceed the market rate applicable to the borrower.

(c) Thin capitalization   In limited circumstances, interest costs may be recharacterized as dividends when debt financing is excessive. In such circumstances, interest costs are not tax deductible. Belgian tax legislation stipulates that interest costs be treated as dividends and, as such, as nondeductible expenses in the following cases:

- When either (1) a company's board member or someone fulfilling the same functions who may be either a individual resident or nonresident or a company (only nonresident) grants a loan to the company or (2) an individual who is a shareholder of the company grants a loan to the company
- When the interest rate exceeds the market rate
- When the total amount of the loans granted by the board member or shareholder in question exceeds the paid-up capital plus retained earnings already taxed—effectively, a 1:1 debt/equity ratio for directors' and shareholders' loans

(d) Source of financing   Specific legislation applies to loans made to a Belgian company by companies established abroad under tax rules different from those under the general law or by entities established abroad in whose hands the interest is taxed under tax rules that are significantly more advantageous than those in Belgium—that is, tax havens. Interest paid to such entities is tax deductible only if the taxpayer is able to provide sufficient evidence for

the tax authorities to convince them that the payments serve an economic purpose and do not exceed an arm's-length rate of interest. In general, if the payments do not meet the two tests described earlier, then the full amount of the interest payments—not just the amount exceeding an arm's-length rate—will be disallowed.

Furthermore, even if the previous conditions are met and if and to the extent the amount of the loan exceeds the amount of the retained earnings plus the paid-up capital of the Belgian company multiplied by seven, interest payments to companies located in countries with a more favorable tax policy are not tax deductible (7:1 debt/equity ratio).

4.2   Equity Finance

Additional funds to acquire the target company or the assets of this target company can be transferred to the Belgian resident acquiring company by means of a capital increase in cash or in-kind.

A contribution in cash or in-kind (special auditor's report required) is subject to a registration duty of 0.5 percent regardless of whether the contribution is qualified as capital or as share premium. The registration duty is deductible for corporate income tax purposes in the hands of the company whose capital is increased.

5.   MERGERS

The Belgian Company Code provides for two types of mergers: merger by acquisition and merger by incorporation of a new company. Both forms of merger have the following characteristics:

- Two or more companies existed before the merger.
- Either the acquired company transfers all of its assets and liabilities to the acquiring company or the merged companies transfer all assets and liabilities to the new company.
- The acquired company or the merged companies are dissolved without being liquidated.
- The shares of the acquiring company or of the new company are immediately allocated to the shareholders of the acquired or merged companies—increased, as the case may be, by an additional cash amount not more than 1/10 of the nominal value or the par value of the issued shares.

5.1   Company-Level Tax Consequences

A tax-free policy generally governed by the principle of tax neutrality is applicable to mergers if the following conditions are met:

- The surviving company must have its registered office or principal establishment in Belgium.
- The transaction must be structured in conformity with the Belgian Company Code.
- The merger transaction must meet legitimate economic or financial needs, which is an antiabuse provision. The antiabuse provision was introduced to avoid purely tax-driven mergers. A ruling can be obtained from the Belgian tax authorities that the transaction meets legitimate economic and financial needs.

If the transaction complies with the aforementioned conditions, the merger will automatically be tax free.

Under the regulations that facilitate tax-free mergers, the following tax-free reserves do not become taxable even if no new shares are issued:

- Nonrealized—but recorded—tax-free capital gains
- Tax-free reserves under the spread taxation regime
- Capital subsidies that have not yet been treated as profit at the time of the merger
- Capital gains that are realized at the time of the merger and deemed capital gains that will result from the merger but not be realized

These reserves are known as the so-called good tax-free reserves. In the administrative commentaries, the tax-free provisions and reductions in value for doubtful debtors are also classified as good tax-free reserves.

The other tax-free reserves—called bad tax-free reserves—of the acquired target company might become taxable upon the merger to the extent that no new shares are issued for the contribution of the absorbed company. If there is full consideration by the issuance of new shares, however, the merger is completely tax free. If there is no full consideration by shares, the merger may be only partially tax free. This can occur when the absorbing company holds shares in the absorbed company—since no new shares may be issued to the extent that the absorbing company holds shares in the absorbed company—or when the surviving company is making a cash payment within the 10 percent limit specified by company law.

All of the assets and liabilities of the absorbed company are transferred to the acquiring company at those shares' net fiscal value for tax purposes—application of the continuity principle. As a result, there would be no increase in the value of the assets after the merger, and the basis for amortization remains the same. Potential amortization, investment deductions, capital losses, or capital gains in the hands of the acquiring entity on elements that have been contributed to this company, together with the paid-up capital, are determined as if the merger had not taken place.

5.2   Shareholder-Level Tax Consequences

As long as the surrendered shares are not held as the shareholder's business (e.g., inventory), capital gain realized on the share exchange is tax free. The shares in the surviving company have a tax value equal to the shares in the acquired target company prior to the share exchange. The gain becomes taxable as business profit when later disposed. If at that time the shares have been held for more than five years starting from the time the shares in the absorbed company were acquired, the gain is taxed at 16.5 percent. Otherwise, the gain is taxed at progressive personal income tax rates. A capital loss is deductible.

With respect to corporate shareholders, the shares in the absorbing company that were received in exchange for the shares in the absorbed company must be recorded at the book value of the exchanged shares. From a taxation viewpoint, any gains realized upon exchange remain tax free. As the result of a subsequent realization of the acquired participation, the gain becomes taxable if participation in the surviving company does not qualify for the exemptions for dividends received. There is no threshold or holding-period requirement. If participation in the absorbed company does qualify for the exemption for dividends received, subsequent realization of the participation does not result in a taxable gain.

6.   OTHER STRUCTURING AND POSTDEAL ISSUES

6.1   Repatriation of Profits and Cash

In the context of the acquisition of a target group, profit is often distributed from the subsidiaries of the target group to higher-tier companies and, ultimately, to the newly incorporated acquisition vehicle. There are several ways the operating subsidiaries can distribute profits.

(a) Dividend distribution either in cash or in-kind   A dividend can be distributed from existing distributable earnings or as an interim dividend.

An interim dividend is an advance payment on the earnings for the year of distribution and cannot be made in the first six months of a financial year. An interim dividend can be distributed only if explicitly stipulated in the bylaws of the distributing company. The amount of the distributed dividend is limited to the earnings available for distribution.

In the hands of the distributing company, the distribution of taxed reserves by means of a dividend will not entail any effective tax liability at the corporate tax level in the hands of the distributing company. A distribution of tax-free reserves, however, results in taxation in the hands of the distributing company—at 33.99 percent.

As a general rule, dividends paid by Belgian companies are subject to a 25 percent withholding tax. However, a 15 percent withholding tax rate applies to dividends on shares (1) that were issued after January 1, 1994, in exchange for contributions of cash and (2) that, since they were issued, have either been registered with the issuer or been subject to an unsecured deposit with a bank, public credit institution, or similar institution in Belgium.

These rates can be reduced under the applicable taxation treaty if dividends are paid to foreign companies or under internal legal provisions in some cases, such as the exemption based on the European Union (EU) parent/subsidiary directive.

In the hands of a Belgian entity, the income from shares is considered as definitively taxed income—that is, Belgian participation exemption—and is, as such, 95 percent deductible from the taxable basis, provided the participation exceeds 10 percent or 1.2 million euros and if other conditions are complied with.

6.2   VAT

The transfer of a universality of goods or of a branch of activity is not considered as a supply of goods or services and therefore is not subject to Belgian VAT, provided certain formalities are complied with. The transferee is deemed to continue in the person of the transferor; that is, the transferee takes over all prospective rights and liabilities with respect to the VAT status of the transferor. Accordingly, no VAT is due provided there has been compliance with the necessary formalities. The buyer, depending upon that buyer's right to deduct VAT, must pay special attention to potential payment of input VAT initially deducted on capital goods—such as immovable property—included in the transfer.

6.3   Preservation of Existing Tax Attributes

In the case of a tax-free merger, Belgian tax law provides for a partial transfer of the tax losses of both the acquired company and the surviving company that have been carried forward. The use of the premerger cumulative tax losses of both the acquiring and the acquired company are limited after the merger in accordance with the following:

$$A \times B/C$$

where

A = carried-forward tax losses of the acquired company before the merger

B = tax net equity of the acquired company before the merger

C = tax net equity of the acquiring company and the acquired company before the merger

or

A = carried-forward tax losses of the acquiring company before the merger

B = tax net equity of the acquiring company before the merger

C = tax net equity of the acquiring company and the acquired company before the merger

In the case of a negative net equity, the net equity is considered to be zero for the purpose of the calculation. As a result, if both of the fiscal net equities are negative, no premerger tax losses may be used to offset postmerger taxable income. If one of the companies has a negative fiscal equity and the other company has a positive fiscal equity, then only premerger tax losses of the company with the positive net equity can be used to offset postmerger taxable income.

A disposal of shares can lead to a change of control of the target company. In the case of a change of control of a Belgian company, the tax losses carried forward and the investment deduction available in that company before the change of control remain available for future utilization only when the change of control meets legitimate financial or economic needs.

Change of control generally refers to an event that results in a change in the legal or de facto power to exercise decision-making authority on nomination of the majority of the directors of the company or on the direction of its management. In brief, this control can be either direct or indirect. If the change of control is effected for the sole purpose of future tax savings, then legitimate financial or economic needs will not be met. Legitimate economic or financial needs can be met if both of the following are true:

- The change of control occurs within a group of companies whose results are consolidated for accounting purposes.
- It concerns a company in difficulties that is able to continue, either entirely or partially, its economic activities and is able to maintain, either entirely or partially, its employment level.

Legitimate needs of a financial or economic nature are in principle deemed to exist, provided jobs and business activities are maintained after the acquisition. Because this is still recent tax law, no tax jurisprudence is available yet.

An advance ruling can be obtained from the Belgian tax authorities to confirm further utilization of tax losses carried forward and investment deduction after a change of control. The granting of such a formal ruling takes three to six months and must precede the transaction.

6.4   Warranties

The tax treatment of a payment made pursuant to an indemnification clause fundamentally differs depending on whether the payment is classified as a purchase price reduction or as an indemnification payment. In general, a Belgian company receiving a payment classified as an indemnity is subject to tax on such amounts, and the seller is entitled to deduct such amounts.

Price adjustments are in principle tax neutral for the acquiring company because the price adjustment is treated as a decrease or increase in the investment value of the shares. For the seller, the price adjustment is treated either as an exempt capital gain if the shares benefit from the dividend received deduction in the case of a price increase or as a nondeductible capital loss in the case of a price decrease.

7.   DISPOSALS

7.1   Stock Disposals

(a) Companies   Any capital gains realized by a Belgian company upon disposal of the shares of a company are tax-exempt up to 100 percent, provided the participation meets the taxation requirement for dividends under the dividend-received deduction rules and to the extent that the capital gain exceeds (old) tax-deductible capital reductions recorded on the shares in the past, if any. This taxation condition is rather complex. In general, it implies that taxation of the dividends at the level of either the distributing company or its subsidiaries has occurred.

Belgian domestic tax law does not provide for any other exemption conditions; that is, no minimum participation requirement is applicable to capital gains on shares, and no waiting period applies in this respect.

If the shares do not meet the taxation requirement, the capital gains on shares are taxed at the general corporate income tax rate of 33.99 percent.

(b) Individuals   As a general rule, Belgian resident individuals holding shares as part of their private estate are exempt from any taxation on the capital gains realized upon the sale of their holding. There are important exceptions to this principle:

- Belgian resident individuals are subject to a 16.5 percent tax charge plus municipal surcharges ranging from 0 to 9 percent on capital gains realized from the sale of shares to a foreign company or foreign entity when such shares are part of a major shareholding in a Belgian company. A shareholding is deemed to be major if the individual shareholder and the shareholder's family own or at any time during the five years preceding the share transfer have owned more than 25 percent of the shares in the Belgian company whose shares are being sold. The sale of the major shareholding is not subject to any capital gains tax if the shares are sold to a Belgian company or individual, unless the shares are subsequently transferred to a foreign company or legal entity within 12 months of the initial sale.

- Belgian resident individuals are subject to tax at a rate of 33 percent plus municipal surcharges if capital gains realized from the sale of a holding are deemed to be speculative. The tax authorities accept that the trading of shares on a stock exchange is not a speculative transaction if it can be considered as the ordinary management of the property. However, the buying and selling of shares in the short term with loaned money could qualify as a speculative transaction.

7.2   Asset Disposal

When the price paid for the acquired assets exceeds the assets' net carrying value, the selling company realizes a capital gain on the sale of the assets equal to such excess. The capital gain is taxable as profit at the general corporate income tax rate of 33.99 percent. This capital gain may be set off by tax-recoverable losses or deduction for investment, provided the purchase price has not been overvalued. Capital losses on the sale of assets are tax deductible.

The selling company can choose to spread taxation for capital gains realized on tangible and intangible fixed assets older than five years—called rollover relief—provided the entire sales price and not only the capital gains are reinvested in new, depreciable fixed assets within three or five years and provided that certain formalities are complied with. Taxation of the capital gains is deferred proportionally over the depreciation period of the new asset.

7.3   Deferred Consideration and Earn-Outs

Earn-out clause refers to a deferred compensation based on the future results of the target in cash or in stock. The share purchase agreement can also provide for adjustments to the purchase price depending on a number of contingencies such as the result of a postclosing audit of the accounts, the outcome of material litigation, or the receipt of a tax assessment.

The fixed purchase price and deferred payment not linked to a contingent obligation determine the amount of the capital gain for the seller, which is taxable as of the signing of the share purchase agreement. The fact that payment of the purchase price is spread over time is not relevant for determining the capital gain for tax purposes because it constitutes a certain and liquid receivable on the date of the sale. The earn-out clause should be recognized only once the contingent event is resolved.

7.4   Payments under Warranties

See Section 6.4.

8.   TRANSACTION COSTS FOR SELLERS

8.1   Transfer Tax

Contributions of property to a Belgian company either at the time of its incorporation or in connection with a capital increase are subject to registration duties at a rate of 0.5 percent of the fair value of the contributed property. However, an exemption of registration duties is applicable within the context of the contribution of a line of business or universal asset transfer in exchange for shares.

If the contribution is not fully remunerated by rights—that is, shares—in the recipient company—that is, when there is a cash payment or when the recipient assumes debts from the contributing entity—the contribution does not qualify for the exemption. In that case, the contribution qualifies as a mixed contribution, to which the following rules apply:

- The capital duty of 0.5 percent is collected only with respect to the rights in the company.
- For the portion of the contribution that is remunerated other than in rights in the company—for example, the amount of cash or debts assumed by the recipient company—the contribution is subject to registration duties fixed for agreements entered into for valuable consideration (e.g., sales) whose subject matter consists of assets of the same nature—that is, 10 or 12.5 percent in the case of a mixed contribution of immovable property, 0 percent for stock and merchandise, and 0.2 percent in the case of the mixed contribution of a lease.

When the mixed contribution includes both immovables situated in Belgium and other assets, the rights in the company and other charges (cash/debt) for the contribution are to be divided proportionally between the value attributed to the immovables and that attributed to other assets. Therefore, the exemption is closely linked to the notions of a line of business or to an entire estate.

8.2   Aspects of Belgian VAT

(a) *Asset disposal*   The contribution or sale of a branch of activities falls out of the scope of VAT, provided that certain conditions are met. Accordingly, no

VAT is due on the contribution or sale of a branch of activity, and the buyer takes over all rights and obligations with respect to VAT from the seller.

However, whether all assets and liabilities constitute a branch of activity for VAT purposes depends on the specific facts of each situation. The European Court of Justice (ECJ) recently ruled that a part of the seller's business—including tangible and intangible elements that together constitute a business or part of a business capable of carrying on an independent economic activity—can be considered a line of business. In addition, for the transfer to be treated as a branch activity, the line of business must be used by the buyer in a manner similar to its use by the seller.

(b) Share disposal The sale of shares is generally exempt from VAT. As a result, the deduction if input VAT was incurred on costs related to the sale is typically subject to limitations, although several optimization possibilities exist.

9. PREPARING A TARGET COMPANY FOR SALE

Before selling the shares of a company, the seller often separates from the business the seller will continue to operate the parts of the business that are to be sold. Several alternatives exist to achieve the separation. Among them are (1) contribution of a part of its assets and liabilities to another company—such as a contributing a branch of activities or a universality of goods, (2) a demerger or a partial demerger (see Section 10), or (3) a taxable contribution.

The tax consequences of the contribution of a branch of activities or a universality of goods are described later.

9.1 Consequences for the Transferor

The seller's transfer of assets generally constitutes a taxable transaction. However, it is possible to exempt the transaction from corporate-level income to the extent the contribution is of a line of business or a universal transfer of assets—for example, the transfer to another company in exclusive exchange for shares. These options are:

- Tax-free contribution
- Taxable contribution

(a) Tax-free contribution If assets are transferred pursuant to a tax-free contribution, the fiscal value of the shares received by the seller in exchange for the contribution is identical to the fiscal value of the assets contributed. The capital gain realized as a result of the contribution—that is, the difference between the value of the shares received and the net carrying value of the assets contributed—is tax free. If capital gains are recognized, they remain tax

free if the gain is booked to a separate reserve account. Any capital loss realized at the time of the exempt contribution is not deductible.

Upon a later disposition of the shares received in exchange, the capital gain is determined on the basis of the net carrying value of the assets originally contributed. Such capital gain realized on the sale of the shares generally qualifies for the capital gain exemption.

The four conditions required to qualify for a tax-free contribution are:

1. The contribution is a line of business or a universal transfer.
2. The company receiving the contribution has its corporate registered office or principal place of business in an EU member state.
3. The sole consideration for the contribution consists of securities in the recipient company.
4. The transaction satisfies legitimate needs of a financial or economic nature.

(i) Line of business or universal transfer   The concepts of *line of business* or *universal transfer* are relevant for income taxation, VAT, and registration duties as well as for the Companies Code procedure.

A line of business is generally defined as being constituted by a whole that, from a technical point of view and organizational perspective, constitutes an autonomous activity—that is, a whole susceptible of operating under its own force. For VAT purposes, the EJC recently ruled that a part of the seller's business—including tangible and intangible elements that together constitute a business or part of a business capable of carrying on an independent economic activity—can be considered a line of business. In addition, for the transfer to be treated as a branch activity, the line of business must be used by the buyer in a manner similar to its use by the seller.

The notion of a universality of goods raises fewer difficulties because it has to do with all of the assets and liabilities of the contributing company, which, as a result of the contribution, becomes a mere holding company.

(ii) Recipient company tax domiciled in the EU.   The expansion of this condition is the result of the adoption into Belgian legislation of the terms of the merger directive by the Act of July 28, 1992.

(iii) Exclusive consideration in the form of rights in the company. A cash payment or assumption of a debt by the transferee of the transferor is not an obstacle to the exemption for corporate tax purposes or for registration duty purposes so long as such cash payment or assumption of debt is generally less than 10 percent of the consideration.

(iv) Transaction must satisfy legitimate needs of a financial or economic nature. This condition can be ruled on in advance by the Belgian tax authorities both for income tax and for registration duties.

With regard to decisions rendered by the rulings commission, filing a ruling request should be considered when the context of the transaction entails certain risks, which is especially the case when the following applies:

- The subject matter of the contribution is a profitable activity, whereas the recipient company is loss making.
- The contributing company intends to resell within a relatively short period all or a significant part of the shares received in exchange for the contribution.
- The tax cost in the event of recharacterization would be significant.

In the case of a contribution or demerger followed shortly thereafter by a sale of the shares, Belgian tax authorities can challenge whether the initial contribution qualifies for tax-free treatment. This may result when the contribution or demerger and the share sale are in fact aimed at transforming a capital gain on assets (taxable) into a capital gain on shares (tax-exempt). In general, the taxpayer should be able to establish sufficient nontax motivations for the overall transaction.

(b) Taxable contribution When the requirements for characterization as a tax-free contribution cannot be met, the transferor is generally taxable on the gains realized pursuant to the contribution. The capital gain so realized can benefit from the deferred-taxation mechanism discussed earlier, as in the case of a sale of assets. Additionally, capital gains realized can be offset against tax losses carried forward.

10. DEMERGERS

The same as it does for mergers, the Belgian Company Code authorizes two types of demergers: demergers by acquisition and demergers by incorporation of a new company.

A demerger by acquisition is a legal act pursuant to which the total assets and liabilities of a company are transferred to different companies as the consequence of a dissolution without liquidation, followed by the distribution of shares in the acquiring companies to the shareholders of the divided company. There may be an additional cash payment not in excess of 10 percent of the nominal value of the distributed shares or, in the absence of a nominal value, the fractional value of the distributed shares.

A demerger by incorporation of a new company consists of the transfer of all assets and liabilities of the divided company to two or more newly incorporated companies as the consequence of a dissolution without liquidation, followed by the distribution of shares issued by the new companies to the shareholders of the divided company. There may also be a cash payment not exceeding 10 percent of the nominal value of the shares issued or, in the absence of a nominal value, the fractional value of the shares issued.

10.1   Classic Demerger

For tax purposes, *demerger* is a collective term covering two different types of breakup restructurings: a split-up, that is, a demerger through dissolution of the divided entity whereby the divided company disappears, and a spin-off, whereby the shares in the divided entity are attributed directly to the shareholders, with no formal exchange of shares. This is referred to as a partial demerger.

(a) ***Consequences for the divided entity***   The liquidation regime is applicable in the case of a demerger either by absorption or by the creation of newly set-up companies. Tax-free treatment is applicable in the case of a merger or demerger and in the case of operations that substantially represent the equivalent of a merger if the following conditions are met:

- The recipient company must issue new shares as consideration for the entire net assets contributed.
- The company absorbing the recipient must be a Belgian resident company.
- The transaction must be carried out in accordance with the provisions of the Companies Code.
- The transaction must satisfy legitimate needs of a financial or economic nature.

Under tax-free treatment, corporate income tax is not imposed on the divided entity with respect to the following:

- The recognition of potential goodwill and capital gain realized as a result of the demerger
- The amounts of certain types of untaxed reserves, so long as the contribution of the assets and liabilities of the divided company is exclusively and fully remunerated by shares in the absorbing companies

If the demerger qualifies for tax-free treatment, Belgian tax law further provides for a partial transfer of the carried-forward tax losses of both the divided entity and the recipient entity. The transfer of the tax losses is not limited when the company is divided into newly set-up companies.

As in the case of contributions of a line of business, a universal transfer of assets, or a merger, an advance ruling with respect to the condition of legitimate needs of a financial or economic nature can be obtained from the Belgian tax authorities.

A Belgian company must meet the following specific procedures set forth within the Companies Code:

- The divided entity must cease to exist (dissolution without liquidation).
- The shareholders of the divided entity must become shareholders of one or more of the beneficiary entities, according to the allocation made in the demerger proposal.
- All of the assets and liabilities of the divided entity must be transferred to the beneficiary companies.

The formalities of a demerger are fairly burdensome and take at least six weeks to be completed.

The transfer of liabilities—including tax liabilities—in a demerger process is strictly addressed by the Companies Code in order to protect the creditors of the company against organized insolvency operations. All assets and liabilities either known or unknown at the time of the demerger must be allocated on the basis of the demerger proposal. If this is not the case, a default allocation applies for the assets in proportion to the net assets attributed to the beneficiary entities and for the liabilities, based on a joint-and-several liability of the beneficiary entities.

The beneficiary entities are also jointly liable for certain and liquid debts existing at the time of the transfer, limited to the net assets attributed to the entity.

(b) Consequences for the recipient entity or entities

(i) Tax capital and tax reserves The fiscal share capital and the tax reserves are divided proportionally on the basis of the net tax carrying value of the contributions made to the recipient companies.

(i) Reserves, capital gains, and exempt provisions Reserves are allocated in the following manner:

- The reserves taken into account to determine the net tax value of the split company must be divided proportionally based on the net value of the contributions.
- The capital gains that have not been taken into account in determining the net tax value of the split company must be attributed to the companies to which the assets, on which such capital gains have been realized, are contributed—such as revaluation reserves.

(ii) Value of the assets contributed   The depreciation, investment deductions, capital losses, and capital gains to be taken into consideration in the hands of the recipient companies are determined as if the split had not taken place.

(c) Consequences for the shareholders of the divided entity

(i) Rollover treatment   The capital gain realized by the shareholder of the demerged entity is considered to be unrealized for tax purposes when the demerger qualifies for tax-free treatment or an analogous treatment for EU-based demerged companies—to the extent that the operation is remunerated by newly issued shares.

Shares received in exchange must be accounted for at the same tax-carrying value as the shares of the divided entity so that the capital gain is not realized from an accounting perspective.

(ii) Tax-free capital gain—risk of reclassification   Shares received in exchange for the demerger can generally be sold by individual shareholders pursuant to the capital gain exemption rules.

As for the contribution, the realization of a tax-free gain on a disposition of shares received in a tax-free demerger raises the possibility that the Belgian tax authorities could reclassify the series of events as a sale of assets, thereby triggering taxation of the gain. Again, the test of sound financial and economic motivation should be demonstrated.

10.2   Partial Demerger, or Spin-Off

A partial demerger occurs when shares in the divided entity are attributed directly to the shareholder(s). Furthermore, the divided entity does not disappear pursuant to the division process.

A similar situation can be achieved by contributing the assets and liabilities of the divided division into a newly set-up Belgian company and distributing the shares in-kind to the shareholders—that is, an operation that does not involve a direct attribution of the shares in the divided entity to the shareholders, which is referred to as a split-off. However, this structure has several disadvantages, including:

- The contribution must qualify as a line of business in order to qualify for tax-free contribution treatment.
- The distribution is subject to corporate law limitations on distributions in-kind—for example, limitation on earnings available for distribution.
- The distribution is treated as a realization event, and the realized gain must be expressed in the accounts of the distributing entity and of the shareholders; that is, the pooling of interests method does not apply.

- The distribution is subject to withholding tax.
- The distribution is treated as a dividend to Belgian shareholders subject to the dividend-received deduction at 95 percent, leaving 5 percent taxable for the shareholders.

To the extent it is considered advantageous for the contributing entity to survive, a partial demerger appears to be an interesting alternative scenario that can offer the following advantages over a classic demerger:

- Preservation of the VAT and commercial register listings of the divided company
- Limitation of the transfer formalities to the divided assets and liabilities, as opposed to the full entity
- Preservation of *delectus personae* contracts of the divided company, which avoids problems from the enforceability of a full demerger process under foreign legislation

In comparison to the contribution of a line of business, a spin-off results in a simplification of the shareholding structure that simplifies the repatriation of the profits from the beneficiary entity.

As far as the sale of shares is concerned, a partial demerger raises the same issue as a classic demerger—that is, that the Belgian tax authorities may assert that the two events should be integrated to treat the transaction as a sale of assets. The potential tax liability in such circumstances is limited, however, to the value of the assets transferred to the newly formed transferee company, as opposed to the entire company in the case of a full division.

(a) Consequences for the divided company The Companies Code that became effective on February 6, 2001, classifies a spin-off as the equivalent of a demerger. Such classification allows a clear differentiation between the spin-off mechanism and the contribution of a line of business.

Equating a spin-off to a demerger implies that the transferred assets do not have to qualify as a line of business for company law or corporate income tax purposes, which was the case before the new Companies Code became effective.

(i) Corporate income tax consequences As the equivalent of a demerger, a spin-off would be subject to the same conditions as for a classic demerger, including, among others, that the transaction must satisfy legitimate needs of a financial or economic nature and should be carried out in accordance with the provisions of the Companies Code. When those conditions are met, the transferring company is not liable for corporate income tax on the recognition of goodwill and on the capital gains that are potential, expressed, or realized at the time of the partial demerger.

However, in contrast to a classic demerger, a taxable spin-off is treated as a partial liquidation of the company, and the tax charge is, consequently, limited to the net equity transferred.

The Belgian Income Tax Code provides a fictional scenario by which the transferring entity is considered as either the divided entity or the beneficiary entity for income tax code purposes. Consistent with that fictional scenario:

- The divided entity is considered as transferring the paid-up capital and taxed and untaxed reserves proportionally to the net fiscal value of the contribution made to the beneficiary, for a classic demerger.
- The tax losses carried forward that are attributable to the transferring entity are attributed to the new entity in proportion to the net fiscal value of the assets transferred.
- The investment deductions are determined in the hands of the transferee entity as if the transaction had not taken place.
- The revaluation reserves are attributed to the company in which the relevant assets are transferred or maintained, whereas the deferred tax reserves and capital grant reserves should be allocated proportionally to the net fiscal value of the assets transferred.

(b) Consequences for the recipient company　In the hands of the shareholders, a legal fiction that an exchange has occurred applies. The demerger is treated as a partial liquidation of the divided entity, and therefore, the tax-free merger regime applies only to the fraction of the assets transferred to the beneficiary entity. The paid-up capital and taxed and untaxed reserves are transferred to the beneficiary entity based on the net tax carrying value of the assets contributed. Depreciation, investment deductions, capital losses, and capital gains to be taken into consideration in the hands of the recipient companies are determined as if the partial demerger had not taken place.

(c) Consequences to the shareholders　Since the shares of the dividend entity are not physically exchanged, a legal fiction is introduced. As in the case of a classic merger, the capital gains recognized on the shares received in the beneficiary entities are, therefore, temporarily exempt, provided that the capital gains are accounted for on a separate reserve account—that is, the so-called intangibility conditions.

(d) Registration duties　If the contribution does not qualify as a line of business, the recipient company does not qualify for the exemption treatment of capital duty. This has the following consequences:

- If the transfer is fully remunerated with rights in the recipient company, the capital duty of 0.5 percent is due.

- If the contribution is not fully remunerated by rights in the company, the capital duty of 0.5 percent is collected only if rights in the company are issued and transferred and if transfer duties of either 10 or 12.5 percent for immovable property, of 1 or 0.5 percent on mortgages, of 0.2 percent for leases, and of 0 percent for stock and merchandise are due on the remaining part in proportion to their market value.

(e) VAT The application of articles 11 and 18 of section 3 of the VAT will require that the assets transferred constitute a separate line of business in the sense of the VAT legislation. If this is not the case, VAT is charged by the contributing company. Furthermore, adjustments of VAT initially deducted on real estate may need to be carried out.

11. LISTINGS AND INITIAL PUBLIC OFFERINGS

The listing or initial public offering (IPO) of a company can be realized by the shareholders' (individual shareholders' or corporate parent's) selling part of their shares to third-party subscribers (the public) or by creating new shares to which external parties may subscribe. In the latter case, 0.5 percent registration duties are due on the capital increase.

Belgian tax law does not provide for special rules related to listings or IPOs.

The tax consequences of an IPO in the hands of the former shareholders of the company—that is, in case existing shares are brought to the market—are covered in Section 7.1.

The listed company itself continues to exist with all of its assets and liabilities, unless some activities, assets, or divisions get removed from the company before the IPO or in case of a partial listing resulting from a spin-off.

However, in the hands of the listed company, it should be verified whether the IPO would entail an actual change of control. If a change of control occurs, there is the risk that article 207, al.3, of the Belgian Income Tax Code applies and that the carried-forward tax losses, if any, of the listed company would be lost. It is, however, very unlikely that article 207, al.3, will apply to a listing, because the business motivation is obvious.

For the sake of completeness, it is important also to note that a tax is due upon subscription to and purchase and sale of securities through a broker or an intermediary acting in the course of business and registered in Belgium. Moreover, a tax is levied upon the physical delivery of bearer securities after such securities have been subscribed or acquired for consideration through an intermediary acting in the course of business. Possible exemptions from these taxes are available.

BRAZIL

INTRODUCTION

This chapter identifies the principal tax issues that are relevant to purchasers and sellers engaged in the transfer of ownership of a Brazilian *limitada* or a Brazilian *sociedade anônima* (S.A., or Brazilian company). Unless otherwise stated, it is generally assumed that all sellers and purchasers are Brazilian companies with limited liability.

Ownership of a business enterprise can be transferred in either of two forms: disposal of a controlling interest of the shares of the company—called a share disposition—or transfer of the assets of a business enterprise that constitute a business establishment or a going concern—called an asset disposition. There are significant differences in the tax consequences of a share disposition and an asset disposition.

Under Brazilian law, a merger is defined as a combination of two or more companies into a surviving company or as the consolidation of two or more existing companies into a new company pursuant to which the survivor or the new company assumes all rights and obligations associated with the former companies. Conversely, an acquisition is not specifically defined under Brazilian law but is generally understood to describe a transfer of shares and/or assets between companies, structured so that the acquiring company obtains an interest in all or a portion of the selling company's shares or assets.

The relevant taxes to be considered in a merger or acquisition are:

- **Corporation tax.** Brazilian corporate taxpayers are subject to a basic corporate income tax rate of 15 percent plus a surtax of 10 percent on taxable income exceeding 240,000 reals. Additionally, a social contribution tax is imposed at the rate of 9 percent on taxable income, although this rate is expected to decrease to 8 percent during 2005. Thus, for 2004 the effective corporate income tax rate is 34 percent. Resident Brazilian corporations are taxed on worldwide income, but they are eligible for tax credits—limited to the amount of Brazilian income tax that is imposed on foreign-sourced income. The Brazilian tax system includes complex provisions for the current taxation of profits earned by controlled non-Brazilian foreign corporations of a Brazilian-controlled group.

  Brazilian companies are taxed on a stand-alone basis even if they are members of a tax group, and, moreover, there are no tax-grouping provisions that enable members of a tax group to offset tax losses among themselves.

- **Withholding taxes.** Brazilian-sourced income distributed to a nonresident company is generally subject to withholding taxes at rates of up to 25 percent unless reduced or eliminated by applicable tax treaty. There is no withholding tax imposed on dividends paid by a Brazilian corporation to nonresident shareholders unless the earnings distributed were accumulated prior to January 1, 1996, in which case withholding tax may apply.

  Recent changes in Brazilian legislation have reduced the withholding rate to 15 percent with respect to technical and administrative services fees paid to nonresident recipients except in cases involving tax-haven recipients, in which case the rate is 25 percent. It is, however, important to note that the Brazilian payer is also required to pay a tax referred to as the CIDE (federal economic intervention contribution) and assessed at the rate of 10 percent on such fees.

  Interest paid to nonresidents is subject to a withholding tax of 15 percent unless the recipient resides in a tax haven, in which case the withholding tax is 25 percent.

- **Capital gains taxes.** Capital gains may be realized on the sale of shares of, reduction of capital in, or liquidation of a Brazilian entity, computed as the excess of the sales price or amount realized over the corresponding book carrying value of the asset or as the value of capital registered with the Brazilian Central Bank—in the case of a sale or transfer of an asset by a nonresident entity. Capital gains recognized by local resident companies are taxed as ordinary income; capital gains recognized by nonresident entities are subject to a withholding tax at a rate of 15 percent, 25 percent if located in a tax haven. In a transaction involving a capital gain realized by an entity resident or domiciled abroad, the responsible party for collecting and remitting the withholding tax is the buyer that is resident or domiciled in Brazil. However, when both the buyer and seller are domiciled abroad, the buyer's legal representative located in Brazil is considered as the withholding agent.

- **Bank transfer tax.** CPMF (contribution on financial transactions) is a contribution levied on withdrawals from bank accounts and assessed at the rate of 0.38 percent on the amount withdrawn. This rate is effective until December 31, 2007, at which time the rate is scheduled to decrease to 0.08 percent. The contribution is deducted from bank accounts weekly and is deductible for income tax and social contribution on net income purposes.

- **Tax on financial operations.** IOF (tax on financial operations) is levied on certain financial transactions such as loans, foreign exchange operations, securities, and foreign exchange instruments. The applicable rate varies depending on the nature of the transaction. IOF of 5 percent is charged on foreign loans with an average maturity of less than 90 days. All other foreign loans are not subject to IOF.

- **State value-added tax (ICMS).** ICMS is a value-added tax on goods, interstate and intermunicipal transport, and communication services. ICMS is a noncumulative state tax assessed at the rate of 7 to 25 percent on the increase in the price of the product or service that occurs in each stage of the circulation process, except for certain categories of sale that are exempt from or outside the scope of the value-added tax (VAT). In general, the credits are computed at the moment the product enters the taxpayer's premises, and the debits are computed at the time the final product exits the establishment. However, the level of recoverability of credits varies from case to case.

- **Federal value-added tax (IPI).** IPI is a noncumulative federal excise tax levied on the production of domestic and imported manufactured goods. It is a tax on the industrialization process and is, therefore, not charged on retail transactions. The rate of tax is imposed equally on imports and Brazilian-made products both at the time of importation and on the sale by the importer. The rate ranges from 10 to 15 percent, although there are many exceptions subject to higher and/or lower rates—in certain cases, exceeding 300 percent. Rates vary according to the tariff classification of each product.

- **Contribution to a federal employees savings program (PIS) and social assistance contribution (COFINS).** PIS and COFINS represent two important transaction-based charges that any Brazilian corporation needs to take into consideration. The PIS and COFINS contributions are monthly federal social contribution charges calculated as a percentage of gross revenue and deductible for income and social contribution tax purposes. PIS and COFINS are calculated at rates of 1.65 percent and 7.6 percent, respectively. It is important to note that PIS and COFINS are also assessed on imported goods or services and that the Brazilian recipient of such goods or services is responsible for the payment of PIS and COFINS. To eliminate the cumulative effect of the contributions, PIS and COFINS are assessed on a noncumulative basis, which allows taxpayers to use credits arising from previous transactions—that is, PIS/COFINS applicable to inputs used in the manufacturing process and goods acquired for resale, including PIS/COFINS paid on imported goods—to offset debits arising on sales.

Certain types of revenue are exempt from the imposition of PIS and COFINS, such as revenues from the sale of permanent assets, including sales of shares, and revenues from export sales and income recorded under the equity pickup method of accounting.

1. ACQUISITIONS

1.1 Asset Acquisitions

In contrast to many tax jurisdictions, a purchaser of a Brazilian business enterprise generally cannot eliminate exposure to preacquisition liabilities by structuring a transaction as an asset acquisition (a successor liability). With respect to successor liability, Brazilian tax law adopts the concept of "the capacity to generate income." Consistent with this concept, the responsibility to pay contingent tax and labor liabilities, both known and unknown, generally follows the ownership of the assets of the business enterprise. This principle is based on the concept that the owner of the operating assets or the acquirer of the business unit retains the capacity to generate income and, therefore, to pay the tax or labor liability. Consequently, whether structuring the transaction as an asset acquisition or as a stock acquisition, the buyer may generally step into the shoes of the previous owner with respect to any obligation to satisfy tax and labor liabilities. Even in situations when the seller and buyer agree to transfer or exclude specified liabilities, the creditor may pursue the seller or the buyer for payment unless there is a formal novation, which is an agreement also involving the creditor pursuant to which the liability is assumed by the buyer, and the creditor agrees to release the seller from any further responsibility for that liability.

Generally, Brazilian labor legislation protects employees on the sale of the assets of a business by providing that the purchaser must assume the current terms and conditions of employment contracts and any labor union agreements.

An asset acquisition generally enables the purchaser to obtain a step-up in the tax basis of assets acquired. (See Section 3.1.) Purchase consideration is allocated among the different assets acquired based on their relative fair market values. In the event that the purchase and sale agreement does not separately allocate the purchase price to the acquired assets, it is recommended that the buyer's allocations be supported by an appraisal prepared by an independent third party. (See Section 3.1.)

Depreciation or amortization expense resulting from the basis step-up is determined by reference to the accounting treatment of the underlying asset—generally, 5 to 20 years, computed on a straight-line basis. Amounts allocated to nondepreciable assets such as land and certain intangibles, however, are not deductible for tax purposes.

1.2   Stock Acquisitions

A stock acquisition results in the purchaser's assuming any historical and prospective ongoing tax and nontax liabilities of the acquired company. Additionally, the acquirer obtains no step-up in the tax basis cost of the company's assets; rather, the net-tax-carrying values of the assets are continued. Notwithstanding the aforementioned, goodwill "paid" as part of a stock acquisition may qualify for tax relief, provided the transaction is properly structured. (See Section 3.2 for the basis of taxation following a share acquisition.)

Since goodwill typically represents a significant portion of the value of the acquired business, it is often beneficial for the purchaser to acquire stock rather than assets in order to benefit from future tax relief attributable to the recorded goodwill.

Another important advantage to acquiring the stock rather than the assets of a target company is that the contracts, licenses, registrations, and tax incentives between the target company and third parties remain in force and do not need to be assigned or renegotiated with the third party, although certain agreements may contain change-of-control provisions that may result in termination or other amendment to the agreement in the event of a change in ownership of the target company.

2.   TRANSACTION COSTS FOR PURCHASERS

2.1   Transfer Taxes

(a) *Stock purchases*   Bank transfer tax (CPMF) of 0.38 percent is imposed on transferred balances held within Brazilian bank accounts. This tax would be charged to the buyer of shares on the payment of the purchase price to the seller.

IOF of 5 percent is charged to the borrower of foreign loans with an average maturity of less than 90 days. IOF of 0.0041 percent per day—with a maximum of 1.5 percent per year—is assessed on the balance of loans among entities domiciled in Brazil.

(b) *Asset purchases*   CPMF of 0.38 percent is imposed on transferred balances held within Brazilian bank accounts. This tax would be charged to the buyer on the payment of purchase price to the seller.

Tax on the sale or transfer of properties (ITBI) is assessed in the range of 2 to 6 percent of the value of the transferred real property depending upon the municipality. ITBI is payable by the purchaser on a sale or transfer of real estate. This tax is imposed on the amount or value of the consideration allocated to land or real estate. ITBI is not imposed on a transfer of stock.

2.2   Value-Added Tax

(a) Stock purchases   Stock transfers are exempt from VAT.

(b) Asset purchases   Generally, the federation and the majority of the states of Brazil adopt VAT legislation consistent with the concept that the sale of business assets that qualify as a transfer of a unified business establishment or that constitute a going concern are exempt from VAT. To qualify for this exemption from VAT, the purchase and sale contract should include all of the assets to be transferred rather than a series of separate purchase and sale contracts.

A transfer that does not qualify as the transfer of a unified business establishment or that does not constitute the transfer of a going concern may or may not be subject to VAT, depending on the state in which the transaction is performed and the nature of the assets transferred. For example, generally no VAT is imposed on a transaction involving selected or individual assets such as separate pieces of machinery, equipment, or land (fixed assets). However, if inventory were to be transferred separately—that is, not as part of a broader transfer—state VAT (ICMS) and federal excise tax (IPI) likely would be imposed at the applicable rates, payable in addition to the purchase consideration. It is important to note that the rules related to ICMS vary by state. Consequently, parties to a transaction should consult a tax professional to verify the applicable legislation in the state in which the transaction is to take place.

When the buyer is subject to VAT independent of any transfer of a business enterprise and is therefore obligated to charge VAT on its sales (outputs) the buyer may recover VAT paid by the seller on purchases (inputs). A purchase of assets on which the seller has previously paid VAT is regarded as an input for the buyer. Therefore, such VAT paid by the seller may be recovered by the buyer—subject to limitations. Note that in some situations, depending on certain VAT-related characteristics of the buyer, the VAT paid on inputs may not always be recoverable in full, and, therefore, such VAT paid would be a real cost to the buyer.

2.3   PIS/COFINS

(a) Stock purchases   Stock purchases are exempt from PIS/COFINS.

(b) Asset purchases   An asset purchase that qualifies as the purchase of a unified business establishment or as a going concern is exempt from PIS/COFINS. However, an asset purchase consisting of specific assets that is subject to PIS/COFINS—payable by the seller but included in the purchase price—in some cases allows the buyer to credit the PIS/COFINS paid.

2.4   Capital Taxes

Capital taxes (e.g., stamp taxes) are not imposed in Brazil on either stock or asset purchases.

2.5   Tax Deductibility of Transaction Costs

The deductibility of a particular expense depends on several factors, including:

- Whether the transaction is structured as a purchase of assets or shares
- The nature of the expense and the reason such expense was incurred

The general rule with respect to deductibility is summarized in the following sections.

(a) Start-up and organizational expenses   Start-up and organizational expenses generally would include professional fees incurred to form an acquisition company and for related legal registrations. Start-up and organizational expenses are classified as deferred costs to be amortized over a period of 5 to 10 years, beginning in the period in which operations commence.

(b) Preoperational expenses   Preoperational expenses generally would include the hiring and training of personnel as well as testing and preproduction costs. Preoperational expenses are classified as deferred costs to be amortized over a period of 5 to 10 years, beginning in the period in which operations commence.

(c) Debt-financing costs   Debt-financing costs generally include bank arrangement fees and professional fees for obtaining such financing. Expenditures incurred with respect to the raising of debt financing are generally deductible at such time as the expenditures are recognized for income statement purposes pursuant to Brazilian generally accepted accounting principles (GAAP) amortizable over no more than five years.

(d) Investigation and due diligence costs   Due diligence and other investigation costs are typically deductible as a period expense in the period in which they are incurred regardless of whether the transaction was completed.

Costs attributable to the acquisition—such as certain costs of incorporating a new entity, registration costs associated with the CVM (the Brazilian equivalent of the US Securities and Exchange Commission), and costs of preparing a prospectus—are generally capitalized as part of the cost of the investment.

(e) VAT treatment of expenses   Professional fees incurred in connection with a transaction, such as financing arrangements and stock issuances, are not subject to VAT in Brazil. Therefore, VAT is generally not imposed with respect to

accounting, legal, financing, and institutional fees generally incurred in connection with an acquisition or transaction.

Furthermore, VAT charged by third parties for the provision of goods and services—such as telecommunications and electricity directly related to the transaction or the issuance of stock may be recoverable in full.

It is important that the description and nature of the costs should be identified separately on invoices to assist with the classification between period costs and capitalized costs.

3.   BASIS OF TAXATION FOLLOWING ASSET OR STOCK ACQUISITIONS

3.1   Asset Acquisitions

The purchaser is entitled to a cost purchase basis of the acquired assets. Aggregate purchase price is allocated to the acquired assets on a relative fair market value basis and generally should be supported by an independent appraisal. As a result of this allocation, capital allowances, or tax depreciation, of 4 percent per year are allowable on a straight-line basis with respect to buildings and building improvements. Also on a straight-line basis, 10 percent per year is allowable with respect to plant and machinery, 10 percent per year is allowable with respect to furniture and fixtures, and 20 percent per year is allowable with respect to computers, autos, and trucks. No depreciation is allowable with respect to the portion of aggregate purchase consideration allocated to inventory or land.

Aggregate purchase price is allocable to purchased intangible assets on the same relative fair market value basis but may not be subject to amortization. Purchased intangibles in the nature of leasehold improvements, author rights, patents, licenses, and trademarks may be amortized over a period that corresponds to their useful life. However, goodwill and other intangibles with an indeterminate useful life are not subject to amortization for tax purposes.

In general, the purchase and sale agreement documenting the transfer of a group of assets should expressly state the allocation of aggregate consideration to each asset transferred, with such allocation binding upon the buyer and seller for tax purposes. In the event the purchase and sale agreement does not provide a separate asset-by-asset allocation, buyers should obtain an independent appraisal to support their purchase price allocation.

3.2   Stock Acquisitions

(a) Purchase price   The tax basis of stock purchased is equal to the purchase consideration paid. The adjusted tax basis in the acquired company's assets is unaffected by the stock purchase, and no election is available to increase the tax basis of assets to reflect the consideration paid for the stock. Under Brazilian

GAAP, the acquisition is reflected in the acquirer's books and records based on the net book value of the acquired company. Any excess of the purchase price over net book value is recorded as goodwill. Accounting goodwill arising on the merger of the acquired company and the Brazilian purchasing company may be tax deductible under certain circumstances. (See Section 6.2.)

(b) *Tax grouping*   Brazil imposes tax on a separate-entity basis and does not recognize the concept of a consolidated tax return. Consequently, operating profits and losses (as well as capital gains and losses subject to some restrictions) arising in the same period cannot be combined and offset between members of the same economic group. The offsetting of profits and losses between members of the same group can be achieved only through a merger.

4.   FINANCING OF ACQUISITIONS

4.1   Debt

The tax treatment of debt and the interest charged on it is as follows:

- Withholding tax
- Deductibility of interest
- Thin capitalization
- Other factors

(a) *Withholding tax*   Interest accruing with respect to indebtedness originating from an offshore lender is subject to a withholding tax of 15 percent. The withholding tax liability becomes due upon the credit of interest and is determined in accordance with the terms of the loan agreement regardless of whether the interest is actually paid. Therefore, withholding-tax liability arises when the borrower defaults after the interest due date and the lender forgives or capitalizes the accrued interest. There are only limited instances when the 15 percent withholding rate can be reduced by virtue of a tax treaty. Moreover, the withholding-tax rate increases to 25 percent with respect to interest that accrues to a lender domiciled in a tax haven—that is, any jurisdiction where the effective tax rate is less than 20 percent. The Brazilian debtor acts as the withholding-tax agent for purposes of collecting and remitting the withholding tax.

Additionally, a withholding tax is imposed on interest accruing between Brazilian entities—excluding interest paid to a financial institution—at the rate of 20 percent.

(b) *Deductibility of interest*   Interest expense related to acquisition indebtedness or interest expense related to operational activities is generally deductible for income tax purposes on an accrual basis.

(c) Thin capitalization   There are no thin-capitalization rules under Brazilian law.

(d) Other factors   The following factors should be considered with respect to debt financing:

- Transfer pricing
- Taxes on loans

(i) Transfer pricing   Interest on foreign related-party loans that are duly authorized by the Brazilian Central Bank are not subject to Brazilian transfer pricing rules. Correspondingly, interest arising from a loan contracted with a foreign related party that is registered but not authorized by the Brazilian Central Bank is deductible only to the extent that the interest rate equals the London Interbank Offered Rate (LIBOR) for six-month deposits plus a 3 percent annual spread. When the interest rate exceeds this threshold, the excess interest can be recharacterized as a nondeductible distribution

(i) Taxes on loans   A federal tax on financial transaction (IOF) is levied on certain financial transactions, including foreign loans and foreign exchange transactions. The current IOF rate for foreign loans with an average maturity of less than 90 days is 5 percent and is 0 percent for foreign loans with an average maturity of more than 90 days. Loans between Brazilian entities are subject to IOF assessed at the rate of 0.0041 percent per day, or approximately 1.5 percent per year. It is important to note that IOF can be changed at any time, subject to a maximum of 25 percent.

4.2   Equity

There is no capital duty tax imposed on the issuance of new stock. Dividends paid on stock are not deductible to the company paying the dividend regardless of whether such stock is ordinary or preferred stock. Under Brazilian law, dividends are not taxable to the recipient. Therefore, a Brazilian company or individual receiving such dividends is not taxed. Additionally, there is no withholding tax on the payment of dividends paid to recipients located in Brazil or paid to offshore recipients, including tax havens.

5.   MERGERS

Under Brazilian law, a transaction described as a merger involves an operation whereby either two or more companies are combined into a surviving company or two or more companies form a new entity, and this company assumes all rights and obligations associated with the former company with regard to tax and labor matters. In neither case is the surviving company entitled to use tax loss carryforwards of the extinct company. For tax purposes, a merger between an acquiring company and a target company that is accounted for at historical net-carrying-book values is a nontaxable transaction.

In a merger transaction, the surviving company, in effect, steps into the shoes of its predecessor company for purposes of succession liability. As a result, the acquiring company becomes primarily liable for any indirect taxes associated with the acquired assets and becomes primarily liable for any labor liabilities associated with employees previously performing services for the acquired company. Moreover, the acquiring company becomes secondarily liable for direct taxes of the target company in cases when the transferred assets have the capacity to generate income, which generally consists of the core operating assets or a division of the acquired company. It is important to note that in a merger, the net operating losses of the merged company are extinguished and cannot be transferred to the survivor. Therefore, a common way to overcome this restriction is to structure the merger in a manner whereby the company with the larger net operating losses survives the transaction.

Generally, the transfer of a unified business establishment is not subject to VAT, whereas the transfer of independent assets may be subject to VAT.

6. OTHER STRUCTURING AND POSTDEAL ISSUES

6.1   Buyer's Preacquisition Structuring

Brazilian law is based on the concept of equality, and foreign investors are generally entitled to the same tax treatment as their local counterparts. However, for purposes of structuring the acquisition of a Brazilian target company by a foreign strategic or financial buyer, it is generally recommended that a Brazilian company rather than a foreign company be utilized as the acquisition vehicle. The primary advantage of using a Brazilian acquisition company is to provide the foreign investor with a basis for recognizing amortization deductions with respect to acquired goodwill for tax purposes.

6.2   Conversion of Recorded Goodwill into a Tax-Deductible Asset

As previously mentioned, it is possible to reduce the effective Brazilian corporate income tax by creating amortization deductions for the premium, or goodwill, paid to acquire the shares of a Brazilian corporation. Under Brazilian law, the acquiring company is generally required to record its investment based on the net book value of the acquired company, and the difference between the price paid and the net book value is recorded as goodwill, in the case of a premium, or negative goodwill, in the case of a discount. It should be noted that the mere recording of goodwill by the acquirer does not enable that company to amortize it for tax purposes. However, depending on the justification for the payment of the goodwill and the postacquisition structure adopted, Brazilian legislation provides that the goodwill paid by an acquiring company may be amortized for tax purposes.

6.3   Preservation of Existing Tax Attributes

An income tax loss is equal to the accounting loss for the year, adjusted for certain items. Income tax losses may be carried forward indefinitely but may not be carried back to a prior period. An income tax loss carried forward may not, however, be used to offset more than 30 percent of the taxable income of the year in which it is utilized. Except during the year incurred, capital losses can be offset only against capital gains. Capital losses are tracked separately from income tax losses and are subject to the same rules governing tax losses with respect to limits on their use and carryforward period.

Tax losses and other, similar tax attributes of the target company generally are not affected by a change of ownership—at least insofar as the change in ownership does not, of itself, cause such tax losses or attributes to be lost. However, when a Brazilian company experiences both a change of control in the amount of 50 percent or more and a change in business activity, the tax losses are extinguished.

6.4   Receipts under Warranties or Indemnities

Generally, payments made by the seller for breach of warranty or under an indemnity provision are taxable to the purchaser. Accordingly, the sales-and-purchase documentation typically contains a clause stipulating that any such payment is to be treated as an adjustment to the consideration offered and received for the transaction. Consequently, in such circumstances, the receipt is not immediately taxable but is instead treated as a reduction of the purchaser's tax basis in the stock acquired.

If the warranties and indemnity payments are made to the target company, they are likely to be subject to tax in the target company.

7.   DISPOSALS

7.1   Stock Disposals

(a) *Companies*

(i) Disposal for cash consideration   Corporate entities are subject to tax on capital gains imposed at the rate of 34 percent on the disposition of stock to the extent that the purchase price is in excess of the tax carrying basis of the stock sold.

To reduce the taxable gain, the selling company may be able to utilize any current year's capital losses or capital loss carryforwards—subject to the limit.

(ii) Exchange of securities for those in another company: stock swap

A transaction in which the shareholders of company A transfer partial or total control of company A to the shareholders of company B in exchange for partial or total control of company B is commonly referred to as a stock swap. Under Brazilian GAAP, such transactions generally require the parties to the exchange to account for any positive or negative goodwill arising from the transaction. Goodwill in this case represents the difference between the net book value of the equity transferred and the net book value of equity received. Positive goodwill would be subject to amortization expense, and negative goodwill would be amortized into income. Various forms of this transaction have become increasingly popular in recent years in order to reduce the tax burden arising from a straight purchase and sale transaction. However, use of the stock swap is based on jurisprudence because the legislation does not specifically address the tax consequences of such a transaction.

There is no VAT on the exchange of shares. As previously noted, stock transactions are exempt from the imposition of PIS and COFINS.

(b) Individuals   Individuals disposing of an interest in stock are subject to capital gains tax. The capital gains tax rate applicable for individuals is 15 percent. The calculation of an individual's taxable gain generally is computed as the difference between sales proceeds less tax basis. There is no distinction between short-term and long-term gains.

7.2   Asset Disposals (Companies Only)

In general, a sale of assets by a company is subject to a capital gains tax imposed at 34 percent on the excess if any between the sales price and the tax basis of the asset. As capital gains are subject to the same tax rate as ordinary income, the distinction between a capital asset and an ordinary asset is less relevant for corporations. The seller can shelter taxable gains against current-year capital losses and capital loss carryforwards—subject to the 30 percent limitation discussed earlier.

It is important to note that any taxable gains recorded by the seller that increase taxable income and, therefore, increase distributable reserves are available for distribution to the shareholders of the seller company in the form of a tax-free dividend. Under this scenario, the proceeds of an asset sale do not remain locked in the company. However, distribution of these proceeds may result in tax liabilities at the shareholder level to the extent that the distribution exceeds the sum of distributable reserves and the tax basis of the shareholder's stock. Shareholder tax treatment depends on the nature of the distribution (e.g., dividend, return of capital, or capital gain).

7.3   Deferred Consideration and Earn-Outs

Generally, if an amount of deferred consideration is fixed and determinable at the time of the disposal, the full amount is included in the tax calculation of the disposal proceeds at the time of the sale. However, if receipt of the deferred consideration is subject to a contingency, for example, determined by reference to formula or future event, the contingent amount is included in taxable income only when it is received by the seller.

7.4   Payments under Warranties or Indemnities

Where the sales-and-purchase documentation contains a clause that any warranty or indemnity payment is to be treated as an adjustment to the consideration offered and received for the transaction, the payment is generally treated for tax purposes as a reduction in the purchase consideration received.

8.   TRANSACTION COSTS FOR SELLERS

8.1   Transfer Taxes

(a) *Stock disposals*   Stock sales are exempt from PIS and COFINS.

(b) *Asset disposals*   Brazilian law stipulates that a transaction involving a Brazilian buyer's purchasing a group of assets that represent a unified business establishment or fixed assets is exempt from the imposition of PIS/COFINS. However, transactions involving the sale of separate assets that do not qualify for one of the exemptions mentioned (unified business establishment or permanent assets) are subject to PIS/COFINS assessed at the rates of 1.65 and 7.6 percent, respectively.

8.2   VAT

(a) *Stock disposals*   A disposal of stock is exempt from VAT.

(b) *Asset disposals*   Asset disposals that are subject to VAT result in the seller's being liable for the collection and payment of such tax. However, because the tax is included in the purchase price of the asset, the buyer bears the economic burden of such tax. It should be noted that in the event the buyer is a VAT taxpayer, the VAT taxes included on the purchase price may be used as a credit to offset VAT taxes payable. (See Section 2.2(b).)

8.3   Tax Deductibility of Transaction Costs

In general, whether or not a particular expense is treated as deductible or as capitalized depends on several factors, including:

- The relationship between the cost and the investment—for example, whether the benefits associated with the cost extend beyond the current tax period
- The reason the expense was incurred

In general terms, the position on corporation tax treatment of expenses can be summarized as follows:

- For companies disposing of shares
- For companies disposing of assets

(a) *For companies disposing of shares*   As a general rule, costs incurred after the decision to dispose of a company has actually been taken are likely to constitute costs of disposing of an investment (e.g., sell-side due diligence) while the costs incurred prior to that point might be regarded as costs of managing investments (e.g., evaluating potential disposal strategies).

Costs related to initial speculative advice on potential disposal possibilities or strategies are generally deductible for tax purposes or, alternatively, capitalized and amortized over a period corresponding to the expected future benefit of that cost and may be written off for tax purposes upon disposal of the related asset.

Costs related to the sales process in general and, particularly, costs related to detailed negotiation with a specific bidder—whether or not such negotiations culminate in the execution of the sale and purchase agreement—are generally considered as period costs and deductible for tax purposes.

(b) *For companies disposing of assets*   Costs incurred as part of the disposal process generally are deductible for the purposes of computing the seller's taxable income.

In computing the corporation tax on chargeable gains on the sale of certain capital assets (see Section 7.2), a deduction may be claimed for certain costs of disposal incurred wholly and exclusively in relation to that asset—for example, asset valuation fees, any costs of transfer, and related legal fees. Expenses incurred as part of the transaction as a whole—for example, the majority of, if not all, legal fees relating to the deal—and those expenses not specifically and solely incurred in relation to that capital asset are likely to be deducted for tax purposes.

9. PREPARING A TARGET COMPANY FOR SALE

9.1 Preacquisition Restructuring: Hive-Down of Assets

It is common in Brazil for a selling corporation to engage in a preacquisition reorganization to achieve the mutual objectives of the buyer and seller. Such transactions typically involve a situation in which the buyer desires to purchase a specific division or a certain group of assets (target assets), or in which a specific liability needs to be excluded from the sale, or in which the seller desires to retain certain assets and, for tax reasons, a stock transaction is preferable to an asset transaction. In these cases, the Brazilian selling company may drop down or spin off the target assets and liabilities to a newly formed subsidiary (Newco) at book value in a nontaxable transaction.

Transactions involving the transfer of a unified business establishment to a subsidiary—a hive-down—are not subject to VAT.

9.2 Intragroup Transfer of Assets Being Retained

Assets may be transferred between members of the same group if it is intended that those assets are to be excluded from an overall sale. Provided that this transfer or drop-down is performed at book value, capital gain is not recognized, and therefore no capital gain tax is imposed.

Transactions involving the transfer of assets between members of a controlled group may be subject to VAT. It is recommended that tax professionals be consulted to verify the tax consequences applicable in the state in which the transaction is to be performed.

9.3 Presale Dividends

Presale dividends paid by the target company to shareholders out of its distributable reserves are exempt from tax.

10. DEMERGERS

10.1 Spin-Offs

A spin-off may be used simply to separate different operating activities in different groups or to partition operating activities between different groups of shareholders.

Under Brazilian law, the corporate law concept of a spin-off involves a transaction under which a single company is split into two or more separate companies or entities and the shares of the spun-off companies are distributed to the shareholders.

A spin-off involves the formation of a new subsidiary by a parent or the use of an existing subsidiary. The parent transfers assets and or liabilities to the wholly owned subsidiary at book value on a tax-free basis. Subsequent to the transfer of assets, the company distributes stock of the subsidiary directly to shareholders. The shareholders continue to hold their original stock but now also directly hold stock in the spun-off subsidiary.

The tax treatment of a demerger (spin-off) can be summarized as follows:

Shareholders	**Brazilian individuals** Distribution is tax free, provided the transaction is performed at book value. The tax basis of the individual shareholder's shares in the distributing company is reallocated to the shares received based on relative net book values. **Brazilian companies** Distribution is tax free, provided the transaction is performed at book value. The tax basis of the corporate shareholder's shares in the distributing company is reallocated to the shares received based on relative net book values.
Distributing company	**Distribution of stock** Exempt from tax on capital gains, provided the transaction is carried out at book value.
Tax attributes	**Net operating losses (NOLs)** Distributing company reduces its balance of NOLs in proportion to the equity transferred, but no NOLs are transferred to the Newco.

11.   LISTINGS AND INITIAL PUBLIC OFFERINGS

11.1   Impact on Tax Status of Listing a Company and Its Subsidiaries

Under Brazilian legislation, only a company classified as a *sociedade anônima* (S.A.) can be a listed public company. The regulatory requirements are more rigorous for an S.A. than for a *limitada*.

11.2   Complete Group Listing or Initial Public Offering

When this occurs, it is common for a new company to be set up as the listed vehicle (Holdco). Forming Holdco can generally be accomplished on a tax-neutral basis.

11.3   Listing or Initial Public Offering of Subsidiary

The immediate implications for the existing parent of a listing of a subsidiary are:

- If the parent sells in the market (i.e., lists) some of its existing stock in a subsidiary, the parent is subject to corporation tax on gains realized on the disposal of stock.
- If a subsidiary issues new stock, the parent has not itself sold any stock. Therefore, no tax charge arises.

11.4   Issue of New Stock by Listed Company

The issue of new stock by the listed company whether a parent or a subsidiary has no tax consequences for the company.

11.5   Disposal of Stock by Existing Shareholders

When the public offering involves a disposal of stock by existing shareholders, the tax consequences to those shareholders are as outlined in Section 7.1.

CANADA

INTRODUCTION

This chapter details the principal tax issues that are relevant to purchasers and sellers engaged in the transfer of ownership of a Canadian trade or business. Unless otherwise stated, it is generally assumed that all sellers and purchasers are Canadian companies with limited liability.

The transfer of ownership of a Canadian business or company may take many distinct forms, the most common being the disposal of shares or the disposal of assets. While there are significant differences in the tax implications of an asset or share sale, nontax considerations must also be considered. The tax implications are discussed in greater detail in the following paragraphs.

The relevant taxes to be considered are:

- **Federal income tax.** Generally, this is a 22.1 percent tax on active business income earned by a company. However, if a company is a Canadian-controlled private corporation that meets certain criteria, the rate may be reduced to 13.1 percent. Canadian companies are taxed on a stand-alone basis even if they are members of an associated group, because there are no provisions to file on a consolidated basis.

- **Provincial and territorial income tax.** All provinces and territories impose income tax on income allocable to a permanent establishment in the province or territory. Income is generally allocated to a province or territory by using a two-factor formula based on gross revenue and on salaries and wages. Provincial and territorial income taxes are not deductible for income tax purposes. Provincial and territorial taxes range from 3 to 17 percent depending on the nature of the income and the province or territory to which it is allocated.

- **Goods-and-services tax.** The federal goods-and-services tax (GST) is levied at a rate of 7 percent. It is a value-added tax (VAT) applied at each level in the manufacturing and marketing chain, and applies to most goods and services. However, the tax does not apply to sales of zero-rated goods, such as exports and groceries, or to tax-exempt supplies, such as certain services provided by financial institutions.

  Generally, businesses pay GST on their purchases and charge GST on their sales and remit the net amount—that is, the difference between the GST collected and the input tax credit for the tax paid on the purchases. Suppliers of zero-rated goods and services are entitled to input tax credits with respect to such goods. Suppliers of tax-exempt goods are not entitled to input tax credits with respect to such goods.

- **Harmonized sales tax.** New Brunswick, Newfoundland and Labrador, and Nova Scotia harmonized their sales tax systems with the GST and impose a single sales tax (HST) that combines the provincial sales tax at a rate of 8 percent and the 7 percent GST. The 15 percent HST is imposed on essentially the same basis as the GST.

- **Retail sales tax.** British Columbia, Manitoba, Ontario, Prince Edward Island, and Saskatchewan levy retail sales tax at rates ranging from 6 to 10 percent on most purchases of tangible personal property for consumption or use in the province and on the purchase of specific services.

  Quebec's sales tax is essentially the same as the GST. Quebec has broadened its sales tax base to include most of the goods and services subject to GST. The general Quebec sales tax rate is 7.5 percent. Quebec administers the GST in that province.

- **Property transfer tax.** Property transfer tax is imposed on the purchaser of real property in the provinces of Alberta, British Columbia, Manitoba, New Brunswick, Nova Scotia, Ontario, Quebec, and Saskatchewan. The rates vary by province but generally range from 1 to 2 percent of the fair market value of the property transferred.

1.   ACQUISITIONS

The purchase and sale of a business have many variables and potential alternatives. Either the shareholder may sell the shares of the company directly to the purchaser, or the shareholder may sell all of the assets or only some of the assets of the business to the purchaser, pay any applicable taxes, and distribute the after-tax profits as dividends.

1.1   Asset Acquisitions

In an asset acquisition, the vendor sells the assets of the corporation to the purchaser, pays any applicable taxes in the corporation (corporate taxes, sales taxes, and transfer taxes), and ultimately distributes the after-tax proceeds to the shareholders.

One advantage of an asset acquisition, from the purchaser's perspective, is that the cost base of the individual assets purchased is the fair market value of each asset included in the purchase price. To the extent that fair market value of the depreciable assets exceeds the net book value or tax cost, there could be an opportunity to obtain a higher tax base for subsequent depreciation claims against future income. To the extent that the aggregate purchase price of assets exceeds the fair market value of the identifiable assets, the excess is treated as purchased goodwill. A total of 75 percent of goodwill acquired in a purchase transaction is amortizable for tax purposes at a rate of 7 percent of the aggregate goodwill per year.

Another advantage to the purchaser in an asset acquisition is the ability to avoid exposure to the risk of any historical liabilities—both recorded and unrecorded—that are not specifically assumed through the sale agreement. Liabilities associated with the business being purchased remain the responsibility of the company that has made the asset sale and do not become the responsibility of the purchaser unless the parties contractually agree that specified liabilities are to be assumed by the purchaser.

Another important nontax consideration is that on a sale of assets, contracts between the seller and third parties may not be automatically assigned to the purchaser. Therefore, it may be necessary for the purchaser either to enter into new contracts with the third parties or to agree with third parties that the existing contracts be assigned from seller to purchaser. This may cause practical difficulties, particularly when there are numerous contracts or when a third party is unwilling to permit assignment.

One significant disadvantage arising out of a purchase of assets is that the sale of the assets is taxable at the selling-company level. Accordingly, capital gains and income inclusion may result to the extent that the value of the assets sold exceeds the tax basis for those assets. Whether or not the seller has to pay tax at the company level depends on the tax attributes of the company. In all likelihood, this will be the case. In addition, distribution of the sale proceeds by the selling company to its shareholders will likely result in taxable income to the shareholder because individual shareholder recipients are further taxed on any dividends received.

1.2   Stock Acquisitions

A share acquisition results in the purchaser's effectively assuming any historical and future ongoing tax and nontax liabilities of the target company. Generally, no step-up in the tax basis of the acquired assets is permitted, and no amortizable asset representing the excess of the consideration paid for the shares over the fair market value of the acquired assets is recognized. However, there are elections that may be made by the seller in the final tax return prior to the acquisition of control to increase the tax cost of certain capital properties in order to use losses that would otherwise expire. To the extent there are historical unused losses, these may be claimed following a change in control, provided the business originally incurring such tax losses continues to be carried on. (See Section 3.2 for the basis of taxation following a share acquisition.)

As a result, from a purchaser's perspective, it is often beneficial to acquire assets rather than shares in order to obtain increased depreciation claims.

From a seller's perspective, if the seller is an individual, the sale of shares may be beneficial because the seller may qualify for the enhanced capital gains exemption, which eliminates tax on the first CAD$500,000 of capital gains on the sale of the shares. This, however, depends on the nature of the company being sold. In addition, for both individual and corporate vendors, only 50 percent of a capital gain is taxable for Canadian tax purposes. Therefore, depending on the seller's province of residence, the tax on the sale of shares could be as low as 19.5 percent—as in Alberta—or as high as 26.5 percent, as in Quebec.

2.   TRANSACTION COSTS FOR PURCHASERS

2.1   Goods-and-Services Tax, Harmonized Sales Tax, and Retail Sales Taxes

(a) Share purchases   Share purchases are generally exempt from GST, HST, and retail sales taxes.

(b) Asset purchases   Ordinarily, GST is collectible by the seller of the assets unless special relieving provisions apply. If both the seller and the purchaser are GST registrants, the corporations may jointly elect to relieve both parties from paying the GST on the sale of a business. This election is applicable only if substantially all of the assets of the business are sold.

If the election is not available, the seller will have to collect and remit GST on the taxable assets of the business that are disposed of by the purchaser. The purchaser may claim the GST paid as an input tax credit. As a result, there should be no GST leakage, but there is normally a timing difference between the GST payable and the GST recovered.

In general, real estate and assets purchased for resale are exempt from retail sales taxes. However, all assets sold should be reviewed in detail by an expert in order to determine the extent of exposure to GST, HST, or retail sales taxes and to ensure that the appropriate taxes are collected and remitted and that all applicable elections are made in a timely fashion.

2.2   Property Transfer Taxes

Property transfer tax applies to the purchaser on registration of the property purchased. The tax is levied in the provinces of Alberta, British Columbia, Manitoba, New Brunswick, Nova Scotia, Ontario, Quebec, and Saskatchewan. The rates vary by province and are generally from 1 to 2 percent of the fair market value of the property transferred. The tax is not deductible, but it can be added to the tax base of the property.

2.3   Tax Deductibility of Transaction Costs

In Canada, transaction costs are deductible only to the extent that they are incurred for the purpose of producing income from a business or property, and they are not deductible to the extent that they are incurred as a capital expenditure. Transaction costs that are capital in nature are added to the cost base of the assets or shares acquired and reduce any gain on their subsequent disposal.

In general terms, this position may be summarized as follows:

- Structuring costs
- Financing costs
- Investigation and due diligence costs
- Other deal costs

(a) Structuring costs   Costs incurred either (1) to organize and form a new company, or (2) in connection with an amalgamation of two or more companies, or (3) in connection with the reorganization of the affairs of a corporation, are generally deductible as eligible capital expenditures (ECE). The tax deduction for ECE is limited to 75 percent of their cost and may be recovered at a rate of 7 percent per year.

(b) Financing costs   Fees incurred in connection with obtaining financing—for example, costs associated with issuing bonds, debentures, and mortgages and with borrowing money for certain business or property purposes—and/or with refinancing or restructuring existing indebtedness are generally deductible over a five-year period.

(c) Investigation and due diligence costs   Due diligence and other investigation costs generally are not deductible unless they can be linked to the issuance of debt. In the event that the costs are not deductible, they can be added to the cost base of the shares or assets acquired as capital expenditures as discussed earlier.

(d) Other deal costs   As noted earlier, items of a capital nature are not deductible. Accordingly, other costs incurred in connection with the acquisition of a business are generally characterized as capital costs that can be added only to the cost base of the assets or shares acquired.

(e) GST treatment of expenses   GST costs incurred by a registered purchaser would be recoverable (i.e., refundable) provided the purchaser is registered for GST purposes prior to incurring the liability.

3.   BASIS OF TAXATION FOLLOWING ASSET OR STOCK ACQUISITIONS

3.1   Asset Acquisitions

In general, the seller and the purchaser negotiate a total price for the assets being purchased. Accordingly, the seller and the purchaser typically negotiate an allocation of aggregate purchase price to each of the various assets. The allocation determines (1) the seller's income tax resulting from the sale, (2) the purchaser's transfer and sales taxes on the purchase price, and (3) the purchaser's future tax deductions deriving from the amortization of the cost of the assets for tax purposes. Because the purchaser and the seller generally have opposing interests in an allocation of the purchase price, the Canada Revenue Agency (CRA) generally accepts a mutually-agreed-upon allocation. However, when the two parties are dealing in a non-arm's-length fashion, the CRA may reallocate the components of the purchase price.

This section addresses tax implications of the purchase price allocation to the purchaser. Section 7.2 addresses implications to the seller.

Typically, accounts receivable are acquired at their net book value or carrying cost. A joint election is generally available to the seller and the purchaser whereby the amount that the seller is allowed as a deduction in the year of sale must be included in the purchaser's income in the year of purchase. In general terms, the joint election allows the seller to deduct any loss incurred on the sale of the accounts receivable—that is, the difference between proceeds received and face value of the accounts receivable—and requires the purchasing company to include the seller's loss in its income. The purchaser may then deal with the accounts receivable for tax purposes as though they had arisen while the purchaser was the owner of the business; that is, the purchaser may claim a reserve for doubtful debts and deduct bad debts. To the extent that the purchaser collects on a receivable that was previously written off by the seller, it must be included in the purchaser's income. Essentially, the joint election ensures income treatment (i.e., inclusion in trading profits)—on the purchase and sale of the accounts receivable.

If the purchaser and the seller are not able to make the joint election, any loss on the sale of the accounts receivable is a capital loss to the seller—and deductible only against capital gains. From the purchaser's perspective, if the election is not made, any gain or loss on realization of the accounts receivable is a capital gain or loss to the purchaser.

Sales of inventory normally are included in the seller's trading profits, and the purchaser receives tax basis equal to the value of the inventory purchased.

With respect to the sale of nondepreciable capital property such as land, the purchaser generally receives a tax basis equal to the value of the land purchased.

With respect to depreciable capital properties, capital cost allowance (tax depreciation) is available on the purchase price paid. Capital cost allowance is calculated based on a pooling of assets. All assets of a certain type, or class, are included in the pool, and then tax depreciation is claimed on that pool. The rates of capital cost allowance vary widely depending on the type of asset. They may be as low as 4 percent per year and as high as 100 percent per year depending on the class of asset. These rates are generally reduced by 50 percent in the year of acquisition. Generally, an asset retains its character when it is purchased and, for the purchaser, is included in the same class it occupied when it was recorded on the seller's tax returns. However, there are certain assets that do not retain their character when they are sold. In these cases, the assets are reclassified with, normally, a less favorable rate of tax depreciation.

A total of 75 percent of purchased intangible assets, including goodwill, are eligible for tax depreciation at a rate of 7 percent per year.

3.2   Share Acquisitions

The purchase price forms the cost base of the purchaser's stock in the acquired company. The underlying cost base in the acquired company's assets is unaffected.

On filing the final tax return prior to acquisition of control by the purchaser, the vendor has the ability to make certain elections to increase the tax basis of certain capital properties in order to use losses that would otherwise expire.

4.   FINANCING OF ACQUISITIONS

4.1   Debt

Specific tax issues related to the overall level of borrowings and the interest charged on the debt used for financing an acquisition are:

- Withholding tax
- Deductibility of interest
- Thin capitalizaton

(a) *Withholding tax*   Canada imposes a 25 percent withholding tax on interest payments to nonresidents, subject to relief under an applicable tax treaty.

Some exceptions exist to the requirement to withhold tax on interest payments to a nonresident. The most common exception applies to interest paid by a Canadian resident corporation to an arm's-length nonresident, pursuant to an obligation wherein the creditor cannot oblige the Canadian debtor to repay more than 25 percent of the outstanding loan principal within five years from the date of issue. This exemption from withholding tax is provided in order to make it easier for Canadian borrowers to obtain medium- and long-term debt financing abroad.

There is no withholding tax on interest payments between Canadian resident companies.

(b) Deductibility of interest In Canada, an amount is considered to be interest if it (1) represents compensation for the use of money, (2) is referable to a principal sum, and (3) accrues on a daily basis.

Generally, interest can be deducted if all of the following requirements are met: (1) the amount is to be paid in the year of deduction or is payable with respect to such year, (2) the amount is paid pursuant to a legal obligation, and (3) the amount of interest is reasonable. As a separate restriction, interest can be deducted only when the taxpayer can demonstrate that the direct purpose of such borrowings is for the production of income. For example, interest paid or accrued with respect to funds borrowed to acquire property can generally be deducted only when the taxpayer can demonstrate that the property was acquired for the purpose of producing income. Therefore, interest that meets the requirements noted earlier is generally deductible when it is paid or payable. If interest compounds (i.e., interest accruing on interest)—it is deductible only when it is paid.

Generally, interest incurred on indebtedness related to purchasing the shares or assets of a target company is deductible because such acquisitions are made with the purpose of producing income.

In addition to the aforementioned requirements that must be met for interest to be deductible, purchasers should be aware that in non-arm's-length lending situations, interest must be paid by the end of the second taxation year following the year in which it was incurred. If the interest is not paid by the end of the second taxation year, the amount is included in the income of the borrower in the third taxation year. Therefore, assuming that the interest meets the requirements noted earlier, it is generally deductible when paid or payable. However, in non-arm's-length situations, the interest deducted must be paid by the end of the second taxation year. If it is not paid by that time, it is included in the income of the borrower in the third taxation year.

(c) Thin capitalization When a Canadian company borrows from a significant nonresident shareholder, there may be a restriction on the interest deduction under the thin-capitalization rules. For the purposes of the thin-capitalization rules, a significant shareholder is someone who owns shares entitling the holder to at least 25 percent of the votes cast at any annual shareholder meeting or who owns shares having a fair market value of 25 percent or more of the fair market value of all of the issued shares of a corporation. The rules can also deem a person to own shares when contingent rights or options exist.

Canadian thin-capitalization rules limit the deduction of interest to the extent that the debt-to-equity ratio exceeds 2:1. These complex rules require a monthly analysis of the ratio and may result in a denial of interest expense. There is no carryforward of these deductions to a subsequent year. As a result, withholding tax may be incurred with no income tax benefits arising on the interest payment.

4.2   Equity

Dividends paid with respect to shares are not deductible by the company paying the dividend regardless of whether the shares are ordinary or preferred shares. A Canadian company receiving such dividends is not taxed on the dividends—except for certain Canadian controlled private corporations owning less than 10 percent of the dividend-paying corporation and the payer corporation gains a tax refund with respect to the payment of dividends. A Canadian individual is taxed on dividends received. There is no withholding tax on the payment of dividends from a Canadian company to Canada residents.

The payment of dividends to a nonresident attracts a 25 percent withholding tax, as discussed in Section 4.1(a). The level of withholding tax may be reduced if the dividend is paid to the resident of a country having a tax treaty with Canada.

5.   MERGERS

Mergers are tax-free combinations of companies within Canada. There are a number of legal alternatives to achieve a tax-free merger, each of which should be carefully reviewed by a professional adviser prior to implementation.

Generally, mergers occur in one of two forms: an amalgamation or a tax-free liquidation.

5.1   Amalgamation

To achieve a tax-free amalgamation of companies resident in Canada, the amalgamating companies must combine their assets and liabilities, and the shareholders must receive new shares in the amalgamated entity. Liabilities existing prior to the amalgamation are assumed by the new amalgamated entity. Assets transfer to the newly amalgamated company at the existing (i.e., carryover) tax basis. The shareholders are treated as exchanging their shares as in a disposition for tax purposes, but generally no tax arises on the exchange—except for nonresident shareholders or shareholders receiving consideration other than shares.

5.2   Tax-Free Liquidation

A tax-free liquidation is permitted in Canada when a parent company dissolves a subsidiary company in which it owns at least 90 percent of the shares, so long as both companies are resident in Canada.

5.3   Income Tax Considerations

Generally, the tax characteristics of companies amalgamating or being liquidated carry over to the resulting company. An amalgamation, however, triggers a year-end for tax purposes, and if there is a change in control, there may be adverse income tax consequences as outlined in Section 6.4. In the case of a tax-free liquidation, no year-end is triggered, but the parent company may not have immediate use of a subsidiary's prior tax losses.

6.   OTHER STRUCTURING AND POSTDEAL ISSUES

6.1   Creation of Local-Country Tax Groups

In Canada, each company is a separate entity for tax purposes. Accordingly, tax consolidation is not available. With proper structuring, however, related Canadian companies may be reorganized to permit utilization of deductions and losses by related profitable companies.

6.2   Repatriation of Profits

Dividends paid within a Canadian group are generally exempt from tax.

To the extent a Canadian company receives dividends from a foreign subsidiary, the Canadian company may claim relief from taxes paid in the foreign country. This relief is normally given by way of a tax credit against Canadian tax payable.

6.3   Cash Repatriation

Cash can be repatriated within a Canadian group by the payment of dividends to the extent there are profits available to be distributed. Dividends paid within a Canadian group are generally exempt from tax.

6.4   Preservation of Existing Tax Attributes

Tax losses and other similar tax attributes of the target company are affected by an acquisition resulting in a change of control of the target company. When control is acquired, a deemed year-end is triggered. For tax purposes, a deemed year-end has the same filing and payment deadlines as a normal year-end. The effects on the existing tax attributes are discussed later.

(a) *Noncapital losses (operating losses)*   The use of noncapital losses is limited after an acquisition of control. Generally, preacquisition noncapital losses are deductible following a change of control only to the extent that such losses arose from ordinary business operations and so long as the businesses that gave rise to such losses are carried on during the year in which the deduction is claimed. In other words, a continuity of business enterprise with respect to post-acquisition utilization of preacquisition noncapital losses is required.

Noncapital losses may be carried forward seven years and carried back three years. A change of control does not eliminate preacquisition noncapital losses.

(b) Net capital losses   Net capital losses that have not been utilized expire on the acquisition of control and are therefore eliminated. Any capital losses incurred after the acquisition cannot be carried back for a refund of income taxes previously paid.

Prior to an acquisition of control, all nondepreciable capital property must be valued. To the extent that such property has declined in value, a capital loss is deemed to be realized. However, the corporation may elect that any capital property that has increased in value from its adjusted cost base be deemed to be disposed of for proceeds of up to the asset's fair market value in order to use any capital losses that would otherwise expire on the acquisition of control.

(c) Depreciable property   When control of a company has been acquired, the tax cost of the depreciable property of each class is deemed to be written down to the fair market value of all of the assets of that class. The excess capital cost is deemed to have been claimed as capital cost allowance for the taxation year ending before the acquisition of control. This calculation is made on a class-by-class basis. As discussed earlier, the company undergoing a change of control may elect to write up the tax-carrying value of any depreciable property that experiences an increase in value.

6.5   Receipts under Warranties or Indemnities

Generally, payments made by the seller for breach of warranty or under an indemnity are taxable to the purchaser. However, the CRA has stated that amounts paid by the seller to honor the assumed warranty liabilities are not deductible expenditures, because they have been made on account of capital. Accordingly, in such circumstances, the receipt is treated as a reduction of the seller's tax basis in the shares acquired.

7.   DISPOSALS

7.1   Stock Disposals

(a) Companies

(i) Disposal for cash consideration   Canadian corporate entities are subject to corporation tax on taxable capital gains attributable to the disposal of shares. The taxable capital gain is generally calculated as 50 percent of the difference between sales proceeds and the tax cost of the shares.

(ii) Share-for-share exchange   The sale of all of the shares in a company in exchange for shares of the purchasing company may be treated as a tax-free transaction to the seller, provided that the appropriate tax elections are filed.

(b) Individuals   Canadian resident individuals disposing of shares are subject to tax on the taxable capital gain. The taxable capital gain is calculated as 50 percent of the sales proceeds minus the original cost base. The rate of tax varies based on the shareholder's province of residence but can be as low as 19.5 percent and as high as 26.5 percent.

The position with regard to share-for-share exchanges is the same as that of companies.

7.2   Asset Disposals

Typically, accounts receivable are deemed sold at their net carrying value for financial reporting purposes. As discussed earlier, a joint election by purchasers and sellers is available whereby the amount that the seller is allowed as a deduction in the year of sale must be included in the purchaser's income in the year of purchase. This ensures that the sale of the accounts receivable is on income account instead of on capital account. If the joint election is not made, the sale of the accounts receivable will be on capital account and only 50 percent of losses will be deductible.

Sales of inventory normally are included in the vendor's trading profits.

Capital assets—excluding assets such as plant or machinery on which capital cost allowance, or tax depreciation, is claimed (see Section 3.1)—are subject to corporate tax on taxable capital gains (50 percent of the capital gain), similar to a share disposal. Any resulting taxable capital gain can be sheltered by capital losses within the seller's company.

When depreciable capital properties are purchased, capital cost allowance (tax depreciation) is available on the purchase price paid. Capital cost allowance is calculated based on a pooling of assets. All assets of a certain type, or class, are included in the pool, and then tax depreciation is claimed on that pool. When depreciable capital property is disposed of, the pool in which that property resides is credited for the lower of original cost or proceeds received. To the extent that the credit to the pool exceeds the balance in the pool, recapture will result. Recapture is subject to tax. To the extent that the proceeds received on the disposition of a depreciable capital property exceed the original cost of that property, a capital gain will result. Only 50 percent of this gain is taxable.

When the proceeds of sale of certain types of capital assets used in the business are reinvested in the acquisition of certain types of new assets for use in the business within one year of the end of the taxation year in which the disposal occurred, an election is available to defer the recognition of income or capital gains on the disposition of the property. The replacement property must be acquired to replace the former property, must have the same use as or a use similar to the former property, and must be used for the purpose of gaining or producing income from the same business or a similar business.

7.3   Deferred Consideration and Earn-Outs

In Canada, the cost-recovery method is generally accepted by the CRA for the calculation of gain or loss on the disposal of shares under an earn-out agreement. Under the cost-recovery method, the selling company reduces its adjusted cost base of the shares, as amounts on account of the sale price become determinable. Once such an amount on account of the sale price exceeds the adjusted cost base of the shares, the excess is considered a capital gain that is realized at the time the amount becomes determinable, and the adjusted cost base is reduced to zero. All such amounts that subsequently become determinable— that is, once they are capable of being calculated with certainty—are treated as capital gains at that time. A capital loss is recognized only at the time the maximum that may be received is irrevocably established to be less than the seller's adjusted cost base.

7.4   Payments under Warranties or Indemnities

When the sales/purchase documentation contains a clause that any warranty or indemnity payment is to be treated as an adjustment to the consideration offered and received for the transaction, the payment would be treated for tax purposes as an adjustment to the purchase consideration received.

8.   TRANSACTION COSTS FOR SELLERS

8.1   Goods-and-Services Tax, Harmonized Sales Tax, and Retail Sales Taxes

(a) Share sales   Share sales are generally exempt from GST, HST, and retail sales taxes.

(b) Asset sales   If both the vendor and the purchaser are GST registrants, the corporations can jointly elect to relieve both parties from paying the GST on the sale of a business. If not, the seller has to collect and remit GST on the taxable assets of the business that are disposed of by the purchaser. The purchaser may claim the GST paid as an input tax credit.

In general, real estate and assets purchased for resale are exempt from retail sales taxes.

However, all assets sold should be reviewed in detail by an expert in order to determine the extent of exposure to GST, HST, or retail sales taxes and to ensure that the appropriate taxes are collected and remitted and all applicable elections are made in a timely fashion.

8.2 Tax Deductibility of Transaction Costs

As noted in Section 2.3, transaction costs are deductible only to the extent they are incurred for the purpose of producing income from a business or property and are not outlays of a capital nature.

In general terms, the position can be summarized as follows:

- Corporation tax treatment of expenses
- GST treatment of expenses

(a) *Corporation tax treatment of expenses*

(i) For investment companies disposing of shares   As a general rule, costs incurred by a seller after the decision to dispose of a company are likely to constitute costs of disposing of an investment, while the costs incurred prior to that point might be regarded as costs of managing investments (e.g., evaluating potential disposal strategies).

Costs related to initial advice on various disposal possibilities or strategies are likely to be deductible for tax purposes. Nevertheless, the CRA may argue that the seller has in fact decided to sell, in which case the expenses are not severable from the costs of disposal, which are capital in nature.

Costs related to the sales process in general and, particularly, costs related to detailed negotiation with a specific bidder whether or not such negotiation culminates in the execution of the sale and purchase agreement are less likely to be deductible for tax purposes. Nevertheless, some of these costs may qualify as costs of disposal in the capital gains tax computation, thereby reducing the capital gain or increasing the loss.

(ii) For operating companies disposing of assets   Costs incurred as part of the disposal process generally are not deductible with regard to computing the seller's operating profits for tax purposes.

In the computation of the corporation tax on capital gains on the sale of certain capital assets (see Section 7.2), a deduction may be claimed for certain costs of disposal incurred wholly and exclusively in relation to that asset—for example, asset valuation fees, any costs of transfer, and related legal fees. But when expenses are incurred as part of the transaction as a whole—for example, the majority of, if not all, legal fees related to the deal—and when those expenses are not incurred specifically and solely in relation to that capital asset, those expenses cannot be deducted in computing the capital gain. If it cannot be argued that the costs incurred are in relation to the capital asset, then the costs are not deductible on capital account, and, as noted earlier, costs incurred as part of the disposal process are generally not deductible on income account. In a case such as this, the disposal costs may not be deductible to the seller at all.

(b) GST treatment of expenses   GST charged by third parties to the seller on transaction costs should be recoverable, provided the seller is registered for GST purposes prior to incurring the liability.

9.   PREPARING A TARGET COMPANY FOR SALE

9.1   Hive-Down of Assets

When the seller is selling only a division or part of a trading business or there is a specific liability that needs to be carved out of the sale, a hive-down method of purchase may be considered.

Hiving down involves the transfer of the specific trade and assets of a company to another group company. Initially, no capital gain is recognized as a result of the hive-down, because the assets are treated as being transferred at their existing tax basis notwithstanding the actual transfer price. The subsequent sale of the hive-down company is taxed as a capital gain, and only 50 percent of such gain is subject to tax.

It is not possible for operating or capital losses to be transferred to the hive-down company.

No GST is payable on a transfer of assets between members of a related group.

9.2   Intragroup Transfer of Assets Being Retained

Assets that are to be excluded from the sale of the target business may be transferred out of group companies. Such transfers are commonly called butterfly reorganizations, and because of their complexity, the advice of a professional is necessary.

In general terms, a butterfly reorganization effects a tax-free reorganization of a company's assets. There are two kinds of butterfly reorganizations that do not attract tax: a spin-off butterfly and a split-up butterfly. Other forms of butterfly transactions such as a purchase butterfly may attract tax and be punitive to the taxpayer. Due to the complexity of these provisions, advance tax rulings are often sought from the CRA before transactions are undertaken. As noted earlier, the advice of a professional is necessary when contemplating one of these transactions.

In a spin-off butterfly, the distributing corporation makes a distribution of property to all of its shareholders and uses Canadian tax provisions to defer tax on the distribution. Generally, this distribution of property is not made directly to the shareholders. Rather, it is made to transferee corporations that are owned by all of the shareholders of the distributing corporation. The distributing corporation can distribute all or only a portion of its assets either to one transferee corporation or to more than one. The shareholders of the distributing corporation may retain a portion of their shares in the distributing corporation, and/or they may exchange their shares in the distributing corporation for shares in the transferee corporation(s). Depending on the transaction's complexity, either the distributing corporation may continue to exist or all of its assets may be distributed to the transferee corporation(s). Therefore, after a spin-off butterfly reorganization has taken place, there are at least two corporations that each have the same shareholders as the original corporation. If assets are retained by the distributing corporation, the distributing corporation will continue to exist and to retain its tax attributes (loss carryforwards and so on). Because the transferee corporations are new entities, they will not have any preexisting tax attributes.

In a split-up butterfly, the distributing corporation makes a distribution of property to some but not all of its shareholders and uses Canadian tax provisions to defer tax on the distribution. This distribution of property can be made either directly to the selected shareholders or through transferee corporation(s) owned by the selected shareholders. The shareholders receiving the distribution can elect to have their shares in the distributing corporation canceled or they can remain as shareholders of the distributing corporation, depending on the value of the property transferred. In a scenario similar to a spin-off butterfly, the distributing corporation can distribute all or only a portion of its assets to one or more transferee corporations. However, unlike the spin-off butterfly, in a split-up butterfly the shareholders of the transferee corporations are not the same as the shareholders of the distributing corporation.

Generally, as long as the distributed property is retained by its respective shareholders, butterfly reorganizations do not attract tax at the corporate or shareholder level. However, if a butterfly is undertaken as part of a series of transactions in order to reduce or eliminate tax on the sale of a corporation or its assets to an arm's-length purchaser—otherwise known as a purchase butterfly— the tax results are punitive and generally involve double taxation of any gain incurred.

No GST is payable on a transfer of assets between members of a related group.

9.3   Presale Dividends

When a disposal of shares is not exempt from capital gains for an individual, this can be a useful planning tool in minimizing tax on capital gains. Antiavoidance legislation exists, however, that may limit any intended utility from a presale dividend. If such antiavoidance legislation applies, any capital gain is adjusted to what it would have been had the value of the target group not been reduced by the presale dividend. This legislation is complex, but in very general terms, dividends paid out of taxed profits would not be subject to the antiavoidance legislation, which is intended to apply to dividends paid out of artificially generated profits that have not been or will not be taxed—for example, revaluations of assets or accounting profits arising from the transfer of assets between two members of the target group.

This strategy is also available to corporate sellers of shares and normally reduces the tax on the resulting capital gain.

10. DEMERGERS

A demerger may be achieved by a hive-down strategy as outlined in Section 9.1 or by a series of hive-downs. Additionally, a demerger may be achieved by using a butterfly reorganization as covered in Section 9.2.

11. LISTINGS AND INITIAL PUBLIC OFFERINGS

11.1 Impact on the Tax Status of a Company and Its Subsidiaries

In Canada the tax status of a company is affected by whether or not it is public. Generally, many tax incentives and low tax rates no longer apply once a company becomes publicly listed. For example, for a listed company, scientific research and experimentation development benefits are reduced and company/ shareholder tax integration is lost.

11.2 Complete Group Listing or Initial Public Offering

In Canada each company is a separate entity for tax purposes. Each public company in a group is listed separately.

11.3 Listing or Initial Public Offering of a Subsidiary

The immediate implications for the existing parent of the listing of a subsidiary are:

- If the parent sells some of its existing shares of stock in a subsidiary, it is subject to corporation tax on capital gains on the disposal of shares. (See Section 7.1 for the tax consequences.)

- If the subsidiary issues new stock for sale in the public market, the parent has not sold any stock and no gain will be recognized. However, if the subsidiary issues sufficient stock to dilute the parent's control, an acquisition of control may occur. (See Section 6.4 for a more detailed discussion of the effect of an acquisition of control on the tax attributes of a company.)

11.4   Issuance of New Stock by a Listed Company

The issuance of new stock by a listed company should have no tax consequences for the listed company. The consideration paid becomes the investors' cost base in the shares.

11.5   Disposal of Stock by Existing Shareholders

When the listing or IPO involves a disposal of stock by existing shareholders, the tax position for those shareholders is as outlined in Section 7.1.

CHILE

INTRODUCTION

This chapter details the principal tax issues that are relevant to purchasers and sellers engaged in the transfer of ownership of a Chilean trade or business. Unless otherwise stated, it is generally assumed that all sellers and purchasers are Chilean companies with limited liability.

Generally, the transfer of a Chilean trade or company takes the form of a disposal of shares or assets. Chilean laws, however, allow for various types of corporate rearrangements, such as mergers and demergers, which can be used to prepare target companies for sale or to structure the deal.

While this chapter generally focuses on the corporate taxation of merger and acquisition transactions, several other types of entities exist. From a tax perspective, there are no special advantages to electing any of the first three structures described later, because all of them are subject to the same total tax burden. Therefore, the final decision should be driven by considerations such as the management of the company, the transfer or sale of the investment, the number of owners, and any other particular issues applicable to the investor. The fourth structure, also described later, is the new holding company established in article 41-D of the Income Tax Law.

The following are types of business entities that exist in Chile:

- **Stock corporations.** A stock corporation is a legal entity formed by a common fund provided by shareholders, who are responsible only for their respective capital contributions, and managed by a board of directors, whose members are essentially revocable.

   Corporations can be open or closed. Open corporations publicly offer their shares in the stock exchange under the Securities Market Law. Similarly, when a corporation has more than 500 shareholders or when at least 10 percent of the subscribed capital belongs to a minimum of 100 shareholders, it is considered by law to be an open corporation.

   Closed corporations are all those that are not open. However, shareholders of closed corporations can voluntarily elect to be subject to the provisions that govern open corporations.

At a minimum, two shareholders are needed for a stock corporation because Chilean law does not allow corporations to be owned by a single owner. Shareholders can be individuals or legal entities, Chilean or foreign. In addition, there is no requirement for maximum or minimum capital. The total capital must be issued and paid within three years. If not, the capital is reduced by law to the amount effectively issued and paid.

- **Limited liability company (LLC).** An LLC is a legal entity created by a contract under which two or more parties agree to make a contribution in common with the purpose of dividing the proceeds arising from such contributions. Each partner's liability is limited to the amount of that partner's capital contribution or to a greater amount specified in the partnership deed.

- **Branch of a foreign corporation.** Chilean commercial law considers a branch as the locally registered office of a foreign corporation. The formation of a branch implies the acquisition in Chile of a fiscal, legal, and commercial presence, and the assets of the branch remain subject to Chilean law, especially to cover the branch's local liabilities.

    A branch is considered to be the same legal entity as the head office. However, it is a permanent establishment that has autonomy and legal capacity to become a partner or shareholder of local partnerships or corporations.

    Unlike an LLC or a stock corporation, a branch may not be established jointly by two different legal entities because it is the local office of one foreign corporation. Therefore, by law, its capital pertains exclusively (100 percent) to its head office.

- **41-D holding company.** Such 41-D holding companies are stock corporations formed in Chile, under Chilean law, with the exclusive purpose of making investments in Chile and abroad. The investments must be made in active business entities. The holding company may also render services to foreign subsidiaries, including financial services. The lending of funds, however, is not allowed.

For income tax purposes, these corporations are treated as non-Chilean residents taxed on Chilean-sourced income only. Foreign-sourced income—dividends, capital gains, service fees—is not taxable in Chile.

Nonresident shareholders are not taxed in Chile on foreign source income distributed to them, except for the portion corresponding to Chilean assets in the equity of the holding company. In addition, capital gains resulting from the transfer of the shares in the holding company are not subject to taxation in Chile.

Shareholders may not be domiciled or resident in tax havens. The capital contributions must be made in freely convertible foreign currency or in capital contributions in-kind of shares of local and foreign entities, as well as participations by foreign entities.

The relevant taxes to be considered are:

- **Corporation tax.** At the company level, income is taxed with first-category tax, payable annually, at a rate of 17 percent on the accrued earnings. At the foreign investors' level, income is taxed with an additional withholding tax of 35 percent at the time of drawing, distribution, or remittance abroad.

  Investors subject to the additional withholding tax are entitled to a tax credit equal to the first-category tax effectively paid (17 percent) on income drawn, distributed, or remitted abroad, which must be added to the basis for calculation of the respective additional withholding tax. Therefore, the total tax burden is 35 percent.

  Investment income, including dividend income after adjustment for inflation, is taxed as ordinary income for residents. Interest earned is taxed after adjustment for inflation. Nonresidents are subject to a flat rate withholding tax of 35 percent on dividend payments. Against this tax, there is the 17 percent credit available on the dividend being distributed, provided the profits out of which the dividend is paid have been taxed with the basic 17 percent income tax at the corporate level.

- **Personal tax.** Individuals are subject to the following taxes at progressive rates of 0 to 40 percent: second-category tax, for dependent services only; surtax, for other income; and additional withholding tax, for nonresidents and nondomiciled individuals.

1.   ACQUISITIONS

1.1   Asset Acquisitions

An asset acquisition generally enables the purchaser to avoid exposure to the risk of any existing liability other than liabilities that are specifically recoverable through the sale agreement. Therefore, those liabilities remain the responsibility of the company that has made the asset sale and do not become the responsibility of the purchaser.

An asset acquisition generally enables a step-up in the tax basis of assets. If the acquisition involves fixed assets, the price would be that contained in the contract or invoice plus the insurance and freight costs. If the acquisition involves inventory, the price would be that contained in the invoice plus, alternatively, the insurance and freight costs. If all of the assets were bought in a bundle, the consideration paid is allocated between the various assets through a valuation made by an expert.

1.2   Stock Acquisitions

A stock acquisition results in the purchaser's effectively bearing any historical and future ongoing tax and nontax liabilities of the target company. The acquisition of stock does not allow a step-up in the tax basis of the underlying assets. The goodwill acquired in the acquisition is not deductible for tax purposes. There is an exception to this rule for mergers (discussed later).

2.   TRANSACTION COSTS FOR PURCHASERS

2.1   Transfer Taxes

(a) Stock purchases   Chile does not impose a transfer tax on stock purchases.

(b) Asset purchases   The only transfer tax applicable to an asset purchase is the tax on the transfer of used vehicles. The tax equals 1.5 percent of the sale price.

2.2   Value-Added Tax

(a) Stock purchases   Stock transfers are exempt from value-added tax (VAT).

(b) Asset purchases   VAT of 19 percent is applicable on the following sales of business assets:

- **Tangible movable assets.** VAT applies if the sale is made prior to the termination of the assets' ordinary useful life or four years, whichever is less. In either case, the seller is a taxpayer who had a right to the VAT tax credit when said assets were acquired or made, and the assets do not form part of the inventory of the business.
- **Immovable property or real estate.** VAT applies when the sale of such assets is made before 12 months have elapsed since their acquisition or construction, as applicable.

2.3   Capital Taxes

There are no capital taxes in Chile applicable to stock or asset purchases.

2.4   Tax Deductibility of Transaction Costs

In general, corporate expenses are deductible for tax purposes when they are necessary for generating income and when they are supported with appropriate documentation.

With respect to expenses incurred in connection with an acquisition, the following concepts generally apply:

- Incorporation costs
- Investigation and due diligence
- Financing costs

(a) *Incorporation costs* Costs incurred in connection with the formation of companies and the obtaining of equity financing may be treated as start-up expenses, and therefore they are deductible over a maximum term of six consecutive financial years, beginning with the year in which the expenses were incurred or in which the company begins to generate revenue from its principal trade or business, whichever is later.

(b) *Investigation and due diligence costs* Costs incurred in connection with the acquisition of an existing company are deductible by the purchaser.

However, the Chilean tax authority—the *Servicio de Impuestos Internos*—may object to the deduction of expenses related to the acquisition of stock in corporations on the grounds that the dividends to be received from the target company will not be subject to corporate tax.

(c) *Financing costs* Interest paid on loans used for acquiring social rights (interests in an LLC) is fully deductible. When the loan is used for acquiring more than 50 percent of the stock in a corporation and when certain other conditions are met, the interest will not be deductible because the capital gain generated from the transfer of stock will not be treated as ordinary income. Nevertheless, the deductibility of financing costs may be challenged by the tax authorities depending on the facts and circumstances of the case.

3.   BASIS OF TAXATION FOLLOWING ASSET OR STOCK ACQUISITIONS

3.1   Asset Acquisitions

Capital allowance, or tax depreciation of fixed assets, excluding land, is allowed on the stepped-up value of the assets. The allowance is calculated via the straight-line method based on the assets' useful lives in accordance with the guidelines of the tax authority. However, the taxpayer may opt for accelerated depreciation for new assets when acquired locally or for new or used assets when imported, provided the normal useful life of such assets is greater than three years. For this purpose, the assets are assigned useful lives equivalent to one-third of the normal life established by the tax authority, excluding fractions of months. Taxpayers may discontinue the use of the accelerated method at any time, but once they do so, they may not begin using the method again.

A recent tax amendment states that the aforementioned accelerated depreciation method is limited to the determination of the applicable first-category tax (corporate income tax). When determining the personal income taxes of the company's partners or shareholders or additional withholding tax in the case of distribution to nondomiciled or nonresident shareholders or partners, a company must use straight-line depreciation.

The tax authority has issued general guidelines on the useful lives of fixed assets for various activities, such as industry, mining, and fishing. However, the regional tax director may, at the request of the taxpayer or the Foreign Investment Committee, modify the applicable depreciation if deemed advisable.

Generally, intangible property is not subject to depreciation or amortization. However, based on administrative jurisprudence, the cost basis may be written off when the asset becomes worthless.

3.2   Stock Acquisitions

(a) Purchase price   The tax basis of the purchaser's stock in the acquired company is equal to the purchase price of the stock. The tax bases of the underlying assets in the acquired company do not change, except in the case of an improper merger. (See Section 5.)

(b) Tax grouping   Chile taxes businesses on a separate-entity basis. Therefore, profit and losses arising in the same period by different entities owned by the same group may not be offset for tax purposes. However, Chilean entities must recognize on an accrual basis the taxable profits or deductible losses accrued by foreign permanent establishments, branches, or 100-percent-owned foreign entities (nonresident entities with only one shareholder that are treated as foreign permanent establishments for Chilean tax purposes).

4.   FINANCING OF ACQUISITIONS

4.1   Debt

Tax issues that are related specifically to the overall level of borrowings and interest charged on acquisition debt are:

- Withholding tax
- Deductibility of interest
- Thin capitalization
- Other key issues

(a) *Withholding tax*   As a general rule, interest payments made from a company in Chile to a party located in another country are subject to a 35 percent withholding tax, which is applied on the total amount of interest payments. Payments of principal are not subject to tax.

Nevertheless, if the lender is a foreign bank or a foreign or international financial institution, the withholding tax would be reduced to 4 percent, which is applied on the total amount of interest payments made abroad. The withholding tax is not deductible for tax purposes.

However, it is important to bear in mind that an amendment to the Income Tax Law has restricted the application of that 4 percent withholding tax rate, introducing new thin-capitalization rules for debt operations made in a so-called related-party scenario.

According to the new legislation regarding intercompany charges, the tax authority is empowered to challenge either the amounts paid or due that are treated as interest by the taxpayer or any other payment related to credit or financial operations agreed to with the parent company, or with a branch of the parent company, or with a financial institution in which the parent company holds a minimum 10 percent capital participation. The same is applicable in the case of a foreign company that participates directly or indirectly in the direction, control, or capital of a Chilean company.

(b) *Deductibility of interest*   As covered in Section 2.4(c), in some cases, capital gain on the disposal of shares is not treated as ordinary income. Therefore, in such cases, interest expense incurred on debt financing used for acquiring the stock may not be deducted for corporate tax purposes. With proper planning, it may be possible to avoid this problem.

(c) *Thin capitalization*   The withholding tax rate for payments of interest to foreign parties is 35 percent (not 4 percent as in the cases described earlier) when the interest payments are remitted abroad to directly or indirectly related entities of the debtor when there is excess indebtedness. A taxpayer is considered to have excess indebtedness when the debt/equity ratio exceeds 3:1. The 35 percent rate applies only to interest payments in excess of the 3:1 ratio.

However, the debtor may deduct, as an ordinary business expense, the difference between the 35 percent rate and the 4 percent rate.

(d) *Other key issues*   Stamp tax is generally levied on credit operations at a rate of 0.134 percent per month, capped at 1.608 percent.

4.2   Equity

There is no capital duty on the issuance of new stock.

Dividends paid on stock are not deductible by the company paying the dividends regardless of whether such stock has any preferences. A Chilean company that receives such dividends is not subject to corporate tax on that income. Once the dividends have been paid to local individuals or to nonresident shareholders (individuals or entities), they are subject to the applicable personal tax or additional tax. The corporate tax paid by the local company generating the taxable profits is deductible by the dividend recipient.

5.   MERGERS

5.1   Legal Forms

Generally, the commercial motive behind a merger is to strengthen the economic position of the parties involved in order to compete more effectively in a given market.

From a legal perspective, the merger of corporations has been defined and regulated in the Law on Stock Corporations. Basically, Chilean corporate law provides that two or more corporations may be united in a single entity that will succeed them in all of their rights and liabilities and into which all of the equity and shareholders of the merged entities are incorporated.

Chilean law recognizes two types of tax-free mergers. The first one, referred to as merger by creation, occurs when the assets and liabilities of two or more extinguished corporations are contributed to a new one that is, therefore, incorporated.

The second type of merger, referred to as an absorbing merger, occurs when two or more extinguished corporations are absorbed by a previously existing one that acquires all of the extinguished corporations' assets and liabilities.

A third special type of merger is referred to as an improper merger (analyzed later). This merger occurs when 100 percent of the stock of a corporation is acquired by a single shareholder.

The Chilean tax authority allows the use of mergers as a reorganization process for companies other than stock corporations as well as between different types of corporate entities.

5.2   Typical Scenarios

In a typical merger by creation, two or more stock corporations contribute all of their assets and liabilities to the creation of a new corporation (Newco) that succeeds the former ones in all of their assets and liabilities.

In an absorbing merger, all of the assets and liabilities of one or more corporations are contributed to an already existing corporation. While the absorbing corporation may be an entity that has been specially incorporated for this purpose, in most cases the absorbing corporation is an entity that is already in operation. In a group reorganization, the decision concerning which entity is to absorb other entities and which is to be merged and will cease to exist often depends on their tax attributes.

Typically, in an improper merger:

- Company A buys all the stock of company B. As a result, the former shareholders of company B receive cash in exchange for their stock, and their interest in company B's, business ceases.
- The shareholders of company B contribute their stock to company A in exchange for shares. As a result, company B shareholders become shareholders in company A.

5.3   Tax Consequences

In a merger by creation, Newco succeeds the entities that are merged in all of their rights and liabilities. The assets of the merged entities are contributed to Newco, and although there is a transfer of ownership, no VAT applies on the transfer of trade tangible assets.

This creates an issue because no VAT credit will be generated for Newco in connection with these assets, and the VAT credits accumulated in the merged entities may not be transferred and used by Newco, which is a new and different taxpayer. In order to avoid this adverse effect, tangible assets often are sold before the merger.

Similarly, carryforward losses and all other tax-related credits existing in the merged entities may not be transferred to Newco. As a result, these tax attributes will not be available for use after the merger.

For income tax purposes, a merger by creation does not trigger taxation on the retained taxable earnings of the merged companies. The earnings are deemed to have been reinvested in Newco. As a result, individual taxation is deferred until these profits are effectively drawn from Newco.

If Newco generates future tax losses and receives taxable profits from the merged entities, it will be able to offset some of its own losses against them and will also be able to recover the corporate tax paid by them. This recovery, however, will be a taxable earning for Newco.

Likewise, the shareholders of the merged companies will not be subject to income tax when they receive the stock in Newco. The tax authorities' view is that the stock in Newco substitutes for the stock held in the companies that have ceased to exist. For capital gain purposes, the stock in Newco is treated as merely replacing the old stock, and its tax base cost is the same as that of the stock in the merged companies.

The Chilean tax authority will not be able to exercise its ability to assess the value of the movable assets transferred as a consequence of the merger—even if the value of the assets is significantly below market prices or below the values used in similar operations—provided that Newco registers them at the same tax value at which they were registered in the merged entities.

The merged entities do not need to go through the formal termination-of-business process before the Chilean tax authorities, provided that in the merger deed, Newco formally declares itself responsible for all tax-related obligations of the merged entities and pays any outstanding taxes due.

In an absorbing merger, the absorbing corporation succeeds to all of the rights and liabilities of the preexisting companies. The general tax effects are the same as those related to a merger by creation. Additionally, if the absorbing corporation has carryforward tax losses and receives taxable profits from the merged entities, it will be able to offset some of its own losses against them and will also be able to recover the corporate tax paid by them. However, this recovery will be treated as taxable income.

An improper merger is the legal consequence of the reunion of 100 percent of the stock or rights in a company in the hands of a single shareholder. When a shareholder is corporate entity A and acquires 100 percent of the stock in company B, all of the assets and liabilities of company B shall become the property of company A.

In this type of merger, the shareholders of company B may generate a capital gain that is subject to the general taxation rules applicable to the transfer of stock or social rights. (See Section 7.) The tax authority is entitled to assess the value at which the stock is sold or contributed if the value used in the transaction exceeds fair market value.

The acquisition of this stock or rights by company A may generate goodwill, which must be distributed among the underlying nonmonetary assets acquired upon the merger. The goodwill so distributed is reflected in the profit-and-loss accounts, following the treatment of each asset. If there are no nonmonetary assets, the goodwill must be kept in a special account and depreciated over six years. Goodwill amortization arises only under these specific conditions. Generally, goodwill is not deductible for tax purposes.

The resulting transfer of the assets from one company to the other is not subject to VAT.

Both taxable profits and nontaxable profits existing in the disappearing company will be registered in the succeeding company. This does not trigger income tax on the former or current shareholders.

The tax losses accumulated in the merged company may not be used by the absorbing company because they are seen as a personal attribute of the taxpayer. If company A has tax losses and acquires taxable profits from company B, company A will be able to offset some of its losses against the profits acquired from company B. It will also be possible to recover the corporate tax paid on those profits. If the corporate tax is recovered, it will be treated as taxable income for company A.

The merged entities do not need to go through the formal termination-of-business process before the Chilean tax authority if, in the merger deed, company A formally declares itself responsible for all tax-related obligations of the merged entities and pays any outstanding taxes due.

6.   OTHER STRUCTURING AND POSTDEAL ISSUES

6.1   Creation of Local-Country Tax Groups

Tax groupings of companies are not allowed in Chile. Each company files and pays its taxes separately.

6.2   Repatriation of Profits

To determine the tax treatment applicable to distributions, the source of the distribution must be determined. There are specific rules that determine the mechanism and order of the distributions.

For distributions from LLCs there is an exception to that rule. If the distribution exceeds the Taxable Profits Fund, it is not taxable until the LLC generates taxable profits. Once the taxable profits are generated, the withholding tax is triggered.

If the distribution is paid to a foreign recipient, it is subject to a withholding tax of 35 percent. This tax is reduced by the first-category tax paid at the corporate level.

6.3   Preservation of Existing Tax Attributes

(a) Asset acquisitions   In an asset acquisition, none of the carryforward losses or other tax credits existing in the target company are transferred to the acquiring entity.

With respect to depreciation, the assets are not treated as new assets. As a result, the accelerated-depreciation method cannot be used by the purchaser.

(b) Stock acquisitions   An acquisition of stock that does not result in a merger implies that all tax attributes remain in the target company.

Recently established provisions disallow the use of carryforward tax losses in certain circumstances in companies that have experienced changes of ownership or in the right to participate in their profits when the new partners acquire, directly or indirectly, at least 50 percent of the social rights, stock, or profit participation.

These new regulations do not apply when the change in ownership occurs among related companies.

6.4   Receipts under Warranties

When the purchaser receives payments from the seller under warranties, the payments affect the tax cost base of the assets or of the shares. Therefore, the purchaser has to make an adjustment to the assets' or shares' registered values.

7.   DISPOSALS

7.1   Stock Disposals

The Income Tax Law establishes three types of taxation on the capital gains generated from the transfer of stock in Chilean corporations:

1. Nontaxable income on the total amount of the capital gain
2. Corporate tax as a sole tax
3. Ordinary taxation, meaning, corporate tax and individual taxation

The following is applicable to both individuals and legal entities:

- Income tax
- VAT

(a) Income tax   With respect to the sale of stock held in closed corporations, ordinary taxation applies if the stock has been held for less than one year. Once the stock has been held for more than one year, it is necessary to determine whether the sale of stock represents a customary operation.

Capital gains generated in customary transfers of stock are subject to ordinary taxation. The tax authority determines whether the operation is customary or not by considering the prior and current circumstances of the operation. In this determination, the tax authority considers formal elements (business purpose of the seller) and material evidence (of other operations).

The sale of the corporation's own stock is deemed to be customary by law.

Capital gains generated in noncustomary operations are subject to corporate tax of 17 percent as a sole tax. Similarly, if the transfer is made between related parties, the capital gain generated in the operation is subject to ordinary taxation.

If the stock transferred is held in an open corporation, no taxation is applicable on the capital gain if the stock was acquired in a stock exchange, and the transfer is made in a stock exchange, and the stock has the stock exchange presence required by the Chilean Securities and Exchange Commission.

If the stock held in an open corporation does not have the required stock exchange presence, the capital gain derived from the transfer is subject to the same taxation applicable to the transfer of stock in closed corporations.

A special situation arises when the sale of stock or of the social rights of an offshore entity allows the purchaser to acquire directly or indirectly a participation in the capital or profits of another company incorporated in Chile. In this situation, if the purchaser is resident in Chile, the capital gain generated in the operation is regarded as Chilean-sourced income.

(b) VAT The transfer of stock is not subject to VAT in Chile. However, commissions earned by stockbrokers are subject to VAT.

7.2   Disposals of Social Rights

(a) Income tax The capital gain generated in the transfer of social rights in LLCs is subject to ordinary taxation. The tax cost base is different, however, depending on whether the transfer is made to a related purchaser or not. If the purchaser is a nonrelated party, the tax cost base is equivalent to the book value of the social rights. If the purchaser is a related party, the tax cost base is the acquisition cost, adjusted by inflation.

(b) VAT The transfer of social rights is not subject to VAT in Chile.

7.3   Asset Disposals

(a) Corporate entities

(i) Income tax The capital gain generated from the sale of assets is subject to ordinary taxation (corporate tax and individual taxes when the corporate income is distributed to shareholders).

The tax cost base of fixed assets is the acquisition cost, net of depreciation, adjusted by inflation. In the case of inventory, the tax cost base is its acquisition cost, adjusted in accordance with general rules if the inventory has been kept for more than 12 months.

(ii) VAT Transfers of fixed assets are subject to VAT only if the operation is made before four years have elapsed since the assets' first acquisition or before the expiration of the operation's ordinary useful life, whichever is less.

The transfer of inventory is normally subject to VAT.

(b) Individuals

(iii) Income tax In general, corporate tax and individual tax are applicable. In the case of an occasional sale of movable assets acquired for personal use, no tax is applicable.

The tax cost base is the acquisition price.

(iv) VAT VAT is applicable only on the sale of movable assets acquired with the purpose of reselling them.

7.4   Deferred Consideration

There is no specific regulation for the sale of shares with an adjustable price. Therefore, such sales should be analyzed on a case-by-case basis.

7.5   Payments under Warranties

There is no specific regulation for the sale of shares with an adjustable price. Therefore, such sales should be analyzed on a case-by-case basis.

8.   TRANSACTION COSTS FOR SELLERS

8.1   Transfer Taxes

See Section 2.1.

8.2   VAT

See Section 2.2.

8.3   Other Costs of the Transaction

Regarding deduction of transaction costs, the nature of the income generated should be considered as follows:

- If the costs are related to tax-exempt operations or income, they may not be deducted from ordinary income.
- If the costs are related to income subject to special taxes such as corporate tax as a sole tax, such costs may be deducted only from said income, as established by the tax authority.
- If the costs are related to income subject to corporate tax and, eventually, to personal taxes, those costs are deductible from the generated income.

9.   PREPARING A TARGET COMPANY FOR SALE

The seller may want to retain certain assets or businesses, and for that purpose, it would be possible to demerge the corporation. As a result of the demerger, assets that the seller wants to retain may be kept in the parent company or transferred to a Newco. The shares of the company holding the assets to be retained would not be sold.

In light of current limitations on the purchaser's use of the tax credits existing in the target company, the inventory is usually sold before the transaction in order to ensure the use of accumulated VAT credits against the debits generated in this sale.

9.1   Intragroup Transfer of Assets Being Retained

(a) General   There is no regulation that prevents the transfer of assets within companies from the same group. The tax authority, however, may assess the value of the operation when it does not respect the arm's-length principle.

However, the tax authorities may not assess the transfer value if the assets are contributed to another corporation to increase its capital or, upon its incorporation, in the scenario of an intragroup reorganization made with a legitimate business purpose. The company making the contributions must remain in existence and no cash flows be received in exchange for the assets. Such assets must be valued and registered at the same tax or book value at which they were registered in the books of the transferor company.

Regarding international transfers, transfer-pricing regulations allow the tax authority to assess the operations when they are not made using market values.

(b) VAT   The sale of assets between related parties has the same tax treatment applicable to transactions between nonrelated parties. Therefore, VAT may be applicable in light of the circumstances discussed earlier.

10.   LISTING ON THE STOCK EXCHANGE

Only open stock corporations may be listed on the stock exchange. Such corporations are subject to Chilean Securities and Exchange Commission supervision.

The tax treatment applicable to the corporation is not modified by the fact that the corporation is listed on the stock exchange market.

10.1   Effect of the Stock Exchange Presence

As discussed in Section 7.1, there is a special tax exemption for shares with stock exchange presence. Provided certain conditions are met, capital gains on listed shares are not taxable.

CHINA

INTRODUCTION

This chapter details the principal tax issues that are relevant to purchasers and sellers engaged in the transfer of ownership of a People's Republic of China (PRC) trade or business. Unless otherwise indicated, it is generally assumed that all sellers are PRC companies and that all purchases are made either by a foreign enterprise (FE) or through a foreign-invested enterprise (FIE) in the PRC.

The relevant taxes to be considered include:

- **Enterprise income tax (EIT).** Generally, PRC companies are taxed on a stand-alone basis. EIT taxes the profits earned by a company at a rate of 33 percent.
- **Withholding tax (WHT).** An FE that has no permanent establishment or place in China but that derives profit, interest, and other income from sources in China is subject to WHT at a rate of 10 percent on such income.
- **Value-added tax (VAT).** This is a sales tax whereby up to 17 percent is added to the sales price charged for goods, except for certain categories of sales that are exempt from or outside the scope of VAT.
- **Business tax (BT).** Generally, a BT of 5 percent is imposed on any transfer of immovable assets, such as land and real estate—and intangible assets, such as trademarks, patents, and copyrights. In addition, an FE that derives interest income from China is also subject to BT at a rate of 5 percent.
- **Deed tax.** This tax is payable by a purchaser at a rate of 3 to 5 percent on the purchase price for land or real estate.
- **Stamp duty.** This tax is payable by both the purchaser and the seller at a rate of 0.03 to 0.05 percent on the equity or asset transfer value.

In addition to the different tax implications of asset sales and share sales, the legal environment in China is also complicated and changing rapidly, especially after China's entry into the World Trade Organization (WTO).

1.   ACQUISITIONS

According to the Provisional Measure for Merger and Acquisition of Domestic Enterprises by Foreign Investors (Provisional Measure), which became effective on April 12, 2003, and which was issued by the Ministry of Foreign Trade and Economic Cooperation (part of the Ministry of Commerce), the State Administration of Taxation (SAT), the State Administration of Industry and Commerce (SAIC), and the State Administration of Foreign Exchange (SAFE), foreign investors are now allowed to acquire PRC companies in any of the following three ways:

1.   Via an acquisition of the equity or shareholdings of a non-FIE by a foreign investor. This acquisition, subsequently, converts the target entity into an FIE, hereinafter referred to as a *stock deal*.
2.   Via an acquisition of the assets of a non-FIE by an existing FIE.
3.   Via an acquisition of the assets of a non-FIE by a foreign investor through the formation of a new FIE, hereinafter referred to as an *asset deal*.

In light of the foregoing, special rules and regulations apply if foreign investors acquire stock in listed Chinese companies. (See Section 11.3.)

The adoption of an asset deal or a stock deal for an acquisition in China depends largely on the regulatory situations as well as on the investors' commercial and tax objectives. For example, in some cases, an asset deal may be the only option for acquiring businesses from Chinese domestic enterprises.

1.1   Asset Acquisitions

In general, an asset acquisition involves the formation of a new company for the purpose of acquiring the assets, liabilities, and business of a target company. However, the formation of a new acquiring company has its own approval requirements.

An asset deal is typically used in order to leave behind some of the inherent risks associated with the target company. An asset acquisition helps restrict the risk to the specific assets, liabilities, and businesses being acquired. Thus, the acquirer generally does not assume any contingent or hidden liabilities of the target company. However, in certain specific situations, an asset deal is not immune from the inherent risk related to the assets acquired. For example, if there is any default on the target company's part of import duty and VAT on the assets acquired, PRC customs could go after the assets, even though the assets have been sold.

Furthermore, the consideration paid for acquiring the assets of a target company is subject to PRC taxes. For example, the transferor is assessed a BT of 5 percent on any transfer of land, building, and intangible assets. A VAT of

17 percent is imposed on any inventory existing at closing that is sold by the target company. The disposal of used equipment is generally exempt from VAT if it is sold at a value not exceeding its original cost. However, used motor vehicles are subject to VAT at a rate of 2 percent if the selling price is higher than the original cost. Although it should be the seller's obligation to pay for these tax liabilities, the seller could require a premium to cover such tax costs if the acquirer decides to do an asset acquisition.

1.2   Stock Acquisitions

According to the Provisional Measure, under a stock acquisition the target company remains a going concern subject to the target's originally approved operating period. The acquirer also inherits the business risk and hidden or contingent liabilities, if any, of the target company. Accordingly, this risk should be addressed by performing due diligence on the target, and/or by adjusting the purchase price, and/or by obtaining contractual warranty from the target's prior shareholders.

In a stock acquisition, there is no change in the legal existence or disruption to the attributes of the acquired PRC company. Thus, the target company cannot revalue its asset basis for Chinese tax purposes.

The transfer of a stock interest in a Chinese entity is subject to stamp duty on the transfer price. Such stamp duty is payable by both the buyer and the seller. Any acquisition expense incurred by the buyer may not be allocated to the target company, and therefore, such expense may not be claimed as a tax deduction in China.

1.3   Acquisition of Shares in Listed Chinese Companies

Domestic Chinese companies may list on one of China's two stock exchanges located in Shanghai and Shenzhen. Two classes of shares are tradable on these stock exchanges: (1) Class A shares, which are restricted to domestic traders and qualified foreign institutional investors (QFIIs), and (2) Class B shares, which are restricted to foreign investors and individual Chinese investors.

There are also two classes of shares that are not traded. These classes are state-owned shares, which are owned directly by the state, and legal-person shares, which are owned by Chinese entities typically controlled by the state. Jointly, these nontrade shares account for 60 percent or more of the total outstanding shares of a listed company.

(a) Acquisition of trade shares Foreign investors have long been allowed to acquire B shares in the Chinese market. However, A shares, which had previously been reserved for domestic investors, became available to foreign investors at the end of 2002, when the China Securities Regulatory Commission (CSRC) and the People's Bank of China jointly issued the QFII rules.

QFII refers to foreign funds management companies, insurance companies, securities companies, and other asset management institutions approved by the CSRC to invest in the PRC securities market within the limitations set by the SAFE.

A QFII is able to invest in A shares, government bonds, convertible bonds, and corporate bonds listed on China's securities exchanges. However, there are various restrictions on the amount of outstanding shares that may be acquired. An investor should check with local counsel to determine the applicable restrictions.

(b) Acquisition of nontrade shares   Before 2003, nontrade shares of listed Chinese companies could be transferred between the state and Chinese legal persons but were off-limits to foreign buyers. On November 1, 2002, the CSRC, the Ministry of Finance, and the State Economic and Trade Commission issued the Notice on Relevant Issues concerning the Transfer to Foreign Investors of Listed Company State-Owned Shares and Legal Person Shares (State-Owned-Share Notice). That State-Owned-Share Notice, effective January 1, 2003, addressed the direct sale of both state-owned and legal-person shares to foreign investors.

There are still a number of uncertainties as to how the State-Owned-Share Notice will be implemented. Therefore, initial foreign investments under this rule will have to be negotiated not only with the selling Chinese company but also with the authorities at several Chinese government agencies.

2.   TRANSACTION COSTS FOR PURCHASERS

2.1   Transfer Taxes

(a) Stock purchase   A stamp duty of 0.05 percent is payable by both the purchaser and the seller on the amount or value of the consideration provided.

(b) Asset purchase   A deed tax of 3 to 5 percent of the amount or value of the consideration provided is payable by the purchaser on transactions related to PRC land or real estate properties. However, according to the latest notice issued by the SAT, a deed tax is not payable if the transfer of land or real estate ownership is caused by a state-owned enterprise restructuring—for example, conversion to a limited liability company—during the period from October 1, 2003, to December 31, 2005.

In addition, under an asset deal, the sale of inventory and fixed assets is subject to a stamp duty at a rate of 0.03 percent on the value set out in the relevant sales contracts. A 0.05 percent stamp duty would be applied on the transfer of immovable or intangible assets. This stamp duty is imposed on both the seller and the buyer.

2.2   Value-Added Tax

(a) Stock purchase   Stock transfers are exempt from VAT.

(b) Asset purchase   From the seller's perspective, generally, the sale or transfer of tangible goods—including machinery and equipment—is subject to VAT—normally, at a rate of 17 percent with valid input VAT deduction. (See Section 8.2.)

From the buyer's perspective, if the buyer is subject to the VAT regime and is obliged to charge VAT on its sales—called output VAT—the buyer may recover VAT paid by it on its own purchases—called input VAT. A purchase of assets on which VAT has been charged by the seller is regarded as an input for the buyer; therefore, VAT charged by the seller may be recovered by the buyer. Note that in some situations, depending on certain VAT-related characteristics of the buyer, the input VAT may not always be recoverable in full, and consequently, such VAT paid would be a real cost to the buyer.

2.3   Capital Taxes

There are no capital taxes in the PRC that are applicable to stock or asset purchasers.

2.4   Tax Deductibility of Transaction Costs

PRC tax laws and regulations have not provided clear stipulations on the deductibility of transaction costs. In general, FIEs are not allowed to take deductions for expense related to feasibility studies, for interest expense on investment loans, for management expense, or for other investment-related expense for EIT purposes. Nevertheless, if an FIE uses noncash assets such as tangible and intangible assets to acquire stock or assets, the difference between the original book value of the noncash assets and the purchasing price of the acquired stock or assets is taxable profit or loss in the taxable period of the transaction.

3.   BASIS OF TAXATION FOLLOWING ASSET OR STOCK ACQUISITIONS

3.1   Asset Acquisitions

(a) Purchase price   Each purchased asset should be recorded on the buyer's books at its actual purchase price. In a case when a lump-sum purchase price is

determined for numerous assets or together with goodwill or business operations and cannot be specified for each purchased item, the buyer should record each purchased asset at the corresponding net value on the seller's books before the transfer. The lump-sum payment, after offsetting against the net book values of the assets, is regarded as the purchase price for goodwill or business operations and is recorded as *intangible assets* on the buyer's books. The balance so recorded can then be amortized evenly over the shorter of ten years or the buyer's remaining operation term.

(b) Loss carryforwards   Tax losses arising prior to an acquisition can continue to be carried forward after the acquisition for any period remaining within the five-year carryforward limit. In addition, the seller and buyer can carry forward only their respective tax losses; they can transfer losses from one to the other through the transfer of all or part of one's assets and business operations to the other.

3.2   Stock Acquisitions

(a) Purchase price   All of the acquired stock should be recorded by the purchaser at its original acquisition cost. No adjustment to the basis of the underlying assets of the company is allowed for PRC tax purposes. (See Section 5.3(a).)

(b) Tax grouping   China has a separate-entity basis of taxation. Therefore, tax groupings are not applicable in China.

(c) Loss carryforwards   Tax losses arising prior to the acquisition can continue to be carried forward after the stock acquisition for any period remaining within the five-year carryforward limit.

4.   FINANCING OF ACQUISITIONS

4.1   Debt

Specific considerations related to the overall level of borrowings and the interest charged on that debt are:

- Withholding tax
- Deductibility of interest
- Thin capitalization
- Foreign debt account

(a) Withholding tax   Interest payments to overseas lenders are subject to WHT at a rate of 10 percent. There is no WHT on interest payments to PRC companies.

(b) Deductibility of interest   For FIEs, interest expense incurred in the current year are generally not deductible from taxable income if the loan is used for investment. Such treatment applies when an FIE does not include its investment income in calculating its tax.

(c) Thin capitalization   According to the prevailing PRC FIE laws and regulations, an FIE should comply with the following debt/equity ratio; that is, the difference between the total investment and registered capital may be financed by debt:

Total Investment (US dollars)	Minimum Registered Capital
Less than 3 million	70% of total investment
3 million to 9.99 million	Higher of 2.1 million or 50% of total investment
10 million to 29.99 million	Higher of 5 million or 40% of total investment
30 million or more	Higher of 12 million or $33^{1}/_{3}$% of total investment

(d) Foreign debt account   An FIE is required to register its foreign debt and to open a foreign debt account under a foreign loan contract. Then the relevant loan amount is remitted or deposited directly into the foreign debt account. Afterward, the foreign loan amount may be used for the specific purposes defined in the loan contract—such as for purchase of fixed assets—after presentation of the relevant documents to the bank.

Regarding the repayment of the loan principal, an FIE should apply for approval with the SAFE. Remittance for the principal repayment could then be made from the FIE's foreign exchange account based on the approval document issued by the SAFE.

The payment of interest on foreign loans is generally regarded as a current item and can be made from an FIE's foreign exchange account through a designated foreign exchange bank after verification by the SAFE. In other words, generally, no approval by the SAFE is required in this case.

4.2   Equity

An increase in capital—including the issuance of new stock—as a method of funding is advantageous in that it will improve the debt/equity ratio and investment cap (see Section 4.3) of the company, which potentially enables additional interest-bearing debt to be issued by the company.

There is no stamp duty on the issuance of new stock. Dividends are not deductible by the company paying the dividend regardless of whether the dividend is paid on listed or nonlisted stock. A PRC company (excluding an FIE) or an individual receiving such dividend is taxable on the receipt of the dividend.

4.3 Investment Cap

The accumulated amount of investments by an FIE should not exceed 50 percent of the FIE's own net assets, excluding a capital increase resulting from the capitalization of profits after the initial investment.

5. MERGERS

5.1 Legal Forms

In China, a merger refers to the combination of two or more enterprises into one enterprise. Such a combination may take the form of an absorption merger or a new-company merger.

- An absorption merger is a merger in which one party continues to exist while other parties to the merger are dissolved.
- A new-company merger is a merger in which all of the parties to the merger dissolve and the investors jointly establish a new enterprise.

5.2 Typical Merger Scenarios

The following illustrate typical merger scenarios:

(a) New-company merger

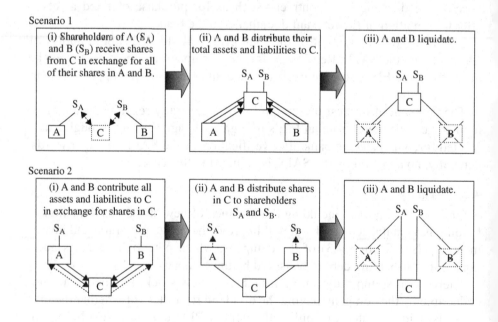

(b) Absorption merger

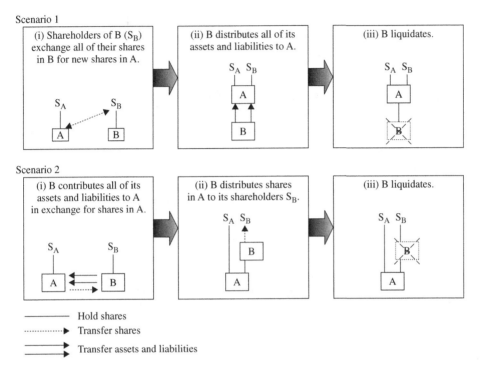

Scenario 1

| (i) Shareholders of B (S_B) exchange all of their shares in B for new shares in A. | (ii) B distributes all of its assets and liabilities to A. | (iii) B liquidates. |

Scenario 2

| (i) B contributes all of its assets and liabilities to A in exchange for shares in A. | (ii) B distributes shares in A to its shareholders S_B. | (iii) B liquidates. |

———— Hold shares
·········▶ Transfer shares
══════▶ Transfer assets and liabilities

5.3   Tax Consequences

For tax purposes, the business operations of the surviving entity are treated as a continuation of the business operations of company A and company B before the merger. For surviving entities that qualify as FIEs, the relevant EIT treatment is discussed in Section 10.2(b). (See Section 6.2.)

(a) Revaluation (step-up in value)   All of the assets, liabilities, and owner's equity of the surviving entity should be recorded at their original cost values as reported on A and B's books before the merger. No step-up in the basis of the assets is allowed as a result of the merger. When adjustments have been made for accounting purposes and the relevant depreciation and amortization are based on such adjusted values (hereinafter referred to as *accounting adjustment*), taxable income is required to be adjusted in the annual EIT filing. The following are the methods that may be adopted to account for such tax adjustment:

- **Actual annual adjustment method—the profit-and-loss approach.**
  The annual taxable income is adjusted by the actual increase or decrease

in the relevant cost or expense resulting from the accounting adjustment for each specific asset item.

- **Consolidated adjustment method—the balance-sheet approach.** All of the balance sheet adjustments for the revalued assets are consolidated—that is, netted off against each other—and spread evenly over a ten-year period for tax adjustment purposes.

The FIE should apply for approval from the relevant tax authority before using either of the foregoing adjustment methods.

The following numerical examples illustrate application of the above two methods. As indicated by the examples, there may be timing differences between the two adjustment methods.

TAX ADJUSTMENT ON REVALUATION UNDER REORGANIZATION

I. Actual annual adjustment method: the profit-and-loss approach

	Original Book Value	Revaluation	Change in Profit and Loss	Annual Tax Adjustment	Total Tax Adjustment
Fixed asset	100	250	–	–	–
Depreciation[a]	(20)	(50)	(30)[b]	30[b]	150 $[= 5 \times 30]$
Stock	100	80	–[c]	–	–
Total					150

II. Consolidated adjustment method: balance-sheet approach

	Original Book Value	Revaluation	Change in Balance Sheet	Annual Tax Adjustment	Total Tax Adjustment
Fixed asset	100	250	150		–
Stock	100	80	(20)		–
Total			130	13[d]	130[e] $[= 10 \times 13]$

[a.] Depreciation is straight line over five years. Because the company is in its first year, no accumulated depreciation is brought forward.

[b.] The same adjustment lasts for five years after the revaluation—inclusive of the revaluation year.

[c.] The adjustment is only for the revaluation year and is assumed to be charged to capital reserve. There is no profit-and-loss impact.

[d.] The same adjustment lasts for 10 years after the revaluation—inclusive of the revaluation year.

[e.] Assuming the illustration is correct, option II appears to be more beneficial. However, the tax authorities may argue that the change of 20 in the balance sheet related to the stock adjustment is not deductible because it has not affected the profit and loss. In this case, the annual adjustment would be 15 over 10 years. This is the same as the adjustment under option I.

(b) Tax holiday If the surviving entity still meets the requirements for a tax holiday, the surviving entity should continue to enjoy the tax holidays to which A and B were entitled before the merger. Specifically, the following rules apply:

- If the tax holiday has already expired before the merger, then no renewal of the tax holiday is allowed for the surviving entity.
- If the tax holiday has not been used up by the time of the merger and if the remaining holiday periods for A and B are the same, then the surviving entity should continue to enjoy the relevant tax holiday until expiration of the remaining holiday period. For example, if both A and B are entitled to a two-year exemption and a three-year 50 percent reduction for EIT purposes and both have enjoyed the benefit of two holiday years before the merger, the surviving entity can obtain only the benefit of the remaining three-year 50 percent reduction holiday period.
- If the remaining holiday periods for A and B are different or if one entity was not entitled to any tax holiday, then the taxable income of the surviving entity should be apportioned for EIT purposes. (See Section 5.3(e).) After such apportionment, the surviving entity should continue to receive the benefit of the relevant tax holiday for the taxable income attributable to the operation entitled to the remaining tax holiday; however, holiday treatment does not apply for any remaining taxable income that is not attributable to the tax holiday.

(c) Tax rate The EIT rates applicable to different operations of the surviving entity are determined according to the locality and the industrial nature of the actual business activities of such operations. When different rates apply, the taxable income of the surviving entity is apportioned based on the rules discussed in Section 5.3(e).

(d) Loss carryforwards Tax losses arising in premerger periods can continue to be carried forward by the surviving entity for any years remaining within the five-year carryforward limitation period.

When different tax holiday treatments or tax rates are applicable to the surviving entity as discussed in Sections 5.3(b) and 5.3(c), an apportionment of taxable income is required for EIT purposes. Losses carried forward from operations entitled to different tax treatments—for example, tax holiday or rate, hereinafter referred to as *tax operations*—may be offset only against the corresponding apportioned taxable income of the surviving entity.

Specifically, when the surviving entity has a net profit or loss, income tax should be levied at the rates applicable to the profit-making operations. For the operations that have been sustaining losses but that turn profitable in a later year, special rules apply in determining the tax rate.

(e) Apportionment of taxable income   When different tax treatments apply to different tax operations in the surviving entity, the taxable income of the surviving entity should be apportioned according to the following methods:

- **Actual basis.** When different tax operations are maintained by the surviving entity and separate accounting books are kept to record the activities of each tax operation, taxable income may be apportioned on an actual basis—that is, based on each operation's own accounting records. The resulting apportionment should still be accurate and reasonable.

- **Deemed ratio.** When the surviving entity does not maintain different tax operations or when the surviving entity maintains different tax operations but is unable to compute the respective taxable income on an accurate and reasonable basis, the surviving entity should apportion its total taxable income among the operations based on certain financial ratios—for example, annual turnover, cost, expense, assets, number of employees, and wages and salaries. The taxpayer may use one or an average of all such ratios—subject to the tax authority's agreement. When the relevant ratios for the year of merger are difficult to determine, the records for the most recent complete tax year before the merger may be used.

6.   OTHER STRUCTURING AND POSTDEAL ISSUES

6.1   Creation of Local-Country Tax Groups

China has a separate-entity basis of taxation. Therefore, tax groupings are not applicable in China.

6.2   Change of Foreign-Invested Enterprise Status

Unless otherwise stipulated, when the ratio of foreign investment in an FIE drops below 25 percent of the total registered capital after an acquisition, merger, or demerger, PRC EIT laws and regulations applicable to FIEs no longer apply to that reorganized entity. Instead, the reorganized entity is treated as a domestic enterprise, as opposed to an FIE, for tax purposes. As a result, any EIT exemption or reduction already enjoyed by the original FIE during its EIT holidays should be treated as follows:

- Foreign investment remains
- Foreign investment withdrawn

(a) Foreign investment remains   If all of the foreign investment in the FIE—which presumably reached 25 percent prereorganization—still remains in the reorganized entity, no clawback of the exempt or reduced EIT is required regardless of the actual operating term of the reorganized entity.

(b) Foreign investment withdrawn   If all or part of the foreign investment in the FIE gets withdrawn or transferred to domestic investors during the reorganization and if the operating term of the reorganized entity does not meet the EIT holiday requirement (normally, ten years), a clawback is required for the previously exempted or reduced EIT amounts.

6.3   Repatriation of Profits

Any after-tax profit remitted by an FIE to its foreign investors is exempt from PRC taxes. However, before an FIE can distribute dividends to its foreign investor, the FIE must meet the following preconditions:

- The registered capital has been duly paid up in accordance with the provisions of the articles of association.
- The company has begun to earn profits—that is, to show profits after covering the accumulated tax losses from prior years if any.
- Either PRC EIT has been paid by the FIE or the company is in a tax-exemption period.
- The statutory after-tax reserve funds (see below) have been provided for.

According to the PRC Equity Joint Venture Law, the foreign equity joint venture company is required to withdraw statutory reserve funds—that is, the general reserve fund (GRF), staff benefit and welfare fund (SBWF), and enterprise development fund (EDF)—before any after-tax profit can be distributed back to its shareholders. The contribution rate to the SBWF is at the discretion of the FIE, and there is no statutory requirement for an FIE to set up an EDF. However, the company must contribute at least 10 percent of its after-tax profits to the GRF until the cumulative amount represents 50 percent of the registered capital. Wholly foreign-owned enterprises are required to provide only GRF and SBWF.

In addition, an FIE is allowed to repatriate its after-tax profits and make after-tax dividend payments in its foreign currency upon presentation of the following documents/certificates:

- Board of directors' resolution on distribution of profits
- Audit report issued by a Chinese certified public accountant certifying the amount of distributable profits
- Relevant tax payment certificates

Generally, profit remittances and dividend payments do not need the approval of the SAFE but can be made by the remitters through their basic foreign exchange accounts in a bank. The remittance amount may also be purchased from designated foreign exchange banks or swap centers by presenting the aforementioned documents/certificates.

7.   DISPOSALS

7.1   Stock Disposals

Gain on the disposal of stock of a Chinese company is China sourced. There-fore, China's tax authorities have the right to tax such gain. When the pro-ceeds are then repatriated to the locality in which the investor is tax resident, the local tax authorities may impose further tax on those same amounts. When there is double taxation, relief may be provided by local tax provisions or by a double-tax treaty if that locality has concluded a double-tax treaty with China.

The following table provides an overview of the PRC tax treatment for a stock disposal by different types of investors.

STOCK INVESTMENT: TAX ON DISPOSAL GAIN

Type of Investor	Taxes	Shares in Nonlisted Company	Shares in Listed Company		
			A Shares	B Shares	Nontrade Shares
QFII	WHT	N/A	Not stipulated in current laws and regulations; may be taxable at 10%	N/A	N/A
FE (other than QFII)	WHT	10% on net transfer gain	N/A	Exempt	Not stipulated in current laws and regulations; may be taxable at 10%
Foreign Individual	WHT	N/A	N/A	Exempt	N/A
Domestic investor (including FIE)	EIT	33% on net transfer gain	33% on net trade gain	N/A	33% on net transfer gain
Domestic individual	IIT	20% on net transfer gain	Exempt	Exempt	N/A

(a) *Companies*   Pursuant to the PRC EIT laws and regulations, any FE that does not have an establishment or place in China but that derives profit, inter-est, and other income from sources in China is subject to a WHT at a rate of 10 percent on such income. However, an FE that receives dividends or derives trading gains from B shares is provisionally exempt from WHT. It should be noted that a QFII would not benefit from this exemption because a QFII is allowed to invest only in A shares.

Gains and losses on the disposition of stock realized by FIEs are generally subject to EIT and should be included in the profit or loss of the FIE in the tax-able period incurred. (See Section 8.3.)

(b) **Individuals** Foreign individual investors receive the same treatment as FEs do regarding their stock disposals; that is, they are exempt from WHT for trading gains derived from B shares.

For PRC domestic individual investors, any gain derived from the sale of shares should be subject to the PRC individual income tax (IIT) at a flat rate of 20 percent. However, gains derived from the sale of shares in domestic listed companies, including A and B shares, are currently exempt from PRC IIT.

(c) **Tax-exempt entities** These are not applicable in China.

7.2 Asset Disposals (Companies Only)

A valuation for state-owned assets is required for any PRC company involved in an asset transfer, exchange, or mortgage procedure. The valuation should be adopted as the pricing basis for the asset disposal. (See Section 9.2.)

Gain arising from the sale of assets is included as taxable income for the seller and is subject to EIT. There is no PRC tax exposure on the transfer of liabilities.

In addition, some of the fixed assets of the seller may have been imported into China free of import duty. For such import-duty-free assets, the customs office imposes a supervising period—generally, a period of five years. In the event that these assets are sold within the supervising period, the relevant portion of the import VAT and duty based on the asset's depreciated value would be required to be paid back before these assets can be sold.

7.3 Deferred Consideration and Earn-Outs

These are not applicable in China.

7.4 Payments under Warranties or Indemnities

These are not applicable in China.

8. TRANSACTION COSTS FOR SELLERS

8.1 Transfer Taxes

Stamp duty is a tax payable by both buyers and sellers on the purchase of shares. (See Section 2.1(a).) In addition, a land appreciation tax is imposed on the seller upon the transfer of land-use rights and building and is assessed at a progressive rate from 30 to 60 percent of the appreciated amount of the land and building.

8.2 VAT/Business Tax

(a) **Stock disposal** The disposal of stock is exempt from VAT.

(b) Asset disposal   Generally, the sale of tangible goods, including, for instance, machinery and equipment, is subject to VAT—normally, at a rate of 17 percent with valid input VAT deduction—which is paid by the seller. However, according to a recent circular, VAT is temporarily exempt on the sale or transfer of used fixed assets if the following criteria are satisfied:

- The equipment was included in the seller's fixed-assets list.
- The equipment has already been used for more than one year.
- The sales price does not exceed the original purchase value.

If all of the foregoing criteria are satisfied and if approval is received by the in-charge tax bureau, the transferred fixed assets may be exempt from PRC VAT. If only the first two criteria are satisfied, then the excess of the sales price over the original purchase value is subject to VAT at an effective rate of 2 percent—without any input VAT deduction.

For the sale of intangible assets—such as patents and land-use rights—and immovable assets such as real estate properties, BT at a rate of 5 percent of the transaction value is imposed on the seller.

8.3   Enterprise Income Tax

(a) Determination of gains or losses   Gains or losses from an exchange or transfer are determined as follows:

$$\text{Transfer Gain or Loss} = \text{Transfer Value} - \text{Transfer Cost},$$

$$\text{where Transfer Value} = \text{Transfer Price} - \text{Allowable Exclusion}$$

Transfer cost refers to the original book value or actual purchase value of the investment being transferred.

Transfer price refers to the gross receipts from the investment transfer, including all cash and in-kind items such as noncash assets and ownership equity.

Allowable exclusion refers to the value of the undistributed retained earnings and reserves (URER) to be transferred. The URER value should not exceed the total book value of the URER to which the transferor is entitled.

Therefore, the formulas can be consolidated as:

$$\text{Transfer Gain/Loss} = \text{Transfer Price} - \text{Allowable Exclusion} - \text{Transfer Cost}$$

(b) EIT treatment of gains   Gains derived from an exchange or transfer by an FIE or an FE are subject to PRC EIT or WHT. However, as illustrated by the foregoing formula, the transfer price attributable to URER is excluded for EIT purposes. The reason for the exclusion is that under the EIT law for an FIE and an FE, undistributed retained earnings are not subject to further taxes when distributed.

(c) EIT treatment of losses   Similarly, losses incurred during a transfer by a Chinese entity, including FIEs, are deductible for EIT purposes. However, it is not clear at the moment whether the allowable exclusion can create a loss. For example, when the transfer price is equivalent to or less than the transfer cost, the authorities are unlikely to allow the exclusion of the URER value (stated in the transfer agreement).

9.   PREPARING A TARGET COMPANY FOR SALE

9.1   Predeal Planning

The foreign investor should view preliminary targets based on the following before taking the first step in conducting the actual tax and regulatory due diligence review:

- **Regulatory efficacy.** Restrictions of the proposed investment under the current PRC laws and regulations
- **Funding option.** Capital contribution requirement and financing options for the proposed investment project
- **Investment evaluation.** Tax attributes and the possible business scope to be approved for the proposed investment
- **Exit strategy.** Options for future disposal of the China investment and the related tax and regulatory considerations

9.2   Valuation of State-Owned Assets

A valuation of the state-owned assets for the entities involved would be required in any of the following situations:

- The restructuring of an entity or a part of an entity into a limited liability company or company limited by shares
- The use of noncash assets for investment purposes
- A merger, division, or liquidation
- A change in the equity holding percentage of the original investors—except for listed companies
- A transfer of all or part of the ownership or equity of a company—except for listed companies
- An asset transfer, exchange, or mortgage

The entities required to obtain a valuation for state-owned assets should engage specialized valuation agencies with relevant qualifications.

In addition, the entities conducting the transactions that require a valuation should use this valuation as the basis for pricing the transaction. In case the actual price has a difference of more than 10 percent compared with the valuation result, such entities should provide the in-charge financial authorities or the group company and other relevant authorities a written explanation for the price difference.

9.3   Antitrust Review

The Provisional Measure has antitrust implications, although the term *antitrust* itself is not used. In certain circumstances, investors are required to report an acquisition of shares or assets. The authorities may prohibit the acquisition if they believe it would create an obstacle to future market competition or would be harmful to consumers' interest. However, the lack of definitions for many terms—such as *market*—suggests that many of the requirements may be difficult to apply.

10.   DEMERGERS

In China, the term *demerger* refers to the split of one entity—referred to hereinafter as *company A*—into two or more entities—referred to as the *surviving entities*—according to relevant PRC laws and regulations.

10.1   Split-Off Demerger and Spin-Off Demerger

Demergers can be classified in two ways:

1. **Split-off demerger.** The shareholders of company A receive shares of newly established surviving entities in exchange for all of their shares in company A. Company A then distributes all of its assets and liabilities to the surviving entities and liquidates afterward. Alternatively, company A may contribute all of its assets and liabilities to the surviving entities in exchange for shares in the latter. Company A then distributes the shares of the surviving entities to the shareholders of company A and liquidates afterward.

2. **Spin-off demerger.** The shareholders of company A receive shares of the newly established surviving entity B or entities in exchange for newly issued shares or for part of their shares in company A. Company A then distributes the corresponding portion of its assets and liabilities to the new, surviving entity. A split-up of company A and company B occurs when the distribution is in exchange for the newly issued shares or a part of the shares in company A. Alternatively, company A may contribute a part of its assets and liabilities to the new, surviving entity B in exchange for shares in the latter. Company A then distributes to its shareholders the shares in the new, surviving entity.

Company A continues to exist as a surviving entity after the demerger.

For both types of demergers, the following applies:

- For split-off demergers, company A does not need to liquidate for tax purposes.
- The shareholders of company A may decide to hold shares in all or some of the surviving entities, including company A after the demerger.
- All of the assets and liabilities of company A should be transferred to or partially remain in the surviving entities after the demerger, according to the statutory procedures and stipulations in the demerger agreement. The relevant shareholders should be able to determine the split ratio for assets and liabilities in the demerger agreement.

10.2   Tax Consequences

For tax purposes, business operations of the surviving entities should be treated as a continuation of the business operation of company A before the demerger. If the surviving entity qualifies as an FIE, the relevant EIT treatment is discussed in Section 10.2(b); otherwise, refer to Section 6.2 for details.

(a) Revaluation (step-up value)   The rules are similar to those discussed in Section 5.3.

(b) EIT preferential treatments   The EIT treatment—including rates and continuation of tax holiday—applicable to each surviving entity should be determined based on the entity's location and business nature, according to the relevant provisions in the EIT law and its detailed rules and regulations.

With regard to a tax holiday, the following rules should be observed:

- **Business nature remains the same.** If the surviving entities assume a business nature that is the same as that of company A for tax purposes, the entities should continue to enjoy tax holidays applicable to company A in the remaining holiday period. No renewal of tax holidays is allowed for the surviving entities.
- **Business nature changes.** When the tax holidays applicable to company A no longer apply to one of the surviving entities due to its business nature, that surviving entity should not continue to enjoy the relevant treatments. That surviving entity may, however, continue to enjoy the tax holidays—starting from the first profit-making year of the original entity A—in the remaining holiday years after the demerger if it qualifies for holiday. For example, if the new business nature allows the surviving entity to enjoy a two-year exemption and a three-year 50 percent reduction and the original entity began to make profits two years before the demerger, then the surviving entity can enjoy the remaining three-year 50 percent reduction holiday period only from the year of demerger.

(c) Loss carryforwards   Tax losses arising prior to the demerger should be split among the surviving entities according to the demerger agreement. Each surviving entity can then carry forward its own portion of the aforementioned losses within the five-year limit. Agreement for the appropriate split of losses should be obtained from the tax bureau.

11.   LISTINGS AND INITIAL PUBLIC OFFERINGS

11.1   Impact on the Tax Status of a Company Being Listed and Its Subsidiaries

The tax status of a company is generally unaffected by listing or initial public offering (IPO).

11.2   Complete Group Listing or IPO

This is not applicable in China.

11.3   Listing or IPO of Subsidiary

This is not applicable in China.

11.4   Issuance of a New Stock by a Listed Company

The issuance of new stock by the listed company would result in a capital increase and would, therefore, trigger a stamp duty at a rate of 0.05 percent of the increased capital.

11.5   Disposal of Stock by Existing Shareholders

If the listing or IPO involves the disposal of stock by existing shareholders, then the tax position for those shareholders is as outlined in Section 7.1.

CZECH REPUBLIC

INTRODUCTION

This chapter details the principal tax issues that are relevant to purchasers and sellers engaged in the transfer of ownership of a Czech trade or business. Unless otherwise stated, it is generally assumed that all sellers and purchasers are Czech companies with limited liability.

On May 1, 2004, the Czech Republic became a member of the European Union (EU), and Merger Directive 434/90/EEC became incorporated into Czech tax law.

Relevant taxes to be considered with respect to merger and acquisition activity are:

- **Corporate income tax.** Generally, this is a 28 percent tax on profits earned by a company in fiscal year 2004, 26 percent in 2005, and 24 percent in 2006 and following.
- **Value-added tax (VAT).** This sales tax adds 19 percent to the sales price charged by a Czech VAT-registered seller for the sale of the majority of goods and services. The reduced rate of 5 percent is applicable to the sales of specific types of goods and services. However, certain categories of sale are exempt from or outside the scope of VAT. A purchaser or recipient of services registered for Czech VAT can generally recover VAT paid if the purchase was incurred in the course of an economic activity. The VAT system was harmonized with the EU directives as of the date of accession of the Czech Republic to the EU.
- **Real estate transfer tax (RETT).** This is payable by a seller at a rate of 3 percent on the purchase price for land and buildings or on the official valuation, whichever is higher.

1. ACQUISITIONS

1.1 Asset Acquisitions

(a) Individual assets An asset acquisition generally facilitates a step-up in the tax basis of assets, allowing the purchaser to depreciate the assets from the (potentially) higher purchase price.

There is no transfer of ownership in the selling company in the case of asset transfer. An asset acquisition enables the purchaser to avoid exposure related to the risk of any historical liabilities that are not specifically recoverable through the sale agreement.

With a sale of assets, contracts between the seller and third parties are not automatically assigned to the purchaser. Therefore, it is necessary for the purchaser either to enter into new contracts with the third parties or to agree with the third party that the existing contract will be assigned from seller to purchaser. In practice, this may often cause difficulties, particularly if there are numerous contracts or if a third party is unwilling to permit assignment. This issue can be solved by a stock transfer or by a contract on transfer of a business or part of one as described later.

(b) Sale of business   The sale of a business represents a specific type of sale-and-purchase contract. Under this arrangement, the business is sold to the purchaser as a going concern. The transferred business includes all assets and liabilities related to the business activities of the company, as well as the employees. If part of a business is sold, it must form an independent organizational unit.

Under the contract on the sale of a business, the purchaser becomes a party to all legal contracts of the seller. In other words, the contracts need not be specifically assigned or renegotiated.

1.2   Stock Acquisitions

In a stock acquisition, the purchaser effectively bears any historical and future ongoing tax and nontax liabilities of the target company. There is no step-up permitted in the tax basis of the company's assets. No goodwill acquired as part of a stock deal is recognized for Czech tax or accounting purposes.

However, as indicated in Section 1.1, an important advantage of a stock acquisition is that contracts between the target company and third parties remain in force and do not need to be assigned or renegotiated with the third party.

2.   TRANSACTION COSTS FOR PURCHASERS

2.1   Transfer Taxes

(a) Asset purchases   Generally, the transfer of real estate is subject to RETT. The seller of the assets pays the RETT, while the purchaser acts as guarantor. The RETT is a tax-deductible cost upon its actual payment.

(b) Transfer of businesses   RETT is payable under the same conditions as in an asset purchase with respect to the real estate assets transferred.

(c) Stock purchases   No fees are payable.

2.2   Value-Added Tax

(a) Asset purchases   In most cases, a purchase of assets is subject to VAT at a rate of 19 percent, which must be paid in addition to the purchase price. When the buying entity is also a VAT payer, it may recover VAT paid on its own purchases, subject to general recovery conditions. Note that in some situations, depending on certain VAT-related characteristics of the buyer, the VAT paid on inputs may not always be recoverable in full or may not be recoverable at all. Therefore, such VAT paid would be a real cost to the buyer.

(b) Transfer of businesses   The sale of a business as a going concern is not subject to VAT. If the buyer is not a registered VAT payer before the purchase of the business, then by operation of law, it will become a registered VAT payer upon the purchase of the business.

(c) Stock purchases   All stock transfers are exempt from VAT. As a result, the seller is not allowed to recover VAT paid on inputs related to the transfer.

2.3   Capital Taxes

There are no capital taxes in the Czech Republic.

2.4   Tax Deductibility of Transaction Costs

In general, whether a particular expense gets treated as deductible varies from case to case. The general test for tax deductibility of an expense is that the expense must be incurred in order to generate, ensure, or maintain revenues that are taxable.

RETT is tax deductible upon payment. Other transaction costs incurred in relation to an asset or business transfer are generally tax deductible on an accrual basis.

The stock transfer transaction costs related directly to acquisition of shares cannot be directly expensed and must be included in the accounting value of the stock. Examples of such costs are fees for brokers and fees for intermediaries.

3.   BASIS OF TAXATION FOLLOWING ASSET OR STOCK ACQUISITIONS

3.1   Asset and Business Acquisitions

In an asset acquisition, acquired tangible assets may be depreciated for tax purposes under general conditions given by tax legislation—that is, from 4 years in the case of cars to 50 years in the case of certain buildings such as hypermarkets and hotels.

The depreciation period of intangible assets should correspond to the length of time for which the company has the right to use it. If such right is given for an indefinite period, the depreciation period is 48 months for software, 60 months for establishment costs of the company, and 72 months for other intangible assets.

In a business acquisition, if the purchase price is set for individual asset items acquired within the acquisition (which is not common), the purchaser records the assets at the assets' individual purchase prices and depreciates them from those prices for both accounting and tax purposes.

If prices are not agreed to regarding individual items of the sold business, the purchaser may decide whether to perform a revaluation of individual acquired assets. In such a case, the buyer depreciates those assets from the acquisition values determined by the revaluation. The difference between the purchase price of the business and the total of revaluated prices of acquired assets reduced by the transferred liabilities creates goodwill—or negative good will, if negative. The goodwill is depreciated over five years for accounting purposes; the tax depreciation period is 15 years.

If individual revaluation is not performed, the purchaser depreciates purchased assets from the book values stated in the accounting records of the seller. The difference between the purchase price of the business and the total of book values of acquired assets reduced by the transferred liabilities results in the so-called valuation difference (positive or negative), which is depreciated for both accounting and tax purposes over 15 years.

3.2   Stock Acquisitions

(a) *Purchase price*   The purchaser records the purchased stock into its accounting records at the purchase price, which also includes other costs directly related to the stock acquisition. (See Section 2.4.)

(b) Revaluation differences

(i) *Stock with neither substantial nor decisive control*   The revaluation differences of a stock that does not represent substantial or decisive control get included in the corporate income tax base if:

- The purchaser revaluates such stock to fair value to the profit-and-loss account—in the case of stock classified into the trading portfolio compared with stock classified into available-for-sale portfolio that is revaluated to equity.
- The stock includes shares traded on the public market. In the case of listing and delisting, the day of sale is decisive.

If the stock is classified into an available-for-sale portfolio that is revaluated to equity or in the case of shares that are not listed on the public market at the sale day, the recognition of revaluation differences is deferred for tax purposes until the disposal of such stock. This applies if the revaluation differences are canceled against the stock; if the revaluation differences are released from equity directly to profit-and-loss account, they do not affect the tax base. For tax treatment of losses from sale of stock, see Section 7.3.

(ii) Stock with substantial or decisive control   Stock representing decisive or controlling interest (generally more than a 20 percent shareholding) is not revalued to fair value. The company may opt for revaluation of (all) stock by the equity method (valuation of the stock at net asset values); otherwise, the stock is held at cost. If the company revaluates the stocks, the revaluation differences are posted to equity. Upon disposal, the revaluation differences are canceled against the stock. For tax treatment of losses from sale of these stocks, see Section 7.3.

(c) Tax groupings   Czech companies are taxed on a stand-alone basis. The concept of tax groupings is not currently incorporated into the Czech tax system.

4.   FINANCING OF ACQUISITIONS

4.1   Debt

Specific tax issues related to the overall level of borrowings and the interest charged on this debt are as follows:

- Withholding tax
- Deductibility of interest

(a) Withholding tax   Interest payments to non-Czech lenders are subject to withholding tax at a rate of 15 percent. This rate can be reduced by double-tax treaties, which the Czech Republic has entered into with most other countries. There is no withholding tax on interest payments between Czech companies. In addition, no withholding tax applies to the interest under the conditions set out in the Interest and Royalty Directive effective for the Czech Republic after accession to the EU on May 1, 2004.

(b) Deductibility of interest   The following rules govern the tax deductibility of interest. All of the following rules have to be complied with for interest to be treated as tax deductible:

- Purpose of the loan
- Thin capitalization
- Transfer pricing

(i) Purpose of the loan   From 2004, the Income Taxes Act explicitly prohibits deduction of interest from loans taken with respect to holding of shares. Any loans taken during the six months preceding the acquisition of shares are considered to have been taken with respect to the holding of shares unless the company can prove otherwise. However, this rule applies only if the shares are held for an uninterrupted period of at least two years and the companies meet the definition of parent company and subsidiary under the parent/subsidiary directive. An amendment to the Income Taxes Act, which is currently pending in Parliament, proposes to apply the prohibition of deduction of interest related to the holding of shares regardless of the two-year period.

(ii) Thin capitalization   For loans from related parties, thin-capitalization provisions apply and may limit the amount of tax-deductible interest. According to the thin-capitalization rules, if the borrower's debt/equity ratio exceeds 4:1, the excess portion of interest paid to the related party represents a non-tax-deductible expense for the borrower, and under certain circumstances—such as when the lender is a non-Czech party—it may be reclassified as a distribution of dividends.

The thin-capitalization rules do not apply in the year of incorporation or for the next three succeeding years. However, only companies incorporated before the end of 2003 can take advantage of this holiday period. Companies incorporated after December 31, 2003, are subject to thin-capitalization rules immediately from their incorporation

(iii) Transfer pricing   If a loan is received from a related party—including brother-sister companies—the rate of interest should be at arm's length to comply with transfer-pricing rules. If the interest rate exceeds arm's length, the excess amount would be nontax-deductible and potentially regarded as a deemed distribution of dividends subject to withholding tax.

4.2   Equity

There is no capital duty on the issuance of new stock. This issuance of equity as a method of funding can be advantageous because it improves the debt/equity ratio of the company for thin-capitalization purposes.

5.   MERGERS

5.1   Legal Forms

The Czech Commercial Code allows, among others, the following methods for the restructuring of companies.

- Fusion (merger, consolidation)
- Absorption (squeeze-out merger)

While the fusion or absorption is legally effective by registration in the Commercial Register, for tax and accounting purposes the concept of decisive day is applied. The decisive day is the starting day of the process and is defined as the day from which the legal actions of the dissolving company—from the corporate income tax and accounting points of view—are considered to be actions made on behalf of and for the account of the legal successor. (That is, for accounting and corporate income tax purposes, the merger is effective from the decisive day.) Thus, if the decisive day is, for example, January 1, 2004, and the merger is registered on September 1, 2004, in the Commercial Register, all actions of the dissolving company from January 1 to September 1, 2004, would, from corporate income tax and accounting points of view, be considered as having been made on behalf of and for the account of the legal successor.

5.2   Typical Scenarios

(a) Fusion

(i) Merger   In a merger, the assets and liabilities of one company (company A) are transferred to an existing company (company B). Company A ceases to exist legally from the moment the merger is registered in the Commercial Register. The companies need not have the same shareholders.

Czech law allows, in a limited way, the fusion of companies with different legal forms, such as a general commercial partnership with a limited partnership or a limited liability company with a joint-stock company.

(ii) Consolidation   In a consolidation, the assets and liabilities of two or more existing companies—say, companies A and B—are transferred to a newly established company—company C—which is the legal successor of companies A and B. Other conditions are the same as they are for a fusion by merger.

(b) Absorption   A special case is the so-called squeeze-out merger, whereby a company can be merged with its majority shareholder that holds more than 90 percent of shares. The squeeze-out merger is most often used in the case of joint-stock companies. The minority shareholders do not acquire any shareholding in the company after the restructuring but are entitled to adequate compensation for their abolished shares.

5.3   Tax Consequences

(a) Corporate income tax   In principle, the aforementioned processes—merger, consolidation, and absorption—are tax neutral. The legal successor

takes a carryover basis in the assets and continues the tax depreciation of the assets of the dissolving company by using the same depreciation method and tax residual value of the assets from the books of the dissolving company. This applies even if revaluation of assets is done according to commercial law; that is, no step-up is generally available for tax purposes.

In these restructuring processes, the tax losses of a dissolving company are not transferable to a legal successor, with the following exception: losses incurred after accession of the Czech Republic to the EU can be transferred to a legal successor in the merger or consolidation process under certain conditions. The transfer of tax losses does not apply to an absorption.

(b) VAT   No VAT is charged on the transfer of assets in the fusion/absorption.

(c) Transfer taxes   The transfer of real estate in a fusion/absorption process is exempt from RETT.

6.   OTHER STRUCTURING AND POSTDEAL ISSUES

6.1   Minimizing the After-Tax Cost of Debt

The conditions for deductibility of interest are described in Section 4. While these conditions are achievable in the cases of asset or business transfers, it may be complicated to achieve tax-deductible interest on a loan for an acquisition of shares. This is due to the prohibition of interest deduction under certain conditions (see Section 4.1) and due to the interpretation by the Czech Ministry of Finance that the interest on a loan for purchase of shares can be deductible only if the shares were purchased with the intent to subsequently sell them; that is, the purchaser will realize a capital gain.

To mitigate the risk of tax nondeductibility, it may be necessary to merge the purchaser and the target company and/or to refinance or restructure the acquisition loan. This issue needs to be specifically addressed on a case-by-case basis.

Interest on a loan for operational purposes should be tax deductible under the general rules described earlier.

6.2   Repatriation of Profits and Cash

There are a number of ways that cash and profit may be passed up to the holding company:

- **Payment of dividends.** In accordance with the current Czech Income Taxes Act, the distribution of dividends by a Czech company to either another Czech company or a non-Czech company is subject to 15 percent withholding tax. The rate can be reduced by a relevant tax treaty.

- **Parent/subsidiary directive.** The parent/subsidiary directive is effective from EU accession on May 1, 2004. Under this directive, dividends paid by a Czech subsidiary to a parent company seated in another EU member state or in the Czech Republic are exempt from withholding tax if the parent company holds a minimum 25 percent share in the subsidiary continuously for at least two years. The tax-free distribution of dividends can be effected before reaching the two-year holding period if this period is achieved subsequently.
- **Intercompany loans.** Rules for the tax deductibility of interest are covered in Section 4.
- **Reduction of share capital.** According to Czech tax legislation, reduction of the share capital of a limited liability company or a joint-stock company is generally not subject to taxation. However, if the share capital was previously increased from the company's own profit or other reserves, that element of the capital decrease would be treated as a distribution of dividends. In this situation, the relevant amount of repaid capital would be subject to 15 percent withholding tax, which may be reduced by an appropriate double-tax treaty.

6.3   Noncore Disposals

There is no such provision in Czech tax law.

6.4   Preservation of Existing Tax Attributes

Tax losses assessed for periods preceding the fiscal year starting in 2004 can be carried forward and deducted from the tax base for the next seven consecutive years. For tax losses assessed for the fiscal year beginning in 2004 and onward, the carryforward period is only five consecutive years, Moreover, if a greater-than-25-percent change of ownership of shares in the company occurs, the tax loss (regardless of the period) can be deducted only if the company continues to achieve at least 80 percent of its revenues from activities carried out the same as before the change of ownership.

The tax loss is not transferable to other entities, with the exception specified in Section 5, Mergers, and Section 10, Demergers, and with the exception of contributions of business as a going concern in line with the Merger Directive.

6.5   Receipts under Warranties or Indemnities

Payments made by the seller for breach of warranty or under an indemnity—that is, contractual penalty—do not, in accordance with Czech accounting law, form a part of the acquisition price for the purchaser. Such payments are taxable revenues in the hands of the recipient.

7.   DISPOSALS

This section details tax aspects of the transfer of individual assets, business, and stock from the seller's point of view.

7.1   Asset Disposals (Companies Only)

The sale of assets is subject to the following taxes:

- Corporate income tax
- VAT
- Real Estate Transfer Tax

(a) *Corporate income tax*   Sales of assets are normally included in the seller's taxable income—at the value of the sold asset. The company is allowed to reduce the taxable proceeds by the acquisition value (tax basis) of the sold assets. However, when two parties are related, special rules exist that allow the assets to be reinstated to market value for tax purposes. The loss incurred generally represents a tax-deductible expense. However, some exceptions exist (land, receivables), in which case the loss from the sale would be treated as a nondeductible cost and could not be utilized in the future.

(b) *VAT*   The sale of assets is generally subject to VAT. In most cases, the basic 19 percent rate is applied. The sale of real estate is generally exempt from VAT, with some exceptions.

(c) *Real Estate Transfer Tax*   The seller is liable for RETT on the sale of its real estate.

7.2   Business Disposals

(a) *Corporate income tax*   Proceeds from the sale of a business are subject to corporate income tax; the seller can reduce the taxable proceeds by the acquisition value (tax basis) of assets. Liabilities belonging to the sold business are written off to revenues and taxed. If the sale of a business results in a loss, the loss is recognized for tax purposes.

(b) *VAT*   The sale of a business is not subject to VAT.

(c) *RETT*   The transfer of real estate under the sale of a business is subject to RETT under the same conditions as described for an asset deal.

7.3   Stock Disposals

(a) *Companies*

(i) *Stock revalued to fair value*   Capital gains or losses from sale of stock that can be revalued to fair value (generally, interests of up to a 20 percent shareholding) are included in the tax base of the seller.

(ii) Other stock   The loss incurred from the sale of stock other than stock revalued to fair value cannot reduce the tax base and, therefore, represents a nondeductible cost for the seller. This includes stock in joint-stock companies with a shareholding of over 20 percent and any share in a limited liability company, limited partnership, or cooperative. The loss on the sale of such stock is determined individually for each stock.

(b) Individuals   Profits from stock disposals—that is, proceeds reduced by acquisition value of the stock—are generally subject to personal income tax at graduated rates. Loss from the sale of stock is not recognized for tax purposes. In some cases, proceeds from the sale may be exempt from taxation as discussed later.

The exemption applies only if the stock was not recorded as part of the business property of the individual—that is, was not acquired in connection with the individual's business activities. Proceeds from the sale of stock are exempt from taxation if the minimum holding period is achieved. This is a period of six months for shares in a joint-stock company and five years for a limited liability company, limited partnership, or cooperative.

7.4   Deferred Consideration and Earn-Outs

The revenue from deferred consideration and earn-outs is taxed on an accrual basis if it is quantifiable. If the revenue cannot be quantified at the time of the disposal, it is included in revenues and taxed at the time when its amount can be estimated or quantified. This means that contingent earn-outs are taxed in the different taxable periods to which they accrue.

7.5   Payments under Warranties or Indemnities

Payments under warranties and indemnities are tax deductible for the seller when they are actually paid, provided the seller can prove they were incurred in order to generate, ensure, or maintain its taxable revenues.

8.   TREATMENT OF TRANSACTION COSTS

8.1   Transfer Taxes

See the discussion in Section 2.

8.2   Value-Added Tax

See the discussion in Section 2.

8.3   Tax Deductibility of Transaction Costs

See the discussion in Section 2.

9.   PREPARING A TARGET COMPANY FOR SALE

Presale planning is a very important phase, especially in mergers, acquisitions, and demergers. Opportunities for planning should be explored on a case-by-case basis.

10.   DEMERGERS

In a demerger process, company A is dissolved without liquidation and all of its assets and liabilities are transferred to two or more legal successors. The successors can be newly established companies, already existing companies (separation by merger), or in the form of a combination of newly established and existing companies. The demerger comes into legal effect upon its registration in the Commercial Register.

Until the day it is deleted from the Commercial Register, the dissolving company acts as a separate legal entity. For corporate income tax and accounting purposes, the concept of decisive day is applied similarly as for fusion or absorption as described in Section 5.

The tax consequences of fusion or absorption described in Section 5 apply similarly for demergers. A tax loss of the demerging company can be transferred to the legal successor only if it is assessed for the fiscal year beginning in 2004 and onwards under the conditions of the Council (Merger) Directive.

11.   LISTINGS AND INITIAL PUBLIC OFFERINGS

The tax status of a company is generally unaffected by a listing or initial public offering (IPO).

DENMARK

INTRODUCTION

This chapter details the principal tax issues that are relevant to purchasers and sellers engaged in the transfer of ownership of a Danish trade or business. Unless otherwise stated, it is generally assumed that all sellers and purchasers are Danish companies with limited liability.

In this chapter a Danish company is defined as a public or private limited company. Other forms of legal entities exist in Denmark, and special caution should be observed if an acquisition involves an entity other than a public or private limited company.

The transfer of ownership of a Danish business or company takes the form of a disposition of shares or assets. There are significant differences in the tax implications of asset deals and stock deals. This chapter does not discuss in detail all of the various nontax considerations.

The relevant taxes to be considered are:

- **Corporate tax.** Generally, this is a 30 percent tax on profits earned by a company. Danish companies are taxed on a stand-alone basis. However, profits and losses arising in the same period can be offset between members of a Danish joint taxation.
- **Value-added tax (VAT).** This is a sales tax whereby 25 percent is added to the sales price charged for goods and services (except for certain categories of sale that are exempt from or outside the scope of VAT). A purchaser or recipient of services can generally recover VAT paid if the purchase was incurred in the course of a commercial activity. However, the level of recoverability depends on the commercial activities performed by the purchaser or recipient of services and therefore varies from case to case.
- **Payroll tax.** Most of the activities exempt from VAT are subject to payroll tax. The payroll tax is calculated as a percentage of the wages paid in the VAT-exempt activities. For some activities the payroll tax is calculated on the basis of both the payroll and the profit or loss regarding the activities. However, profit or loss in relation to a closing down or sale of activities is not subject to payroll tax.
- **Land registration fee.** This is payable by a purchaser at DKK1,400 plus 0.6 percent on the purchase price for land or real estate. The land registration fee applies only in connection with an asset purchase.

1.   ACQUISITIONS

An acquisition takes the form of an acquisition of shares or assets. In addition, the acquisition can take the form of either a tax-free or taxable merger or a contribution of assets, which can also be either tax free or taxable.

1.1   Asset Acquisitions

An asset acquisition generally enables the purchaser to avoid exposure related to any historical liabilities. Liabilities associated with the business being purchased remain the responsibility of the company making the asset sale and do not become the responsibility of the purchaser unless the parties agree that specific liabilities are being transferred to the purchaser.

For tax purposes, an asset acquisition is effective from the date the sales agreement is signed without significant reservations. Profit from the business is taxable to the purchaser from that date even though the purchase price is based on the value at a previous date or at any agreed-to effective date.

Generally, an asset acquisition allows the purchaser to step up the tax basis of assets. The consideration paid should be allocated between different assets in the sale documentation. By and large, the Danish tax authorities accept such allocations as the new tax basis for the acquired assets if the seller and purchaser have opposing interests in the allocation.

Acquired goodwill can be depreciated over seven years on a straight-line basis. Certain restrictions regarding the depreciable value of goodwill apply in case of intragroup transactions. Costs related to purchase of patents, know-how, and rights to utilize such intangibles can be either fully expensed in the year of acquisition or depreciated over seven years on a straight-line basis.

1.2   Stock Acquisitions

In a stock acquisition, the purchaser effectively bears all historical and future ongoing tax and nontax liabilities of the target company. No step-up is permitted in the tax basis of the company's assets. Any goodwill allocated as part of a share deal is not deductible for tax purposes. (See Section 3.2.) Therefore, from a purchaser's tax perspective, it is often advantageous to acquire assets rather than stock.

In Denmark there is a potential conflict between the preferences of the purchaser and those of the seller because the seller's disposal of stock may be exempt from tax on capital gains if certain criteria are met. (See Section 7.1.) There is no such exemption on a disposal of assets. Therefore, a purchaser may want to acquire assets, and a seller may prefer to sell stock.

2.   TRANSACTION COSTS FOR PURCHASERS

2.1   Transfer Taxes

(a) Stock purchases   No transfer tax is payable by the purchaser as a result of a stock purchase.

(b) Asset purchases   The purchaser must pay a land registration fee equal to 0.6 percent of the value of land or real estate acquired. If different types of assets are acquired, only the consideration allocable to land and real estate is subject to the land registration fee. However, the basis for calculating the land registration fee cannot be smaller than the latest public assessment of the land or real estate.

If a company owns land, no land registration fee is payable if only the stock of the company is acquired—with the land remaining in the ownership of the company.

2.2   Value-Added Tax

(a) Stock purchases   Stock transfers are exempt from VAT.

(b) Asset purchases   A transfer of business assets that qualifies as a transfer of a going concern is not subject to VAT. Other asset purchases are subject to VAT at a rate of 25 percent, which is payable in addition to the purchase consideration.

If the buying entity is subject to VAT and is obliged to charge VAT on its sales—called outputs—it may recover the VAT it paid on its own purchases, called inputs. A purchase of assets on which the seller has charged VAT is regarded as an input for the buyer; therefore, VAT charged may be recovered by the buyer. In some situations, depending on certain VAT-related characteristics of the buyer, the VAT paid on inputs may not be fully recoverable, and the VAT paid represents a real cost to the buyer.

2.3   Capital Taxes

No capital taxes apply to stock or asset purchases in Denmark.

2.4   Tax Deductibility of Transaction Costs

In general, all expenses incurred during a year to obtain, ensure, or maintain the income are tax deductible. In contrast, expenses incurred to obtain or ensure the capital base are not deductible unless the tax deduction is stated in a specific tax provision.

Whether or not a particular transaction expense gets treated as deductible depends on several factors, including:

- Whether the transaction is a purchase of assets or a purchase of stock
- Why the expense is incurred and to whom the expense is paid
- How the debt financing is structured

In general terms, the position can be summarized as follows:

- Finance costs
- Investigation and due diligence costs
- Other transaction costs
- VAT treatment of expenses

(a) Finance costs Generally, the costs incurred to form a company or to raise equity financing are not deductible. At best, such costs can be added to the tax basis of the acquired company and reduce capital gains on a subsequent disposition.

Costs related to obtaining debt financing are generally deductible on an accrued basis—that is, amortized over the life of the loan.

No deduction is allowed for the capital loss incurred when a Danish borrower repays a loan amount at a premium over par.

(b) Investigation and due diligence costs Generally, due diligence and other investigatory costs are not deductible unless the costs are tax deductible according to the general tax deduction principles or solely to the extent that such costs are paid to auditors or lawyers for the purpose of establishing or extending an existing business.

In general, due diligence and other investigatory costs are not deductible in connection with a stock acquisition. However, a recent ruling by the Danish Supreme Court has relaxed that general rule somewhat with regard to costs paid to auditors and lawyers.

(c) Other transaction costs Costs incurred to acquire assets may be deductible either as direct charges to profit and loss or as additions to the basis for depreciation of the assets. The determination is made on a case-by-case basis.

(d) VAT treatment of expenses Fees charged for making arrangements for loans and for issuing stock usually are not subject to VAT in Denmark, but the case law regarding financial transactions is not clear. Therefore, bank and institutional fees generally are not subject to VAT. Professional fees charged to local

customers by advisers based in Denmark, however, usually are subject to VAT even if the fees are related to the sale or issue of stock or to loan financing.

Input VAT—which is VAT charged by third parties for goods or services provided—that is related directly to the issue of stock to Denmark or European Union (EU) counterparties may not be recovered.

VAT on professional fees incurred for a transaction other than that related directly to the issue of stock can be treated as an overhead expense of the group and is recoverable in full, unless the group is subject to the partial-exemption method.

It is important that costs be identified separately on invoices so that input VAT can be attributed accurately to the issue of stock and to other matters.

VAT on costs related to an asset transfer is fully recoverable if the business transferred is fully subject to VAT. If the asset transfer is not a transfer of a going concern, the deductibility for costs depends on the assets transferred; no deduction is available if it concerns immovable property or shares.

3.   BASIS OF TAXATION FOLLOWING ASSET OR STOCK ACQUISITIONS

3.1   Asset Acquisitions

Generally, an asset acquisition allows the purchaser to step up the tax basis of assets. The consideration paid should be allocated between different assets in the sale documentation. By and large, the Danish tax authorities accept such allocations as the new tax basis for the acquired assets if the seller and purchaser have opposite interests in the allocation.

Tax depreciation of up to 25 percent annually on a declining-balance basis is available for plant, machinery, and office equipment acquired—based on the price paid for those assets.

Tax depreciation of up to 5 percent annually on a straight-line basis is available for industrial buildings and fixtures. Office buildings, buildings for residential purposes, and such buildings as hotel apartments, hospitals, and human care buildings do not qualify for tax depreciation.

Purchased intangible assets and goodwill are amortized over seven years on a straight-line basis. Intangible assets other than goodwill can be amortized over the remaining protection period if other laws protect the intangible assets for less than seven years.

As an alternative, acquired know-how and patents can be written off in the year of acquisition.

The sale agreement must include an allocation of the purchase price on the assets subject to tax depreciation. At a minimum, the allocation must be shown on machinery and equipment, buildings, fixtures, and goodwill and other intangible assets.

Normally, sales of inventory are included in the seller's operating income, and the purchaser receives a tax basis equal to the purchase price. Similar rules apply to work in progress.

Usually, trade receivables are acquired at net book value. If one of the receivables is fully or partially uncollectible, a bad-debt deduction is allowed.

If trade receivables are acquired at net book value, the purchaser cannot deduct the VAT if the receivables prove uncollectible. Deduction for VAT on bad receivables is possible only if the receivable is acquired at nominal value.

3.2   Stock Acquisitions

(a) Purchase price   The purchase price becomes the purchaser's basis in the acquired stock. The underlying basis of the acquired company's assets is not changed, and there is no election available to step up the tax basis of assets. Accounting goodwill arising on the consolidation of the company in the financial statements of the Danish parent is not tax deductible.

Costs incurred to acquire stock, which are not tax deductible at the time incurred, can be added to the basis of the stock acquired.

(b) Tax grouping   Denmark has a separate entity basis of taxation. However, profits and losses arising in the same period can be offset among members of a Danish joint taxation. (See Section 6.2.)

4.   FINANCING OF ACQUISITIONS

4.1   Debt

Specific tax issues related to the overall level of debt and the interest charged on that debt are:

- Withholding tax
- Deductibility of interest
- Thin capitalization
- Transfer pricing
- Transparent entities
- Key nontax issues

(a) Withholding tax   As the main rule, there is no withholding tax on interest payments even if the payments are between Danish companies or to companies outside Denmark.

However, newly adopted rules make certain intercompany interest payments and capital losses on intercompany loans subject to 30 percent withholding tax. Only interest payments and capital losses paid to a group company that is resident in a low-tax country with which Denmark has no tax treaty are subject to withholding tax.

(b) Deductibility of interest   In Denmark, interest expense is generally deductible on an accrual basis.

Unless the lender is able to provide documentation that sufficient assets are available to cover all liabilities, there is a restriction that interest is deductible only when paid—rather than on an accrual basis—if the interest accrued in previous periods has not been paid,

As a general rule, interest is not subject to VAT.

(c) Thin capitalization   Danish thin-capitalization rules apply when a Danish resident entity has a loan with a related legal entity or with an independent lender if the loan is secured by a related legal entity (controlled debt). Debt is considered controlled if the loan is provided for (or secured) by a legal entity that owns, directly or indirectly, more than 50 percent of the share capital of the Danish borrower or controls more than 50 percent of the voting rights.

If the Danish company in question is thinly capitalized, it will no longer be allowed to deduct (for tax purposes) interest payments to related lenders.

However, the limitation of deductions for tax purposes is applicable only if:

- The controlled debt exceeds a threshold of DKK10 million.

- The loan could not have been obtained from an independent lender on similar terms. The company has the burden of proof.

- The debt/equity ratio exceeds 4:1.

A Danish lender is not taxed on interest payments or on capital gains made by a related Danish borrower that has had its deduction limited for thin-capitalization reasons.

Equity is calculated at year-end as the fair market value of the assets (including nonbooked assets such as goodwill) minus debt at year-end. Debt consists of all debt, controlled and uncontrolled, and is also valued at market value at year-end.

If the 4:1 ratio is exceeded, only interest deductions and capital gains allocated to that part of controlled debt, which should have been converted into equity to meet the 4:1 ratio, are limited for tax purposes.

The interest payments are not reclassified as dividend payments.

If several Danish companies—including some non-Danish companies that make up part of a Danish joint taxation—are controlled—that is, more than 50 percent of the notional share capital or more than 50 percent of the voting rights is in the hands of the same group of shareholders—then the 4:1 ratio might apply to those companies on a consolidated basis. In that case, shareholdings, debts, and claims between the consolidated companies will be eliminated.

Capital contributed to a Danish company to avoid a thin-capitalization position must be maintained in the company for at least two years.

(d) Transfer pricing Loans between a Danish company and a group company must be on an arm's-length basis; otherwise, transfer-pricing rules may apply to restrict the interest deductions.

Danish tax authorities can use transfer pricing to challenge intercompany loans even if the Danish company, from an overall perspective, has an acceptable debt-to-equity ratio. A risk of transfer pricing adjustment also exists when the debt is provided by a third party but guaranteed by a foreign group company.

(e) Transparent entities According to newly adopted rules, Danish entities, which are otherwise separate and autonomous entities for Danish tax purposes, are considered transparent for Danish tax purposes under certain conditions.

The new rules apply only if:

- The Danish entity is controlled by a foreign entity—that is, the foreign entity owns, directly or indirectly, more than 50 percent of the nominal share capital or voting rights of the Danish entity.
- The Danish entity is treated as transparent for local tax purposes in the relevant foreign country.
- The Danish entity's income is included in the income of the controlling foreign entity.
- The foreign company is resident in an EU or European Economic Area member state or in a country with which Denmark has a double-taxation treaty.

If the Danish entity is considered transparent for Danish purposes, the Danish entity is not entitled to deduct payments made to the foreign entity or to other transparent entities, because the payments are considered payments made within the same legal entity. Instead, the controlling foreign entity becomes subject to a limited Danish tax liability on the Danish entity's taxable income.

(f) Key nontax issues The rules regarding financial assistance are intended to maintain share capital for the protection of creditors and to prevent, for example, the purchase of stock in a company using the proceeds of a loan from that company, or the company providing security in its assets to secure external

borrowings that were used to fund the purchase of the company's stock. Lawyers and other competent professionals should always be consulted on these matters.

The general rule is that if a person is acquiring or is proposing to acquire stock in a company, it is not lawful for the company or any of its subsidiaries to provide financial assistance directly or indirectly for the purpose of that acquisition. If a person has already acquired stock, the company may not provide "financial assistance" for the purpose of reducing or discharging any liability of the purchaser or anyone else incurred for the purposes of the acquisition.

The criminal and civil consequences of a breach of the financial assistance rules can be serious. In addition, any transaction entered into in breach of the rules is void.

4.2   Equity

There is no capital duty on the issuance of new stock.

Dividends are not deductible by the company paying the dividend. Dividends received by a Danish company are not taxable if the shareholder owns at least 20 percent of the payer's stock for at least the 12-month period in which the dividends are paid. Otherwise, 66 percent of the received dividend is taxable. A Danish individual is taxed on dividend income.

Dividend distribution from a Danish company is subject to a 28 percent withholding tax. The withholding tax can be avoided or reduced if the recipient company is resident in the EU or in a state having a double-tax treaty with Denmark.

Equity financing is advantageous because it improves the debt-to-equity ratio of the company, thereby potentially enabling additional interest-bearing debt to be issued by the company. (See Section 4.1(c).)

VAT on costs related to the issuing of new stock is not deductible if the stock is sold or becomes listed.

5.   MERGERS

5.1   Legal Forms

From a legal perspective, a merger can be consummated in two ways:

1. One company absorbs another company, and the absorbed company ceases to exist in legal terms.

2. Two or more existing companies merge into a newly established common company, and both existing companies cease to exist following the merger into the newly established company.

Mergers can be vertical or horizontal without any legal requirements as to which party should be the continuing company.

However, regardless of the specific form of the merger, all preexisting liabilities—whether tax or nontax, actual or contingent—are transferred to the successor company.

5.2   Typical Scenarios

From a tax perspective, mergers can be either tax free or taxable. In either case, the merger can have retroactive effect.

(a) Taxable merger   In a taxable merger, all assets and liabilities are transferred from one company to another, which afterward will be the continuing company.

The amount of tax the company transferring all assets and liabilities to the continuing company is subject to is the amount of tax the company would have been subject to if the company had been liquidated. (See Section 5.3(a).)

A taxable merger may be preferable when one of the merged companies has tax-loss carryforwards, because such tax losses will be lost in a tax-free merger.

Further, a taxable merger may be preferable if the merged companies have specific interest in a merger date that could not be obtained under the provision of a tax-free merger. Finally, a taxable merger could be preferable if the merged companies cannot or do not wish to fulfill the specific requirements for a tax-free merger.

(b) Tax-free merger   In a tax-free merger, the successor company assumes the tax position of the predecessor company in all aspects. The assets and liabilities of the predecessor company are transferred to the successor company and in every aspect are treated the same way as in the predecessor company in terms of holding period, basis, purpose of acquisition, and special tax conditions connected to assets and liabilities.

A tax-free merger is generally the preferable model if neither of the merged companies have tax losses to carry forward and if it is the intention to complete a merger without any tax consequences in any of the merged companies. Generally, in a tax-free merger, all tax losses that are carried forward in the merged company are lost permanently.

The legal requirements for a taxable or a tax-free merger are the same both in terms of documents to be filed for legal purposes and in terms of filing deadlines to be observed. Additionally, a tax-free merger requires the filing of documents with the Danish tax authorities. The documents to be filed depend on the specific circumstances of the tax-free merger because some tax-free mergers require an approval from the tax authorities.

5.3   Tax Consequences

(a) Taxable merger   A taxable merger requires that all assets and liabilities be transferred at fair market value to the continuing company. A valuation of the predecessor company is, therefore, required.

The taxable merger allows for a step-up in basis for tax depreciation if a fair market valuation exceeds the current tax values.

In the predecessor company, the taxable merger results in a taxable disposition of all of the assets and liabilities. This is similar to liquidation taxation. Thus, capital gains on the assets are taxed based on a sales value equal to the fair market value.

Whether a taxable merger results in actual tax payments in the predecessor company depends on the amount of tax losses carried forward.

(b) Tax-free merger   In some cases, a tax-free merger requires an approval from the Danish tax authorities. If the tax authorities do not approve the tax-free merger, then the merger is considered taxable if consummated. The Danish tax authorities will not approve a tax-free merger if the only purpose is tax avoidance.

The following circumstances always require an approval for a tax-free merger from the Danish tax authorities:

- A parent company wishes to merge with a subsidiary, but the parent company has owned the shares in the subsidiary for less than three years.
- Any of the merged companies have acquired assets from a group company outside the normal course of business within a period of three years from the effective date of the merger.
- Any of the merged companies have been established within a year of the final decision to merge the companies, or the ownership of the shares or voting rights in any of the companies has changed by more than 50 percent within the past year prior to the final decision to merge the companies.

If none of the aforementioned circumstances applies to the merger, then a tax-free merger can be completed without an approval. However, consultation with tax professionals is recommended.

The tax authorities can deny the application, issue a blanket approval, or give approval with qualifications. An approval with qualifications requires that the merged company fulfill during the period the requirements stated in the qualification; otherwise, the merger becomes a taxable merger.

It is required that shares in the successor company be issued to the shareholders in the predecessor company equal to the contribution of equity in the merged company. The requirement for issuing shares does not apply to a vertical merger.

5.4   VAT Consequences

Generally, although the transfer of a going concern is not subject to VAT, the transfer of independent assets is subject to VAT unless both transferor and transferee are part of the same VAT group.

There is no VAT on a transfer of stock.

6.   OTHER STRUCTURING AND POSTDEAL ISSUES

6.1   Minimizing After-Tax Costs of Debt

As part of overall debt funding within the target group after the acquisition has been completed, the following methods may be used as tax-efficient means of pushing deductible interest expense into Denmark. Danish thin-capitalization rules (see Section 4.1(c)) should be considered.

(a) *Borrowing to pay a dividend*   A loan is obtained to fund the payment of a dividend out of distributable reserves. In general, the tax deduction for the interest expense is not challenged if thin-capitalization rules at the group level are observed and the loan is established on arm's-length terms. (See Section 4.2 for information on withholding tax on dividend payments.)

(b) *Inserting a debt-funded new Danish holding company*   A new Danish company is set up within the buyer's group (DK Holdco). DK Holdco then purchases the Danish target companies for cash from their current parent company(ies). A mixture of debt and equity funds DK Holdco, which must comply with Danish thin-capitalization rules at the group level. The tax issues arising are broadly similar to those covered in Section 4.1(a).

A Danish joint taxation is then established between DK Holdco and the target group and allows the interest expenses related to the acquisition sum to be offset against profits in the target groups. Careful tax planning must be observed regarding the timing and method of the incorporation of DK Holdco.

6.2   Creating Local-Country Tax Groups

(a) *Creating Danish joint taxation*   For group relief purposes whereby the losses of one group company can be used to offset the profits of another, a Danish joint taxation could be formed. A Danish joint taxation generally requires that a 100 percent shareholding relationship be created. A Danish joint taxation can also include foreign subsidiaries.

Ownership can be direct or indirect. In the case of indirect ownership, it is required that all shareholders be included in the Danish joint taxation. For example, if company A owns 60 percent of company C and 100 percent of company B and if company B owns 40 percent of company C, then company C can be part of a Danish joint taxation only if both companies A and B are included in the Danish joint taxation.

Besides the shareholder requirement, there are a number of other requirements for a company to be part of a Danish joint taxation.

All members of the joint taxation are jointly liable for the joint taxation group's tax liability.

Danish joint taxation is particularly relevant in the year of acquisition because it may provide the possibility to offset the interest expense incurred as a result of the acquisition against the profits in the acquired companies. For the purchaser to receive the full benefit of Danish joint taxation, some timing issues concerning the incorporation of a Danish acquisition vehicle need to be considered. Competent professionals should always be consulted on these matters prior to establishing the acquisition structure.

(b) Recapturing foreign tax losses   Danish joint taxation provides the possibility of including a non-Danish company. However, if losses in a foreign jointly taxed company are offset against profits in other jointly taxed companies, then a deferred tax liability in relation to recapture of the tax losses arises.

Generally, the utilized tax losses from foreign companies in the joint taxation are subject to recapture (become taxable) in the Danish parent company in the year the joint taxation is discontinued—regardless of whether the discontinuation is due to reasons related to the Danish parent company or due to reasons related to the foreign company.

In addition to the discontinuation of a joint taxation, intragroup transfers of assets or business activities trigger the balance of foreign tax losses to become taxable in the Danish parent.

In general, the balance of foreign tax losses is increased by foreign tax losses utilized in the Danish joint taxation and is reduced by subsequent profits from the foreign company, which are taxed in Denmark under the Danish joint taxation.

(c) VAT   Two or more companies that are engaged solely in VAT-registered activities can be members of a domestic VAT group. Furthermore, the authorities can allow two or more companies that carry out activities that are both subject to and exempt from VAT to be members of a domestic VAT group. In the latter case, the rules in Denmark allow only companies that have full

control—that is, 100 percent of shares—to become members of a VAT group. The only exception to the rule on full control is that certain preference shares can be issued to employees. In effect, doing so decreases the ownership ratio for the parent.

When joining a VAT group, the taxable entity must be established in Denmark as, for example, a branch or a company. A fiscal representative of a foreign company cannot be a member of a domestic VAT group.

When there is a VAT group, no VAT is charged on intragroup supplies of goods or services. However, consideration should be given prior to making a group VAT election—especially if some of the group companies provide non-taxable supplies, because this can reduce the group's right to recover VAT on its own purchases. All members of the VAT group are jointly liable for the group's VAT liability.

6.3   Repatriating Profits

Dividends received by a Danish company are not subject to tax if the recipient company owns at least 20 percent of the stock of a subsidiary for a period of 12 months in which the dividend is paid. Otherwise, 66 percent of the dividend amount is subject to 30 percent tax.

Dividends received from a company resident in a tax haven, which has mainly financial activities, are subject to corporation tax on the full amount unless the underlying income is already taxed in Denmark as a consequence of Danish controlled-foreign-company legislation.

A Danish company may claim double-tax relief. This relief is normally given by way of a credit against Danish tax payable.

6.4   Disposing of Noncore Entities

The sale of a subsidiary by a Danish company after acquisition—including, for example, capital contribution—may be exempt from corporate tax if the entire share capital of the subsidiary has been held for at least three years. If the exemption is not available, then the sale is subject to capital gain taxation at 30 percent. If the sale results in a capital loss, then the loss can, in the future (indefinitely), offset only capital gains arising from disposition of stock also with less than three years of ownership.

Any intended postacquisition disposition should be reviewed carefully to ensure that it will not give rise to hidden tax liabilities—such as when the balance of recaptured foreign tax losses becomes taxable. (See Section 5.3.)

6.5   Preservation of Existing Tax Attributes

(a) *Restrictions in utilizing tax losses due to change of ownership*   Tax losses and other similar tax attributes of the target company and its subsidiaries are subject to certain restrictions in the utilization of the tax losses following a change in ownership.

Existing tax losses in the target company and its subsidiaries can offset only income from normal trade. The tax losses cannot offset financial income, dividend income, capital gains, and certain lease income.

The restrictions apply if more than 50 percent of the share capital or 50 percent of the voting rights have changed owners within a year. The restrictions also apply if the change in ownership takes place in a company above the Danish company. That is, a change in ownership in a foreign company that owns a Danish company imposes a restriction on the utilization of tax losses in the Danish company too, even if the direct ownership of the Danish company has not changed.

(b) Reducing tax losses due to forgiveness of debt   The forgiveness of debt either as an agreement with the Danish company's creditors, or as a debt conversion, or as a capital injection followed by a repayment of debt to group companies may reduce the balance of tax losses carried forward.

The same reduction applies to intercompany debt if the remission of debt implies a write-off of the debt to an amount less than the market value for the creditor.

The forgiveness of debt and the implication for the tax loss carryforwards always require careful tax planning, and a tax adviser should be contacted.

6.6   Receipts under Warranties or Indemnities

Generally, payments made by the seller for breach of warranty or under an indemnity are taxable in the hands of the purchaser. Accordingly, usual practice is for the sale-and-purchase documentation to contain a clause stipulating that any such payment is to be treated as an adjustment to the consideration offered and received for the transaction.

The Danish tax authorities in general accept that in such circumstances the receipt will not be immediately taxable but will, instead, be treated as a reduction of the purchaser's tax basis in the stock acquired.

If warranties and indemnity payments are made to the target company, they are subject to tax in the target company.

7.   DISPOSITIONS

7.1   Stock Dispositions

(a) Company   A corporate entity is subject to corporation tax on chargeable gains on the disposition of stock unless the disposed stock has been held for at least three years. If the disposed stock includes both stock held for less

than three years and stock held for at least three years, then the portion of stock held for less than three years is subject to corporate tax.

The calculation of chargeable gain is, broadly, sales proceeds minus original costs including capital contributions, further reduced by costs related to the sale and acquisition of stock, unless the expenses have already been deducted for tax purposes.

Frequently, the sale-and-purchase agreement includes a working capital or net asset adjustment that will affect the final cash amounts passing between the parties. Usually, such a cash transfer is explicitly referred to in the sale-and-purchase agreement as an adjustment to the purchase price and will therefore be included in the seller's chargeable gains calculation.

(b) Individual An individual disposing of an interest in stock is subject to capital gains tax. If the individual has held the stock for less than three years, the capital gains are subject to tax at the individual's respective marginal rate of tax, which is up to 59 percent.

Stock held for at least three years is also subject to capital gains tax, but the gain is treated differently for tax calculation purposes, and the tax rate is up to 59 percent.

Stock held for at least three years in a company listed on an approved stock exchange is not subject to taxation when sold if the total market value of the listed stock held has not exceeded DKK133,700 (2004) or DKK267,300 (married couples for 2004) in the last three years prior to the sale. The market value of the stockholding is assessed at every year-end whenever listed stock is bought and whenever listed stock is sold.

In certain circumstances, taxation of individual directors and employee shareholders may differ from that described.

(c) Tax-exempt entity In general, some Danish entities are not subject to tax. This includes certain pension funds, certain investment funds, local authorities, and the state of Denmark and its institutions.

7.2 Asset Dispositions

A disposition of assets is subject to corporation tax on the gain. In general, the gain equals the sales value less the tax basis of the assets. The calculation of the taxable gain may depend on the specific asset. Therefore, a firm opinion of the tax consequences following the disposal of assets requires tax assistance.

7.3 Deferred Consideration and Earn-Outs

Generally, consideration for a disposition is included in the tax calculation of the proceeds at the time of the sale even if the cash receipt of the consideration is deferred.

If uncertainty surrounds the deferred consideration in relation either to duration of the agreement or to the amount of annual consideration, then the capitalized value of the deferred consideration is still taxable at the time of the sale.

The tax authorities require that a deferred consideration agreement be included in the tax returns of both seller and purchaser, stating capitalized value, capitalization rate, and the specific assets financed with a deferred consideration.

Both seller and purchaser establish a balance, with the capitalized value of the assets involved as the opening balance. Both balances should be reduced by any actual consideration paid by the purchaser. If the balances become negative—that is, the actual payments exceed the capitalized value—the payments are subject to corporation tax in the selling entity and are tax deductible in the acquiring company.

Actual payments exceeding the capitalized value are subject to corporate tax even if the original disposition was tax free—that is, disposal of stock held for at least three years. Careful tax planning must be observed if a tax-exempt disposition is desired with deferred consideration.

If the agreement of deferred consideration is terminated while the balance is positive, the remaining balance is tax deductible in the selling entity and considered taxable in the acquiring entity.

The seller could be granted an extension of time for payments of tax following the disposition of intangible assets such as goodwill and patents. The payments the seller receives must first be used to pay the tax attributable to the disposition of the intangible assets until the entire tax debt is paid.

An agreement providing deferred consideration does not affect the purchaser's tax depreciation on the assets acquired. The basis for tax depreciation will be the capitalized value.

7.4   Payments under Warranties

If the sales and purchase documentation contains a clause that any warranty or indemnity payment is to be treated as an adjustment to the consideration offered and received for the transaction, the payment is treated for tax purposes as a reduction of the purchase consideration received.

8.   TRANSACTION COSTS FOR SELLERS

8.1   Transfer Taxes

No transfer taxes are payable by the seller on disposition of assets or shares. A land registration fee is payable by the buyer on the disposal of buildings or real estate.

8.2   VAT

(a) *Stock disposals*   The disposal of stock is exempt from VAT.

(b) *Asset disposals*   A transfer of business assets that qualifies as a transfer of a going concern is not subject to VAT. Other asset purchases are subject to VAT at a rate of 25 percent, which is payable in addition to the purchase consideration.

8.3   Tax Deductibility of Transaction Costs

All transaction costs incurred by the seller are deductible. Either they are deductible directly in the calculation of the taxable income, or, if the transaction costs are related to disposal of stock or specific assets, they are included in the calculation of capital gain taxation.

Because some transaction costs related to the disposition of stock and to the disposition of certain assets can be deducted only in the capital gain calculation, the deduction may be without any tax value if the transaction itself is not subject to tax.

In addition, if the transaction costs create or increase a capital loss on a disposition of assets, the capital loss could be difficult to utilize, and therefore the deduction could effectively be without value.

8.4   VAT Treatment of Expenses

VAT charged by third parties to the seller on transaction costs should be recoverable subject to the partial-exemption method applicable to the seller, provided (1) that the costs relate to a service provided for that seller, (2) that the service is not directly attributable to an exempt supply made by the seller—for example, a sale of immovable property, stock, or loan notes—and (3) that the service is attributable to the seller's business activities that are subject to VAT.

It is important that costs be identified separately on invoices in order to facilitate the allocation of input VAT to, for example, the disposal of stock and other matters.

9.   PREPARING A TARGET COMPANY FOR SALE

Presale planning could be important if the purchaser wants to buy only specific assets or if the seller wishes to retain certain assets; for example, the seller wishes to sell its trading activities but also wishes to retain the securities and available funds. Splitting the assets into trading activities and available funds could be done tax efficiently by means of a tax-exempt demerger whereby the company's assets and liabilities are transferred to two or more new companies. Alternatively, dividend payments of the distributable funds to the shareholder before the sale could be a tax-efficient way of preparing the company for sale.

Also, reduction of the registered capital followed by cash payments to the shareholders could prove to be tax efficient.

10.   TAX-EXEMPT DEMERGER OR SPIN-OFF

A demerger and a spin-off differ in that while the contributing company still exists following the spin-off (partial demerger), the contributing company ceases to exist following a demerger (full demerger).

If the seller is selling only a division or part of a company, such as the trading activities, or there is a specific liability that needs to be kept out of the sale, a demerger or a spin-off is a method to consider.

A demerger or a spin-off involves a transfer of specific assets and liabilities to another company. The receiving company assumes the contributing company's tax position in terms of tax basis, holding period, and purpose of acquiring the assets.

Any tax losses carried forward in the contributing company and in the receiving company cannot be carried forward in the receiving company after a demerger or spin-off. However, tax losses carried forward in the contributing company that survives a spin-off can be carried forward as usual even after the spin-off. Special and more-favorable rules apply if the companies in question are part of a joint taxation.

The shareholders in the contributing company should receive stock in the receiving company following the demerger, which is contrary to the tax-free contribution of assets, whereby the transaction does not involve the shareholders. (See Section 10.1.)

The stock that shareholders receive in the receiving company will have the same holding period as the existing stock, and therefore a disposition of stock in the receiving company will be tax free if the stock in the contributing company has been held for more than three years. (Tax-free disposal after three years applies only to company shareholders. The tax consequences of a disposition of stock by an individual are outlined in Section 7.1(b)).

A demerger or spin-off always requires approval by the Danish tax authorities.

Approval by the tax authorities for a spin-off can be obtained only if the assets and liabilities transferred to the receiving company constitute an entire business activity that can function by its own means or if all of the assets of a company are subject to a full demerger as defined earlier. The contribution of a business activity that is dependent on intercompany funding or finance guaranteed from other group companies does not constitute a business activity that can function by its own means. A demerger or spin-off of individual assets— for example, a single customer—does not qualify as a tax-free demerger or spin-off.

If a tax-free demerger or spin-off cannot be approved, then the transfer of assets is considered as a disposition of assets and liabilities subject to corporation tax and capital gains tax, depending on the assets involved.

10.1   Tax-Free Contribution of Assets

A tax-free contribution of assets has the same consequences as a tax-free demerger or spin-off, with several differences: The contributing company becomes a shareholder in the receiving company. A tax-free contribution of assets also requires approval by the Danish tax authorities. And contributed assets must constitute an entire business activity.

A contribution of assets could be preferred to a demerger because the legal requirements related to a demerger are stricter than those related to a contribution of assets. From a legal perspective, the contribution of assets is considered a contribution in-kind.

10.2   Intragroup Transfer of Assets Being Retained

Intragroup transfers of assets outside the scope of a tax-free demerger or tax-free contribution of assets are deemed to be regular dispositions of assets.

The disposition of assets is subject to capital gains taxation—depending on the nature of the assets—to the extent described in Section 7.2.

No VAT is payable on a transfer of assets between members of a VAT group. If the transferor and transferee are not part of the same VAT group, VAT is still not payable if the transfer of assets constitutes a transfer of going concern.

11.   LISTINGS AND INITIAL PUBLIC OFFERINGS

11.1   Impact on the Tax Status of the Company

The tax status of the company is largely unaffected by listings or initial public offerings (IPOs).

11.2   Complete Group Listing or IPO

On a listing of an entire group, it is common to set up the existing parent company as the listed company and to sell newly issued stock in the market together with existing holdings of stock.

11.3   Listing or IPO of a Subsidiary

The immediate implications for the existing parent of a listing of a subsidiary are:

- If the parent sells in the market—that is, lists—some of its existing stock in a subsidiary, then the parent is subject to corporation tax on chargeable gains on the disposal of stock unless the stock has been owned for more than three years, in which case the disposition is exempt from tax. (See Section 7.1(a).)

• If the subsidiary issues new stock, then the parent has not itself sold any stock, and no tax charge arises.

VAT on costs related to listing is not recoverable, and generally only a small part is tax deductible.

11.4   Issuance of New Stock by a Listed Company

The issuance of new stock by a listed company should not have any tax consequences for the company if the listed company is the parent of the group. In the case of a subsidiary that is being listed, the issuance of new stock results in that subsidiary's leaving a tax group, with potential consequences as noted in Section 6.2(b).

The consideration paid becomes the investors' basis in the stock.

11.5   Disposition of Stock by Existing Shareholders

If the listing or IPO involves a disposition of stock by existing shareholders, the tax position for those shareholders is as outlined in Section 7.1.

FRANCE

INTRODUCTION

This chapter details the principal tax issues that are relevant to purchasers and sellers engaged in the transfer of ownership of a French trade or business. Unless otherwise stated, it is generally assumed that all sellers and purchasers are French companies with limited liability.

The transfer of a French business or company may take the form of a disposal of shares or assets. In France, share transactions are far more common than asset transactions. A stock purchase is simpler and, from a tax perspective, less costly than an asset sale. However, acquirers may prefer an asset purchase if they suspect undisclosed liabilities or wish to avoid the risks of litigation or other exposures to which the target is a party. The choice between acquiring stock in a company or acquiring a company's assets is also influenced by the treatment of such transactions for tax purposes.

The relevant taxes to be considered are:

- **Corporate income tax (CIT).** CIT applies to the profits realized in France by companies subject to CIT[1] either by reason of their form or upon election. The standard rate of 33 percent is increased with surtaxes, resulting in a statutory tax rate in the range of 34 percent to 35.43 percent. All companies with CIT liability exceeding €763,000 before surtaxes are subject to the maximum rate of 35.43 percent. CIT at the reduced rate of 19 percent may apply to long-term capital gains—for example, on the sale of stock held at least two years and on royalties for the use of patents. Including surtaxes, the maximum reduced rate of CIT applicable to long-term capital gains is 20.2 percent.
- **Registration duties (RDs).** RDs are payable by the purchaser. They are levied at rates of up to 4.8 percent on the transfer price of certain assets—such as business as a going concern, goodwill, trademarks, and leasehold rights—and 4.89 percent on real properties also applicable to the acquisition of shares in companies whose assets constitute more than 50 percent

---

1. CIT may also apply, by virtue of French antiabuse, controlled-foreign-companies provisions (Article 209 B of the French tax code), to profits realized either by the foreign establishment or by the direct or indirect foreign subsidiary (if the French-based company owns 10 percent or more of the vote or the value of its stock) of a French-based company.

of real estate properties. Acquisitions may be structured in ways that significantly reduce RDs to the payment of a fixed duty of €230.

- **Value-added tax (VAT).** VAT is a noncumulative tax imposed at each level of the production and distribution cycle at a rate of 19.6 percent.[2] The discussions in this chapter assume that the purchaser is subject to VAT. Only sales of inventories, tangible assets, and, under very limited circumstances, intangibles are likely to be subject to VAT. VAT is seldom a key issue in most merger and acquisition transactions. The purchaser can recover VAT that has been charged regularly by the seller. The recovery rate varies from case to case.

1. ACQUISITIONS

An acquisition may take the form of an acquisition of either shares or assets. In addition, the acquisition can take the form of either a tax-free merger or a taxable merger. This chapter addresses only the key features of the two main types of acquisitions. The specific tax consequences of those types are detailed further in the sections that follow.

1.1   Asset Acquisitions

An asset acquisition generally enables the purchaser to avoid any historical liabilities that might not be covered by the sale agreement. Liabilities associated with the business remain the responsibility of the seller and do not become the responsibility of the purchaser unless otherwise agreed. The purchaser cannot be held responsible later for settlement of so-called hidden liabilities that would have been attached to the assets purchased but that were left undisclosed by the seller.

Another issue to be considered is that, on a sale of assets, contracts in force between the seller and third parties such as customers, suppliers, and service providers do not get automatically assigned to the purchaser. This causes practical difficulties—particularly if there are numerous contracts—and is a reason that stock acquisitions frequently are preferred to asset transactions.

From a labor law perspective, due to specific provisions, the purchaser is legally bound to hire all employees attached to the business and to do so under the employees' current terms and conditions of employment (Article L. 122-12, al. 2 of the French Labor Law Code).

An asset acquisition generally results in a step-up in the tax basis of assets. In France, however, no tax deduction is allowed for depreciation of a number of intangible assets such as client list, going concern, goodwill, trademarks,

---

2. Rates other than the aforementioned standard rate may be applicable on certain transactions. They are not dealt with in this chapter.

and trade names. Only those intangible assets that have a limited life span either for legal reasons such as patents or for economic reasons such as movie rights may be amortized for tax purposes. Therefore, the step-up in basis concerns primarily fixed tangible assets. Depreciation for tangible assets is effected either on a straight-line basis or on a declining-balance basis.

1.2　Stock Acquisitions

In a stock acquisition, the purchaser bears any historical and future ongoing tax and nontax liabilities of the target company. The stock purchase agreement generally covers areas that might give rise to liabilities in the future, and it provides for an appropriate indemnification of the purchaser. The indemnification may be done via a reduction of the original sale price or via compensation of the target company itself. The choice depends primarily on the tax status of the seller and that of the target company.

From a purchaser's perspective, the absence of any step-up in the basis of the company's assets is balanced by the fact that in a stock acquisition, all contracts entered into by the target company remain in force and need not be assigned or renegotiated—apart from *intuitu personae* contracts that would be terminated in the event of a change of control of the target company.

In a stock acquisition, the target company retains its carryforward tax losses. However, in an asset acquisition, the losses remain within the company that is selling its assets. An asset sale may, at times, forfeit the right of the selling company to use part or all of its tax loss carryforward. (See Section 2.3(b).)

From a tax perspective, a stock transaction is generally less costly for both the seller and the purchaser than an asset transaction is. For the seller, the sale of stock held for more than two years is treated as a long-term capital gain and is taxed at the reduced rate of CIT: 19 percent plus surtaxes. The gain recognized on the sale of other assets is subject to the standard rate of CIT—that is, 33 percent. For the purchaser, the acquisition of stock in a corporation[3] attracts RDs that are capped at €3,049, while the acquisition of business assets qualifying as a going concern are taxed at 4.8 percent. (See Section 6.2.)

Both types of transactions permit leveraging. Tax groupings permit offsetting the taxable profits of the target against the tax losses of the French acquisition vehicle. (See Section 6.1.)

---

3. A corporation (*société anonyme* [SA]) or a simplified corporation—*société par actions simplifiées* [SAS]), as opposed, for registration tax purposes, to a limited liability company (*société à responsabilité limitée* [SARL]), a general partnership (*société en nom collectif* [SNC]), and a limited partnership (*société en commandite simple* ([SCS]).

2.   TRANSACTION COSTS FOR PURCHASERS

2.1   Stock Acquisitions

(a) *Registration duties*   Acquisition of stock in a corporation such as an SA or an SAS is subject to RDs at the rate of 1 percent of the transfer price, subject to a cap of €3,049. If the stock of the company is listed, the 1 percent duty is levied only if the transaction is stated in a deed.

The transfer of shares in other types of companies such as an SARL and an SNC is subject to a transfer duty of 4.8 percent levied on a transfer price exceeding €23,000 regardless of whether the sale is stated in a deed or not.

If the target is nonlisted and if its assets consist primarily of real estate properties, RDs are then levied at the rate of 4.89 percent, which is the rate applicable to the acquisition of real property.

In both cases, unless otherwise stipulated in the legal documentation, RDs are due from the purchaser.

(b) *Value-added tax*   Stock transactions are exempt from VAT.

(c) *Tax on stock exchange operations*   The acquisition of securities traded on the stock exchange is subject to a special tax of 0.3 percent on the portion of the transaction price below €153,000 and of 0.15 percent on a transaction price of €153,000 or more. The total tax liability for each transaction is capped at €610 and is the amount to be paid by both the purchaser and the seller—that is, €1,220 per transaction.

2.2   Asset Acquisitions

(a) *Registration tax*   Asset acquisitions may consist of:

- Acquisition of a business as a going concern (*fonds de commerce*): French law gives no definition of a going concern. A going concern is a business unit to which a clientele is attached. It may consist of intangible assets—that is, clientele, leasehold rights, goodwill, trademarks, and trade names—and tangible assets—that is, equipment, furniture, and inventories. Such acquisitions are subject to registration taxes that are assessed on the transfer price[4] of the clientele/goodwill, equipment, and other fixed assets—exclusive of inventories—at a rate of 4.8 percent.[5]

- Acquisition of isolated assets—versus acquisition of a business unity— is subject to its own tax rules as follows:

    o Acquisition of tangibles other than real estate has no registration duty—subject to VAT.

---

4. Where the transfer price does not reflect the fair market value, the French tax authorities may raise assessments.

5. The 4.8 percent duty applies to the portion of the price in excess of €23,000.

- Acquisition of real estate property is subject to a 4.89 percent transfer duty on the acquisition price.
- Acquisition of inventories is subject to VAT, which is recoverable in the hands of the purchaser, provided the purchaser is subject to VAT.
- Acquisition of a patent is subject to a fixed €75 transfer duty.
- When the acquisition of isolated assets results in the transfer of the clients attached to those assets, it is treated by the tax authorities as the transfer of a going concern and is subject to the 4.8 percent duty.

(b) VAT Acquisition of inventories is subject to VAT at the normal rate of 19.6 percent. Lower rates may apply depending on the nature of the goods transferred.

The acquisition of assets separately (as opposed to the acquisition of the entire business as a going concern) is subject to VAT at the normal rate of 19.6 percent.

2.3   Transaction Costs

Transaction costs consist primarily of bank fees, lawyer's fees, and consultant's fees. However, they can be split into two different categories:

1. Advisory costs such as those connected with banks acting as advisers, lawyers, auditors, transaction support, and consultants
2. Financial costs such as bank commissions related to the acquisition process and to the execution of the transaction itself and bank fees for coordination work

(a) Corporate income tax treatment For tax purposes, advisory fees are permitted to be fully deducted as expenses in the year of acquisition or are permitted to be capitalized and amortized over two to five years depending on the accounting treatment chosen.

Bank commissions must be amortized over the duration of the loan.

(b) VAT treatment Advisory costs are subject to VAT at the standard rate; financial costs are exempt from VAT.

All agreements and invoices must be examined for proper allocation in light of their exact nature, such as financial costs versus advisory costs. VAT charged on advisory costs is recoverable by the acquiring company, provided it carries out VAT-able activities and therefore acts as a services company—such as by providing support functions—for the other companies of the target group.

It is therefore crucial that a number of conditions be met and a number of documents be drafted carefully:

- Articles of incorporation, board meeting minutes, and any other relevant documents must state that it is within the acquiring company's corporate purpose to render services in order to prove that the company's purpose from the date of incorporation is, in addition to holding shares, to perform VAT-able activities.
- Management services agreements—accounting, payroll, marketing, commercial strategy, legal and tax services, and so on—are to be entered into by the acquiring company with its direct and indirect subsidiaries (French and foreign companies) and are to be effective as of the date of the closing.
- The acquiring company needs to demonstrate the reality of the services rendered (substance). This means that certain employees—previously in charge of these matters within the target group companies—may have to be transferred to the acquiring company.

Provided these conditions are met, input VAT charged on the acquisition costs is, in principle, recoverable.

However, the acquiring company must carry out a VAT-able activity exclusively. Should it also perform a VAT-exempt activity such as making loans to affiliates, the right to recover VAT would be reduced proportionally—that is, application of a recovery ratio equal to the total turnover subject to VAT divided by the total turnover (VAT-able turnover plus VAT-exempt turnover)—unless the direct attribution method can be applied.

Note that the salary tax (*taxe sur les salaires*) would be due if the acquiring company performs VAT-exempt activities and/or receives dividends falling outside the scope of VAT. The computation of this tax is based on the amount of salaries paid by the company times a ratio. The ratio is equal to: total revenues (including dividends and revenue otherwise outside the scope of VAT) divided by total VAT-able turnover]. The result is then multiplied by the progressive rate of the salary tax—an average rate of approximately 13 percent.

3.   BASIS OF TAXATION FOLLOWING ASSET OR STOCK ACQUISITIONS

3.1   Arm's-Length Principle

One overriding principle is that all transactions must be performed at arm's length. If the transaction takes place between unrelated parties, it is likely, absent fraud, that the sale price is at market value. Transactions between related parties are subject to more scrutiny by the tax authorities. Tax authorities may make CIT adjustments on the vendor's side and RDs adjustments on the buyer's side if the transaction is not at arm's length.

3.2   Cost Basis of Assets

In the acquiring company, the tax basis of assets is the historical cost, or purchase price. When a single price is paid for the acquisition of an entire business, the tax basis must be allocated in the transaction documents to each asset that is forming part of the business. Such allocation of the purchase price enables the acquiring company to identify the depreciable cost basis of each asset.

The acquiring company is entitled to a tax deduction for depreciation of tangible assets—exclusive of land. Because the useful life of certain intangibles such as clientele list/goodwill, trademarks, and leasehold rights is not limited in time, such intangibles are not depreciable for tax purposes. Amortization is available for intangibles—such as patents—whose useful life is limited.

(a) Tangibles   Several depreciation methods are available:

- The straight-line basis, or basic method, is available whereby the yearly depreciation equals the basis of depreciation divided by the useful life of the asset.
- The declining-balance basis is available for certain assets—for example, heavy production and handling equipment—that are purchased new and have a useful life of at least three years. Real property is excluded from this method unless it consists of industrial plants with an expected maximum useful life of 15 years.

(b) Inventories   The purchaser receives a tax basis equal to the value of inventory as paid. Similar rules apply to work in progress.

(c) Trade receivables   Typically, receivables debts are acquired at net book value. The acquiring company may write down debt that is fully or partially uncollectible. Such a reserve is tax deductible, provided certain tests are met.

3.3   Cost Basis of Shares

In the balance sheet of the acquiring company, shares are booked at their acquisition price. At fiscal year-end, the proper valuation mechanism, depending on the category of portfolio investments, is as follows:

- Shares acquired for temporary investment purposes
- Participating stock

(a) Shares acquired for temporary investment purposes

- For quoted shares, the average quotation over the last month of the fiscal year
- For unquoted shares, the likely realizable value, which must reflect, as much as possible, the fair market value

Any decrease in value of the shares may be booked as a reserve for temporary impairment. For tax purposes—provided such impairment can be demonstrated—the reserve is deductible from operating profits. Otherwise, the reserve so booked must be added back into the taxable profits.

(b) Participating stock   French law does not provide a straightforward definition for participating stock. The test is met if the stock concerned gives the stockholder the right to participate in control of the company and to exert influence over the company's assets. Also, in the statutory accounts, such stock must be distinctively booked as participating stock. Stock representing 5 percent of the vote or value or having a cost basis of €22.8 million or more is deemed to be participating stock.

Based on the rules of French generally accepted accounting principles, the actual value of a participating stock at year-end must be determined on the basis of its economic value—that is, the value that the parent company would be paying for the acquisition of the said stock from a third party.

When the actual value of shares at year-end is different from the acquisition cost of those shares, the following tax treatment applies. When the difference is positive—that is, if the actual value is higher than the acquisition cost—the built-in gain is ignored for both tax and accounting purposes.

When the difference is negative, that difference may be booked as a reserve for temporary impairment. For tax purposes, this reserve is treated as a long-term capital loss regardless of the holding period (more or less than two years). Section 7.1(a) covers the tax treatment of long-term capital gains and losses.

4.   FINANCING OF ACQUISITIONS

4.1   Debt Financing

Broadly speaking, the tax consequences of debt financing vary depending on whether the debt is provided by the direct shareholder of the borrower (as a company) or by any other person (third party or affiliate).

French law does not provide for thin-capitalization rules unless debt financing comes from a direct controlling (French or nonresident) shareholder of the borrower.

Conversely, interest accrued on acquisition debt provided by third parties is normally deductible for tax purposes if the debt financing constitutes a normal management act and if certain other tests are met.

The French tax authorities currently contemplate the possibility of reforming their thin-capitalization rules. While such reform is highly probable, it seems that the new rules would not be effective prior to January 1, 2006, at the earliest.

(a) Shareholders loans   A tax deduction for interest accrued on loans granted by direct shareholders is allowed but is subject to three restrictions. The first two conditions/restrictions that follow apply to any direct shareholder; the third concerns only direct controlling shareholders.

1. **Fully paid-up capital.** The acquiring company is eligible for a tax deduction only if its share capital is fully paid up.

2. **Maximum interest rate.** The interest rate must not exceed the annual average of effective rates applied by credit organizations or banks on floating-rate loans for more than two years. The rate is published at the beginning of each year by the tax administration. The maximum rate for 2004 was 4.58 percent.

3. **Debt/equity ratio.** This test involves only loans or facilities granted by shareholders with legal or effective management control or by those owning more than 50 percent of votes *or* the financial rights in the company. Interest accrued on the portion of such loans exceeding 1.5 times the share capital is not deductible (debt/equity ratio of 1.5:1). As an exception, such limitation does not apply even on loans granted by direct shareholders, provided the share/stockholder qualifies as a parent company in the sense of the French participation exemption rules. (See Section 6.2.)

French tax authorities have long held that nonresident companies cannot qualify as parent companies. Interest payable by French borrowers on loans from nonresident stockholders was, therefore, subject to the 1.5:1 ratio. This discriminatory treatment was struck down by the French Supreme Administrative Court in two decisions dated December 31, 2003, which ruled that this provision is not compatible with:

1. The nondiscrimination clause contained in the French-Austrian double-tax treaty: The same approach is to be applied to any other double-tax treaty with a nondiscrimination clause that follows the Organization for Economic Co-operation and Development (OECD) model income tax treaty, unless the treaty expressly provides for application of French thin-capitalization rules.[6]

---

6. SA Andritz decision, Supreme Administrative Court, December 31, 2003.

2. Article 43 of the Treaty of Rome regarding freedom of establishment within European Union (EU) member states.[7]

Following these decisions, French thin-capitalization rules are from now on stripped of their essential content, which explains why a reform is contemplated. It is still too soon to speculate on the nature of any future reform efforts.

Under current legislation, excess interest—that is, interest that exceeds the aforementioned restrictions—is usually recharacterized as deemed dividends. If excess interest is recharacterized as a distribution and the recipient of it is a non-French resident, a 25 percent withholding tax is payable. However, that rate may be reduced by tax treaty depending on whether or not the definition of *dividend* in the applicable treaty also refers to *distributed income.*

(b) *Loans from related companies other than shareholders*   The deduction of interest on debt provided by related parties who are not shareholders is not expressly limited by thin-capitalization rules and is treated as interest on third-party loans.

(c) *Third-party loans*   The deduction of interest accrued on third-party loans is not limited by thin-capitalization rules. French law does not give a safe harbor for a maximum debt/equity ratio.

The French tax authorities have frequently tried to refer to the 1.5:1 debt/equity ratio as a guideline to apply to third-party loans but have been consistently contradicted by recent court decisions. Higher ratios may be defended, provided the debt-financed company is in a position to demonstrate it can service the interest and principal of the loan.

The decision to finance the acquisition by debt must constitute a normal management act. The interest rate must also be at arm's length. The deduction is then restricted at what is considered to be a true arm's-length financing arrangement structure.

(d) *Restricted deduction of interest borne by the head company of a tax unity*   Article 223 B of the French tax code (*Amendement Charasse*) aims primarily at preventing investors from combining leveraged acquisition benefits together with election for tax consolidation treatment. (See Section 6.1.) Under such antiabuse provisions, deduction of financial expense incurred by the member companies of a tax unity is disallowed if the following occurs:

- The French acquisition vehicle belongs to the same group as the seller; that is, the vehicle is under the control (direct or indirect) of the seller or the shareholder of the seller.
- The target company or group of companies has elected to become a member of the French acquirer's tax consolidated group.

---

7. Coreal Gestion decision, Supreme Administrative Court, December 31, 2003.

The disallowed interest expense of the tax unity members is calculated as:

$$\frac{\text{Price Paid for Acquisition of the Target Company}}{\text{Average Indebtedness of Tax Unity Members Companies per Year}}$$

This mechanism applies over 15 fiscal years inclusive of the acquisition's fiscal year. It ceases once the target company leaves the group—say, through a sale or a merger.

(e) Withholding tax   Interest paid to non-French residents is subject to a domestic withholding tax (WHT) of 25 percent. In most cases, the domestic WHT rate is capped by a tax treaty.

According to French law (Article 13—*quater* of the French tax code), no WHT is payable on interest paid to non-French residents, provided all the following conditions are met:

- The loan agreement is in writing.
- The loan agreement is entered into prior to the transfer of funds.
- The loan agreement sets forth the amount of the loan, the repayment date, and the interest rate.

(f) Payment of interest expense   The French acquisition vehicle may need cash to pay the interest expense on the acquisition financing. Cash may be moved up to the French holding company:

- Dividend income received by French companies qualifying for the participation exemption rules (see Section 6.2) is 95 percent tax-exempt regardless of whether the distributing company is French based or not.
- Management fees can be received in consideration for services (support functions) provided for group companies. These services need to be supported by relevant transfer-pricing documentation to secure the tax deduction for the payer whether in France or outside France.
- Licensing of trade names and trademarks—that is, royalties received by a French company for the right to use its trade name and/or trademark—is fully taxable.

Cash may be remitted by French companies to their foreign parents or affiliates under the same mechanisms if justified. If not, the payments are generally treated as deemed dividends.

- Interest expense paid on loans is most often exempt from withholding tax under domestic rules. (See Section 4.1(e).)
- Intra-EU dividend payments may be exempt under the parent/subsidiary directive.

- France's treaty network includes more than 100 treaties that allow for a reduced rate[8] of taxation on royalty payments.

4.2   Equity

In the formation of a French company, there is no capital duty on contributions made in exchange for shares if one of the following contributions is made:

- By a company subject to corporation tax to another company subject to corporation tax
- By a company not subject to corporation tax or by an individual to a company not subject to corporation tax

Conversely, contributions—consisting of real property, client list, business assets as a going concern, or leasehold rights—that are made by a taxpayer not subject to corporation tax to a company subject to corporation tax may attract a 4.8 percent registration duty unless the contributor undertakes to hold for at least three years the shares issued.

When applicable, the 4.8 percent duty is assessed on the transfer value of the contributions in excess of €23,000. That threshold does not apply for contributions of real property.

Any later equity contribution for new shares is treated as described earlier, except that a registration duty of €230 substitutes for the total tax exemption.

4.3   Key Nontax Issues

(a) *Financial assistance*   France has financial assistance rules. Under Article L. 225-216 of the French commercial code (formerly Article L. 217-9), a company may not advance funds or grant loans or securities in view of the subscription or purchase of its own shares by a third party. Financial assistance is an offense, and there is no whitewash procedure available. Lawyers and other competent professionals always should be consulted on these matters.

5.   MERGERS

5.1   Mergers and Other Assimilated Transactions

From a legal perspective, a merger may consist of the absorption of one or more companies into an existing company or of one or more companies being merged in a newly incorporated company. The absorbed companies are dissolved. The merger results in the complete transfer of assets and liabilities from one company to another.

From a tax perspective, the merger is a taxable event both for the transferring company (recognition and taxation of capital gains) and the acquiring

---

8. Most often 5 percent.

company (RDs). However, the French tax code permits a variety of corporate reorganizations to be effected on a tax-free basis both to the shareholders and to the corporation when neither capital gains taxation nor RDs are levied.

The tax-free treatment covers a wide range of transactions ranging from statutory merger to exchange of stock for stock, asset drop-down for stock, division, and dissolution without liquidation of a 100-percent-owned subsidiary. Similarly, cross-border merger transactions may also enjoy tax-free treatment. The criterion common to all of these transactions is that they result in the transfer for stock of some or all of the assets and liabilities of one company to another.

Certain stock-for-stock exchanges that involve a substantial stockholding (a minimum of 50 percent of the capital or giving at least 30 percent of the voting rights to the recipient) may be treated as mergers for tax purposes.

Hereinafter, *acquiring company* means the company to which the assets or qualifying stock is carried over. *Transferring company* means either the company that contributes its assets or stock for stock or the company that is dissolved or merged into the acquiring company.

5.2   Fiscal Definition

Until 2002, transactions likely to benefit from the tax-free merger treatment provided by Article 210 A of the French tax code—which is inspired by the EU parent/subsidiary directive—were only those qualifying as mergers or spin-offs for corporate law purposes.

For 2002 onward, a specific fiscal definition was introduced in the law so that French law complies with the EU directive. A merger is from now on defined as a transaction whereby one or several companies transfer—through and upon their dissolution without being followed by proper liquidation—all of their assets and liabilities to the absorbing company in exchange for shares of the latter (Article 210-0 A of the French tax code).

Many more corporate transactions that were previously outside the scope of the merger definition provided under corporate law are now likely to be eligible for tax-free-merger treatment—for example, upstream dissolution without liquidation of a 100-percent-owned subsidiary as referred to by Article 1844-5 al. 3 of the civil code. Similarly, cross-border corporate merger transactions in compliance with the definition may also be eligible for tax-free treatment.

5.3   Tax Treatment of Standard Mergers

If the transaction does not comply with the fiscal definition of mergers as set forth previously or if the parties do not wish to avail themselves of the statutory tax-free-merger treatment, the merger is treated as a mere liquidation of the absorbed company. The fiscal treatment is then identical to that imposed on a disposal of assets and liabilities.

(a) Immediate taxation of built-in gains and operating profits   The liquidation of the absorbed company is a taxable event and therefore leads to the immediate taxation of operating profits, built-in gains on all fixed assets (tangibles and intangibles), tax-free reserves, and liquidation proceeds.

Such gains and profits are taxable at the standard rate of CIT: 33 percent plus surtaxes. Only capital gains recognized on the transfer of stock that has been owned for at least two years and profits from patent licensing are taxed as long-term gains—that is, at 19 percent plus surtaxes—provided the net after-tax profit is booked as a reserve at year-end. However, the future distribution of this net after-tax profit, as part of the liquidation proceeds, triggers an additional taxation that brings the whole taxation up to 33 percent plus surtaxes.

The upstream distribution of net income derived by the absorbed company after completion of the liquidation process may benefit from the participation exemption rules. (See Section 6.2.)

(b) Registration taxes   Mergers, divisions, and asset drop-downs for shares are viewed as transfers of assets and liabilities and therefore are taxable according to the set of rules described in Section 2.2(a).

5.4   Tax-Free Mergers (Article 210 A of the Tax Code)

(a) Tax relief   Tax relief available under the tax-free-merger rules involves primarily corporate tax and RDs.

(i) Corporate tax   No taxation is levied on net capital gains recognized by the absorbed company on assets transferred to the absorbing company, provided the absorbing company meets a set of tests and commitments as follows.

When a merger is effected under the tax-free-merger rules, the only immediate taxation relates in theory to the absorbed company's operating profits that have been realized between the first day of the merger fiscal year and the date at which the merger is voted. The absorbed company must then file a tax return and pay the corresponding corporate tax within 60 days. In practice, though, most mergers are made with retroactive effect as of the first day of the fiscal year in which the merger is executed. Operating profits or losses realized by the absorbing company until the date of merger completion are merged into the taxable income basis of the absorbing company. If the absorbing company's fiscal year ends later than the absorbed company's fiscal year, the merger will be effective no sooner than the first day of the absorbing company's fiscal year.

The capital gains exemption also applies to other corporate transactions that comply with the fiscal definition of a merger. As covered in Section 9, such transactions include assets or stock contribution for stock, divisions or spin-offs, distribution of stock following an asset or a stock contribution for stock, and dissolution—without liquidation—of a fully owned subsidiary.

(ii) Registration duties   Generally, mergers and other, similar transactions between companies subject to corporate tax—as opposed to partnerships or flow-through entities—give rise to a flat registration duty of €230, provided the consideration received for transfer of assets consists, at the minimum, of 90 percent in shares. When assets are transferred not only in exchange for shares but also for cash, bonds, or any payment other than shares[9] and when such payment is more than 10 percent of the par value of the shares to be issued, the transfer is, in due proportion, characterized as a sale of assets and may be taxed as described in Section 2.2(a).

(b) Conditions   There are various accounting and tax rules that are common to mergers and other qualifying corporate transactions whereby all participants are subject to corporate tax in France. Additionally, there are rules regarding cross-border transactions. Detailed coverage of those rules is beyond the scope of this discussion. Professional advisers should be consulted in connection with any contemplated mergers because each transaction has its own specific requirements.

(c) Consequences for shareholders
(i) Gain on share-for-share exchange   Taxation of capital gains recognized by both corporate and individual shareholders of the absorbed or divided company (spin-off) at the time of the share-for-share exchange is deferred until the fiscal year in which the shares received are sold. If the consideration received includes both shares and cash, the cash payment must neither exceed 10 percent of the par value of shares nor, for corporate shareholders only, more than 10 percent of the capital gain. If the cash payment is 10 percent or less of the capital gain, that portion is immediately taxable. When the cash payment exceeds that 10 percent threshold, the whole capital gain is taxable.

Even though the deferred taxation mechanism is applicable automatically for individual shareholders, corporate shareholders may elect immediate taxation.

When the deferred taxation mechanism applies, the capital gain on future disposition of shares must be computed as the difference between the sale price and the cost basis of the shares exchanged. For corporate shareholders, that gain or loss may be eligible for long-term-capital-gain treatment. (See Section 2.2(a).) Both parties must comply with requirements as prescribed by

---

9. Liabilities to be transferred through the merger and their future settlement by the recipient are never viewed as a cash payment.

Article 54 septies, sections I and II. (See filing requirements in Section 5.4 (b).)

For individual shareholders, the deferred-taxation mechanism applies automatically.

(ii) Issuance of shares: Not a taxable event   The issuance of shares by the recipient company in consideration for the net worth of assets transferred through the merger is not viewed as distributed income and triggers no taxation.

(d) Impact on tax loss carryforwards   From 2004 onward, there is no longer any distinction to be made between ordinary losses (to be carried forward over five years) and deferred depreciation (to be carried forward with no limit in time). Tax losses derived by companies may be carried forward indefinitely.

(i) Tax loss carryforwards of the absorbed company   According to the general rules, premerger losses carried forward by the absorbed company cannot be carried over to the absorbing company and are lost for both parties to the transaction unless, as noted later, an advance ruling is obtained.

The carryback tax receivable of the company absorbed may be transferred to the absorbing or acquiring company regardless of the tax treatment applied to the merger (standard or tax free). The receivable is transferred on the basis of its face value.

According to the special rules allowing for the transfer of tax loss carryforwards (advance ruling), when the merger or any similar corporate transaction is effected on a tax-free basis, the tax loss carryforward of the transferring or absorbed company may be carried over to the absorbing or acquiring company if approved by the tax authorities prior to the transaction (advance ruling). That advance ruling is automatically granted, provided the following tests are met:

- The transaction is effected on the basis of Article 210 A provisions.
- The transaction is effected for business reasons and is driven by other than purely fiscal purposes.
- The business activity from which the said losses have been originated must be pursued for at least three years.

Assuming these tests are met, when the transaction involves the transfer of one business division, then the transfer of the tax losses is limited to the proportion that the net worth of the business division transferred bears to the rest of the transferring company.

If a merger takes place between two foreign-based companies and the absorbed company has a French branch, an advance-ruling request could be filed to transfer the losses of the French branch of the absorbed company to the French branch of the absorbing company.

A similar ruling could be requested if a foreign-based company absorbs its French subsidiary, assuming that all conditions for cross-border transactions are met and that all properties of the French subsidiary are carried over to the French branch (permanent establishment) of the foreign company.

(ii) Carryforwards of the absorbing company or recipient   Premerger losses carried forward by the absorbing or recipient company are not altered by the transaction, provided the transaction does not involve a change in the business activity conducted by the company.

Premerger losses are likely to be altered when the merger involves such fundamental changes in the nature of the business carried out by the absorbing company that it cannot any longer be viewed as running the same business. In such cases, the absorbing company is likely to lose the right to use its carryforward tax losses.

5.5   Other Qualifying Reorganizations

See Section 9.

5.6   Anti-Tax-Avoidance Rules

Mergers should not be used to avoid taxes. The French tax authorities increasingly cite the concepts of abnormal act of management and abuse of law. To attack on the grounds of the abuse of law, the tax authorities try to demonstrate that the merger was driven purely or mainly by tax-avoidance or tax-basis-reduction purposes.

Following are some examples of transactions under the tax authorities' scrutiny.

(a) Merging a company with losses with a profitable company   As covered in Section 5.4(d)(i), losses carried forward by the absorbed company are definitely lost unless there is a business reason to ask for a ruling to carry them over to the absorbing company. This is why the tax authorities usually attack mergers in which the loss-making company is chosen to be the absorbing company, particularly when the absorbed company is of larger size, preserving its carryforward losses for future use. The tax authorities may argue that such a decision was made only so that the absorbing company's carryforward losses can be used against the absorbed company's future profits, thereby avoiding future corporate taxation.

However, the Supreme Administrative Court has ruled that if the merger itself is driven by a legitimate business purpose, the parties may always choose the less costly tax treatment. Taxpayers may utilize the precedent, provided that both the absorbing and the absorbed companies engage in similar activities. It is crucial for future use of carryforward tax losses that after the merger, the absorbing company can still be viewed as engaging in the same activity as it did beforehand. The merger of two companies with different activities— such as manufacturing versus distribution—would prevent the absorbing company from using its premerger losses against future profits.

(b) So-called quick mergers and financial assistance   Banks often advocate the merger of the target into the leveraged holding once the acquisition is completed. This is the best alternative to maximize their guarantees, facilitate immediate repatriation of profits from the target, and rapidly utilize the holding's preconsolidation losses.

Such quick mergers have been the subject of extensive discussions for a number of years. Lawyers and other competent professionals always should be consulted on these matters.

6.   OTHER STRUCTURING AND POSTDEAL ISSUES

6.1   Setting Up a Tax-Consolidated Group (or Tax Unity)

Companies subject to corporate income tax in France may elect the tax consolidation treatment. Qualifying subsidiaries are those owned directly or indirectly at 95 percent (both voting rights and rights to profits) by the head company. These rules allow the tax unity to be headed by the French branch of a foreign company.

The acquisition of 95 percent of a French company therefore allows the purchaser (through the French acquiring company) to form a tax unity with the target company and any of the target company's qualifying subsidiaries.

The tax consolidation treatment allows for a pooling of all member companies' taxable income and losses. Such treatment is available upon election by both the parent company, which is to be acting as the pooling company, and the subsidiaries.

The election for the tax-grouping mechanism by each member company must be made within the first three months of the current fiscal year so that it will be effective as of the first day of the current fiscal year. The tax unity treatment is then valid for a five-year period and is renewable by tacit consent. During the five-year period, the parent company may exclude any of its direct or indirect subsidiaries from the tax-consolidated group. This must be done within the first three months of the fiscal year to be effective as of the first day of the current fiscal year.

A member company automatically exits from the tax unity if at year-end the ownership percentage of the head company is less than 95 percent. The exclusion of the member is deemed effective as of the first day of the fiscal year during which the exclusion occurs.

6.2   Participation Exemption (Dividends)

If the purchaser (company) acquires at least 5 percent of the vote or value in the target company, it may be eligible for the French participation exemption. This treatment allows a 95 percent exemption on dividends received from eligible subsidiaries if the parent company has subscribed the shares upon issuance or, when purchased, has undertaken to hold them for a minimum of two years.

A total of 5 percent of the gross dividend (dividend plus attached tax credit, if any) remains taxable at the standard rate of corporate tax in the hands of the parent company as *quote part de frais et charges,* which is allegedly deemed to cover the cost of the portfolio management.

Within a tax-consolidated group, the 5 percent taxation of the intragroup dividend is neutralized at the level of head company.

Up to December 31, 2003, a tax credit (*avoir fiscal*) was attached to any dividend paid by a French company. The tax credit was equal to 50 percent of the net dividend for individual shareholders and for those corporate shareholders qualifying for participation exemption treatment (10 percent for nonqualifying corporate shareholders).

The *avoir fiscal* mechanism has been repealed by the Finance Bill for 2004. The new legislation is binding with regard to distributions paid from January 1, 2005. From that date, dividend distributions will no longer give rise to any tax credit in the hands of corporate shareholders.

As for individuals, as a replacement of *avoir fiscal,* they will henceforth be entitled to a 50 percent relief that is deductible from the dividend income itself.

6.3   Distribution Tax: Exceptional Levy of 25 Percent on Dividends Distributed in 2005

Until 2003, the distributing company had to pay an equalization tax (*précompte*) on dividends if dividends were paid out of profits that had not been subject to French corporate income tax at the standard rate or, although initially taxed, that had been generated more than five years prior to the distribution. Equalization tax, which was equal to 50 percent of the net dividend distributed, while not deductible for tax purposes, reduced the dividend to be distributed.

According to the Finance Bill for 2004, equalization tax has been repealed. In order to cover the cost associated with such reform, an exceptional levy of 25 percent of dividend distributions is to be substituted for equalization tax.

The exceptional levy applies on dividends distributed from January 1 to December 31, 2005, only.

Like the *précompte*, the exceptional levy of 25 percent will be based on the net amount of distributions paid out of profits that have not been subject to corporate income tax at the standard rate or those that are more than five years old. In return, the taxpayer will receive a tax credit for the same amount. One-third of it will be usable against the corporation tax liability of each of the three following fiscal years. The excess tax credit, after payment of the annual tax liability, will be reimbursable.

7.   DISPOSITIONS

7.1   Seller's Costs

The most significant tax cost borne by the seller is the taxation of capital gains upon sale. In addition, the transaction may have a number of other tax consequences, such as an impact on the seller's tax loss carryforwards (for corporate bodies only).

(a) Stock sales   Under French law, capital gains and losses may be split into several distinct categories:

- Short-term capital gains or losses are characterized as operating profits and are therefore taxed at the standard corporate income tax rate of 33 percent plus surtaxes. Short-term capital gains are netted against short-term capital losses. Should this result in a net short-term loss at year-end, the loss can be offset against ordinary income indefinitely. The net short-term loss may also be carried back over the previous three fiscal years.

- Long-term capital gains are taxed at the reduced rate of corporate income tax: 19 percent plus surtaxes. Long-term capital gains or losses derived within a given fiscal year are offset against each other. Long-term loss may be carried forward for 10 years. The 19 percent reduced rate is available only if the net after-tax gain is posted to a special retained-earnings account, the *réserve spéciale des plus-values à long-terme*.[10] The scope of the long-term rate of taxation[11] has become restricted over the past ten years and is henceforth applicable solely to gains from the

---

10. Any distribution that would be paid out of the reserve triggers additional taxation, the purpose of which is to bring the effective taxation up to 33 percent plus surtaxes.

11. Profits derived from patent rights licensing are also eligible for long-term tax treatment.

sale of qualifying shares—see definition in Section 3.3(b)—and venture capital shares.

A capital gain or loss is the difference of the sale price over the cost basis of stock. The taxation treatment depends first, on the nature of shares sold, and second, on the holding period. For tax purposes, a distinction must be made between participating stock and portfolio (temporary) investment. (See definition in Section 3.3.)

Only stock or shares qualifying as participating stock—see definition in Section 3.3(b)—that have been owned for more than two years are eligible for long-term tax treatment (taxed at 19 percent plus surtaxes), provided the net after-tax profit is booked as a reserve at year-end. Otherwise, they are treated as short-term gains or losses at 33 percent plus surtaxes. The same treatment applies regardless of whether the shares are owned in a French or non-French company.

(b) Asset sales   As described earlier, any capital gain derived from assets transferred out of the company is taxable as operating profit at the standard rate of corporate income tax regardless of the holding period prior to the sale. A massive sale of assets—even though it cannot be viewed as a transfer of assets as a going concern—may trigger adverse tax consequences related to the future use of carryforward tax losses. (See Section 7.2(b).)

7.2   Target-Side Issues: Impact on Tax Loss Carryforwards

(a) Stock acquisitions   There are no tax consequences for the target company that arise either from the acquisition of the target company's shares by another company or from the transfer of ownership of a significant stock (no winding-up mechanism, no challenging of its carryforward tax losses).

(b) Asset acquisitions   There are no circumstances under which the acquiring company can utilize tax losses of the selling company. Carryforward tax losses can be used only within the selling company and only if the selling company may be viewed, after the assets' transfer, as still being engaged in the same business activity. Otherwise, the company will no longer be entitled to use any of its carryforward tax losses.

8.   PREPARING A TARGET COMPANY FOR SALE

Presale planning could be important if the purchaser wants to buy only specific assets or if the seller wishes to retain certain assets, such as when the seller wants to sell its trading activities but wishes to retain the securities and available funds.

8.1   Hive-Down of Assets in Exchange for Shares

If the seller is selling one division or a part of a trading business, a hive-down method of purchase may be considered. This may be achieved either through a drop-down of assets in exchange for shares or through a division or spin-off.

For corporation tax purposes, such reorganizations may—under conditions described in Sections 9.1(a) and 9.1(c)—be effected on a tax-free basis. However, to benefit from this favorable treatment, the transferring company must hold the stock issued in exchange for the drop-down of assets for at least three years. This means that a drop-down of assets immediately prior to the sale of the shares received in exchange cannot be achieved tax free and will be treated merely as a disposal of assets resulting in the taxation of built-in gains at the rate of 33 percent plus surtaxes.

Nevertheless, an advantage of the hive-down method may be to reduce the RDs cost, for which there is no holding-period requirement. While the direct sale of a business as a going concern is subject to RDs assessed on the transfer price at a rate of 4.8 percent (to be paid by the purchaser), sales of shares in a corporation are capped at €3,049. (See Section 1.2.)

8.2   Presale Dividend

Any presale dividends paid by the target from its distributable reserves to its shareholders are subject to the participation exemption rules covered in Section 6.2. A presale dividend may therefore be a useful tool to minimize capital gains tax.

The magnitude of the presale dividend strip depends on the reserves available for distribution within the target group. For 2005, it should mean those reserves that can be distributed without triggering the exceptional levy of 25 percent. As discussed in Section 6.3, this levy should no longer be applicable on dividend distributions made as of January 1, 2006.

9.   DEMERGER OR SPIN-OFF

9.1   Corporate Reorganizations Qualifying for the Tax-Free Merger Regime

(a) *Drop-down of assets in exchange for shares*   The *apport partiel d'actif* is a transaction whereby one company contributes to a different one (either existing or newly formed) part of its assets and connected liabilities in exchange for stock. As a result of the assets drop-down, the business unit that used to be one division among others in the company prior to the reorganization becomes a separate and distinct subsidiary of the transferring company.

The transaction results in a partial division of the transferring company. The assets and connected liabilities are allocated between those being transferred out and those remaining with the transferring company. Such reorganization can be executed on a tax-free basis for corporate tax and RD purposes if all properties transferred constitute a whole and autonomous business unit on their own. The autonomy is deemed effective if, for instance, the business unit has its own distinct clientele, its own employees, its own accounts, and so on.

A thorough analysis should be performed to determine whether tax-free treatment might be achieved.

(b) Distribution of shares received in exchange for a drop-down or contribution   The distribution by a company to its shareholders of the shares received in exchange for a drop-down is a taxable event both for the company (taxation of capital gain) and for the company's shareholders (distributed income).

However, such distribution may be effected tax free subject to obtaining an advance ruling. For this purpose, the following conditions must be met:

- The distribution of stock must be made within one year subsequent to the assets drop-down.
- Both the asset contribution and the ensuing stock distribution must be driven by business purposes—for example, simplification of the ownership structure for concentration on the core business. Any of the companies involved in the assets drop-down (contributor and acquirer) must, after the transaction, be in a position to run a real and autonomous activity on its own. This means that no ruling could be obtained if, as result of the transaction and the ensuing distribution of stock, the contributing company would own only nonsignificant participations or isolated assets.
- The assets contribution for stock must be effected under the tax-free-merger treatment.
- The stock distribution must be pro rata to each stockholder in the contributing company.
- Stockholders of the contributing company must hold their former and new stock for at least three years.

(c) Division or spin-off   A spin-off is defined as a transaction in which one company (the divided company) is divided into two or more companies—already existing or to be incorporated for that purpose—to which all properties get transferred in exchange for stock. Because the divided company no longer exists after the spin-off, the stockholders of the divided company directly receive the newly issued shares.

This transaction may be executed on a tax-free basis (capital gains taxation deferral) if the following conditions are met:

- The divided company must, at a minimum, have two separate, autonomous business units, each of them run autonomously.
- Each acquiring company receives one or more of the business units.
- The stockholders of the divided company undertake to own the shares in the acquiring company for at least three years. This commitment is required only from those stockholders (1) having at least 5 percent of voting powers in the divided company at the date the spin-off is decided or (2) having 0.1 percent but also having participated in the management or direction of the company in the previous six months prior to the spin-off if those stockholders hold altogether at least 20 percent of the share capital.

If these conditions are not met prior to the transaction, the spin-off may be executed on a tax-free basis if approved by the French Ministry of Economy and Finance. (See Section 5.4(d).)

Cross-border spin-offs may consist of:

- **Division of a French company owned by non-French resident shareholders.** If foreign shareholders are among those in the so-called decision makers college, they must own the shares for the minimum three-year holding period. Failing that, the French tax authorities may seek payment of the aforementioned penalties from the French-based companies resulting from the division. These companies are jointly liable for the payment of such penalties.
- **Division of a French company into two or more foreign-based companies.** Such a transaction should be treated as the merger of a French company into a foreign-based company. The tax authorities would therefore require that all properties of the divided company be carried over to the French permanent establishment of the foreign acquiring companies.

(d) Dissolution—without liquidation—of a wholly owned subsidiary   The *dissolution par confusion de patrimoines* is the upstream transfer of all properties (assets and liabilities) from a fully owned subsidiary to its parent company through the dissolution of the subsidiary. While for legal purposes this transaction is not a merger, it meets the fiscal definition as introduced in the tax code in 2002. (See Section 5.2.) It may from then on be executed on a tax-free basis.

The main difference between this transaction and a statutory merger is the simplicity of the applicable legal procedure. There is no need either for an appraisal of the net worth of assets by an independent appraiser or for a merger agreement setting forth the terms and conditions of the transaction. Instead of a shareholders meeting to be held in the company dissolved, only a single decision from the parent company is required.

From 2002 forward, cross-border transactions with non-French-resident companies are also eligible for the tax-free system. The conditions for eligibility are:

- The foreign-based parent company must reside in a country that has entered into a double-tax treaty with France, and this tax treaty must provide for an antiavoidance mutual agreement. (See Section 5.4 (b).)
- A prior ruling from the French Ministry of Economy and Finance must be obtained.

Such advance ruling is automatically granted when each of the following conditions are met:

- The foreign-based company has or recognizes a permanent establishment to which all assets of the French company are being allocated.
- The foreign-based company, by the intermediary of its French branch, meets the provisions of Article 210 A of the tax code. (See Section 5.4 (d).)

10.   LISTINGS AND INITIAL PUBLIC OFFERINGS

10.1   Impact on Tax Status of Listing a Company and Its Subsidiaries

The tax status of a company is generally not affected by a listing or initial public offering (IPO).

10.2   Listing or IPO of a Complete Group

In the listing of an entire group, a new company may be set up as the listed vehicle (Holdco). The stock in the existing parent company may be transferred to Holdco via a share-for-share exchange. It should be possible to carry out this share-for-share exchange on a tax-neutral basis.

10.3   Listing or IPO of a Subsidiary

The immediate implications for the existing parent of a listing of a subsidiary are:

- If the parent sells in the market—that is, lists—some of its existing stock in its subsidiary, then the parent becomes subject to corporation tax of 33 percent, plus surtaxes, on the resulting gains. This occurs if the shares have been held for less than two years. If the shares were held for more than two years, the parent will become subject to tax at 19 percent, plus surtaxes, on the resulting gain, provided the net after-tax gain of 81 percent is booked as a reserve at year-end.

- If the subsidiary issues new stock, no tax charge arises, because the parent has not sold any stock. The issuance of stock is not a taxable event.

One of the indirect effects of a listing or IPO may be to reduce the parent's shareholding below 95 percent, in which case the listed subsidiaries may no longer be part of the tax unity headed by the parent. This may result in degrouping charges. (See Section 6.1.)

If the parent's shareholding is reduced to below 5 percent, the participation exemption treatment of dividends (see Section 6.2) is no longer available. Therefore, any dividend income received by the parent from the listed subsidiaries becomes fully taxable.

GERMANY

INTRODUCTION

This chapter details the principal tax issues that are relevant to purchasers and sellers engaged in the transfer of ownership of a Gersman trade or business. Unless otherwise stated, it is generally assumed that all sellers and purchasers are German companies with limited liability.

The transfer of ownership of a German trade or legal entity takes the form of a disposal of assets or shares. While there are significant differences in the tax implications of an asset or share sale, nontax considerations must also be considered. Indeed, it is very common for parties to the transaction to have determined the form of the deal even before the tax implications have been considered. Both German commercial law and German tax law provide for legal mergers (with one business being the surviving entity), for demergers, for changes of legal forms, and for share-for-share transactions—without triggering a capital gains tax charge.

The relevant taxes to be considered are:

- **Corporation tax.** Generally, this is a 25 percent (26.5 percent in 2003 and then again 25 percent thereafter) tax plus a 5.5 percent solidarity surcharge on a company's taxable income. German companies are taxed on a stand-alone basis. However, if they are members of a tax group, the parent is taxed according to the group's total income. German partnerships are look-through entities for income tax purposes, and income tax is levied at the level of the partners.

- **Trade tax.** Trade tax is levied on the income of a German business or a trade carried out in Germany regardless of whether the trade is carried on by an individual, a partnership, or a company. It is levied by the local municipality and is a deductible expense. Therefore, the effective rate is an amount of 15 to 20 percent depending on where the business is located.

- **Overall statutory tax rate.** The overall statutory tax rate—including trade tax, corporate tax, and solidarity surcharge—amounts to 38 to 40 percent.

- **Value-added tax (VAT).** This sales tax is added to the sales price charged for goods or services at a rate of 16 percent, except for certain categories of sale that are exempt from or outside the scope of VAT or that are taxed at a lower rate of 7 percent. A purchaser or recipient of services can generally recover VAT paid if the purchase took place in the course of a commercial activity.

- **Real estate transfer tax (RETT).** This tax is charged at a rate of 3.5 percent on the purchase price of land or real estate when the legal title of German property changes hands, and at a rate of 3.5 percent on a special estate value where at least 95 percent of the shares in a company are transferred or unified or at least 95 percent of the shares in a partnership are transferred.

1.   ACQUISITIONS

1.1   Asset Acquisitions

Generally, an asset acquisition enables the purchaser to avoid exposure to the risk of any historic liabilities that are not specifically recoverable through the sale agreement. Liabilities associated with the purchase remain the responsibility of the company that has made the asset sale and do not become the responsibility of the purchaser unless the parties agree that specified liabilities will transfer to the purchaser. Even if the seller and buyer agree to transfer specified liabilities, the creditor may pursue the seller for payment unless there is a formal novation (an agreement also involving the creditor under which the liability is assumed by the buyer and the creditor agrees to release the seller from any further responsibility for that debt). However, it should be noted that the buyer might be secondarily liable for so-called business taxes if the vendor fails to pay them.

Another important nontax consideration is that on a sale of assets, contracts between the seller and third parties are not automatically assigned to the purchaser. Therefore, it is necessary for the purchaser either to enter into new contracts with the third parties or to agree with a third party that the existing contract can be assigned from seller to purchaser. This often causes practical difficulties—particularly when there are numerous contracts or when a third party is unwilling to permit assignment—and frequently is a reason that stock transactions are preferred to asset transactions.

Note also that there are regulations that protect the employees on the sale of a business (Section 613, a *Burgerliches Gesetzbuch*). Such regulations generally provide that the purchaser must take on employees on employees' current terms and conditions of employment if a whole business or a business segment is acquired.

An asset acquisition generally enables a step-up in the tax basis of assets. Based on the assets' market value, the consideration paid is allocated between different assets, including goodwill, and these allocations are accepted as the new tax basis in those assets.

However, a disadvantage will accrue to the shareholders of the seller company in that the proceeds of an asset sale will remain locked in the seller company. Therefore, distribution of these proceeds may result in double taxation. The company will already have been subject to tax on the sale of assets. In addition, the distribution of the sale proceeds by the company to its shareholders may result in taxable income to the shareholder depending on who the shareholder is. This will affect, in particular, shareholders who are German resident individuals, because such individuals are subject to income tax on 50 percent of dividends received.

1.2   Stock Acquisitions

In an acquisition of company shares, the purchaser effectively bears any historical and future ongoing tax and nontax liabilities of the target company. Without careful planning, there is no step-up permitted in the tax base cost of the company's assets. Any goodwill acquired as part of a stock deal generally does not qualify for tax relief.

Therefore, from a purchaser's perspective from a tax viewpoint, it is often beneficial to acquire assets rather than stock.

When partnership interests are acquired, a step-up of the underlying assets is permitted under partnership taxation principles. (See Section 3.2 (a).)

An important advantage of a stock acquisition is that contracts between the target company and third parties remain in force and do not need to be assigned or renegotiated with the third party. However, some contracts may contain change-of-control provisions that might result in termination of or other amendment to the contract in the event of a change in ownership of the target company. There is a potential conflict between the preferences of purchaser and seller because of the availability of the participation exemption to corporate sellers, under which a disposal of shares in a company is exempt from tax on capital gains. There is no such exemption on a disposal of assets or partnerships. (See Section 7.1 for details on the capital gains tax.) Therefore, in principle, if the conditions are met, a purchaser may want to acquire assets, and a seller will prefer to sell stock. Therefore, the tax impact of the acquisition structure can be a key factor in pricing negotiations with the seller.

2.   TRANSACTION COSTS FOR PURCHASERS

2.1   Transfer Taxes: Real Estate Transfer Tax

(a) *Asset acquisitions*   In the case of an asset deal, RETT of 3.5 percent is charged on the transfer of the land and building's legal title. Basis for the tax is the arm's-length purchase price.

The tax is to be borne jointly by the seller and the buyer where the land's legal title is transferred. However, most sale-and-purchase agreements provide that the buyer pay the tax.

(b) Stock acquisitions   RETT at 3.5 percent is triggered if at least 95 percent of the shares in a company owning German property are transferred directly or indirectly to one acquirer or to a group of related acquirers. The basis for the RETT charge is a special estate value, which generally equals 60 to 80 percent of the property's market value.

In the case of the transfer of shares in a partnership, the tax becomes due when at least 95 percent of the partnership interests are transferred directly or indirectly to new partners at once or even within a period of five years. The basis for the RETT charge is a special estate value, which generally equals 60 to 80 percent of the property's market value.

The tax is to be borne by the following parties under the following circumstances:

- The acquirer, if at least 95 percent of the shares in a company are unified in the hand of one acquirer for the first time

- The seller and buyer in other cases of the transfer of at least 95 percent of the shares in a company; however, most sale-and-purchase agreements provide that the buyer pay the tax

- The partnership, if at least 95 percent of partnership interests change hands

2.2   Value-Added Tax

(a) Asset acquisitions   Transfers of business assets that qualify as transfers of a business or business segments as going concerns are outside the scope of VAT. Otherwise, a purchase of assets is generally subject to VAT at 16 percent, which must be paid in addition to the purchase consideration. The sale of land or real estate and accounts receivables is exempt from VAT. However, the seller can opt for a VAT charge.

When the buyer is itself subject to the VAT regime and is obliged to charge VAT on its sales—called outputs—the buyer may recover VAT paid by it on its own purchases—called inputs—including the VAT on the acquisition of assets. Some exemptions may apply.

(b) Stock acquisitions   Both stock transfers and the transfer of partnership interests are exempt from VAT. However, the seller can opt for a VAT charge.

The buyer may recover the VAT paid to the vendor on the sale of the stock, though some exemptions might apply.

2.3   Capital Taxes and Stamp Duties

There are no capital taxes and stamp duties in Germany that are applicable to stock or asset purchases.

2.4   Tax Deductibility of Transaction Costs

In general, transaction costs, regardless of the kind of deal, have to be capitalized as acquisition costs and do not qualify for tax relief.

In general terms, however, the position can be summarized as follows:

- Finance costs
- Investigation and due diligence costs
- Other deal costs
- RETT

(a) Finance costs   Costs incurred on the formation of companies and on raising equity finance generally qualify for tax relief.

Costs related to the raising of debt financing should be available for tax relief. However, relief is limited to 50 percent for trade tax purposes in the case of financing costs related to long-term debt. Relief is normally given for such costs when they are taken to the profit-and-loss account, pursuant to German generally accepted accounting principles (GAAP). Such costs include bank arrangement fees and professional fees for securing that financing. Costs are, however, disallowed if they are related to tax-exempt income. To the extent they are related directly to tax-exempt dividend income or capital gains from the disposal of shares in the hands of a corporation, 5 percent of the dividend or the capital gain will be deemed to qualify as a nondeductible expense.

(b) Investigation and due diligence costs   Due diligence and other investigation costs that are related to the acquired target are generally not deductible unless and to the extent that it can be argued that such work was necessary to obtain debt financing.

(c) Other deal costs   Only those costs incurred that relate to the raising of debt financing for the acquisition are deductible for tax purposes.

(d) RETT   RETT is to be capitalized as acquisition costs of the property if the land's legal title changes hands. In other cases (transfer of shares), RETT should be tax deductible.

3. BASIS OF TAXATION FOLLOWING ASSET OR STOCK ACQUISITIONS

3.1 Asset Acquisitions

Capital allowances (tax depreciation) of 20 percent per year on a reducing-balance basis are available with respect to plant and machinery as well as to other movable assets acquired—based on the price paid for those assets. Alternatively, depreciation can be taken over the assets' remaining economic lifetimes and on a straight-line basis.

Allowances (depreciation) of 3 percent are available on the purchase of buildings. However, the rate and/or amount of these allowances depends on the age of the building. Land and shareholdings cannot be depreciated.

Purchased intangible assets are eligible for tax depreciation in line with the accounting treatment. Goodwill is to be amortized over a period of 15 years on the tax books.

Sales of inventory normally are included in the seller's trading profits, and the purchaser receives tax basis equal to the value of stock as paid.

Similar rules apply to work in progress.

Typically, trade receivables are acquired at net book value (i.e., nominal value). When the amount subsequently received is equal to the net book value, no taxable profit or loss arises. If any of the debts prove to be irrecoverable whether in full or in part, it should be possible to obtain a tax deduction to the extent that the debt is not recovered.

3.2 Stock Acquisitions

(a) Purchase price The purchase price forms the base cost of the purchaser's stock in the acquired company. The underlying base cost in the acquired company's assets is not changed, and there is no election available to step-up the tax basis of assets. Accounting goodwill arising on the consolidation of the company in the financial statements of a German parent is not tax deductible. A step-up of the underlying assets might be achieved only if careful planning is considered.

Acquiring partnership interests results in a step-up of the underlying assets in the buyer's tax books, including noncapitalized items such as goodwill. The acquisition of partnership interests is therefore similar to an asset deal. The buyer's base costs amount to the partnership's net asset value as allocated to the individual partner's tax books—that is, acquisition price minus depreciation/amortization plus profit allocation and contributions minus withdrawals.

(b) Tax grouping Germany has a separate-entity basis of taxation. However, operating profits and losses and capital gains and losses arising in the same period can be offset between German residents if a German parent holds more than 50 percent of the voting rights in the subsidiaries. (See Section 6.1.)

4.   FINANCING OF ACQUISITIONS

4.1   Debt

Specific tax issues related to the overall level of borrowings and to the interest charged on this debt are:

- Withholding tax
- Deductibility of interest
- Thin capitalization

(a) Withholding tax   Under domestic rules, interest payments to German and overseas lenders are generally not subject to any withholding tax. If a loan is guaranteed by German real estate or by German boats that are registered or when a loan is profit participating, withholding tax may be required for payments to an overseas lender.

(b) Deductibility of interest   Generally, interest expense is deductible in Germany. There is, however, a 50 percent disallowance for interest expense on long-term debt (12 months or more) for trade tax purposes.

Under German partnership taxation principles, interest expense charged by a partner are completely disallowed at the level of the partnership. The partner's interest expense that is related directly to their partnership share are, however, deductible at the partnership level.

Interest expense is disallowed if it is linked directly to tax-exempt income. When the participation exemption on dividends or on capital gains applies (see Section 6.2 and 7.1), 5 percent of the dividend or capital gain is deemed to result in nondeductible expenses.

Generally, related-party loans must be based on arm's-length conditions to avoid any restrictions on their deductibility, and thin-capitalization rules limit the leveraging of German companies.

(c) Thin capitalization   Thin-capitalization rules apply to German companies for corporate tax purposes if the interest charge is made by a more-than-25-percent shareholder, a related party, or a third party with recourse (e.g., guarantees). The rules provide for a debt/equity ratio of 1.5:1. Equity is determined by the commercial balance sheet at the beginning of the German company's accounting period and is reduced by the book value of investments in the case of operating entities that do not qualify as a holding company. A company generally qualifies as a holding company if it holds shares in at least two companies. In the case of loans granted to a partnership with a 25-percent-or-more corporate partner, special rules apply.

In the case of third-party loans with recourse, thin-capitalization rules should apply only in case of back-to-back financing. According to the German tax authorities, back-to-back financing is deemed to exist if the payments made to the third party are linked to a consideration paid directly or indirectly to the corporation, the shareholder, or any affiliated party for long-term deposits.

Interest on profit-participating loans does not qualify for any tax relief at all. The same applies to a loan secured to acquire the shares of a company from a related party.To the extent the debt/equity ratio is exceeded, the excess interest is recharacterized as a nondeductible, or hidden, distribution. Withholding tax of 20 percent on the hidden distribution is to be reduced either to zero under the European Union (EU) parent-subsidiary directive or to the amount specified under the respective tax treaty.

4.2   Equity

There is no capital duty on the issuance of new stock.

Dividends paid on stock are not deductible by the company paying the dividend regardless of whether such stock is ordinary or preferred stock. A German company receiving such dividends is not taxed on them. However, because 5 percent of the dividend is deemed to result in nondeductible expenses (see Section 4.1(a)), effectively 95 percent of the dividend is tax-exempt in the hands of a corporate shareholder. A German individual is taxed on 50 percent of the dividend income. There is a 20 percent withholding tax on the payment of dividends, which is credited at the level of the shareholder.

The issuance of equity as a method of funding is advantageous in that it will improve the debt/equity ratio of the company. This potentially enables additional interest-bearing debt to be granted to the company. (See Section 4.1(c).)

5.   MERGERS

Both German company law and tax law enable a German company to legally merge into another corporate entity and to issue new shares in the surviving entity to the shareholders of the other entity. Alternatively, a merger can be achieved by a transfer of trade and assets either by transferring the trade and assets from one company to another company or by transferring the trade and assets of both companies to a Newco. Another form of merger involves the combining of two groups previously held by separate sets of shareholders.

5.1   Legal Forms of Mergers

(a) *Legal merger*   German partnerships and companies can be merged if one entity (the transferor) transfers all of the assets and liabilities to either an existing entity or a newly set-up entity for the purpose of issuing new shares or partnership interests in the surviving entity to the stakeholders of the transferor. An upstream merger does not require the issuance of new shares in the surviving entity. As a result of the merger, the transferor is dissolved without liquidation, and the surviving entity becomes the legal successor of the transferor.

There is currently no method under German law for executing a cross-border merger involving a German company and an overseas company when the latter is the surviving entity.

(b) Transfer of trade and assets   A German company or a German partnership can transfer its trade or part of its trade to either an existing or a newly set-up company or partnership, with the latter issuing new shares as a contribution in kind or a demerger.

Legally, a demerger requires documents similar to those required for a merger, plus a division report, which is a comprehensive written report and which, among other things, describes and justifies the division legally and economically.

(c) Exchange of shares   Shareholders can transfer their shares in a German company or a partnership to another German company or partnership, with the latter issuing new shares. If GmbH (*Gesellschaft mit beschrankter Haftung*) shares are transferred, the transfer is to be notarized by a German public notary.

5.2   Typical Scenarios

All types of reorganizations take place in Germany. However, most types are limited to those within one group or within a joint venture—for example, following an acquisition or prior to a disposal. Mergers are, therefore, either upstream mergers, in which a subsidiary is merged with its parent and the parent is the surviving entity, or vice versa: downstream mergers. Side-step mergers normally take place between companies held by the same shareholder. In these cases, the shares issued to the shareholder do not normally reflect the market value of the transferor.

5.3   Tax Consequences

German tax law has long since removed many of the potential tax barriers that otherwise would have hindered necessary or desirable group internal reorganizations. The provisions of the Reorganization Tax Act apply especially to domestic mergers and to conversions of business enterprises, which may be accomplished at existing book values subject to the overriding provision that Germany's right to ultimately tax the capital gain realized on a subsequent third-party sale is not restricted. Furthermore, the partial transformation of the

EU merger directive into German domestic law has opened new possibilities for tax-free contributions of businesses located abroad and for tax-free share exchanges. The tax burden on such transactions, which previously was often prohibitive, may, in many cases, be deferred indefinitely.

In particular, the following reorganizations may be carried out free of a capital gain tax charge:

- Conversion of a partnership into a corporation and vice versa
- Mergers and demergers of German companies
- Hive-down of a division into a new subsidiary
- Transfer of individual assets to a partnership
- Exchange of shares of EU companies and hive-down of branches in EU countries in exchange for shares in EU companies

In any case, German RETT and the safeguarding of existing tax attributes will have to be managed. (See Section 6.4.)

Typically, a merger transfers the tax attributes—for example, net operating losses and holding periods—of the transferor to the surviving entity. A merger loss or a merger gain is, in general, not tax effective. However, a merger loss can have a negative side effect for statutory accounts purposes because the loss reduces distributable reserves and earnings and therefore restricts the possibility of making dividend distributions.

In 1992, the EU merger directive was incorporated into German tax law. The rules provide that shares of an EU company or the net assets of an EU branch can be contributed at book values (i.e., without realization of a taxable gain) in exchange for shares in another EU company if the company that receives the contribution holds the majority of the shares after the contribution. The shareholder of the EU company whose shares are contributed may be either a corporate or an individual taxpayer and may also be resident outside the EU. However, it should be noted that a practical problem sometimes arises if the contribution is reflected at book value at the receiving entity. Some jurisdictions—for example, the UK—do not apply the strict book value concept and therefore require the shares contributed to be capitalized at fair market value.

Similar provisions for a domestic share-for-share transaction (transfer at book value without a capital gain tax charge) exist for a German resident corporate or individual shareholder transferring shares into a German company or partnership in exchange for shares or partnership interest in that company. Transferring shares into a corporation requires again that the entity that receives the contribution hold the majority of the shares after the contribution, whereas the contribution into a partnership requires that one partner contribute all of the shares in a company.

6. OTHER STRUCTURING AND POSTDEAL ISSUES

6.1 Creation of Local-Country Tax Groups (*Organschaften*)

(a) Corporate and trade tax A corporate and trade tax group requires that a parent hold more than 50 percent of the voting rights in a German company (financial integration) and that both parent and subsidiary agree to a profit-and-loss pooling agreement.

The parent in an *Organschaft* can be a German company, a German partnership, or the registered branch of an overseas company and even, in some cases, an individual. The greater-than-50-percent stake in the German subsidiary must be held from the subsidiary's accounting period onward. Indirect shareholdings can be considered under certain conditions.

The profit-and-loss pooling agreement must be concluded for a minimum of five years. It must be notarized by a German public notary and entered with the German commercial register before the end of the first *Organschaft* accounting period of the subsidiary. The agreement provides for the subsidiary's annual profits to be allocated to the parent, which requires an actual cash payment or, when this is not intended, a loan arrangement regarding the profits that currently belong to the parent. If the subsidiary suffers losses, either the parent must make a corresponding cash payment to the subsidiary or loan arrangements must be made. When the parent does not hold all of the shares in the subsidiary, guaranteed dividend payments generally have to be made to the minority shareholders.

For tax purposes, each entity of a tax group files its own tax returns. The taxable income or the loss is, however, allocated to the parent, which is the sole taxpayer in the group. The subsidiary is secondarily liable if the parent fails to pay the tax.

Within a trade tax group, there is no 50 percent add-back for interest on intragroup long-term debt. (See Section 4.1(b).)

(b) VAT In a VAT group, the subsidiary must be financially, economically, and organizationally integrated with the parent. While only German companies can be integrated in a VAT group as subsidiaries, the parent can be any kind of entrepreneur—even a foreign entrepreneur.

While the corporate group and trade tax group are financially integrated (see Section 6.1(a)), economic integration requires the subsidiary to support the business activities of the parent. Organizational integration is achieved if the parent's will is carried out at the level of the subsidiary—for example, through binding guidelines or a domination agreement or when the managing director of both parent and subsidiary is the same person. Note that the parent must qualify as an entrepreneur within the meaning of the VAT code.

Within a VAT group, VAT on all of the services and sales made by the group is paid by the parent, which can recover input VAT paid by one of the group members. Sales and services within the VAT group are not subject to VAT.

6.2   Repatriation of Profits

Effectively 95 percent of dividends paid to a German company are not subject to corporate tax. There is neither a minimum holding period nor a stake nor double-tax relief for overseas taxes paid on the dividend.

In the hands of an individual, a total of 50 percent of the dividend income must be taxed.

Dividends received by a partnership are 95 percent tax exempt for corporate partners and 50 percent tax-exempt for individuals.

Ninety-five percent of the dividends received by a German shareholder are free of trade tax if the shareholder held at least a 10 percent stake at the beginning of the calendar year.

Interest income and royalties derived are subject to normal German tax rates. Double-tax relief is available on withholding tax on interest or royalties, with a country-by-country limitation.

6.3   Noncore Disposals

See Section 7.1 for details on the taxation of capital gains arising from the disposal of company shares and partnership interests.

6.4   Preservation of Existing Tax Attributes

(a) Partnership   The trade tax losses of a partnership are cancelled if the partnership shares change hands, if the partnership stops its business activities, or if a significant change in business activities takes place. It should be noted that since a partnership is a look-through entity for corporate tax purposes, there are no corporate tax losses at a partnership.

(b) Economic identity   German loss restriction rules deny loss relief when the profitable business is seen as having a different identity from that under which the loss originally occurred. In general terms, loss relief is denied if both of the following conditions exist:

1. More than 50 percent of the shares in the company change hands.
2. The company continues or resumes its business activities with mainly new assets.

Transfer of more than 50 percent of the shares does not have to occur as a single act. However, if it does not, the individual share transfers should be seen as occurring within the same temporal context. This is assumed when the owner-ship of more than 50 percent of the issued share capital is transferred during the course of a five-year period.

The business is considered to have continued or resumed with mainly new assets when new assets of more than the gross assets (balance sheet total) at the time the shares were transferred are contributed to the company by the share-holders or are acquired from the proceeds of related or third-party finance. As with the transfer of the shares, five years is the period during which such an increase can occur. It should also be noted that intangible assets, as well as hid-den reserves—for example, off-balance-sheet goodwill or appreciation of real estate value—should be taken into account in this regard, even if the relevant items cannot be taken up in the financial statements.

Once a company has lost its economic identity under this definition, it has no way of reviving the loss relief that was cancelled.

An injection of assets solely for the purpose of restoring solvency is not harmful. The additional assets must benefit that business from which the loss arose. It is also a requirement that this business be carried on in a similar scale for an additional five years.

(c) Merger   In the case of a merger of a loss company with another entity, the loss company's losses can be carried forward at the level of the surviving entity only if the loss business is carried on in a comparable way for a mini-mum period of at least five years.

(d) Other tax attributes   Other special tax rules—such as special deprecia-tion allowances, tax-exempt subsidies, and incentives—can be endangered if the respective requirements to apply them are not reviewed. This need to review is relevant to all forms of special tax treatments and must also be pur-sued with respect to all other incentives and subsidies granted by federal, state, or municipal authorities.

6.5   Receipts under Warranties or Indemnities

Generally, payments made by the seller for breach of warranty or under an indemnity are taxable in the hands of the purchaser. Accordingly, the usual practice is for the sales-and-purchase documentation to contain a clause stip-ulating that any such payment is to be treated as an adjustment to the consid-eration offered and received for the transaction. In such circumstances, the receipt is not taxable but instead is treated as a reduction of the purchaser's tax basis in the stock acquired. If the warranties and indemnity payments are made to the target company, these are likely to be subject to tax in the target company.

7.   DISPOSALS

7.1   Stock Disposals

(a) Companies   A capital gain from the disposal of shares in a company by a German corporation is generally tax-exempt under the German participation exemption. As 5 percent of the capital gain is deemed to result in nontax-deductible expenses (see Section 2.4 (a)), effectively 95 percent of the capital gain is tax-exempt. No special conditions, such as a minimum holding period or a minimum stake, are required for the participation exemption to apply. The capital gain is, however, not exempt if it compensates a previously tax-effective write-down. It basically also does not apply to shares issued in consideration of the tax-free transfer of a business, a business segment, or partnership interests as a contribution in kind within the past seven years, which results in so-called tainted shares.

According to the tax authorities, the participation exemption does not apply for trade tax purposes if shares are sold by a partnership.

The disposal of partnership interests is subject to both trade tax and corporate tax. The latter is, however, not triggered when the gain from disposing partnership interests is related to shares held by the partnership.

(b) Individuals   An individual's capital gain from selling shares is completely tax-exempt if shares of less than 1 percent were held within a period of five years prior to the sale and if the sale takes place at least one year after the acquisition of the shares. In other cases, 50 percent of the capital gain has to be taxed.

When shares are tainted and have been issued as a contribution in kind in a tax-free reorganization within the past seven years, the capital gain from their disposal has to be taxed at normal tax rates.

The disposal of partnership interests by an individual is free of trade tax, but it is subject to income tax limited to 50 percent of the gain related to shares that are held by the partnership. Special income tax rates may be applied.

7.2   Asset Disposals (Companies Only)

The disposal of assets other than stock is subject to corporation tax and trade tax. Capital gain is the difference between the assets' base cost (book value) and their fair market value.

When the proceeds of the sale of certain types of capital assets used in the trade are reinvested in the acquisition of certain types of new assets for use in the trade of that company—either in the accounting period of the disposal or in the period before—the gain accruing on the sale of the old asset may instead be deferred. Rather than the gain's crystallizing, the tax basis of the new asset is reduced by the amount of the gain. This is principally relevant to land and buildings.

7.3   Deferred Consideration and Earn-Outs

Deferred consideration results in discounting the deferred amount. The discounted part of the consideration is included in the tax calculation of the disposal proceeds at the time of the sale even if receipt of this amount is contingent. Likewise, if the deferred consideration is determined by a formula but subject to an upper limit on the amount payable, that maximum amount is discounted and included in the disposal proceeds figure. However, this is subject to adjustments if the maximum is not paid eventually. The remaining part results in interest income. If the seller is a trade, that interest income is taxed annually. In the case of an individual seller, the interest income is taxed at the time payment is made.

A right to contingent future consideration that is unquantifiable—for example, a formula with no upper-limit earn-outs—should completely be included in the disposal proceeds figure as a retroactive adjustment once the amount can be quantified.

7.4   Payments under Warranties or Indemnities

When the sales-and-purchase documentation contains a clause that any warranty or indemnity payment is to be treated as an adjustment to the consideration offered and received for the transaction, the payment would be treated for tax purposes as having been deducted from the purchase consideration received.

8.   TRANSACTION COSTS FOR SELLERS

Generally, expenses can be deducted if they are not related directly to tax-exempt income. Therefore, when assets are disposed of, expenses will be allowed at the level of the seller. In the case of a share deal, transaction costs may reduce the seller's capital gain.

8.1   Transfer Taxes

RETT is shared by the seller and the buyer. However, most sales-and-purchase agreements require the buyer to pay this tax.

8.2   VAT

See Section 2.2.

9.   PREPARING A TARGET COMPANY FOR SALE

The introduction of the participation exemption a few years ago has made pre-sale tax planning less relevant. However, presale planning is important if the purchaser wants to buy only specific assets or if the seller wishes to retain certain assets, or if the disposal is not sheltered from tax by the participation exemption.

9.1   Hive-Down of Assets

Whereas past business philosophy often advocated building up conglomerates to spread risks, the trend now seems increasingly to concentrate on the core business. Noncore business activities are therefore being sold, transferred to a joint venture, or at least maintained separately. If the noncore business is not ready for an immediate sale, it may be transferred to a separate company by means of a spin-off, a split-up, or a hive-down. A tax-neutral reorganization is permitted if the business transferred and the business retained each qualify as a separate business segment (*Teilbetrieb*) before the reorganization. In legal terms, a *Teilbetrieb* is an investment in a partnership or a 100 percent shareholding in a company.

Antiabuse regulations prohibit spin-offs and split-ups if the purpose of the spin-off or split-up is merely to facilitate a subsequent sale of the resulting shareholding. Such abuse is deemed to occur if shares in either of the companies involved are sold within a period of five years following the demerger, and these represent 20 percent or more of the value of the shares in the company before the spin-off. In this case, the reorganization will be taxed as a disposal of assets. Note that shares issued in the course of a hive-down are tainted within the parameters covered in Section 7.1(a).

A hive-down, or transfer of individual assets that do not qualify as a business unit, is a taxable event. The difference between the assets' fair market value and their book value is subject to standard tax rates unless the hive-down qualifies for a transfer of assets under partnership taxation principles.

To facilitate the restructuring of partnerships, assets may be transferred between partners and their partnerships if the ultimate taxation of the hidden reserves contained in the assets is not endangered. Specifically, the following tax-free transfers are possible:

- Transfer of business assets from a partner to the partner's partnership and vice versa
- Transfer of assets from a partnership to the collective ownership of one or more of the individual partners or vice versa
- Transfer of assets used in the partnership from one partner to another partner in the same partnership
- Transfer of assets from one partnership to another partnership with the same partners

However, such transfers are not tax free if another corporation is a partner in the partnership.

RETT is to be managed if German real estate is involved. VAT does not become due on the hive-down if the assets qualify as *Teilbetrieb*.

9.2   Intragroup Transfer of Assets Being Retained

Assets may have to be transferred out of group companies that are to be sold if it is not intended that the assets are to be included in the sale package. As long as they do not qualify for a transfer of assets under partnership taxation principles as covered earlier (in Section 9.1), they have to be transferred at fair market value so that a capital gain will be taxed. RETT will have to be managed. No VAT is payable on a transfer of assets between members of a VAT group.

9.3   Presale Dividends

Presale dividends can be used to reduce the value of a target company. The tax treatment in the hands of the recipient of any presale dividends paid by the target group out of its distributable reserves is covered in Section 6.2.

10.   DEMERGERS

The commercial rationale for a demerger is based on creating value for the shareholders. Demergers may be used simply to separate different trading activities in different groups or to partition trading activities between different groups of shareholders.

In Germany, corporate law covers the corporate demerger concept—that is, that a single company is split into two or more separate companies or entities. A transferor can split up its assets and is dissolved without liquidation or it can split off one or more parts of its assets. (See Section 9.1.)

The demerger does not trigger any capital gain tax charge in the cases of separate business units. (See Section 9.1.)

11.   LISTINGS AND INITIAL PUBLIC OFFERINGS

On the German market, the trend is to list enterprises on a German stock exchange, and many venture capitalists are searching for appropriate candidates for such listings.

Some of the important reasons for going public are:

- Obtaining new capital to finance future growth
- Fungibility of the shares
- Sale of the company in installments
- Qualified management
- Capital market discipline and transparency

The success of a listing depends on the earnings history and on the preparation, structuring, execution, and timing of the listing. While tax questions certainly are not top-priority items when going public, complete disregard of their impact usually leads to irrevocable disadvantages. With respect to tax issues, some of the main concerns are:

- Tax-neutral reorganization prior to the listing
- Utilization of net operating losses
- Tax treatment of capital gains arising from the initial public offering (IPO)
- Tax deductibility of procurement costs
- Exit taxation of investors

11.1   Reorganization

Legally, only shares in a company limited by shares (*Aktiengesellschaft*, or AG) or in a commercial partnership limited by shares (*Kommanditgesellschaft auf Aktien*, KGaA) can be listed. Therefore, either existing enterprises must be converted into an AG or a KGaA prior to the listing or the shares in existing entities must be transferred to an AG/KGaA.

A KGaA is a hybrid entity that combines elements of a partnership and a corporation. A KGaA is in fact a corporation with a general partner and with shareholders. As far as the general partner is concerned, partnership principles are applied. However, for the company side and the shareholders, company rules apply. Only the capital of the shareholders can be floated.

The taxation of a KGaA takes place in two steps. With regard to the general partner, partnership taxation principles apply such that the proportional income of the partner is taxed for income tax purposes at the partner level rather than at the KGaA. The income of the KGaA is subject to corporate tax at the level of the company. Dividends paid to the shareholders are taxable by the recipients unless the dividend exemption rules apply: 95 percent exemption in the case of corporate shareholders, 50 percent exemption in the case of individuals.

The taxation treatment of an AG is the same as that for a GmbH: trade tax and corporate tax are levied at the level of AG. Dividends will have to be taxed at the level of the shareholders unless the dividend exemption rules apply.

Under the provisions of German tax law, it is generally possible to transform a German partnership or a GmbH into an AG or a KGaA without triggering a tax charge. Even in cases involving German real property, no RETT will become due. However, the conversion of a partnership results in a capital gain tax charge if the shares are not held by a German tax resident.

The transfer of existing shares to a newly set-up AG or KGaA follows normal rules. (See Section 7.1.) For the rules if a transfer is not carried out as a share-for-share transaction, see Section 5.3.

11.2   Net Operating Losses

In the course of the transfer of shares in a partnership or company to a newly set-up AG/KGaA, the normal German loss rules apply. (See Section 6.4.) The conversion of a GmbH into an AG/KGaA does not generally affect the tax attributes of the corporate entity—for example, in terms of tax losses. However, the conversion of a partnership into an AG or KGaA does result in the cancellation of a trade tax loss carryforward of the partnership.

If more than 50 percent of the shares in an AG/KGaA are listed/floated, German loss restriction rules apply. (See Section 6.4.)

11.3   Capital Gains from the IPO

For corporate shareholders, disposing of the shares in an AG/KGaA is 95 percent tax-exempt under German participation exemption rules. In the hands of an individual shareholder holding at least 1 percent of the shares or when the disposal takes place within one year after the acquisition of the shares, 50 percent of the capital gain is taxed. (See Section 7.1.)

When a partnership is converted into a corporate vehicle, the shares of the company are tainted for seven years. A capital gain from their disposal is either 95 percent tax-exempt or subject to the 50 percent exemption, as applicable, on the expiration of the seven-year period. Therefore, if the business intends to go public, it should be organized from the beginning as a separate corporate entity rather than as a partnership or a business unit or division within a company. In the case of the hive-down of a business unit, the seven-year holding period also applies. (See Section 9.1.)

11.4   Tax Deductibility of Costs

Costs related to issuing new shares—such as consulting fees, printing costs, and capital procurement costs—are deductible expenses for accounting and tax purposes. Under German GAAP, these costs cannot be capitalized; they must be expensed. Furthermore, it is not permissible to set off these expenses against a share premium. While there are clear advantages to incurring wholly tax-deductible expenses, the incidence of these costs in any one year might seriously depress earnings.

Other costs such as those related to the listing of existing shares must be paid by the shareholders and may reduce the seller's capital gain.

VAT issues should be considered and managed.

11.5   Investor's Exit

Taxation of the investor's exit follows the rules described in Section 7.1.

HONG KONG

INTRODUCTION

This chapter details the principal tax issues that are relevant to purchasers and sellers engaged in the transfer of ownership of a Hong Kong trade or business. Unless otherwise stated, it is generally assumed that all sellers and purchasers are Hong Kong companies with limited liability.

The transfer of ownership of a Hong Kong business can take the form of a transfer of shares or assets. Because Hong Kong company law does not contain the concept of *merger*, business combination is generally implemented by transferring assets from one company to another or by transferring the assets of two companies to a third one.

The relevant taxes to be considered in the context of a merger and acquisition transaction in Hong Kong are:

- **Profits tax.** Hong Kong imposes a profits tax on a person carrying on a trade or business in Hong Kong with respect to the assessable profits sourced in Hong Kong from that trade or business. Gains arising from the disposal of capital assets and income of non-Hong Kong sources are not subject to a profits tax. For the year of assessment 2004-05, the profits tax rates for incorporated and unincorporated businesses are 17.5 percent and 16 percent, respectively.

- **Stamp duty.** Stamp duty at progressive rates of up to 3.75 percent applies on conveyances of immovable property. The rate for the transfer of Hong Kong stock, when the transfer of shares is required to be registered in Hong Kong, is 0.2 percent, which is payable by the seller and purchaser in equal shares of 0.1 percent each. The level of duty is computed by reference to the higher of consideration or the market value of the assets being transferred.

- **Capital duty.** Capital duty of 0.1 percent applies to increases in authorized share capital—capped at HKD$30,000 per case—of a company.

- **Withholding taxes.** Withholding taxes are charged only on royalties or similar payments to a nonresident party. The rate at which withholding tax applies is either 5.25 percent or 17.5 percent depending on the relationship between the payer and the payee and on whether the intellectual property in question has ever been owned by another person in Hong Kong. The withholding rate is reduced to 5 percent under Hong Kong's comprehensive double-tax treaty with Belgium, Hong Kong's only such treaty. Hong Kong does not impose withholding taxes on dividends or interest.

- Other taxes: There are currently no goods-and-services taxes or value-added taxes or turnover taxes in Hong Kong.

The rules apply equally to Hong Kong incorporated entities—generally, limited liability companies—and foreign entities that conduct business in Hong Kong through a branch.

The principal forms whereby a company can conduct business in and through Hong Kong are:

- A company incorporated in Hong Kong can be private or public. The latter normally is listed on the Hong Kong Stock Exchange.
- Branch of a foreign company.
- Representative or liaison office of a foreign company.
- Partnership.
- Unincorporated joint venture.

Private companies and branches of foreign companies are the business entities most commonly used by foreign investors because limited liability is usually desirable. The use of a Hong Kong company is generally the simpler option, but for certain foreign investors there may be tax advantages in using a branch of a foreign company. While Hong Kong-incorporated companies are required to prepare, maintain, and file with the local authorities their audited statutory accounts on an annual basis, such requirements do not apply to branches of overseas companies.

1.　ACQUISITIONS

1.1　Asset Acquisitions

Subject to the fulfillment of certain statutory requirements, an asset acquisition generally enables the purchaser to avoid exposure to the risk of any historical tax liabilities that are not specifically recoverable through the sale agreement. Liabilities associated with the business being purchased remain the responsibility of the seller and do not become the responsibility of the purchaser unless the parties contract to transfer specified liabilities to the purchaser.

In the case of an asset deal, a Hong Kong profits tax deduction may be obtained for financing costs if certain conditions are met. In principle, interest on financing obtained from a Hong Kong or overseas financial institution is deductible, but interest on financing from a nonfinancial institution is generally deductible only if the interest is subject to Hong Kong profits tax in the hands of the recipient—unlikely in the case of interest payments to an overseas company.

In certain cases, deductions may also be available for interest paid on loans solely to finance the acquisition of inventory and fixed assets and on debentures and marketable instruments.

It should be noted that there are various antiavoidance provisions designed to prevent abuse by disallowing interest deductions for back-to-back financing arrangements with financial institutions and for other arrangements whereby interest indirectly flows back to related parties and whereby the taxpayer is seeking to gain an interest deduction through the creation of artificial interest streams by issuing debentures or other commercial papers and then subscribing for them through their associates. Any arrangements designed to circumvent these restrictions are increasingly at risk of being challenged by the local tax authorities.

An asset transaction may also allow the purchaser to step up the costs of the underlying business assets for tax depreciation purposes although no tax deduction is available for goodwill.

One issue that will interest the seller in an asset deal is the apportionment of consideration, particularly in relation to assets qualifying for tax depreciation. For fixed assets other than buildings, these assets may be depreciated over a shorter period for tax purposes than for accounting purposes, and therefore a disposal at accounting book value could give rise to a clawback of tax depreciation—that is, a taxable balancing charge. This is advantageous if the seller has available tax losses to utilize, especially since the purchaser in turn inherits the higher tax bases for future depreciation purposes.

The following points may also be noted in relation to asset valuations:

- Real estate should be transferred at market value; otherwise, the value for stamp duty purposes may be challenged.
- The tax authorities have the power to deem transfer of assets between connected persons for tax purposes at market value.
- Subject to consideration of general antiavoidance rules, inventory may be assigned at any chosen value—regardless of whether the parties are connected persons—if the transfer results from a cessation of business and the purchaser can claim a Hong Kong tax deduction for the inventory cost. Otherwise, market value should apply.
- Payments for intangibles are generally not tax deductible, although in certain cases, payments for patents and technical know-how are. As previously noted, payments for goodwill are not tax deductible.

1.2   Share Acquisitions

Generally, a purchaser has a variety of considerations to bear in mind—apart from the basic commercial and financial implications of the chosen method of acquisition. Factors that may offset the usual concerns over the unknown liabilities that might be locked in a company include:

- Loss preservation in the target company: While tax losses may generally be carried forward indefinitely to offset a company's future taxable profits, there is a provision in the tax legislation that may restrict the carryforward of tax losses in the target company if the sole or dominant purpose of the change in shareholding of the company is to use up those losses. This provision is unlikely to be invoked for a commercially driven company acquisition or restructuring.
- Real estate in the target company, which would result in a significantly higher stamp duty cost if an asset purchase takes place.
- Potentially higher tax bases for depreciable assets.
- Simplified transaction formalities, such as contracts the target company previously entered into that may remain undisturbed.

For both Hong Kong and foreign-based investors, investments in Hong Kong either in the target company or in the Newco to which the target's assets have been transferred are often structured through a holding company in a tax haven or low-tax jurisdiction, such as the British Virgin Islands. In the absence of withholding taxes or tax on capital gains, this involves no additional tax cost and may provide flexibility for stamp duty planning. Some investors also believe that such a structure mitigates political risk.

Subject to the clawback of any tax depreciation allowances previously claimed in respect of the relevant depreciable assets and the impact of any stamp duty cost, a Hong Kong seller of a Hong Kong company often is neutral about whether to sell the company's shares or assets, because gains on both shares and capital assets should generally not be taxable, while the distribution of retained profits after an asset sale is similarly nontaxable. The following issues should also be considered:

- The issue of what constitutes a capital asset has been the subject of many court decisions in Hong Kong. Therefore, it would be prudent to ascertain the true nature of such an asset before deciding on the type of deal to enter.
- A non-Hong Kong seller also has foreign tax considerations to take into account. In Hong Kong many investments are made through holding companies based in low-tax jurisdictions, in which case a share disposal may be preferred if the capital gains derived from the disposal by the holding company are treated more advantageously under the tax legislation of the ultimate owner's home tax jurisdiction.

2.   TRANSACTION COSTS FOR PURCHASERS

2.1   Transfer Taxes

(a) Asset purchases   Stamp duty at progressive rates of up to 3.75 percent applies on conveyances of immovable property.

Stamp duty is also chargeable on the transfer of Hong Kong stock.

(b) Share purchases   The rate for the transfer of Hong Kong company shares—which are required to be registered in Hong Kong—is 0.2 percent and is payable by the vendor and purchaser in equal shares of 0.1 percent each.

Exemption from stamp duty may apply for the conveyance of an interest in immovable property or, if certain conditions are satisfied, for the transfer of Hong Kong stock between companies with a 90 percent common shareholding.

2.2   Value-Added Tax

Hong Kong does not impose a value-added tax.

2.3   Capital Taxes

There are no capital taxes in Hong Kong applicable to the transfer of shares or assets.

2.4   Tax Deductibility of Transaction Costs

In general, a business expense is treated as deductible if it is incurred in the production of Hong Kong assessable profits and is not capital in nature. Whether or not certain transaction costs are deductible therefore depends on a number of factors, including:

- Whether the purchaser or seller is carrying on business in Hong Kong and derives income sourced in Hong Kong. It should be noted that dividends are generally not subject to profits tax in Hong Kong, and expenses incurred in generating such dividend income are not eligible for tax deduction.
- Whether the purchaser or seller incurs the expenditure in producing such Hong Kong assessable profits.
- Why the expenditure is incurred. Capital expenditure is generally not tax deductible.

In general terms, the position can be summarized as follows.

(a) Financing costs   Interest is deductible in Hong Kong only if it is incurred for the purposes of producing assessable profits and if it meets one of a number of specified conditions. Therefore, while interest paid on debt incurred for the purposes of acquiring shares from which nonassessable dividends will be derived is not tax deductible, interest on debt incurred under an asset deal should at first view be tax deductible.

Share dealers and venture capitalists who carry on business in Hong Kong could, however, be treated differently. On one hand, they normally are not allowed to claim profits from a share disposal as being capital and nontaxable. On the other hand, they should be allowed a tax deduction on interest on debt used for acquiring such shares. Share dealers and venture capitalists who do not carry on business in Hong Kong and who are not subject to tax on profits from the disposal of shares would not be able to obtain a tax deduction for any interest costs.

(b) Due diligence and other deal costs   On one hand, for share dealers and venture capitalists who carry on business in Hong Kong and derive Hong Kong assessable profits from the trading of their investments, the due diligence and other deal costs should prima facie be deductible. On the other hand, if the due diligence and other deal costs are incurred in relation to the acquisition of a capital asset held for investment purposes, no deduction is available.

3.   BASIS OF TAXATION FOLLOWING ASSET OR STOCK ACQUISITIONS

3.1   Asset Acquisitions

In an asset acquisition, the purchaser is eligible to claim initial allowances (tax depreciation) with respect to qualifying capital expenditure incurred on the acquisition of plant and machinery items (at 60 percent of qualifying cost). Annual allowances—at 10, 20, or 30 percent—are also available each year on a reducing balance basis.

Initial allowance at 20 percent is available on qualifying capital expenditures incurred by the purchaser on the acquisition of a new industrial building or structure. Annual industrial building allowances and annual commercial building allowances are also available each year at 1/25 or 4 percent of the qualifying capital expenditure. For the acquisition of secondhand industrial buildings or structures and other commercial buildings or structures, the purchaser is eligible to claim annual allowances only on the qualifying capital expenditure, and the amounts of annual allowances are subject to the age of the building.

Goodwill is not eligible for tax depreciation or deduction. Tax deductions are generally available to the purchaser on the acquisition of patent rights or technical know-how, even though the expenditure incurred is of a capital nature. There is, however, a specific provision in the legislation that prohibits the claiming of deductions when the transfer is made between affiliated parties.

In a transfer of a trade or business wherein the seller ceases to carry on the trade or business, the purchaser normally receives tax basis for the inventory equal to the value of consideration being paid and regardless of whether the parties are related if the purchaser carries on the business of the seller and the purchaser can claim a Hong Kong tax deduction for the inventory cost. In other cases, when the purchaser is unable to claim any Hong Kong tax deductions for the cost of the inventory, the inventory should be treated as being transferred at market value as of the date of cessation of the business by the seller. Similar rules apply to the transfers of works in progress.

Typically, trade debtors are acquired at net book value. If the amount subsequently received is equal to the net book value, no taxable profit or loss arises. If one of the debts proves irrecoverable (whether in full or in part), there are provisions in the tax legislation that prevent the purchaser from claiming a tax deduction in the event that the debt is not recovered.

3.2   Share Acquisition

In a share acquisition, there generally is no change of tax base for either the purchaser or the target company. However, there are provisions in the legislation that may restrict the carryforward of unutilized tax losses in the target company if the sole or dominant purpose of the transfer is to utilize such losses.

As there is no tax consolidation or similar group relief regime in Hong Kong, profits and losses arising in different companies of the same group have to be managed carefully to minimize profits tax on a group basis.

4.   FINANCING ACQUISITIONS

There are no formal debt-equity restrictions in Hong Kong. However, there are stringent conditions for the deductibility of interest, which may effectively restrict the use or method of overseas debt financing.

There are no government consents required to approve the financing unless the debt in question is publicly marketable on the Hong Kong Stock Exchange.

5.   MERGERS

As noted previously, Hong Kong company law does not contain the concept of *merger*. A merger can be achieved by a transfer of trade and assets—either from one company to another company or by transferring the trade and assets of both companies to a third one.

6.   OTHER STRUCTURING AND POSTDEAL ISSUES

Not applicable.

7.   DISPOSALS

As indicated earlier, profits derived from the sale of long-term investments—such as interest in an associated company or in a subsidiary company—should not be taxable in Hong Kong.

A buyer is concerned mainly with (1) structuring the investment (and minimizing Hong Kong and overseas taxes on any exit), (2) how to finance the investment, and (3) the different transaction costs of the alternative routes. Careful planning from the outset should assist in maximizing the buyer's rate of return on its acquisition.

ITALY

INTRODUCTION

This chapter details the principal tax issues that are relevant to purchasers and sellers engaged in the transfer of ownership of an Italian trade or business. Unless otherwise stated, it is generally assumed that all sellers and purchasers are Italian stock-joined companies.

The transfer of ownership of an Italian trade or company can take the form of a disposal of shares or assets for consideration or of a contribution in-kind. It could also take the form of a merger or demerger transaction. While there are significant differences in the tax implications of an asset or share deal, nontax considerations must also be considered.

Effective as of January 1, 2004, Italy implemented a significant reform of the corporate income tax system aimed at bringing the Italian taxation system into line with the others in Europe. In particular, in shaping the new corporate income tax regime, authorities referred to the prevailing European tax model with a view to:

- Introducing a participation exemption system for capital gains on disposal of shareholdings
- Abolishing the former dividend tax credit imputation system and replacing it with a participation exemption system
- Introducing thin-capitalization rules and other regulations disallowing a tax deduction for borrowings in certain cases
- Introducing domestic tax consolidation
- Having the possibility, mainly for Italian resident listed companies, of setting up a global tax consolidation
- Introducing consortium relief, allowing holding companies to treat as transparent for tax purposes their investments in companies that they do not control
- Abolishing the 19 percent substitute tax on certain corporate reorganizations' tax step-up basis
- Reducing IRES (corporate income tax) to 33 percent (corporate income tax rate)

Past merger and acquisition transactions, debt-financed structures, and leveraged buyouts have been significantly affected by the tax reform.

The relevant taxes to be considered are:

- **Corporation tax (IRES).** This is a 33 percent national tax on profits earned by a company. A further 4.25 percent regional tax (IRAP) is, in general, applicable on trading profits—normally, gross financial charges (namely, interest on debt) and labor costs. Specific IRAP provisions are applicable to banks and financial companies.
- **Value-added tax (VAT).** VAT is a sales tax whereby 20 percent is added to the sales price charged for goods and services—except for certain categories of sale that are exempt from or outside the scope of VAT. A purchaser or recipient of services can generally recover VAT paid if the purchase was incurred in the course of a commercial activity. However, the level of recoverability varies from case to case. Substantial VAT recoverability restrictions apply to pure holding companies with no structure directed at managing the investment.
- **Stamp duty land tax.** Normally, this is payable by a purchaser at a rate of up to 18 percent on the purchase price for land or real estate, and up to 0.14 percent on the purchase price for stock.

Antiabuse and antiavoidance provisions allow the Italian tax authorities to disregard tax advantages obtained by means of certain transactions—among others, mergers, demergers, transfers and contributions in-kind of business and of shares, and distributions of equity reserves other than profits—in case a tax reduction or refund is obtained in the absence of valid and sound economic reasons.

1.   ACQUISITIONS

1.1   Asset Acquisitions

Carrying out an asset transaction implies three main effects.

1. The purchaser is not responsible for risks linked to historical liabilities of the selling company; however, the purchaser is jointly liable with the seller for any tax liability that refers to the tax period of the deal and the two previous ones up to the value of the business acquired.
2. Agreements entered into by the business transferred are normally transferred to the purchaser, unless differently regulated by the parties.
3. Labor law safeguards the acquired rights of workers and employees of the business transferred.

Asset acquisitions in exchange for consideration do not create major issues from a corporate law perspective because the direct sale does not require an expert opinion on the value of the assets and/or business transferred.

An asset acquisition could also be executed if a contribution in-kind is exchanged for shares by means of capital increase of the receiving company. Contribution in-kind is strictly regulated by corporate law provisions.

An asset acquisition could also be executed if contribution in-kind is exchanged for owned shares of the receiving company without capital increase of the latter.

In an asset acquisition for consideration, the price paid by the purchaser results in tax basis (see Section 3.1), because the seller is subject to capital gains tax. (See Section 7.2.)

An asset-contribution-in-kind acquisition does not necessarily allow the receiving company to obtain book values recognized for tax purposes (see Section 3.1), because capital gains realized by the contributing company may not necessarily be taxed. (See Section 7.2.)

1.2   Stock Acquisitions

Stock acquisitions can occur for consideration or via contribution in-kind in exchange for shares by means of a capital increase of the receiving company or in exchange for owned shares of the receiving company without any capital increase.

In a stock acquisition, the purchaser risks being responsible for any tax and nontax liability related to the company acquired. The purchase price cannot be reflected other than in the cost of the stock but will not be reflected in any step-up of the assets acquired. (See Section 3.2.)

An important advantage of a stock acquisition is that contracts between the target company and third parties remain in force and do not need to be assigned or renegotiated with the third party. However, some contracts may contain change-of-control provisions that may result in termination of or other amendment to the contract in the event of a change in ownership of the target company.

Conflicts may arise between the purchaser's and seller's interests when share disposal for consideration is compared with asset disposal for consideration. Purchase price negotiation may combine the seller's interest to achieve the benefits of participation in an exemption regime (see Section 7.1) and the purchaser's interest to obtain tax recognition of the price paid—as allowed by the asset deal for consideration.

2.   TRANSACTION COSTS FOR PURCHASERS

2.1   Transfer Taxes

(a) *Stock purchase*   A stock disposal is subject to stock transfer tax at a maximum of 0.14 percent of the sale price.

(b) Asset purchase   A business transfer is outside the scope of VAT and is subject to the registration tax of 3 percent calculated on the sale price, including the goodwill. The Tax Administration may carry out adjustments to the value of goodwill declared.

Registration tax of up to 7 percent plus the land registry tax of 1 percent and the mortgage tax of 2 percent is payable on the acquisition of real estate (for land, the tax rate is 8 to 15 percent) included in the business; liabilities included in the business are attributed to real estate and other assets in proportion to their value for the purposes of the application of the different tax rates.

2.2   Value-Added Tax

(a) Stock purchase   Stock transfers are exempt from VAT.

(b) Asset purchase   A transfer of business assets that qualifies as a transfer of a business is outside the scope of VAT. Otherwise, a purchase of assets is normally subject to VAT at 20 percent, which must be paid in addition to the purchase consideration.

When the buyer is subject to VAT and is obliged to charge VAT on its sales—called outputs—the buyer may recover VAT paid on purchases—called inputs. Note that in some situations, depending on certain VAT-related characteristics of the buyer, the VAT paid on inputs may not always be recoverable in full and, therefore, such VAT paid would be a real cost to the buyer.

2.3   Capital Taxes

There are no capital taxes in Italy applicable to stock or asset purchases.

2.4   Tax Deductibility of Transaction Costs

(a) Existing regime   In general, under current tax treatment, whether a particular expense is treated as deductible depends on several factors, including:

- Whether the transaction is for the purchase of assets or shares
- The actual connection of the expense incurred with the company trade (so-called *principio di inerenza*)

The identity of the business to which the expenses were paid is not relevant at all, provided that the recipient is not a business resident in a tax haven jurisdiction.

Expenses related to the management of shares that qualify for the participation exemption remain 100 percent tax deductible even if the related dividend flow is partially (95 percent) exempt.

In general terms, current legislation can be summarized as:

- Financing costs
- Investigation and due diligence costs

(i) Financing costs   Costs incurred to form companies and to raise equity financing qualify for corporate tax relief as intangible goods; amortization is spread over five years, which is the period that costs are normally taken to the profit-and-loss account.

Costs incurred to obtain debt financing should be available for corporate tax relief. The costs are generally recovered over the life of the loan. Interest payable is generally available for corporate tax relief unless the thin-capitalization rules (see Section 4.1(c)) or the interest pro rata restriction (see Section 4.1(d)) applies. Relief is normally given for such costs when they are taken to the profit-and-loss account pursuant to Italian generally accepted accounting principles. Such costs include bank arrangement fees and professional fees related to securing the provision of the financing.

(ii) Investigation and due diligence costs   Due diligence and other investigation costs are generally deductible according to the general principles set out earlier, provided that the *principio di inerenza* is fully complied with. Official instructions are needed from the tax authorities in order to ascertain the tax treatment, under the approved tax reform, of transaction costs incurred if the tax authorities claim such costs should have been capitalized as ancillary costs over the cost of investment. For example, investigation and due diligence costs might, at a later stage, not be deductible because they are related to shares qualifying for a participation exemption regime.

(b) VAT treatment of expenses   Fees charged for intermediary activities for loans and for the issuance of stock are not subject to VAT in Italy; therefore, bank and institutional fees generally do not carry VAT. Professional fees charged to Italian customers by advisers, however, are subject to VAT even when the fees are related to the sale or issue of stock or loan finance.

Input VAT (VAT charged by third parties for goods or services provided) that is related directly to the issuance of stock to Italian or European Union counterparties may not be recovered.

VAT related to professional fees incurred for a transaction other than a transaction that is related directly to the issuance of stock can be treated as an overhead expense and is recoverable in full, unless the company is subject to the partial-exemption method.

On invoices it is important to identify costs separately so as to facilitate the allocation of input VAT to the issuance of stock and to other matters.

3.   BASIS OF TAXATION FOLLOWING ASSET OR STOCK ACQUISITIONS

3.1   Asset Acquisitions

The purchase price paid in cash for the business forms the taxable base for the purchaser; amortization is determined according to fixed tax depreciation rates. This also applies to goodwill recorded in the purchasers' books, which is depreciable, with a maximum 10 percent rate on a yearly basis for tax purposes.

Under certain conditions, a special neutrality regime can be elected for contributions in-kind. In this case, the accounting base and the tax base could differ from that recorded in the purchaser's books. An ad hoc reconciliation chart, between accounting and tax values, is required.

As per tax reform, further relief is likely with respect to group taxation; the disposal or contribution of assets between group companies that have elected to choose group taxation could benefit—at their request and under specific conditions—from a particular tax neutrality regime. (See Section 6.1.)

3.2   Stock Acquisitions

After the stock deal has been performed, the base cost for the purchaser is represented by the purchase price. No election for the step-up of the taxable basis of the assets of the acquired company exists. Capital loss upon disposal is tax deductible only if participation exemption is not applicable. (See Section 7.1.)

The tax cost base of qualified holdings acquired by means of a contribution in-kind is subject to detailed rules. (See Section 7.1.)

4.   FINANCING OF ACQUISITIONS

4.1   Debt

Specific tax issues related to the overall level of borrowings and the interest charged on this debt are:

- Withholding tax
- Deductibility of interest
- Thin capitalization
- Asset pro rata rules
- Combination of provisions
- Transfer pricing
- Recharacterization as divided
- Additional withholding tax
- Hybrid financial instruments

(a) Withholding tax   Cash interest payments to overseas lenders are subject to a withholding tax of 12.5 percent; payments to foreign lenders resident in tax haven jurisdictions are subject to a withholding tax of 27 percent.

The withholding tax can be reduced to lower rates according to the provisions of double-tax treaties signed by Italy.

There is no withholding tax on interest payments between Italian companies and between Italian and foreign banks.

Italy has not yet implemented the interest royalties directive, which allows the payment of interest and royalties withholding free if certain specific conditions are met between related parties.

(b) Deductibility of interest   Interest expense forms part of the calculation of the taxable profit and is generally deductible on an accruals basis. When insufficient current-year profits exist to offset all current-year deductible interest, the interest may be carried forward as part of the company's trading losses and set against the future trading profits of the company in which the interest arose.

Interest expense is not deductible for the purpose of the 4.25 percent regional tax. However, banks and finance companies are normally allowed to deduct interest expense.

Interest deductibility restrictions apply according to the principles set forth in the thin-capitalization rule, in the asset pro rata rule, and in the further taxable/exempt rule.

(c) Thin capitalization   To reduce excessive debt financing of Italian resident companies, thin-capitalization rules are introduced to limit the deduction in computing the taxable income of interest paid to qualifying shareholders and related parties.

The new rules provide that all or part of interest on loans made by a qualifying shareholder or a related party (group finance) is not deductible in computing profits subject to corporation tax—to the extent that the ratio between the group finance and the shareholder's equity exceeds 4:1. In the first year in which thin-capitalization rules apply—the first accounting period beginning on or after January 31, 2004—the ratio is 5:1.

It is therefore necessary to compare the total group finance with the total equity attributable to the qualifying shareholders (first test). If the ratio exceeds 4:1 (or 5:1 for the first year), the thin-capitalization rules apply at the single-qualifying-shareholder level (second test) such that the relevant interest is not deductible in computing profits subject to corporation tax, and the qualifying shareholder is liable for tax on the deemed distribution of dividends.

The definition of debt is broad and includes all loans made by a qualifying shareholder or a related party as well as debt guaranteed by a qualifying shareholder or related party.

Loans are defined as borrowings, deposits of money, or any other financial arrangement. Further guidance from the tax authorities determines whether the definition covers such arrangements as cash pooling, financial leases, and factoring arrangements.

When the 4:1 ratio (5:1 for the first accounting period) is exceeded, exemption from the thin-capitalization rules nevertheless applies when the borrower is able to demonstrate that the amount of the group finance is justified by its own credit capacity and that consequently, the loans could have been made by an independent third party exclusively on the basis of the security provided for by the borrower's share capital.

(d) Asset pro rata rules   Restrictions exist to limit the deduction for interest expense used in financing the acquisition of shareholdings when the company paying the interest owns shares in subsidiaries, since the disposal of such shares would qualify for the participation exemption.

This pro rata is calculated as:

$$\text{Net interest payable} \times \frac{\text{Excess of book value of investment over net equity of the parent company}}{\text{Total balance sheet assets of the parent less net equity less business payables}}$$

The restrictions on asset pro rata interest expense deductions apply to any remaining interest that is deductible after the application of the thin-capitalization general rule.

The scope of this specific restriction is to prevent a deduction's arising from computation of the taxable base of the costs (interest expenses) related to assets (shareholdings) that generate exempt income under the participation exemption regime. (See Section 7.1.) The interest deduction restriction may be removed as a result of:

- Merging the target (subsequently) into the purchasing company
- Electing to use the domestic tax consolidation regime (See Section 6.1.)
- Electing to use the tax transparency regime (See Section 6.1.)

(e) Combination of provisions   Legislation in force provides that, given a certain amount of accrued interest expense, the amount of interest that is deductible must be calculated according to the general thin-capitalization rule (Section 4.1(c)); in addition, the deductible amount so determined must be netted according to the asset pro rata rules (Section 4.1(d)); moreover, the deductible amount must be further netted according to the taxable/exempt income rule. The last rule provides that (1) interest expense shall not be deductible up to the amount of interest or other revenue that is tax-exempt—mainly from old

public bonds—and (2) interest expense shall be deductible in an amount corresponding to the ratio between the amount of gross revenue and other receipts included in the taxable profit and the total amount of all revenues and receipts. Detailed rules exist to determine the exact ratio.

(f) Transfer pricing   Interest charges on loans between an Italian company and a foreign related party must be on an arm's-length basis. Otherwise, transfer-pricing rules that restrict interest deductions may apply.

(g) Recharacterization as dividend   If the interest expense is in excess of the 4:1 (or 5:1) debt equity ratio set forth in Section 4.1(c), it is recharacterized as dividend income to the related party.

(h) Additional withholding tax   Many tax treaties with Italy contain a clause stipulating that when there is a "special relationship" between lender and borrower and when the borrower pays more interest than would be required in the absence of such a special relationship, the excess interest may not be eligible for the reduced rate of withholding tax under the treaty.

(i) Hybrid financial instruments   Legislation provides that remunerations of hybrid financial instruments allowing participation in the borrower's profit— for example, participating loans—are not deductible from the borrower's taxable profit.

4.2   Cash Repatriation

The acquiring group's holding companies are likely to require cash to finance the ongoing interest on bank debt that they have borrowed to make the acquisition. There are a number of ways that cash may be passed up through the structure to Italian holding companies to achieve this:

- **Dividends.** Dividends may be paid by Italian companies if available profits and distributable reserves exist; dividends from foreign shareholdings may be partially or totally subject to tax in Italy. (See Section 6.2.)
- **Intercompany loans from other Italian companies.** Interest on such loans should be tax neutral because an expense that arises in one company (assuming no restrictions on deductions exist) gets matched by income in another company. Alternatively, such loans could be made interest free, subject to corporate law analysis. However, this is subject to thin capitalization and other related issues covered in Section 4.1.
- **Intercompany loans from non-Italian companies.** Any non-Italian interest charged on such loans is deductible in Italy on an accruals basis.

However, this is subject to thin capitalization and other related issues covered in Section 4.1.

- **Payments for services provided for group companies.** These need to be supported by relevant transfer-pricing documentation when the provider is resident outside Italy, demonstrating that the charge is at arm's length.
- **Capital reductions or redemptions.** Assuming civil law provisions are fully complied with, the capital reduction or redemption is not considered as dividend distribution, as far as and to the extent to which no profit reserves were previously transferred to capital as capital increases or other profit reserves.

Cash may be paid by Italian companies to foreign parent companies by the same methods, although care should be taken to ensure withholding tax is correctly calculated on interest and on any other relevant payments such as royalties. If upstream loans are made to foreign companies, it is important that interest be charged on such loans to ensure that companies are in compliance with Italian transfer-pricing rules and corporate law provisions.

4.3 Equity

There is no proportional capital duty on the issuance of new stock.

The use of equity as a method of funding may be advantageous in that it improves the debt/equity ratio of the company and potentially enables additional interest-bearing debt to be issued by the company. (See Section 4.1(c).)

4.4 Key Nontax Issues

(a) Government consents Generally there are no government consents required in relation to an acquisition or the raising of financing—other than those of the antitrust authorities.

(b) Abuse-of-law provisions Italian civil code stipulates (contract in fraud of law) that the *causa* of the contract is unlawful when it provides the means to evade the application of a mandatory provision.

(c) Financial assistance Corporate lawyers and other competent professionals always should be consulted on these matters.

5. MERGERS

In Italy a merger can be carried out as follows:

- **A merger created by establishing a Newco.** This occurs when two or more companies join their own structures (trade as well as assets and liabilities), and the beneficial entity is a company set up specifically for this purpose.

- **A merger created by absorption.** This occurs when two or more companies join their own structures (trade as well as assets and liabilities), and the beneficial entity is an existing company.

5.1   Tax Impact of a Merger Transaction

The neutrality principle is applicable in merger transactions. According to this principle, the successor company steps into the shoes of its predecessor company, and assets qualifying for capital allowances are transferred at tax written-down value without requiring a balancing of profits/losses on those assets.

No realization of capital gains or losses on the merged assets—including inventories and, if any, goodwill—takes place as a result of the merger transaction, but at the same time, the tax value of all merged companies' assets/liabilities has to be maintained by the recipient company.

Generally, tax losses can be carried forward only for national corporate income tax purposes and only for five years.

The carryforward of the tax losses of companies participating in the merger is subject to certain conditions. Among those conditions is that the tax losses carried forward cannot exceed the net equity book value of the relevant company as shown in the most recently approved financial statements, excluding any capital contribution made during the previous two years.

Equity reserves that are subject to tax deferral shown in the financial statements of the merged company have to be included in the income of the successor company if they are not included in the financial statements of the successor company.

The transfer of assets, including inventories, related to a merger transaction is not subject to VAT. However, a transfer of independent assets is subject to VAT.

The merger deed is subject to the registration tax at a fixed amount of €29.11.

5.2   Exchange of Shares for Merged Company's Shareholders

Exchange of the old shares in the merged company for the new ones issued by the successor company is not treated as a disposal by the merged company's shareholder, and the new shares in the successor company that are received are treated for capital gains tax purposes as the original shares in the merged company.

The exchange of shares is not subject to the stamp duty and is not a VAT-relevant transaction.

6.   OTHER STRUCTURING AND POSTDEAL ISSUES

6.1   Creation of Local-Country Tax Groups

(a) *Tax group*   Each Italian resident company that forms a group is entitled to opt for the national tax consolidation. Nonresident parent companies and subsidiaries are allowed to participate in the tax consolidation only if:

- They are resident in a country with which Italy has concluded a double-taxation treaty and if an instrument on mutual assistance procedure exists.
- They have a permanent establishment in Italy to which the shareholdings in subsidiaries have been attributed.

The effects of the consolidation are:

- The parent company makes a single computation for the group's taxable profits and losses.
- The subsidiaries still need to prepare a return, but this is given to the parent company, which may then file a single return with the tax authorities. The return represents the mathematical sum of all of the subsidiaries' profits and losses.
- Dividends paid by group members to others are excluded from the group's taxable profits.
- Taxes on sales of assets, other than stocks of finished or semifinished products, and on sales of business divisions between group members are also excluded from the computation of profits and losses until either the assets are sold to third parties, the fiscal consolidation is dissolved, or the option is not renewed.
- The subsidiary companies included within the domestic tax group are excluded in calculating the pro rata for nondeductible interest. (See Section 4.1.)

The option for tax consolidation applies irrevocably for a minimum period of three accounting periods. Clawback rules apply if there is no longer any control, in which case:

- The parent company needs to recalculate interest expense deducted within the pro-rata parameters for the part of the past three-year period.
- The departing company needs to calculate the tax due on any gain on previous intragroup sales that were treated as tax neutral.

Regardless of the shares held, all (100 percent of) profits and losses of each subsidiary must be consolidated.

Tax losses are treated as follows:

- Tax losses carried forward from periods prior to entry into the tax group may be utilized only by the company that incurred the loss.
- Losses incurred during periods in which the tax group option is in force may be offset against the profits of other group members, and excess can be carried forward by the group leader in accordance with the normal rules on tax loss carryforwards.

Italian resident companies may also elect to apply international tax consolidation. The option is available only for companies and entities:

- Whose securities are traded on a regulated capital market
- That are controlled by the state, by other public entities, or by individuals resident in Italy who do not control (including via related parties) other resident or nonresident companies or entities

Only the top Italian company in a chain can exercise the option.

Under international tax consolidation, the subsidiaries' profits or losses are attributed to each shareholder proportionally to such shareholder's share in the profits regardless of whether the profits are distributed. This differs from domestic consolidation, whereby all of the profits and losses of the subsidiary are to be ascribed to the parent company regardless of the percentage of ownership. Unlike domestic consolidation, the all-in, all-out principle applies.

The option may not be revoked for a period of five years—as opposed to three years for the domestic tax consolidation.

(b) Consortium relief   Italian resident companies may opt to apply transparent taxation rules to the profits and losses of other Italian resident companies in which they hold shares. The election is available to shareholders who hold at least 10 percent but not more than 50 percent of the voting rights in companies that are resident in Italy or that, if not resident, are entitled to make distributions of profits without withholding of tax at the source—for example, dividends to qualifying parent companies resident in other European Union jurisdictions. All of the shareholders must satisfy the same requirements; for example, shareholders must be no less than 2 and no more than 10.

If the option is exercised, then profits and losses of the subsidiary are attributed to the shareholder according to their shareholdings during the shareholders' fiscal year that includes the year-end of the subsidiary. The option is irrevocable for three of the subsidiary's accounting periods.

Dividends paid among companies in the tax-transparency regime are exempt.

Losses by a subsidiary that arise during the transparency period are allocated to the shareholders based on detailed rules and limitations.

(c) VAT group taxation   Group companies can generally elect to carry out the periodical VAT settlement at the group level; nevertheless, they remain separate VAT taxable entities, each with an individual VAT identification number. When this is done, VAT credits deriving from the members of the VAT group can be utilized by the parent company to offset other VAT debts. Members of the VAT group that are transferring VAT credits are, along with the parent company, jointly and severally responsible for their VAT liability.

6.2   Repatriation of Profits

Since January 1, 2004, participation exemption rules have been applicable to distribution of dividends. These rules provide for a 95 percent exclusion of dividends from taxable income, including liquidation profits, on dividends distributed by both Italian and non-Italian companies. Therefore, in the hands of the Italian companies, only 5 percent of the dividends received are subject to national tax. Moreover, only 5 percent of the dividends distributed are taxable— at an effective rate of 1.65 percent—except for shareholdings held in controlled foreign companies located in black-list jurisdictions as identified in a list published by the tax authorities.

Dividends paid by one Italian company to another Italian company are not subject to withholding tax.

Italian companies receiving dividends from a foreign subsidiary may claim, proportionally to the taxable amount of the dividend, the tax credit for the foreign tax paid abroad against Italian tax that is also payable.

6.3   Preservation of Existing Tax Attributes

When an Italian company carries on trading activities and incurs a tax loss, generally such tax loss can be carried forward for five years. This applies only for national income corporate tax purposes. Tax losses accrued in the first three tax periods by a newly incorporated company can be carried forward indefinitely.

Losses carried forward can be lost if both of the following conditions are met:

- Fifty percent or more of voting rights in the company's shareholders meeting change ownership—except if such change involves group entities

- The activity carried on by the company is changed in the two years prior to the ownership change or will change within two years after the ownership change.

6.4   Receipts under Warranties or Indemnities

Generally, payments made by the seller for breach of warranty or under an indemnity are taxable to the target company (the purchased entity). Consequently, the usual practice is for the sales-and-purchase documentation to contain a clause stipulating that any such payment is to be treated as an adjustment to the consideration offered and received by the purchaser. In such circumstances, the receipt is treated as a reduction of the purchaser's tax basis in the stock acquired.

Indemnity payments made to the target company are likely to be subject to tax in the target company.

7.   DISPOSALS

7.1   Stock Disposals

(a) Disposal for cash   Generally, a 33 percent national income tax is applicable to gains realized by corporate entities on stock disposals. The gain may be recognized for tax purposes over a period of five years if the stock disposed of is recorded among the financial immovable assets on the statutory financial statements for at least the prior three years.

Taxable gain is calculated as the difference between the consideration paid—including all purchase price adjustments—minus the tax basis recorded in the books of the seller.

Beginning January 1, 2004, tax reform provides that corporate entities are subject to corporation tax on gains upon disposal of stock unless requirements of the participation exemption rules are met. In this case, the disposal is fully exempt from tax. The participation exemption requirements are:

- *The shares must have been held without interruption from the first day of the 12th month prior to the month of the sale.* In the event that the shares are sold in several installments, those purchased more recently are deemed to be sold first (last-in, first-out basis). This rule is discretionary in the event that all of the purchases comply with the requirements.
- The shares are classified among financial fixed assets in the selling company's first financial statements ended during the period of ownership.

- *The subsidiary is not located in a black-list country.* The black list is a list of countries identified by the Tax Ministry that are in jurisdictions that have favorable tax regimes. This requirement holds unless a ruling request is filed with the tax authorities.
- *The subsidiary carries out a commercial activity.* This condition does not apply to real estate holding companies other than companies that trade or construct real estate or companies that own real estate for the purpose of conducting a commercial activity.

Those conditions—namely, the location of the subsidiary in a nonblack-list country and the subsidiary's conduct of a commercial activity—must be met from the beginning of the third accounting period prior to the date of disposal of the shares without interruption.

When shares are held through holding companies whose activities are exclusively or mainly to own shares, the conditions described in A and B above must be met with regard to the shares owned in the holding company. The conditions described in C and D must be met by the indirect subsidiaries. Furthermore, the current value of the majority of the indirect subsidiaries must exceed 50 percent of the current value of the holding company's net equity— this likely means an absolute majority—taking into account any goodwill both positive and negative even if not recorded in the financial statements.

(b) Disposal by means of contribution in-kind   If the stock disposed represents a controlling stake, meaning, more than 50 percent of the voting rights, or represents a connection stake, which means more than 20 percent of the voting rights, the capital gain is subject to the ordinary 33 percent tax rate if the participation exemption does not apply. (See Section 7.1(a).) The contributing company and the receiving company may agree—from a direct tax standpoint—on the amount of capital gain to be entered in the general accounting records.

(c) Disposal by means of share-for-share exchange   Under certain conditions, stock disposals of a controlling stake in exchange for shares of the recipient company without a capital increase may be effected under the neutrality rules. In this case, no capital gains are realized.

7.2   Asset disposals

The disposal of a business for cash generates a capital gain for the seller. This capital gain is subject to corporate tax at a rate of 33 percent. At the transferor's option, the capital gain may be taxed in its entire amount in the year in which it is realized or in five equal installments if the business transferred has belonged to the transferor for at least three years.

The income tax provisions applicable to contributions in-kind allow the taxpayer the possibility of choosing between alternative tax treatments:

- **Fiscal neutrality.** In this case, transfer of the assets and liabilities of the business must be executed on the basis of the tax written-down values on the books of the seller company.

- **Ordinary taxation (values recognized for tax purposes).** Tax on the capital gain is payable over a period of no longer than five years, with the application of corporate tax at a rate of 33 percent, provided that the transferred going concern has belonged to the transferor for at least three years. Any capital loss is recognized immediately. The contributing company and the receiving company may agree—from a direct tax standpoint—on the amount of capital gain to be entered in the general accounting records.

Group taxation exemption may be applicable for assets and business disposals as well as for contributions in-kind. (See Section 6.1.)

7.3   Deferred Consideration and Earn-Outs

Generally, if an amount of deferred consideration is ascertainable at the time of the disposal but the receipt of that amount is contingent or if an agreement for the sale of stock in a company includes the right to receive deferred consideration unascertainable at the time of the agreement (usually because it depends on the future profitability of the company), such receipts are booked as extraordinary income when definitively accrued. A general principle in the determination of business income is that revenues and expenses, which, in the relevant tax period, are not yet certain or the amount of revenues and expenses that are not yet objectively determinable shall be included in the business profit of the tax period in which such conditions are met.

Careful analysis must be made of the wording of the agreement, and professionals should be consulted on these matters.

7.4   Payments under Warranties or Indemnities

When the sales-and-purchase documentation contains a clause that any warranty or indemnity payment is to be treated as an adjustment to the consideration offered and received for the transaction, the payment would, for tax purposes, be deducted from the purchase consideration received.

8.   TRANSACTION COSTS FOR SELLERS

8.1   Transfer Tax

Transfer tax is normally but not necessarily payable by buyers on the purchase of shares. (See Section 2.1(a).) Likewise, transfer land tax is normally payable by purchasers of real estate.

8.2   VAT

(a) Stock disposal   The disposal of stock is exempt from VAT.

(b) Asset disposal   The transfer of business assets that qualifies as a transfer of a business is outside the scope of VAT. Otherwise, a purchase of assets would attract VAT at a rate of 20 percent that would have to be paid in addition to the purchase consideration.

8.3   Tax Deductibility of Transaction Costs

In general, under current tax treatment, whether a particular expense is deductible depends on several factors. (See Section 2.4(a).)

(a) Corporation tax treatment of expenses

(i) For companies disposing of shares   Costs related to the sales process in general and, particularly, costs related to detailed negotiations with a specific bidder in relation to shares that qualify for a total exemption from taxation under the participation exemption rules are not regarded as deductible.

Costs incurred prior to the disposal of qualified shares might be regarded as the deductible costs of managing investments—for example, evaluating potential disposal strategies. However, this treatment could be disputed and has to be clarified by the administrative practice.

(ii) For companies disposing of assets   Under existing legislation, provided that general rules (see Section 2.4(a)) are complied with, no restrictions on transaction expense deductions exist.

Costs incurred—for example, asset valuation fees, costs of transfer, or related legal fees—as part of the disposal process generally are deductible for the purposes of computing the seller's trading profits for tax purposes.

(b) VAT treatment of expenses   VAT charged by third parties to the seller on transaction costs should be recoverable, subject to the partial-exemption method applicable to the seller and provided that the costs involve a service provided for that seller, that the service is not directly attributable to an exempt supply made by the supplier—for example, a sale of stock, or loan notes—and that the service is attributable to the seller's taxable business activities. VAT charged by third parties to the seller and related to group reorganization activities may, however, be recovered.

It is important that invoices separately identify costs so as to facilitate the attribution of input VAT to the issue of stock and to other matters.

9.   DEMERGERS

A corporate demerger is an operation involving a transfer of assets—which can include shares—that splits a single company into two or more separate companies or entities.

Demergers may be used simply to separate different trading activities in different entities or to partition trading activities between different groups of shareholders.

In Italy a demerger transaction is regulated by the Civil Code, which defines different kinds of operations as follows:

- **Total demerger.** The demerged company transfers all of its assets and liabilities to more than one so-called recipient company (also newly established) and ceases to exist.
- **Partial demerger.** The demerged company transfers to one or more recipient companies part of its assets and liabilities and does not cease to exist.

As a result of a demerger transaction, the shareholders of the demerged company receive new shares issued by the recipient company(ies) in substitution for the preexisting shares of the demerged company, which will be cancelled. In this respect, the Italian Civil Code provides that a demerger transaction can be defined as follows:

- **Proportional demerger.** The demerged company's shareholders receive shares of the recipient companies in direct proportion to their rights in the capital of the demerged company.
- **Nonproportional demerger.** The demerged company's shareholders receive shares of the recipient companies in a different proportion from their rights in the capital of the demerged company. However, the total value of the new shares received must equal the value of the shares held in the capital of the demerged company.

9.1   Tax Impact of a Demerger Transaction

The neutrality principle is applicable to a demerger. Consequently, a demerger does not give rise to the realization or distribution of capital gains or losses on the assets—including inventories and, if any, goodwill—of the demerged company. Also, in this case, the historical tax written-down value of all of the demerged company's assets and liabilities transferred must be retained by the recipient company(ies).

If certain conditions are met—that is, the same limitations established for the merger transaction covered in Section 5.1—then fiscal losses of the demerged entity and of the beneficiary entity can be carried forward.

Equity reserves subject to tax deferral shown in the financial statements of the demerged company must be included in the income of the recipient company(ies) in proportion to the demerged company's net worth received, if they are not included in the financial statements of the relevant recipient company.

The transfer of assets, including inventories, related to a demerger transaction is not subject to VAT.

The demerger deed is subject to registration tax, which is a fixed amount of €129.11.

9.2   Exchange of Shares for a Demerged Company's Shareholders

Exchange of the old shares in the demerged company for new ones issued by the recipient company(ies) is treated as not involving a disposal by the demerged company's shareholders, and the new shares in the recipient company(ies) that shareholders receive are treated for capital gains tax purposes as the same asset as their original shares in the demerged company.

The exchange of shares is not subject to stamp duty and is not a VAT-relevant transaction.

10.   LISTINGS AND INITIAL PUBLIC OFFERINGS

10.1   Impact on the Tax Status of a Company Being Listed and on Its Subsidiaries

The tax status of a company generally is unaffected by a listing or initial public offering (IPO).

10.2   Listing or IPO of a Subsidiary

For the existing parent of the listing of a subsidiary, the immediate implications are:

- If the parent sells in the market, that is, lists, some of its existing stock in a subsidiary, then that parent is subject to corporation tax on chargeable gains on the disposal of stock unless requirements for the participation exemption are met, in which case the disposal is exempt from tax. (See Section 7.1.)
- If the subsidiary issues new stock, the parent has not sold any stock, and no tax charge arises.

However, the impact of a listing may be to reduce the parent's shareholding below 51 percent, in which case the subsidiary may no longer be part of relevant tax groups. (See Section 6.1.)

10.3   Issuance of New Stock by a Listed Company

If the listed company is the parent of the group, the issuance of new stock by the listed company should not have any tax consequences for the company. If the listed company is a subsidiary, the issuance of new stock may result in that subsidiary's exiting a tax group. (See Section 6.1.)

10.4   Disposal of Stock by Existing Shareholders

If the listing or IPO involves a disposal of stock by existing shareholders, the tax position for those shareholders is as outlined in Section 7.1.

JAPAN

INTRODUCTION

This chapter details the principal tax issues that are relevant to purchasers and sellers engaged in the transfer of ownership of a Japanese trade or business. Unless otherwise stated, it is generally assumed that all sellers and purchasers are Japanese companies with limited liability.

A change in the ownership of a Japanese company or business can occur via a disposal of shares or assets or through legal merger. Transactions are normally subject to the Japanese Commercial Code (JCC) and take one of the forms prescribed therein. The forms of transaction envisaged by the tax law generally, though not identically, follow the JCC.

Nontax considerations such as regulatory and licensing issues as well as employment law normally play major roles in determining the form taken by Japanese merger and acquisition transactions. Some of those considerations are noted in this chapter when appropriate.

The most-significant and most-relevant taxes related to mergers and acquisitions are:

- Corporate income tax
- Consumption tax
- Income tax
- Withholding income tax
- Stamp tax
- Registration and license duties
- Local real estate acquisition tax
- Local-inhabitants and -enterprise taxes
- Depreciable-fixed-assets tax

Other taxes that would be relevant but that are currently temporarily suspended include:

- Land value tax
- Special land-holding tax

1.   ACQUISITIONS

For the purposes of corporate taxation, there is (1) no distinction between the taxation of capital gains and of trading profits and (2) there is no form of participation exemption. Nevertheless, several differences exist between asset and stock acquisitions.

1.1   Asset Acquisitions

An asset acquisition generally allows the purchaser to avoid exposure to historical liabilities. Historical liabilities remain with the vendor unless they are contractually assumed by the purchaser under the sale-and-purchase agreement.

However, asset acquisitions are more likely to encounter regulatory difficulties. Many sectors of industry are subject to one or more forms of regulation or licensing. Obtaining consent to transfer licenses—or, perhaps more accurately, to obtain a new license—can be a long process.

Employment law can also be a key issue, because the transfer of employees in an asset or business transfer requires each transferring employee's individual consent.

From a tax perspective, an asset purchase at greater than historical tax basis (note that this is not guaranteed given Japan's deflationary environment) allows a step-up in tax basis. Goodwill, in particular, may then be amortized on a straight-line basis over five years, provided it has also been recognized for financial accounting purposes. Obtaining tax relief for any premium of the purchase price over the underlying assets' tax bases is far more difficult in the case of a stock purchase.

One point of detail to note in the case of an asset acquisition has to do with provisions for retirement benefits. Japanese companies often operate unfunded pension arrangements when provisions are simply set up on the companies' own balance sheets. These provisions are generally not tax deductible. In the event of a business disposal by means of an asset transfer, the purchaser may be paid by the seller to assume these pension liabilities. This payment would represent taxable income for the purchaser in the period in which it is received; the purchaser would receive no immediate tax deduction for setting up a corresponding provision on its own balance sheet. Therefore, without further planning, the purchaser may suffer an unexpected up-front tax liability.

The result in a nonqualified demerger—that is, a spin-off or hive-down not qualifying for the tax-free treatment discussed in Section 10—is broadly similar to an asset acquisition and may be the preferred option in some cases, because, for example, individual employee consents are not required.

1.2   Stock Acquisition

In a stock acquisition, the purchaser effectively bears the target company's historical liabilities. In practice, outright purchases of large Japanese companies are
still uncommon. More common transactions might involve:

- The purchase of a less-than-50-percent stock interest in a Japanese group
- A Japanese group separating part of its business into a subsidiary by one
  mechanism or another prior to sale of the subsidiary's stock

In the first situation, because at least some former shareholders remain
involved, the value of warranties or indemnities with respect to historical liabilities might be increased. In the second situation, the target company may
have owned the target business for only a short period of time, and the historical liabilities borne by the target company therefore depend on the mechanism
by which it acquired the target business.

2.   TRANSACTION COSTS FOR PURCHASERS

2.1   Transfer Taxes

(a) Asset purchase   Asset acquisitions may attract stamp duty, although, generally, at de minimis rates of duty. More significant registration and license duties
may also arise. When real property is transferred in an asset acquisition, the rate of
registration duty payable is currently 1 percent of the official rated land value.
This is expected to rise to 2 percent on April 1, 2006. Local real property acquisition tax may also be due at 3 percent on the official rated land and building value.
This tax is expected to rise to 4 percent on April 1, 2006. Lower rates apply in the
case of asset transfers by merger.

(b) Stock purchase   Registration and license duties are not applicable to
stock acquisitions. Neither should stamp duty arise, provided the transaction is
properly documented.

2.2   Consumption Tax

(a) Asset purchase   Asset acquisitions may be subject to consumption tax
depending on the assets transferred. There is no exemption for the transfer of a
whole business as in certain other countries. However, provided the purchaser is
registered for consumption tax and conducts a fully chargeable business, any such
consumption tax should be recoverable. Note also that the transfer of land—as
distinct from any buildings on the land—is not subject to consumption tax.

The transfer of assets in the course of a merger or demerger is free of consumption tax. In the case of contributions in-kind, the total amount of consumption tax

payable is calculated on the basis of the net value of the contribution in-kind and is then allocated across the consumption-taxable assets transferred.

(b) Stock purchase   Consumption tax is not applicable to stock transactions.

2.3   Capital Taxes

(a) Share capital registration duty   Share capital registration duty arises when new share capital is issued—for example, when an acquisition company is incorporated and funded in order to perform an asset acquisition. The rate of duty is 0.7 percent—or 0.15 percent in the case of a capital increase in the course of a merger equal to the former share capital of the disappearing company.

In the case of increasing an existing company's share capital, it may be possible to record 50 percent—or in some circumstances perhaps 100 percent—of a capital increase as additional paid-in capital—meaning, share premium or contributed surplus—that is not liable to registration duty.

(b) Local-enterprise tax levied by reference to share capital   Effective as of April 1, 2004, for companies with share capital exceeding ¥100 million, local enterprise tax is not based solely on profitability but also includes amounts charged by reference to other value-added factors, such as staff wages and share capital. The tax rate applied to share capital plus capital reserves is generally 0.2 to 0.21 percent per year.

2.4   Tax Deductibility of Transaction Costs

Transaction costs may generally include lawyers' fees, any costs required to conclude the purchase agreement, arrangement fees, acquisition finance costs, investment advisory fees, valuation fees, other advisory fees, and transaction taxes. Arrangement fees, valuation fees, and transaction taxes are generally deductible; other costs are generally regarded as capital expenditures.

3.   BASIS OF TAXATION FOLLOWING ASSET OR STOCK ACQUISITIONS

3.1   Asset Acquisitions

Tax-deductible depreciation is available for tangible fixed assets other than land as well as for several types of intangible fixed assets, including patent rights, trademarks, and goodwill. However, this tax deduction can neither exceed nor precede recognition of a corresponding depreciation expense in the profit-and-loss account of the financial statements. While tangible fixed assets may be tax depreciated by either the straight-line method or on a reducing-balance basis, intangibles are tax depreciated on a straight-line basis. The maximum permissible rate of tax-depreciation for each category of asset is set forth in the tax law. In particular, goodwill is tax depreciated on a straight-line basis over five years.

In general, Japanese tax law does not require segregation, or ring fencing, of acquired businesses from any other business operations of the purchaser. Consequently, a purchaser with tax loss carryforwards would normally be permitted to offset taxable profits against such losses.

3.2   Stock Acquisitions

(a) Tax basis   The purchase price generally establishes the purchaser's tax basis in the acquired stock. The tax basis in the underlying assets is not changed, and there is no possibility to elect to equalize the inside and outside bases. Accounting goodwill arising in consolidated group financial statements is not tax deductible in Japan.

(b) Tax grouping   Historically, Japan has had a separate entity basis of taxation for all purposes. However, since April 2002, tax consolidation has been possible for national corporate income tax purposes. (See Section 6.1.)

4.   FINANCING OF ACQUISITIONS

4.1   Debt

The principal tax issues in connection with acquisition debt are:

- Withholding tax
- Thin capitalization
- Deductibility of interest

(a) Withholding tax   Interest paid to a Japanese corporate lender is not subject to withholding tax. Interest paid to a nonresident lender is subject to a 20 percent withholding tax unless this liability is reduced by an applicable tax treaty. Japan's tax treaties typically provide for a 10 percent treaty rate of withholding on interest—with certain limited exceptions, such as a 0 percent rate for interest received by sovereign bodies and financial institutions in the new US-Japan treaty effective as of July 2004 with respect to provisions related to withholding tax.

Corporate bonds issued outside Japan may qualify for a 0 percent rate of withholding tax under Japanese domestic tax law, subject to the satisfaction of various conditions.

(b) Thin capitalization Japanese rules that restrict deductibility of interest for thinly capitalized companies are:

- If the average balance of total interest-bearing debt is not greater than three times the Japanese company's equity, then no thin-capitalization restriction will arise.
- If the average balance of total interest-bearing debt is greater than three times the Japanese company's equity, then to the extent the average balance of interest-bearing debt owed to a foreign related party exceeds the equity in the Japanese company owned by that particular foreign related party, a thin-capitalization disallowance will arise with respect to the proportion of the interest that relates to the excessive element of the debt. (Note: A foreign related party is a foreign party that owns directly or indirectly 50 percent or more of the Japanese company's capital, is under 50 percent or more common ownership of the Japanese company, or can effectively decide the business policies of the Japanese company.)

The thin-capitalization rules do not apply under these circumstances if it can be proved that similar unrelated parties have higher debt/equity ratios.

Interest that is subject to ordinary rates of Japanese tax in the hands of the foreign related party—most commonly when it is loaned through a Japanese permanent establishment—is excluded from the calculation. Interest on back-to-back loans is included in the calculations. Interest on third-party loans guaranteed by a foreign related person is not automatically included in the thin-capitalization calculation.

For purposes of the thin-capitalization calculation, equity may be calculated by using the higher of:

- Average month-end assets: Average month-end liabilities determined under the rules of Japanese generally accepted accounting principles
- Capital (share capital) plus capital surplus (share premium) determined under Japanese tax rules

Recent changes to the JCC permit the creation of treasury stock. It is currently not clear how such stock is taken into account for purposes of the thin-capitalization rules. The prevailing view, however, is that treasury stock should be considered equity for purposes of the thin-capitalization rules.

(c) Deductibility of interest Interest is generally deductible on an accrual basis. Note that withholding tax on interest is generally triggered by actual

payment of interest. When interest is paid late, there are no specific late-payment rules restricting deductibility. It is possible to choose to capitalize acquisition debt into the cost of an investment, which may be beneficial when the alternative would give rise to tax losses that are not expected to be utilized within their five-year life.

4.2   Equity

Issues related to equity financing include:

- Registration duty
- Treasury stock
- Use of foreign stock as acquisition stock

(a) Registration duty   See Section 2.3.

(b) Treasury stock   It has recently become possible under the JCC for Japanese companies to hold treasury stock (i.e., for companies to reacquire their own stock).

(c) Use of foreign stock as acquisition currency   Japanese tax law does not allow shareholders in a Japanese company to exchange their stock for stock in a foreign company on a tax-free basis unless the shareholders benefit from a tax treaty providing for exemption of capital gains from Japanese taxation.

4.3   Tokumei Kumiai

Tokumei kumiai (TK) is a Japanese form of silent partnership wherein a TK investor provides financing for a TK operator in return for a share of the pretax profits of part or all of the business conducted by the TK operator. Such a relationship is contractual in nature and does not constitute an equity investment. The TK investor receives neither shareholding in the TK operator nor ownership rights.

Under domestic Japanese tax law, the share of the TK operator's pretax profits paid to the TK investor (the TK profit share) is tax deductible by the TK operator. Nonresident TK investors are generally subject to withholding tax at the rate of 20 percent, although this may be reduced if the TK profit share is treated as "other income" under an applicable tax treaty. Such arrangements have been used aggressively by foreign businesses but have recently come under attack by Japanese tax authorities.

5.   MERGERS

5.1   Overview

Japanese tax law contains two separate regimes potentially allowing tax-free treatment for various noncash transactions. The two regimes are:

1. Rules permitting tax-free share exchanges when such share exchanges are effected between Japanese companies pursuant to the JCC's *kabushiki koukan* or *kabushiki iten* provisions and 100 percent ownership of the target company is transferred

2. The corporate reorganization rules dealing with:

- Mergers (discussed in this Section)
- Various forms of corporate division (discussed in Section 10, although some forms may be relevant to purchasers as well as to sellers)

In all of the transactions described previously, it is necessary to consider the characterization and requirements of both tax law and the commercial code.

Under the JCC, two or more Japanese corporations may merge upstream, downstream, or sideways without a common ownership requirement. In general, shares in the surviving corporation are issued to former shareholders in the disappearing corporation based on a merger ratio that reflects the relative value of the merging corporations. In the case of an upstream merger of a wholly owned subsidiary into its parent, no share issuance is required. For accounting purposes, the disappearing corporation's assets may be taken over by the surviving corporation at their existing book value or at fair market value. Any merger gain—that is, any excess of the surviving corporation's resultant increase in net assets over the amount of new share capital issued—is generally recorded as a capital reserve within the shareholder's funds. However, to the extent the disappearing corporation has distributable reserves prior to the merger, the merger gain may be credited instead to the surviving corporation's distributable reserves at the option of the parties.

Note that in a merger the disappearing company must have positive net assets.

5.2   Taxable (Nonqualified) or Tax Free (Qualified)

For tax purposes, mergers may be either of the following:

- Qualified, in which case the disappearing corporation's assets and liabilities are transferred to the surviving corporation on a tax-free basis and to all parties with no change in tax basis
- Nonqualified, in which case the disappearing corporation recognizes a taxable disposal of its assets, and its shareholders receive a deemed dividend with respect to the disappearing corporation's accumulated profits

Note that comments in this Section involve only income tax/corporate income tax. (See Section 8 for transfer and consumption taxes.)

The conditions that must be met for a merger to be qualified differ depending on the shareholding relationship between the disappearing and surviving corporations. Those conditions are:

- If 100 percent common ownership exists, no cash consideration is permitted and there must be an intent to continue such ownership for the foreseeable future.

  If greater than 50 percent but less than 100 percent common ownership exists, no cash consideration is permitted, as above; the main business of the disappearing corporation must be taken over; there must be an expectation on the part of the surviving corporation to continue to employ at least 80 percent of the employees of the disappearing corporation; and at the time of the merger, such common ownership must not be expected to drop to 50 percent or less in the foreseeable future. (The last condition is irrelevant to certain joint business situations.)

- Finally, if the shareholding relationship is 50 percent or less, then in addition to the requirements with respect to the main business and employees of the disappearing corporation mentioned earlier, the merger must be executed to enable the creation of a joint business. In a joint business (1) the businesses of the surviving and disappearing corporations are similar in nature and in magnitude or at least one managing director of both the disappearing and surviving companies is a managing director in the surviving company postmerger and (2) the aggregate number of the shares held by shareholders, who are expected to hold the entire shares received upon the merger, is at least 80 percent of the total number of the issued shares of the disappearing corporation.[1]

5.3   Carryover of Premerger Tax Losses

(a) No-more-than-50-percent shareholding relationship between merging companies Ignoring transitional rules, the premerger tax losses of both the surviving and disappearing companies remain available postmerger in the case of a qualified merger when the shareholding relationship is not more than 50 percent.

(b) More-than-50-percent shareholding relationship between merging companies Ignoring transitional rules, in order for premerger tax losses of both the surviving and disappearing companies to remain fully available postmerger,

---

1. This condition would be exempt if the number of shareholders of the disappearing corporation is 50 or more.

the merger must be qualified and all of the conditions in either (1) through (3), or in (1) and (4) below must be satisfied.

1. The businesses of the merging companies must be relevant to each other. For example, a manufacturer and its distributor in the same industry would be considered relevant to each other, but a manufacturer and a distributor in different industries probably would not.

2. The relative sizes of the merging companies or the merging companies' businesses must be within a ratio of five, measured on some suitable basis of the taxpayers' choosing, such as sales, capital, or number of employees.

3. The sizes of the merging companies or the merging companies' businesses must not have changed by more than a factor of two between creation of the more-than-50-percent shareholding relationship and the merger, measured on the same basis as condition (2).

4. At least one managing director of each merging company must be a managing director of the surviving company at the time of creation of the more-than-50-percent shareholding relationship.

If none of the conditions set forth in (1) through (3) or in (1) and (4) are satisfied, then premerger tax losses remain available postmerger only if it can be demonstrated that at the time the greater-than-50-percent shareholding relationship arose, unrealized gains on assets held by each company exceeded the carried-forward tax losses.

6. OTHER STRUCTURING AND POSTDEAL ISSUES

6.1 Creation of Local-Country Tax Groups

Since 2002, Japanese tax law has allowed the filing of consolidated tax returns by a Japanese company and its 100-percent-owned Japanese subsidiaries. Non-Japanese companies, partly owned subsidiaries (with very minor exceptions to allow the effects of employee share plans to be ignored) and Japanese subsidiaries that are owned by an intermediate foreign company cannot be included. Similarly, Japanese companies owned by a common foreign shareholder cannot be consolidated.

Tax consolidation is possible only for national corporate income tax purposes. For local-tax purposes, the existence of a consolidated tax group has some relatively minor effects on the calculation of taxable profit but does not eliminate the need to file separate returns and, crucially, does not permit the offset of profits and losses arising in different companies.

A number of measures exist to minimize the revenue shortfall resulting from the introduction of tax consolidation, including:[2]

- With very limited exceptions, for national corporate income tax purposes, the only tax losses incurred preconsolidation that can be utilized against consolidated profits are those of the parent company of the consolidated group.

- When groups have been formed within the past five years, it may be necessary to perform a taxable revaluation of certain assets of the subsidiary members of the consolidated group immediately prior to their joining the group so that any profits or losses get taxed separately in each company. Japanese authorities are still considering whether internally generated goodwill is one of the categories of assets requiring such revaluation.

6.2   Repatriation of Profits

(a) Dividend-received deduction   Provided that shares are not purchased within one month prior to the dividend record date and sold within two months after such date, dividends paid by a Japanese company to another Japanese company or to a Japanese permanent establishment qualify for an offsetting dividend-received deduction equal to:

- A total of 100 percent of the dividend income in the case of shareholdings of at least 25 percent held for at least six months
- A total of 50 percent of the dividend income in other cases

However, in the period in which the dividend income is received, any interest expense of the shareholder related to financing such shareholding is nondeductible.

(b) Withholding tax   Dividends paid by a Japanese company are subject to a 20 percent withholding tax. If the shares are held for the entire period to which the dividend relates, then the withholding tax is creditable against the recipient's tax liability in situations when the dividends are paid either to a Japanese company or to a Japanese permanent establishment holding shares in the Japanese company paying the dividend.

Japan's tax treaties typically provide for treaty withholding tax rates of 5 to 10 percent on dividends. Note that the new US-Japan treaty, effective as of July 1, 2004, with respect to provisions related to the withholding tax, provides for a 0 percent treaty rate of withholding on certain types of intragroup dividends.

---

2. The 2 percent surtax has been abolished and would not apply to fiscal years commencing on or after April 1, 2004—that is, fiscal year 2005 for a December-end company.

6.3   Noncore Disposals

Disposals are discussed generally in Section 7. With respect to the disposal of noncore assets following an acquisition, in addition to the general discussion in Section 7, the following points should be noted:

- If the purchaser's initial investment was effected through a tax-free reorganization such as a merger, then various antiavoidance provisions potentially apply to postreorganization asset disposals.
- If the purchaser has formed a Japanese tax consolidation and the noncore asset consists of stock in a consolidated subsidiary, then upon disposal, the subsidiary is treated as leaving the group as of the day of the disposal and takes its share of unutilized consolidated tax losses with it. The tax basis in the shares of the departing subsidiary being disposed reflects the subsidiary's profits or losses during the period of consolidation.

6.4   Preservation of Existing Tax Attributes

In the context of stock acquisitions, Japanese tax statutes impose no change-of-ownership restrictions on the use of a target company's preacquisition tax losses against its postacquisition profits other than the normal five-year loss expiry rule.

However, when a loss company is acquired with the specific intention of injecting or starting a new profit-generating business into the loss company in order to use the tax losses, use of such losses may be denied. The value to be attributed to the preacquisition tax losses of a target company by prospective purchasers depends on the extent of intended changes to the target company's business and on the projected timing of taxable profits.

6.5   Receipts under Warranties or Indemnities

Receipts under seller warranties or indemnities can be treated as price adjustments—that is, reductions of the base cost of the acquired assets, if relevant—if the purchase agreement is appropriately drafted to that effect. Otherwise, such receipts are immediately taxable.

6.6   Establishing Acquisition Companies

In Japan, acquisitions of shelf companies are uncommon. Accordingly, prospective purchasers desiring to establish a Japanese company so as to make a stock or asset acquisition generally have two choices:

1. Purchase a previously active company with the attendant due diligence and historical liability implications.
2. Incorporate a new company—a process that typically takes several weeks.

It is important to note that the JCC imposes some restrictions on postestablishment transfers, (cash subscription for share capital in a newly formed *kabushiki kaisha* (KK), the most common form of company) followed by the use of the subscribed funds to purchase assets. The restrictions are:

- In general, a court-appointed inspector is required to preapprove the terms of any purchase worth 5 percent or more of the share capital of a newly formed KK unless the purchase consideration represents not more than 20 percent of the KK's share capital and unless such consideration is not more than ¥5 million.

- The requirement for a court-appointed inspector is waived when an appraisal report is prepared for the KK by lawyers, accountants, or tax accountants and when the report provides evidence that the value of the purchased assets at least equals the proposed purchase price.

Similar restrictions apply to contributions in-kind—that is, transfers of assets in exchange for shares—to both a newly formed and an existing KK.

7.   DISPOSALS

7.1   Stock Disposals

(a) Companies

(i) Disposal for cash consideration   A capital gain or loss on disposal of shares is generally fully taxed, with no distinction being made between such capital gains or losses and trading profits and losses.

Note that under Japanese domestic tax law, a disposal of the following by a nonresident can be made tax free:

- Less than 5 percent of the shares in a Japanese company within a single year
- Any disposal of less than 25 percent

In each case, the percentage interests are judged on a group basis.

Other disposals by nonresidents are subject to Japanese taxation unless an applicable tax treaty dictates otherwise.

(ii) Share-for-share exchanges   The share-for-share exchange is regarded as a chargeable disposal unless all of the following conditions and approaches are satisfied and observed:

- The exchange is performed under the JCC's *kabushiki iten* or *kabushiki koukan* procedures and involves a Japanese purchaser's acquisition of 100 percent of the shares of a Japanese target company.

- The tax basis of the target shares in the hands of the purchaser is equal to the aggregate basis of the shares in the hands of the selling shareholders if there are fewer than 50 selling shareholders or to the net asset book value of the target—as measured under tax rules—if there are 50 or more selling shareholders. If the purchaser gives a mixture of cash and shares to the selling shareholders, the cash element must not exceed 5 percent of the total consideration.

(b) Individuals   An individual's capital gains from the sale of stock are taxed separately from other income. There is no distinction between short- and long-term gains. Capital losses are offset only against capital gains arising from the sale of stock, and any net gains are taxed separately from other income.

In principle, net capital gains are subject to a flat 15 percent national tax and an additional, nondeductible local tax of 5 percent, for a total of 20 percent. By contrast, normal individual income tax rates are graduated from 16 to 50 percent.

For sales of publicly traded securities on or after January 1, 2004, individual shareholders are taxed at the 20 percent rate unless they qualify for the special 10 percent rate.

For periods beginning January 1, 2003, through December 31, 2007, individual shareholders are to be taxed at a favorable, 10 percent rate (7 percent national tax and 3 percent local tax) on capital gains generated from the sale of publicly traded securities—whether listed, as defined, on an exchange in Japan or elsewhere—when the shares are sold through a registered Japanese brokerage firm. If these conditions are not met, individual shareholders are taxed at 20 percent on the net gain.

Under special provisions, if the stock was acquired on or before September 30, 2001, the taxpayer may elect to report the acquisition cost as 80 percent of the stock market price as of October 1, 2001. This is to benefit individuals who have not retained records of their stock purchase costs.

Furthermore, capital gains are exempt from tax if all of the following circumstances are satisfied:

- The stock was purchased between November 30, 2001 and December 31, 2002.
- The stock is sold between January 1, 2005 and December 31, 2007.
- The total purchase price was ¥10 million or less.
- The stock is listed stock and is sold through a Japanese registered brokerage firm.
- An application is submitted to the tax office on filing the individual's income tax return.

For years beginning on or after January 1, 2003, net losses from the sale of publicly traded securities through a registered Japanese brokerage firm can be carried over three years and used to offset future capital gains.

(c) Tax-exempt entities Profits and gains recognized by tax-exempt state-owned companies are not subject to tax, although transaction taxes—for example, consumption tax or stamp duty—may apply unless exemptions apply.

Charities are taxable on any profits derived from for-profit business activities.

In principle, pension funds are subject to corporation tax at the rate of 1 percent of the pension fund balance per year, but this tax is currently suspended.

7.2   Asset Disposals (Companies Only)

Asset disposals generally are subject to both national corporate income tax and local corporate income tax. There is no distinction in Japanese corporate tax law between revenue and capital profits. Accordingly, the profit or loss from any asset disposal is taxed together with the seller's other income or losses.

Transfer taxes and registration and license duties generally are chargeable to the purchaser. However, output consumption tax must be accounted for on the disposal of certain categories of assets, including buildings but excluding land.

In the case of asset disposals by nonresident companies, the following rules apply:

- Under Japanese domestic law:
  - Both national and local corporate income taxes arise if the asset is held through a Japanese permanent establishment.
  - If assets are not held through a Japanese permanent establishment, taxation is limited to national corporate income tax on profits from the disposal of Japanese shares or Japanese real estate.
- Some Japanese tax treaties are exempt from source-country-taxation capital gains in certain categories of assets.

7.3   Deferred Consideration and Earn-Outs

Subject to certain conditions, when a known purchase consideration is paid in installments, the seller may defer capital gain or loss recognition, while the purchaser receives immediate tax basis in the acquired assets, meaning, equal to the total purchase consideration.

Depending on future satisfaction of certain conditions, when additional contingent consideration is paid, such additional consideration is normally treated as a purchase price adjustment.

7.4   Payments under Warranties or Indemnities

If properly structured, payments under warranties or indemnities should be tax deductible.

8.   TRANSACTION COSTS FOR SELLERS

8.1   Transfer Taxes

All registration and license duties are generally payable by the purchaser rather than the seller. If stamp duty is imposed on a document that both parties are liable to produce, the parties may share the tax costs.

8.2   Consumption Tax

In principle, business and asset transfers are subject to consumption tax, although specific assets, such as receivables and land, are exempt. The treatment of consumption tax on the transfer of taxable assets depends on the parties' tax registration and recoverability status as follows:

- If the purchaser is registered for consumption tax and not operating on the simplified filing basis, such purchaser is allowed to claim an input-tax credit. If the purchaser is not registered, the consumption tax is not recoverable.
- If the seller is registered for consumption tax, such seller needs to account for output tax under normal consumption tax reporting. If the seller is not registered, such seller is allowed to retain the collected consumption tax for its own account.
- If the purchaser is a partially exempt supplier—for example, a bank, an insurance company, or a property company—it is unlikely that the purchaser can recover full input consumption tax.

Note that the question of whether the purchaser or the seller is registered for consumption tax has no bearing on whether the transfer price contains a consumption tax element. As a result, it is possible for a mismatch to occur if only one party is registered for consumption tax.

9.   PREPARING TARGET COMPANY FOR SALE

9.1   Presale Dividends

Section 6.2(a) explains that dividends paid from one Japanese company to another or to a Japanese permanent establishment may in effect be partly or wholly non-taxable, subject to certain conditions. Through the use of a presale dividend, there may be clear incentive for a seller to extract the maximum possible value from a subsidiary prior to its disposal. It should be noted that under the JCC, KKs can pay dividends only as follows:

- Dividends are either annual dividends, which need to be approved at the annual general shareholders' meeting, or interim dividends, which require directors' approval and also need to be provided for in the articles of incorporation.
- Dividends are restricted to the extent of the distributable reserves as defined under the JCC. Dividends may not be distributed unless either a legal reserve equal to 25 percent of share capital has first been created or an amount equal to 10 percent of the declared dividend is credited to the legal reserve at the time of declaration.

9.2   Separation of Assets to Be Disposed and Retained

Tax consolidation is the only form of tax grouping applicable to national corporate income tax that is possible in Japan. Consequently, asset transfers within the seller's group prior to a disposal are subject to consumption tax as well as stamp, registration, and license duties in the same manner as a sale to a third party. National and local corporate income taxes also arise unless the transfer is within a tax consolidation, in which case some deferral is possible depending on the type of asset transferred.

It should be noted also that various types of intragroup tax-free reorganizations will not be available if at the time of reorganization the party receiving the assets intends to leave the group at a later time. Detailed rules for determining whether such intention exists at a particular point in time do not currently exist in Japan. The tax authorities instead form a view based on all available evidence.

10.   DEMERGERS AND SIMILAR REORGANIZATIONS

Section 5 covers tax-free mergers by virtue of the rules governing tax-free corporate reorganization. These rules also allow various other types of tax-free reorganizations, including:

- **Contribution in-kind.** Transfer of assets in exchange for shares
- **Postestablishment transfer.** Transfer of assets to a recently incorporated company, paid for by using share subscription proceeds
- **Hive-down.** Drop-down of a business to the form of a subsidiary in exchange for a share issue to the transferor
- **Spin-off.** Transfer of a business to another company in exchange for a share issue to the transferor's shareholders

In some sense, all of these reorganizations can be characterized as involving the transfer of assets in exchange for a share issue by the transferee, and therefore they are grouped together in this section. In several cases, the same economic result can be achieved by more than one of these types of reorganization, but the legal procedures and requirements may differ.

10.1   Conditions for Tax-Free Corporate Treatment

For contributions in-kind, for hive-downs, and for spin-offs, the conditions for tax-free treatment are:

- If a 100-percent-ownership relationship exists, no cash or other nonshare consideration can be given, and there must be no intention at the time of the transfer to terminate the 100-percent-ownership relationship.
- If a greater-than-50-percent-but-less-than-100-percent-ownership relationship exists, no cash or other nonshare consideration can be given. In addition, the transferee of the transferred business must continue the transferred business posttransfer, must take over the main assets and liabilities of the transferred business, and must intend to continue the greater-than-50-percent-ownership relationship. Moreover, the transferee must continue to employ posttransfer at least 80 percent of the pretransfer employees of the transferred business.
- If a not-more-than-50-percent-ownership relationship exists, then in addition to the conditions for the greater-than-50-percent-ownership situation, the reorganization must be for the purpose of establishing a joint business—that is, a joint venture. This condition requires that:
  - The transferred business and the transferee's existing business must be relevant to each other in nature.
  - In general, either the relative size of the transferred business and the transferee's existing business must be within a ratio of 1:5 in either direction as measured on some suitable measure such as sales volume, number of employees, or amount of capital, or at least one director or similar executive from each of the transferor and transferee companies must be a managing director of the transferee company posttransfer.
  - The shares issued in payment for the transferred business continue to be held by the shareholders posttransfer.

Further detailed guidance exists on many of the aforementioned points but is somewhat beyond the scope of this discussion. However, the following should be noted:

- The joint-business condition cannot be satisfied when the transferee is a new company, such as an acquisition vehicle, because it will have no existing business.

- In the case of the requirements for continuity of ownership, no particular time period has yet been established. The fundamental principle is that the intention at the time of the reorganization must be for continuity. However, if genuinely unanticipated future events occur requiring that, for example, shares be sold or the transferred business be discontinued, such events will not likely cause the reorganization to lose its tax-free status. In such cases, the burden of proof is on the taxpayer.

Postestablishment transfers differ slightly from the other types of reorganization discussed in this section because they involve cash payment for the transferred business or assets. When the transferred assets are transferred from the transferee's shareholder, the economic result is indistinguishable from a contribution in-kind.

The key conditions for tax-free treatment of a postestablishment transfer are that the transferee must be 100 percent owned by the transferee and that there must be no intention at the time of transfer to discontinue such ownership.

10.2   Carryover of Tax Losses

In general, it is not possible to transfer tax losses in the course of a spin-off, hive-down, contribution in-kind, or postestablishment transfer. In the specific case of a tax-free spin-off involving liquidation of the transferor, tax losses may be transferred in a manner similar to a tax-qualified merger transaction. (See Section 5 for further requirements.)

10.3   Consumption Tax

No consumption tax arises as a result of a hive-down or spin-off. The transfer of assets in a postestablishment transfer results in consumption tax in the same way as an ordinary asset transfer. In the case of a contribution in-kind, consumption tax arises; however, it is calculated based on the value of the shares issued in exchange for the transferred assets and liabilities.

10.4   Stamp Duty, Registration, and License Taxes

The company issuing share capital has to pay registration tax on a share capital increase at the following rates:

- Spin-off
  - Share capital increase not exceeding the share capital decrease of the transferor company: 0.15 percent
  - Share capital increase to the extent it exceeds the share capital decrease of the transferor company: 0.7 percent
- Hive-down or contribution in-kind: 0.7 percent.

In addition, registration and license duties also are payable—at the following rates—on the official rated value of land and buildings transferred in the course of the reorganization:

- Spin-off or hive-down: 0.2 percent (increasing to 0.4 percent as of April 1, 2006)
- Contribution in-kind or postestablishment transfer: 1 percent

10.5   Other Issues

(a) JCC issues   Contributions in-kind are subject to court-appointed inspection as discussed in Section 6.6. Spin-offs and hive-downs require fulfillment of the legal procedures, which may take time.

(b) Employment issues   The consent of each individual transferring employee is required in the case of contribution in-kind and postestablishment transfer. However, such consent is not required in the case of spin-offs and hive-downs.

LUXEMBOURG

INTRODUCTION

This chapter details the principal tax issues that are relevant to purchasers and sellers engaged in the transfer of ownership of a Luxembourg trade or business. Unless otherwise stated, it is generally assumed that all sellers and purchasers are Luxembourg companies with limited liability.

During the past seven to eight years, many multinational companies have extended their business organization to Luxembourg, which has emerged as a choice jurisdiction in which to structure acquisitions. The acquired businesses, whether within Europe or outside Europe, are usually acquired by Luxembourg holding or financing companies, facilitating an efficient tax structure and providing exit alternatives.

Moreover, as of May 12, 2004, a new fund structure, the *société d'investissement en capital à risque* (SICAR), is available in Luxembourg for investments in private equity. Given the important flexibility and attractive tax policies attributed to the SICAR (whose description is beyond the scope of the present chapter), the SICAR targets all types of investors who can commonly be found in venture capital investments, from specialized high-net-worth individuals to traditional institutional investors.

The relevant taxes to be considered are:

- **Corporation tax.** Generally, this is a 30.38 percent tax on profits earned by a company.
- **Value-added tax (VAT).** This is a sales tax whereby 15 percent is added to the sales price charged for goods or services except for certain categories of sale that are exempt from or outside the scope of VAT. A purchaser or recipient of services can generally recover VAT paid if the purchase was incurred in the course of a commercial activity. However, the level of recoverability varies from case to case.
- **Net wealth tax.** Generally, the net assets of the company are taxed annually at a rate of 0.5 percent.
- **Registration duty.** Registration duties are levied according to varying rates from 0.01 to 14.4 percent depending on the nature of the assets transferred.
- **Capital duty.** A 1 percent capital duty is levied on contributions made to Luxembourgian companies at the time of their incorporation as well as on further recapitalizations. However, the law provides for two major

exemptions that would generally apply to the transactions described in this chapter.

1.   ACQUISITIONS

An acquisition may take the form of a purchase of either the assets or the shares of the target company. The choice of one or the other may depend on numerous factors, including but not limited to current business organization of the acquiring group, economics surrounding the transactions, legal constraints, and culture of the acquiring group.

1.1   Asset Acquisitions

An asset acquisition generally enables the purchaser to avoid exposure related to historical liabilities that are not specifically recoverable through the sale agreement.

Liabilities associated with the purchased business remain the responsibility of the company that has sold the assets and do not become the responsibility of the purchaser unless the parties agree that specified liabilities will transfer to the purchaser.

Commercial companies are allowed to contribute assets as a contribution in-kind.[1] However, the contribution does not allow for an automatic transfer of rights and obligations attached to those assets. A bill of law amending the law on commercial companies was filed before the Luxembourgian parliament in July 2002.[2] One of the amendments proposed in the bill would allow the contribution of branches of activity under Luxembourgian commercial law, with automatic transfer of rights and obligations to the beneficiary entity. However, as of January 1, 2005, there was no indication as to whether or when this bill will be passed.

1.2   Stock Acquisitions

A stock acquisition results in the purchaser's effectively bearing any historical and future ongoing tax and nontax liabilities of the target company. There is no step-up permitted in the tax basis of the company's assets.

It can be assumed that as a general rule, an acquisition of shares is more straightforward in the sense that fewer legal transfer formalities are required. An acquisition of shares might therefore be chosen for practical reasons, especially when the acquisition of the target company needs to be completed within a short time frame.

---

1. Loi du 10 août 1915 concernant les sociétés commerciales (Law of August 10, 1915, relating to commercial companies).
2. Projet de loi n° 4992 (government bill number 4992).

2.   TRANSACTION COSTS FOR PURCHASERS

2.1   Registration Duty

(a) Stock purchases As a general rule, no transfer tax is due if the shares of a Luxembourgian company are purchased.

(b) Asset purchases Registration duties are levied according to rates varying from 0.01 to 14.4 percent depending on the nature of the assets sold. The transfer of real estate generally triggers a 7 percent registration duty. The rate increases to 10 percent if the real estate is located in Luxembourg City. However, this duty does not become due if the real estate changes hands within the framework of the transfer of a branch of activity or universality of goods, such as a merger or a demerger.

2.2   Value-Added Tax

(a) Stock purchases The transfer of shares is exempt from VAT. However, special attention should be given to the VAT treatment of advisory fees and other transaction costs borne by the seller or the acquirer in relation to the disposal or acquisition of the shares: place of supply, VAT liability, deductibility.

(b) Asset purchases In principle, Luxembourgian VAT is due on the transfer of inventories and assets—other than land and buildings for which the seller has not opted for VAT—should the place of supply be deemed to be in Luxembourg. The standard rate of VAT is 15 percent. Reduced rates of VAT—3, 6, or 12 percent—might apply to specific types of assets.

However, the transfer can be outside the scope of VAT if the transfer—in the form of a sale or a contribution—is made between VAT payers and if it relates to a line of business or to a totality of assets, provided certain conditions are met and some formalities are complied with. In this last case, special attention should be given to the deductibility of VAT incurred on advisory fees and on other transaction costs in relation to this transfer.

2.3   Tax Deductibility of Transaction Costs

As a general rule, under Luxembourg's tax law, costs incurred by a Luxembourgian company are deductible from the company's taxable basis, provided that the costs relate to the company's professional activity.

However, there is an exception to the general rule of tax deductibility. Costs that are connected directly to exempt income such as dividends cannot be deducted from the taxable basis.[3] Only the costs for services rendered directly and

---

3. Costs/expenses expressly listed in articles 12 and 48 of the Luxembourgian tax law are not tax deductible.

exclusively for the benefit of the Luxembourgian company are tax deductible—for example, legal or tax advisers' fees.

In addition, it is worth noting that these costs are tax deductible only if they have been posted in the profit-and-loss accounts of the Luxembourgian company. If the costs are capitalized for book purposes, they are not deductible for tax purposes.

3.   BASIS OF TAXATION FOLLOWING ASSET OR STOCK ACQUISITIONS

3.1   Asset Acquisitions

(a) Tax consequences for the acquiring company   The assets acquired are booked at their acquisition cost in the books of the acquiring company.

This acquisition cost also constitutes the tax basis for the depreciation of the depreciable assets acquired. Although there are a limited number of exceptions, the annual depreciation charge booked in the accounts is tax deductible, entitling the acquiring company to deduct the annual depreciation charges and therefore to offset income. In other words, as a general principle, tax depreciation generally equals book depreciation.

In the event that an entire business is acquired, the acquiring company might recognize goodwill. This goodwill can be depreciated over a period of ten years for tax purposes. Depreciation over a shorter period of time—a minimum of five years—might be accepted from a tax point of view, provided it is demonstrated to the tax authorities that such accelerated depreciation is economically justified.

3.2   Stock Acquisitions

(a) Tax consequences for the acquiring company   The shares acquired are booked for their acquisition cost in the books of the acquiring company. The underlying tax cost of the assets does not change.

(b) Tax grouping   Luxembourgian companies can apply for tax unity. (See Section 6.1.)

4.   FINANCING OF ACQUISITIONS

4.1   Debt Financing

Specific tax issues related to the overall level of borrowings and the interest charged on this debt are:

- Withholding tax on interest
- Deductibility
- Thin-capitalization rules

(a) Withholding tax on interest   Interest payments are not subject to with-holding tax under Luxembourgian domestic tax law. The only exception relates to interest on profit-participating bonds.[4]

(b) Deductibility of interest   Interest paid on debt financing is deductible from the taxable base of Luxembourgian companies on an accrual basis, as opposed to a cash basis. The tax deductibility is, however, subject to the rate of interest being set at arm's length and to the fulfillment of thin-capitalization rules. (See Section 4.1(c).)

There is an exception to the general rule for acquisition debt. If a company used debt to acquire shares and dividends, such shares would be tax-exempt. However, interest expense related to the debt, up to the amount of the dividend, is not tax deductible. Any interest in excess of the tax-exempt dividend is tax deductible.

Additionally, a Luxembourgian company may be required to recapture acquisition interest expense if it sells the underlying shares. If the capital gain on the sale is tax exempt, then interest expense related to the acquisition of the shares must be recaptured for all preceding years, up to and including the year of the sale.

Such a recapture of tax-deducted interest is, however, globally tax neutral.

(c) Thin-capitalization rules   Luxembourgian tax law does not provide for thin-capitalization rules. Therefore, there is no provision in Luxembourgian tax legislation preventing a company from being incorporated with minimum share capital or from financing its activities mostly by debt

The Luxembourgian tax authorities nevertheless require that a debt/equity ratio of 85:15 be complied with for intragroup financing of shareholdings. Where external financing is granted to the Luxembourgian company for acquiring shares, this ratio does not apply.

Noncompliance with this ratio may result in the recharacterization of that portion of debt exceeding the stated debt/equity ratio. If such a recharacterization occurs, the portion of the interest related to the excess debt is recharacterized as non-tax-deductible dividend payments. Dividend payments are subject to 20 percent withholding tax unless a reduced rate applies under a double-tax treaty or under the European Union (EU) parent/subsidiary directive.

It is worth noting that alternative thin-capitalization structures have been developed to allow maximum flexibility in financing plans while preserving the interest of the tax authorities.

4.2   Equity

Funds required to purchase assets or shares may be provided for the acquiring company by way of a share capital increase that may be paid in kind or in cash.

---

4. Interest paid on profit-participating loans is in principle not subject to withholding tax.

Upon a Luxembourgian company's incorporation or thereafter, share capital contributions made to the company are subject to a 1 percent capital duty. Capital duty is assessed on the market value of the assets contributed.

Capital duty costs are tax-deductible expenses for income tax purposes for the entity benefiting from the contribution.

The EU directive of July 17, 1969, concerning indirect taxes on the raising of capital (69/335/EEC) has been introduced in Luxembourgian law. The directive provides for some exemptions from capital duty. Two major exemptions are:

1. Contribution to a Luxembourgian company of shares of an EU joint-stock company representing at least 65 percent of the share capital of the contributed company or a contribution in which the percentage held in said company is increased, so that the 65 percent threshold is reached. If the 65 percent threshold is reached over a period of time, only the contributions made after the threshold is met are exempt.

2. Contribution to a Luxembourgian company of all of the assets and liabilities or of a branch of activity of an EU company.

These exemptions require that the contributions be remunerated by shares only, although a cash payment is allowed if the amount of cash does not exceed 10 percent of the nominal value—or the par value if no nominal value—of the attributed shares.

With respect to the first exemption, it should be noted that the Luxembourgian company must retain the shares received under the contribution and any other shares in the contributed company that were acquired before the exempt contribution. This must occur during a five-year period. Failing this, the capital duty would become due. There are, however, exceptions to this recapture of capital duty.

5.   MERGERS

5.1   Legal Form

Luxembourgian-company law defines two types of mergers: merger by acquisition and merger by incorporation of a new company.

In the case of a merger, as opposed to a mere asset acquisition, Luxembourg's commercial-company law provides for automatic legal transfer—to the absorbing entity—of the rights and obligations attached to the assets of the entity being merged. As a result, the legal formalities of the asset transfer are significantly simplified because, for example, it is not required that every creditor of the entity being merged be notified.

5.2   Tax Consequences

Even if a merger as defined by Luxembourgian-company law does not induce the liquidation of the company being absorbed, the tax law equates a merger to a liquidation.

(a) Corporate income tax

(i) In the hands of the absorbed company   Because the merger is regarded as a liquidation of the absorbed entity for tax purposes, the latter's liquidation profit is taxable. Such profit is equal to the difference between the fair market value and the book value of the assets of the company and is taxable at the standard corporate income tax rate of 30.38 percent for Luxembourg City. Tax reserves that were temporarily immune from tax cease to be immune and thus become taxable.

Any tax losses or credits that exist may be used to reduce the resulting tax liability.

Luxembourg has introduced in its internal legislation the EU directive on mergers of companies resident in different EU member states. These rules also apply when both of the merging entities are Luxembourgian fully taxable joint-stock companies.

Under this legislation, the gain or loss from the liquidation of the absorbed entity would not be currently recognized, provided the following conditions are met:

- The transfer of assets and liabilities must be carried out in return for either an issue of shares by the absorbing company to the shareholders of the contributing company—with a possible cash payment of up to 10 percent of the nominal value of the attributed shares or the accounting price if there is no nominal value—or, if the absorbing company already held shares in the contributing company, the cancellation of that shareholding.

- The latent capital gains should remain subject to further potential taxation in Luxembourg at a later date: this requirement assumes that the merger is carried out at book value such that the absorbing company takes over the assets and liabilities of the absorbed entity for the book value these had in the absorbed entity's books.

Under such a tax-free merger, tax reserves temporarily immune continue to be immune if the absorbing company acquires them.

(ii) In the hands of the absorbing company   If the absorbing company held no shares in the absorbed entity:

- The absorbing company takes over the assets and liabilities of the absorbed company and may realize a step-up in basis on the assets so acquired. Such a step-up in basis would allow the absorbing company to depreciate the assets based on the higher value. A new holding period would start in the absorbing company with respect to the participations previously held by the absorbed company.

- There is no step-up in basis in a tax-free merger, but the participations previously held by the absorbed company would be deemed held by the absorbing company based on the original acquisition date—that is, no new holding period.

If the absorbing company held shares in the absorbed entity:

- The shares held by the absorbing company will be cancelled due to the merger. The shares will be replaced with the assets and liabilities of the absorbed entity. The cancellation of shares creates a capital gain or loss.
- This gain is calculated based on the difference between the tax cost base of the shares cancelled and the market value of the assets and liabilities transferred. Should this difference generate a profit, the profit will benefit from an exemption under the same conditions as required under the participation exemption applicable to dividends.

In a tax-free merger, the same principles apply, with the exception that if the absorbing company held shares that represented at least 25 percent of the share capital of the absorbed company, such profit is exempt in all cases.

Should the difference generate a loss, the loss should be tax deductible.

(iii) In the hands of the shareholders of the absorbed company
At the shareholder level, the merger results in replacement of the shares held in the absorbed company with shares in the absorbing company and eventually, with cash. An exchange of shares, like any other exchange of assets, entails in principle the realization of latent capital gains or losses attached to this asset. (See Section 7.2 for the tax consequences of a disposal of shares in a Luxembourgian company.)

If the shareholder is a Luxembourgian resident individual or company:

- The exchange of shares resulting from the merger may be tax neutral at the level of the shareholder under certain conditions. The tax neutrality is left at the option of the shareholder, who is free to renounce it.
- Such neutrality applies if the merging entities are either joint-stock companies—this also applies to foreign joint-stock companies—or companies tax resident in an EU member state and listed in Annex 3 to the EU merger directive. It is therefore worth noting that the tax neutrality also applies if the merging entities are exempt entities, provided they are joint-stock companies.

If the shareholder is a non-Luxembourgian tax-resident individual or company:

- There are only few circumstances under which a Luxembourgian non-resident individual or company might be taxed in Luxembourg upon a disposal of shares. Indeed, in addition to the limited cases in which Luxembourgian internal tax law provides for such taxation, double treaties concluded by Luxembourg generally grant the power to tax capital gain realized on the disposal of Luxembourgian shares to the state of which the seller of the shares is a tax resident.
- When the treaty would grant to Luxembourg the power to tax or—in the absence of a tax treaty signed with the state of which the shareholder is a tax resident—tax neutrality claimed by the non-Luxembourgian shareholder in case of a merger could be questioned.

It should be noted that such an issue would possibly arise only if the shareholders were not residents of an EU member state.

(iv) In the hands of the shareholders of the absorbing company

The absorbing company has to issue shares to the shareholders of the absorbed company as consideration for the merger. As a result, the previous shareholders of the absorbing company end up with a lower stake in the absorbing company—that is, a dilution.

Depending on the magnitude of the stake's reduction and on the circumstances, this could have the following tax consequences:

- Capital duty recapture will arise only when the Luxembourgian shareholder acquired shares within the past five years under a capital-duty-exempt share-for-share transaction and when, as a result of the merger, its stake in the absorbing company is diluted below 65 percent.
- The 20 percent withholding tax—possibly reduced under double-tax treaties or by virtue of the parent/subsidiary directive—becomes due on dividends distributed by the absorbing company in the future if the stake of the previous shareholders is reduced to less than 10 percent in case the acquisition price of its stake in the Luxembourgian company was less than €1.2 million. Similarly, dividends received by the previous shareholders as well as capital gain derived upon sale of the absorbing company become taxable. For the capital gain, this becomes taxable only if its stake in the absorbing company—now reduced to less than 10 percent—was initially acquired for less than €6 million.
- If the absorbing company was part of a fiscal unity with its parent company, it will cease to benefit from it if the stake of its previous shareholders is reduced to less than 95 percent.

Tax losses carried forward and any tax credits available to the absorbed entity cannot be transferred to the absorbing company. Therefore, if the absorbed company has significant tax losses carried forward and available tax credits, it may be desirable to realize a taxable merger rather than a tax-free merger. A taxable merger enables the absorbed entity to utilize its tax losses and tax credits to offset latent capital gains and allows the absorbing company to realize a step-up in basis on the assets and liabilities transferred. Tax losses are therefore regenerated at the level of the absorbing company by way of a higher depreciation basis.

However, it should be noted that tax credits are creditable only on corporate income tax and not on municipal business tax. It may therefore be wise to structure the transaction so that it falls within the conditions for a tax-free merger where carryforward losses would not be sufficient to offset latent capital gains entirely.

As an alternative, when possible, the absorbing company should be the entity that has the highest tax losses carried forward and/or tax credits in order to preserve them to the greatest extent possible.[5]

(b) VAT   A transfer of total assets or of a branch of activity is not considered a supply of goods or services and therefore is not subject to Luxembourgian VAT, provided certain conditions are met and some formalities are complied with. The transferee is deemed to step into the shoes of the transferor in terms of adjustment of VAT initially deducted on acquisition of capital goods. As covered in Section 2.2, special attention should be given to the deductibility of VAT incurred on advisory fees and other transaction costs related to this transfer.

Since a merger can be considered to be the transfer of a universality of goods, no VAT is due if parties to the transaction have complied with the necessary formalities.

(c) Registration duties   A merger under which new shares are to be issued by the absorbing company is not subject to capital duty. This falls under the scope of the all assets and liabilities capital duty exemption.

In addition, even if real property is transferred within the framework of a merger, the registration duty normally levied on the transfer does not become due, because the transfer takes place within the transfer of a branch of activity or universality of goods.

---

5. Under current Luxembourgian tax law, this does not constitute a per se abuse of law. The general antiabuse provisions of Luxembourgian law remain applicable.

6.   OTHER STRUCTURING AND POSTDEAL ISSUES

6.1   Creation of Local-Country Tax Groups

If the shares acquired are shares of a Luxembourgian resident company, the Luxembourgian acquiring company may apply for a tax unity. It should be stressed that this is not an accounting consolidation and that the system is quite complex.

Tax unity would be available under, among others, the following conditions:

- The acquiring company and the target company whose shares have been acquired are fully taxable Luxembourgian resident joint-stock companies, and they have the same accounting periods.
- The acquiring company holds directly or indirectly shares representing at least 95 percent of the share capital of the acquired company,[6] although 75 percent might be exceptionally accepted by the Ministry of Finance.
- The tax unity regime is applied for a minimum of five years.
- The tax unity regime allows the acquiring company to offset its tax profits or losses with those of the target company. As a general rule, losses incurred by the target company prior to its acquisition by the acquiring company may offset only its own future taxable profits.

Under current legislation, the tax unity regime is limited to income taxes—namely, corporate income tax and municipal business tax on income. While it does not yet extend to net wealth tax, some planning may be implemented in order to mitigate the net wealth tax charge to both the acquiring company and the target company.

6.2   Repatriation of Profits

(a) Dividends in cash or in-kind   In principle, dividends are fully taxable at the standard corporate income tax rate of 30.38 percent. However, a dividend tax exemption may apply under, among others, the following conditions:

- The Luxembourgian subsidiary whose shares are acquired is a joint-stock company—that is, a *société anonyme, société à responsabilité limitée, société en commandite par actions*—fully liable to tax.

---

6. *Indirectly* means that the shares in the subsidiary may be held by way of either a Luxembourgian joint-stock company or a foreign company subject to a tax similar to the Luxembourgian corporate tax—that is, taxation of at least 11 percent on a basis similar to the Luxembourgian corporate tax basis—as well as through tax-transparent entities.

- The Luxembourgian acquiring company is a fully taxable joint-stock company.

At the date on which the dividend is paid, the acquiring company held or undertakes to hold the participation for an uninterrupted period of at least 12 months, and during this period the holding rate does not fall below 10 percent; nor does the acquisition price fall below €1.2 million.

This dividend exemption also applies to a number of other dividends receipts—notably, in the case of shares that are held in non-Luxembourgian subsidiaries.

If the holding period condition of 12 months is not met, the acquiring company may claim an exemption of 50 percent of the dividend.

Dividends distributed by a Luxembourgian company are subject to a 20 percent withholding tax. This rate of withholding tax may be reduced by application of a double-tax treaty or under the EU parent/subsidiary directive.

A withholding tax exemption on dividends distributed applies if the following conditions, among others, are met:

- The distributing company is a fully taxable Luxembourgian joint-stock company.
- The parent company is another EU resident joint-stock company or a Luxembourgian permanent establishment of such an EU company or of a joint-stock company resident in a state with which Luxembourg has concluded a double-taxation treaty.
- The date on which the dividend is put at disposal, the shareholder held or undertakes to hold the participation for an uninterrupted period of at least 12 months, and during this period the holding rate does not fall below a threshold of 10 percent or the acquisition price below €1.2 million.

(b) Capital reduction or repayment of share premium   Repayments of share capital and/or share premium representing initial capital contributions made by the shareholders are not subject to withholding tax.

Such repayments may, however, be recharacterized into dividend distributions if they are not justified by sound economic reasons. It is assumed that such repayments lack sound economic reasons when the company has reserves available for distributions in case reserves have been incorporated to the share capital up to the amount of capitalized reserves.

This assumption may, however, be reversed if it can be demonstrated that there are sound economic reasons to do so.

In all other cases, it is necessary to demonstrate that the repayment is motivated by purposes other than tax reasons.

(c) Company buyback of its own shares A company buyback of its own shares might be subject to different tax treatments depending on the manner in which the redemption is completed:

- If all the shares held by a shareholder are redeemed and cancelled consecutively against the share capital of the redeeming company, the company redeeming its own shares is deemed partially liquidated in proportion to the shares redeemed. As a consequence, no withholding tax is levied on such a redemption if shares have been redeemed according to at-arm's-length standards.

- If a few shares are redeemed to a given shareholder and cancelled against the share capital, the allocation paid might either be exempt from withholding tax as a share capital reduction motivated by genuine economic reasons or be subject to dividend withholding tax at a rate of 20 percent—possibly reduced under a double-tax treaty or under the EU parent/subsidiary directive.

- If shares are redeemed and activated on the balance sheet of the redeeming company under the conditions provided by Luxembourgian commercial company law, no withholding tax would be levied on the allocation paid to the shareholder.

6.3 Preservation of Existing Tax Attributes

Tax losses and other similar tax attributes of the target company are generally not affected by a change of ownership. However, the availability of tax losses and credits after a change in ownership could be challenged if the business of the target company has been radically modified. For example, a radical modification would be a change in the activity of the company such as a switch from an operational activity to a financial activity or to a totally different operational activity. In such a case, the tax authorities could argue that there is no economic identity between the taxpayer that generated the losses and the taxpayer that has the ability to make use of them.

6.4 Receipts under Warranties or Indemnities

Indemnification payments received by a Luxembourgian company pursuant to a warranty clause are generally taxable in the hands of such company. However, the Luxembourgian company paying such indemnity is in principle entitled to deduct such payments.

The tax treatment is different if the indemnity might be regarded as a price adjustment. A price adjustment is a decrease or increase in the investment value of the assets acquired and is therefore tax neutral for the acquiring company.

In the hands of the seller, the adjustment price either increases or decreases the capital gain or loss realized upon the sale and follows the same tax treatment.

7.   DISPOSALS

7.1   Asset Disposals

Assets must be sold for their market value according to arm's-length standards. The seller might therefore realize capital gains upon the sale of the assets. Capital gains are taxable at the standard corporate income tax rate of 30.38 percent.

Capital gains may be offset by any existing loss carryforwards or credits. Losses may be carried forward indefinitely.

Capital gains realized on some specific assets might be rolled over under certain conditions, thereby allowing deferred taxation of the capital gain. Basically, such a rollover of capital gains is available when nondepreciable assets or real estate has been held by the seller for at least five years and provided the seller reinvests the sale proceeds into newly acquired assets.

When a loss is realized upon disposal of the assets, that loss is tax deductible from the seller's taxable basis.

(a) Corporate income tax consequences with respect to the pricing   Assets must be sold, from a tax point of view, for their fair market value and according to at-arm's-length principles.

If the price is not arm's-length, the tax authorities might challenge the selling price if the transaction takes place between related parties and results in a transfer of profit from Luxembourg to another jurisdiction. This could result in a change of the taxable basis of the seller and/or recharacterization of the transaction as a hidden distribution of profit. A hidden dividend distribution would in principle be subject to a 20 percent withholding tax,[7] which could be reduced under a double-tax treaty concluded with the state of the purchaser or under the EU parent/subsidiary directive.

When both the seller and the acquiring company are Luxembourgian tax residents, it could be questioned whether the tax authorities would have legal grounds to challenge the transaction. In practice, as long as the price does not harm the tax authorities' interests on a global basis, there is low probability that this will be questioned.

7.2   Stock Disposals

Luxembourgian tax policy applicable to disposals of shares differs depending on the identity of the seller.

---

7.   The rate will be 25 percent should the dividend be grossed up.

(a) Seller is a Luxembourgian resident individual   The tax regime applicable to the disposal of shares forming part of the private estate of a Luxembourgian resident individual depends on the circumstances.

(i) Shares are disposed of within six months following their acquisition
The seller is taxable on the capital gain realized regardless of the percentage it holds or held in the share capital of the company. Capital gains realized within six months following the acquisition qualify as speculative profits and as a general rule, do not benefit from any advantageous tax regime. However, speculative profits realized in 2004 benefit from a sale deduction.[8]

The seller is taxable on speculative profits at a rate corresponding to seller's marginal tax rate—up to 38.95 percent. In addition, if the seller is subject to Luxembourgian social security, a 1 percent dependency contribution is due.

If the sale gives rise to a capital loss, such loss may be offset against speculative profits and then against sale profits of the same year.

(ii) Shares not forming part of an important shareholding are disposed of more than six months following the acquisition   If the individual sells owned shares in the acquired company more than six months after their acquisition, the potential capital gain realized upon the disposal should not constitute a taxable income. This holds true as long as the seller had not held an important shareholding in the share capital of the acquired company.

If the sale gives rise to a capital loss, such loss is not tax deductible.

(iii) Shares forming part of an important shareholding are disposed of more than six months after the acquisition   A shareholding is deemed important when the seller—either alone or together with seller's spouse and/or underage children—has held either directly or indirectly at a time over the past five years at least 10 percent of the share capital of the company.

If the individual sells shares forming part of an important shareholding more than six months after the acquisition, the capital gain realized is taxable as a sale profit.[9] Sale profits benefit from favorable rules—for example, from actualization of the acquisition price for the determination of the capital gain and the application of a sale deduction. In addition, unlike speculative profits, sale profits are taxed pursuant to a favorable tax equal to half of the seller's normal tax rate—that is, a maximum of 19.475 percent. In addition, if the seller is subject to Luxembourg's social security plan, a 1 percent dependency contribution is due.

---

8. According to a bill of law not yet passed, this exception may be renewed so as to apply to speculative profits realized up to December 31, 2007.
9. The actualization rate is determined according to a decreasing scale that takes into account the year during which the asset was acquired—that is, the older the acquisition, the larger the actualization rate.

If the sale gives rise to a capital loss, such loss can be offset against sale profits and then against speculative profits earned during the same year.

(b) Seller is a non-Luxembourgian resident individual There are a limited number of circumstances under which nonresident individuals might be taxable in Luxembourg upon disposal of shares held in a Luxembourg company.

In principle, when the shareholder is a tax resident in a country with which Luxembourg has signed a tax treaty for the avoidance of double taxation on income, the power to tax would ultimately be granted to the state of which the seller is a tax resident.

There are, however, some exceptions to these rules. Therefore, it is worth considering under which circumstances Luxembourg may tax a nonresident individual upon disposal of shares that form part of an important shareholding in a Luxembourgian company.

(i) Shares forming part of an important shareholding are disposed of within six months following their acquisition A shareholding is deemed important if the seller—either alone or together with seller's spouse and/or underage children—has held either directly or indirectly at a time over the past five years at least 10 percent of the share capital of a company.

Compared with the taxation rules described for Luxembourgian residents, it should be noted that a minimum tax rate applies to nonresidents: 15.375 percent. The dependency contribution is not due.

If the seller had not held an important shareholding in the share capital of the Luxembourgian company whose shares are sold, the timing of the disposal is not relevant: the seller is not taxable in Luxembourg upon disposal of the seller's shares.

(ii) Shares forming part of an important shareholding are disposed of more than six months following their acquisition Nonresident individuals may be taxed upon disposal of shares forming part of an important shareholding even if those shares are sold after the above-mentioned six-month period if they had been tax residents in Luxembourg for more than 15 years and ceased to be Luxembourg tax residents less than 5 years prior to the sale.

It should be noted that a minimum tax rate applies to nonresidents: 15.375 percent. The dependency contribution is not due.

(c) Seller is a Luxembourg resident company In principle, a Luxembourgian fully taxable company is taxable on capital gains realized upon disposal of shares held in another Luxembourgian company at the standard rate of taxation: 30.38 percent for Luxembourg City. If the sale of the shares results in a capital loss, such capital loss is fully tax deductible and may offset other taxable income and/or create tax losses that may be carried forward without any time limit.

However, Luxembourgian tax law provides for a full exemption of capital gains on shares under, among others, the following conditions:

- The Luxembourgian subsidiary whose shares are sold is a joint-stock company fully liable to tax.
- The Luxembourgian seller is a fully taxable joint-stock company.
- At the date on which the sale takes place, the seller held the participation for an uninterrupted period of at least 12 months, and during this period the holding rate does not fall below a threshold of 10 percent, or the acquisition price below €6 million.

This capital gains exemption also applies to a number of other share disposals—notably, in the case of disposal of shares held in non-Luxembourgian subsidiaries.

A recapture system exists under which the exempt amount of the gain is reduced by the sum of expenses—mainly, interest expense linked directly to the participation and not offset by corresponding taxable dividends—derived from the participation and any write-down in the value of the participation to the extent that they have reduced the taxable base of that year or previous years.

The purpose of the system is to avoid the taxation vacuum that could arise if the deductibility of expenses and write-downs connected to the participation was allowed when the income arising from the participation was tax-exempt.

In the worst case, the recapture is tax neutral. In the best case, expenses deducted in the past have permitted the deferred taxation of other taxable income derived by the Luxembourgian company.

(d) Seller is a non-Luxembourg resident company   As discussed earlier with respect to non-Luxembourgian resident individuals, nonresidents may be taxed in Luxembourg upon disposal of shares held in a Luxembourgian company at the current rate of 22.88 percent. There are, however, a limited number of circumstances under which such individuals would be subject to tax.

In principle, if the shareholder is a tax resident in a country with which Luxembourg has signed a tax treaty for the avoidance of double taxation on income, the power to tax would ultimately be granted to the state of which the seller is a tax resident.

There are, however, some exceptions to these rules, since some treaties provide for taxation in the state of which the company whose shares are sold is a tax resident. The state of which the seller is a tax resident has the obligation to provide the seller with a corresponding tax credit.

(i) An important shareholding is disposed of less than six months after its acquisition   If it is determined that the nonresident seller is taxable

in Luxembourg, the applicable rate is 22.88 percent. For a corporation, an important shareholding refers to a shareholding of at least 10 percent.

(ii) An important shareholding is sold more than six months after its acquisition   A nonresident company may be taxed upon disposal of an important shareholding—even if the shareholding was sold after six months—if the company has been a tax resident in Luxembourg for more than 15 years and ceased to be a Luxembourg tax resident less than 5 years prior to the sale. From a practical point of view, this rule is unlikely to apply to non-Luxembourgian resident companies.

7.3   Deferred Considerations and Earn-Outs

The purchase agreement can provide for deferred payments if the acquirer cannot directly pay the full amount of the purchase price, or if the payment is linked to contingencies such as the result of a postclosing audit of the accounts, or if the payment is related to the future results of the target (earn-out clause).

The fixed purchase price and deferred payments not linked to a contingent obligation are taken into account to determine the capital gain realized and are taxable as of the date of the sale. Payments made under the earn-out clause become taxable only once the contingency has been resolved.

7.4   Payment under Warranties

See Section 6.4.

8.   TRANSACTION COSTS FOR SELLERS

8.1   Registration Duty

(a) Stock purchase   As a general rule, no transfer tax is due if the shares of a Luxembourgian company are purchased.

If the seller is a Luxembourgian resident company, capital duty may be due upon the sale of the shares. This will arise only if the Luxembourgian company acquired the shares within the past five years under a capital-duty-exempt share-for-share transaction.

(b) Asset purchase   The buyer is responsible for registration duty and VAT associated with an asset purchase.

8.2   Tax Deductibility of Transaction Costs

See Section 2.3.

9.   PREPARING A TARGET COMPANY FOR SALE

Prior to the acquisition, the seller may wish to isolate from the rest of its activities the part of the business that the seller wants to sell. This might be realized in different ways. Among the possibilities are a contribution of a branch of activities to another company and a partial demerger. (See Section 10.)

The tax consequences of a contribution of a branch of activities or of a universality of goods are described in the following sections.

9.1   Consequences for the Transferor

(a) Corporate income tax   As described in Section 7.1, the assets must be contributed for their market value, entailing the realization of a taxable capital gain for the transferor.

When the assets transferred constitute either an independent line of business[10] or a universality of goods—that is, all of the assets and liabilities of the entity—and are contributed to a Luxembourgian fully taxable joint-stock company or to a Luxembourgian permanent establishment of an EU company, Luxembourgian tax law provides for a tax-free transfer. The taxation of any latent capital gains attached to the transferred assets is deferred and transferred to the acquiring company.

(i) Tax-free contribution   The law provides for a tax-free transfer under, among others, the following conditions:

- At least one line of business or a universality of goods is contributed.[11]
- The transfer of assets and liabilities must be carried out in return for an issuance of shares by the acquiring company to the transferor. Only cash payments of less than 10 percent of the nominal value of the attributed shares can be made.
- The transfer must be carried out at book value.

The original acquisition date of the assets carries over to the acquiring company. The acquisition date of the shares received upon contribution by the transferor is, however, the actual date of the contribution. In other words, the transferor has to wait 12 months before selling the shares in the acquiring company in order to benefit from the capital gain participation exemption—or at least in order to maintain a 10 percent shareholding or an acquisition price of at least €6 million in the acquiring company for 12 months.

---

10. Some additional, unrelated assets could be contributed along with the independent line of business without jeopardizing the tax-free transfer.
11. As previously indicated, unrelated assets might be contributed along with the independent line of business.

The concept of a line of business—usually defined as "constituted by a whole that, from a technical point of view and organizational perspective, constitutes an autonomous activity, that is, a whole susceptible of operating under its own force"—may raise some difficulties, and parties to the transaction should be careful to ensure that the assets transferred fall within the definition before claiming the benefit of the tax-free contribution.

However, the Luxembourgian tax authorities usually approach this issue with a certain degree of flexibility.

(ii) Taxable contribution When the conditions of a tax-free contribution are not satisfied, then in accordance with the general tax law provisions, the transferor is generally required to pay tax on the gains realized upon the contribution. There is no special tax regime applying to the transfer of a line of business or of a universality of goods; each asset therefore regarded as being sold on a stand-alone basis. The capital gain so realized can, however, benefit from the participation exemption and from the deferred taxation mechanism as in the case of a sale of assets. Again, the capital gains might be offset either totally or partially by tax losses carried forward.

(b) Registration duties A contribution of universality of goods or of a line of business with issuance of new shares is not subject to registration duties even if real property is transferred.

No capital duty will be due as long as either a line of business or a universality of goods is contributed; that is, capital duty exemption is available in such cases. Only the contribution of the line of business or of the universality would benefit from the capital duty exemption. The contribution of any other assets along with the line of business would entail the levy of the capital duty up to 1 percent of the fair market value of the additional contributed assets.

(c) VAT A transfer of totality of assets or of a branch of activity is not considered as a supply of goods or services and therefore is not subject to Luxembourgian VAT, provided certain conditions are met and some formalities are complied with. The transferee is deemed to step into the shoes of the transferor in terms of adjustment of VAT initially deducted on acquisition of capital goods. As stated earlier, special attention should be given to the deductibility of VAT incurred on advisory fees and other transaction costs related to this transfer.

10. DEMERGERS

Luxembourgian-company law defines two types of demergers: demerger by absorption and demerger by incorporation of new companies.

Under both types, all of the assets and liabilities of a company are transferred to different existing or newly incorporated companies as a consequence of dissolution without liquidation, followed by the issuance of shares by the acquiring companies to the shareholders of the divided entity. There may be an additional cash payment not in excess of 10 percent of the nominal value of the distributed shares or, in the absence of a nominal value, not in excess of the par value.

Additionally, Luxembourgian company law does not allow spin-offs with direct attribution of shares in the beneficiary company to the shareholders of the contributing company. At this time, it is unclear whether the aforementioned bill will introduce the spin-off of activities, as already provided for in the tax law.

Therefore, from a company law perspective, a spin-off needs to be structured as a contribution of assets in exchange for shares in the acquiring company, followed by an immediate transfer of the newly issued shares to the shareholders of the contributing company. Such transfer could take place in the form of a distribution in-kind or as a capital reduction, as legally required.

10.1   Classic Demerger

(a) Consequences for the demerged entity   As with mergers, a demerger either by absorption or by incorporation of new companies is regarded for tax purposes as a liquidation of the divided entity. This entails the realization and potential taxation of any capital gain inherent in the assets. Potential capital losses are deductible.

However, a tax-free option is available if the following conditions are met:

- The transfer of assets and liabilities must be carried out in return for either an issuance of shares by the absorbing company to the shareholders of the contributing company—with a possible cash payment of up to 10 percent of the nominal value of the attributed shares or the accounting price if no nominal value—or, when the absorbing company already held shares in the contributing company, the cancellation of that shareholding.
- Shareholders of the divided entity must receive shares in the absorbing companies in proportion to the shares they held in the divided entity.
- Latent capital gains must remain subject to further potential taxation in Luxembourg at a later date. This requirement supposes that the demerger is carried out at book value such that the absorbing companies take over the assets and liabilities of the absorbed entity for the book value those assets and liabilities had in the absorbed entity's books.
- The assets and liabilities transferred must constitute an enterprise or at least a branch of activity. This requirement must be met in the hands of the divided entity and in the hands of the absorbing companies—that is, before and after the transfer. This means that the assets of the demerged

entity should encompass at least two independent lines of business prior to the demerger.

Regarding tax losses existing at the time of the demerger (as for mergers), the tax law does not provide for a transfer of tax losses from the divided entity to the acquiring companies.

(b) Consequences for the recipient entity   The consequences of a demerger in the hands of the recipient company are exactly the same as they are for mergers. (See Section 5.2(a)(ii).)

(c) Consequences for shareholders of the demerged entity   Again, the consequences for shareholders of the demerged entity are the same as if a merger had occurred. (See Section 5.2(a)(iii).)

10.2   Spin-Off

As indicated earlier, Luxembourgian company law does not currently allow a spin-off of assets with direct attribution of shares in the beneficiary company to shareholders of the contributing company. Therefore, from a company law perspective, a spin-off must be structured as a contribution of assets in exchange for shares in the acquiring company, followed by an immediate transfer of the newly issued shares to the shareholders of the contributing company. The transfer could take place in the form of a distribution in-kind or as a capital reduction, as legally required.

(a) Consequences for the divided entity   For the tax consequences of the first step of a spin-off—that is, a contribution of assets in exchange for shares in the acquiring company, see Section 9.1.

(b) Consequences for the recipient company   These are the same consequences as those discussed in Section 5.2(a)(ii).

(c) Consequences for shareholders   The contributing company's transfer to its shareholders of the shares issued by the acquiring company may be accomplished in different ways. The Luxembourgian tax treatment depends on how such transfers are structured.

If the transfer of shares does not imply a reduction of capital in the contributing company, the shares received are viewed in the hands of shareholders as an income derived from the shareholders' participation in the contributing company. Distributions in-kind are treated, for tax purposes, as a cash dividend. The tax treatment of such distribution in-kind in the hands of the shareholders is therefore the same as if the shareholders had received a dividend in cash. (See Section 6.2.)

If the transfer of shares is accomplished through a share capital reduction at the level of the contributing company, it should not be subject to withholding tax unless the reduction of capital cannot be justified by sound economic reasons. (See Section 6.2(b).)

In a share capital reduction, some attention should be paid to potential capital duty issues if the shareholders are Luxembourgian resident companies and acquired the shares in the contributing company under a share-for-share exempt contribution.

(d) Registration duties   Neither registration duties nor capital duty should be due. (See Section 9.1(b).)

(e) VAT   If a totality of assets is transferred, no VAT is due if the necessary obligations are fulfilled and formalities are complied with.

As stated earlier, special attention should be given to the deductibility of VAT incurred on advisory fees and other transaction costs related to this transfer.

11.   LISTINGS AND INITIAL PUBLIC OFFERINGS

Luxembourgian tax law does not provide for special rules related to listings or initial public offerings (IPOs).

The tax consequences of a listing or IPO in the hands of former shareholders of the company therefore follows the requirements of a disposal of shares.

Should the listing or IPO of a Luxembourgian company be realized, at least partly, through the issuance of new shares—as opposed to sale of the existing stock—the 1 percent Luxembourgian capital duty could become due. Under current tax law, there is no exemption foreseen for cash contributions—even in the context of the listing or IPO of a company.

MALAYSIA

INTRODUCTION

This chapter details the principal tax issues that are relevant to purchasers and sellers engaged in the transfer of ownership of a Malaysian trade or business. Unless otherwise stated, it is generally assumed that all sellers and purchasers are Malaysian companies with limited liability.

Malaysia operates a unitary tax system on a territorial basis. Tax residents of Malaysia (corporations or individuals) are taxed on income accruing in, derived from, or received in Malaysia from an outside source. Resident companies are exempt from income tax on foreign-sourced income remitted to Malaysia, except for those carrying on banking, insurance, or sea or air transport operations. Resident companies are taxed on a worldwide basis. Effective as of 2004, income remitted into Malaysia by a resident individual is also exempt from income tax. Nonresidents are taxed only on income accruing in or derived from Malaysia.

In the structuring of merger and acquisition transactions, income tax (including impact on tax incentives), stamp duty, and real property gains tax implications should be considered in addition to commercial factors. Nontax considerations, such as exchange control and foreign equity participation requirements, also affect transactions. The relevant taxes to be considered with respect to Malaysian mergers and acquisitions are:

- Corporate tax
- Withholding tax
- Indirect taxes

Corporate Tax

The corporate tax rate for resident and nonresident corporations is 28 percent. From 2000 onward, the basis of income assessment has been changed from the preceding year to the current year. With regard to companies, a self-assessment system (SAS) of taxation was introduced in stages beginning in 2001. Under the SAS, the responsibility of correctly assessing a company's tax liability rests with the taxpayer. Taxpayers are now required to file a tax return and compute their own tax liability. The return is an assessment that is deemed to have been served on the taxpayer.

Beginning in 2004, companies resident in Malaysia with paid-up capital not exceeding RM2.5 million are subject to income tax at the rate of 20 percent on chargeable income up to and including RM500,000. The remaining chargeable income will continue to be taxed at 28 percent.

Branches of foreign corporations are subject to a corporate tax at a rate of 28 percent.

Withholding Tax

Malaysian income tax legislation provides for withholding tax to be deducted at the source on certain payments made to nonresidents. The withholding tax rates are:

Payment Type	Nontreaty Rate (%)	Treaty Rate (%)
Interest	0–15	0–15
Royalty	10	0–10
Management/technical fees*	10	0–10
Rental of movable properties	10	0–10

* Effective as of September 21, 2002, payments to nonresidents with respect to management/technical services rendered abroad are not subject to the 10 percent withholding tax.

Appropriate double-tax treaties may reduce withholding tax rates. Malaysia has a comprehensive network of double-tax treaties.

Malaysia also imposes withholding tax at the following rates on payments made to nonresident contractors with respect to services rendered in Malaysia:

- A rate of 10 percent of contract payment on account of tax that is or may be payable by the nonresident contractor
- A rate of 3 percent of contract payment on account of tax that is or may be payable by employees of the nonresident contractor

Indirect Taxes

Currently, Malaysia does not have a comprehensive value-added tax (VAT) or a goods-and-services tax. However, the following taxes or duties are imposed on goods and services. One or more of the following types of duty and tax could be imposed on goods:

- Customs duties at specific rates or ad valorem rates of up to 200 percent or composite rates on dutiable goods imported into Malaysia
- Sales tax at specific rates or ad valorem rates of 5, 10, 20, or 25 percent on taxable goods that are either manufactured in or imported into Malaysia
- Excise duties at specific rates or ad valorem rates of up to 100 percent on goods subject to excise duty that are either manufactured in or imported into Malaysia.

With regard to services, service tax is chargeable on taxable services provided by taxable persons—except intragroup services. The taxable services and taxable persons are prescribed by way of regulations. The rate of service tax is 5 percent ad valorem.

Service tax and sales tax will be replaced with a single broad-based goods-and-services tax. It is proposed that goods-and-services tax be implemented on January 1, 2007. Goods-and-services tax is a multistage tax, as opposed to the current service tax and sales tax on taxable services and goods, which are single-stage taxes.

1. ACQUISITIONS

An acquisition can be defined as the act of acquiring control. In the case of a corporation, it would involve an acquisition of shares in or assets and/or liabilities of another entity. The benefits and drawbacks of either an asset or share acquisition depend on various factors, including the tax attributes of the target, the acquiring company, and the business fit between the target and the buyer.

1.1 Asset Acquisitions

In an asset acquisition, any tax attributes—for example, unabsorbed tax losses, tax incentives, and dividend franking credits—remain with the target and cannot be transferred to the buyer.

1.2 Stock Acquisitions

In a stock acquisition, tax attributes such as unabsorbed tax losses, tax incentives, and dividend franking credits remain with the target company. This is generally the main advantage of a share acquisition. In a share acquisition, the buyer may be exposed to liabilities in the target company. As a result, the buyer in a share acquisition may wish to carry out an even more thorough due diligence exercise on the target company's business compared with that required in an asset acquisition. Also, if the target company is entitled to any tax incentives or exemptions, the conditions attached to the incentives or exemptions should be examined to ensure that a change in ownership will not affect the target's entitlement to such incentives or exemptions.

2. TRANSACTION COST FOR PURCHASERS

2.1 Transfer Taxes

(a) *Stock purchase* Malaysia imposes stamp duty on certain transactions. In a share purchase, Malaysian stamp duty is computed at a rate of 0.3 percent on the consideration paid or market value of the shares—whichever is higher—and is payable by the buyer.

(b) Asset purchase   In an asset purchase, stamp duty ranges from 1 to 3 percent, is computed on the market value of the dutiable properties transferred under the instrument, and is payable by the buyer.

(c) Exemptions   Specific stamp duty exemption is available, provided certain stipulated conditions are met—for example, in transfers involving companies that are at least 90 percent related or in the case of the restructuring or amalgamation of a company, when the consideration for transfer is satisfied by issuance of at least 90 percent of shares in the transferee company.

3.   BASIS OF TAXATION FOLLOWING ASSET OR STOCK ACQUISITIONS

3.1   Asset Acquisitions

In a purchase of assets, the buyer would generally be treated as having acquired the assets at the assets' acquisition price. The buyer can claim initial and annual allowances on the acquisition price. It may be possible to achieve a step-up in the cost base of the assets acquired. When assets are transferred between companies under common control, the tax provisions would deem the transfer of fixed assets to be at their tax written-down values.

With respect to acquired industrial buildings—for example, a factory—capital allowances for the buyer are restricted to annual allowances, and the qualifying expenditure would be based on the residual tax written-down value. It was announced in the 2005 budget that with effect from year of assessment 2005, the current purchase price of a used industrial building will be taken as the qualifying expenditure for the purpose of computing capital allowances.

It is important to note that goodwill is not tax deductible.

3.2   Share Acquisitions

In general, the acquisition price is the tax cost base of the shares. If the shares acquired are shares in a real property company (RPC), the shares would represent a chargeable asset, and any subsequent gain on disposal of the shares would attract real property gains tax. An RPC is a controlled company that owns real property, with a defined value of not less than 75 percent of its total tangible assets constituting real property. The purchase price of RPC shares would be determined, under certain circumstances, by a statutory-defined formula. It is therefore important to ascertain whether or not the shares acquired are RPC shares.

4.   FINANCING OF ACQUISITIONS

4.1   Debt

Specific tax issues related to the overall level of borrowings and interest charged on debt are:

- Withholding tax
- Deductibility of interest
- Thin capitalization

(a) **Withholding tax**   Withholding tax is applicable only if the acquisition is financed by funds borrowed from an overseas lender. However, there is no withholding tax if interest is paid to a Malaysian or Labuan bank.

(b) **Deductibility of interest**   Interest incurred on funds used for acquiring a business under an asset deal should be fully tax deductible.

In a share deal, interest expense incurred from money borrowed for the acquisition of shares is deductible to the extent that dividend income is received in the same year. This could result in a tax refund to the shareholder company. For example, assume that a Malaysian company receives a dividend of RM100 from its Malaysian subsidiary in the same year that the Malaysian company has RM90 of interest expense. The following example reflects the treatment of such a transaction as it relates to a Malaysian company:

	RM
Dividend (gross)	100
Interest expense, say	(90)
Net dividend	10
Tax on net dividend	2.8
Tax paid (imputation system)	(28.0)
Tax to be refunded	25.2

It is important to time the payment of interest with the flow of dividends so as to maximize the interest deduction and, correspondingly, to maximize the tax refund. It should be noted that excess interest costs are not eligible for offset against other income and cannot be carried forward to offset future dividend income.

(c) *Thin capitalization*   There are no thin-capitalization rules in Malaysia for tax purposes. Subject to the implications of interest restriction rules noted earlier, the acquiring company can maximize the amount of debt to fund the acquisition.

However, pursuant to exchange control regulations, the Malaysian Central Bank may impose restrictions on the amount of local borrowings. If the acquirer is a nonresident controlled company, short-term trade financing facilities are permitted, provided that the term of the credit is not more than 12 months and the domestic borrowing does not exceed RM50 million in the aggregate. Otherwise, prior approval from the Malaysian Central Bank is required. If approval is sought, the nonresident controlled company must comply with a 3:1 debt/equity ratio for amounts above RM50 million.

4.2   Equity

All proposed acquisitions of assets, including a subscription of shares, or any interests, mergers, or takeovers of a Malaysian business or company require strict approval by the Foreign Investment Committee (FIC), which is responsible for the coordination and regulations of such matters under the Regulation of Acquisitions, Mergers, and Takeovers.

Generally, acquisitions of assets or interests of more than RM10 million in value or acquisitions involving 15 percent or more of the voting rights in a Malaysian company by foreign interest require FIC approval. The FIC may impose foreign-ownership restrictions normally limited to 70 percent when 30 percent is to be allocated to Bumiputra, which defines Malay individuals who profess the religion of Islam, habitually speak the Malay language, and conform to Malay custom.

It may be possible to approach the FIC for a concession if it can be demonstrated that significant benefits accrue to Malaysia. However, this concession is granted very sparingly.

5.   MERGERS OR TAKEOVERS

In Malaysia, there is no statutory concept of a merger or a takeover. Generally, the term *merger* refers to any transaction involving:

- Amalgamation of two or more local companies to be incorporated into a new local company
- Amalgamation of two or more companies without the incorporation of a new local company

The term *takeover* refers generally to any transaction involving the transfer of more than 50 percent of the voting rights in a local company or group of local companies from one party to another.

However, the mode of merger or takeover in Malaysia involves either the acquisition of shares in an existing Malaysian company or an acquisition of the assets and liabilities of another entity. The taxation treatment is as stated under Section 1.

6.   OTHER STRUCTURING AND POSTDEAL ISSUES

6.1   Minimizing After-Tax Cost of Debt

When the seller transfers at cost its intercompany debts due by a target, such transfers are considered capital in nature and are tax neutral to the seller. For the buyer who acquires the shares of the target, the purchase price of the shares in the target would be reduced, but the debt assumed that subsequently becomes worthless is generally not tax deductible by the buyer.

If the seller forgives its intercompany debts due by a target, the tax consequences will depend on the nature of the liabilities. When the liabilities relate to business expenses payable to the seller that have previously been allowed as tax deductions by the target, the forgiveness of such liability is taxable to the target. When the intercompany loan is capital in nature, the forgiveness should not result in any tax consequences to the target. In relation to the write-off, a tax deduction is granted only if it is a trade debt and the obligee has attempted to recover the debt.

6.2   Tax Groups

Currently, group relief in Malaysia is limited to food production companies. Losses incurred by companies engaged in approved food production projects are allowed as deductions against the income of other companies in the same group, subject to certain stipulated conditions.

However, the 2004 budget proposes that group relief be extended under a prepackaged scheme to forest plantations, including rubber plantations, and for selected products in the manufacturing sectors, such as biotechnology, nanotechnology, optics, and photonics.

6.3   Repatriation of Profits

The common methods of repatriation of profits are through payments of dividends, interest, royalties, and management fees.

The ability of a company to pay dividends to shareholders (resident or non-resident) depends on the availability of retained earnings, dividend franking credits, and exempt tax credits. Companies with insufficient dividend franking credits or exempt tax credits suffer additional tax charges to the extent of the shortfalls in franking or exempt credits.

Payments of interest and royalties to nonresidents generally are subject to withholding tax at rates that may be reduced under a relevant double-tax treaty.

As for management and technical fees, if all of the services are performed outside Malaysia, there is no withholding tax on the payment of such fees.

6.4   Cash Repatriation

With respect to dividend repatriation, there is no restriction for exchange control purposes on dividend distributions by Malaysian companies to nonresidents. However, for amounts in excess of RM50,000, a statistical form required by the Malaysian Central Bank must be completed.

6.5   Preservation of Existing Tax Attributes

Unabsorbed tax losses, unutilized tax deprecation, tax incentives, and dividend franking credits remain with the target company. These can be carried forward indefinitely. No carryback of tax losses is allowed.

Under current Malaysian law, notwithstanding a change in ownership or nature of business, the tax losses of the target company can be carried forward indefinitely for offset against future business income. Therefore, a profitable business operation could be injected into the target company. However, to avoid possible challenge by the tax authorities under antiavoidance provisions, the company must ensure that the injection of new activities is bona fide and supported by commercial justifications.

Unutilized tax depreciation and tax incentives can also be carried forward indefinitely but can be used only to offset future income of the same business source. Accordingly, these unutilized balances cannot be applied against the income of a new business source.

Under an asset deal, unabsorbed tax losses, unutilized tax deprecation, tax incentives, and dividend franking credits cannot be transferred to the acquiring company.

6.6   Receipts under Warranties

The tax treatment depends on the particular circumstances, but payments received under warranties in relation to the acquisition of assets/shares—when the recipient is not in the business of trading in shares—are generally not taxable.

7.   DISPOSALS

7.1   Share Disposals

Unless the seller is in the business of dealing in shares, profits on the sale of shares should not be subject to income tax, because such profits are considered capital in nature. Malaysia does not have capital gains tax, except for the real property gains tax (RPGT). When the shares represent interests in a real property company (RPC), the gains from the disposal thereof are subject to RPGT. RPGT is levied at rates that scale from 30 to 5 percent depending on the duration of ownership.

7.2   Asset Disposals

(a) By companies Generally, the sale of real property—land and buildings—is subject to RPGT.

However, exemptions are available under the Real Property Gains Tax Act of 1976. The most notable exemptions involve the transfer of real property between companies in the same group. It is possible to apply for an exemption from RPGT on the transfer of assets between companies in the same group if the asset is transferred to bring about greater efficiency in operations.

The exemption may also cover the following types of assets:

- Assets transferred between group companies under any scheme of reorganization, reconstruction, or amalgamation
- Assets distributed by a liquidator in the case of a liquidation made under any scheme of reorganization, reconstruction, or amalgamation

In both of the aforementioned situations, the exemption applies only when the scheme is in compliance with certain government policies in particular industries.

Transactions in these categories would require prior approval by the tax authorities.

With respect to the sale of trading stock, the gain is subject to income tax because it is considered part of business income.

Any gain on the sale of fixed assets is not subject to income tax. For transactions between unrelated parties, a balancing adjustment (balancing charge or allowance) arises. If the transfer value exceeds the tax written-down value of the asset, then the difference, known as a balancing charge, is taxable to the transferring company. The balancing charge is restricted to the amount of allowances previously claimed. If the transfer value is less than the tax written-down value of the asset, then the shortfall, known as the balancing allowance, is deductible against the adjusted income of the company. If the transaction is between related parties, no balancing adjustment arises for the seller, because the assets are deemed to be transferred at their tax written-down value.

Currently, there are no indirect tax consequences related to the disposal of real property—for example, factories, office premises—or for the sale of machinery or equipment and trading stocks when import duty and/or sales tax has been paid.

If the seller has any facility that qualifies for exemption from import duty and/or sales tax—including any facility for licensed manufacturers licensed under the Sales Tax Act in Malaysia—the following indirect tax implications may apply:

- The sale of exempt dutiable and/or taxable machinery or equipment—inclusive of spare parts—and raw materials may result in import duty and/or sales tax, unless the seller or buyer is able to obtain from relevant authorities an exemption of import duty and/or sales tax for the sale or purchase of the said machinery or equipment and raw materials.
- With respect to sales of tax-free raw materials, taxable work-in-progress, and taxable finished goods manufactured by a seller that is a licensed manufacturer under the Sales Tax Act, there are provisions in the Sales Tax Act to allow the buyer to purchase these items free of sales tax, subject to certain conditions. Namely, the buyer has to be a licensed manufacturer as well. Otherwise, sales tax is due and payable by the seller upon sale.

(b) By individuals   Generally, the disposal of shares is not taxable unless the individual habitually trades in shares.

7.3   Deferred Consideration and Earn-Outs

In an earn-out, consideration to the seller may be:

- An immediate payment in cash or shares of the buyer
- A deferred payment contingent upon the target's future earnings

These payments generally are not subject to tax, because such receipts by the seller are considered capital in nature.

7.4   Payments under Warranties

Payments under warranties related to the disposal of assets or shares are generally tax deductible.

8.   TREATMENT OF TRANSACTION COSTS

Generally, expenses such as the cost of drawing up agreements and deeds, expenses related to the acquisition capital assets, costs incurred in issuing convertible notes, costs incurred for increasing or reducing share capital, and so on, are considered capital in nature and are not tax deductible.

9.   PREPARING A TARGET COMPANY FOR SALE

In a deal's preparation, it would be expedient for the seller to identify the income tax and RPGT impact on any gains arising from a share or asset deal. When possible, the tax costs should be quantified, and the potential tax exposure minimized. Positive tax attributes including the availability of loss carryforwards, unutilized tax depreciation, and tax franking credits should be considered and used as bargaining tools in negotiations with the buyer.

9.1   Intragroup Transfer of Assets Being Retained

In the preparation for a sale of assets, it is important to identify the assets being transferred and the assets' associated costs and to engage an independent professional appraiser to value the assets.

9.2   Presale Dividend

The ability of a company to pay dividends—other than those paid out of exempt income—prior to a sale depends on the availability of retained earnings and dividend franking credits. Generally, there are no adverse tax consequences related to a presale dividend.

10.   DEMERGERS

In Malaysia, there is no statutory concept of a demerger. A demerger in Malaysia typically involves either a disposal of shares or assets to another party or a distribution in specie of the shares or assets to the shareholders via either dividend distribution or capital reduction exercise.

The taxation treatment of a disposal is as stated under Section 1.

When the demerger is by way of a dividend in specie, the company paying the dividend must have sufficient franking or exempt tax credits when shares or assets are distributed. The shareholders receiving the distribution are taxed on the dividend distributed.

When the demerger is effected through a return of capital via a capital reduction exercise, shareholders generally are not taxed on the capital distribution (unless the shareholders are treated as share dealers).

11.   LISTINGS AND INITIAL PUBLIC OFFERINGS

There should be no income tax liability related to an initial public offering (IPO) if the shares have been held as long-term investments and are non-RPC shares.

The terms *IPO* and *listing* are synonymous.

Typically in an IPO, certain conditions must be satisfied. For example, equity conditions are imposed on companies seeking listing on Bursa Malaysia Berhad (Malaysian Stock Exchange). One condition requires that at least 30 percent of the equity be allocated to Bumiputra upon listing.

MEXICO

INTRODUCTION

This chapter details the principal tax issues that are relevant to purchasers and sellers engaged in the transfer of ownership of a Mexican trade or business. Unless otherwise stated, it is generally assumed that all sellers and purchasers are Mexican companies with limited liability. The acquisition of a business is usually carried out by the purchase of shares or assets. It is also common practice to conduct pre or postacquisition restructurings aimed at streamlining the resulting corporate structures or even at obtaining additional business or tax benefits. Under certain circumstances, Mexican law allows for tax-free mergers, demergers, and intragroup transfers.

The relevant taxes to be considered are:

- **Income tax.** Income tax is a federal tax obligation; there are no local or state income taxes. Companies are required to pay income tax on all income regardless of location or source. In 2005, the federal corporate income tax rate is 30 percent. This rate will decrease 1 percent each year until it reaches 28 percent in 2007 that is, 29 percent in 2006 and 28 percent in 2007.
- **Asset tax.** A minimum tax, asset tax is payable at the rate of 1.8 percent of the value of the assets of the taxpayers. It supplements the federal income tax; that is, it is payable and increases the overall tax burden only if it exceeds regular income tax.
- **Value-added tax (VAT).** VAT is generally imposed on all entities that sell goods or render services. The VAT rate is generally 15 percent (10 percent along the US-Mexican and southern Mexican borders).
- **Real property transfer tax.** The sale or transfer of real property (land and buildings) is subject to a local property transfer tax. The rate depends on the Mexican state in which the property is located.
- **Statutory employees' profit sharing.** Although profit sharing is not a tax, every Mexican business with employees is required to distribute a portion of its annual profits among all of its employees except directors and the general manager. The amount of profit to be distributed is equal to 10 percent of the business's taxable income, with certain modifications. According to new rules applicable from January 1, 2005, statutory employees' profit sharing paid in 2006 and based on the 2005 calendar

year taxable income will be 100 percent deductible for Mexican income tax purposes.

1.   ACQUISITIONS

1.1   Asset Acquisitions

Buyers may prefer purchasing assets in order to obtain a step-up in the tax basis of the purchased assets and to try to avoid liabilities the seller may have generated. The basis step-up may allow the buyer to deduct, over time, a significant portion of the purchase price.

Asset purchases can be particularly challenging for the following reasons:

- Sellers would prefer to sell stock if the sale results in a lower tax liability.
- Buyers generally attempt to obtain a basis step-up in the assets purchased so that they can deduct or amortize as much of the purchase price as possible. For this reason, a proper allocation of the purchase price should be made among the assets acquired.

When the company's inside basis in its assets is lower than the shareholder's outside basis in the company's stock, the seller would prefer a stock deal to avoid paying income tax and statutory employees' profit sharing on the taxable income derived from the sale of assets. Thus, a buyer wishing to purchase assets often must work with the seller to ensure that both parties meet their goals.

Generally, the excess of the purchase price over the fair market value of the assets acquired is considered nondeductible for Mexican tax purposes. Goodwill is also nondeductible for income tax purposes.

It should be noted that asset purchases deemed to be purchases of a going concern may result in joint liability for the buyer for the tax contingencies arising during the time the business was in the hands of the previous owner. Any such joint liability will be limited to the value of the going concern acquired. Thorough due diligence exercises are therefore strongly recommended even in the case of asset purchases.

1.2   Stock Acquisitions

A stock acquisition is a common way to enter the Mexican market. Sellers usually prefer this type of transaction because they generally retain no liabilities. That is, the purchaser acquires all tax and legal contingencies arising from previous years because the target company, as an existing legal entity, continues to be responsible for any obligation incurred prior to the acquisition.

The statute of limitations is five years under Mexican law, which implies that the Mexican tax authorities are empowered to conduct tax audits and make the corresponding assessments for that five-year period.

According to the Mexican Federal Tax Code, the shareholders of a company—that is, the purchasers—are jointly liable with respect to any tax liability arising from the company's operations.

However, that joint liability is limited as follows:

- It applies only if (1) the company is not registered at the Federal Tax-payers Registry, (2) the company has changed its domicile without filing the corresponding notification and the change was made after it was notified of the initiation of a tax audit and before it was notified of the audit's resolution or if the change took place after it was notified of a tax assessment and before it covered that assessment or before it is declared without effect, or (3) the company failed to keep accounting records or accounting records were hidden or destroyed.
- If applicable, the stockholders are jointly liable for the portion of the tax liability not guaranteed by the company's assets.
- The resulting joint liability will not exceed the amount of the stockholders' ownership of the capital stock of the company.

In Mexico, the sale of the beneficial ownership of shares is treated as a sale of the shares themselves.

2.   TRANSACTION COSTS FOR PURCHASERS

2.1   Transfer Taxes

(a) Stock acquisitions   There is no transfer tax or other stamp duty on the sale of stock.

(b) Asset acquisitions   The sale or transfer of real property (land and buildings) is subject to the local property transfer tax. While the rate depends on the Mexican state in which the property is located, it generally averages 2 to 4 percent. Including the notary fees, the cost of the sale could equal 5 to 6 percent of the value of the real property.

2.2   Value-Added Tax

(a) Stock acquisitions   Stock transfers are exempt from VAT.

(b) Asset acquisitions   Generally speaking, the gross proceeds from the sale of assets are subject to a 15 percent VAT. The value of land, however, is exempt. VAT paid on the purchase of assets is recoverable either as a credit against future VAT collected—or, in some cases, by offsetting any overpayment against income tax or asset tax—or as a refund.

It is important to point out that in general terms, because a nonresident company is not allowed to credit input VAT derived from an asset acquisition, this tax would become an additional cost. However, if the purchaser is a Mexican company, this entity would be entitled to recover the VAT paid.

In the case of goodwill—because goodwill is considered to be nondeductible—any VAT paid that is related to goodwill is unrecoverable. Additionally, the VAT paid on goodwill or other nondeductible items is also considered to be a nondeductible expense.

2.3   Capital Taxes

There are no capital taxes in Mexico applicable to stock or asset purchases.

2.4   Tax Deductibility of Transaction Costs

(a) Corporate income tax deductions   Generally speaking, transaction costs such as financing, notary, legal, and due diligence expenses are deductible for income tax purposes. In the case of stock purchases, such costs should be deducted by the company acquiring the stock. This could make it difficult to fully utilize those tax deductions because in most cases, the acquisition vehicle has no taxable income to offset them. In this scenario, consideration should be given to either filing consolidated tax returns, or merging the operating company and the acquisition company, or implementing any other strategy to channel taxable income to the holding company.

Pro rata expenses are nondeductible. Therefore, if the transaction costs were incurred abroad and subsequently are charged to Mexico on a pro rata basis—that is, based on income, assets, labor, and so on—the Mexican tax authorities could challenge the deductibility of those expenses.

(b) VAT treatment of expenses   Legal and due diligence fees are typically subject to 15 percent VAT. If the purchasing entity is resident in Mexico, that input VAT may be recovered either by crediting against future output VAT or by petitioning for a VAT refund.

When those fees are charged to a nonresident entity, either of the following could occur:

- The process is completed successfully and the Mexican target company is acquired. In this case, the fees would be subject to VAT, which would become an additional cost for the nonresident company because the nonresident company would not be entitled to recover that VAT.

- The purchase is not completed. In this case, the fees could be deemed as exported services not subject to VAT.

Therefore, it would be advisable for the expenses to be paid by a Mexican company whenever possible so that they can be deductible for income tax purposes and creditable for VAT purposes or so that a refund can be requested. If the operation is carried out and the expenses are invoiced to a foreign entity, VAT becomes an additional cost.

3. BASIS OF TAXATION FOLLOWING ASSET OR STOCK ACQUISITIONS

3.1 Asset Acquisitions

(a) *Fixed and intangible assets* The acquiring company may deduct the fixed assets via depreciation. That depreciation should be computed by applying the following maximum annual percentages specified in the income tax law to the amount paid for the assets:

- Five percent for buildings
- Five percent for deferred charges: that is, intangible assets represented by goods or rights allowing for a decrease in operating costs or for improving the quality or acceptance of a product for an unlimited period depending on the lifetime of the item in question
- Fifteen percent for deferred expenses; that is, intangible assets represented by goods or rights allowing for a decrease in operating costs or for improving the quality or acceptance of a product for a limited period that is less than the lifetime of the item in question
- Ten percent for office furnishings and equipment
- Twenty-five percent for automobiles
- Thirty percent for computers, and so forth

The selling entity must provide the purchaser with an invoice for the assets acquired; otherwise, the buyer is not entitled to deduct the cost allocated to those assets.

(b) *Inventories* Until 2004, inventories were fully deductible in the year in which they were acquired. However, as of 2005, the acquisition of inventory is no longer deductible for income tax purposes. In this case, the deduction of purchased merchandise is replaced by the deduction of cost of goods sold. The cost of goods sold will be deductible in the year in which the income arising from the sale of goods is earned.

3.2 Stock Acquisitions

The amount at which the stock is acquired creates in the stock of the target company a tax basis that can be utilized in the event of future disposal of the company. The tax basis is restated for inflation.

4. FINANCING OF ACQUISITIONS

4.1 Debt

(a) Withholding tax   As a general rule, the payment of interest by a Mexican company to a nonresident lender is subject to withholding tax in Mexico. The rate of withholding tax depends mainly on the residence of the lender and on whether the interest payments derive from a bank loan or from intercompany debt, as follows:

- A 10 percent withholding tax rate applies on interest paid to the following entities as long as the entities are registered at the Mexican Revenue Service and provide the service with all information requested under the general rules established for loans made to entities domiciled in Mexico:
  - ○ Financing entities of foreign governments domiciled abroad when they are the beneficial owners of the interest
  - ○ Foreign banks, as long as they are the beneficial owners of the interest
  - ○ Entities investing or placing capital in Mexico arising from credit instruments issued by them that are publicly traded abroad in accordance with the general rules issued by the Mexican Revenue Service
- The 10 percent rate is also applicable to interest paid to entities domiciled abroad on credit instruments placed abroad through banks or brokerage houses, provided that the documents involved in the financing operation are registered at the Special Section of the National Securities and Intermediaries Registry.
- A 4.9 percent withholding tax rate applies to the interest paid to foreign banks registered before the Mexican Revenue Service as long as the beneficial owner resides in a country with which Mexico has a tax treaty in place.
- A 15 percent withholding tax rate applies to interest paid to reinsurance companies.
- A 21 percent withholding tax rate applies to interest paid by Mexican banks to nonresidents, as well as to interest paid by Mexican residents to nonresident suppliers of machinery and equipment.
- Thirty percent (28 percent for fiscal year 2007) applies to interest arising from intercompany debts. However, if the party receiving the payment is resident in a country with which Mexico has signed a tax treaty, then generally speaking, the provisions contained in the treaty overrule the provisions contained in local legislation, and, therefore, taxpayers may opt to apply the rates stated in the tax treaty in force, which usually benefits them the most in each particular case. Mexico has tax treaties

in which the withholding tax ranges from 10 to 15 percent for intercompany loans.

- There is no withholding tax on interest paid to Mexican lenders.

(b) Deductibility of interest   Accrued interest that is set at fair market value is deductible. Otherwise, the excess is not deductible.

If the interest is paid to a party resident abroad, any tax payable on receipt of the interest income by third parties must be withheld by the payer and remitted to the tax authorities. Alternatively, those third parties may provide documentation attesting to payment of the tax.

Information returns must be filed that report on operations carried out with parties resident abroad (including interest payments) on the officially approved forms.

(c) Inflationary gain and loss   Operating profits must be modified by applying certain provisions designed to recognize the effects of inflation by recognizing gain or loss from the reduction in the purchasing power of currency (monetary correction). Taxpayers are required to calculate an inflationary gain or loss on an annual basis by applying the percentage increases in the National Consumer Price Index to the difference between the average of all liabilities and the average of certain assets. If the liabilities are larger, the result must be declared as income for tax purposes; if the assets are larger, the difference is considered a deductible expense.

(d) Thin capitalization   When the debt of Mexican taxpayers exceeds three times their shareholder equity, the interest generated by excess debt is not deductible. This rule applies to both nonresident related and unrelated parties and in some cases, to domestic lenders.

In calculating the debt/equity ratio mentioned earlier, the total amount of the loans contracted by the company must be considered, with the exception of certain mortgages.

The thin-capitalization rules are not applicable to financial-sector companies that comply with the capitalization rules pertaining to their sector. Furthermore, Mexican entities that have an excessive debt/equity ratio due to loans with related parties can apply for a ruling from the tax authorities on the arm's-length nature of the loan in order to maintain the excessive ratio. An authorization is also possible for excesses attributable to unrelated-party loans if the arm's-length nature of the taxpayer's operations with its related parties is also reviewed by the tax authorities.

These formalities (to have the nondeductible excess interest waived) require certification by an independent accountant.

A five-year transition rule was enacted that allows taxpayers to reduce their debt proportionately, in equal parts, in each of those years until they reduce their debt to meet the 3:1 ratio mentioned earlier. If, at the end of that term, the ratio of liabilities continues to be higher than the allowable amount, then the interest paid from January 1, 2005, arising from debts exceeding three times the book equity, is not deductible.

(e) *Transfer pricing*   Interest payable must be stated at fair market value; otherwise, the tax authorities could challenge the respective deduction in the event of a tax audit. Therefore, it is necessary to gather sufficient evidence to prove that the interest charged complies with the arm's-length principle. For this purpose, Mexican taxpayers may obtain a transfer-pricing study to support the fact that the transactions are at arm's length.

(f) *Reclassification of interest as a dividend*   Mexican income tax law reclassifies interest payments as nondeductible dividends under certain circumstances. Such reclassifications can occur in related-party situations, including, but not limited to the following:

- The loan agreement provides that the debtor unconditionally promises to repay the loan at any time determined by the creditor.
- The interest is not deductible because the interest rate is not stated at fair market value.
- In the event of default, the creditor has the right to intervene in the administration of the debtor's business.
- Interest payment is conditioned on the availability of profits or the amount is determined based on profits.
- The interest is derived from a back-to-back loan.

A back-to-back loan is defined for this purpose as any operation under which one party provides cash or goods for an intermediary that in turn provides cash or goods for a related party or for the original party. Furthermore, back-to-back loans are those provided by an intermediary and guaranteed with cash or cash deposits by a party related to the borrower or by the borrower—to the extent that it guarantees the loan.

(g) *Additional withholding tax*   Some of the tax treaties signed by Mexico contain a rule restricting the provision concerning the taxation of interest in cases when, by reason of a special relationship either between the payer and the beneficial owner or between both of them and some other party, the amount of the interest paid exceeds the amount that would have been agreed upon by the payer and the beneficial owner had they agreed to the amount at fair market value. This rule provides that in such cases, the provision applies

only in the second instance and that the excess portion of the interest is taxable under the laws of the two contracting states.

4.2   Equity

There is no capital duty on the issuance of new stock.

It should also be mentioned that there is no withholding tax obligation on dividend payments; however, Mexican companies distributing non-CUFIN dividends (the after-tax earnings account (CUFIN) is described in Section 6.3) pay an additional corporate income tax (30 percent in 2005, 28 percent in 2006, and 28 percent in 2007) to be determined by applying the corresponding income tax rate to the dividend payment multiplied by a gross-up factor of 1.4286 provided for in Mexican income tax law (1.4085 in 2006).

5.   MERGERS

5.1   Tax Consequences

Until 2003, mergers were tax free, provided the surviving company filed tax returns for the year and filed the related information returns for the merged company, which included payment of the related tax. Additionally, the regulations of the Mexican Federal Tax Code required the surviving company in a merger to file notification of the merger no later than one month following the date on which the merger was carried out and to specify the names of the merged company(ies) and the date on which the event took place.

However, the rules governing the taxation of corporate mergers and split-ups—that is, demergers—were significantly modified in 2004. New and more complex requirements must be fulfilled in order for mergers and split-ups to avoid being taxable.

A one-year continuity-of-business requirement is now imposed on the merged entities. This requirement is waived in certain situations when the activity of the merged entities consists of leasing operations carried out between them, the income of the merged entities prior to the merger was sufficiently similar, or the surviving entity is liquidated within a year of the merger. Furthermore, if a merger is to take place before five years have elapsed since the most recent merger or split-up, authorization must first be obtained from the tax authorities.

5.2   Legal Issues

While the Corporations Law (*Ley General de Sociedades Mercantiles*) regulates corporate mergers, it does not define the concept. The *New Mexican Legal Dictionary*[1] defines a merger as "the joining of two or more companies

---

1. *Nuevo Diccionario Jurídico Mexicano*, Editorial Porrúa, T. D-H, p. 1779.

to form a single company, with the other(s) being dissolved and transferring their capital and assets to the company surviving in the merger" (free translation). The shareholders of the merged company are given stock in the surviving company in exchange for their stock in the merged company.

The Corporations Law specifies that merger agreements must be registered at the Public Commerce Registry and published in the *Official Gazette* for the jurisdiction in which the merging companies have their domicile. Each company must also publish its last balance sheet, and the merged companies must publish the manner in which their liabilities are to be paid off.

It is important to consider that in accordance with the Corporations Law, a merger is effective three months after the date on which it is registered at the Public Commerce Registry. During this period, creditors are allowed legally to object to the merger, unless (1) an agreement is reached for total payment of all the debts of the merging companies; or (2) the amount of the companies' debts is deposited at a bank; or (3) the creditors consent to the merger, in which case the merger is effective from the date it is registered at the Public Commerce Registry.

6.   OTHER STRUCTURING AND POSTDEAL ISSUES

6.1   Financing an Acquisition in Mexico

There are structures that can be implemented to help maximize the tax benefits of the investment. Each structure should be analyzed on a case-by-case basis because a number of tax issues could arise from the implementation—for example, withholding tax, interest deductibility, and transfer-pricing rules.

6.2   Tax Consolidation

Mexican income tax law contains provisions that allow certain holding companies to file a consolidated income tax return with their majority-owned subsidiaries. Tax consolidation is applicable only for income tax and asset tax purposes.

In general terms, the consolidation rules allow certain benefits, such as offsetting losses incurred by one company against the profits of another controlled company.

From 1999 to 2004, only 60 percent of the controlling company's interest in the controlled companies was allowed to be consolidated for income tax purposes. Also, all holding companies were allowed to consolidate only 60 percent of their results. For the remaining 40 percent interest, holding and controlled companies were required to determine their tax result on a nonconsolidated basis and were subject to formal filing and compliance requirements.

As of 2005, Mexican income tax law states that tax consolidation will be determined based on 100 percent of the shareholding that a holding company has directly or indirectly in a subsidiary during a given tax year. Also, the holding companies will consolidate 100 percent of their tax result with that of their subsidiaries.

The principal advantages of filing a consolidated return are:

- The possibility of deducting (at the consolidated level) the tax losses incurred by the subsidiaries owned by the holding company.[2]
- The filing of a consolidated asset tax return for the entire group, thus optimizing the determination of the respective tax liabilities by allowing excess income tax credits of one company to be offset against the net asset tax liabilities of other companies within the group.
- Tax-deferred flow of dividends in excess of the net previously taxed income—to the extent that the dividend flow remains within the consolidation group.

To qualify as a holding company, the principal requirements are that the company must be a Mexican tax resident and no more than 50 percent of the holding company's shares are held by other companies regardless of their country of residence. However, shares that qualify as having been placed among the general investing public and nonvoting shares are not regarded as company owned for this purpose. Unfortunately, this rule precludes the possibility of filing a consolidated return for a Mexican group of companies that would otherwise qualify if more than 50 percent of the holding company's shares are held by a foreign corporation, unless the foreign corporation is a resident in a country that has executed a comprehensive agreement for the exchange of tax information with Mexico. At present, Belgium, Canada, Chile, Czech Republic, Ecuador, Finland, France, Israel, Italy, the Netherlands, Norway, Romania, Singapore, South Korea, Spain, Sweden, and the United States have agreements of this nature with Mexico, and other agreements or tax treaties that might contain such an agreement are awaiting ratification or being negotiated.

6.3   Preservation of Existing Tax Attributes

In a stock acquisition, the tax attributes remain with the company, which allows the new stockholder to utilize them in any further tax planning.

Typically, the tax attributes of a company are:

- **The after-tax earnings account (CUFIN).** This represents the company's retained earnings already taxed at the corporate income tax rate. The CUFIN balance can be distributed to the stockholders with no additional corporate income tax at the level of the distributing entity.

---

2. In the case of tax losses incurred before the consolidation, the deduction may be applied only up to the amount of the controlling or controlled company's individual taxable income in the period in question.

- **The capital contributions account.** This measures the amount of capital stock plus premiums contributed to an entity. Its balance represents the amount that can be distributed to the stockholders on a tax-free basis in the event of a capital redemption or liquidation of the company.
- **Tax-loss carryforwards.** For Mexican tax purposes, a corporation is entitled to carry forward tax losses for a period of 10 subsequent years and use those losses to offset future taxable profits. Tax losses are subject to adjustment for inflation.
- **Asset tax paid in prior years.** This may be recovered if the company pays income tax in any of the following 10 years. A refund of this tax can usually be requested, or it can be offset against other taxes.

In an asset purchase, the tax attributes are not transferred to the purchaser.

7.   DISPOSALS

7.1   Companies

When a foreign corporation sells or transfers stock issued by a Mexican corporation, the source of income is generally considered to be located in Mexico. As a result, the transaction is taxable in Mexico. A 25 percent income tax rate is applied to the gross sales price without any deduction for basis and is withheld by a Mexican purchaser or by a nonresident purchaser with a permanent establishment in Mexico. If the acquirer is a foreign resident without a permanent establishment, the seller must remit the tax to the Mexican tax authorities.

In addition, gain from the sale of shares is considered Mexican-sourced income when more than 50 percent of the book value arises directly or indirectly from real property located in Mexico, including when the shareholding is structured in different levels.

Note that the results of such transactions may be different for non-Mexican sellers resident in countries that have a tax treaty with Mexico. Understanding the applicable treaty provisions is therefore vital.

A taxpayer may elect to pay 30 percent income tax (IT) on the net gain (29 percent in 2006 and 28 percent in 2007). This alternative applies when the seller appoints a legal representative in Mexico and legalizes the appointment in both Mexico and the other country. In any event, the transaction must be carried out at fair market value, and the tax basis must be calculated under Mexican tax rules.

Additionally, the legal representative must file:

- The tax return and must remit the corresponding tax within 15 business days of the sale

- A notice advising the authorities that a tax report (*dictamen*) will be prepared and filed by a certified public accountant within 15 business days of filing the tax return
- A tax report within 30 days of filing the tax return

Sellers resident in a tax haven or a country with a territorial taxation system cannot elect to be taxed at the 30 percent rate on the gain.

If a Mexican company sells stock, gains on the sale of shares are wholly includable in gross income. Losses on the sale of shares are deductible only if the acquisition and sale or other dispositions comply with the general rules established by the tax authorities. The deductible amount is limited to the amount of gains from similar transactions in the same year or the following five fiscal years. These losses are not deductible against ordinary income.

7.2   Individuals

Individuals receiving income from the sale of stock may deduct the adjusted tax basis in the stock from the income arising from the sale.

In general terms, annual tax is calculated by applying to the profit arising from the sale of the stock the rate established in the income tax law, considering the number of years the stock was held.

Estimated income tax payments should be calculated as 25 percent of the gross amount of the operation and must be withheld by the purchaser when the purchaser is a resident of Mexico or a resident of another country with a permanent establishment in Mexico.

However, the individual may elect to pay income tax on the net gain, in which case a tax report must be issued by a certified public accountant, stating that the capital gain or loss and the corresponding tax, if any, were duly determined according to Mexican income tax law.

8.   TRANSACTION COSTS FOR SELLERS

8.1   Transfer Taxes

(a) *Stock acquisitions*   There is no transfer tax or other stamp duty on the sale of stock.

(b) *Asset acquisitions*   The sale or transfer of real property (land and buildings) is subject to the local property transfer tax. While the rate depends on the Mexican state in which the property is located, it generally averages 2 to 4 percent. Including the notary fees, the cost of the sale could equal 5 to 6 percent of the value of the real property.

8.2   VAT

(a) Stock acquisitions   Stock transfers are exempt from VAT.

(b) Asset acquisitions   Generally speaking, gross proceeds from the sale of assets are subject to a 15 percent VAT. The value of land, however, is exempt. VAT paid on the purchase of assets is recoverable either as a credit against future VAT collected—or, in some cases, by offsetting any overpayment against income tax or asset tax—or as a refund.

It is important to point out that in general terms, because a nonresident company is not allowed to credit input VAT derived from an asset acquisition, this tax would become an additional cost. However, if the purchaser is a Mexican company, that entity would be entitled to recover the VAT paid.

Since goodwill is nondeductible for tax purposes, any VAT paid related to goodwill is unrecoverable. Additionally, the VAT paid on goodwill or on other nondeductible items is also considered to be a nondeductible expense.

8.3   Capital Taxes

There are no capital taxes in Mexico applicable to stock or asset purchases.

8.4   Tax Deductibility of Transaction Costs

(a) Corporate income tax deductions   Generally speaking, such transaction costs as financing, notary, legal, and due diligence expenses are deductible for income tax purposes. In the case of stock purchases, those costs should be deducted by the company acquiring the stock. This could make it difficult to fully utilize those tax deductions, because in most cases, the acquisition vehicle has no taxable income to offset them. In this scenario, consideration should be given to filing consolidated tax returns, merging the operating company and the acquisition company, or implementing any other strategy that would channel taxable income to the holding company.

Pro rata expenses are nondeductible. Therefore, if the transaction costs were incurred abroad and subsequently are charged to Mexico on a pro rata basis—that is, based on income, assets, labor, and so on—the Mexican tax authorities could challenge the deductibility of those expenses.

(b) VAT treatment of expenses   Legal and due diligence fees are typically subject to 15 percent VAT. If the purchasing entity is resident in Mexico, that input VAT may be recovered either by crediting against future output VAT or by petitioning for a VAT refund.

When those fees are charged to a nonresident entity, either of the following could occur:

- The process is completed successfully and the Mexican target company is acquired. In this case, the fees would be subject to VAT, which would become an additional cost for the nonresident company, since the company would not be entitled to recover that VAT.

- The purchase is not completed. In this case, the fees could be deemed as exported services not subject to VAT.

Therefore, it would be advisable for the expenses to be paid by a Mexican company whenever possible so that they can be deductible for income tax purposes and creditable for VAT purposes or so that a refund can be requested. If the operation is carried out and the expenses are invoiced to a foreign entity, VAT becomes an additional cost.

9.   DEMERGERS AND SPLIT-UPS

In general terms, a number of requirements established in the Corporations Law must be complied with for the purpose of accomplishing a tax-free demerger or split-up. These include registering the split-up agreements at the Public Commerce Registry and publishing those agreements in the *Official Gazette* for the city in which the company is domiciled.

The split-up is considered effective once 45 calendar days have elapsed from the registration and publication of the split-up agreement. In this case, the split-up procedure could require two or three months.

Until 2003, a split-up was tax free if the shareholders holding at least 51 percent of the stock of the original and spun-off company remained the same for a period of two years from the time immediately preceding the date on which the split-up was carried out. However, as of 2004, the continuity-of-interest requirement was modified. The 51 percent shareholding of the voting stock must be maintained for three years, beginning one year prior to the split-up, as opposed to the previous two-year requirement. More important, the holders of 51 percent of the voting stock must also maintain the same proportion in the capital of the resulting entities as they had in the original entity prior to the split-up. It could be interpreted that this requirement shifts the continuity test from a pure vote test to both a vote test and a value test. It is also important to note that under prior law, limited voting stock was expressly exempt from applying the continuity-of-interest requirement. The current Mexican Federal Tax Code (MFTC) does not exempt limited voting stock; however, it excludes the stock held by the general investing public. Finally if a split-up is reclassified as a capital reduction under the Mexican IT Law, it will qualify as a taxable sale.

Also, under the current MFTC, when a merger or split-up is part of a corporate restructuring, the other requirements provided in the income tax law must be met. Split-ups complying with all such requirements are generally considered to be tax free and will not generate either adverse or favorable consequences for the companies involved or for their shareholders.

10.   OTHER PERTINENT ISSUES

10.1   Payments on Income under a Preferential Tax Treatment

Income received by foreign residents that is subject to preferred tax regimes is subject to a withholding tax rate of 40 percent on gross income without any deduction. The withholding should be applied by the Mexican resident (or permanent establishment of nonresidents) payer.

Through December 31, 2004, Mexican tax law subjected Mexican taxpayers to immediate taxation on income generated indirectly in tax-haven jurisdictions. The list of tax-haven countries is enumerated and included as an appendix to the law.

As of January 1, 2005, Mexican taxpayers are subject to immediate taxation on foreign-sourced income that arises in subsidiaries or from any other investment vehicle when the income is subject to an effective foreign tax rate of less than 75 percent of the Mexican tax to which the same income would have been subject had it been generated under Mexican income tax rules.

This is a significant focus shift in the determination of which income indirectly generated by Mexican taxpayers should be subject to immediate Mexican taxation.

These new rules have two significant effects:

1. They require that Mexican taxpayers with foreign investments calculate the effective rate of tax on all of their investments in order to determine whether the income must be immediately reported and taxed in Mexico.

2. They require Mexican taxpayers that make payments of Mexican-sourced income to determine whether the income will be preferred-tax-regime income in the hands of the payee and, if so, withhold at a punitive, 40 percent rate.

However, preferred tax regime (PTR) income will be exempted when:

*   It arises in a country with a broad exchange-of-information agreement in place with Mexico and the income is not passive income.

*   It arises from a business activity and at least 50 percent of the total assets of such entities are composed of fixed assets, land, and inventory used in such business. However, this exception may not be applied to such income as dividends, rents, royalties, interest, and certain capital gains—that is, passive income—when such income represents more than 20 percent of the total income generated by the Mexican taxpayer.

10.2   Social Security

If an asset deal is carried out and the employees are transferred to the new company under a so-called employer replacement, the former employer (the seller) is jointly liable for the obligations of the new employer for the six months following the replacement.

After that term elapses, the only party responsible for any obligation arising from the social security law is the new employer, even when those liabilities arise from years prior to the acquisition.

NETHERLANDS

INTRODUCTION

This chapter details the principal tax issues that are relevant to purchasers and sellers engaged in the transfer of ownership of a Dutch trade or business. Unless otherwise stated, it is generally assumed that all sellers and purchasers are Dutch companies with limited liability.

1.   ACQUISITIONS

1.1   Asset Acquisitions

In an asset deal, the historical tax liabilities of the transferor company do not transfer to the purchaser. It should be noted, however, that certain tax claims or issues of a recurring nature effectively may follow the transferred assets—for example, tax issues related to employee benefits that cannot easily be modified or revoked—because amending the relevant provisions in an employment contract may prove to be cumbersome.

The gain realized by a Dutch company on the sale of its assets generally is subject to an immediate tax at a corporate income tax rate of 34.5 percent. Note that pending legislation would reduce the corporate tax rate to 31.5 percent effective January 1, 2005, then to 30.5 percent effective January 1, 2006, and finally to 30 percent effective January 1, 2007.

It is possible to defer taxation of the capital gain realized upon disposal of a business asset by forming a so-called reinvestment reserve. The capital gain may be placed in the reinvestment reserve if it is intended that such a gain be reinvested. Absent special circumstances, the capital gain must be reinvested within three years following the year in which the reserve was formed. Otherwise, the reserve should be included in taxable income. If it is neither possible nor preferable to form a reinvestment reserve, the capital gain in excess of available tax losses is subject to tax.

For the purchaser, an asset acquisition permits a step-up in the tax basis of the acquired assets, including goodwill and assuming that the target's assets have in fact appreciated in value.

1.2   Stock Acquisitions

If the transaction is structured as a stock acquisition, then the purchaser effectively bears any historical tax liabilities of the acquired target company because such a target generally remains liable for historical tax claims. One important exception to this rule applies if the acquired Dutch target company was part of a fiscal unity for Dutch corporate tax purposes as defined in Section 6.1. The parent company of the fiscal unity is responsible for the reporting and payment of tax for all fiscal unity members; that is, only one taxable entity is recognized for Dutch corporate tax purposes. In such a case, tax liabilities related to the period during which the target was a member of the fiscal unity remain with the parent company of the fiscal unity. For tax collection purposes, however, Dutch tax law stipulates that the fiscal unity members are jointly and severally liable for any Dutch corporate tax claim for periods during which they were included in the fiscal unity. Furthermore, other charges—for example, value-added tax (VAT) or wage tax—to companies that are or were part of the fiscal unity may, for tax collection purposes, be set off against a claim with respect to tax or other charges that a fiscal unity member has against the tax authorities.

A step-up in the tax basis of a company's assets generally is not permitted in the context of a purchase of that company's stock; that is, in Dutch tax law, there is no concept similar to a Section 338 election under US tax law. Significantly, however, Dutch tax law contains several provisions that in some cases effectively transform a share deal into an asset deal from a corporate income tax perspective. These provisions must be taken into account by the parties when the parties are contemplating acquisition of the stock of a Dutch company, since they may affect the depreciable tax basis of the target company's assets—and, therefore, the purchase price paid for the target.

For example, assume that a member of the same corporate income tax fiscal unity as the target had previously transferred hidden reserves[1] and/or goodwill to the target within six years—or in some cases, three years—preceding the sale of target stock to an unrelated purchaser. In such case, a taxable revaluation of the previously transferred assets, which were transferred at book value, will take place, resulting in the imposition of corporate income tax on the parent company of the fiscal unity. Correspondingly, the tax basis of the previously transferred assets will be stepped up in the hands of the transferee member—in this illustration, the target.

As another illustration of these rules, if the Dutch target company was formed through a tax-free merger or a split-off and if the shares of that target were subsequently transferred to a nonrelated party within three years after the merger or split-off, the merger is—though this can be rebutted—presumed not to have been based on business motives. This may trigger a tax on the previously exempt profit

---

1. A transfer of hidden reserves to the target would occur if the other member of the fiscal unity transferred fixed assets to the target at book value under circumstances in which the fair market value of those assets exceeded such book value. Such excess would constitute the hidden reserves.

at the level of the transferring member company, with a corresponding step-up in the tax basis of the target's assets to fair market value as indicated on the books of the target company. (See Section 5.)

2.   TRANSACTION COSTS FOR PURCHASERS

2.1   Transfer Taxes

A transfer tax is payable on the acquisition of real estate located in the Netherlands. The transfer tax is payable by the purchaser of the real estate in an amount equal to 6 percent of the greater of the purchase price paid for such real estate or the fair market value of such real estate. The acquisition of shares in a qualifying real estate company—that is, a company 70 percent or more of whose assets consist of real estate located in the Netherlands—also is subject to the 6 percent transfer tax.

2.2   Value-Added Tax

VAT is payable by the purchaser of assets in an amount equal to 19 percent of the fair market value of the transferred assets, including transferred goodwill. VAT becomes an actual cost only if it is due from an entity that does not fall within the scope of VAT—for example, a pure holding company—or from an entity that is not subject to VAT—for example, a group finance company. In other words, the VAT status of the purchaser determines whether such VAT is creditable or recoverable.

The transfer of an entire business or independent part (division) thereof, or the transfer of shares, is outside the scope of VAT.

2.3   Capital Taxes

No capital tax is payable on the acquisition of assets or shares except in some situations in which the acquired company was formed through an exempt share-for-share transaction. A disposal by the seller within five years after such a formation may result in a recapture of capital tax for the full amount for which an exemption previously was claimed (the clawback). Note that a disposal of shares within the framework of a subsequent capital-tax-exempt merger or internal reorganization does not trigger this claw back.

For a description of the 0.55 percent capital tax imposed on contributions to capital, see Section 4.2.

2.4   Tax Deductibility of Transaction Costs

(a) *Finance costs* As a rule of thumb, debt financing costs—including exchange rate losses and other costs incurred in obtaining a loan—normally are deductible for corporate income tax purposes so long as the interest on such debt is tax deductible. (See Section 4.1(c).)

(b) Other deal costs   In anticipation of legislation to be introduced to overturn a 2002 ruling by the Dutch Supreme Court, the tax treatment of costs related to the acquisition of shares can be summarized as follows:

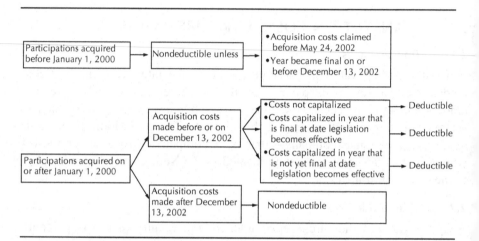

Costs incurred by newly incorporated companies related to the companies' establishment, such as for capital taxes and the costs of a civil law notary, are deductible for Dutch corporate income tax purposes.

(c) VAT   Even though the sale of shares is a VAT-exempt transaction, VAT on costs incurred by a seller in connection with the sale of shares in a company can be deducted if the seller was involved in the management of the company and if consideration was paid for the performance of those management services.

In principle, Dutch VAT is due on the transaction costs incurred by a purchaser. Depending on the VAT status of the purchaser, these VAT costs may be deducted. In general, a Dutch acquisition company will be a mere holding company and therefore will not be in a position to reclaim the input VAT incurred. In order to reclaim such input VAT, the Dutch acquisition company should be included in a VAT group with the Dutch target company or should itself qualify as an entity whose activities fall within the scope of VAT.

The chart on page 339 summarizes these rules.

3.   BASIS OF TAXATION FOLLOWING ASSET OR STOCK ACQUISITIONS

3.1   Asset Acquisitions

The taxpayer has discretion with regard to the depreciation method chosen for acquired assets so long as the depreciation method selected (1) conforms to the

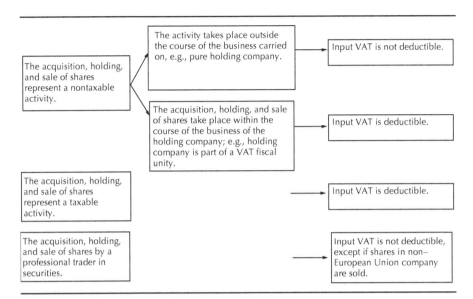

standard of sound business practice, (2) is supported by sound business reasons, and (3) is not intended to yield an incidental tax benefit. In general, goodwill acquired on asset purchases may be depreciated.

3.2   Stock Acquisitions

(a) Purchase price   The purchase price paid for stock is not recoverable through depreciation deductions. While a step-up in the tax basis of a company's assets generally is not permitted in the context of a purchase of that company's stock—that is, under Dutch law, there is no concept similar to a Section 338 election under US tax law—certain clawback rules will trigger an increase in the tax basis of the acquired company's assets in certain cases.

(b) Tax grouping   See Section 6.1 for a discussion of the fiscal unity concept in the Netherlands, which functions in a manner similar to the US consolidated-return tax rules.

4.   FINANCING OF ACQUISITIONS

4.1   Debt

(a) Withholding tax   The Netherlands does not impose withholding tax on interest payments.

(b) Deductibility of interest generally   Interest paid on debt incurred to finance the acquisition of a company from a third party generally is deductible for tax purposes so long as the terms and conditions of the debt are at arm's length. This is the case even if the Dutch participation exemption is available.

(c) Deductibility of interest: special rules for certain related-party loans   In some cases, certain base erosion rules may operate to restrict the deductibility of related-party interest expense. A company or individual that owns at least a one-third interest in a Dutch taxpayer company is treated as being related to that Dutch taxpayer company. Similarly, if a Dutch taxpayer company owns at least a one-third interest in another company, that other company and the Dutch taxpayer company are treated as related. Finally, if the Dutch taxpayer company and another company have a mutual direct or indirect shareholder that owns at least a one-third interest in each company, then those two companies are treated as related.

(i) Ultimate ownership of the transferred company does not change. If a transfer of shares is financed by related-party debt and the transfer does not change the ultimate ownership or control of the transferred company, the deductibility of interest paid on that debt is denied. This restriction on the deductibility of interest is not imposed if the taxpayer demonstrates to the satisfaction of the tax authorities that (1) the indebtedness and share transfer are supported by overriding sound business reasons or (2) the interest is effectively taxed in the hands of the recipient on a basis and at a rate comparable to Dutch taxation.

(ii) Acquired Dutch company joins a fiscal unity with the purchaser. If a transfer of shares in a Dutch company is financed with a related-party loan and a fiscal unity subsequently is formed between such company and the purchaser, then the deduction of interest expense by the fiscal unity is deferred for an eight-year period unless the taxpayer demonstrates to the satisfaction of the tax authorities that:

- The related-party indebtedness ultimately is funded by a loan obtained by the related-party creditor from a nonrelated person, such as a third-party financial institution, for the purpose of effectuating the stock acquisition, *and*

- The interest income on the related-party indebtedness is included in the related creditor's taxable income in the financial year in which such interest accrued or in the following financial year. It is *not* necessary, however, that the interest be subject to tax at a rate comparable to the Dutch rate.

Consequently, if all of the relevant criteria for tax-deductible acquisition financing are satisfied, it still is possible to utilize a creditor entity resident in a low-taxed jurisdiction. The second of the aforementioned two conditions is important to US companies, which commonly use a Dutch fiscal unity as a tax-planning tool. In a typical structure, a Dutch company (the parent in a Dutch fiscal unity) incurs intercompany debt to fund an acquisition, with the objective of utilizing the interest expense thereon to offset the profits of Dutch subsidiaries included in the same fiscal unity. The related creditor usually is a US entity. In this context, the purchaser may seek to avoid a current US tax on the creditor's receipt of interest income by utilizing US entity classification rules (the check-the-box regulations) to treat the US creditor as a disregarded entity. If the result of such an election is that the interest income is not taxed in the creditor's juris-diction, then the deductibility of the corresponding interest payments will be drastically limited during an eight-year period. Alternative structuring may then be required. Note that the use of hybrid financing instruments also may run afoul of this second condition.

(d) Thin capitalization Effective January 1, 2004, thin-capitalization rules have been enacted for Dutch corporate income tax purposes. These rules apply to all Dutch corporate taxpayers that form part of a domestic or international group of companies. The term *group* is defined as an economic entity whereby legal entities and corporations are related from an organizational point of view. The element of control is decisive and is determined on the basis of legal and benefi-cial control; for example, the voting rights of shares might not be in the hands of respective shareholders as a result of a deed of pledge. Consequently, the requirement of having to consolidate the results of one entity with another forms a guideline in establishing whether an entity is part of a group for thin-capitalization purposes. The deductibility of interest paid on genuine third-party loans will not, however, be limited by the thin-capitalization rules.

If the average level of debt does not exceed three times the average tax equity of the Dutch corporate taxpayer, no limitation is imposed on the deduct-ibility of interest expense; that is, a 3:1 safe harbor ratio exists. In the determi-nation of the average debt position for this purpose, the balance of loans payable and loans receivable is taken into account, but loans on which no interest is due (for business reasons) and loans on which the interest is not deductible because of other anti-tax-abuse rules are excluded.

If the 3:1 ratio is exceeded, then the interest paid on borrowings—including the costs of borrowings—will be disallowed proportionally in relation to the por-tion of the loans exceeding the safe harbor ratio, less a threshold of €500,000.

In Dutch acquisition structures, the Dutch fiscal unity concept typically is relied on to offset the acquisition interest costs against the Dutch target's prof-its. If a fiscal unity is formed between the Dutch acquisition company and the Dutch target company, then the tax equity of the fiscal unity is calculated through consolidation of the balance sheet of all member companies of that particular fiscal unity and adjusted for any differences between the commercial and tax valuations if any. In other words, the goodwill that is included in the purchase price of the shares in the Dutch target company must be eliminated for purposes of calculating the tax equity of the fiscal unity (taxpayer).

Alternatively, the group ratio may apply at the request of the Dutch corporate taxpayer if the commercial consolidated debt/equity ratio of the ultimate parent company of the group to which the Dutch corporate taxpayer belongs exceeds the commercial debt/equity ratio of the Dutch corporate taxpayer.

4.2   Equity

If a Dutch acquisition company is capitalized with equity, a 0.55 percent Dutch capital tax is due in an amount equal to 0.55 percent of the greater of the value of the contribution to the Dutch company or the nominal value of the shares issued by the Dutch company. The capital tax is a transaction in nature and is paid each time capital is put into a company. This capital tax is deductible for Dutch corporate income tax purposes. Note that various exemptions to the capital tax exist, including exemptions for hybrid financing instruments.

5.   MERGERS

Because of the Dutch participation exemption (covered in Section 7.1), most share transactions take the form of a sale of shares. Profits realized on the disposal of a participation qualifying for the Dutch participation exemption are not subject to corporate income tax.

A business merger or demerger may be executed on a tax-free basis if:

- The transfer is made at tax book value.
- All companies involved use the same method of calculating their profit for corporate income tax purposes.
- All companies involved cannot have losses that are available for carry-forward.
- The predominant reason for the transaction is not the avoidance or deferral of tax (the business motives test).

Under the business motives test, tax-free rollover treatment is available only if the transaction is motivated predominantly by valid business considerations—for example, rationalization of the activities of the entities involved in the transaction. A transaction is arguably presumed not to be motivated predominantly by valid business considerations if the shares in the contributing/dividing and/or acquiring company are sold to a nonrelated party within three years after the transaction. The taxpayer may rebut that presumption by demonstrating to the satisfaction of the tax authorities that the business motives test was in fact satisfied. It is also possible to request an advance ruling on this issue.

A merger or demerger also may trigger a 0.55 percent Dutch capital tax, but an exemption may be available. In the case of a demerger, the exemption may be recaptured if the business motives test is not met.

Due to the participation exemption most share transactions take place via sale-and-purchase agreements. Profits realized on the disposal of a qualifying participation are not subject to corporate income tax. If the participation exemption is not available, a share-for-share merger may be a solution. A company's acquisition of shares in another company in exchange for its own shares is regarded as a share-for-share merger. If certain criteria are met, the disposing shareholder does not report any gain realized from the disposal of the shares. The existing book values of the disposed shares are shifted to the newly acquired stock (rollover facility). If all shares have been acquired, a fiscal unity can be established.

If a transaction is executed through a business merger or demerger and if a transfer of hidden reserves and/or goodwill previously took place, certain clawback rules may apply to cause an adjustment to the basis of assets.

6.   OTHER STRUCTURING AND POSTDEAL ISSUES

6.1   Creation of Local-Country Tax Groups

The typical acquisition structure in the Netherlands is as follows: A Dutch acquisition company is organized with a combination of equity and (shareholder) debt. (See the chart on page 344.)

The Dutch fiscal unity concept is relied on to offset the acquisition interest expenses against the Dutch target's profits. Because the members of a fiscal unity are treated as a single taxable entity for Dutch corporate income tax purposes, profits and losses of companies within the fiscal unity can, in principle, be immediately offset in a manner similar to the US consolidated-return tax rules. Utilized in the acquisition context, the fiscal unity mechanism effectively permits the target company to finance its own acquisition.

The requirements that must be satisfied in order for a parent company to include a direct or indirect Dutch resident subsidiary in a fiscal unity as of a particular starting date are that (1) the parent company must have full ownership of at least 95 percent of the shares (by vote and by value) of the Dutch subsidiary; (2) the Dutch subsidiary must have the same financial year as the parent; and (3) within three months of the desired starting date, the companies must file with the tax authorities a request for fiscal unity status. Note that under certain conditions, a branch of a foreign company can become part of a Dutch fiscal unity—either as a parent company or as a subsidiary.

Achieving such a fiscal unity structure maximizes the opportunities for utilizing debt financing costs to reduce the corporate income tax costs of the new group and therefore to reduce that group's effective tax rate.

6.2   Repatriation of Profits

Dividend distributions within a fiscal unity are not subject to Dutch (dividend withholding) tax and are neither deductible by the payor nor taxable to the

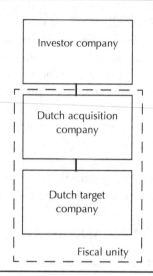

recipient. Further, under the Dutch participation exemption, dividend payments received from Dutch subsidiaries are not subject to withholding tax even if the subsidiaries are not part of the fiscal unity.

In other cases, dividend distributions—including redemptions treated as dividend distributions—generally are subject to a 25 percent Dutch dividend withholding tax. In addition to potential relief from this withholding tax pursuant to an applicable tax treaty, the European Union parent/subsidiary directive reduces the withholding rate to zero if the European Union investor company holds 25 percent of the shares of the Dutch distributing company—reduced to 10 percent in certain circumstances—for a period of 12 months.

6.3   Participation Exemption for Corporate Shareholders

For a discussion of the Dutch participation exemption, see Section 7.1.

6.4   Preservation of Existing Tax Attributes

Tax losses may be lost in the event of a substantial change of 30 percent or more in the ultimate ownership or control of a loss company. In the event of such a change, prechange tax losses cannot offset postchange profits unless both a passive-investment test and an activity test are satisfied.

- **Passive-investment test.** For a period of at least nine months in both the year of the loss and the year to which the loss is to be carried, no more than 50 percent of the group's assets may consist of portfolio investments.

- **Activity test.** Immediately prior to the change in ultimate control, the loss company's business activities must not have been reduced by more than 70 percent compared with its business activities at the beginning of the first year in which tax losses were incurred. In addition, at the time of the change in ultimate control, there must be no intention to reduce the loss company's business activities by more than 70 percent compared with its business activities at the beginning of the first year in which tax losses were incurred (scale-down of operations).

6.5   Receipts under Warranties or Indemnities

If a seller makes a payment to the purchaser due to a breach of warranty or pursuant to an indemnity provision, such payment is treated as a modification to the purchase price if the purchase agreement specifies such treatment and if the Dutch participation exemption applies to the purchaser's ownership of shares acquired pursuant to the purchase agreement.

7.   DISPOSALS

7.1   Disposals at the Dutch Acquisition Company Level

The following illustrates a disposal at the Dutch acquisition company level.

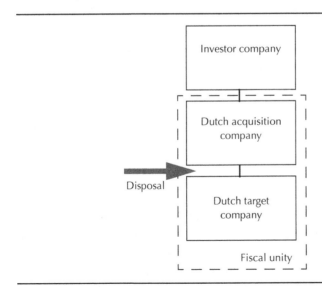

In general, any capital gain realized by a Dutch acquisition company upon the sale of Dutch or non-Dutch subsidiaries is exempt from tax under the Dutch participation exemption.

To qualify under the Dutch participation exemption, several requirements must be satisfied. First, at least 5 percent of the nominal issued and paid-in share capital of the subsidiary's shares must be held by the Dutch company. Second, the shares must not be held as stock—that is, no cash-box company. Based on case law and discussions in Parliament, shares of a subsidiary are considered held as stock if (1) they are acquired for the sole purpose of subsequently disposing of them; (2) the subsidiary does not conduct an active trade or business; and (3) either (a) the majority of the subsidiary's assets consist of cash and/or assets that without delay can be converted into cash without realizing a considerable loss or (b) the subsidiary has no assets.

If the subsidiary at issue is not a Dutch company, two additional requirements must be satisfied. First, the shares must not be held as a passive portfolio investment. Second, the subsidiary must be subject to a tax on its profits. Note that the focus of the second requirement is on whether the subsidiary is subject to tax, *not* on whether it is actually required to pay tax.

The principal advantages of the Dutch participation exemption rules compared with other such rules are that no minimum holding period requirements are imposed and that all benefits, including dividends and capital gains, are fully tax-exempt.

Note that because the term *benefits* includes all positive and negative results from a qualifying shareholding—a loss with respect to a qualifying participation generally is not deductible for tax purposes. In some circumstances, however, a loss suffered by a Dutch company upon the liquidation of a subsidiary is excluded from the Dutch participation exemption and as a consequence, may be tax deductible.

7.2   Disposal at the Investor Company Level

The chart on page 347 illustrates a disposal at the investor company level.

A disposal at the investor company level generally is not subject to capital gains taxation in the Netherlands. However, care must be taken when a non-Dutch investor company—for example, a British Virgin Islands resident partnership—holds more than 5 percent of the shares in the Dutch acquisition company and the exit takes the form of a sale of the shares of that Dutch company. If the non-Dutch investor company cannot demonstrate that it held its shares in the Dutch company as part of the investor's active business—that is, that the investor company was actively involved in the management of the Dutch company—then all of the profits (including capital gains, dividends, and interest) arising out of that share ownership may be subject to Dutch corporate income tax under Dutch substantial-interest legislation. By contrast, if the shares were held as part of the investor's active business, a capital gain on the disposition should not be subject to Dutch tax. Note that this potential Dutch tax cost may be

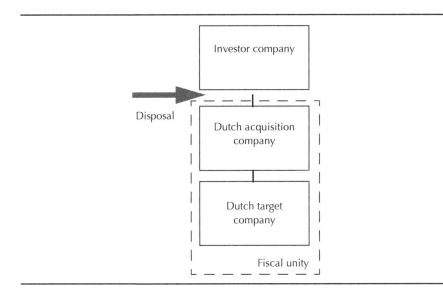

reduced under an applicable tax treaty between the Netherlands and the investor company's country of residence.

7.3   Deferred Consideration and Earn-Outs

An agreement qualifies as an earn-out for corporate income tax purposes if the seller and purchaser agree that the acquisition price depends in part on the target company's future profits. Changes in the value of the earn-out receivable are covered by the Dutch participation exemption for the seller. From the standpoint of the purchaser, changes in the value of the earn-out liability increase or decrease the purchase price if the Dutch participation exemption applies to the shareholding.

   If the participation exemption does not apply, then any future value changes to the estimated amount of the earn-out receivable (for the seller) and the estimated amount of the earn-out liability (for the buyer) are not covered by the participation exemption for the seller and do not increase or decrease the acquisition cost for the buyer. The valuation of the earn-out receivable or liability at the time of the sale and purchase is, therefore, crucial, since that valuation fixes the basis for a possible future tax-deductible loss and/or a taxable profit for the seller and buyer, respectively.

7.4   Payments under Warranties or Indemnities

Payments made by the seller due to a breach of warranty or pursuant to an indemnity provision are covered by the Dutch participation exemption, if applicable. If not, such payments would be deductible—and receipts would be taxable.

8.   PREPARING A TARGET COMPANY FOR SALE

Usually, presale planning is not relevant due to the Dutch participation exemption covered in Section 7.1. However, presale planning *is* important if the purchaser wants to buy only specific assets, or if the seller wishes to retain certain assets, or if the disposal is not sheltered from tax by the Dutch participation exemption.

If the seller is selling only a division or part of a trading business or if a specific liability must be excluded from the sale, a hive-down method of purchase may be considered.

Hiving down involves the transfer of specific trade and assets of a company to another newly formed group company. Such a transfer may be accomplished by way of a tax-free rollover, resulting in the deferral of corporate income tax on value in excess of the book value of the transferred assets. (See Section 5.)

If such a hive-down is accomplished within a fiscal unity, the sale may trigger a revaluation of transferred assets and liabilities to fair market value as determined at the moment immediately prior to separation of the fiscal unity or to fair market value at the moment the assets were transferred.

9.   DEMERGERS

See Section 5.

10.   LISTINGS AND INITIAL PUBLIC OFFERINGS

In the Netherlands, no special tax rules apply to an acquisition of shares that is accomplished by way of an offer to the public.

The immediate implications to an existing parent as a result of a listing of its subsidiary are:

- If the parent sells some of its existing subsidiary shares to the public, that sale generally is not subject to capital gains taxation in the Netherlands due to application of the Dutch participation exemption. For requirements associated with the Dutch participation exemption, see Section 7.1.

- If the subsidiary issues new shares to the public, the parent will not itself have sold any stock and so will not be subject to a tax charge. Such an issuance of new subsidiary shares may, however, cause the subsidiary to cease being part of a fiscal unity with its parent due to the parent's reduced percentage of ownership. The requirements for fiscal unity are covered in Section 6.1.

The issuance of new shares by the listed company is subject to a 0.55 percent Dutch capital tax.

NEW ZEALAND

INTRODUCTION

This chapter details the principal tax issues that are relevant to purchasers and sellers engaged in the transfer of ownership of a New Zealand trade or business. Unless otherwise stated, it is generally assumed that all sellers and purchasers are New Zealand companies with limited liability.

The main taxes to be considered are:

- **Income tax.** This is a 33 percent tax on profits earned by a company. Companies with common shareholding can transfer tax losses among themselves and elect to be taxed on a group basis.
- **Goods-and-services tax (GST).** This is a transaction-based tax and is levied on the supply of goods and services in New Zealand. The main rate of GST is 12.5 percent. However, some transactions are not subject to GST: principally, the transfer of a going concern and supplies to nonresidents. In addition, some supplies of financial services are exempt from GST.

There is no capital gains tax in New Zealand. However, income tax may apply to the sale of specific capital assets and to sales when the asset was acquired with the purpose of resale or as part of a business or a moneymaking plan.

1.   ACQUISITIONS

1.1   Asset Acquisitions

From a purchaser's perspective, it is often beneficial to acquire assets rather than shares. In an asset deal, the purchaser is able to cherry-pick the sought-after assets from the target company and leave behind those assets and liabilities that are not desired.

Additionally, in an asset deal there is opportunity to optimize the allocation of the purchase price so as to maximize postacquisition tax deductions.

An asset acquisition generally enables the purchaser to avoid exposure related to any historical liabilities of the target company. Liabilities associated with the target company remain the responsibility of the vendor and do not become the responsibility of the purchaser unless the parties agree to the transfer of specific liabilities.

1.2   Share Acquisitions

From a purchaser's perspective a share acquisition is generally less attractive than an asset purchase. There is generally no step-up permitted in the tax basis of the target company's assets. In addition, a share acquisition may result in the purchaser's effectively bearing all historical and future ongoing tax and nontax liabilities of the target company.

When the target company has tax losses and imputation credits (see Section 4.2) brought forward, these will be extinguished unless sufficient shareholder continuity is maintained—generally measured through to the ultimate individual shareholders. Forty-nine percent continuity must be maintained to retain losses, and 66 percent continuity for imputation credits.

Therefore, a purchaser may require comprehensive warranties and indemnities from the vendor. Additionally, the purchaser is likely to require a more detailed due diligence review for a share acquisition.

As indicated in Section 1.1, an important commercial advantage of a share acquisition is that contracts between the target company and third parties may remain in force and do not need to be assigned or renegotiated with the third party, although some contracts may contain change-of-control provisions that may result in the termination or other amendment to the contract in the event of a change in ownership of the target company.

2.   TRANSACTION COSTS FOR PURCHASERS

2.1   Income Tax

In general, acquisition expenses receive the same treatment as the assets purchased.

For a share acquisition, therefore, the costs generally constitute a nondeductible capital item unless the purchaser is in the business of buying and selling shares. By comparison, an asset acquisition allows for such expenses to be allocated to the assets purchased. Therefore, the expenses add to the basis of the assets and are deductible to the purchaser in determining gain or loss at the time of disposal. Furthermore, to the extent that those assets are depreciable, a tax deduction is available over time for the acquisition costs.

2.2   Goods-and-Services Tax

(a) Asset acquisitions In principle, the sale of assets constitutes a taxable supply for GST purposes, imposing GST at a rate of 12.5 percent.

However, when the assets are sold as a going concern, no GST applies. A going concern is generally a group of assets that, on their own, constitute a trade or business. Both the vendor and the purchaser must agree in writing that the transfer will be a going concern.

If GST is charged on the supply and the purchaser makes or will make supplies subject to GST, then the GST charged by the vendor can be recovered. GST is an absolute cost to the purchaser only when the purchaser makes any supplies that are not subject to GST.

(b) Share acquisitions There is no GST tax on the sale and purchase of shares. Furthermore, there is no GST input tax credit available to the purchaser on nondeductible expenditures incurred in relation to the purchase of shares.

2.3   Duties

There is generally no stamp duty or capital duty on the transfer of real and personal property in New Zealand. However, stamp duty does apply in certain very limited circumstances.

Gift duty is levied progressively on transactions that involve consideration at other than market value—up to a rate of 25 percent. It is generally accepted that a commercial transaction between third parties has no element of gift, and therefore is not subject to gift duty.

3.   BASIS OF TAXATION FOLLOWING ASSET OR STOCK ACQUISITIONS

3.1   Asset Acquisitions

(a) Depreciable assets The purchaser is able to step up the value of depreciable assets to maximize depreciation claims, provided that (1) the stepped-up value is the amount agreed between the vendor and purchaser, (2) the value can be supported by a valuation, and (3) the vendor is not a related party. When there is no purchase price allocation agreed between the parties, a step-up may still be available if supported by an appropriate valuation.

(b) Treatment of goodwill Goodwill is generally not deductible for tax purposes. Certain specific types of intangible property may, however, be depreciated. To be depreciable, such property must have a fixed legal life and therefore usually involves the right to use something for a fixed period. Examples of such depreciable property include the right to use a copyright, a patent or trademark, or a premium upon acquisition of a leasehold interest in land.

(c) Inventory Inventory is transferred on revenue account such that the sale is included in the vendor's profit and the amount paid becomes the basis of the inventory for the purchaser—subject to antiavoidance provisions when inventory is transferred at other than market value.

(d) Debt As a general principle, when debt receivables are sold as part of the transfer of a business, they represent a capital asset. As a result, any subsequent loss or gain on realization is on capital account. When debts are held on capital

account, a deduction for bad debts is not available. However, various potential solutions are available.

(e) Other assets and liabilities   Liabilities and provisions transferred are generally on capital account, and payments made by the purchaser to meet the liabilities are generally not deductible. One exception to this general rule is employee liabilities transferred between associated parties. Although buyer's payment of seller's liabilities may not result in a deduction for the buyer, the assumption of liabilities should increase the step-up in asset basis available to the buyer.

3.2   Share Acquisitions

(a) Purchase price   The purchase price forms the base cost of the purchaser's shares in the target company. The underlying base cost in the target company's assets does not change, and there is no step-up available in the tax basis of assets. However, some exceptions apply when the target company was previously a member of a tax-consolidated group. Accounting goodwill arising in the financial statements is not tax deductible.

(b) Tax groupings

(i) Income tax   Companies in a wholly owned group can elect to enter a tax-consolidated group, which enables the group to be treated as a single taxpayer for income tax purposes. The primary advantages of tax consolidation are that assets transferred between group members are ignored for tax purposes, and compliance requirements are simplified.

However, companies with a common shareholding of 66 percent or greater can offset losses between each other without forming a tax-consolidated group.

(ii) GST   Companies with a common shareholding of 66 percent or greater can group register for GST purposes. The impacts of GST group registration are that taxable transactions between companies in the GST group are ignored and that only a single GST return is filed by the representative member of the group for the group as a whole.

4.   FINANCING OF ACQUISITIONS

4.1   Debt

Specific tax issues related to the overall level of borrowings and the interest charged on this debt are:

- Withholding tax
- Deductibility of interest
- Thin capitalization
- Transfer pricing

- Specific antiavoidance
- Accrual rules

(a) Withholding tax

(i) Resident withholding tax   Interest paid to New Zealand residents is subject to resident withholding tax (RWT) at 19.5, 33, or 39 percent. The applicable rate of RWT depends on whether the recipient has supplied an Inland Revenue Department (IRD) number to the payer and whether an election has been made to apply a certain rate to a particular source of interest income. However, companies generally adopt a 33 percent RWT rate.

RWT does not apply when the lender and borrower are in a group—that is, 66 percent or more common shareholding—or when the lender has a certificate of exemption. A certificate of exemption can be obtained in a variety of circumstances, but these include situations in which the lender is a bank or has turnover exceeding NZD$2 million New Zealand.

(ii) Nonresident withholding tax (NRWT)   Interest paid or accrued to nonresidents is subject to Nonresident withholding tax (NRWT) at rates of 0, 10, or 15 percent depending on whether the payer is registered under the approved-issuer levy regime or whether New Zealand has a double-tax agreement with the recipient jurisdiction.

The rate of withholding tax imposed on interest is a minimum tax in the case of nontreaty countries and related-party lenders.

The NRWT tax can be reduced to 0 percent if interest is paid to a nonrelated party, and the security and borrower are appropriately registered with the IRD. In that case, approved-issuer levy is payable on the gross interest amount instead, at a rate of 2 percent. The levy is deductible to the payer.

(b) Deductibility of interest

In general, interest incurred by companies is deductible subject to thin-capitalization rules, transfer-pricing rules, and specific antiavoidance rules.

Some further restrictions apply to interest deductions for closely held companies that elect to become qualifying companies (as a result, they are treated in a similar manner to partnerships) and those that derive certain types of exempt income.

(c) Thin capitalization

New Zealand resident companies controlled by a single or associated nonresident or nonresidents (50 percent or greater ownership interest) are subject to thin-capitalization rules. Under the rules, a deduction for interest is partially denied when the taxpayer's total interest-bearing debt/gross asset ratio exceeds 75 percent and 110 percent of the worldwide group ratio.

All interest-bearing debt is included in the calculation—that is, not just related-party and/or overseas borrowings. Gross assets are measured principally by using financial accounting recognition policies. Noninterest-bearing liabilities are not netted off the gross asset figure. An on-lending concession can be applied to reduce both debt and assets when the funds are subsequently lent to a third party.

(d) Transfer pricing The New Zealand transfer-pricing rules are based on principles of the Organization for Economic Co-operation and Development (OECD) and require cross-border related-party transactions to result in an arm's-length return.

When loans between a New Zealand company and an overseas related party are not on an arm's-length basis, the transfer-pricing rules may apply to restrict interest deductions.

(e) Specific antiavoidance When New Zealand borrowing is undertaken that is used for investing in non–New Zealand subsidiaries, antiavoidance rules apply:

- To deny an interest deduction when the borrowing is from a related party overseas and the dividends received from the overseas subsidiary are fully tax relieved in New Zealand, or
- To reduce New Zealand tax relief related to overseas investments when New Zealand is a conduit and borrowings are regarded as excessive.

(f) Accrual rules Specific rules apply to debt instruments in New Zealand. These act to treat amounts that might not otherwise be regarded as interest as if they are interest. Examples include certain foreign exchange gains and losses and the difference between face value and acquisition costs for discounted securities.

4.2   Equity

In New Zealand there is no tax or duty imposed on the issuance of new shares.

Dividends paid on shares are not deductible to the company paying the dividend. The dividend imputation system applies to all dividends paid by New Zealand resident companies. It allows tax paid by resident companies to flow through to shareholders in the form of credits attaching to dividends paid. Imputation credits are generated through the payment of tax to the IRD at 33 percent and can be carried forward by companies from year to year, provided that 66 percent continuity of shareholding is maintained.

Dividends between wholly commonly owned companies are exempt income to the recipient.

Resident individual shareholders in receipt of dividends with imputation credits attached may offset these credits against their personal tax liability; individual tax rates range from 19.5 to 39 percent. Resident corporate shareholders in receipt of dividends with imputation credits attached may offset these credits against their liability, except when the dividend is exempt from income tax.

Nonresident shareholders may also benefit from dividend imputation under the foreign investor tax credit regime when the nonresident investor receives the same cash amount that a resident investor would despite the dividend's having been subject to NRWT.

This is achieved by a company's paying a supplementary dividend in addition to the original dividend. The supplementary dividend equals the liability to NRWT when dividends are fully imputed. Its payment entitles the company to a tax credit of an equivalent amount.

4.3   Key Nontax Issues

(a) Foreign ownership restrictions   A nonresident must obtain approval from the Overseas Investment Commission if the proposed investment exceeds NZD$50 million. For certain types of investments (particularly land), approval may be required for smaller investments. Approval is usually forthcoming because the process is generally considered a formality. There are also certain infrastructure companies wherein foreign ownership is restricted, but these are relatively rare.

(b) Commerce commission   The Commerce Act of 1986 restricts acquisitions that are likely to have the effect of substantially lessening competition in a particular market or industry. A clearance or authorization may need to be sought from the Commerce Commission when a dominant position is likely to arise from an acquisition.

5.   MERGERS

New Zealand has a set of tax and company-law rules—known as the Amalgamation Regime—which governs mergers of companies. When two or more companies amalgamate, then from the date of amalgamation, the company— either one of the amalgamating companies or a completely new company— nominated by shareholders succeeds to all rights and obligations of the others. The other companies are struck off the Companies Register.

Wholly owned groups of companies can be amalgamated by means of a simple short-form procedure. Groups of companies not wholly owned must amalgamate under a more complicated procedure referred to as a long-form amalgamation.

Amalgamation is an alternative to a share purchase or can be used as part of a subsequent restructuring.

As a general rule, the amalgamated company steps into the shoes of each amalgamating company and takes over all rights and responsibilities from both commercial and tax perspectives.

It should be noted, however, that some contracts have antiavoidance clauses that dictate that an amalgamated company does not automatically succeed to the rights and responsibilities under that contract.

Tax implications arising on amalgamation depend largely on whether or not the transaction is a qualifying amalgamation. Qualifying amalgamations can normally be carried out tax free. In particular, there is no transfer of assets or liabilities for tax purposes, since they are assumed to have been held throughout by the same party.

A qualifying amalgamation is defined as any amalgamation in which:

- Each of the amalgamating companies and the amalgamated company are New Zealand tax resident.
- No company party to the amalgamation derives only exempt income.
- An election to treat the amalgamation as a nonqualifying amalgamation is not filed.

An amalgamation that is not a qualifying amalgamation may give rise to a number of tax issues, including that assets can be deemed to be transferred from the amalgamating company at their market value, which may result in obtaining a step-up in the tax basis and increased depreciation deductions in the amalgamated company and, conversely, a clawback of depreciation deductions to the amalgamating companies.

6.   OTHER STRUCTURING AND POSTDEAL ISSUES

6.1   Creation of Local-Country Tax Groups

(a) Income tax   Refer to Section 3.2(b).

(b) GST   Refer to Section 3.2(b).

6.2   Repatriation of Profits

There are a number of ways to repatriate funds to holding companies outside New Zealand. They include:

- **By repaying loans.** No New Zealand tax cost
- **By paying interest.** Subject to thin-capitalization and transfer-pricing restrictions as noted earlier and subject to NRWT
- **By paying dividends.** No net New Zealand tax cost if fully imputed. Generally, this means paid out of tax-paid reserves.
- **By return of capital.** Generally, no New Zealand tax cost so long as the return meets certain minimum requirements: 15 percent of the market value of the company returned, reduced to 10 percent if approved by the tax authorities

- **By advance to shareholders.** Interest should be charged to meet transfer-pricing rules; interest received is taxable in New Zealand; and foreign tax withheld from interest payments is generally creditable in New Zealand.

Refer to Sections 4.1 and 4.2 for further details on the tax treatment of interest and dividends, respectively.

6.3   Noncore Disposals

As noted earlier, New Zealand does not have a capital gains tax. There are no specific rules regarding the disposal of noncore acquisitions. The treatment depends on the intentions of the acquirer at the time of acquisition. If there was a purpose of disposal at the time of acquisition or the shares or assets were acquired as part of a profit-making scheme or a business operation—that is, a share trader—any gain on sale will be taxable.

Note that in making this decision, it is the intention of the *direct* acquirer that is important. Therefore, if the noncore business is in a subsidiary of the company that has been the subject of the recent sale transaction, what is important is the intention of the direct holding company at the time that it originally acquired the shares in the subsidiary.

6.4   Preservation of Existing Tax Attributes

(a) Tax losses   Losses can be carried forward by companies (including branches of overseas companies), provided there is at least 49 percent continuity of ultimate ownership from the time the losses are incurred to the time they are utilized. There are no ownership continuity provisions for the carryforward of losses for individuals. Losses cannot be carried back.

There is no same-business test for the carryforward of losses.

Losses incurred by companies can also be used to offset income of other companies in the same group when there is at least 66 percent commonality of shareholding.

There are certain potential planning opportunities available to freshen or utilize losses before a shareholding change.

There are current provisions applying to special partnerships—basically, limited liability partnerships—that prevent resident but not nonresident special partners from offsetting losses against other income. The government has introduced legislation to repeal this restriction. The proposed changes are expected to apply retrospectively from April 1, 2004.

(b) Imputation credits   Imputation credits can be carried forward by companies, provided there is at least 66 percent continuity of ownership.

6.5   Receipts under Warranty or Indemnity

Amounts received by a purchaser of shares and resulting from a warranty or indemnity with the vendor are generally considered to be a nontaxable capital receipt. This position is usually protected by specifically stating that payment is an adjustment to purchase price. Payments related to an asset acquisition or paid to the company that has been acquired can be considered taxable income depending on the underlying reason for the payment; that is, if the cost is deductible, the warranty claim is generally taxable.

The situation is usually dealt with by including a gross-up clause in a sale-and-purchase agreement, stipulating that if a warranty payment is subject to tax in the hands of the purchaser, the vendor must gross up the payment at the prevailing tax rate.

7.   DISPOSALS

7.1   Share Disposals

A vendor usually prefers the sale of shares because of the opportunity to obtain a tax-free receipt and because of its relative simplicity.

As noted earlier, New Zealand does not have a specific capital gains tax. Consequently, profit on the sale of shares is not subject to income tax, provided the shares are held by the vendor as capital assets. This applies to all taxpayers, including companies and individuals.

However, profit on the sale of shares may be subject to income tax if the shares were held on revenue account or if the vendor is in the business of dealing in shares. The government has introduced legislation to benefit nonresident investors who are currently subject to tax in New Zealand on share sale transactions that are not taxable in their home country. To qualify for the exemption, nonresidents must be exempt from tax in their own jurisdiction and resident in an acceptable country; this should include the majority of countries with which New Zealand has a double-tax agreement. The proposed changes are expected to apply retrospectively from April 1, 2004.

As noted in Section 1.2, on a share disposal the purchaser generally takes over any historical and future liabilities of the target company. Accordingly, comprehensive warranties and indemnities may be required from the vendor.

There are a number of specific antiavoidance provisions that address share-dealing transactions. The share-dealing provisions are designed to counter dividend stripping and loss-utilization arrangements.

7.2   Asset Disposals

On an asset sale, a portion of the sale proceeds may be subject to income tax.

The sale of revenue assets generates taxable income to the vendor.

As noted earlier, inventory is held on revenue account so any amount received is taxable income.

The sale of fixed assets results in a taxable recovery of previously claimed depreciation. Proceeds in excess of original cost generally—although not always—give rise to a nontaxable capital gain.

Gains resulting from the sale of real property—that is, land and buildings—and personal property, including shares, acquired for the purpose of resale or as part of a dealing operation are subject to income tax. Profits on the sale of real property also may be taxable in certain other circumstances.

The disposal of goodwill is generally not subject to income tax. Therefore, the vendor usually wants to attribute as much of the sale proceeds as possible to goodwill.

Other amounts recovered generally give rise to nontaxable capital gains—subject to specific provisions related to assets acquired for the purpose of resale or as part of a business or money-making plan.

Following an asset disposal, the proceeds are locked into the company. These can generally be returned to the shareholder effectively tax free to the extent that tax has been paid on the income generated. When the income is a nontaxable capital gain, it can be returned to New Zealand resident shareholders tax free on a liquidation of the vendor company. In other circumstances some form of withholding tax generally applies when funds are returned to shareholders.

7.3   Deferred Consideration and Earn-Outs

In general, the tax implications from earn-outs payments and receipts are complex.

Depending on their wording, some earn-out clauses may constitute deferred property settlements. As a result, there may be an imputed interest element.

If the parties do not intend that there be an interest element in earn-out payments, it is usual to insert an appropriate clause in legal agreements to ensure that no interest is imputed. This is usually referred to as a lowest-price clause.

7.4   Payments under Warranties or Indemnities

As noted in Section 6.5, it is usual to include a clause in a sale-and-purchase agreement so that amounts paid by a vendor in relation to a warranty or indemnity are treated as deductible from the purchase consideration received.

8.   TRANSACTION COSTS FOR SELLERS

8.1   Income Tax

In general, costs incurred by a seller in relation to the sale of shares are non-deductible unless the share sale is taxable. In an asset sale, costs can usually be allocated across the assets sold and be treated the same as the asset to which they are allocated. In addition, a specific deduction is allowed for employment-related costs—for example, redundancy payments and transferred employee provisions—unless the parties are related.

8.2   GST

Refer to Section 2.2

8.3   Duties

Refer to Section 2.3

9.   PREPARING A TARGET COMPANY FOR SALE

9.1   Hive-Down of Assets

When the vendor is selling only a division or part of a trading business or when there is a specific liability that needs to be excluded from the sale, a hive-down method of purchase may be considered.

Due to various specific rules that apply to transfers between associated parties (as covered in Section 9.2), such a hive-down does not generally create any specific tax advantages.

In addition, there is a significant risk that the shares in the hive-down entity are acquired with the purpose of disposal such that any gain on the sale of the shares is taxable. However, in some circumstances, a hive-down may be preferred for commercial reasons.

9.2   Intragroup Transfer of Assets Being Retained

It may be desirable to transfer assets out of the group companies prior to sale if the assets in question are not to be included in the sale.

(a) General rules   In general, the tax implications arising from the transfer of assets follow the nature of the asset transferred. As such, the transfer of revenue assets generates taxable income to the transferor, whereas the transfer of capital assets results in nontaxable gains. However, in the case of capital assets, the transferor may have a taxable recovery of previously claimed depreciation.

GST is imposed on the transfer of assets between companies unless the supply constitutes a going concern (see Section 2.2) or the companies are within the same GST group (see Section 6.1).

There is no stamp duty payable; however, gift duty may require consideration (see Section 2.3).

The tax consequences arising from the sale and acquisition of assets are further outlined in Sections 1.1 and 7.2.

(b) Transfers between related parties   In general, the transfer of assets between related parties is deemed to occur at market value. An exception applies to transfers of trading stock or revenue account property that is deemed to have been transferred at cost when market value is less than cost.

(c) Transfers between consolidated group members   When an asset is transferred between members of a consolidated group, the transferee is deemed to have acquired the asset for the same amount and at the same time as it was acquired by the vendor.

Effectively, the transferee steps into the shoes of the transferor. As a result, fixed assets can be transferred between consolidated-group members without creating depreciation recapture or requiring new cost bases to be calculated.

Additionally, no gift duty is payable on asset transfers within consolidated groups.

Specific antiavoidance rules act to limit the benefits of consolidation when a company joins a consolidated group, or transfers an asset to a group member, or exits the consolidated group—for instance, by way of sale.

9.3   Presale Dividends

The tax treatment of dividends is covered in Section 4.2. This can be a useful planning tool prior to a share sale, especially in passing imputation credits to shareholders. Imputation credits are otherwise forfeited upon the change in shareholding. It also facilitates the removal of excess cash from the sale company.

A potential alternative when there is insufficient cash to fund a dividend is to undertake a taxable bonus issue of shares. This is deemed to be a dividend, but if imputation credits are attached, there is no tax payable by a corporate shareholder. This has the effect of converting excess imputation credits to capital, which can later be returned to shareholders tax free on liquidation or under specific capital reductions.

10.   DEMERGERS

In New Zealand there are no specific company-law provisions allowing demergers that result in a single company's being split into two or more entities. However, it is possible to achieve effective demergers through the process of transferring assets to a subsidiary and then transferring the shares in the subsidiary to shareholders.

A demerger involves a company's initially transferring appropriate assets to a subsidiary and then distributing shares in the demerged subsidiary directly to shareholders. The shareholders continue to hold their shares in the original company and also directly hold shares in the demerged subsidiary.

Usually, the shares are distributed to the shareholders in one of the following ways:

- In specie distribution of the shares in the subsidiary company
- Reduction of capital, which involves a company's reducing its own capital but not the number of shares on issue and then applying the funds to the acquisition of shares in the subsidiary company on behalf of the company's shareholders

10.1   Tax Treatment of Shareholders

The tax treatment to shareholders depends on how the demerger has been carried out.

When the demerger is effected by an in specie distribution, shareholders receive a taxable dividend. Furthermore, the cost base for the shares acquired in the demerged company is equal to the amount of the dividend received.

A demerger under the reduction-in-capital method involves a return of capital to shareholders. Consequently, when the value of the demerged business is equal to the capital returned and subject to meeting certain specified requirements, there are no immediate tax consequences to shareholders who hold the shares in the parent company on capital account. If the shares in the parent company were held on revenue account or if the demerged business has a higher value than the paid-up capital returned, a tax cost arises to the shareholders. Under the reduction-in-capital scenario, the cost base is split between the subsidiary company and the demerged company.

Any subsequent disposal of the new shares will not give rise to taxable income if the shares in the parent company are held on capital account and the shareholder is not in the business of share dealing.

10.2   Tax Treatment of the Distributing Company

The tax implications arising from the initial transfer of assets from the demerged company into the subsidiary company are the same as those for hive-down of assets as covered in Section 9.2

The tax treatment of distributing the shares to shareholders depends on how the demerger has been carried out. In the case of an in specie distribution, the distributing company determines the level of imputation credits to attach to the dividend paid and, therefore, the tax that the ultimate shareholders will have to pay.

A capital reduction reduces the paid-up capital (as calculated for tax purposes) in the distributing company, which reduces the amount that can later be returned to shareholders tax free. The reduction is offset by an equivalent increase in available subscribed capital in the demerged subsidiary.

10.3   Tax Treatment of the Distributed Subsidiary

With respect to the initial transfer of assets, the subsidiary company generally takes over the transferred assets and liabilities at their transfer values. Some limitations apply—for example, in relation to the cost base of depreciable assets.

There should be no direct tax implications for the company being distributed on a direct demerger.

11.   LISTINGS AND INITIAL PUBLIC OFFERINGS

11.1   Impact on the Tax Status of the Company

The tax status of a company is generally unaffected by a listing or initial public offering (IPO). However, tax attributes such as losses and imputation credits will be forfeited unless sufficient shareholder continuity is maintained: 49 percent for losses and 66 percent for imputation credits.

11.2   Complete Group Listing or IPO

On a listing of a group, it is not uncommon for a new company to be incorporated as the listed vehicle and for the shares in the existing parent company to be transferred into the new company. This structure has limited tax implications.

11.3   Flotation of a Subsidiary

Any profit derived from the parent company from the flotation of a subsidiary is not taxable unless the parent company is in the business of dealing in shares or has originally acquired the shares to resell them or as part of a profit-making plan.

If the subsidiary was a member of a tax-consolidated group (see Section 6.1), it will automatically leave the group when it is listed, and, consequently, deferred tax liabilities may crystallize on certain intragroup property transfers.

11.4   Issuance of New Shares by a Listed Company

The issuance of new shares by a listed company should not have any direct tax consequences for the company when the listed company is the parent of the group. But if a subsidiary is being listed, the issue of new stock may result in that subsidiary's leaving a tax group, with consequences as noted in Section 11.3.

The consideration paid becomes the investors' base cost in the stock.

The new issuance of shares increases the paid-up capital, which can later be returned to shareholders tax free under specific circumstances.

11.5   Disposal of Shares by Existing Shareholders

When the listing/IPO involves a disposal of shares by existing shareholders, the tax position for those shareholders is as outlined in Section 7.1.

NORWAY

INTRODUCTION

This chapter details the principal tax issues that are relevant to purchasers and sellers engaged in the transfer of ownership of a Norwegian trade or business. Unless otherwise stated, it is generally assumed that all sellers and purchasers are Norwegian companies with limited liability.

There are two categories of Norwegian companies with limited liability: *Aksjeselskap* (AS) and *Allmennaksjeselskap* (ASA). The tax rules are the same for these two categories of limited companies. Special tax rules applicable to shipping, electricity, and oil production businesses are beyond the scope of this discussion.

Significant changes in the tax law for 2004–2006 were proposed in 2004. The proposed tax law changes were expected to be acted upon by the Parliament in December 2004, and some of the proposed changes will come into force for the income year 2004. Comments on the proposed legislation are included in this chapter.

Ownership of a Norwegian company may be transferred in the form of a transfer of either stock or assets. Because the tax implications affecting these two forms differ significantly, the transaction structure should be considered during an early stage.

Norwegian tax law contains rules for tax-free mergers as well as for demergers. A merger or demerger entails a transfer of assets, rights, and liabilities from one company to another, according to which the shareholders in the transferor company exchange shares. Norwegian tax law generally does not recognize the concept of a tax-free share-for-share exchange.

The taxes that must be taken into account in connection with the transfer of a Norwegian company are:

- **Corporation tax.** The ordinary tax rate for companies is 28 percent. While Norwegian companies are taxed on a stand-alone basis, group contribution rules make it possible to transfer taxable income between companies within a tax group.
- **Value-added tax (VAT).** A sales tax of 24 percent is added to the sales price charged for goods and services; the proposed tax legislation would increase the rate to 25 percent effective January 1, 2005. Certain categories of sales are not subject to VAT.

- **Stamp duty.** When the deed that transfers the ownership of land and buildings is registered, the purchaser must pay a stamp duty equal to 2.5 percent of the property's fair market value.
- **Reregistration duties.** Reregistration duties on certain assets, such as vehicles, may be applicable.

Proposed tax legislation 2004-2006 are:

- **Tax exemption for corporate sales of shares.** Corporations would be exempt from tax on capital gains realized with respect to sales of shares after March 26, 2004. From the same date, it is proposed that corporate losses on such sales would not be deductible.
- **Tax exemption for dividends.** Dividends with respect to stock of corporations generally would be exempt from taxation effective January 1, 2004. Foreign corporate shareholders within the European Union/European Economic Area (EU/EEA) also would be exempt from Norwegian withholding tax.
- Exceptions to the proposed tax-exemption rules:
  - Gains or losses realized on shares in companies resident in low-taxed countries outside the EU/EEA still would be taxable or deductible.
  - Gains realized on shares in companies resident in countries outside the EU/EEA still would be taxable, provided that the shareholder has continuously owned less than 10 percent of the shares during the preceding two years.
  - Losses realized on shares in companies resident in countries outside the EU/EEA would not be deductible if the shareholder and/or closely related persons have continuously owned less than 10 percent of the shares during the preceding two years.
  - Dividends from companies resident in countries outside the EU/EEA would be taxable, provided that the shareholder has continuously owned less than 10 percent of the shares during the preceding two years.
- **Shareholder model.** Individuals would be taxed on dividends exceeding an after-tax, fixed, risk-free rate of interest based on the interest level for five-year government securities; the 2004 after-tax fixed risk-free interest rate was 3.3 percent. Capital gains on shares in excess of the risk-free interest rate amount during the ownership period would be taxed at a 28 percent rate, effective as of January 1, 2006.

1. ACQUISITIONS

1.1 Asset Acquisitions

An asset acquisition generally results in a step-up in the tax basis of the acquired assets. The consideration paid must be allocated between the different acquired assets.

Most tangible assets other than land are depreciable on a declining-balance method pursuant to rules specified in the depreciation system. Goodwill is also depreciable under these rules. Other intangible assets generally are not depreciable unless an obvious decrease in value can be demonstrated or the intangible asset has been acquired for a limited period of time. (See Section 3.1 for additional details on depreciation deductions for acquired assets.)

After an asset sale, the shareholders of the selling company have the option either of dissolving the company or of retaining it in existence. If the company is dissolved, the shareholders generally will be in the same net tax position as if the shares had been sold due to a system—the so-called RISK regulation—under which the shareholders obtain a step-up in the tax basis of their shares—generally measured by reference to the company's after-tax profit.

The proposed tax legislation would abolish the RISK system: it is proposed that from 2006 forward, a new shareholder model come into force. Under that model, *individual* shareholders would be taxed on the return on their investments in excess of an after-tax fixed-interest rate. Under a transitional rule that would be effective January 1, 2006, the RISK regulation could be used as a basis for estimating the tax-free dividend or the tax-free part of the gain. Under the new rules, dividends exceeding the risk-free interest rate simply may not be distributed, and the company is retained in existence. If the shareholder is a corporation, however, it is proposed that dividends and capital gains on shares would be exempt from taxation.

If the shareholders of the selling company choose to retain the company in existence following the asset sale, it is possible to defer taxation of the gain pursuant to rules specified in the depreciation system. However, a correction tax is imposed on the company if the untaxed portion of the gain is distributed as a dividend. The correction tax can be avoided by limiting dividends to the taxed portion of the gain. Correction tax that actually gets triggered will be neutralized when the gain is taxed under the rules governing deferred taxation of gains. For example, assume that a business asset is sold and that a capital gain of 1,000 arises. Of that gain, 20 percent (200) will be taxed in year one. In year two, 20 percent of the remaining gain of 800—that is 160—would be taxed, and so on until the entire gain is taxed. In year one, a correction tax arises if more than 200 is paid out as dividends. If, for example, the dividend amount is 300, a correction income on100 and a correction tax of 28 will arise. In year two, only 60 is paid out as dividends. After year two, 360 of the gain is paid out as dividends, and 360 of the gain is taxed. In year two, the correction income taxed in year one will be deducted. The Ministry of Finance has stated that the correction tax rules will be reviewed due to the shareholder model scheduled to come into force effective January 1, 2006. The correction tax rules likely will be abolished.[1]

1.2   Stock Acquisitions

If the transaction is structured as a stock acquisition, the purchaser cannot claim depreciation deductions with respect to the cost of the purchased shares. In addition, a step-up in the tax basis of the target company's assets is not permitted (i.e., Norwegian tax law has no concept similar to a Section 338 election under US tax law).

Sellers that owned their shares before certain tax law changes went into effect in 1992 may have been eligible for a step-up in the tax basis of their shares. However, certain restrictions prevent such a taxpayer from fully utilizing such tax basis in the event that the shares are disposed of at a loss. In addition, it may not be possible to fully utilize such tax basis in a case in which the company sells its assets and liquidates. Depending on the specific circumstances, such a shareholder, therefore, may prefer a stock sale rather than an asset sale. Other cases also may exist in which, due to the particular shareholder's individual tax position, it is more favorable to structure the deal as a stock sale rather than as an asset sale.

Under the proposed tax reform legislation, corporations would not be taxed on capital gains realized with respect to shares, and capital losses would not be deductible. It is proposed that these rules would come into force effective March 26, 2004. Thus, under the proposed legislation it may be more favorable for a corporate shareholder to structure a sale as a sale of shares rather than as a sale of assets.

Shareholders (including related parties) that are active in the company and that own, in the aggregate, directly or indirectly, shares carrying the right to two-thirds of the dividends or that otherwise are entitled to two-thirds of the dividends are subject to tax under special taxation rules that take into account the portion of the company's income attributable to the shareholder's work. Under these rules, capital income is segregated pursuant to certain rules, and the remaining income is taxed as personal income. If the conditions for the imposition of these special taxation rules are met for at least two months in a

---

1. The numbers used in this example are illustrative and not intended to represent a specific currency.

year, the special taxes are levied on the basis of the company's income for the full year. Shareholders subject to tax under these rules have the right to be reimbursed by the company for any such taxes. Purchasers of shares in companies that are liable for reimbursement of such taxes should take this liability into account in negotiating the purchase agreement.

Under the proposed tax reform legislation, these special taxation rules would be repealed effective as of 2006 and would be replaced by the shareholder model described earlier.

2. TRANSACTION COSTS FOR PURCHASERS

2.1 Transfer Taxes

(a) Stock purchases No stamp duty is payable on the transfer of stock.

(b) Asset purchases A stamp duty payable by the purchaser is imposed on a transfer of land and buildings in an amount equal to 2.5 percent of the fair market value of the transferred assets.

2.2 Value-Added Tax

(a) Stock purchases Stock transfers are not subject to VAT.

(b) Asset purchases A transfer of business assets that qualifies as the transfer of a business as a going concern is exempt from VAT (with input credit). Otherwise, a purchase of assets is subject to VAT in an amount equal to 24 percent of the purchase price. This tax must be paid in addition to the purchase consideration. The proposed tax legislation would increase the rate to 25 percent effective January 1, 2005.

When the buying company is itself subject to the VAT rules and is obliged to charge VAT on its sales—called outputs—it may recover VAT paid by it on its own purchases—called inputs. More particularly, a purchase of assets on which the seller has charged VAT is regarded as an input for the buyer. When the buyer is registered for VAT, the buyer may recover VAT paid on its own purchase (inputs), subject to certain limitations.

2.3 Capital Taxes

Limited companies are not subject to capital taxes.

2.4 Tax Deductibility of Transaction Costs

In an assessment of the tax treatment of transaction-related expenses, relevant factors include:

- Whether the cost is deductible as part of the ordinary conduct of a business or otherwise has the necessary connection to taxable income

- Whether the cost should be capitalized as part of the purchase price and if so, which asset it should be linked to
- Whether the cost is borne by the right person—that is, shareholder versus company cost

Under the proposed tax legislation, companies would be exempt from capital gains tax on shares, effective as of March 26, 2004. Correspondingly, expenses related to a company's acquisition of shares would not be deductible.

(a) Finance costs   Costs related to financing, including costs related to assistance in obtaining debt financing, are deductible.

Costs related to the formation of a company, as well as costs related to the issuance of new shares, also are deductible.

(b) Investigation and due diligence costs   Acquisition costs—such as costs related to analyses, contract negotiations, and due diligence review—are deductible.

As a general rule, costs related to an asset acquisition must be allocated among the various acquired assets and capitalized as part of the tax basis of such acquired assets. Similarly, costs related to a stock acquisition must be capitalized as part of the tax basis of the acquired stock. Under the proposed tax legislation, a corporation would be exempt from capital gains tax on shares, and the costs of acquiring shares would not be deductible.

(c) VAT treatment of expenses   Fees charged for assistance in obtaining debt financing or issuing stock are not subject to VAT. Therefore, bank and institutional fees generally do not carry VAT. In general, however, professional fees charged to Norwegian customers by advisers based in Norway *are* subject to VAT, even when the fees are related to debt or equity financing.

Norwegian VAT directly related to the issuance of stock that is charged to a VAT-registered Norwegian purchaser should be deductible under the regular rules.

3.   BASIS OF TAXATION FOLLOWING ASSET OR STOCK ACQUISITIONS

3.1   Asset Acquisitions

The tax treatment of capital assets discussed below applies to business assets and equipment used in taxable activity.

The tax basis of tangible assets other than land is depreciable. The declining-balance method is mandatory. The depreciation groups and percentage rates are:

(a)	Office machines, etc	30%
(b)	Acquired goodwill/business value	20%
(c)	Trucks, buses, taxicabs, vehicles for the disabled	20%
(d)	Cars, tractors, other vehicular machinery, instruments, fixtures, and furniture, etc.	20%
(e)	Ships, vessels, offshore rigs, etc.	14%
(f)	Aircraft, helicopters	12%
(g)	Power plants and constructions for distribution of electricity	5%
(h)	Buildings and construction, hotels, hostels, inns, etc.	4%[a]
(i)	Office buildings	2%

[a] While 4 percent is the general rule, under certain circumstances the rate could be 8 percent.

The foregoing rates are maximum rates; taxpayers may choose to use lower rates. In addition, taxpayers are also allowed to vary the rate from year to year, subject to the maximum rate cap.

As a general rule, the tax basis of intangible assets is depreciable only if an obvious decline in value can be demonstrated. Intangible assets with a limited life—such as patents or rights acquired for a limited period of time—may be depreciated on a straight-line basis over their useful lives. Acquired goodwill is depreciated up to 20 percent annually under the declining-balance system, as indicated in the table above.

It should be noted that on several occasions in the past few years, the tax authorities have questioned the amount of the purchase price allocated to goodwill, asserting that a portion of such amount should instead be allocated to nondepreciable assets such as brand names, trademarks, or government concessions.

3.2   Stock Acquisitions

(a) Purchase price   The purchase price paid for stock—including costs capitalized as part of the purchase price—is not recoverable through depreciation deductions. In addition, the acquired company retains its historical tax basis in its assets; no election is available to step up the tax basis of the acquired company's assets. Consequently, the acquisition does not give rise to additional depreciable tax basis at the level of the acquired company.

The present taxation of companies is based on a principle of full integration. This means that the company's profits are to be taxed only once, taking into account both the company and its shareholders. Double taxation of capital gains on shares is avoided through the opening-value-adjustment method—that is, the RISK method. This method takes into account the tax paid on retained profits during the ownership period. Each year, the opening value of the shares is to be adjusted upward or downward according to changes in the company's retained earnings during the ownership period. The opening value is increased if the company retains taxed profits. The opening value is reduced if dividend distributions exceed the current year's profit.

Under the proposed tax legislation, a transitional rule would permit individuals to use the RISK-adjusted value as the opening value under the shareholder model, which would come into force effective January 2006.

(b) Tax groupings   Although a consolidated system for the taxation of group companies, along the lines of a US consolidated-return group, does not exist, a group relief system applies to Norwegian corporations that are under common control. Two or more Norwegian corporations are under common control for this purpose if a common ultimate parent either Norwegian or foreign directly or indirectly owns stock of each corporation that represents more than 90 percent of such corporation's capital and voting power. The group relief system permits the transfer of taxable income to unprofitable group members, including to a new, debt-financed parent. (See Section 6.1(b) for a more detailed discussion of the group relief system.)

4.   FINANCING OF ACQUISITIONS

4.1   Debt

(a) Withholding tax   Norway does not charge withholding tax on interest payments regardless of whether the lender is a foreign person or a Norwegian. Dividend payments, by contrast, currently are subject to withholding tax. Under proposed tax legislation, dividends paid to corporate shareholders resident in EEA countries would be exempt from withholding tax, effective for payments on or after January 1, 2004.

Under corporate law, all material agreements between group companies must be in writing. When a loan agreement is executed, it is important that it possess the necessary characteristics of a loan rather than of an equity interest, so that interest payments thereon are not subject to potential recharacterization as dividends subject to withholding tax. Accordingly, the loan agreement must document that the instrument is in fact a loan and not equity or another form of capital contribution that in some circumstances may be taxable, such as an operating subsidy.

(b) Deductibility of interest   Interest expense incurred by the company on its indebtedness generally is deductible on an accrual basis regardless of the purpose of the loan. If the creditor is foreign, certain additional documentation related to interest expense must be included in the company's tax return.

If the company conducts a foreign activity that is exempt from Norwegian tax pursuant to a tax treaty, a limitation is imposed on the deductibility of interest expense based on the value of Norwegian assets compared with the value of assets based outside of Norway.

(c) Thin capitalization   If a Norwegian borrower is thinly capitalized, a portion of its indebtedness may be reclassified by the tax authorities as equity, in which case the interest on the reclassified portion is not tax deductible and may even be treated as a dividend for withholding tax purposes. This is why the relevant tax law does not expressly differentiate related party loans from third-party loans.

The tax law does not contain a minimum debt/equity ratio or some other safe-harbor rule. The decisive criterion is what a similarly situated company would be able to borrow—and on what terms—from an independent third party. A debt/equity ratio of 4:1 often is acceptable, provided that the debtor can service the debt without financial support from affiliates. Therefore, shareholder-guaranteed loans extended by third parties might be reclassified as equity.

Although Norway currently has no specific transfer-pricing regulations, the tax law contains a general arm's-length provision requiring intercompany transactions to be carried out under the same terms and conditions as would have been agreed upon between unrelated parties. The arm's-length standard has relevance both to the debt/equity ratio and to the other terms and conditions of the loan agreement.

4.2   Equity

No capital duty is imposed on the issuance of new shares.

Dividends paid on stock are not deductible by the payer company. The tax consequences of the repatriation of profits are addressed in Section 6.2.

5.   MERGERS

5.1   Legal Forms

Pursuant to the Public Limited Liability Companies Act and the Limited Liability Companies Act (PCA/CA), a merger is a transaction in which a company—called the transferee company—takes over the assets, rights, commitments, and obligations of another company—called the transferor company—and in which the shareholders of the transferor company receive as consideration either shares in the transferee company or shares together with an additional, nonstock payment, provided that such nonstock payment does not exceed 20 percent of the total consideration.

For groups as defined in Section 3.2(b), the share consideration may consist of shares in the group's parent company or shares in another—more-than-90-percent-owned—subsidiary within the group. The latter alternative is not used in practice because tax-free merger treatment is not available in such a case.

A more simplified formal process is available for mergers within a group: subsidiaries can be merged into a parent, and sister companies can be merged without the issuance of new shares.

5.2   Typical Scenarios

In practice, mergers are commonly used as practical means of amalgamating businesses without the imposition of a current tax at either the company level or the shareholder level. Mergers also are commonly used in postdeal restructurings.

The most typical merger scenario is one in which one or more companies are merged into another existing company. Alternatively, a new company may be formed as part of the merger process, so that none of the original companies survive the merger. Also, a merger in which shares of the group's parent company are issued as consideration is commonly used. The transferor company is liquidated as a final step in the merger process.

5.3   Tax Consequences of Typical Scenarios

Provided that the corporate law, accounting, and tax rules applicable to mergers are followed, a merger can be undertaken without any immediate taxation of the companies and their shareholders. Additional payments of cash are treated as dividends.

In principle, any failure to follow the formal requirements for a merger will cause the transaction to be taxable. In practice, the tax authorities have stated that a relatively minor breach of the formal requirements may not cause the transaction to be taxable.

For accounting purposes—and regardless of which company is the formal survivor from a corporate law point of view—the larger of the merged enterprises is considered the acquirer of the smaller enterprise. Mergers of companies under common control or of companies of approximately the same size may be made with continuity in the accounting values of assets.

In order for a merger to qualify for tax-free treatment, all of the merging companies generally must be Norwegian. The Ministry of Finance may, however, grant a ruling permitting tax-free treatment even if one or more of the merging companies is foreign. The most common such case is a merger of foreign companies that have Norwegian shareholders. Provided that those companies are situated in countries with which Norway has entered into a double-taxation treaty, it is often possible to obtain a favorable ruling. If a favorable ruling is issued for a merger involving foreign companies, then at the ministry's discretion, special conditions may be imposed on the companies and their shareholders.

The transferee company in a merger assumes the tax attributes of the transferor company—for example, tax bases of assets and loss carryforwards. At the level of the transferor company's shareholders, the tax basis in the old transferor company shares carries over to the transferee company shares received in the merger.

The merger is effective for tax purposes as of the beginning of the year in which the merger is registered as completed by the Register of Business Enterprises.

5.4 Transfer Taxes

The general exemption from VAT that applies to the transfer of a going concern also applies to a merger. Similarly, a merger is exempt from stamp duty on land and buildings.

6. OTHER STRUCTURING AND POSTDEAL ISSUES

6.1 Creation of Local-Country Tax Groups

(a) Transfer of taxable income Norwegian companies are treated as separate taxpayers even though they are included in a group as defined in Section 3.2(b) and even though each company files its own tax return. Nevertheless, losses by unprofitable companies within the group may be offset by the income of profitable group members via a group contribution. A group contribution is deductible by the contributing member and taxable to the recipient group member. Whether the recipient group member is unprofitable or has a loss carryforward is irrelevant to the analysis.

Note that these rules apply without regard to whether the parent corporation is a Norwegian company, so long as the requisite ownership requirements are satisfied. However, if foreign entities are included in the chain of ownership, a group contribution may result in a deemed dividend in one or more intermediate jurisdictions. Therefore, transfers from a non–check-the-box entity to a check-the-box entity may trigger income at the shareholder level in the shareholder's jurisdiction.

Under Norwegian corporate law, group contributions are treated in a manner similar to dividends in that the transferring company must have the necessary equity—for accounting purposes—to support a distribution. Under these rules, it is also possible to transfer after-tax profits between the companies in a group.

(b) Transfer of assets Provided that the group requirements are met, assets can be transferred between companies in a group on a rollover basis in exchange

for shares or cash. The recipient company inherits the tax basis of the transferor company.

If the group requirements are not satisfied—for example, if the recipient or the transferor company leaves the group, and assuming that the assets previously transferred in the rollover transaction have not already been disposed of outside the group—then the transferor company is taxed on the difference between (1) the fair market value of the assets at the time the recipient company leaves the group and (2) the tax basis of such assets at the time the intercompany transfer occurred. In that event, a corresponding adjustment is made to the tax basis of the assets in the hands of the recipient company.

(c) VAT Norwegian companies and, under certain circumstances, foreign companies may elect to account for VAT as if they were a single person (VAT group), provided that at least 85 percent of the shares of each member of the VAT group is owned by one or more of the members of the group and that the companies cooperate in their business activity. A VAT group does not affect and is not affected by the tax grouping described in Section 3.2(b).

If the election is made, no VAT is charged between the companies in the VAT group. All VAT-group companies are jointly and severally liable for the group's VAT liability.

A VAT group should in all cases be reviewed, particularly if some VAT-group companies conduct business activity outside the VAT scope.

6.2   Repatriation of Profits

The profits of a target company or group may be distributed to a parent company in the form of dividends, that is, taxed profits, or in the form of group contributions, that is, a transfer of taxable income. The rules governing the distribution of group contributions are summarized in Section 6.1(a).

In principle, dividends paid by a Norwegian company to another Norwegian company are subject to corporate tax at a 28 percent rate. However, under the current imputation system, the shareholder receives a credit for the underlying corporate tax paid by the subsidiary so that the effective consequence generally is that the dividend is tax free. Note, however, that such a credit is available only if the distribution was made legally and under the applicable corporate law.

If the recipient shareholder has insufficient profits in a taxable year to use the credit, such credit carries forward for up to ten years.

Under proposed tax legislation, dividends paid to companies would be exempt from taxation effective January 1, 2004, subject to certain exceptions described earlier in the Introduction. For individuals, effective 2006 dividends exceeding an after-tax risk-free interest rate would be taxable.

The repayment of paid-in share capital and premium is tax free. If share capital previously was increased by fund emission, then a corresponding amount is classified as the first repaid dividend.

Paid-in capital is measured on a per-share basis. When capital is repaid in the form of a capital decrease, the amount paid with respect to each individual share must be determined in order to identify the portion of the payment that properly is treated as a repayment of capital and the portion if any that properly is treated as a dividend. Since dividends effectively are tax free for Norwegian shareholders due to the imputation system, the distinction between repayment of capital and dividend is of practical importance only for foreign shareholders subject to the 25 percent withholding tax or to a reduced, tax-treaty rate. Under the proposed tax legislation, effective January 1, 2006, the distinction between repayment of capital and dividend also would be of practical importance to individual Norwegian shareholders.

A domestic subsidiary's dividends and repayments of capital serve to reduce the tax basis of that subsidiary's shares pursuant to the RISK regulation. The RISK regulation is discussed in more detail in Section 7.1(a).

A redemption of shares in connection with a repayment of capital is treated as a realization of the redeemed shares, and a capital gains tax will apply. However, under the proposed tax legislation, companies would be exempt from capital gains taxation on shares, effective as of March 26, 2004.

Broadly speaking, only taxed profits can be paid out of the company in the form of a dividend or as an after-tax group contribution without triggering correction tax at the company level. Such correction tax will reverse in later years when the company has sufficient taxed reserves.

Currently, dividends received by a Norwegian company from a foreign subsidiary generally are taxable at a rate of 28 percent. A tax credit is available for the underlying foreign corporate tax and foreign withholding tax paid by the subsidiary, but the benefit of the credit is capped at the 28 percent Norwegian tax rate. In order to be eligible for such a tax credit, the Norwegian company must hold at least 10 percent of the foreign subsidiary's stock and of the votes at the general meeting. Unused tax credits can be carried forward for ten years.

Pursuant to certain older tax treaties—such as, the tax treaties between Norway and Malaysia and between Norway and Thailand—dividends paid by foreign subsidiaries may be exempt from Norwegian taxation.

Under the proposed tax legislation, companies would be exempt from taxation on dividends, effective as of January 1, 2004.

6.3 Noncore Disposals

Any contemplated postacquisition disposal of assets should be examined carefully in order to ensure that such disposal does not trigger an unexpected tax liability. If the assets previously were transferred within an acquired group in a tax-deferred rollover transaction (see Section 6.1(b), the postacquisition disposal of such assets may trigger taxable gain to the transferor in that prior intercompany transaction.

6.4   Preservation of Existing Tax Attributes

A company's tax attributes generally are not affected by a change in ownership.

Losses can be carried forward for a period of up to 10 years. If business activity ceases or the company liquidates, losses may be carried back against profits earned in the prior two years. A change in the ownership of a company generally does not impair the company's ability to carry its existing losses forward. However, if the main reason for the merger or the acquisition is to transfer the losses of a company to another entity, then the carryforward of losses may be denied. Under the proposed tax legislation, if the main motive of a transaction is the exploitation of a company's tax attributes, such exploitation may not be allowed.

6.5   Receipts under Warranties or Indemnities

Generally, payments made by the seller for breach of warranty or pursuant to an indemnity provision cause an adjustment to the purchaser's tax basis in the acquired property in an amount equal to the amount of the repayment. Accordingly, the usual practice is for the purchase agreement to contain a provision expressly stating that any such payment is to be treated as an adjustment to the consideration paid and received in the transaction. The clear position of the tax authorities in such circumstances is that such a payment will not be immediately taxable to the purchaser but instead will be treated as a reduction of the purchaser's tax basis in the acquired stock or nonstock property as the case may be.

Note, however, that such payments, if made to the target company, are likely to be subject to tax at the target company level.

7.   DISPOSALS

7.1   Stock Disposals

(a) *Companies*   Under current tax rules, companies that recognize taxable gain on the disposal of stock are subject to tax at the ordinary tax rate of 28 percent. Gain or loss is calculated as sales proceeds minus the seller's tax basis in the shares sold. Sales costs are also deductible. The first-in, first-out method applies to a sale of shares, so that the shares held by the seller for the longest time are treated as having been sold first.

Broadly, the tax basis of a share of stock consists of the following items:

- The original cost of the share, including costs related to the purchase of the share that were required to be capitalized as a part of the original cost

- Increases in paid-in capital made by the shareholder (capital contributions)
- Increases in tax basis to avoid the double taxation of company profits—pursuant to the RISK regulation. Under this system, the tax basis of a share is increased to reflect an allocable portion of the company's after-tax profits each year end.

Example: Income 100 − Tax 28 =

RISK regulation basis adjustment to company shares of 72 [2]

- Decreases in tax basis to reflect dividends, group contributions without tax effect, and capital reductions: such decreases may result in a total negative tax basis in the shares.

The somewhat complicated RISK system, as well as various other events, may cause additional adjustments to the tax basis of a company's shares, particularly in the context of group companies. The company history should be examined closely in order to accurately determine tax basis in a sale context.

Companies that could have made a tax-free sale of a subsidiary's shares prior to certain 1992 tax law changes were permitted to step up the tax basis of those shares. However, limitations were imposed on the deductibility of subsequent losses attributable to such a tax basis step-up. (See Section 1.2.)

As noted in the Introduction, as of March 26, 2004, proposed tax legislation would provide a tax exemption for dividends and capital gains on shares and would prohibit a tax deduction for losses on such shares.

(b) Individuals   The current rules for sales of shares by individuals are basically the same as those for companies as discussed immediately above.

Under the proposed tax legislation, beginning in 2006 only the portion of the gain in excess of an after-tax risk-free rate during the ownership period is subject to tax. As noted in Section 3.2(a), the RISK-adjusted value can be used as the opening value under the new tax regime.

(c) Tax-exempt entities   A number of public and nonprofit institutions are not subject to tax. These may also include pension funds and mutual funds.

7.2   Asset Disposals (Companies Only)

Generally, gains if any on the sale of business assets are taxable in the year of sale.

However, there is an election available that would defer current-year recogniton of the gain. For assets included in the depreciation groups *a* through *d* of

---

2. The numbers used in this example are illustrative and not intended to represent a specific currency.

the declining-balance system as shown in Section 3.1—for example, office machines, acquired goodwill, trucks, and cars—the seller may instead reduce its balance in the particular depreciation group. In that case, the gain is taxed through lower depreciation amounts in subsequent periods. If the balance becomes negative, the seller must take the negative balance into taxable income at a rate at least similar to the depreciation rate for the group.

If a sale involves goodwill, the goodwill amount reduces the seller's acquired goodwill balance. If the balance becomes negative, the negative balance is transferred to the seller's gain-and-loss account, the consequences of which are discussed immediately below.

Gains or losses on assets in depreciation groups e through h of the declining-balance system—for example, ships, aircraft, buildings, and office buildings—together with any negative balance in goodwill, are transferred to the seller's gain-and-loss account. In addition, gains or losses on other business assets and equipment not included in the declining balance-system, such as land and trademarks, are transferred to the seller's gain and loss account. A total of 20 percent of the balance either is taken to income or, in the case of a loss, is expensed annually on a declining-balance basis.

7.3   Deferred Consideration and Earn-Outs

Generally, if the amount of deferred consideration is ascertainable at the time of the sale, the full amount is included at that time in the calculation of taxable gain recognized, even if the receipt of that amount is contingent. If, ultimately, the entire amount is not received, a retrospective adjustment is made to the capital gain calculation, and tax is refunded as appropriate.

7.4   Payments under Warranties or Indemnities

Payments made by the seller for breach of warranty or pursuant to an indemnity provision cause an adjustment to the purchaser's tax basis in the acquired property in an amount equal to the amount of the repayment, and the usual practice is for the purchase agreement to contain a provision expressly stating that any such payment is to be treated as an adjustment to the consideration paid and received in the transaction. The clear position of the tax authorities in such circumstances is that the seller's taxable income for the year of sale must be reduced even if the seller makes the repayment in a subsequent taxable year.

8.   TRANSACTION COSTS FOR SELLERS

8.1   Transfer Taxes

Stamp duty on the transfer of land and buildings is payable by the purchaser, not the seller.

8.2 VAT

(a) Stock disposals Stock transfers are not subject to VAT.

(b) Asset disposals As covered in Section 2.2(b), a transfer of business assets that qualifies as the transfer of a business as a going concern is exempt from VAT—with input credit. Otherwise, the seller must charge VAT in the manner described in Section 2.2(b).

8.3 Tax Deductibility of Transaction Costs

Costs related to the sale of a company (stock or assets) are deductible as part of the calculation of gain or loss recognized.

Costs related to a sale that ultimately does not occur are deductible as trade or business expenses.

As discussed in the Introduction, as of March 26, 2004, proposed tax legislation would provide an exemption from capital gains tax on shares and, correspondingly, would deny a loss with respect to such shares. Another consequence of that legislation is that costs related to a sale of stock would not be deductible regardless of whether the sale ultimately occurred.

9. PREPARING A TARGET COMPANY FOR SALE

9.1 Hive-Down (Presale Disposition) of Assets

If the seller is selling only a division or part of a trade or business or if the purchaser is unwilling to assume or take assets subject to a specific liability, a hive-down transaction to remove specific items from the target company may be necessary. Various techniques may be used. For example, assets can be removed in a taxable transaction. Alternatively, the provisions for a tax-free transfer between group companies may be used, but the transferee company in such a transaction will be taxed if the transferor subsidiary subsequently leaves the tax group. (See Section 6.1(b).) Through the merger and demerger provisions, it is also possible to effectively hive down assets without immediate taxation, but such a transaction does not result in a step-up in the tax basis of assets.

No VAT is payable on a transfer of assets between members of a VAT group. Otherwise, an asset transfer generally is subject to VAT unless it constitutes the transfer of a business as a going concern. (See Section 2.2(b).)

9.2 Intragroup Transfer of Assets Being Retained

For a discussion of tax-free transfers of assets between group members, see Section 6.1(b). See also Section 6.1(c) (VAT consequences of transfers within a VAT group) and Section 2.2(b) (general VAT consequences of asset sales other than within a VAT group). For utilization of the demerger provisions to effect an intracompany asset transfer, see Section 10.

If the purchaser of a target company does not wish to acquire buildings and land owned by the target, one structuring option would be to retain the target company that holds only the buildings and land, thereby avoiding stamp duty on a transfer of those assets out of the target.

9.3   Presale Dividends

Under the RISK regulation, the payment of a dividend by a domestic company prior to a sale of the shares of that company generally should result in the same tax consequences to the shareholder or seller as if the dividend had not occurred, because the amount of the dividend reduces the shareholder or seller's tax basis in the company's shares. The same is true if the presale event is in the form of a repayment of share capital and premium.

However, proposed tax legislation would exempt companies from dividend taxation as of January 1, 2004, and as of March 26, 2004, would provide a tax exemption for capital gains on shares.

Dividend payments from foreign companies are currently taxable but may carry a foreign tax credit. (See Section 6.2.) However, in order to obtain such a tax credit, the shareholder must own the shares at the end of the year in which the dividends are received. The proposed tax legislation indicates that dividends from foreign companies generally would be exempt from tax.

10.   DEMERGERS

10.1   Legal Forms

Pursuant to the PCA/CA, a demerger is a transaction in which a company's assets, rights, and obligations are divided between the company itself (the transferor company) and one or more transferee companies and in which the shareholders of the transferor company receive as consideration either (1) shares in the transferor company or in one or all transferee companies or (2) such shares together with an additional (nonstock) payment, provided that such nonstock payment does not exceed 20 percent of the total consideration.

A transaction in which a transferor company is dissolved in connection with a merger and in which its assets, rights, and obligations are divided between two or more transferee companies also constitutes a demerger.

For groups as defined in Section 3.2(b), the share consideration may consist of shares in the group's parent company or of shares in another, more-than-90-percent-owned subsidiary within the group. The latter alternative is not used in practice, because tax-free demerger treatment is not available in such a case.

In practice—and depending on the type of demerger—a demerger often takes three to five months to complete due to creditor-notice-period and registration requirements. However, the demerger is binding between the parties when the demerger plan has been approved at the general meeting of the companies by at least two-thirds of the vote and share capital present.

10.2   Typical Scenarios

A typical demerger scenario is one in which the shareholders split the company's real estate activities and other activities—possibly in preparation for the sale of the business. The non–real estate activities are demerged into a new company with the same shareholders, whereas the real estate activities are retained within the transferor company.

Another typical demerger scenario is one in which groups of shareholders separate, with each shareholder or shareholder group receiving the shares of one company and with the assets split between the companies.

10.3   Tax Consequences

Provided that the corporate law, accounting, and tax rules applicable to demergers are followed, a demerger can be undertaken without any immediate taxation of the companies and their shareholders. Additional payments of cash are treated as dividends.

The conditions that must be satisfied in order for a demerger to be tax free are much the same as those applicable to mergers, as covered in Section 5. A special condition for demergers is that the nominal and paid-in share capital must be split in the same way as the net value is split between the companies. This rule ensures that the tax basis of the shares is split in a manner that is proportionate to value so that gain or loss as determined for tax purposes in the event of a later sale of shares in one of the companies appropriately reflects the real gain or loss.

11.   LISTINGS AND INITIAL PUBLIC OFFERINGS

11.1   Impact on the Tax Status of the Company and Its Subsidiaries

The tax status of the company and its subsidiaries generally is unaffected by a listing or initial public offering (IPO).

11.2   Complete Group Flotation

It is probably most common to list the existing holding company in a complete group listing or IPO. A transfer of shares in an existing group parent to a new holding company—that is, a share-for-share exchange—is a taxable event.

11.3   Flotation of a Subsidiary

If the parent company sells some of its existing subsidiary shares in the market, then the sale is a taxable event under current law, and gain and loss are calculated under the ordinary rules covered in Section 7. However, if the proposed tax legislation is enacted, such a sale would be tax free.

The issuance of new stock in the subsidiary is not a taxable event for either the parent or the issuing subsidiary. However, when such a subsidiary leaves the group in connection with a listing (or otherwise), a member of the selling group may recognize gain that had been deferred on a prior transfer of assets to that subsidiary—pursuant to tax-deferred rollover rules summarized in Section 6.1(b).

11.4   Issue of New Stock by a Listed Company

The issuance of new stock by a listed company is not taxable to the company.

11.5   Disposal of Stock by Existing Shareholders

The tax consequences of a disposal of stock by existing shareholders are covered in Section 7.1.

POLAND

INTRODUCTION

This chapter details the principal tax issues that are relevant to purchasers and sellers engaged in the transfer of ownership of a Polish trade or business. Unless otherwise stated, it is generally assumed that all sellers and purchasers are Polish joint stock companies or Polish companies with limited liability.

Polish law is subject to frequent and extensive amendments as Poland attempts to harmonize Polish law with the legislation of the European Union (EU).

A transfer of ownership of a Polish business or company may take the form of a stock deal or an asset deal. An acquisition may also take the form of a merger if it is structured in a manner consistent with the Commercial Companies Code—that is, merger *per unionem*, or merger *per incorporationem*. Similarly, the Commercial Companies Code also covers available forms of demergers. A transfer of ownership of shares or assets may also be accomplished through an in-kind contribution to a company in exchange for shares in that company.

The relevant taxes to be considered are:

- **Corporate income tax (CIT).** A company with its legal seat or place of management in Poland is taxed on its worldwide income regardless of the source of such income. The company and its shareholders are taxed separately. The CIT rate is 19 percent. There are no specific tax rules with regard to capital gains.

- **Value-added tax (VAT).** Generally, VAT applies to the sale of goods and the provision of services. The standard VAT rate is 22 percent; however, there are three available reduced rates of 0 percent, 3 percent, and 7 percent. The purchaser of goods or the recipient of services can generally recover VAT if the purchase or receipt was made in the course of a commercial activity and was made in order to generate goods that are creditable VAT supplies.

- **Civil law activities tax (CLAT).** Formerly the stamp duty tax, the CLAT is a transfer tax applicable to civil law transactions, including but not limited to contracts for the sale of assets and property rights, loan agreements, the formation of a company, or a share capital increase. The sale of real estate or perpetual right to the use of land and tangible assets is generally subject to a 2 percent tax. The sale of certain property rights—for example, sale of shares—is taxed at a rate of 1 percent. Loan agreements are generally subject to a 2 percent tax although certain exemptions and preferential rates are available. As a rule, CLAT is not due when VAT applies to a given transaction. The formation of a company or an increase of share capital is taxed at an effective rate of 0.5 percent.

Business activity in Poland can be carried out by an individual, or by a corporate entity such as a limited liability or a joint stock company, or by a commercial law partnership such as a general partnership, a limited partnership, or a limited joint-stock partnership. Foreign investors may also establish representative offices and branches.

1.   ACQUISITIONS

1.1   Asset Acquisitions

An asset acquisition may be structured in any of the following ways:

- A sale of specific assets
- A sale of an enterprise as a going concern—that is, generally, including all of the assets and liabilities of a selling company
- A sale of a part of a business as a going concern—also called an organized part of an enterprise—defined in the CIT law as a complex of tangible and intangible components, including liabilities, that are organizationally and functionally separated within an existing enterprise and that form an independent enterprise fulfilling specific economic tasks on its own

The tax implications of a given transaction may be dramatically different depending on the object of the transaction—that is, specific assets, an enterprise, or an organized part of an enterprise. Because the tax regulations are unclear with regard to many of the definitions, the proper classification of the object of the transaction can become an issue of vital importance.

An asset acquisition generally enables the purchaser to obtain a step-up in the tax basis of the acquired assets. (See Section 3.1 for tax basis following an asset acquisition.) If the acquisition is structured as the purchase of an enterprise or an organized part of an enterprise, then the purchaser may allocate a portion of the purchase price to goodwill or other intangible assets. Usually, both of these structures would require an investor to establish a new company first, unless the investor already has some kind of legal presence in Poland. In the case of an acquisition of selected assets, the purchaser cannot create goodwill on the transaction but does obtain a step-up in the basis of the acquired assets.

As a result of an asset deal, the acquirer undertakes joint and several liability, together with the seller, for tax liabilities connected with the acquired business or for assets that arose before the date of the acquisition. The scope of this liability is limited to the value of the acquired assets, enterprise, or organized part of an enterprise. In practice, under certain conditions, such liability may be minimized if not totally excluded.

1.2　Stock Acquisitions

The main advantages of a stock acquisition are the simplicity of the transaction and the relatively short time required to complete the acquisition. Specifically, a share acquisition requires the execution of a written contract. In the case of an acquisition of shares in a limited liability company, a confirmation of the signatures on the contract by a notary is also required. If a target holds real estate, a permit from the Ministry of Interior and Administration may be required. In certain cases, antitrust approval may also be required.

However, apart from the short time required to complete the transaction, a stock acquisition does not offer many other benefits to the purchaser. In particular, a stock acquisition does not allow a purchaser to obtain a step-up in the basis of the assets held by the target or to recognize any goodwill. Consequently, the majority of the price paid for the acquisition cannot generally be deducted for tax purposes until the future disposal of those shares.

Moreover, when acquiring shares, a purchaser effectively bears any potentially hidden tax liabilities of the target company. There is no formal way to eliminate the responsibility for these potential liabilities. Therefore, the acquirer may strive only to limit the negative consequences of such responsibility through certain indemnity clauses in a civil law agreement. Additionally, in certain circumstances, an acquirer of shares may also assume responsibility for the tax obligations of the seller of the shares—that is, the shareholder(s) of the target. This responsibility can, however, be limited or eliminated by application of specific procedures prescribed by the Polish Tax Ordinance.

The acquisition of real estate by a foreign purchaser requires a permit from the Ministry of Internal Affairs and Administration. Such an acquisition refers to any transaction, by which, as a result of the transaction, ownership of real estate is transferred to a foreigner—for example, an acquisition of shares in a Polish target company owning real estate. The Act on Acquisition of Real Estate by Foreigners defines *foreigner* broadly. The definition covers not only foreign nationals and entities registered abroad but also Polish companies directly or indirectly controlled by a foreign entity or foreign nationals. However, this requirement to obtain a permit does not apply to purchasers registered in the European Economic Area or to Polish entities with EU-based shareholders, unless the Polish entity holds agricultural land. The process of obtaining the permit can usually be completed within two to three months.

2.   TRANSACTION COSTS FOR PURCHASERS

2.1   Transfer Taxes

(a) Stock purchases   Unless the tax authorities confirm in a ruling that a specific transaction is subject to VAT (for further discussion see Section 2.2 (a)), a sale of shares in a Polish company is subject to a 1 percent CLAT on the market value of the shares. Both parties to the sale are jointly and severally liable for payment of CLAT, but it is customarily agreed that it is the purchaser who pays the tax.

A sale of shares to a brokerage house or a bank conducting brokerage activity as well as a sale of shares using brokerage houses and banks conducting brokerage activity as intermediaries is exempt from CLAT.

(b) Asset purchases   Generally, the acquisition of an enterprise is subject to CLAT at a 2 percent rate, which is imposed on the market value of real estate, tangible assets, perpetual right to the use of land and certain specifically listed property rights to premises that compose the enterprise. A CLAT rate of 1 percent, however, would apply to other property rights such as intangibles and shares.

(c) Purchase price   The tax base for CLAT purposes is the market value of the shares and assets sold. When the purchase price applied by the parties to an asset is significantly different from the market value of such an asset, the authorities are entitled to restate the value of the asset, taking into account any third-party valuation. If the purchase price of the shares or assets is understated, an additional CLAT liability along with a penalty may be assessed. Both parties can be held liable for understating the tax regardless of any agreement between the parties as to which party will bear the costs of CLAT.

2.2   Value-Added Tax

(a) Stock purchases   Under new VAT law that became effective on May 1, 2004, there is uncertainty regarding whether or not a sale of shares is subject to VAT. In addition, the tax authorities have neither passed laws nor put forth established practices to address this issue. Nevertheless, if a sale of shares is subject to VAT, the sale would qualify as an exempt transaction and therefore no VAT obligation would arise. In addition, as covered in Section 2.1(a), if a sale of shares is subject to VAT, the transaction would not be subject to CLAT. Therefore, no transfer tax would be assessed; however, a ruling should be obtained before taking this approach.

(b) Asset purchases   For VAT purposes, a sale of assets qualifying as the delivery of goods or the provision of services—as in case of intangibles, for

instance—is subject to VAT. The standard VAT rate is 22 percent; however, the applicable rate depends on the particular asset sold. Generally, a sale of assets that do not qualify as the delivery of goods or the provision of services is subject to CLAT rather than VAT. In some cases, the sale of a secondhand asset may be exempt for VAT purposes.

The sale of an enterprise or a part of an enterprise that prepares its own balance sheet is outside the scope of Polish VAT. However, the sale of an organized part of an enterprise is regarded as a sale of the particular assets composing such an organized part of an enterprise. Therefore, the sale of an organized part of an enterprise is subject to VAT. VAT is generally charged on the transfer price; therefore, for invoicing purposes, there should be a split between the portion of purchase price related to the delivery of goods and any remaining portion of the purchase price not related to the delivery of goods.

Because the sale of an enterprise and the sale of an organized part of an enterprise involve different VAT implications, the proper classification of an acquisition is of vital importance. For example, the potential reclassification of the sale of an organized part of an enterprise, which is subject to VAT, into the sale of an enterprise, which is not subject to VAT, could result in the tax authorities' disallowing the recovery of input VAT incurred by the purchaser. As a result, the purchaser could be held liable for tax on the understatement of its VAT liability or the overstatement of its VAT refund plus a penalty of 30 percent plus interest—currently at an annual rate of 13.5 percent.

(c) Recovery of VAT   Provided the transaction is subject to VAT and the buyer is a registered VAT payer delivering VAT-able supplies, the buyer may generally recover VAT incurred on the acquisition. In some situations, however, VAT incurred by the acquirer may not always be recoverable in full—for example, the acquired assets are used by the buyer to perform VAT-able activities and/or activities exempt from VAT. Unrecoverable VAT would be tax deductible for CIT purposes unless either it increases the initial value of the acquired fixed assets established for tax depreciation purposes or it relates to an expenditure that is not tax deductible for CIT purposes.

2.3   Capital Taxes

There are no specific capital tax rules in Poland. Any gain earned on the disposal of property is taxed under the standard CIT rules.

2.4   Tax Deductibility of Transaction Costs

(a) Financing costs   Costs incurred on the formation of companies and in raising equity generally do not qualify for corporate tax relief. At best, such costs can be taken into account in a calculation of the tax basis of the acquired company on a subsequent disposal.

Costs related to the raising of debt financing generally should be deductible for CIT purposes. Certain restrictions are covered in more detail in Sections 4.1(b) and 4.1(c).

(b) Investigation and due diligence   There are no clear regulations regarding the deductibility of expenditures incurred with respect to due diligence and other investment-related consulting. However, in light of recent interpretations by the Ministry of Finance, these types of expenses may be deducted for tax purposes. It should be noted that the position of the Ministry of Finance is subject to frequent change; therefore, this issue should be analyzed on a case-by-case basis.

(c) Other costs   Other direct costs of acquisition—including CLAT and legal fees—generally should be capitalized and deductible only through depreciation if incurred in an asset deal or upon the disposal of shares in a stock acquisition.

3.   BASIS OF TAXATION FOLLOWING ASSET OR STOCK ACQUISITIONS

3.1   Asset Acquisitions

Generally, payments related to the acquisition of assets become tax deductible under the rules set by the CIT law. In particular, expenditures for the acquisition of assets defined in the CIT law as fixed assets and some categories of intangibles should be capitalized and are deductible only through the allowance of depreciation.

With the exception of land, investments in process, and prepayments if any, the acquirer is allowed to take deductions for tax depreciation on the acquired fixed and intangible assets. Goodwill created as the result of a contribution in-kind and contributed know-how would also not be subject to tax depreciation. Certain acquired fixed assets may qualify as used assets and be subject to specific higher depreciation rates.

Goodwill created upon the purchase of an enterprise or its organized part may be depreciated for tax purposes on a straight-line basis for a minimum period of five years. There are specific regulations for the calculation of goodwill for tax purposes. In an acquisition of an enterprise or an organized part of an enterprise, the method for determining the initial value of the acquired assets depends on whether or not goodwill was created in the transaction.

In the acquisition of either an enterprise or an organized part of an enterprise, the value of the acquisition should be established at a market level. An independent valuation is recommended. Obtaining a valuation minimizes the risk that tax authorities will question the price of the transaction and, in particular, the basis established for tax depreciation deductions.

3.2 Stock Acquisitions

(a) *Purchase price* The purchase price of the shares forms the base cost of the purchaser's basis in the stock of the acquired company. Expenditures incurred on the acquisition become tax deductible at the moment the shares are sold. The book value of assets owned by a target cannot be revalued to their market value—that is, cannot be stepped-up in base value; therefore, tax depreciation deductions remain unchanged. Generally, the purchaser would not be able to take advantage of the CIT law provisions allowing applying individual or accelerated tax depreciation rates. No tax-depreciable goodwill is created on a stock acquisition.

(b) *Tax groupings* The general rule is that each Polish entity is taxed separately. However, Section 6.1 contains a further discussion of this matter.

4. FINANCING OF ACQUISITIONS

4.1 Debt

(a) *Withholding tax and civil law activities tax* According to existing regulations, reduced withholding tax (WHT) rates apply only to payments of interest made to foreign corporations and individuals. Payments of interest are taxed according to the double-taxation agreement between Poland and the applicable foreign jurisdiction. If no such treaty exists, interest payments are taxed at a 20 percent withholding rate. Application of the treaty rate is possible only if at the moment of the interest payment a Polish remitter of tax is in possession of a certificate—issued by the tax authorities—confirming the tax residence of an interest receiver.

According to the EU directive on a common system of taxation applicable to interest and royalty payments made between associated companies of different member states, interest payable to beneficial owners that are resident in an EU member state should be exempt from WHT. However, Poland has been granted a transitional period of eight years for implementation of this directive.

Loans are typically subject to CLAT at a rate of 2 percent, although some types of loans are exempt from CLAT. Importantly, loans to a company from a direct shareholder are exempt from CLAT. Loans made by banks, including non-Polish entrepreneurs whose business activities consist of granting loans and providing credit, are also exempt from this tax. In addition, specific exemptions exist for loans granted with the purpose of financing a start-up or running business activities if certain formal requirements are met.

(b) **Deductibility of interest**   The CIT law generally states that costs become tax deductible only in the year to which they relate and can be matched against related revenue. If such cost appropriation is not possible, the costs are deductible in the year in which they were incurred.

Unlike in many other jurisdictions, interest on loans is generally recognized on a cash basis—that is, when payments are actually made or when interest is capitalized. This general rule does not apply to interest on loans drawn in order to purchase fixed or intangible assets depreciable for tax purposes or acquired as components of an enterprise or as organized parts of an enterprise. Interest accrued up to the moment an asset is placed in service should be capitalized into the initial value of that asset.

Due to unclear regulations, there have been certain discussions about the timing of deductibility of interest on loans drawn in order to finance the acquisition of shares. According to the currently binding position of the Ministry of Finance as confirmed by the Supreme Administrative Court, such interest should not be capitalized into the base cost of the shares acquired. Rather, it should become deductible under the general rule—that is, when paid.

(c) **Thin capitalization**   The Polish CIT law restricts interest deductions on loans received from qualified lenders if the debt/equity ratio exceeds 3:1. A qualified lender is defined as:

- A company holding directly at least 25 percent of the debtor's shares
- Two or more companies' directly holding together at least 25 percent of the debtor's shares
- Sister companies, if the same entity holds directly at least 25 percent of the shares in the creditor and the debtor company

All of the percentage ratios are defined in the regulations in accordance with the number of voting rights to which the shareholders are entitled. The establishment of this ratio should be made each time interest payments on qualifying debt are made by the company. For the purposes of the Polish tax regulations, the term *equity* refers solely to registered share capital. In addition, share capital should be calculated without taking into consideration the following items:

- The part of the capital that has not been paid in
- The part of the share capital that was covered by contributions of shareholders' loans and by the interest on these loans (debt/equity swap)
- The part of the share capital that was covered with intangibles not subject to tax depreciation deductions—for example, know-how

(d) **Transfer pricing**   Prices established between related parties may be scrutinized by the tax authorities with respect to the related parties' arm's-length

nature. If the conditions of a related-party transaction differ from the conditions applied in a third-party transaction and the related parties are unable to prove that the difference results from valid commercial reasons, the tax authorities may challenge such arrangements and assess additional tax liabilities.

Effective from January 1, 2001, taxpayers are obliged to provide the tax authorities—within seven days of request—formalized transfer-pricing documentation for related-party transactions whose value exceeds certain thresholds—for example, €30,000 for the provision of services. If a taxpayer is not able to present the appropriate documentation within the aforementioned deadline and the authorities assess additional income related to the transaction, that income would be subject to CIT at a 50 percent rate, as opposed to the standard 19 percent.

4.2   Equity

The minimum share capital requirement for a Polish limited liability company is PLN50,000, of which 100 percent must be paid up. The minimum share capital for a joint stock company is PLN500,000, of which 25 percent must be paid up.

Equity funding is subject to CLAT at a rate of 0.5 percent. The taxable base may, however, be reduced by certain specifically listed costs related to raising capital—for example, court fees. The contribution by the investor may be made either in cash or in-kind. The company may, however, also be provided with nonequity capital such as additional payments or a loan, subject to certain restrictions. (See Section 6.2 for a discussion of the treatment of dividends.)

5.   MERGERS

5.1   Legal Forms and Typical Scenarios

Under the Commercial Companies Code, there are two methods provided for merging companies:

1. Merger *per unionem,* whereby all of the property of the target companies is transferred to a newly created company, after which the target companies cease to exist.
2. Merger *per incorporationem,* whereby one of the target companies survives and all of the property of the other target companies is transferred to the surviving company. Thereafter, all of the target companies, except the surviving company, cease to exist.

In both types of mergers, the property of the target companies is transferred in exchange for new shares issued to the target companies' shareholders.

In the case of a merger *per incorporationem*, there may be different directions that the merger might take:

- A vertical merger applies in the case of a parent-subsidiary relationship between the entities to be merged.
- A horizontal merger applies when one or more sister companies or non-related companies are merged into the other.

For clarity of presentation, in the discussion that follows, the term *surviving company* covers both the entity surviving the merger *per incorporationem* and the newly incorporated entity in the case of a merger *per unionem*.

In a merger, the Commercial Companies Code introduces a general succession rule. In other words, the surviving company acquires all rights and obligations of the target companies unless other regulations specifically stipulate otherwise. Consequently, decisions and concessions granted to the target companies after January 1, 2001, when the Commercial Companies Code was introduced, are automatically transferred to the surviving company upon the merger. There are no clear regulations with respect to concessions and permits granted before that date. Therefore, the transferability of any such rights would need to be analyzed on a case-by-case basis.

The Tax Ordinance provides for a similar general succession rule (see Section 5.2(c)) with respect to tax rights and obligations. With respect to labor law implications, the employees of the target companies would be automatically transferred to the surviving company upon the merger.

5.2 Tax Consequences

Although a legal merger is, in general, tax neutral for the entities involved and for their shareholders, it is necessary to consider other tax consequences such as the general succession rule, the recovery of losses, and the depreciation of assets.

(a) Corporate income tax implications In general, no immediate taxable income is recognized either for the merging companies or for their shareholders.

As a rule, a positive difference between the value of the target company's assets received by the surviving entity over the nominal value of the shares issued to the shareholders of the target company does not constitute taxable income for the surviving entity. However, one exception to this rule applies when the surviving entity is a shareholder of the target company holding less than 25 percent of the target company's shares. However, these rules apply exclusively to entities that are resident in Poland or the EU.

From the perspective of the shareholder of the target company, a surplus of the nominal value of the shares of the surviving entity received in the merger over the shareholder's basis in the shares in the target company would not constitute taxable profit for the shareholder until the future disposal of the shares received in the surviving entity. Such gain on the future disposal of such shares could be exempt from tax in Poland depending on the provisions of the relevant double-tax treaty between Poland and the shareholder's (or shareholders') country of residence.

Based on a specific antiavoidance rule, the foregoing exemptions from taxation under CIT do not apply if the merger is undertaken for tax avoidance purposes rather than for valid economic reasons. Therefore, the consequence of the tax authorities' successfully applying the antiavoidance provision would be the potential taxation of the surviving entity and its shareholder. However, disputes between taxpayers and the tax authorities with respect to the tax implications of merger transactions based on the antiavoidance provision are not very common.

A merger would not allow for any step-up in the tax basis of the target company's assets. Those assets have to be recorded by the surviving entity at their book values—that is, the gross book value will be carried over. Depreciation, in the surviving entity's hands, should continue to be based on the depreciation principles used by the target company, taking into consideration the accumulated depreciation and depreciation rates the target used prior to the merger. In addition, no goodwill subject to tax depreciation is created as a result of the merger.

(b) Transfer taxes   The provisions of the VAT law do not include any specific rules applicable to the transfer of assets in a merger transaction. The definition of a VAT-able transaction does not include a transfer by merger; therefore, a merger transaction should not be subject to VAT.

A merger would be subject to CLAT at the rate of 0.5 percent on the increase of share capital of the surviving company. The tax base would, however, be reduced by the amount of any share capital that was subject to CLAT before the merger.

(c) General succession rule; recovery of losses   Under the general succession rule of the Polish Tax Ordinance, in a merger, the surviving company acquires all of the tax rights and obligations of the target company, including any potential tax arrears, unless otherwise stipulated by specific regulations.

One such exemption to the general succession rule is provided for by the CIT law. This exemption provides that the surviving company in a merger may utilize only its own losses incurred prior to the merger and may not utilize any of the losses of the target company. Thus, the tax losses of the target company are effectively lost. Consequently, in the case of a merger *per unionem*, there would be no possibility for the utilization of tax losses brought forward from previous years.

As a result of the general succession rule, while the surviving entity is responsible for any VAT obligations of the target company, it also has the right to any recovery of the target company's available input VAT.

6.   OTHER STRUCTURING AND POSTDEAL ISSUES

For general comments regarding the tax treatment of loans, see Section 5.

6.1   Creation of Local-Country Tax Groups

Two or more corporate entities having a registered headquarters in Poland may form a tax group that effectively treats the group as a single taxpayer for purposes of CIT.

The basic conditions that must be met by companies forming a tax group include:

- A tax group consists of a parent company and its dependent subsidiaries. All of the companies included in the group must be either limited liability or joint-stock companies, with a registered headquarters in Poland.
- The average share capital per company should not be less than PLN1 million.
- The parent company must hold directly no less than 95 percent of the shares of the dependent subsidiaries.
- The dependent subsidiaries cannot hold shares in other members of the tax group.
- The companies included in a tax group cannot have any tax arrears in state budget taxes—that is, practically all taxes except stamp duties, real estate tax, and minor tax burdens.
- The companies included in a tax group cannot benefit from CIT waivers.
- The companies included in a tax group must not have any non–arm's-length situations with companies outside the tax group; that is, the tax group cannot have any transactions with nongrouped companies on terms and conditions different from those found on the free market.
- Once established, the tax group cannot be extended to include other companies.
- In each year of its existence, the tax group must have a tax profitability ratio of at least 3 percent—that is, the ratio of taxable income to taxable revenue for all of the group members combined.

Due to strict requirements related to the formation and operation of these tax groups, there is a lack of taxpayer interest in this form of organization in Poland. Additionally, the taxpayer's probability of losing tax group status is high, and the consequences of a retroactive loss of status may be severe—for example, tax arrears for the group members. There is also no established practice by the Polish tax authorities with respect to the verification of combined returns or with respect to the taxation of income generated by companies included in a tax group.

6.2   Repatriation of Cash

(a) Dividend payments   Based on the CIT law, dividends are subject to a WHT that is remitted by the Polish entity making a dividend distribution. The CIT law provides for a 19 percent WHT rate; however, an applicable double-tax treaty may reduce this rate. In order to benefit from the lower tax rate provided by treaty, the remitter of the tax—that is, the Polish entity—must possess a valid certificate issued by the respective tax authority of the country of the dividend recipient. The certificate confirms that the dividend recipient is a resident of that country for tax purposes.

Effective May 1, 2004, the Polish CIT law was amended to introduce EU parent/subsidiary directive relief. Accordingly, dividends payable to EU members in cases in which the EU member holds more than 25 percent of the shares of a Polish subsidiary for more than two years are exempt from Polish WHT.

(b) Loans   See the discussion of debt in Section 4.1.

(c) Royalties   Generally, royalties are payments for the use of intangible assets such as the copyright of literary, artistic, or scientific work; patents; trademarks; and know-how. Royalties paid for the use of technology, recipes, methodologies, or other intangibles that have no registered trademark would require proof of substance.

Royalties paid by a Polish entity to a foreign recipient are subject to a 20 percent WHT. This rate may be reduced if a relevant double-tax treaty applies. In order to benefit from the lower tax rate provided by the double-tax treaty, the remitter of the tax –that is, a Polish entity—must possess a valid certificate of tax residency that is issued by the respective tax authorities in the country of the recipient and that confirms that the recipient is a resident of that country for tax purposes.

According to the EU directive on interest and royalty payments made between associated companies of different member states, royalties payable to beneficial owners resident in an EU member state should be exempt from WHT. Poland has been granted an eight-year transitional period for implementation of the directive.

(d) Redemption of shares   Generally, under CIT law, a payment made to a shareholder as a result of redemption of shares reduced by the basis in the

shares redeemed is treated as income from the participation in profits of a legal entity. Such a redemption payment is subject to a 19 percent WHT. This rate may be reduced when a relevant double-tax treaty applies. In order to benefit from the reduced WHT rate provided by the relevant double-tax treaty, the company distributing the payments must possess a certificate of tax residency that is issued by the respective tax authorities in the country of the shareholder and that confirms that the shareholder is a resident of that country for tax purposes. EU parent/subsidiary directive relief does not apply to a redemption of shares.

However, gains from the redemption of shares received in exchange for a contribution in-kind of a business as a going concern are treated as earned from the related business activities; therefore, such gains are subject to CIT and not to WHT.

(e) Service charges   A Polish entity may also make cash payments for services rendered directly by its parent company or for services rendered by other foreign entities for the benefit of the Polish entity.

Generally, the CIT law does not include any specific restrictions on the tax deductibility of such service charges. Therefore, fees for services rendered by a service provider are tax deductible for a service recipient if properly documented costs of services were incurred by the taxpayer in order to generate taxable revenue for the service recipient. If a foreign entity provides services for a Polish company through the foreign entity's personnel present in Poland, there is a risk that the foreign entity will create a permanent establishment in Poland and, as well, create a reverse-charge VAT obligation. In addition, transfer-pricing regulations should be observed in order to determine the appropriate fee for services rendered.

Effective January 1, 2004, a WHT of 20 percent is generally due on revenues earned by foreign providers for the provision of services in the fields of consulting; bookkeeping; market research; legal, advertisement, management, and control services; data processing services; recruitment of employees and personnel; and granting of guaranties and sureties as well as of other services of a similar nature.

In most cases, services rendered by foreign providers are sheltered from taxation in Poland by the respective double-tax treaties if the Polish company—that is, the service recipient—at the moment of distributing the service charge, possesses a certificate of tax residency that was issued by the respective tax authorities in the country of the service provider and that confirms that the service provider is a resident of that country for tax purposes.

(f) Cost-sharing agreements   Under a cost-sharing agreement, a foreign company would charge a Polish company for a portion of the costs—such as head office costs and costs of marketing—incurred in relation to the latter's activities.

The discussion in Section 6.2(e) regarding service charges would also apply to any cost-sharing agreement.

6.3 Noncore Disposals

See Section 7.2.

6.4 Preservation of Existing Tax Attributes

A stock acquisition does not affect the tax position of the target company. In particular, the target company is entitled to continue to utilize its tax losses and to continue its VAT rights.

In the case of an asset acquisition, the acquirer is not entitled to utilize the tax losses of the target corporation regardless of whether a going concern is or is not transferred. In addition, there is no succession of VAT rights—for example, recovery of excess input VAT—in the case of an asset deal.

6.5 Receipts under Warranties or Indemnities

On one hand, as a rule, payments made by the seller to the purchaser for breach of warranty or under an indemnity are treated as taxable revenue in the hands of the purchaser. On the other hand, the tax deductibility of such payments for the seller may be questioned by the tax authorities. The tax treatment of warranty payments should be analyzed on a case-by-case basis.

7. DISPOSALS

7.1 Stock Disposals: CIT Treatment

(a) Companies Any consideration received on the disposal of stock should equal the fair market value of the shares sold. If the price applied by the parties differs significantly from the market value of such shares, the tax authorities are entitled to restate the value of the shares, taking into account any valuation provided by a third party.

The seller realizes taxable income on the sale of shares based on the difference between the sales price of the shares and the tax basis of such shares. Such taxable income realized is subject to tax at the regular CIT rate of 19 percent.

The basis of the shares sold depends on the manner in which the shares were historically acquired. In the case of shares that are purchased, the basis should be equal to the expenditures incurred on their acquisition. In the case of shares received in exchange for in-kind contribution, the basis depends on what was contributed. If the shares were received in exchange for the contribution of an enterprise or of an organized part of an enterprise, the basis is the book value of the enterprise or its organized part at the time the shares are received. The basis cannot be higher than the nominal value of such shares on the day they were received. If the shares were received in exchange for the contribution of assets or shares, the basis is equal to the nominal value of the shares issued in exchange for the contribution.

Income from the sale of shares is regular business income for a Polish seller. Accordingly, that income may be offset against CIT losses, if any, carried forward from prior years. Similar rules apply to gain realized on the sale of shares by a foreign shareholder. In that case, generally, a foreign shareholder should declare a capital gain with the Polish tax authorities and pay the CIT due. However, in many cases, this gain is protected from Polish taxation by appropriate provisions in a relevant double-tax treaty concluded by Poland and the country of the vendor's tax residence.

The same rules apply in the case of a share-for-share exchange—that is, an exchange in which shares in a company are exchanged for shares in the latter. The consideration in a share-for-share exchange equals the nominal value of new shares received. However, under certain conditions, taxation on a share-for-share exchange between a Polish entity and another EU-resident company may be deferred until the future disposition of the shares received in the exchange.

(b) Individuals   An individual recognizes taxable income from the disposal of shares based on the difference between the sales price of the shares and the basis of such shares sold at the moment of the disposal of the shares. This income is subject to personal income tax at progressive rates; the maximum personal income tax rate is 40 percent. However, if the seller is an individual who is involved in business activities and who made an election for preferential taxation, then such income would generally be subject to tax at a rate of 19 percent. As noted in Section 7.1(a), the sales price of the shares should be the market value of such shares. (See the discussion in Section 7.1(a) concerning determination of the basis of the shares sold.)

Gain earned on the sale of shares listed on a stock exchange and acquired in a public offering before December 31, 2003, is exempt from personal income tax; otherwise, the gain is subject to tax at a 19 percent rate.

(c) Tax-exempt entities   The CIT law lists a number of entities exempt from CIT in Poland. These entities include investment funds and pension funds. Income earned by certain entities—for example, charities—that is related to their statutory activity as specified by the CIT Act—for example, cultural and scientific activity—is also exempt from CIT.

7.2   Asset Disposals for Companies

The timing of the taxation of gains on an asset sale depends on the type of transaction. A sale or contribution in-kind of assets that do not qualify as a going concern is subject to immediate taxation. However, taxation of a contribution in-kind of an enterprise is deferred until the future disposition of the shares received in the contribution in-kind. (See Section 7.1.)

Generally, the gain realized on a taxable asset sale is equal to the proceeds from the transaction reduced by the basis of the assets sold. This gain is subject to taxation at a standard CIT rate of 19 percent at the moment of the transaction.

Generally, proceeds from the sale of assets, the sale of an enterprise, or the sale of an organized part of an enterprise equal the sales price, which should equal the market value of the property sold. If the price applied by the parties differs significantly from the market value, the tax authorities are entitled to restate the value, taking into account any valuation by a third party. In the case of a contribution in-kind of assets that do not qualify as a going concern, the sale proceeds are established as the nominal value of the shares received in the contribution in-kind.

In a sale or contribution of assets that do not qualify as a going concern, the tax basis is generally the net tax value of the assets sold. In a case of the sale of a going concern, the basis would be decreased by the amount of the liabilities transferred with the business.

Income realized on an asset deal is regular business income for a Polish seller. Therefore, this income may be offset with CIT losses, if any, carried forward from prior years.

Generally, the sale of an enterprise is outside the scope of Polish VAT; that is, no obligation to charge VAT on this transaction arises. Because VAT taxpayers are generally allowed to deduct input VAT incurred on the acquisition of goods and services purchased for the purpose of conducting VAT-able activities, there is a risk that the seller's right to deduct input VAT incurred on the purchase of assets that are sold as components of an enterprise and therefore not subject to VAT may be lost. This risk is generally minimized if, prior to the sale of an enterprise, the goods such as fixed assets have been used to generate VAT-able supplies—that is, the production of goods or provision of services subject to VAT.

The sale of assets that do not qualify as an enterprise should not have an impact on the seller's right to deduct input VAT incurred on the acquisition of assets because such a sale transaction is generally subject to VAT.

7.3   Deferred Consideration and Earn-Outs

These are not applicable in Poland.

7.4   Payments under Warranties or Indemnities

As a rule, if the seller makes a warranty payment to the buyer under a purchase-and-sale agreement, that payment should not be treated as tax deductible for the seller. Instead, the payment, generally, represents an adjustment to the purchase price for the assets or stock. However, treatment should be assessed on a case-by-case basis.

8.   TRANSACTION COSTS FOR SELLERS

8.1   Transfer Taxes

See Sections 2.1 and 2.2.

8.2   CIT Treatment of Costs

See Section 2.4.

9.   PREPARING A TARGET COMPANY FOR SALE

No additional discussion is necessary.

10.   DEMERGERS

10.1   Forms of Demergers

Under the Commercial Companies Code, a corporation may be divided into two or more companies; however, partnerships cannot be divided. Moreover, neither a company in liquidation that has started distributing its assets nor a company in bankruptcy may be divided.

A demerger can take any of the following forms:

- A transfer of all of the assets of the divided company into other companies in exchange for shares of the bidding company; the shares are then received by the shareholders of the divided company—that is, demerger by takeover.
- The formation of new companies to which all of the assets of the divided company are transferred in exchange for shares in the new companies—that is, demerger by formation of new companies.
- A transfer of all of the assets of the divided company to an existing company and a newly formed company or companies—that is, demerger by takeover together with formation of a new company or companies.
- A transfer of a portion of the assets of the divided company to an existing company or a newly formed company—that is, demerger by separation or a spin-off.

In the case of the first three of the types of demergers, the tax consequences are the same. Therefore, for the sake of clarity, in the following discussion, the term *demerger* refers to any of the first three listed, while the fourth type of demerger is referred to as a spin-off.

10.2   General Remarks

Generally, the tax implications of a demerger or spin-off depend on whether the assets transferred out in the demerger and, in the case of a spin-off, the assets left in the divided company constitute an organized part of an enterprise. In the following discussion, a transaction that meets the foregoing requirement is referred to as a qualifying demerger or spin-off. A nonqualifying demerger or spin-off occurs when either the assets transferred out or left in the divided entity do not meet the definition of an organized part of an enterprise.

10.3   Tax Treatment of Shareholders

A qualifying demerger or spin-off is a tax-neutral transaction. In other words, no taxable income is recognized by the shareholders of the divided company at the moment of the demerger or spin-off. Taxation is deferred until the moment of future disposal of the shares received as a result of the transaction.

However, if, as a result of the demerger or spin-off, the shareholders receive cash payments in addition to any shares, such cash payments are subject to a 19 percent WHT rate upon receipt. In the case of foreign shareholders, the respective double-tax treaty could apply to reduce the tax rate if the divided company possesses the appropriate certificate of tax residency as of the date of the demerger. EU parent/subsidiary directive relief is available for shareholders resident in the EU.

In the case of nonqualifying demergers or spin-offs, the shareholders recognize taxable income at the moment of the transaction. It is equal to the difference between the nominal value of the shares received as a result of the transaction and the shareholders' basis in the shares of the divided company. Such capital gains are taxed at the general 19 percent CIT rate. EU parent/subsidiary directive relief does not apply in this case.

10.4   Tax Treatment of a Divided Company

A qualifying demerger or spin-off should be tax neutral for a divided company. However, in the case of a nonqualifying demerger or spin-off, the divided company would recognize taxable income equal to the difference between the market value of the assets spun off and the tax basis of such assets.

10.5   Tax Treatment of Existing or Newly Formed Companies Receiving Assets

For the existing or newly formed companies that receive assets of the divided company in the demerger, the demerger or spin-off remains tax neutral regardless of whether the demerger or spin-off is a qualifying or nonqualifying transaction. As a result, no gain is recognized on the difference between the value of the assets received and the nominal value of the shares issued to the shareholders of the divided company unless the company receiving the assets of the divided company is a shareholder of the divided company holding less than 25 percent of the shares of the divided company. However, this rule applies only to shareholders that are resident in the EU.

10.6   Tax Basis

As the result of a qualifying demerger, the acquiring company takes a carryover basis with respect to the transferred assets. Accordingly, the acquiring company records the acquired assets and liabilities of the divided company on its books at the same initial values as recorded in the books of the divided company. Consequently, no step-up in value of the transferred assets or creation of goodwill or other intangible assets occurs as a result of the transaction. Nevertheless, the application of this basis rule in the case of a spin-off should be analyzed on a case-by-case basis.

In the case of a nonqualifying demerger or spin-off, the initial value of the assets acquired should equal their fair market value. Therefore, the acquiring company obtains a step-up in the basis of the assets received.

10.7   Transfer Taxes

The provisions of the VAT law do not include any specific rules applicable to a demerger or spin-off transaction. Since the definition of a VAT-able transaction does not include such a transfer, a demerger or spin-off should not be subject to VAT.

Since a demerger increases the share capital of the acquiring company, CLAT is levied at the rate of 0.5 percent of the increase. The tax base would, however, be reduced by the amount of share capital that was subject to CLAT before the demerger.

10.8   Antiavoidance Rule

A qualifying demerger or spin-off is not tax neutral for shareholders of the divided company and acquiring companies in cases when, based on a specific antiavoidance rule, the demerger or spin-off is not undertaken for valid economic reasons but has as its main objective the avoidance of taxation. Application of the antiavoidance rule by the tax authorities could result in the potential taxation of the shareholders and acquiring companies.

10.9   General Succession Rule

In the case of a qualifying demerger or spin-off, under the general succession rule the acquiring companies take over the tax rights of the divided company according to the demerger plan unless other regulations stipulate otherwise. One such exception to the general succession rule provided in the CIT law occurs in a demerger or spin-off of entities with carryover tax losses. The acquiring entity is entitled to utilize its losses incurred before the transaction; however, any tax losses of the divided company are effectively lost. Nevertheless, the companies are jointly and severally responsible for potential tax arrears of the divided entity. This responsibility for tax arrears cannot be allocated to the acquiring companies in the demerger plan, and there is no possibility of mitigating it.

The Polish Ministry of Finance challenges the succession of tax rights in the case of a spin-off regardless of whether the spin-off does or does not qualify. However, based on the current regulations, it appears that such succession may be secured if the transferred assets form a unit that prepares its own financial statements.

10.10   Succession of VAT Rights

Currently, VAT succession depends on whether the transferred parts of a divided company have been registered as individual VAT payers. If this condition is fulfilled, the acquiring companies succeed to the VAT rights and obligations related to the operations of their respective parts of the divided entity. However, effective as of January 1, 2005, this rule will be waived. Under the new rules, the company acquiring the majority of the assets connected with the activities subject to VAT inherits all of the VAT rights and obligations.

11.   LISTINGS AND INITIAL PUBLIC OFFERINGS

Under Polish tax law, the tax status of a company is generally unaffected by listings or initial public offerings (IPOs). The tax consequences of acquisitions and disposals of shares are discussed in Sections 1 and 7.

RUSSIA

INTRODUCTION

This chapter details the principal tax issues that are relevant to purchasers and sellers engaged in the transfer of ownership of a Russian trade or business. Unless otherwise stated, it is generally assumed that all sellers and purchasers are Russian companies with limited liability.

The most-common legal entities in Russia are the limited liability company (OOO), the closed (private) joint-stock company (ZAO), and the open (public) joint-stock company (OAO). With respect to each of these entities, shareholder liability is limited to the amount of contributed capital, although in certain circumstances the shareholders may also be liable for the amount of declared but unpaid capital. The tax treatment of each of these entities is similar. However, joint-stock companies (ZAOs and OAOs) may be subject to additional reporting to the Federal Securities Commission.

Russian civil legislation recognizes five types of corporate reorganization:

1. Merger
2. Absorption (merger into)
3. Division (demerger)
4. Split-off
5. Change in the form of business entity

In the course of any corporate reorganization, the company undergoing reorganization is required to notify both its creditors and its contract holders, which then have the right to withdraw from existing contracts. As a result, commercial as well as tax issues must be considered prior to undertaking a reorganization.

The relevant taxes to be considered include:

- **Corporate tax.** Russian legal entities and branches of foreign corporations operating in Russia through a permanent establishment are subject to a federal profits tax rate of 24 percent on their worldwide income. A portion of this federal tax is credited directly to the regional budgets. There are no separate state (regional) or local income or profits taxes.
- **Withholding tax.** The general withholding tax rate is 20 percent, with special rates applying to freight (10 percent) and dividends (15 percent).

The rate may be reduced under a relevant double-taxation treaty. Capital gains recognized by a foreign corporation on a disposal of shares in a Russian company are not subject to withholding tax unless the shares are in a company having more than 50 percent of its assets represented by immovable property. Double-taxation treaties may provide for additional exemptions from withholding tax applicable to capital gains.

- **Taxation of dividends.** Domestic dividends received by a Russian legal entity are subject to income tax of 6 percent, with a credit for tax on those dividends paid previously. Beginning January 1, 2005, the domestic dividend withholding tax increases to 9 percent. Dividends paid to an offshore parent are subject to 15 percent withholding tax, which may be reduced to as little as 5 percent under a relevant double-tax treaty.

- **Value-added tax (VAT).** VAT is levied on certain goods and services at the current rate of 18 percent on the total price of goods delivered or services provided. A 10 percent rate applies to certain food, publications, and medical goods. The supply of certain services is exempt from VAT. Certain services—such as consulting and advertising—supplied to or by foreign entities may also not be subject to Russian VAT based on place-of-supply rules. Exports of goods are not subject to VAT. Input VAT on purchases of goods or services related to VAT-able sales may be credited against output VAT. Surplus input VAT may be carried forward against future output VAT liabilities or refunded in cash. If income payable to a foreign company is subject to Russian VAT, this tax should be withheld and remitted to the budget by the Russian payer of income. There is no separate VAT registration.

- **Capital tax.** Initial shares issued by a company are exempt from capital taxes. Additional shares issued by a joint-stock company, however, are subject to 0.2 percent securities tax, which is capped at RUB100,000. It is anticipated that this securities tax will be abolished beginning January 1, 2005.

1.   ACQUISITIONS

Generally, an acquisition can be structured as a purchase of discrete assets, as a transfer of an entire business, or as a share purchase. From the buyer's perspective, a share purchase can be structured in one of two different ways: by purchasing the shares directly from the shareholders of the target company or by forming an acquisition vehicle—a newly established Russian or foreign company—to purchase the shares of the target company. In most asset acquisitions, the purchaser typically forms a new Russian entity—often, a limited liability company—to acquire the assets.

1.1   Asset Acquisitions

An acquisition of assets has several advantages from the buyer's perspective as compared with the acquisition of shares. These include:

- Minimal exposure to preacquisition liabilities of the seller's business, with the exception, possibly, of customs tax liability
- The ability to allocate the aggregate purchase consideration to the various acquired assets for later recovery through depreciation and amortization deductions

Prices used in the asset acquisition generally do not require an independent appraisal.

Special rules apply to the acquisition of assets made in the form of a purchase of a business as an enterprise (or property complex) within the framework of Article 559 of the Russian Civil Code. For accounting purposes such a purchase may result in goodwill that is based on the difference between the acquisition price and the net book value of the assets. If the legal form of the transaction is structured differently—for example, as a separate sale of assets and transfer of liabilities—no goodwill is recognized.

Russian tax legislation does not have provisions that would specifically allow recognition and amortization of goodwill for tax purposes. As a result, no amortization of goodwill is allowed in the event recognized pursuant to statutory accounting.

To avoid the effective loss of deductibility of goodwill for profits tax purposes—in case the purchase price of the purchased business exceeds its net assets—specific values need to be assigned to the assets in the enterprise sale agreement.

The purchase of a business as an enterprise creates significant complications from a VAT perspective. As a general rule, VAT liability is determined based on the net book value of the assets adjusted by a special index that depends on the relationship between the purchase price and the value of the property. The value of the property is the value of the assets without reduction for liabilities. Accordingly, the value of property for VAT purposes may exceed the enterprise sale price even when this exceeds the net assets of the enterprise purchased.

Additional VAT complications may result from the transfer of receivables and liabilities as part of the enterprise. The purchase of a business as an enterprise also requires an auditor's opinion on the composition and value of assets composing such an enterprise.

The purchase of a business as an enterprise is rarely used in Russia and should be considered a very complicated transaction from both tax and legal perspectives.

1.2   Stock Acquisitions

The advantages of a share purchase from the buyer's perspective include:

- Carryover of cumulative historical tax losses incurred by the target business; such losses can be used to offset postacquisition tax profits of the target business.
- The purchase of shares does not attract VAT, whereas an asset deal does.

2.   TRANSACTION COSTS FOR PURCHASERS

2.1   Transfer Taxes

Currently there are no stamp duties or transfer taxes on the transfer of stock or assets for the acquiring entity other than securities tax applicable in 2004 to certain share issues. (See Introduction and Section 2.3.)

2.2   Value-Added Tax

(a) Stock purchase   An acquisition of shares in a stock purchase is not subject to VAT.

(b) Asset purchase   The purchasing entity is subject to VAT in an asset acquisition based on the purchase price paid for the assets. The acquirer may incur a cash flow cost if sufficient output VAT does not exist to immediately recover the VAT it incurs on the purchase of assets. The budget rarely grants large cash refunds without litigation or delays. Input VAT on purchased fixed assets is technically subject to recovery when the asset is put into use.

2.3   Capital Tax

Initial shares issued by a company are exempt from capital taxes. However, additional shares issued by a joint-stock company are subject to 0.2 percent securities tax, which is capped at RUB100,000.

Shares issued by a limited liability company are not subject to capital tax.

2.4   Tax Deductibility of Transaction Costs

Typically nondeductible, acquisition expenses may become part of the capital cost base for calculating profit on future disposals and for calculating depreciation on depreciable assets. Allocation of costs incurred by other legal entities—for example, by a centralized financing entity of a group of companies—is normally not deductible.

However, certain expenses, such as interest and consulting services, can be expensed as period costs. Such expenses normally include those defined in the Russian Tax Code as *other expenses incurred in connection with realization* or as *nonrealization expenses*.

3.   BASIS OF TAXATION FOLLOWING ASSET OR STOCK ACQUISITIONS

3.1   Asset Acquisitions

The buyer is entitled to depreciate assets based on the acquisition price, including capitalized transaction costs discussed earlier. This approach also applies to free-of-charge asset transfers between companies (see Section 4.2) other than transfers between a parent and a subsidiary, though such a transfer generally results in taxable income for the recipient of assets.

Accordingly, the buyer may obtain a full increase in the cost basis of the assets based on the acquisition price so long as the acquisition is not pursuant to a transfer between a parent and a subsidiary.

Free-of-charge asset transfers between a parent and a subsidiary likely render the assets nondepreciable in the hands of the subsidiary. For this reason, such free-of-charge transfers between the parent and the subsidiary are uncommon.

Russia has very restrictive rules in terms of the possibility of recognizing and amortizing an intangible asset for tax purposes. Such items as customer lists or customer relationships cannot be recognized as intangible assets.

Goodwill may appear in statutory accounting solely in the acquisition of assets made in the form of a purchase of a business as an enterprise as the difference between the acquisition price and the net book value of the assets. Russian tax legislation does not have provisions that would specifically allow recognition and amortization of goodwill for tax purposes. Further, goodwill amortization, recognized in statutory accounting, is not deductible for tax purposes.

3.2   Share Acquisitions

The tax basis for purchased shares is determined by the amount paid for the shares, including capitalized transaction costs.

4.   FINANCING OF ACQUISITIONS

4.1   Debt

(a) Withholding tax   Interest paid to a foreign legal entity is subject to Russian withholding tax at the rate of 20 percent. Interest that is reclassified as a dividend under Russian thin-capitalization rules discussed in Section 4.1(c) is subject to a 15 percent withholding tax. Russia has an extensive double-tax treaty network, and most treaties either reduce or eliminate the withholding tax imposed with respect to interest.

(b) Deductibility of interest   Interest may generally be deducted for income tax purposes regardless of the type of loan or issuing entity, provided that the

interest expense is incurred with respect to income-producing activities. This normally includes both loans for the purchase of assets that are subsequently used for business purposes and loans for the purchase shares.

Generally, interest can be deducted at a maximum interest rate of 15 percent per annum with respect to a loan granted in foreign currency. Similarly, interest denominated in rubles is generally deductible to the extent of a multiple of 1.1 times the current Russian Central Bank's refinancing rate—effectively, 14.3 percent per year as of July 1, 2004. The law is expected to lower the foreign currency maximum rate from 15 percent to 13 percent effective January 1, 2005.

(c) Thin capitalization   A Russian company cannot deduct excessive interest on debt provided from a direct or indirect foreign parent owning more than 20 percent of the Russian subsidiary if the debt/equity ratio exceeds 3:1. The limitation applies regardless of whether the interest is considered market rate. Such excessive interest is recharacterized as a dividend. At the time of this writing, this limitation does not apply to loans between affiliated foreign sister companies or from another Russian company.

4.2   Equity

(a) Charter capital contribution   Initial contributions to the statutory charter capital of a Russian legal entity are free from income tax at the company level. Initial in-kind contributions of production equipment to the statutory charter capital of a Russian company may be granted exemption from import VAT and customs duties.

(b) Free-of-charge transfers   A contribution subsequent to the initial formation of a Russian company is respected only as a contribution to capital and therefore is free from income tax when formal registration procedures are observed; that is, shares are executed against contributions received. Conversely, the tax consequences of informal contributions—that is, when assets are contributed to the company free of charge with no formal registration procedures undertaken—vary as follows: Cash can be transferred to a greater-than-50-percent-owned subsidiary without tax on the transfer. The parent will not receive any tax basis for informal contributions, and there will be no tax-efficient mechanism for repatriating the contributed cash at a later date.

Other informal contributions to the capital of a Russian company—a free-of-charge transfer of assets—may be subject to certain taxes, including VAT. The receipt of assets by a greater-than-50-percent-owned subsidiary should not be subject to Russian income tax, provided these assets are not disposed of within one year of transfer.

5. MERGERS

Russian tax legislation contains provisions regarding the taxation of reorganizations. Little guidance, however, exists with respect to how these rules should apply in practice. Also, many areas related to the process of reorganization are not specifically covered in the tax law, thus leaving room for different interpretations and potential claims by the tax authorities.

The existing tax legislation provisions apply to all five types of reorganizations—that is, merger, absorption, division, split-off, change in the form of business entity.

For tax purposes, the transfer of assets in the course of a corporate reorganization is not treated as a sale. Consequently, no increase in tax basis is available as a result of a reorganization, and all historical tax bases continue subsequent to the reorganization; that is, all assets and liabilities of the merged company are transferred to the surviving company at the book value. Consequently, no gain or loss is recognized in connection with the merger. At the shareholder level, there is no deemed dividend or any other type of gain or loss recognized with respect to liquidation of the remainder company or companies.

The surviving company is the legal successor to the tax assets—including any carryforward of historical tax losses of the merged companies—and liabilities. However, a merger may affect the local tax concessions, if any, since local legislation often contains provisions allowing local authorities to revoke or even claim back-tax concessions in the case of a corporate reorganization. Additionally, the reorganization may result in some negative VAT and other tax implications that should be taken into consideration. Typically, a reorganization results in the commencement of a tax audit.

In the case of a share-for-share exchange wherein new shares are issued, there should be no income recognized for the company that issues the shares and receives shares of another company in return.

The shareholder that exchanges existing shares should determine capital gain based on general rules applicable to determining income on disposal of shares.

6. OTHER STRUCTURING AND POSTDEAL ISSUES

6.1 Creation of Local-Country Tax Groups

Russian legislation does not provide for group consolidation or loss sharing among affiliated entities.

6.2   Repatriation of Profits

In general, a Russian company is limited in the amount it may distribute as dividends to the current year's net earnings. In certain circumstances, retained earnings of prior years may also be distributed as dividends.

6.3   Noncore Disposals

Noncore disposals can be achieved in several ways. The assets can simply be sold or contributed to the capital of a subsidiary on a tax-free basis, followed by a sale of the shares of the transferee subsidiary—the most common approach because of its simplicity. Alternatively, a reorganization in the form of a split-off can be undertaken. This gives the added flexibility of transferring an entire business, including liabilities. Split-off transactions are gaining in popularity as the technique becomes more widely accepted by practitioners. A split-off, however, is a complex transaction that needs to be well planned to mitigate tax risks that may arise as a result of ambiguity in the legislation with respect to treatment of such deals.

6.4   Preservation of Existing Tax Attributes

Tax losses can generally be carried forward for ten years to offset future tax profits. Utilization of tax losses cannot exceed 30 percent of current-year profits. Tax losses attributable to either (1) regular operating activity—that is, ordinary losses, (2) a sale of marketable securities, or (3) a sale of nonmarketable securities are calculated separately and gains with respect to one category cannot be used to offset the losses of another. There is no provision for a carryback of tax losses.

A change in ownership of the shares of a company does not affect the company's utilization of available tax loss carryforwards or any other tax asset, such as tax refunds due from the budget. In a share purchase transaction, the balance sheet value of the assets carries over.

6.5   Receipts under Warranties or Indemnities

A purchaser's receipt of a payment under a seller's warranty against unrecorded liabilities is generally taxable as ordinary income. Typically, since such payments cannot be identified as liabilities up front, they cannot be used as subsequent adjustments to purchase price.

7.   DISPOSALS

7.1   Stock Disposals

(a) Corporate shareholders   Russian tax law separates ordinary income or loss from capital gains or losses on marketable (traded) securities and from capital

gains or losses on nonmarketable securities. Gains or profits from one category cannot be used to offset losses in other categories. However, each of the three categories is taxable in the hands of a Russian corporate shareholder at the rate of 24 percent.

A capital gain for profits tax purposes is calculated as the difference between the sales proceeds and the cost bases of the investment, including the acquisition and disposal costs. If share sale proceeds deviate by more than 20 percent from the market value, then the market value is used to calculate the taxable gain. For nonmarketable securities, the relevant share of the net assets may be used as an approximation of the market value of the shares for this purpose. This implies that the Russian tax authorities may have the right to adjust the securities sale price for tax purposes even when the price is established at arm's length.

Capital gains recognized by a nonresident investor on the sale of shares in a Russian company are generally not subject to withholding tax unless either (1) the sale relates to a foreign company's permanent establishment in Russia or (2) the shares are in a company more than 50 percent of whose assets are represented by real property. A taxation treaty may override the latter limitation.

Capital gains of a corporate shareholder attributable to a sale of shares are exempt from any other withholding taxes.

(b) Individual shareholders   Resident Russian individuals are subject to capital gains tax at a rate of 13 percent. Capital gains are computed as the excess of sales consideration (net of selling expenses such as broker fees) over the individual's tax basis in the shares.

The taxable base with respect to securities for personal income tax purposes is determined separately for transactions with marketable (traded) securities, transactions with nonmarketable securities, transactions with derivative instruments, transactions with unit trusts, and transactions with securities placed under fiduciary agreement. Similar to profits tax, gains or profits from one category cannot be used to offset losses on other categories. Taxable base with respect to shares that are not securities—such as shares in limited liability companies—is calculated similar to income from the sale of property and separately from the taxable base with respect to securities.

In addition to deduction of actual selling expenses incurred, the Tax Code technically provides for the possibility to apply a predetermined deduction in the amount of:

- Up to RUB125,000 in case shares were owned for less than three years prior to the sale
- Share sale proceeds in case shares were owned for three years or more

This deduction, however, may be applied only to securities such as shares in joint-stock companies in case the expenses incurred in relation to the share transactions cannot be supported by relevant documents.

No clear guidance exists on what precisely this provision means, and its practical applicability is questionable. Tax authorities tend to challenge the aforementioned deduction tied to the three-year rule in case the actual expenses are potentially identifiable, which would normally be the situation with purchased securities. The prudent approach is to deduct the actual expenses incurred in relation to the securities.

Technically, the aforementioned limitation of standard deduction does not apply to the sale of shares that are not securities, such as shares in limited liability companies.

It is expected that as of January 1, 2005, the aforementioned standard deduction will not be applicable to the sale of shares—both in joint-stock companies and in limited liability companies.

7.2   Asset Disposals

A company that sells any of its assets, including its entire business, is subject to income tax on any gain derived from such a sale. Generally, gain is calculated as the excess of the proceeds received over the tax book value of the assets.

Any losses resulting from the sale of fixed assets are depreciated over the remaining useful life of the disposed asset.

A sale of tangible and intangible assets is usually subject to VAT based on the assets transferred.

The VAT rules for sale of an entire business are complex. As discussed earlier, the VAT liability in this case is determined based on the net book value of the assets adjusted by a special index that depends on the relationship between the purchase price and the value of the property. The value of property is equal to value of the assets without reduction for liabilities. Accordingly, the value of property for VAT purposes may exceed the enterprise sale price even when the enterprise sale price exceeds net assets of the purchased enterprise.

7.3   Deferred Consideration and Earn-Outs

Any deferred consideration, which can be quantified as a fixed and determinable amount as consideration for the assets transferred at the time of the sale, is recognized as part of the sales proceeds when the title is transferred—regardless of when payment is made—as long as this is clearly specified in the sale agreement. The VAT liability may be deferred until the cash is received if the seller is on a cash basis for VAT purposes.

If the amount of additional or deferred consideration is speculative and cannot be quantified at the time of title transfer, then such additional consideration becomes taxable when it becomes quantifiable. If properly documented, such later amounts are treated as additional sales proceeds for profits tax purposes in the hands of the seller. The buyer, however, may have difficulties in capitalizing these additional costs into the purchase price of the assets.

7.4   Payments under Warranties or Indemnities

Payments made by a party to a merger pursuant to a warranty against unrecorded liabilities—tax or otherwise—should technically be deductible if the seller received a separate fee for providing the original warranty for the purchase; that is, the expense is deducted under general deductibility rules as being related to income-producing activities. Normally, since such payments cannot be identified as a liability up front, they cannot be used to effect a subsequent adjustment to purchase price.

8.   TRANSACTION COSTS FOR SELLERS

Direct expenditures incurred in connection with a disposition of assets or shares should generally be deductible against the sales proceeds in a calculation of the taxable gain for both share and asset disposals. General (indirect) costs should be deductible if specifically provided by the Russian Tax Code. Deduction of indirect expenses that are not specifically mentioned in the Russian Tax Code will likely be challenged by the Russian tax authorities.

9.   PREPARING A TARGET COMPANY FOR SALE

Although Russian law generally exempts from corporate tax both (1) in-kind contributions to capital and (2) asset transfers between parent and subsidiary, the governing legislation applicable to a distribution or split-off of assets to be retained by the selling group member is ambiguous. The exemption for asset transfers between parent and subsidiary applies only if the assets transferred (other than cash) are not disposed of by the transferee within one year.

9.1   Hive-Down of Assets

Certain assets of a target company to be sold may be transferred to a new or existing subsidiary on a tax-free basis, the stock of which may then be sold to a purchaser. Capital gains recognized by a parent on the sale of subsidiary stock would then be subject to a capital gains tax. (See Section 6.3.)

9.2   Intragroup Transfer of Assets Being Retained

So long as the assets (other than cash) transferred between a parent and a subsidiary are retained for at least one year by the transferee, the initial asset transfer is exempt from tax. Accordingly, the assets of a subsidiary to be retained may be distributed to its parent on a tax-exempt basis so long as the parent does not dispose of the transferred assets within one year.

9.3   Presale Dividends

Special rules with respect to presale dividends do not exist. Accordingly, the general rules with respect to dividends apply. Consequently, the dividends in joint-stock companies are normally limited to the current year's earnings. In certain cases, however, unrestricted retained earnings of prior years may also be distributed.

10.   DEMERGERS

In a demerger, assets and liabilities of the surviving entities are determined based on the separation balance sheets and formal acts of transfer. As with other types of corporate reorganizations, no gain or loss should be recognized by either of the corporate parties to the demergers or their shareholders, respectively. However, if a court determines the demerger was initiated in order to avoid a payment of taxes, then each of the surviving entities may be jointly and severally liable for the tax liabilities of the original entity.

11.   LISTINGS AND INITIAL PUBLIC OFFERINGS

There are no special tax laws or regulations applicable to capital gains arising from a public offering of shares in Russia.

Accordingly, proceeds from the issue of shares during an initial public offering (IPO) should generally not be subject to Russian profits tax or VAT. If an existing entity issues shares during an IPO, the proceeds should be subject to a securities tax of 0.2 percent, which was capped at RUB100,000 during 2004.

If existing shares are sold during an IPO, such sales of stock are taxed similarly to other stock disposals by the company or its shareholders.

Historically, most new listings by Russian companies other than those listed on Russian stock exchanges during the privatization process have been made primarily through foreign stock exchanges.

SINGAPORE

INTRODUCTION

This chapter details the principal tax issues that are relevant to purchasers and sellers engaged in the transfer of ownership of a Singaporean trade or business. Unless otherwise stated, it is generally assumed that all sellers and purchasers are Singaporean companies with limited liability.

The transfer of ownership of a Singaporean business can take the form of a disposal of stock or assets. While there are significant differences in the tax implications of an asset or stock sale, it may be possible to reorganize the companies postacquisition in order to maximize the tax benefits that may be associated with an asset deal.

A number of incentives are available for industries and activities encouraged by the Singaporean government. A detailed list of incentives can be seen in Section 12.

The relevant taxes to be considered are:

- Corporate tax
- Withholding tax
- Goods-and-services tax
- Stamp duty tax

Corporate Tax

The general income tax rate for resident and nonresident corporations—that is, branches of foreign companies—is 20 percent. However, beginning with the 2002 tax year, three-fourths of the first SGD10,000 of chargeable income—that is, the amount on which tax is imposed—and one-half of the next SGD90,000 of chargeable income is exempt from tax. Therefore, for the first SGD100,000 of chargeable income, SGD52,500 is exempt from tax. The remaining portion of the chargeable income is subject to tax at the prevailing corporate tax rate.

Dividends received from Singaporean companies are not to be taken into account in a computation of the aforementioned exemption.

Singapore imposes income tax on income derived in Singapore and on income received in Singapore from outside Singapore. The following income is deemed to be income received in Singapore from outside Singapore:

- Any amount remitted to, transmitted to, or brought into Singapore
- Any amount applied in or to satisfaction of any debt incurred with respect to a trade or business carried on in Singapore
- Any amount used to purchase any movable property that is brought into Singapore

However, as of June 1, 2003, provided certain conditions are met, the following categories of foreign-sourced income received in Singapore by Singaporean tax residents are exempt from taxation:

- Dividends derived from any territory outside Singapore
- Trade profits earned by a branch of a Singaporean resident company located in a foreign territory
- Foreign-sourced service income (service income is considered to be foreign sourced if the service is rendered in the course of trade, business, or profession through a fixed place of operation in a foreign jurisdiction).

The exemption is available if the following conditions are met:

- In the year in which the income is received in Singapore, the headline tax rate—the highest corporate tax rate of the foreign jurisdiction but not necessarily the effective tax rate—in the foreign jurisdiction is at least 15 percent.
- The relevant foreign income has been subject to tax, including withholding tax, in the foreign jurisdiction from which it was paid. However, effective as of July 30, 2004, this condition will be considered met even if no taxes were imposed in the relevant foreign jurisdiction as the consequence of a tax incentive for carrying out substantive business activities in that jurisdiction.

Capital gains are not subject to tax. However, gains derived from the ordinary course of business or from a transaction entered into with the intention of realizing a profit should be treated as ordinary income and should be subject to tax.

Withholding Tax

Interest, loan fees, royalties, management fees, and technical assistance fees paid to nonresidents of Singapore may be subject to withholding tax:

	Nontreaty Rate	Treaty Rate
Interest, loan fees, royalties,* leases	15%	0–15%
Management fees and technical fees	20%	0–20%

* Nontreaty rates reduced to 10 percent, effective January 1, 2005. The reduced rate also applies to treaty rates if such rates are higher than 10 percent.

When services related to the derivation of certain payments such as loan fees and technical service fees are performed entirely outside Singapore and the payments are at arm's length, such payments are not subject to withholding tax. Management fees paid to related entities, which are charged at cost by the recipient, are also not subject to withholding tax.

In addition, payments of interest, royalties, and licensing fees may also be exempt from tax under a relevant tax concession granted to a payor.

Singapore has a comprehensive network of double-tax agreements that reduce withholding tax and that exempt business profits derived by a company resident in a treaty country that does not have a permanent establishment in Singapore.

A nonresident entity that conducts its operations in Singapore through a permanent establishment may obtain a waiver—subject to the satisfaction of certain conditions—from withholding tax on income.

Goods-and-Services Tax

The goods-and-services tax (GST) rate is 5 percent. However, certain goods or services, such as transfer of shares, are exempt from GST. The transfer of a business that satisfies certain conditions is also exempt from GST.

Stamp Duty Tax

Singapore imposes stamp duty—at a rate of 0.2 percent—on documents related to the transfer of shares and transfers of real estate—at ad valorem rates of up to 3 percent.

1.   ACQUISITIONS

Singapore does not have detailed legislation dealing with the tax treatment of acquisitions. Accordingly, general principles of taxation would apply in the structuring of a deal and in the choice between an acquisition of assets or of stock.

Whether a deal is structured as a stock deal or an asset deal may depend largely on commercial considerations. A stock deal may, however, be subsequently restructured as an asset deal to allow it to be completed on a more-tax-efficient basis.

1.1   Stock Acquisitions

Generally, it is less expensive for a purchaser to acquire the business under a stock deal. The stamp duty on the transfer of stock is 0.2 percent of the consideration, whereas the transfer of real property under an asset deal is subject to a maximum duty of 3 percent of the property's value.

(a) Preservation of tax losses and tax concessions Because there are no provisions for transferring losses from one entity to another, if a target company has accumulated losses carried forward and the buyer wishes to preserve the losses, the buyer has to acquire the business by means of a stock deal. In addition, for such losses to be carried forward and offset against future income, the target company would need to seek a waiver from the Ministry of Finance to comply with the continuity-of-substantial-ownership test. Generally, if the acquisition price is not affected by the availability of the losses, the waiver should be granted.

If a target company has been granted a tax concession, the buyer has to acquire the stock of the company in order to preserve the concession and seek prior approval from the relevant government body to continue to benefit from the concession.

(b) Continuity of tax incentives If the target enjoys any tax incentives, it may be necessary to obtain approval from the authority granting the incentive to ensure the continued applicability of the incentive.

1.2 Asset Acquisitions

An asset deal allows a purchaser to select the desirable assets to be acquired and to transfer assets between one or various entities, including offshore entities, in order to optimize future intragroup payments.

If a vendor insists on a stock deal, the purchaser may restructure the target after the acquisition by selling the business to a subsidiary. This maximizes both the step-up base of certain assets and the deductibility of interest costs.

2. TRANSACTION COSTS

2.1 GST

The GST rate is 5 percent. GST is collected by a GST-registered service provider (seller) and is payable by the end user (purchaser). However, certain goods or services, such as transfer of shares, are exempt from GST. The transfer of a business that satisfies certain conditions is also exempt from GST.

2.2 Stamp Duty Tax

Singapore imposes stamp duty on documents related to the transfer of shares—at a rate of 0.2 percent—and transfers of real estate—at ad valorem rates of up to 3 percent. The stamp duty is payable by the purchaser.

(a) Concessions Related to Mergers and Acquisitions The Income Tax Act, GST Act, and Stamp Duty Act provide for certain concessions when a company

is being reorganized:

- For income tax purposes, with respect to sales of tax-depreciable assets to a related party, the transferor and transferee may elect to transfer these assets at the tax written-down value without giving rise to the previously allowed tax depreciation's being recharged to the transferor. Parties are related if the buyer controls the seller or vice versa or if they belong to the same group of companies.

- For GST purposes, the transfer of a business as a going concern would not be regarded as a taxable supply and would therefore not be subject to GST. For a transfer to qualify as a transfer of a going concern, the assets must be used by the transferee to carry on the same kind of business as that of the transferor. When only part of a business is transferred, that part must be capable of operating the same kind of business in order for the transfer to meet the going-concern requirement.

- Corporate reconstructions and amalgamations may be exempt from stamp duty on the transfer of shares or real estate, because stamp duty is not applicable on the transfer of other assets if the following conditions are met:

  o The transfers are in connection with a plan to reconstruct companies.
  o A transferee company has been incorporated or has increased its capital in order to acquire the business or to acquire not less than 90 percent of the issued share capital of the transferor company.
  o At least 90 percent of the consideration for the acquisition consists of shares of the transferee company.

Stamp duty concession may be available when the restructuring occurs in connection with an initial public offering.

2.3   Tax Deductibility of Transaction Costs

Acquisition expenses are generally not tax deductible to the buyer in Singapore, with the exception of expenses that may be attributed to the purchase of inventories. Therefore, if appropriate, it is preferable to book the nondeductible expenses in a country in which an appropriate tax deduction may be available.

3.   BASIS OF TAXATION FOLLOWING ASSET OR STOCK ACQUISITIONS

3.1   Asset Acquisitions

An asset deal often allows the buyer to step up the cost basis of acquired assets for tax purposes. This would enable the buyer to maximize tax benefits through allocating, if possible, higher costs to inventory, depreciable assets, and intellectual property. Generally, the costs of plant and equipment may be depreciated over their respective useful lives via the straight-line method. Alternatively, their costs may be depreciated on a straight-line basis over a period of three years. The costs of automated or similar equipment may be fully depreciated in the first year.

A company that purchases certain types of intellectual property is entitled to claim a deduction on a straight-line basis over a period of five years. The types of intellectual property eligible for the deduction include patents, copyrights and related rights, trademarks, registered designs, geographic indications, layout designs of integrated circuits, and protection of confidential information. The conditions for the deduction are:

- The capital expenditure for the acquisition of the intellectual property is incurred on or after November 1, 2003 (approval required prior to this date).

- The intellectual property must have commercial value and be used in the company's trade or business.

- The cost eligible for deduction excludes legal fees, registration fees, stamp duty, and other costs related to acquisition of the intellectual property.

- The company must have legal ownership of the intellectual property.

- Third-party valuations are required if the value of the intellectual property acquired exceeds SGD2 million or SGD500,000 for related-party transactions.

No tax deduction is available for the amortization of goodwill. Therefore, the purchase price on an asset deal should, if appropriate, be allocated as much as possible to inventory, depreciable capital assets, and other items such as intellectual property that will generate a tax deduction.

4.   FINANCING OF ACQUISITIONS

4.1   Thin Capitalization

There are no thin-capitalization rules in Singapore. The determination of an appropriate debt/equity ratio is generally governed by commercial considerations. However, if a company is set up to take advantage of a tax concession or requires a special license from the government—for example, banking, insurance, or telecommunications—the regulatory body may require the company to comply with certain ratios.

4.2   Deductibility of Interest

(a) Stock deals If a Singaporean company is used for acquiring a target company, the interest expense would have tax-deductible value only if the company receives franked dividends. (See Section 6.1.) Otherwise, dividend income received from companies that have moved to the one-tier system is exempt from tax, and no deduction would be allowed for the interest expense. To obtain a tax deduction for the interest cost, after the stock deal, the business of the target company should be transferred to a new company and the debt should be pushed down to the new-company level for the new company to obtain a tax deduction for the interest expense.

(b) Asset deals Interest incurred on funds used to acquire a business under an asset deal should be tax deductible. Since Singapore does not have a debt/equity ratio requirement for tax purposes, it is possible to maximize the amount of debt used to acquire a business.

If, however, the business acquired consists of assets that may not produce regular returns, interest would not be tax deductible if no income is derived from such assets in a particular year. Therefore, in an asset deal, the assets may be acquired by separate entities and the debt/equity may be appropriately structured to maximize the interest deduction.

5.   MERGERS

Singaporean tax law contains no specific provisions related to mergers. Specifically, the transfer of carried-forward losses and unabsorbed capital allowances may not be made from the merging entities to the merged entity. Therefore, if a company has substantial tax losses or unutilized capital allowances, subject to commercial considerations, the profit-making company should be merged into the loss-making company.

5.1   Types of Mergers

In the Singaporean context, a merger could take place as a transfer of trade and assets from one company to another company or as a stock swap.

(a) Transfer of trade and assets from one company to another company The following illustrates one type of transfer of trade and assets from one company to another company:

In this example, the business and assets of company A are transferred to company B in consideration for stock of company B being issued to company A.

The following illustrates another structure for this transaction:

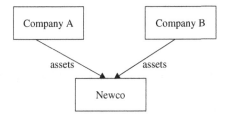

In this example, stock in Newco would be issued to company A and company B in proportion to the respective value of the assets transferred. The tax implications would be the same as in the case of an asset deal. (See Section 1.2.)

(b) Stock swap In one type of stock swap, the following occurs:

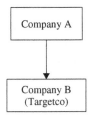

In this example, stock in company B would be transferred to company A, which will issue new shares to the shareholders of company B.

The following illustrates another type of stock swap:

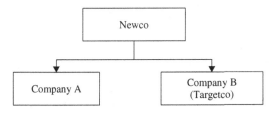

In this example, stock in Newco would be issued to shareholders of company A and company B in proportion to the respective value of the stock transferred.

If, as a result of the stock swap, there is a substantial change (more than 50 percent) in the shareholding of the transferor company, a waiver must be obtained from the tax authorities for the carryforward and utilization of unabsorbed tax losses and capital allowances. Additionally, prior approval from the relevant government body may be required for the continuation of tax concessions granted to the transferor company.

The transferee company would normally be liable to pay stamp duty at the rate of 0.2 percent on the higher of the consideration or market value of the stock of the transferor company. (See Section 2 for a discussion of the relevant transaction costs.)

6.   OTHER STRUCTURING AND POSTDEAL ISSUES

6.1   Repatriation of Profits

Singapore does not impose any restrictions on the repatriation of profits. Since January 1, 2003, Singapore has been operating a one-tier corporate tax system. Under the system, tax collected from corporate profits is final and all dividends paid by companies in Singapore are tax-exempt in the hands of the shareholder regardless of the shareholder's tax residence status or legal form.

Prior to January 1, 2003, to avoid double taxation at corporate and shareholder levels, Singapore adopted an imputation system for the taxation of dividends. Under the imputation system, income tax paid by a Singaporean resident company is imputed to the dividends paid to the company's shareholders such that the shareholders are deemed to have paid the tax equivalent to the underlying tax paid by the company.

To enable resident companies to make full use of unutilized dividend-franking credits as of December 31, 2002 the Minister for Finance introduced a five-year transitional period from January 1, 2003, to December 31, 2007 for such companies to pay franked dividends out of their unutilized dividend-franking credits as of December 31, 2002. During this period, shareholders will continue to receive these dividends with tax credits attached and will be entitled to offset the tax credits against their tax liability. Companies also have the option of making an irrevocable election to opt into the one-tier tax system at any time during this transitional period.

Companies that repurchase their shares—limited to the maximum of 10 percent of share capital—are considered to have paid a dividend out of distributable profits with respect to the amount paid in excess of the contributed capital: paid-up capital and share premium, if any. Similarly, payment out of a share capital reduction exercise or payment for redemption of redeemable preference shares in excess of the relatable capital contribution would be treated as a dividend distribution. All such dividends would carry franking credits or be treated as exempt dividends under the one-tier system.

There are various avenues whereby the profits of the target company may be repatriated to the home country by means other than dividends. These include the payment of license fees, royalties, interest, and management fees. However, the payment of such amounts may be subject to withholding taxes.

Appropriate tax treaties may reduce the withholding tax rates. For example, payment of interest to a Mauritian entity is not subject to withholding tax, provided certain conditions are met. Management fees in consideration for services rendered outside Singapore that are recharged should not be subject to withholding tax or should not be taxed if an appropriate double-tax agreement operates to exempt the fee from tax—due to the nonexistence of a permanent establishment in Singapore. Singaporean tax legislation does not have any specific antitreaty shopping provisions, and if an arrangement with commercial substance takes advantage of a tax treaty, the reduced rate provided under that treaty should generally apply.

6.2   Losses Carryforwards and Unabsorbed Capital Allowance

Operating losses may be carried forward indefinitely and applied against income in future years. A corporation may utilize its loss as long as its shareholders, on the last day of the year in which the loss was incurred, are substantially the same as the shareholders on the first day of the year of assessment in which the loss is to be utilized. The shareholders are considered to be substantially the same if 50 percent or more of the shareholders at the two points in time are the same.

Unused capital allowances may also be carried forward indefinitely if the corporation carries on the same business and the shareholders on the last day of the year in which the allowances arose are substantially the same as the shareholders on the first day of the year of assessment in which the unused allowances would be used.

A waiver to comply with the foregoing ownership requirements may be obtained from the Minister for Finance if the substantial change in shareholdings is not for the purpose of obtaining a tax benefit. Losses, which would otherwise be forfeited, may then be utilized, but generally only against income from the same business that incurred the losses.

6.3   Continuity of Tax Incentives

In general, any tax incentives available to the target would be lost when the business is transferred through an asset deal. However, it may be possible to obtain approval from the authority granting the incentive to ensure the continued applicability of the incentive to the transferred business.

Tax concessions available to a target are generally preserved through a stock deal unless prior approval is required as a condition of the initial granting of such a concession to the target.

6.4   Group Relief

Beginning with the 2003 year of assessment (companies with financial years ending from January 1, 2002 to December 31, 2002), a company's tax losses may be used to offset the profits of another group company under the group relief system. The group relief system recognizes group companies as a single entity by allowing a company's current year's unabsorbed capital allowances, trade losses, and donations—collectively known as loss items—to offset the assessable income of another company belonging to the same group. Group companies are those Singaporean incorporated companies that have a common equity shareholding of at least 75 percent held directly or indirectly by the same Singaporean corporate shareholders. In the determination of whether the minimum 75-percent-shareholding threshold has been achieved, equity interest held through foreign companies and shares with fixed dividend rights are to be ignored. Additionally, the companies must be able to demonstrate that they are beneficially entitled directly or indirectly to at least 75 percent of residual profits and assets (in case of liquidation) available for distribution to all equity holders.

The following graphically illustrates group relief:

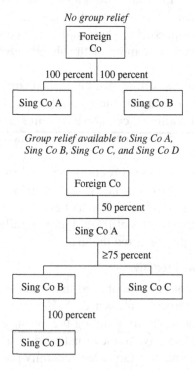

To be eligible for group relief, the companies in question must have a common year-end, and the shareholding requirement must be fulfilled for a continuous period that ends on the last day of the common accounting period. If the continuous period ends on the last day of the accounting period but does not actually cover the entire accounting year, then only the loss items attributable to that continuous period may be transferred.

6.5   Receipts under Warranties or Indemnities

Generally, payments made by the seller for breach of warranty or under an indemnity are treated as adjustments to the purchase price.

7.   DISPOSALS

Singapore does not have detailed legislation dealing with the tax treatment of acquisitions. Accordingly, general principles of taxation would apply in the structuring of a deal and in the choice between a disposal of assets or stock.

7.1   Stock Disposals

(a) Profit on sale of stock   Generally, unless the vendor is a share dealer or a venture capitalist, profits derived from the sale of shares should not be subject to tax, because such profits should be of a capital nature. As a result, it is generally preferable, from the seller's perspective, to sell stock.

(b) Distribution of profits   Under the one-tier system (see Section 6.1), all profits, including capital gains, which have not been subject to tax, may be distributed as tax-free dividends to the shareholders.

7.2   Asset Disposals

(a) Profits on sale of assets   In an asset deal, any price received for the sale of goodwill, including self-generated intellectual property that has been used in the business, should not be subject to tax in the hands of the seller. However, any profits on the sale of inventories or tax-depreciable assets—that is, to the extent of the tax depreciation recouped—should be subject to tax in the hands of the seller.

A corporate seller should be prepared to enter into an asset deal if the company has tax losses or unutilized tax depreciation or if the sales price of the inventories and the tax-depreciable assets is not substantially higher than their book value.

In the allocation of the price for the assets sold, the value allocated to inventories and tax-depreciable assets should be on an arm's-length basis. Otherwise, it is subject to challenge by the tax authorities.

(b) Distribution of profits   Under the one-tier system, all profits, including capital gains, which have not been subject to tax, can be distributed as tax-free dividends.

7.3   Deferred Compensation and Earn-Outs

Contingent consideration is not included in the purchase price until the contingency has materialized and the amount of additional payment has been made.

8. TRANSACTION COSTS FOR SELLERS

8.1 GST

The GST rate is 5 percent. GST is collected by a GST-registered service provider (seller) and is payable by the end user (purchaser). However, certain goods or services, such as transfer of shares, are exempt from GST. A transfer of a business that satisfies certain conditions is also exempt from GST.

8.2 Stamp Duty Tax

Stamp duty is generally payable by the purchaser unless otherwise stated in a contract.

8.3 Concessions Related to Mergers and Acquisitions

See Section 2.3.

8.4 Tax Deductibility of Transaction Costs

Generally, transaction costs are not tax deductible to the seller in Singapore except for any expenses that may be attributed to the sale of inventory.

9. PREPARING A TARGET COMPANY FOR SALE

9.1 Transfer of Assets Being Retained to Another Company within the Group

For income tax purposes, with respect to sales of tax-depreciable assets to a related party, the transferor and transferee may elect to transfer these assets at the tax bases. As a result, prior tax depreciation is not assessable income of the transferor. Parties are related if the buyer controls the seller or vice versa or if they belong to the same group of companies.

9.2 Declaration of Dividend prior to the Sale

One of the means of extracting surplus cash from a company that is identified for sale is through dividends. When the company identified for sale has imputation balance, franked dividends should be declared to the maximum extent. The imputed tax may, in certain circumstances—such as in a loss situation or group relief—be offset.

10. DEMERGERS

Under Singaporean tax law, there are no specific provisions related to demergers. A demerger usually takes place through the sale of assets or of business. It is important to note that any loss carryforwards or unabsorbed capital allowances may not be transferable. The implications for a demerger would be the same as those for an asset deal. (See Section 1.2.)

11. LISTINGS AND INITIAL PUBLIC OFFERINGS

After acquiring a target, a financial buyer generally looks for an exit strategy involving either a sale or an initial public offering (IPO). Since a financial buyer's objectives are to maximize return on investment and optimize exit multiples, any profits derived from an exit by means of an asset or stock sale are generally regarded as income subject to tax. To realize profits in a tax-efficient manner, an appropriate structure should be put in place to effect the acquisition.

If a company is seeking a listing on the Singapore Stock Exchange, the listed vehicle, which can also be the acquisition vehicle, should be incorporated in Singapore.

Generally, profits derived from an IPO by a financial buyer may be subject to tax in Singapore because the gains are regarded as income. However, if the shares are held through a company resident in, for example, Mauritius, the gain should not be taxable in Singapore, as provided under the Mauritius-Singapore double-tax agreement.

For financial buyers that require a good exit multiple achievable through an IPO, any goodwill needs to be housed in an appropriate vehicle to avoid diluting the group profits on which the IPO price may be based. There are no restrictions on the transfer of goodwill to an entity outside Singapore. Goodwill may be packaged such that a foreign acquirer may obtain a tax deduction for the purchased goodwill and charge the Singaporean company a fee for benefiting from use of the goodwill.

12. INCENTIVES

12.1 Tax Incentives

As mentioned in the Introduction, a number of tax incentives are granted for doing business in Singapore. They include:

- Pioneer enterprise
- Export enterprise
- Headquarters (HQ) incentive
- Finance and treasury center
- Approved fund managers
- Approved international shipping enterprise
- Global trader program
- Venture capital companies
- Research and development (R&D) and intellectual property
- Management hub scheme

Entities carrying on approved activities may take advantage of a concessionary tax rate ranging from 0 to 15 percent for a specified period (generally, 5 to 10 years) depending on the types of tax incentive.

12.2 HQ Incentive

The HQ incentive is available with respect to the following activities:

- Strategic business planning and development
- General management and administration
- Marketing control, planning, and brand management
- Intellectual property management
- Corporate training and personnel management
- Research, development, and test bedding of new concepts
- Shared services
- Economic or investment research and analysis
- Technical support services
- Sourcing, procurement, and distribution
- Corporate finance advisory services

Depending on the scale of investment and the level of operation, an HQ set up in Singapore may qualify for either a regional HQ (RHQ) award or an international HQ (IHQ) award.

(a) RHQ award   Under this incentive, a company is entitled to pay tax at a concessionary tax rate of 15 percent on qualifying income for five years. Qualifying income includes management fees, sales/trading income, and royalties. There are a number of criteria that the applicant must meet by the end of the third year of the incentive period, such as minimum total business spending of at least SGD2 million.

This incentive is attractive to companies looking for a base to conduct exploratory forays into the Asia-Pacific region. It allows such companies to enjoy concessionary tax treatment while they evaluate the viability of using Singapore as a base or as they take the initial step to expand, thereby qualifying for further incentives such as the IHQ award.

(b) IHQ Award   Under this incentive, a company is entitled to pay tax at a concessionary tax rate of 0, 5, or 10 percent on incremental qualifying income for 5 to 20 years. Tax rates are customized based on commitment level. Qualifying income includes management fees, sales/trading income, and royalties. This award is suitable for companies with a commitment substantially higher than that required under the RHQ award.

12.3   Research and Development and Intellectual Property Management Hub Plan

This plan provides an exemption from tax on foreign-sourced royalty and interest income received in Singapore, where such foreign income is deployed for research and development (R&D) activities. The incentive is applicable for a period of five years from the date of the approval. There are detailed rules governing the mechanics of the plan, and there are various conditions. Among others, the latter includes commercialization of the resulting intellectual property by the company and a requirement that at least 20 percent of R&D be performed in Singapore.

SLOVAK REPUBLIC

INTRODUCTION

This chapter details the principal tax issues that are relevant to purchasers and sellers engaged in the transfer of ownership of a Slovak trade or business. Unless otherwise stated, it is generally assumed that all sellers and purchasers are Slovak companies with limited liability.

The Slovak Republic became a member of the European Union (EU) on May 1, 2004. Further to the accession treaty concluded between the Slovak Republic and the EU, some 80,000 pages of community law were required to be implemented within Slovak legislation by that date. This includes all EU law with respect to taxation, notably the value-added tax (VAT), merger, and parent/subsidiary directives. Legislation regarding the Interest/Royalty Directive is expected to be introduced by May 1, 2006. Slovak tax law has been simplified, and a variety of minor taxes such as gift tax have been eliminated. The harmonization process has also brought about significant changes in Slovak company law, as well as new Income Tax Acts.

The Slovak tax and legal system recognizes several types of business reorganizations. Currently, the following basic methods can be used to reorganize a business:

- **Merger.** This is the process whereby existing legal entities are wound up without liquidation, and a surviving entity takes over their assets and liabilities.
- **Acquisitions.** The following types of acquisitions are commonly used: asset acquisitions (either the acquisition of individual assets or business assets constituting a going concern) or share acquisitions.

The main taxes that need to be considered in the acquisition of a Slovak company include:

- **Corporate income tax.** This is a tax on profits earned by a company. The corporate and income tax rate is currently 19 percent.
- **VAT.** This is a tax charged on the taxable supply of goods and services in the Slovak Republic on the import of goods and on occasional international bus transport. Certain supplies are exempt or fall outside the scope of Slovak VAT. A unified VAT rate of 19 percent is applicable on all taxable supplies.

1.   ACQUISITIONS

1.1   Asset Acquisitions

Asset acquisitions may take the form of the acquisition of individual assets or the acquisition of assets constituting a business that is a going concern.

(a) Acquisition of individual assets   An acquisition of individual assets generally enables the purchaser to avoid exposure related to the risk of any historical liabilities that are not expressly purchased as part of the assets.

On an acquisition of individual assets, contracts between the seller and third parties, as well as employment contracts, are not automatically assigned to the purchaser. The purchaser, therefore, needs to either enter into new contracts or agree to have the old contracts assigned to them as required. (Note that employment contracts may need to be renegotiated upon such a change.) The cancellation of contracts may result in certain seller economic costs and may become a negotiating point in a potential transaction.

The consideration for each individual asset needs to be determined in the sale-and-purchase agreement (SPA). The consideration paid for an asset becomes its new acquisition price for a purchaser. As a result, a step-up in the tax basis of the assets can be achieved.

(b) Acquisition of a business or part of a business as a going concern   Slovak legislation defines *business as a going concern* as a group of tangible assets, intangible assets, and personal assets constituting a discrete operating unit. The tangible-property element is represented by material features of the business, such as tangible fixed assets and accounts payable and receivable. The intangible elements include property rights or goodwill related to the business operations, among other items. Finally, the personal element is represented by the employees of the business. A part of a business that forms a separate identifiable organizational division within a larger business may also be transferred.

Under the contract for sale of a going concern, certain carryover features occur that follow what would likely occur in a share sale and purchase. For example, certain commercial contracts between the seller and the seller's customers and suppliers are transferred automatically to the purchaser. Employment contracts also are transferred automatically with the transferred business.

The transferred employees should be notified about the transfer, and the conditions agreed to in their original employment contracts would remain unchanged in the short term. From an administrative point of view, the seller should deregister all transferred employees for social security purposes, and the purchaser should register the employees. Any rights and obligations arising from any collective bargaining agreements—for example, additional bonuses—are also automatically transferred to the purchaser. However, the purchaser is not obliged to renew such transferred agreements once they have expired.

Existing liabilities attached to the business or a part of a business are transferred to the purchaser. It is not possible to exclude unwanted liabilities from the transfer; that is, no cherry picking is allowed. In general, the contingent and unknown liabilities remain with the seller.

The purchased assets together with attached liabilities are registered by the purchasing entity in its balance sheet at their fair value that is represented by fair market value, value determined by a court-approved valuation expert, or acquisition price depending on which value is available. If the purchase price paid for the business differs from fair value, the difference represents goodwill—or negative goodwill when the assessed value is higher than the purchase price paid by the purchaser. The depreciation of such goodwill (or negative goodwill) arising on the acquisition of a business as a going concern is tax deductible (or taxable) over a period of up to five years. The annual tax depreciation charge of the goodwill (or negative goodwill) should equal the accounting depreciation charge.

1.2   Stock Acquisitions

In a stock acquisition, the purchaser effectively bears any historical and future liabilities, including ongoing tax liabilities of the purchased company. Therefore, from a purchaser's perspective, it is often beneficial to purchase assets rather than shares.

Contracts between the purchased company and third parties generally remain in force and do not need to be assigned or renegotiated with the third party.

2.   TRANSACTION COSTS FOR PURCHASERS

2.1   Transfer Taxes

No transfer taxes apply in the Slovak Republic.

2.2   Value-Added Tax

(a) Asset acquisitions

(i) Acquisition of individual assets   A transfer of assets in the Slovak Republic is subject to Slovak VAT with the exception of land, cash, receivables, and liabilities that fall outside the scope of Slovak VAT. If the seller of individual assets is a Slovak VAT payer, then a VAT of 19 percent is charged on the selling price of the assets. The transfer of land, with exception of land used for construction purposes, is exempt as a VAT supply. The transfer of receivables and cash for nominal value is not subject to VAT.

The purchaser can recover the input VAT paid if it is, or becomes at any point in the future, registered for Slovak VAT.

It should be noted that special rules apply when a claimant subsequently becomes registered for Slovak VAT. For example, the input VAT related to purchased tangible fixed assets, material, inventory, and intangible fixed assets might be claimed, but the amount recoverable is reduced by depreciation claimed prior to VAT registration. Further, VAT related to the assets sold during the period while the purchaser was not a Slovak VAT payer cannot be reclaimed.

The input VAT recovery might be restricted when the purchaser provides the VAT-exempt supplies—for example, provision of loans or transactions with securities.

(ii) Acquisition of a business or part of a business as a going concern
The transfer of a business or part of a business as a going concern is not subject to Slovak VAT if both the seller and the purchaser of the business are registered Slovak VAT payers.

Note that purchasers of a Slovak-based business/going concern that are not registered automatically become so registered upon the purchase. However, if the purchaser is an entity that provides VAT-exempt supplies such as a bank, the transfer of business or part of a business as a going concern is subject to Slovak VAT.

(b) Stock acquisitions   The transfer of shares is exempt from Slovak VAT.

2.3   Capital Taxes

There are no capital taxes in the Slovak Republic that are applicable either to stock purchases or to asset purchases.

2.4   Tax Deductibility of Transaction Costs

The transaction costs of stock or asset acquisitions can be summarized as:

- Financing costs
- Investigation, advisory, and due diligence costs
- VAT treatment of transaction costs

(a) Financing costs   Costs related to the procurement of equity financing generally form part of the tax base of the shares and currently are not deductible.

(b) Investigation, advisory, and due diligence costs   Legal and advisory costs related to the formation of a company can be capitalized and depreciated for tax purposes over a period of up to five years.

Due diligence and other investigation and advisory costs are not deductible in aborted transactions. Transaction costs are deemed to be shareholder costs and therefore are not tax deductible by the target company.

(c) VAT treatment of transaction costs   All fees charged by banks are VAT-exempt supplies. Therefore, no input VAT is due on receipt of bank services.

Advisory fees are subject to VAT at 19 percent if the advisers are Slovak VAT payers. Certain advisory services that are provided by Slovak advisers for an overseas entity may be subject to VAT at a 0 percent rate. A reverse-charge mechanism has been introduced as of May 1, 2004. Advisory fees charged to a Slovak VAT payer are subject to self-assessment at a rate of 19 percent. However, no cash costs should arise, because the Slovak VAT payer is entitled to recover any self-assessed VAT in the same VAT return.

If the recipient of the service is not a Slovak VAT payer, no self-assessment applies. However, any foreign VAT charged on the services rendered may not be recoverable.

Input VAT related to transaction costs is usually recoverable by the purchaser that is a Slovak VAT payer in the case of an acquisition of individual assets or of a business or part of a business. If shares are purchased, input VAT on advisory services is not recoverable by the purchaser.

3.   BASIS OF TAXATION FOLLOWING ASSET OR STOCK ACQUISITIONS

3.1   Asset Acquisition

(a) Acquisition of individual assets   If individual assets are purchased, the purchase price as detailed in the SPA represents the base cost of the purchased assets in the purchaser's books.

The purchaser depreciates the purchased fixed assets for tax purposes based on the price paid for the assets net of VAT if the VAT can be recovered. There are two tax-depreciation methods for tangible fixed assets: the linear method and the reducing-balance method. The taxpayer can choose which method to apply to each individual fixed asset. The depreciation period varies from 4 to 20 years depending on the type of the fixed asset.

The purchased intangible fixed assets must be fully written off within five years following their acquisition.

Investments, material, and inventory purchased are recorded on the purchaser's books at the purchase price agreed to in the SPA. Receivables are purchased at their net book value; payables and cash are purchased at their nominal value.

(b) Acquisition of a business or part of a business as a going concern   If an allocation of the purchase price paid for individual assets exists in the SPA, then the tax basis of the assets acquired as part of the business as a going concern would be set up in the same manner as in the case of an acquisition of individual assets. (See Section 3.1(a).) Alternatively, a valuation of the purchased business and individual items may be obtained from a court-approved valuation expert. Such valuation would then form the tax basis of the assets purchased as part of the business.

For tax purposes, the purchaser calculates depreciation of the purchased fixed assets based on the assets' allocated tax basis. (See Section 3.1(a).) Purchased goodwill is depreciated equally for accounting and tax purposes for up to five years. Investments, material, and inventory purchased are entered into the purchaser's books at their tax basis determined as stated earlier in this section. Receivables are purchased at their net book value; payables and cash are purchased at their nominal value.

3.2   Stock Acquisitions

The purchase price of the purchased shares represents the base cost of the shares in the purchaser's books. Goodwill arising on the consolidation of the company into the financial statements of the parent company is not tax deductible.

4.   FINANCING OF ACQUISITIONS

4.1   Debt

(a) Withholding tax   Interest paid to overseas lenders other than banks is subject to withholding tax of 19 percent. The withholding tax rate can be reduced according to relevant double-tax treaties. The EU interest and royalty directive will become applicable beginning May 1, 2006. Under the directive, interest paid between EU residents should in general be tax free. There is no withholding tax on interest paid to a Slovak borrower.

(b) Deductibility of interest   Interest is generally tax deductible on an accruals basis. Nonbank interest accrued but unpaid in periods before December 31, 2003, is tax deductible on a cash basis.

Interest on acquisition debt is not tax deductible unless it is capitalized in the costs of the shares acquired. In order to obtain a tax deduction of acquisition debt, it may be necessary to merge the acquisition and target companies. Subsequently, it is advisable for the acquisition debt to be refinanced by newly drawn debt.

(c) Thin capitalization   No thin-capitalization rules apply in the Slovak Republic on interest accrued after January 1, 2004.

Previously, a 4:1 debt/equity ratio restricted the deductibility of interest on related-party debt. Such restrictions are still applicable on interest on related-party debt that has been accrued but that remained unpaid before December 31, 2003. A 6:1 ratio was applicable in the case of related-party loans provided by banks or by insurance companies.

Interest accrued but unpaid before December 31, 2003, on related-party debt in excess of the thin-capitalization ratio is reclassified as a dividend. A withholding tax of 19 percent is applicable on payment of excess interest after April 1, 2004. The rate of withholding tax may be reduced by an applicable double-tax treaty. Provided the excess interest is paid to an EU resident who directly owns at least 25 percent of the shares in the Slovak entity at the moment of paying the excess interest, no withholding tax is applicable.

(d) Transfer pricing   Interest charged on loans between related parties must be on an arm's-length basis. Otherwise, transfer-pricing rules may apply so as to restrict interest deductions.

Any related-party interest that was accrued but remained unpaid by December 31, 2003, in excess of the arm's-length (usual market) price is treated as a dividend. If excess interest that was accrued by December 31, 2003, is paid to the related party on or after April 1, 2004, it is subject to 19 percent withholding tax. The withholding tax rate may be reduced by a relevant double-tax treaty. If the recipient of the excess interest accrued by December 31, 2003, is a direct shareholder that has its seat in an EU member state and owns at least 25 percent of the shares in the interest-paying company, no withholding tax is applicable.

(e) Key nontax issues

(i) Government consents   There are generally no government consents that are required in the Slovak Republic with regard to making an acquisition or raising financing.

(ii) Abuse-of-law provisions   The Slovak Republic has no abuse-of-law provisions.

(iii) Other key nontax issues   In the Slovak Republic, there are no financial assistance rules. A Slovak company may finance the acquisition of its own shares.

4.2   Equity

There is no capital duty on the issuance of new shares.

Dividends are not deductible by the company paying the dividend. Dividends received are not taxable in the hands of Slovak recipients of dividends. Dividends declared out of pre-2004 profits that were received by a Slovak parent company prior to March 31, 2004, are fully taxable at a rate of 19 percent.

Distribution of profits generated after January 1, 2004, is tax free, and no withholding tax is applicable on such dividends.

Distribution of pre-2004 profits is subject to withholding tax of 19 percent if paid on or after April 1, 2004. The withholding tax rate may be reduced by a relevant double-tax treaty. No withholding tax is applicable on dividends paid from pre-2004 profits if the recipient of the dividend is a direct shareholder that has its seat in an EU member state and owns at least 25 percent of the shares in the distributing company.

5.   MERGERS

5.1   Legal Forms

There are several forms available for combining existing legal entities. These include:

- **Merger.** A merger occurs when an existing entity takes over the assets and liabilities of two or more existing companies that are being wound up without liquidation. Both upstream and downstream mergers are legally possible.
- **Amalgamation.** An amalgamation occurs when a new, surviving entity is created from the process of winding up without liquidation of existing legal entities.

The surviving entity is the legal successor of the dissolved entity or entities.

5.2   Tax Consequences

Any capital gain or loss arising from a merger or an amalgamation is not subject to tax in the Slovak Republic.

Any restructuring of the entities that reside in the EU countries should be tax neutral. The Slovak Commercial Code in its current form does not, however, allow cross-border mergers, and any changes to the code have not been proposed.

Upon merger, the assets and liabilities of dissolved companies are transferred to the surviving entity at the merger date at their carrying values, that is, the tax written-down values of the transferred assets in the books of the dissolved entity. No goodwill or negative goodwill may arise as the result of a merger.

In an amalgamation, the transferred assets and liabilities must be revalued for accounting purposes in the closing books of the dissolved entity to their fair value—that is, either a professional estimate or valuation by an independent expert. The surviving company takes over the assets and liabilities from the closing balance sheet of the predecessor at their revised value. Alternatively, the difference between the restated value and the carrying value may be recorded as goodwill or negative goodwill. Such revaluation of asset and liability values and goodwill or negative goodwill is ignored for corporate income tax purposes.

For tax purposes, in both a merger and an amalgamation, the surviving entity continues with the prior method of tax depreciation of depreciable fixed assets: using the same tax basis for depreciation and the same depreciation method as used by the dissolved company. In the year of merger or amalgamation, the dissolving entity can claim proportional amounts of annual depreciation charges attributable to any whole calendar month prior to the merger. The surviving entity can claim depreciation charges attributable to the remainder of the tax year.

The dissolved entity must release any reserves and provisions that are not taken over by the surviving entity. Any income arising as a result of release of such reserves and provisions is taxable unless their creation was not tax deductible. The surviving entity takes over any reserves and provisions carried forward. The release of the reserves and provisions created by the dissolved entity by the surviving entity would be taxable unless their creation in the dissolved entity's books was not tax deductible.

Investments, inventory, material, works in progress, and receivables are taken over by the surviving entity at their net book values. Cash is transferred at its nominal value.

In mergers, the surviving entity can utilize the tax losses of its legal predecessor.

In mergers between related companies, the successor company can proportionally apply certain types of tax credits that had been applicable by the dissolved company before the merger. However, no further tax credits are available after January 1, 2004, unless the tax credit has already been claimed before January 1, 2004.

Generally, amalgamation enables the surviving entity to use any prior tax losses of its legal predecessors (wound up without liquidation). This was not the case prior to 2004. Amalgamation disqualifies the surviving company from claiming any tax credit or tax incentive that was applied by the dissolved entity.

Upon the reorganization of a Slovak entity that is a registered Slovak VAT payer, the surviving entity or entities automatically become Slovak VAT payers.

5.3   Exchange of Securities for Those in Another Company

If shareholders of existing companies swap the shares in those companies for stock or debentures in a merged company, the exchange may be treated as not involving a disposal by the shareholders. New stock in the merged company is treated for tax purposes as the same asset as their original stock in the dissolved companies. The tax-base cost of the merged-company stock is the same as was the tax-base cost in the dissolved company previously held. Effectively, any in-built gain or loss on the merged company stock is deferred from tax until the date of any future sale of the stock in the merged company.

6. OTHER STRUCTURING AND POSTDEAL ISSUES

6.1   Creation of Local-Country Tax Groups

No tax groups exist in the Slovak Republic.

6.2   Minimization of After-Tax Cost of Debt

Because no tax grouping exists in the Slovak Republic, in order to achieve an effective debt push down, it is necessary to merge the leveraged holding company with the target company. It is also advisable to refinance any acquisition debt following the merger to obtain a tax deduction on any interest. Alternatively, the target company may be converted into a partnership that is tax transparent.

6.3   Repatriation of Profits

The following methods of repatriating profits or withdrawing cash from a Slovak company may be used:

- **Distributions.** Distributions of dividends are allowable to the extent of profits and distributable reserves. No Slovak withholding is levied on dividends for profits or distributable reserves originating after January 1, 2004. Distributions of pre-2004 profits are subject to withholding tax of 19 percent if paid on or after April 1, 2004. The withholding tax rate may be reduced by a relevant double-tax treaty. No withholding tax is applicable on dividends paid from pre-2004 profits if the recipient of the dividends is a direct shareholder that has its seat in an EU member state and owns at least 25 percent of the shares in the distributing company.

- **Share buybacks or redemptions.** Share capital reduction may be carried out if all losses of the Slovak subsidiary have been recovered. Redemption of share capital is tax free.

- **Upstream or cross-stream loans.** Intercompany loans may be issued by the Slovak subsidiary to a foreign affiliate. Interest must be charged at least at arm's length and would be taxable at the standard Slovak income tax rate of 19 percent.

- **Cross-chain sales.** The acquisition of affiliates such as cross-chain sales may be financed.

- **Intercompany service payments.** Intercompany service payments may be made, although the payments must be charged out at arm's length and need to be supported by relevant transfer-pricing documentation.

- **Licenses.** Royalty payments may be made, provided that they are substantiated and are charged at arm's length. Royalties are subject to withholding tax of 19 percent. The withholding tax rate may be reduced under a relevant double-tax treaty.
- **Intercompany debt allocation.** Interest can be charged to the Slovak company on loans used to finance business activities of the Slovak company.

No foreign exchange permission is generally required to make payments abroad. However, the Slovak National Bank may need to be notified.

6.4   Noncore Disposals

The general rules governing either disposal of assets, a business as a going concern, or shares should be followed.

6.5   Preservation of Existing Tax Attributes

The change in ownership of shares does not affect the ability of the target company to carry forward its tax losses or the entitlement to any special tax credit regime awarded or other tax incentives granted to the target company if the target company still meets the conditions to be eligible for such incentives. The tax losses as well as the tax incentives are attached to the entity in which these arose. Accordingly, tax losses and tax incentives generally are not transferred to the buyer in individual asset, partial business, or going-concern purchases.

With respect to mergers, demergers, and amalgamations, the surviving entity or entities can utilize the tax losses of the legal predecessor. In a merger with a related company, the successor company can proportionally apply certain types of tax incentives that had been applicable by the dissolved company prior to the merger. Amalgamation, however, disqualifies the surviving company from claiming any tax incentive awarded to the dissolved entity.

6.6   Receipts under Warranties or Indemnities

Any adjustment to the purchase price under warranties or indemnities should generally be recognized when entitlement to such adjustments arises. If any claim that gives rise to a liability under a warranty arises in the year of the sale of shares, then any adjustment to the purchase price can be reflected in the tax basis of the shares—rather than being taxed.

7.   DISPOSALS

7.1   Asset Disposals (Companies)

(a) Disposal of individual assets   Gains arising on the sale of assets that form part of business profits are subject to corporate tax at the rate of 19 percent.

Losses realized on disposal of individual assets generally—with the exception of receivables and securities—are fully tax deductible. Special rules apply to aggregate losses on sales of quoted shares if deductions are allowed, provided that the acquisition or selling price of each share sold is not lower than 90 percent of the average share price on the day of purchase or sale on the relevant stock exchange. Losses on the sale of participations are not tax deductible. Further, losses on the assignment of receivables are not tax deductible.

Sellers are not entitled to claim any tax-depreciation charges with respect to fixed assets sold in the year of sale. The tax bases of these depreciable fixed assets are fully deductible in a calculation of capital gain or loss arising on the sale of fixed assets.

(b) Disposal of a business or part of a business as a going concern   Capital gains arising on the sale of a business as a going concern are amalgamated with the business profits of the seller and are subject to corporation tax of 19 percent. Losses on the sale of a business as a going concern are fully deductible for the seller. The capital gain or loss on the sale is the difference between the purchased price adjusted by any transferred liabilities and cash and the tax value of the transferred assets.

As with the sale of individual assets, the seller is not entitled to claim any tax-depreciation on assets subject to sale. The tax bases of the fixed assets transferred are deducted from the sales proceeds in the calculation of the capital gain or loss arising on the sale.

Sale proceeds arising from the disposal of individual assets or of businesses as going concerns can be distributed to shareholders either through distribution of dividends to the extent of existing distributable reserves or through liquidation.

7.2   Stock Disposals

(a) Companies   Capital gains are taxed as part of business profits and are subject to corporate tax of 19 percent. Generally, capital losses arising on the sale of shares are not tax deductible unless the seller is a securities dealer. Losses on sales of quoted shares are tax deductible, provided the acquisition or selling price of each share sold is not lower than 90 percent of the average share price on the day of purchase or sale on the relevant stock exchange. This condition must be met for all sales of quoted shares in a tax year. Losses on sales of participations in companies other than joint-stock companies are not tax deductible.

Capital gain or loss is the difference between the selling price and the base cost of the shares. Base costs of the shares in a company include the acquisition value of those shares or the value of the initial and subsequent capital injection (including any capitalized shareholder debt) into the share capital and share premium and value of debt being swapped to share capital. Any capital injection above the registered share capital does not form part of the base cost of the shares.

Capital gains on the sale of shares in a Slovak company by nonresidents are taxable in the Slovak Republic if either the seller or the purchaser has a Slovak permanent establishment. The majority of double-tax treaties that the Slovak Republic has entered into eliminate the taxation of capital gains arising on the sale of shares by nonresidents.

(b) Individuals   Slovak resident individuals are liable to pay income tax of 19 percent on capital gains arising on a sale of shares. Capital losses incurred by individuals are ignored for tax purposes and therefore cannot be carried forward or offset against gains earned from other kinds of income such as entrepreneurial income.

(c) Tax-exempt entities   In general, all legal entities carrying out business activities in the Slovak Republic through either a Slovak legal entity or the Slovak branch of a foreign entity are liable for Slovak corporate income tax.

7.3   Deferred Consideration and Earn-Outs

Any deferred consideration payable on a sale of shares is recorded in the books of the seller at the time when the value of such consideration is known. Any deferred consideration received is taxable income when accrued. Generally, if an amount of deferred consideration is ascertainable at the time of the disposal, the full amount is included in the tax calculation of the disposal proceeds at the time of the sale if the receipt is confirmed before the end of the respective tax year.

7.4   Payments under Warranties or Indemnities

Any adjustments to the purchase price under warranties or indemnities should be recorded when the warranty claim is made and the liability arises. If any claim that gives rise to a liability under the warranty arises in the year of the sale of shares, then adjustments to the purchase price can be reflected in the calculation of the capital gain or loss. The actual amount of the liability claimed must be known prior to approval of the financial statements.

8.   TRANSACTION COSTS FOR SELLERS

8.1   Transfer Taxes

There is no stamp duty in the Slovak Republic.

8.2 VAT: Asset Disposals

(a) Disposal of individual assets   The sale of individual fixed assets (including real estate but excluding land), material, and inventory is regarded as a taxable supply that is subject to Slovak VAT. VAT must be charged by the seller that is registered for the Slovak VAT. The VAT rate is 19 percent. Land is generally exempt from Slovak VAT, but the sale of land used in construction is subject to Slovak VAT.

The transfer of receivables and liabilities falls outside the scope of Slovak VAT.

The transfer of either securities (including shares) or participations (investments) is regarded as a VAT-exempt taxable supply—that is, no output VAT should be charged—affecting input VAT recoverability of related input supplies.

(b) Disposal of businesses as going concerns   The sale of a business or part of a business as a going concern is generally not subject to Slovak VAT if both the seller and the purchaser are Slovak-registered VAT payers.

The sale of a business as a going concern is subject to Slovak VAT if the business is sold to an entity that provides mainly VAT-exempt supplies with no right to recover input VAT—such as banks and insurance companies. In such a case, VAT is charged as in the case of a sale of individual assets.

8.3 Stock Disposals

Disposals of stock (shares) are exempt from VAT.

8.4 Tax Deductibility of Transaction Costs

In general, all of the costs that have been incurred to make the sale and therefore to generate the taxable income from it should qualify as tax-deductible expenses.

(a) Advisory, legal, and valuation fees   Advisory, legal, and valuation fees related to disposal of both assets and shares should be deductible in the year in which they were accrued.

(b) VAT treatment of transaction costs   Input VAT with respect to transaction costs incurred on the sale of a business as a going concern is not recoverable. Input VAT with respect to the service purchased in order to carry out the sale of shares (which do not consititute VAT-able supply) is not recoverable, because the service is used for rendering VAT-exempt supply.

9.   PREPARING A TARGET COMPANY FOR SALE

9.1   Hive-Down of Assets

If the seller is selling only a division or part of a trading business or if there is a specific liability that needs to be excluded from the sale, a hive-down may be considered. Hiving down involves the transfer of specific assets of a company to another group company in exchange for shares or cash. If the specific business is transferred in exchange for shares, then a court-approved valuation of assets (trade) to be transferred is required. The value of in-kind contribution cannot exceed the court-approved value.

Hive-down of the business or assets is treated the same way as the sale of individual assets or of a business as a going concern.

Subsequent to the hive-down, shares in the subsidiary can be sold to third parties.

9.2   Intragroup Transfer of Retained Assets

Assets may be transferred out of group companies that are to be sold if it is not intended that these assets are to be included in the sale package.

A new company would be incorporated that would acquire the assets or business or part of the business from the group companies to be sold. As with the hive-down, the same rules that apply to a sale of individual assets or of a business as a going concern apply in this case.

9.3   Presale Dividends

Distributable reserves may be distributed as dividends. However, it is not possible to pay interim or special dividends.

10.   DEMERGERS

In the Slovak Republic, commercial legislation recognizes a demerger (split-up). A demerger occurs when a single company is wound up without liquidation and split into two or more separate companies or entities. The surviving entities take over all of the assets and liabilities of the dissolved company. The tax value of the transferred assets and liabilities represents the tax base of the acquired assets and liabilities for the surviving entities. The tax consequences of demergers are generally the same as the tax consequences of mergers and amalgamations.

The dissolved entity needs to release any reserves and provisions that are not taken over by the surviving entity. Any income arising as a result of release of such reserves and provisions is taxable unless the reserve has not previously been deducted for tax purposes.

The surviving entities continue with the same method of tax depreciation of depreciable fixed assets by using the same basis for depreciation as that used by the dissolved entity. In the year of demerger, the dissolving entity can claim a proportional amount of annual depreciation charge attributable to any whole calendar month prior to the demerger. After the demerger, the surviving entities claim depreciation charges attributable to the remainder of tax year—that is, during which time the assets were held in the surviving entity's register.

The balance of tax loss carryforward should be split among the surviving companies by using the same proportion that was used to split the predecessor's equity into those companies. Such losses may then be offset against future profits of the surviving entities for up to five years.

11. LISTINGS AND INITIAL PUBLIC OFFERINGS

11.1 Impact on Tax Status of Company

The tax status of a company is generally unaffected by a listing on a stock exchange.

11.2 Complete Group Listing or Listing of Subsidiary

No specific tax provisions governing either group listing or subsidiary listing exist in the Slovak Republic. In practice it is not common to float a Slovak company on the Bratislava Stock Exchange. Usually, a foreign holding company is introduced above the Slovak company and is then floated on a foreign stock exchange.

SPAIN

INTRODUCTION

This chapter details the principal tax issues that are relevant to purchasers and sellers engaged in the transfer of ownership of a Spanish trade or business. Unless otherwise stated, it is generally assumed that all sellers and purchasers are Spanish companies with limited liability.

The transfer of ownership of a Spanish business or company can take the form of a disposal of shares or assets. While there are significant differences in the tax implications of an asset or share sale, nontax considerations must also be taken into account. Unfortunately, it is very common for the parties to a transaction to have determined the form of the deal before considering the tax implications.

The relevant taxes to be considered are:

- **Corporate tax.** Generally, this is a 35 percent tax on profits earned by a company. Spanish companies are taxed on a stand-alone basis unless a tax-grouping treatment applies, in which case the group is the tax payer.
- **Value-added tax (VAT).** A 16 percent sales tax is generally added to the sales price charged for goods or services, except for certain categories of sale, which are exempt from or outside the scope of VAT. A purchaser or recipient of services generally can recover VAT paid if the purchase was incurred in the course of a commercial activity. However, the level of recoverability varies from case to case.
- **Transfer tax.** This is payable by a purchaser at a general rate of 6 or 7 percent on the purchase price for land or real estate.

1. ACQUISITIONS

1.1 Asset Acquisitions

An asset acquisition generally enables the purchaser to avoid exposure to the risk of any historical liabilities that are not specifically recoverable through the sale agreement. Liabilities associated with the purchased business remain the responsibility of the company that sold the asset and do not become the responsibility of the purchaser unless the parties agree that specified liabilities will transfer to the purchaser.

Nevertheless, in the event that the seller fails to settle those tax debts, a business transfer may result in the purchaser's being jointly and severally liable for tax debts that are settled or pending settlement and attributable to the business. The insolvency of the seller is no longer required. Therefore, guarantees should be requested and obtained from the seller.

An important nontax consideration is that on a sale of assets, contracts between the seller and third parties are not automatically assigned to the purchaser. Therefore, it is necessary for the purchaser either to enter into new contracts with the third parties or to agree with them that the existing contracts can be assigned from seller to purchaser. This often causes practical difficulties, particularly if there are numerous contracts or if a third party is unwilling to permit assignment. This frequently is a reason that stock transactions are preferred to asset transactions. In fact, each item—asset, liability, contract, right, obligation, and legal action—contained in the purchased business must be transferred. This involves a large number of formalities and procedures for the seller and purchaser as well as uncertainty, in that the counterparties to such agreements may deny their consent or call for special negotiations or even a change of conditions.

As a result of the purchase, there would be a change of employer. This may have significant effect with respect to employees' rights, which should be analyzed and handled carefully.

An asset acquisition generally facilitates a step-up in the tax basis of assets. In effect, the price paid is reflected in both assets and goodwill. Therefore, a significant advantage of a purchase of assets is that new values are established for future tax depreciation charges. This is especially relevant if there are significant built-in gains on fixed assets.

The purchaser would also be allowed to apply accelerated depreciation on assets that cannot be classified as new.

Amortization of goodwill is allowed for tax purposes up to a maximum annual limit of 1/20 (5 percent) of the amount of the goodwill. Nevertheless, it should be noted that goodwill arising in an intragroup transaction cannot be amortized by the purchaser unless it can be proved that there is an irreversible decline in the value of that goodwill.

However, a disadvantage arises for the shareholders of the selling company in that the proceeds of an asset sale will remain locked in that company. Distribution of those proceeds may result in double taxation. The company will already have been subject to tax on the sale of assets. In addition, the distribution of the sale proceeds by the company to its shareholders may result in taxable income to the shareholder, depending on the shareholder. This may affect, in particular, shareholders who are Spanish resident individuals because they are subject to income tax on dividends received or liquidation proceeds, in the latter case, unless the shares have been held for the reguisite holding period. (See Section 7.1.) If the shareholder is a company that owns a substantial shareholding in the selling company, then the distribution of the sales profit as a dividend should not trigger further taxation to the shareholder, because the dividend will be exempt. In fact, this exemption takes the form of a tax credit amounting to 35 percent of the dividend. (See Section 6.2.)

1.2   Stock Acquisitions

In a stock acquisition, the purchaser effectively bears any historical and future ongoing tax and nontax liabilities of the target company. However, the purchaser is liable only up to the amount of the net worth of the company acquired. The seller should, therefore, be required to provide guarantees during the negotiation of the deal.

An important advantage of a stock acquisition is that contracts between the target company and third parties remain in force and do not need to be assigned or renegotiated with the third party, although some contracts may contain change-of-control provisions that might result in the termination of or other amendment to the contract in the event of a change in ownership of the target company.

The purchase price forms the base cost of the purchaser's stock in the acquired company. The underlying base cost in the acquired company's assets is not changed, and there is no election available to step up the tax basis of assets. Similarly, goodwill is not tax deductible.

Regardless, the step-up in the tax basis of the underlying assets can sometimes be achieved if the target is merged into the purchaser company by means of an upstream merger. As a result of this type of merger, the difference between the price paid for the stock and the accounting value of the underlying assets is allocated first to built-in gains of those assets. The remainder is allocated to goodwill, which can be amortized. Note that when the seller is an individual, this allocation is allowed to the extent that the gain obtained by the individual on the sale of the shares in the target was taxed.

In this kind of merger, there is a risk that the Spanish Tax Administration may challenge the application of the special tax treatment for restructuring operations on the grounds that the upstream merger has not been carried out for valid economic reasons such as the restructuring or rationalization of the activities of the companies involved in the merger.

With respect to goodwill arising from the acquisition of a stake in a foreign company, a merger would not be necessary, because the tax amortization of the financial goodwill—that is, the goodwill embedded in the price of the shares— is allowed if the target qualifies for the substantial shareholdings exemption and if the amount has not benefited from the tax credit for export activities.

Foreign financial goodwill can be amortized over 20 years regardless of whether the amortization has been recorded as an accounting expense. This is in line with the Spanish government's efforts to promote investment in foreign companies.

The stockholder is allowed to enter provisions for the decline in value of the target shares, which, as long as they relate to losses in the target, may be considered deductible.

The possibility might also exist of applying a tax credit for export activities derived from the acquisition of stock in foreign entities. There is a 25 percent tax credit on an investment related to the formation of a foreign branch or to the acquisition of a stake of at least 25 percent in a foreign entity linked to export activities or to tourist services in Spain.

2.   TRANSACTION COSTS FOR PURCHASERS

2.1   Value-Added Tax

(a) Stock purchases   Stock transfers are exempt from VAT.

(b) Asset purchases   The transfer of all of the assets and liabilities of a company to a single purchaser that continues to exercise the same activity as the seller is outside the scope of VAT. However, this can trigger transfer tax on the real estate transferred—normally, at the rate of 6 to 7 percent—which must be paid by the purchaser.

The transfer of a separate business within a company does not give rise to the right to the exemption, in which case VAT—normally, at the rate of 16 percent—becomes applicable. Second and subsequent transfers of real estate are exempt from VAT and are therefore subject to transfer tax. However, it is possible to opt for VAT, provided that certain requirements are met, thereby avoiding the cost of transfer tax.

When the purchasing entity is subject to VAT and is obliged to charge VAT on its sales, it may recover VAT paid on its own purchases. Therefore, VAT charged on a purchase of assets may be recovered by the buyer. Note that in some situations, depending on certain VAT-related characteristics of the buyer, the VAT paid may not always be recoverable in full. Consequently, VAT paid would be a real cost to the buyer. Despite the fact that VAT paid is recoverable by the buyer, the financial impact should be considered. An inconveniently long time may elapse before VAT is recovered in the event that not enough output VAT is generated to absorb the VAT paid on the asset purchase—for example, in the case of exempt activities being carried out. At the end of the year, the remaining excess of VAT on inputs can be claimed.

2.2 Transfer Tax

(a) Stock purchases There is an exemption from transfer tax on the transfer of shares. This exemption does not apply when, as a result of the transfer, the buyer obtains control of an entity whose assets are made up of at least 50 percent real property located in a Spanish territory. In this case, the transfer of stock is subject to transfer tax—as if a transfer of real property were involved—at a rate normally from 6 to 7 percent depending on the location of the real estate.

(b) Asset purchases Transfer tax on real estate is discussed in Section 2.1.

2.3 Capital Taxes

There are no capital taxes in Spain applicable to stock or asset purchases.

2.4 Tax Deductibility of Transaction Costs

In general, the tax deductibility of a particular expense depends on several factors, including whether the transaction is for the purchase of assets or the purchase of shares.

In general terms, the position is summarized in the following sections.

(a) Financing costs Financing costs are deductible for corporate tax purposes. See Section 4.1(c) for thin-capitalization rules.

(b) Investigation and due diligence costs Due diligence and other investigation costs related to an asset purchase may be capitalized as start-up costs and amortized at a minimum rate of 20 percent, which allows for full amortization in the year of the transaction. This expense would generally be considered deductible for tax purposes.

Costs related to a share purchase would increase the consideration paid for the shares and would not be considered ordinary deductible expenses.

(c) Other deal costs In general, any cost incurred that is related to an asset or share purchase would follow the rules set forth in Section 2.4(b).

(d) VAT treatment of expenses Fees charged for loans and for the issuance of stock generally are exempt from VAT in Spain. Therefore, bank and institutional fees generally do not carry VAT. However, professional fees charged to Spanish customers by advisers based in Spain are subject to VAT.

If a holding company buys stock, then the VAT charged by third parties in connection with the purchase process may be recoverable under some circumstances. Typically, a deduction may be claimed when the purchaser is an active holding company providing services (administrative, management, and/or financial) for the target company and other companies. However, Spanish tax authorities often consider this issue to be controversial.

3. BASIS OF TAXATION FOLLOWING ASSET OR STOCK ACQUISITIONS

3.1 Asset Acquisitions

Tax depreciation is available with respect to fixed assets. The percentage rates depend on the type of asset and on the activity developed by the company.

Normally, purchased intangible assets, including goodwill, are eligible for tax amortization over a period of 20 years unless purchased from group companies.

Usually, sales of inventory are included in the seller's trading profits, and the purchaser receives tax basis equal to the value of stock as paid.

Typically, trade debts are acquired at net book value—that is, nominal value. When the amount subsequently received is equal to the net book value, no taxable profit or loss arises. If any of the debts prove to be irrecoverable whether in full or in part, it should be possible to obtain a tax deduction to the extent that the debt is not recovered.

3.2 Stock Acquisition

As covered in Section 1.2, the purchase price forms the base cost of the purchaser's stock in the acquired company. The underlying base cost in the acquired company's assets is not changed, and there is no election available to step up the tax basis of assets. Similarly, goodwill is not tax deductible.

The step-up in the tax basis of the underlying assets may be achieved through a merger.

4. FINANCING OF ACQUISITIONS

4.1 Debt

The following sections cover specific tax issues related to the overall level of debt and to the corresponding interest expense.

(a) Withholding tax Cash interest payments to European Union (EU) countries are not subject to withholding tax. However, lenders are subject to withholding tax at 15 percent (18 percent before 2003) unless a tax treaty establishes a lower rate.

Interest payments between Spanish companies are subject to a refundable withholding tax of 15 percent unless a tax grouping applies.

(b) Deductibility of interest Interest expense is generally deductible from a corporate tax point of view regardless of the purpose of the loan. Nevertheless, transfer-pricing rules should be kept in mind with respect to intercompany loans.

When insufficient current-year profits exist to offset all current-year interest, the accumulation of tax loss carryforwards may be avoided either through tax groupings or through a merger of the target into the vehicle that borrowed the funds for the acquisition. In the latter case, it should be noted that the special treatment for mergers is applicable only when the merger has been carried out for valid economic reasons.

(c) Thin capitalization   Spanish legislation establishes a debt/equity ratio of 3:1. This ratio is exceeded when the net direct or indirect borrowing by an entity from related persons or entities that are not resident in Spanish territory, excluding banking institutions exceeds the stated debt/equity ratio. If exceeded, the accrued interest on the excess is treated as dividends. Both the net borrowings and fiscal capital are determined based on their average level during the tax period.

Nevertheless, as a consequence of the European Court of Justice's judgment in the Lankhorst-Hohorst case, thin-capitalization rules are no longer applicable to loans made by EU companies. Notwithstanding this, general arm's-length rules remain applicable.

4.2   Equity

There is a capital duty of 1 percent on the issuance of new stock.

Dividends paid on stock are not deductible by the company paying the dividend. A Spanish company receiving such dividends is taxed on the receipt of such dividends. However, a tax credit normally is available, provided that the recipient has a substantial shareholding in the subsidiary. (See Section 6.2.)

This issuance of equity as a method of funding is advantageous in that it improves the debt/equity ratio of the company, thereby potentially enabling additional interest-bearing debt to be issued by the company. (See Section 4.1.)

5.   MERGERS

5.1   Definitions

According to Spanish legislation, a merger is considered to be as follows:

- One or several companies (the transferring companies), on dissolution, transfer *en bloc* to another already existing company (the receiving company) their respective assets and liabilities. The shareholders of the transferring companies receive shares in the receiving company.
- Two or more companies (the transferring companies), on dissolution, transfer *en bloc* to another new entity (the receiving company) their respective assets and liabilities. The shareholders of the transferring companies receive shares in the new company.

- A company (the transferring company), on dissolution, transfers all of its assets and liabilities to the company that owns all of its share capital (the receiving company). This is a so-called upstream merger.

5.2   Tax Benefits

Mergers can be carried out on a tax-neutral basis with no capital gains arising for either the shareholders, the transferring companies, or the receiving companies. The tax values of the assets and shares remain unchanged—that is, as if the transaction had not taken place.

Mergers under the special regime are exempt from capital formation tax and transfer tax, which includes transfers of real estate. These operations are also exempt from VAT.

The taxpayer determines whether the merger regime will apply. The taxpayer's decision must be communicated to the Ministry of Economy and Finance after registration of the pertinent deed.

When, as a consequence of administrative verification, it is proved that the merger was not carried out for valid economic reasons, the right to the regime discussed in this chapter is forfeited and the Tax Administration will correct the taxpayers' tax situation.

5.3   Substitution in Tax Rights and Obligations

Because a merger entails universal succession, the transfer takes place with respect to the tax rights and obligations that refer to the goods and rights transferred. The receiving company assumes compliance with the requirements for preserving or confirming the tax incentives of the transferring company.

Generally speaking, the tax losses that have not yet been offset in the transferring entity may be fully transferred to the receiving company unless current or previous shareholders have indirectly taken advantage of such losses through a portfolio provision or a capital loss.

5.4   Legal Aspects

Transfers of assets, liabilities, contracts, rights, obligations, and legal actions are practically automatic under the so-called universal succession principle— transfer *en bloc*.

Another advantage of mergers is that the business is integrated into a single legal entity, which involves some savings in terms of the administration costs associated with maintaining legal entities.

However, if different jurisdictions and, therefore, different regulations are involved, there can be certain procedural and formal differences that require proper coordination. Therefore, the operation may be complex and time-consuming.

Adequate attention should also be given to special or key contracts containing clauses whereby a merger might trigger adverse effects, such as termination, price increases, or price reductions—typically, contracts and agreements with key customers, suppliers, banks and finance parties, as well as those related to real property leases or outsourcing. In the same way, similar effects might have an impact on government permits and product registration or approvals.

There are also employment implications. As a result of the merger, there would be a change of employer. Therefore, issues with respect to employees' rights should be analyzed and handled carefully in connection with the merger.

6.   OTHER STRUCTURING AND POSTDEAL ISSUES

6.1   Creation of Local-Country Tax Groups

(a) Corporate tax   A Spanish tax group can be formed when a Spanish parent company has a direct or indirect 75 percent shareholding interest in the Spanish subsidiaries at the beginning of the tax year. After the acquisition of a company, this implies that the purchased company cannot be part of the purchaser's group until the beginning of the next tax year.

A permanent establishment may qualify as the controlling company if its head office is resident in a country that has signed a tax treaty with Spain with an exchange of-information clause. All treaties except the Switzerland-Spain tax treaty contain such a clause.

The tax grouping must be approved by the shareholders at a meeting of all of the group companies, and the decision has to be reported to the Spanish Tax Administration.

The main consequences of tax grouping are:

- The group is the taxpayer; that is, it has its own taxable income, tax credits, and so forth.
- The profits and losses of the group companies can be offset against each other. Therefore, the interest expense connected with the debt arranged by an acquisition company can be offset against profits of the target, subject to thin-capitalization rules. The only limitation is that pregrouping losses can be used only to offset income by the company that accrued them. This is normally relevant for interest accrued by a company in the year of the acquisition of the target. However, an effective deduction of this interest can be achieved through a merger of the target into the acquisition company. This can also help achieve the deductibility of the goodwill, provided that there are valid economic reasons for the merger other than tax savings (antiabuse regulation).

- Intercompany income is not taxable until it is sourced from third parties.
- Tax credits can be used by the tax group. Reinvestment requirements for the application of the tax credit for reinvestments can be met by any company in the group. (See Section 7.1.)

(b) VAT   Tax grouping for VAT purposes is not available in Spain.

6.2   Repatriation of Profits

Dividends paid by one Spanish company to another are initially taxable at the 35 percent ordinary tax rate. Nevertheless, a tax credit equal to 35 percent of the dividends is available if the recipient has held a substantial shareholding—that is, at least 5 percent of the share capital, directly or indirectly—in the subsidiary for a continuous 12-month period. This can be achieved before or after the dividend payout. In most cases, the tax credit is equivalent to an exemption.

If a Spanish company receives dividend income from a foreign company, it is normally exempt, provided that the following requirements are met:

- The recipient of the dividends has held a substantial shareholding for a continuous 12- month period immediately before the dividend.
- The subsidiary is subject to and not exempt from corporate tax analogous in nature to Spanish corporate tax.
- The subsidiary carries out entrepreneurial activities abroad. Passive income does not qualify for the exemption.

Finally, when distribution of the dividends triggers a decline in value of the shares in the subsidiary, the tax credit or exemption is sometimes not available. However, the dividend is then offset by the tax deduction of the related provision.

6.3   Preservation of Existing Tax Attributes

(a) Losses and tax credits   In general, tax losses and other, similar tax attributes of the target company are not affected by a change of ownership. The only exception is when the purpose of the transaction is to make those losses available to the purchaser. Broadly speaking, the losses may be forfeited or reduced when the following applies:

- The purchaser becomes the majority shareholder of the target and had a stake of less than 25 percent in the tax year when the losses were obtained.
- The target has been a dormant company for the six months prior to the date on which the purchaser becomes the majority shareholder.

In general, there are no other limitations on the availability of losses. Specifically, the nature of the loss (a trading or capital loss) is irrelevant.

(b) Management expense   Nontrading companies nevertheless incur expenses in the course of their activities, and tax deductions normally are available with respect to such expenses. In this discussion, such a company is referred to as a holding company. Under the tax-grouping treatment (see Section 6.1), management expense can be used to offset other taxable profits of either that company or other group companies. Any unutilized management expense can be carried forward by the company and can be offset against income of any nature during the following 15 years.

6.4   Receipts under Warranties or Indemnities

Generally speaking, payments made by the seller to the purchaser for breach of warranty or under an indemnity are regarded as an adjustment (reduction) of the purchase price. Therefore, such payments are not taxable in the hands of the purchaser. Rather, they trigger an increase in the gain in the event of a sale.

Warranties and indemnity payments should be made to the purchaser and not to the target company.

In some cases, indemnity payments are connected with a tax-deductible loss or expense for the target. Accordingly, the sale-and-purchase agreement often includes a clause that reduces the indemnity payment by the amount of the tax savings arising from the tax deduction of the loss or expense by the target.

7.   DISPOSALS

7.1   Stock Disposals

(a) Companies

(i) Disposal for cash consideration   The calculation of the chargeable gain is, generally speaking, sales proceeds minus tax cost (equal to the original cost minus the provisions for the decline in value of the shares, if any). Frequently, the sale-and-purchase agreement includes a working capital or net asset adjustment that affects the final cash amounts paid between the parties. Such a cash transfer should be regarded as an adjustment to the purchase price and should therefore be included within the seller's chargeable gains calculation.

The taxation of chargeable gains on the disposal of stock depends mainly on the residence of the company being disposed of. If the company being sold is resident in Spain, the chargeable gain is initially taxed at the ordinary rate of 35 percent. However, the consideration for the stock often includes undistributed profits generated by the company being sold. In order to avoid further taxation of those profits (already taxed in the company being disposed of), a tax credit equal to 35 percent of those profits is available if the seller company has held a substantial shareholding—that is, at least 5 percent of the share capital in the company being sold—for a continuous 12-month period immediately before the sale.

The goodwill embedded in the consideration cannot be sheltered. However, the effective tax rate on this gain can be reduced to 15 percent if the sales proceeds are reinvested by the seller company in tangible or intangible assets or in shares representing a stake of at least 5 percent during the year before or the three years after the disposal. If tax grouping applies, the reinvestment can be made by any group company, and the tax credit can be used by the group.

When the company being sold is not resident in Spain, the chargeable gain is fully exempt if the following requirements are met:

- The selling company has held a substantial shareholding for a continuous 12-month period immediately before the sale.
- The target has been subject to corporate tax that is analogous in nature to Spanish corporate tax.
- The target must carry out entrepreneurial activities abroad.

Despite the exemption, corporate tax is charged on a clawback of the provision for the decline in value of the shares deducted by the seller company before the sale and the amortization of the foreign financial goodwill (see Section 1.2) to the amount of the gain.

Finally, any losses available to the selling company can be used to offset the taxable gains

(ii) Share-for-share exchange   A transfer of the stock representing a company's share capital—when, as a result of that transfer, the acquiring company becomes the majority shareholder of the subsidiary—may be treated as a tax neutral transaction to the seller if a motive test is passed—that is, assurance that the transaction is being carried out for bona fide commercial reasons and does not form part of a plan to avoid tax.

A share-for-share transaction in which the acquiring company does not become the majority shareholder of the subsidiary may, under some circumstances, also qualify for a tax deferral.

(b) Individuals   Individuals disposing of an interest in stock are generally subject to personal income tax. The chargeable gain is sale proceeds minus original base cost. Taper relief, which reduces the gain depending on the length of ownership of the stock, is available for shares purchased before 1995 and provides that each year of ownership prior to December 31, 1994, reduces the gain by 14.28 percent (11.11 percent when the target owns mostly real estate).

The gain is taxed at the ordinary rate of 15 to 45 percent—depending on the seller's income—if the stock has been held for one year or less or at a 15 percent flat rate if the stock has been held for longer than one year.

Finally, no relief is provided for the avoidance of double taxation of the retained earnings of the company being disposed.

(c) Asset-holding companies   A new treatment for asset-holding companies was introduced in 2003. Broadly speaking, an asset-holding company is a company normally used by individuals for conducting passive investments in stock, real estate, and so forth. As a consequence, these companies are in some situations taxed as individuals if, for example, chargeable gains on the disposal of stock are taxed at the 15 percent rate—without the need to reinvest the sale proceeds as required for companies under the ordinary treatment—when the stock has been held for longer than one year. This advantage may be outweighed by the fact that asset-holding companies are not entitled to any relief for the avoidance of double taxation of the target's retained earnings.

It is not clear when a holding company owning substantial shareholding will be treated as an ordinary company or as an asset-holding company. This uncertainty could trigger lengthy discussions with the Spanish Tax Administration, since the consequences can vary greatly depending on the circumstances involved. As a general approach, one could conclude that a holding company that owns substantial shareholdings will be treated as an ordinary company if it exercises—through its directors—its shareholder rights: attendance at shareholders' meetings, collection of dividends, and so on.

(d) Tax-exempt entities   Some Spanish entities can take advantage of reduced rates or exemptions on the disposal of stock. Among other things, venture capital companies can benefit from an exemption of 99 percent of the capital gain if the disposal takes place from the beginning of the 2nd year and until the 15th year after the takeover. The period can be extended to 20 years under some circumstances. Investment funds are taxed at the rate of 1 percent, and pension funds are exempt.

7.2   Asset Disposals (Companies Only)

Gain on the disposal of assets is subject to corporate tax. The calculation of the gain is sale proceeds less tax basis of the assets, or original cost less depreciation of the assets. An inflation allowance is available for real estate depending on the period of ownership. Any resulting chargeable gain can be sheltered without limitation by any losses—not only capital losses but also trading losses.

The gain is taxed at the ordinary 35 percent rate. If the proceeds are reinvested in qualifying assets, then a tax credit amounting to 20 percent is available to the seller, thereby bringing down the effective tax rate to 15 percent. (See

Section 7.1.) Since the reinvestment generally has to be maintained over three to five years, the sale proceeds will be locked in the seller company unless the seller company has other funds, even from loans, available for the reinvestment.

Distribution of the sales profits may result in further tax liabilities for the shareholders, thereby giving rise to an element of double taxation. This depends on the nature of the shareholder (individual, company, tax-exempt) and the method of distribution—for example, liquidation or dividend. If the shareholder is a company that owns a substantial shareholding in the seller company, the distribution of the sales profit as a dividend should not trigger further taxation to the shareholder, because the dividend will be exempt. In fact, as covered in Section 6.2, this exemption takes the form of a tax credit amounting to 35 percent of the dividends.

7.3 Deferred Consideration

When the deal involves an amount of deferred consideration, payment of tax on the related capital gain is also deferred until the payment takes place. Alternatively, the taxpayer could opt for paying taxes on an accrual basis.

There are no specific rules concerning the treatment of deferred consideration determined by formula or dependent upon certain conditions. However, in most cases, this deferred consideration is treated as a separate gain that accrues when the right to receive the deferred consideration arises. However, specific situations should be analyzed on a case-by-case basis.

7.4 Payments under Warranties or Indemnities

Any warranty or indemnity payment is to be treated as an adjustment to the consideration offered and received for the transaction, and therefore the payment should be treated for tax purposes as having been deducted from the purchase consideration received.

8. TRANSACTION COSTS FOR SELLERS

8.1 VAT

(a) Stock disposals The disposal of stock is exempt from VAT.

(b) Asset disposals The transfer of all of the assets and liabilities of a company to a single purchaser that continues to exercise the same activity as the seller is outside the scope of VAT. However, this can trigger transfer tax—normally, at the rate of 6 to 7 percent—on the real estate transferred. However, this tax has to be paid by the purchaser.

The transfer of a separate business within a company does not give rise to the right to an exemption, in which case VAT—normally, at the rate of 16 percent—becomes applicable. This leads to a VAT cash-flow impact for the purchaser.

(See Section 2.1.) A hive-down of the assets to be sold may help overcome this, subject to antiavoidance provisions. (See Section 9.1.)

8.2   Transfer Taxes

If applicable, transfer tax on the purchase of shares is payable by the buyers and not the sellers. (See Section 2.2.)

For information on transfer tax on real estate, see Section 8.1.

8.3   Tax Deductibility of Transaction Costs

(a) Corporate tax treatment of expenses

(i) For holding companies disposing of shares   Broadly speaking, any expenses incurred during the sales process—such as vendor due diligence costs; legal, tax, and accounting fees; and valuation services—are regarded as costs of disposal and should be deducted from the sales price in order to calculate the capital gain, thereby reducing the gain or increasing the loss. Being resident in Spain reduces the tax liability of the selling company; if the target company is foreign, the deduction of the expenses from the sales price does not have any tax effect because the capital gain is generally fully exempt. (See Section 7.1.)

Costs related to initial speculative advice may be deemed tax-deductible ordinary expenses if the transaction does not crystallize. If the deal is completed, the Spanish Tax Administration will probably consider those expenses to be disposal costs, particularly if the company being sold is not resident in Spain. This issue is not as relevant when the target is resident in Spain, because disposal costs reduce the tax liability.

(ii) For trading companies disposing of assets   Costs incurred in connection with the sale of assets are deductible in computing the seller's taxable profits.

However, expenses connected directly with certain assets—for instance, real estate valuation fees—should be deducted from the sales price of those assets in a calculation of the chargeable gain. However, this is normally not an issue because the seller will benefit from the expenses either as tax-deductible ordinary expenses or as deductions from the sales price.

(iii) VAT treatment of expenses   If a holding company disposes of stock, VAT charged by third parties in connection with the sales process may under some circumstances be recoverable. Typically, a deduction may be claimed when the seller has been an active holding company providing services (administrative, management, financial) for the company being disposed of and for other companies. However, this is always a gray area that is likely to trigger lengthy discussions with the Spanish tax authorities.

A trading company that sells should normally be entitled to deduct the input VAT on the services received from third parties during the sales process, subject to the general rules that cover the deduction of input VAT.

9.   PREPARING A TARGET COMPANY FOR SALE

Normally, presale planning is necessary if the purchaser wants to buy only specific assets and when the seller wishes to retain certain assets. Other situations may also require presale planning, but this need should be ascertained with regard to each specific transaction.

9.1   Hive-Down of Assets

When the seller is selling only a division or part of a trading business, a hive-down may be considered.

Normally, a hive-down in Spain involves the seller company's contributing the assets to another group company (a Newco) in exchange for shares that are subsequently sold to the purchaser.

The contribution of the assets could be tax neutral because the tax value of the shares in the hive-down company received by the seller company is equal to the tax value of the assets transferred. Moreover, the transaction is VAT exempt, and the share capital increase in the hive-down company is exempt from capital formation tax. All of this is subject to the applicability of the special regime for restructuring transactions—very similar to that of the merger directive. The subsequent sale of the shares in the hive-down company will trigger a capital gain for the seller company, not the hive-down company.

Overall, the main advantage of the hive-down is the avoidance of any VAT on the transaction. This is relevant in order to avoid the impact of VAT cash flow or VAT costs when the purchaser is not entitled to the deduction of VAT because of the application of pro rata regulations. Notwithstanding these principles, the Spanish tax authorities very well might challenge the application of the special regime for the restructuring of transactions on the grounds that it is tax driven.

A similar outcome can be achieved by means of a spin-off of the assets that are to be sold. (See Section 10.)

9.2   Intragroup Transfer of Retained Assets

Assets may be transferred out of the target if the intention is to exclude some assets from the sales package. This often happens when the purchaser does not wish to purchase certain assets—normally, real estate—or because one part of the business is not included in the deal. Normally, the transfer to a seller's group company of the assets being retained can be achieved by a sale of assets or by a spin-off.

If a sale of assets is carried out, fair market value applies. This implies that both the goodwill and the built-in gains in the assets are taxable. The tax consequences are the same as those outlined in Section 7.2. Moreover, the goodwill cannot be amortized by the group company purchasing it, which makes this transaction highly inefficient when a substantial amount of goodwill is involved.

The taxation of both the goodwill and the built-in gains can be eliminated if both seller and purchaser belong to a tax group. The deferred gain normally arises when either the seller or the purchaser leaves the tax group or when the assets are sold to a third party.

Another drawback of the intragroup sale of assets is that such a sale is subject to VAT. (See Section 8.1.)

In light of the disadvantages of the sale of assets, the seller company may well decide to carry out a spin-off of the unwanted assets from the company being sold. (See Section 10.)

9.3   Presale Dividends

The tax treatment in the hands of the recipient of any presale dividends paid by the target group out of its distributable reserves is outlined in Section 6.2. Generally, very similar rules apply to dividends and capital gains, and therefore presale dividends are not useful tax planning tools in Spain. Nevertheless, a presale dividend may be used to reduce the price that the seller has to reinvest in order to take advantage of the tax credit for reinvestments.

10.   DEMERGERS

In Spain, a spin-off is normally used to separate different trading activities or assets from a company in the context of a corporate restructuring within a group.

A spin-off can be total or partial as follows:

- In a total spin-off, a company (the transferring company) on dissolution divides its assets and liabilities into two or more parts and transfers them to two or more existing or new companies (the receiving companies). The shareholders of the transferring company receive shares in the receiving companies.

- In a partial spin-off, a company (the transferring company) segregates one or more parts of its assets, forming a branch of activity—that is, a separate business activity—and transfers them to two or more new or existing companies (the receiving companies).

The transferring company reduces its share capital and reserves by the appropriate amounts, while the receiving company issues shares to the shareholders.

These transactions can be carried out on a tax-neutral basis, with no capital gains arising for the shareholders, the transferring company, or the receiving companies. The tax values of the assets and the shares remain unchanged, as if no transaction had taken place. Furthermore, spin-offs are exempt from VAT and from capital formation tax. Nevertheless, this tax neutrality is available only when the spin-offs are carried out for valid economic reasons, such as the restructuring or rationalization of the activities of the companies involved in the transaction. Therefore, a spin-off as part of a presale restructuring might in some cases be challenged by the Spanish Tax Administration on the grounds that it is tax driven.

11.   LISTINGS AND INITIAL PUBLIC OFFERINGS

Initial public offerings (IPOs) and listings are regulated by securities market legislation. However, there are no specific tax regulations regarding listings or IPOs. A company's tax status is not affected by listing or by an IPO, and therefore, the general comments made earlier on the disposal of stock, restructuring transactions, tax grouping, and so on should normally apply.

SWEDEN

INTRODUCTION

This chapter details the principal tax issues that are relevant to purchasers and sellers engaged in the transfer of ownership of a Swedish trade or business. Unless otherwise stated, it is generally assumed that all sellers and purchasers are Swedish companies with limited liability.

The purchase and sale of a Swedish company may take the form of a transfer of stock or a transfer of assets. The tax implications of these two forms differ significantly, and various nontax considerations must also be taken into account. Unfortunately, in actual practice, it is very common for parties to a transaction to determine the form of the deal before considering the tax implications.

The relevant taxes to be considered are:

- **Corporation tax.** Generally, this is a 28 percent tax on profits earned by a company. While Swedish companies are taxed on a stand-alone basis, group contribution rules make it possible to transfer taxable income between companies within a tax group.
- **Value-added tax (VAT).** A sales tax of 25 percent is added to the sales price charged for goods and services. Certain categories of sales are not subject to VAT or are subject to tax at a reduced rate.
- **Stamp duty land tax.** A purchaser of land and buildings must pay a stamp duty equal to 3 percent of the purchase price or of the tax assessment value, if higher.

1. ACQUISITIONS

1.1 Asset Acquisitions

Generally, an asset acquisition enables the purchaser to avoid exposure to the risk of any historical liabilities that are not assumed by the purchaser pursuant to the purchase agreement. Such liabilities remain the responsibility of the selling company and do not become the responsibility of the purchaser.

Also in general, an asset acquisition results in a step-up in the tax basis of the acquired assets. The consideration paid is allocated between the various acquired assets in the manner specified in the sale documentation. (See Section 3.1 for additional discussion of tax basis following an asset acquisition.)

Usually, the tax authorities accept these allocations as the new tax basis in the acquired assets.

Depreciation is permitted for acquired goodwill and intangibles, such as know-how, under a declining-balance method, which allows for a maximum depreciation rate of 30 percent. A straight-line method at a yearly rate of 20 percent also is available. Either method can be chosen, and the method can be changed from year to year.

For the shareholders of the selling company, one of the disadvantages of an asset sale is that a distribution of the sales proceeds by the selling company to its shareholders may result in double taxation. In this regard, shareholders who are Swedish resident individuals are subject to income tax on dividends received.

1.2   Stock Acquisitions

If the transaction is structured as a stock acquisition, the purchaser effectively will bear any historical and future ongoing tax and nontax liabilities of the target company. In addition, a step-up in the tax basis of the target company's assets—such as goodwill—is not permitted; that is, Swedish tax law contains no concept similar to a Section 338 election under US tax law. (See Section 3.2 for the basis of taxation following a stock acquisition.) Consequently, from a tax point of view, it is often beneficial from the purchaser's perspective to acquire assets rather than stock.

With regard to the relative merits of a stock or an asset deal, one potential conflict that may arise between a corporate seller and the purchaser involves the availability of a participation exemption. In particular, a corporate seller's capital gain on a *stock* sale is exempt from tax if certain criteria are satisfied. (See Section 7.1 for details on the exemption.) No such exemption is available for an asset sale. If the participation exemption is available, a corporate seller may oppose the purchaser's desire to structure the deal as an asset deal rather than as a stock deal. Consequently, the tax impact of the acquisition structure may be a key factor in pricing negotiations between the parties.

2.   TRANSACTION COSTS FOR PURCHASERS

2.1   Transfer Taxes

(a) Stock purchases   No stamp duty is payable on the purchase of stock.

(b) Asset purchases   A 3 percent stamp duty is imposed on the acquisition of land and buildings. The base for the stamp duty is the higher of the consideration paid or the tax assessment value. If the stock of a company holding land is sold with the land and/or buildings remaining in the company, no stamp duty is imposed.

No other stamp duties are imposed.

2.2   Value-Added Tax

(a) *Stock purchases*   Stock transfers are not subject to VAT.

(b) *Asset purchases*   A transfer of business assets that qualifies as a transfer of a business as a going concern is outside the scope of VAT. Otherwise, a purchase of assets is subject to VAT in an amount equal to 25 percent of the purchase price. This tax must be paid in addition to the purchase consideration.

When the buyer is itself subject to the VAT rules and is obliged to charge VAT on its sales—called outputs—the buyer may recover VAT paid by it on its own purchases—called inputs. Note that in some situations, depending on certain VAT-related characteristics of the buyer, the VAT paid on inputs may not always be recoverable in full, in which case the VAT paid would be a real cost to the buyer.

2.3   Capital Taxes

Asset or stock purchases are not subject to capital taxes.

2.4   Tax Deductibility of Transaction Costs

In general, whether or not a particular expense is deductible by the purchaser depends on several factors, including (1) the nature of the transaction—that is, a purchase of assets or shares—and (2) the reason the expense was incurred. The identity of the persons to whom the expenses were paid is of less significance.

(a) *Finance costs*   Costs incurred on the formation of companies and in obtaining equity financing generally are not currently deductible. At best, such costs can be taken into account in a calculation of the tax basis in the stock of the company for purposes of determining capital gain on a subsequent disposal, but in light of the participation exemption, such tax basis is not of any use in most cases.

Costs incurred in obtaining debt financing generally are deductible for tax purposes when they are reflected in the profit-and-loss account pursuant to Swedish generally accepted accounting principles. Such costs include bank arrangement fees and professional fees incurred in obtaining the financing.

(b) *Investigation and due diligence costs*   Due diligence and other investigation costs generally are not deductible except to the extent it can be successfully argued that such costs were necessary in order to obtain debt financing.

(c) *Other deal costs: structuring*   Costs incurred in structuring an acquisition are deductible for tax purposes.

(d) *VAT treatment of expenses*   Fees charged for assistance in obtaining debt financing or issuing stock generally are not subject to VAT in Sweden.

Therefore, bank and institutional fees generally do not carry VAT. In general, however, professional fees charged to Swedish customers by advisers based in Sweden *are* subject to VAT, even if the fees are related to debt or equity financing.

Input VAT (VAT charged by third parties for goods and/or services provided that is related directly to the issuance of stock) may be recovered under certain circumstances. For example, VAT related to the new issuance of shares can, according to recent case law, be recovered. Note, however, that this decision has been appealed to the Supreme Administrative Court of Appeal.

In order to assess whether input VAT is deductible, it is important to identify costs separately on invoices.

3.   BASIS OF TAXATION FOLLOWING ASSET OR STOCK ACQUISITIONS

3.1   Asset Acquisitions

Plant and machinery normally are depreciated according to a declining-balance method, which allows for a maximum depreciation rate of 30 percent. A straight-line method allowing for 20 percent depreciation per year also is available. Either method can be chosen, and the method can be changed from year to year.

If the method is changed from one year to another, the change will affect the depreciation of all machinery and equipment. The best result normally is achieved by starting with the declining-balance method and then, after four years, changing to the straight-line method. Goodwill, as well as several other types of intangibles such as patents and trademarks, may be amortized according to the same methods that apply to plant and machinery. For buildings, only the straight-line method is allowed. The depreciation rates vary from 2 to 5 percent per year.

Sales of inventory normally are included in the seller's trading profits, and the purchaser receives a tax basis equal to the consideration paid for the inventory.

Typically, trade debts are acquired at net book value so that no taxable profit or loss arises if the amount subsequently received is equal to the net book value. If an acquired debt proves to be unrecoverable whether wholly or in part, it should be possible to obtain a tax deduction to the extent that the amount ultimately recovered is less than the net book value amount. Capital losses on debt to related parties are not deductible for tax purposes—a consequence of the participation exemption on shares.

3.2   Stock Acquisitions

(a) Purchase price   The purchase price paid for stock is not recoverable through depreciation deductions. In addition, the acquired company retains its

historical tax basis in its assets; no election is available to step up the tax basis of the acquired company's assets. Consequently, the acquisition does not give rise to additional depreciable tax basis at the level of the acquired company. For example, accounting goodwill arising in the financial statements of a Swedish parent on the consolidation of the company is not depreciable.

(b) Tax grouping   Swedish companies are not taxed on a consolidated basis. Rather, each company files its own return based on its own net profit or loss. It is possible, however, to effectively use the operating losses of one member of a group (as defined below) against the operating profits of another group member through the use of group contributions.

Subject to the following conditions, group contributions are deductible by the payer company and are taxable income to the recipient company:

- The companies must be subject to Swedish taxation.
- The parent company, which may be a foreign corporation not subject to Swedish tax, must hold more than 90 percent of the subsidiary by vote and by nominal share capital.
- The subsidiary must have been so held for the entire financial year or from the date it started the business.

4.   FINANCING OF ACQUISITIONS

4.1   Debt

Specific tax issues related to the overall level of debt and the interest charged on such debt are:

- Withholding tax
- Deductibility of interest
- Thin capitalization
- Restrictions on interest deductions under an arm's-length standard

(a) Withholding tax   No withholding tax is imposed on interest payments to foreign lenders.

(b) Deductibility of interest   So long as the interest rate is set at arm's length, no restrictions are imposed on the deductibility of interest expense.

(c) Thin capitalization   Sweden has no thin-capitalization rules.

(d) Restrictions on interest deductions under an arm's-length standard: Certain interest payments recharacterized as nondeductible distributions   Loans between a Swedish company and a foreign related party must be made on an arm's-length basis. If not, transfer-pricing rules may apply to restrict interest

deductions. Such rules do not serve as a basis for a thin-capitalization challenge because Sweden has no thin-capitalization rules.

If the interest rate exceeds a normal arm's-length rate, the excess interest may be recharacterized as a nondeductible distribution. Depending on the residence of the recipient, that nondeductible distribution may be subject to withholding tax.

Special rules also may treat an interest payment on debt as a nondeductible distribution if the interest payment is dependent on the borrower's financial results.

4.2   Equity

No capital duty is imposed on the issuance of new shares.

Dividends paid on stock are not deductible by the distributing company. As long as the shares with respect to which such dividends are paid are held for business reasons, a Swedish company receiving such a dividend generally is eligible for a participation exemption so that such dividends will be exempt from tax. (See Section 6.3.) By contrast, Swedish individuals are taxed on dividend income.

Depending on the status and residence of the shareholder, a withholding tax may be imposed on the payment of dividends.

5.   MERGERS AND SHARE-FOR-SHARE EXCHANGES

5.1   Mergers

A merger (*fusion*) is a reorganization in which one or more companies are dissolved and cease to exist as legal entities—without going into liquidation—while at the same time another surviving company, or a new company formed for the purpose of the merger, acquires all of the assets and assumes all of the liabilities and commitments of the dissolved companies.

Provided that certain requirements are satisfied, a merger can be implemented with no severe or immediate tax consequences. The surviving or new company inherits the tax position(s) of the dissolved company or companies.

5.2   Share-for-Share Exchanges

A shareholder may defer the taxation of its capital gain on a transfer of shares in a target company if the transfer is structured as a share-for-share exchange. For this purpose, *share-for-share exchange* generally is defined as a transaction in which one company—say, company X—acquires the shares of the target in exchange for company X shares. A small portion—a maximum of 10 percent of nominal value on shares received—of the consideration also may consist of cash. In order for the target shareholder to be eligible for deferral of its gain on such an exchange, company X must own more than 50 percent of the voting rights in the target at the end of the calendar year in which the share-for-share exchange occurs. Certain additional requirements also must be satisfied, such as that the acquiring company must be a qualified company. For example, a Swedish limited company, Sw. Aktiebolag or AB, is considered a qualified company for this purpose.

In the event of a qualifying share-for-share exchange, an individual shareholder takes a tax basis in company X shares equal to such shareholder's tax basis in the Target shares surrendered.

Transfers of stock are not subject to VAT.

6.   OTHER STRUCTURING AND POSTDEAL ISSUES

6.1   Creation of Local-Country Tax Groups

Companies are not taxed on a consolidated basis. Each company files its own tax return based on its own net profit or loss. As covered in Section 3.2(b), however, it is possible to effectively use the operating losses of one group member to offset the operating profits of another group member via group contributions.

6.2   Repatriation of Profits

As covered in more detail in Section 6.3, a corporate seller of stock held for business reasons generally is eligible for a participation exemption. Pursuant to this exemption, capital gain on the stock sale is exempt from tax. For dividends received during financial years commencing on or after January 1, 2004, the participation exemption also is available for dividends on such shares. By contrast, Swedish individuals are taxed on dividend income.

6.3   Participation Exemption for Corporate Shareholders

Capital gains recognized by corporate shareholders upon the disposition of shares held for business reasons generally are exempt from tax pursuant to a participation exemption. The participation exemption also is available to a foreign corporate shareholder resident in the European Economic Area, provided that such a foreign corporate shareholder conducts business from a permanent establishment in Sweden and that the shares at issue are allocable to that permanent establishment. Foreign corporate shareholders resident outside the European Economic Area also may be eligible for a participation exemption pursuant to a tax treaty containing a nondiscrimination clause, provided that the permanent establishment requirements summarized earlier are satisfied. Sweden does not tax foreign shareholders on the disposition of shares unless the foreign shareholder has a permanent establishment in Sweden and the shares are allocated to that permanent establishment.

With regard to the requirement that the shares be held for business reasons, unquoted (unlisted) shares always are considered to be so held. Quoted shares are considered held for business reasons if they have been held for at least one year and either (1) the particular corporate shareholder is at least a 10 percent shareholder as measured by reference to voting power or (2) the shares are held by that corporate shareholder in the ordinary course of business.

Shares in foreign companies also may satisfy the held-for-business-reasons requirement pursuant to the aforementioned rules.

An exception to the participation exemption applies in the case of capital gain recognized with respect to the stock of a shell company. A company is a shell company if the fair market value of its cash, shares, other marketable instruments and similar assets but not including shares held for business reasons exceeds 50 percent of the consideration paid for the shares. Further, unless certain conditions and formalities are satisfied, the gross consideration received on the sale of such a shell company is subject to capital gains tax; that is, the shareholder's tax basis in its shares of the shell is disregarded.

One consequence of the participation exemption is that capital losses on shares held for business reasons no longer are deductible.

The capital gains tax exemption does not apply to shares held by partnerships, but restrictions nonetheless apply to the deduction of losses in a partnership upon a disposal of shares—and also to a deduction upon a disposition of an interest in a partnership to the extent the loss is dependent upon a decline in the value of shares held by the partnership.

6.4   Preservation of Existing Tax Attributes

Unused losses incurred by a Swedish company in a financial year normally carry forward to the next succeeding taxable year to offset the taxable profits in that subsequent year. If the taxable profits are insufficient to cover the losses from the previous year, then the remaining unused loss carries forward to the next financial year and so on, indefinitely. Losses must be utilized against profits as soon as profits are available. Losses may not be carried back.

Losses may be forfeited and/or unusable until a certain period of time has elapsed if there is a more than 50 percent change—measured in terms of voting power—in the ownership of the loss company. In such a case, the amount of preacquisition tax losses that may be utilized to offset taxable gains subsequent to the ownership change is limited to 200 percent of the purchase price paid for the shares that together compose the controlling interest that triggered the ownership change. Further, the permitted preacquisition loss generally cannot offset group contributions from the new owner until a six-year barring period elapses. The total purchase price as computed for this purpose must be reduced by capital contributions or injections received by the loss company during the portion of the ownership change financial year that precedes the change and the two preceding financial years.

6.5   Receipts under Warranties or Indemnities

Payments made by the seller for breach of warranty or pursuant to an indemnity provision are taxable in the hands of the purchaser unless the purchase agreement contains a provision stating that any such payment is to be treated as an adjustment to the consideration paid and received in the transaction. In such a case, the receipt is not immediately taxable to the purchaser but, instead, is treated as a reduction in the purchaser's tax basis in the acquired property.

Note, however, that such payments, if made to the target company, are likely subject to tax at the target company level.

7.   DISPOSALS

7.1   Stock Disposals

(a) Companies For corporate shareholders, dispositions of stock in a corporation normally are exempt from tax pursuant to the participation exemption rules. (See Section 6.3.) If not exempt, the disposals are taxed at the corporate income tax rate of 28 percent.

(b) Individuals Individuals disposing of an interest in stock are subject to tax on their taxable capital gain at a 30 percent rate. The taxable gain on the sale of shares is the net profit—that is, the sales price less the average purchase price for all shares of the same kind. Losses on a sale of shares may be offset against gains on share sales. Normally, only 70 percent of any remaining losses on stock sales is deductible.

Special rules apply to the taxation of capital gains on the sale of shares in closely held companies—that is, generally, companies in which a few individuals hold more than 50 percent of the stock by voting power and are active in management.

7.2   Asset Disposals (Companies Only)

Gains on the disposition of assets, including goodwill, are subject to corporation tax. Gains can be sheltered by loss carryforwards.

If the proceeds of a corporate-level asset sale are distributed by the selling corporation to its shareholders, another layer of tax may be imposed at the shareholder level depending on the nature of the shareholder—individual, corporation, or tax-exempt entity—and the method of distribution—for example, liquidation, capital distribution, or dividend.

7.3   Deferred Consideration and Earn-Outs

Generally, if the amount of deferred consideration is ascertainable at the time of the disposition, the full amount is included in the taxable gain calculation as of the time of sale, even if the receipt of this amount is contingent. If the deferred consideration is not ascertainable at the time of the disposition, such deferred consideration will be taxed when the consideration becomes ascertainable.

7.4   Payments under Warranties or Indemnities

Payments made by the seller for breach of warranty or pursuant to an indemnity provision are treated as reductions in the purchase consideration received if the purchase contains a provision stating that any such payment is to be treated as an adjustment to the consideration paid and received in the transaction.

8.   TRANSACTION COSTS FOR SELLERS

8.1   Transfer Taxes

While stamp duty on the transfer of land and buildings is the joint liability of the seller and the purchaser, the parties generally agree in the purchase agreement that the stamp duty will be paid by the purchaser.

8.2   VAT

(a) Stock disposals   Stock transfers are not subject to VAT.

(b) Asset disposals   As covered in Section 2.2(b), a transfer of business assets that qualifies as the transfer of a business as a going concern is not subject to VAT. Otherwise, the seller must charge VAT in the manner described in Section 2.2(b).

8.3   Tax Deductibility of Transaction Costs

In general, whether a particular expense is currently deductible depends on several factors, including whether the transaction is in the form of a sale of assets or a sale of stock.

(a) Corporate sellers

(i) Disposal of shares   If the capital gain on a disposition of shares is subject to the participation exemption, the associated costs are not deductible. In the event that the sale is not actually concluded, such costs are currently deductible as a business expense.

If the capital gain on a disposition of shares is subject to tax, the associated costs reduce the amount of taxable gain or increase the loss. Note, however, that any such loss may be offset only against capital gains on the disposition of shares or similar instruments.

(ii) Disposition of assets   Costs incurred in connection with the disposition of assets are currently deductible.

(b) VAT treatment of expenses   VAT charged by third parties to the seller on transaction costs related to the disposition of assets should be recoverable. The tax authorities take the position, however, that VAT charged by third parties to the seller on transaction costs related to the disposition of shares is not recoverable. This issue currently is being litigated, but a resolution is not expected in the near future.

In order to assess whether input VAT is recoverable, it is important to separately identify costs on invoices.

9.   PREPARING A TARGET COMPANY FOR SALE

Introduction of the participation exemption in 2003 has made presale tax planning less relevant in the context of a corporate seller. However, presale planning is important if the purchaser wants to buy only specific assets, if the seller wishes to retain certain assets, or if the disposal is not sheltered from tax by the participation exemption.

9.1   Hive-Down of Assets

If the seller is selling only a division or part of a trade or business or if the purchaser is unwilling to assume or take assets subject to a specific liability, a hive-down transaction to remove specific items from the target company may be necessary.

Hiving down involves the transfer of specific assets of a company to another group company in a transfer below market value; that is, the consideration may not exceed the tax basis of the transferred assets. If certain requirements are satisfied, such a hive-down can be undertaken without adverse tax consequences.

Stamp duty on land and buildings is payable on a hive-down transfer. (See Section 2.1 for additional detail on the stamp duty.) Payment of the stamp duty can be deferred if the assets are transferred between associated companies but is triggered when the group relationship between the companies no longer exists—for example, when the shares of the transferor or transferee company are sold to a third party or the real estate as such is sold outside the group.

VAT is not imposed if the hive-down transfer consists of a line of business.

9.2   Intragroup Transfer of Assets Being Retained

Assets may be transferred out of group companies that are to be sold if the purchaser does not wish to acquire or the seller does not wish to sell such assets. If certain requirements are satisfied, such a transfer can be undertaken without adverse tax consequences as long as the consideration does not exceed tax basis.

Stamp duty on land and real estate is payable on such an intragroup asset transfer. (See Section 2.1.) Payment of the stamp duty can be deferred if the assets are transferred between associated companies but is triggered when the group relationship between the companies no longer exists. VAT is not imposed if the hive-down comprises a business line.

9.3   Presale Dividends

For the tax treatment of dividends, see Section 4.2 and Section 6.2. A presale dividend may benefit the buyer by reducing the necessary funding—for example, not paying cash for cash.

10.   DEMERGERS

Typically, the commercial rationale for a demerger is the creation of value for shareholders. Demergers may be used to separate different business activities in different groups or to partition business activities between different groups of shareholders.

Under Swedish corporate law, *demerger* is not a defined term. Instead, *demerger* is a term of art referring to a certain form of restructuring involving a transfer of assets, which can include shares, to another, existing company or a transfer of shares in subsidiaries to existing shareholders.

In the demerger of a group, it is important to consider various associated tax costs, such as income tax costs to shareholders, capital gains tax costs to both the company and the shareholders, and stamp duty costs.

11.   LISTINGS AND INITIAL PUBLIC OFFERINGS

11.1   Impact on Tax Status of Listing a Company and Its Subsidiaries

The tax status of a company and its subsidiaries generally is unaffected by listing or initial public offering (IPO).

11.2   Complete Group Listing or IPO

If an entire group is to be listed, it is common for a new company to be organized as the listed vehicle (Holdco). The stock in the existing parent company can be transferred to Holdco on a tax-neutral basis if certain requirements are satisfied.

11.3   Listing or IPO of a Subsidiary

If a parent corporation sells some of its existing stock in a subsidiary in the market (i.e, lists), the parent generally is exempt from tax pursuant to the participation exemption. However, should the parent's stock ownership in the subsidiary fall short of the 10 percent voting power threshold required for the application of the participation exemption in the case of quoted shares, subsequent disposals may be subject to tax. (See Section 6.3.)

If a subsidiary issues new stock, no tax charge is imposed.

11.4   Issuance of New Stock by a Listed Company

The issuance of new shares by a listed company should have no adverse tax consequences if the listed company is the parent of the group. If the subsidiary is being listed, the issuance of new stock may cause the subsidiary to cease to be a member of the group.

11.5   Disposal of Stock by Existing Shareholders

The tax consequences in the event that the listing or IPO involves a disposal of stock by existing shareholders are outlined in Section 7.

SWITZERLAND

INTRODUCTION

This chapter details the principal tax issues that are relevant to purchasers and sellers engaged in the transfer of ownership of a Swiss trade or business. Unless otherwise stated, it is generally assumed that all sellers and purchasers are Swiss companies with limited liability or Swiss tax resident individuals.

This chapter reflects the laws and rules currently in effect, including the provisions of the new Federal Act on Mergers, Demergers, Transformations and Asset Transfers (Merger Act), which entered into force on July 1, 2004. The Swiss federal tax authorities have issued a circular letter detailing how the tax authorities intend to apply these new rules in practice. The following comments discuss the application of these rules as described in the circular letter. It should be noted that the cantons have been granted a transition period until June 30, 2007, when not otherwise stated, to incorporate the legislative changes into their cantonal tax law. Note that the cantons, therefore, may apply their existing rules, which may deviate from the rules under the Merger Act—particularly with respect to demergers—until adaptation of their tax laws.

The aim and purpose of the Merger Act is to close gaps in corporate law, which in the past had to be filled by doctrine and practice. As a result, the generally liberal treatment granted by the Commercial Registries and the tax authorities with respect to the commercial law requirements regarding the tax neutrality of transactions such as restructurings and reorganizations has been codified into law.

Overview of the Swiss Tax System

The Swiss federation consists of 26 sovereign cantons and approximately 3,000 independent municipalities. According to the Swiss constitution, the cantons have fiscal sovereignty and the full right of taxation to the extent the right to tax a particular source is not exclusively allocated to the federal government in the federal constitution.

As a result, Switzerland has two—and in some cases even three—levels of taxation: the federal level and the cantonal/communal levels. A harmonization of the cantonal tax laws has recently taken place due to the required implementation of the federal Tax Harmonization Law by the cantons on or before January 1, 2001. While the Tax Harmonization Law requires harmonization of tax liability, taxable income, deductions, tax periods, assessment procedures and so on, the cantons are still free to set the applicable tax rates. Therefore, the tax burden of a company may vary considerably depending on the canton in which it is located.

Corporate income and capital taxes are deductible for purposes of computing taxable income. Income and capital taxes for corporations and self-employed individuals are generally assessed based on the statutory financial statements. Therefore, if the assessing tax authorities have made no adjustments, then the taxable income and taxable equity are equal to the income and equity shown in the statutory financial statements.

The cantons grant tax advantages to companies that carry out certain types of activities (i.e., the holding-company and mixed-company tax privileges). Advantageous tax status is given to holding companies as discussed below. A company qualifies as a holding company for tax purposes if two-thirds of its assets consist of participations in other companies or if two-thirds of its income is earned from participations—for example, dividend income.

Holding companies are exempt from cantonal and communal income taxes. This exemption applies not only to participation income but also to all other income received by a holding company, such as interest and royalty income. However, the exemption does not apply to income from Swiss real estate. Therefore, this income is taxable in most cantons. Additionally, a qualifying holding company is not allowed to have an active business in Switzerland. This privilege does not exempt holding companies from paying federal income taxes. However, companies holding at least 20 percent of the share capital of another company or holding shares in another company that has a market value of at least CHF2 million can benefit from participation relief on dividend income.

Capital gains relief is also available on the disposition of participations that (1) make up at least 20 percent of the share capital of the company, (2) have been held for at least one year, and (3) were purchased on or after January 1, 1997. This relief reduces the income tax in proportion to the ratio of net income from qualifying participations to total net income. Capital gains resulting from the disposition of participations acquired before January 1, 1997, will benefit from capital gains relief from January 1, 2007, onward if the participation transferred constitutes at least 20 percent of the share capital.

Another advantageous tax status is given to mixed companies that carry out their business mainly abroad. *Mainly abroad* means that at least 80 percent of the company's income must come from foreign sources. Some cantons also require 80 percent of the expenses to come from foreign sources. The non-Swiss-source income of a mixed company may be partially exempt from cantonal and communal income taxes but not from federal income tax. The overall effective tax rate of a mixed company may vary from approximately 9 to 11 percent.

In Switzerland it is possible to discuss the tax consequences of a proposed transaction or a special tax status in advance with the appropriate tax authorities and to receive a binding tax ruling regarding the matter. The relevant taxes at the federal level to be considered are:

- **Corporate income tax.** This is an 8.5 percent, statutory-rate tax on profits earned by a company.

- **Income tax for individuals.** The income tax rates for individuals are dependent on income and marital status: married or other. The overall maximum income tax rate is 11.5 percent, but marginal income tax rates can be as high as 13.2 percent.

- **Value-added tax (VAT).** VAT is a sales tax of 7.6 percent added to the sales price charged for goods or services, except for certain categories of sales that are exempt from or outside the scope of VAT. Purchasers or recipients of services who qualify as VAT taxpayers can generally recover VAT paid. However, the level of recoverability varies from case to case.

- **Stamp taxes.** A 0.06 to 0.12 percent tax (issuance stamp tax) is levied on the issuance of CHF bonds, foreign bonds, or bondlike financing instruments. A 1 percent tax is levied on the original issue of capital— the first CHF250,000 is exempt—and on any increase in capital. It is also levied on capital contributions either in kind or in cash made by shareholders without a formal increase of the company's capital. For reorganizations, exemptions are available if certain conditions are met. Securities transfer tax is due on the transfer of CHF bonds and foreign bonds as well as on the purchase, sale, or exchange of Swiss (0.15 percent) and foreign (0.3 percent) securities by registered professional securities dealers acting for their own account or as intermediaries. The same rule applies to Swiss-domiciled companies, which disclose taxable securities at a value of more than CHF10 million in their balance sheets.

- **Withholding tax.** A 35 percent tax is levied on dividend distributions as well as on interest payments on bonds, bondlike loans, and deposits accepted by Swiss banks from nonbank clients.
  The relevant taxes at the cantonal/communal levels to be considered are:

- **Corporate income tax.** A 6.5 to 33 percent, statutory-rate tax is imposed on profits earned by a company. The tax rate varies depending on the canton and community of residency.

- **Corporate capital tax.** In addition to taxes on income, corporations are also assessed annually a tax on net assets. This capital tax—0.07 to 0.8 percent for ordinary taxed companies—is normally determined by reference to the company's net equity—that is, paid-in capital, reserves, and retained earnings.
- **Income tax for individuals.** The income tax rate for individuals depends on the canton and the community. Furthermore, level of income and marital status are also factors in determining the income tax. In 2003, the maximum income tax for the capital cities of the cantons varied from 11 to 30 percent.
- **Net wealth tax for individuals.** An annual net wealth tax is levied. The net wealth tax varies depending on the canton and the community of residence as well as on marital status and level of wealth. The maximum net wealth tax for the capital cities of the cantons in 2003 varied from 0.2 to 0.9 percent of taxable net wealth.
- **Real estate gains tax.** This tax is levied at a rate ranging from 30 to 48 percent—depending on where the real estate is located—on the gain realized on the transfer of real estate. In most of the cantons, the real estate gains tax may be reduced, depending on the length of ownership of the real estate. Usually, the transfer of shares of a real estate company is taxed as well. For reorganizations, exemptions are available if certain conditions are met. Under the Merger Act, cantons with the monistic system—that is, cantons that levy real estate gains tax from individuals and corporations—must refrain from levying this tax if the restructuring is free of income tax under the Merger Act.
- **Real estate transfer tax.** This tax is levied at a rate ranging from 0.5 to 3 percent—depending on where the real estate is located—on the transfer of real estate. Usually, the transfer of shares of real estate companies is taxed as well. For reorganizations, exemptions are available if certain conditions are met. Under the new Merger Act, cantons and communities are not allowed to levy real estate transfer taxes in the case of privileged restructurings. Note that cantons have a transition period until June 30, 2009, to incorporate this change into their law.

1.   ACQUISITIONS

In the past, acquisitions were structured contractually as either stock transactions, or asset transactions, or a combination of both. The Merger Act now allows a taxpayer to structure acquisitions differently because the Merger Act provides for new institutions, such as demergers. For example, an acquisition may be structured as a demerger followed by subsequent sale of the demerged entity's stock. Other possibilities exist as well.

1.1 Asset Acquisitions

(a) Nontax issues An asset acquisition generally enables the purchaser to avoid exposure to the risk of any historical liabilities that are not specifically recoverable through the sale agreement. When a seller and purchaser agree to transfer an entire business with all assets and liabilities, the seller remains jointly and severally liable with the purchaser for all transferred liabilities for three years. This three-year period starts from the publication date of the acquisition. Although unclear, it appears that a new result of the Merger Act is that all contracts between the seller and third parties are automatically assigned to the purchaser; that is, basically no consent of the third party is required for the transfer. However, due to the uncertainty surrounding this result, it is advisable to seek the third party's consent in advance with regard to the transfer of any material contracts.

Note also that certain regulations protect employees on the sale of a business. They generally provide that the purchaser becomes the new employer by law and that unless the employees object, has to take on the employees under the employees' current terms and conditions of employment.

The Merger Act contains new provisions designed to protect creditors and employees in the case of a transfer of assets. In particular, the Merger Act states that the companies involved in a merger must consult employees' representatives before execution of the transaction.

(b) Tax issues An asset acquisition generally enables the purchaser to obtain a step-up in the tax basis of the assets acquired. (See Section 3.1 for a discussion of the basis of taxation following an asset acquisition.) Generally, the purchaser and seller agree with regard to allocation of the purchase price among the assets. If the purchaser and seller agree upon an allocation, the tax authorities will accept that allocation among the different assets as the new tax basis of those assets.

However, one disadvantage for the shareholders of the selling company is that the proceeds from the asset sale will remain locked in that company. Depending upon the circumstances, the selling company may either (1) distribute as a dividend to its shareholders the capital gain recognized on the asset sale or (2) liquidate. Under the first scenario, the dividend received by a shareholder is either taxed at the shareholder's level—for example, the shareholder is a Swiss individual—or may qualify for participation relief—for example, the shareholder is a corporation. In the case of liquidation, the liquidation proceeds are taxed at the shareholder level, though participation relief may be available for a corporate shareholder.

Furthermore, tax loss carryforwards of the selling company can be used to offset the selling company's capital gains realized on the asset sale. However, any remaining tax loss carryforwards would not be available for future use if the selling company does not have any other activities. (See Section 7.2.)

1.2   Stock Acquisitions

In a stock acquisition, the purchaser effectively bears any historical and future ongoing tax and nontax liabilities of the target company. There is no step-up permitted in the tax basis of the company's assets. Any goodwill acquired as part of a stock deal does not qualify for tax relief. (See Section 3.2 for a discussion of the basis of taxation following a stock acquisition.) In a stock acquisition, the target company remains subject to taxation. As a result, the target can use its tax loss carryforwards in the future.

Therefore, from a purchaser's perspective, it is often beneficial to acquire assets rather than stock for tax reasons.

There is a potential conflict between the preferences of the purchaser and those of the seller because of the availability of participation relief for substantial shareholdings for Swiss resident corporate sellers and the availability of achieving a tax-free capital gain for Swiss resident individuals holding the stock to be disposed of as private assets. (See Section 7.)

Generally, while a seller will prefer to sell stock, a purchaser may want to acquire assets. Thus, the tax impact of the acquisition structure can be a key factor in pricing negotiations with the seller.

2.   TRANSACTION COSTS FOR PURCHASERS AND SELLERS

2.1   Transfer Taxes

(a) Securities transfer tax   Securities transfer tax is levied if the seller, the purchaser, or the intermediary qualifies as a Swiss securities dealer for Swiss stamp tax purposes. In general, every entity that qualifies as a bank according to Swiss banking law or that holds taxable securities—for example, shares—with a book value exceeding CHF10 million as its assets qualifies as a Swiss securities dealer. The securities transfer tax will be levied on the consideration at a rate of 0.15 percent for Swiss shares and 0.3 percent for non-Swiss shares and has to be paid by the Swiss securities dealer. If both the seller and the purchaser qualify as Swiss securities dealers, each party is responsible for half of the securities transfer tax.

In a stock purchase transaction, the securities transfer tax is levied on the purchase price if a Swiss securities dealer is involved. In an asset acquisition, the securities transfer tax is levied if the assets include taxable securities—for example, shares—and a Swiss securities dealer is involved.

Under the Merger Act, transfers of taxable securities that occur in connection with an intercompany restructuring are no longer subject to the securities transfer tax, and transfer of the stock in a group company is exempt from the securities transfer tax if at least 20 percent of the nominal share capital is transferred.

(b) Other transfer taxes   There are certain other transfer taxes such as real estate transfer tax and stamp tax on documents and similar legal fees. However, because these transfer taxes are regulated by cantonal and/or communal law, no general comments can be made. Each individual case has to be reviewed to determine whether additional transfer taxes will arise.

2.2   Value-Added Tax

(a) Stock transfers   Stock transfers are exempt from VAT.

(b) Asset sales   VAT is levied on the sale of assets at a rate of 7.6 percent. However, VAT liability is settled in a notification procedure—that is, no payment of output VAT and recovery of input VAT—if the seller and the purchaser qualify as VAT taxpayers and the assets transferred qualify as a going concern.

2.3   Issuance Stamp Tax

Issuance stamp tax is covered in Sections 4.2 and 10.3.

2.4   Tax Deductibility of Transaction Costs

In general, transaction costs qualify as tax-deductible expenses if they are commercially justified. Whether a particular expense qualifies as commercially justified depends on whether the expense incurred is a shareholder expense or a company-related expense.

It does not make any difference whether an economically justified cost is charged directly to a Swiss-domiciled entity or indirectly through a group company. However, invoices should clearly detail the company to which the services have been provided and the nature of the services supplied. Furthermore, any documentation regarding the cost allocation—for example, breakdown calculation or background information—should be made available within a short period of time.

In general terms, the tax deductibility of transaction costs can be summarized as:

- Financing costs
- Investigation and due diligence costs
- Legal costs and professional fees
- Transfer taxes

- Capitalizing of transaction costs versus immediate deduction
- VAT treatment of expenses

(a) Financing costs　Financing costs related to Swiss entities should, in principle, be tax deductible for Swiss corporate income tax purposes.

(b) Investigation and due diligence costs　Due diligence costs should, in principle, be tax deductible for Swiss corporate income tax purposes.

(c) Legal costs and professional fees　Legal costs and other professional fees should be deductible for Swiss income tax purposes if the work performed relates to the Swiss structure—for example, mergers of Swiss-domiciled entities and formation of Newcos—and not to the shareholder structure.

(d) Transfer taxes　The transfer taxes described in Section 2.1 are deductible for Swiss corporate income tax purposes.

(e) Capitalizing of transaction costs versus immediate deduction　In principle, transaction costs cannot be capitalized and must be deducted immediately. However, Swiss accounting principles permit the capitalization of incorporation, capital increase, and organization costs resulting from the establishment, expansion, or reorganization of a business. Capitalized reorganization costs have to be amortized over a maximum period of five years. The annual amortization should be deductible for Swiss corporate income tax purposes. However, the decision on whether or to what extent the transaction costs described earlier can be capitalized must be discussed with the auditors.

(f) VAT treatment of expenses　Bank and institutional fees charged for making arrangements for loans and for the issuance of stock are generally not subject to VAT in Switzerland. However, professional fees charged to Swiss customers by advisers based in Switzerland are subject to VAT even when the fees are related to the sale or issuance of stock or loan financing. Professional fees charged to Swiss customers by advisers based outside Switzerland may be subject to the reverse-charge mechanism in Switzerland.

It is likely that input VAT that is related directly to the finance activities may not be recovered.

It is important that costs be identified separately on invoices to facilitate the allocation of input VAT to the issuance of stock and to other matters.

3.　BASIS OF TAXATION FOLLOWING ASSET OR STOCK ACQUISITIONS

3.1　Asset Acquisitions

Depreciation of tangible fixed assets is allowed if it is commercially justified. For tax purposes, the straight-line method or the declining-balance method may be used. Depreciation and amortization not recorded in the statutory accounts are not deductible for tax purposes. The federal tax authorities have issued guidelines with regard to the maximum annual rates of amortization and depreciation that are permitted.

In the declining-balance method of depreciation, immovable assets can be depreciated at an annual rate ranging from 2 percent (for houses built by real estate companies) to 20 percent (for railway sidings; water, gas, and electricity mains for industrial purposes; storage tanks; and so on) on the net book value.

Movable assets can be depreciated at an annual rate ranging from 25 percent (for office furniture and machines, storeroom equipment, and so on) to 40 percent (for hardware and software, automatic control systems, security equipment, and so on) on the net book value.

Purchased intangible assets and goodwill can be depreciated at an annual rate of 40 percent on the net book value.

In the straight-line method, the depreciation rates are half of those of the declining-balance method.

3.2   Stock Acquisitions

(a) Purchase price   The purchase price becomes the purchaser's basis in the acquired company's stock. The underlying basis in the acquired company's assets does not change. There is no election available to step up the tax basis of assets in the acquired company. Any accounting goodwill that arises in the financial statements of a Swiss parent from the consolidation of the company is not tax deductible.

(b) Tax consolidation   See Section 6.1.

4.   FINANCING OF ACQUISITIONS

4.1   Debt

Specific tax issues related to the overall level of borrowings and the interest charged on these debts are:

- Withholding tax
- Deductibility of interest
- Thin capitalization

(a) Withholding tax   Usually, no Swiss withholding tax is levied on interest from loans granted by Swiss banks. However, a Swiss withholding tax of 35 percent is levied on interest from bonds and bondlike loans of Swiss debtors. Swiss withholding tax on interest payments to a foreign-domiciled recipient may be refunded under the provisions of the applicable double-tax treaty in force.

There is generally no withholding tax on interest payments on intercompany loans.

(b) Deductibility of interest A corporation may generally deduct all interest paid or accrued during a business year if the underlying borrowing is made on an arm's-length basis.

The federal tax administration regularly issues guidelines regarding maximum interest rates on intercompany loans. (See Section 4.1(c).) Interest payments at rates in excess of those stated in these guidelines may be treated as hidden profit distributions. The excess amount of interest paid is not tax deductible and is subject to a 35 percent withholding tax. However, if the taxpayer can prove that the interest payments are on an arm's-length basis, higher rates may be charged.

(c) Thin capitalization According to a circular published in 1997 by the federal tax authorities, the maximum debt financing on assets—in the case of intercompany financing—is restricted for tax purposes to a certain percentage of the fair market value of the assets a company owns—that is, the safe-harbor amount of debt. The amount of capitalization required depends on the type of assets that are financed. However, the company has the right to prove that an amount of capitalization lower than the safe-harbor amount is on an arm's-length basis. Any third-party debt would not qualify as hidden equity for this purpose.

Furthermore, the federal tax authorities usually issue on a yearly basis certain guidelines covering the maximum interest rates that may be charged by affiliated companies—that is, the safe-harbor interest rate. Interest payments that are in line with those guidelines are tax deductible. However, higher rates may be charged if the taxpayer can prove that the rate charged represents an arm's-length amount. The guidelines also set forth the minimum rates applicable to interest that needs to be charged to related parties.

Interest paid on related-party loans that exceed safe-harbor interest rates is not tax deductible. However, to the extent that the interest rate on related party loans is lower than the safe harbor interest rate, the allowable interest deduction is determined by multiplying the safe-harbor interest rate by the safe-harbor amount of debt. Only interest that has been deducted in excess of this amount is added back into taxable income.

4.2   Equity

An issuance stamp tax of 1 percent is levied on the issuance of new stock. The first CHF250,000 is exempt.

Dividends paid on stock are not deductible by the company paying the dividend. Dividends received by a Swiss company from qualifying equity investments—that is, investments of at least CHF2 million market value or 20 percent of the subsidiary's capital—in Swiss or foreign companies will benefit from participation relief. Dividends received by a Swiss individual are taxed as income.

5.   MERGERS

5.1   General

In Switzerland, a merger in the broadest sense of the term can be carried out either by a full merger of entities or by a share-for-share transaction—a mergerlike transaction.

There are two types of full mergers: merger by absorption and merger by amalgamation. In a merger by absorption, all assets and liabilities are transferred to the absorbing company and the absorbed company is extinguished. In a merger by amalgamation, all of the companies involved are wound up, and their assets and liabilities are transferred to a newly incorporated company. For both types of merger, Swiss law requires the surviving company to become the universal successor to the assets and liabilities of the extinguished company; that is, the surviving company assumes the legal rights and responsibilities of the company that has been extinguished in its entirety. Although the tax consequences of mergers by absorption and mergers by amalgamation are, in general, the same, mergers by amalgamation are infrequent, and therefore they are not discussed further here.

In general, mergers by absorption in Switzerland may be structured in such a way that they are exempt from taxes if all assets and liabilities remain subject to Swiss taxation and if the assets are transferred at book value; that is, no step-up is made.

Mergers between two Swiss resident companies can be carried out free of income tax and, basically, free of withholding tax consequences. A tax-neutral, domestic share-for-share transaction can also be undertaken.

Under the Merger Act and according to the circular letter issued by the Swiss federal tax authorities, issuance stamp duty will be levied on a share-for-share transaction if:

- The increase in the nominal share capital exceeds the nominal share capital of the merged company. Exemptions are possible in the case of a foreign company with a high equity but with a very low nominal share capital.
- There is a contribution of less than 50 percent of the voting rights of the merged company.

Inbound cross-border mergers can be carried out free of income and dividend withholding tax consequences if the Swiss company is the surviving company and if no substance is transferred out of Switzerland. In general, for Swiss income tax purposes, a tax-neutral, inbound share-for-share transaction can be undertaken.

Income-tax-neutral, outbound, cross-border mergers in which the Swiss entity does not survive can be undertaken only if the Swiss business and, accordingly, its substance are not transferred out of Switzerland; for example, a permanent establishment exists in Switzerland after the merger. For withholding tax purposes, such an outbound cross-border merger qualifies as a liquidation and is subject to a 35 percent withholding tax. This withholding tax is levied on the difference between the fair market value of the company's assets and the nominal share capital. Depending on the applicable tax treaty, this withholding tax can be either fully or partially reclaimed.

Outbound share-for-share transactions can be carried out income tax free if a qualifying investment—for example, 20 percent of the share capital—is transferred and if the Swiss shareholder or a Swiss group company controls at least 50 percent of the voting rights in the foreign company.

With the advent of the Merger Act, opportunities for a squeeze out have been expanded. Minority shareholders may elect to receive shares in the surviving company or to receive a settlement in the merger agreement between the merging companies, or the parties may agree that minority shareholders must accept a settlement if a resolution is passed by shareholders owning a 90 percent majority of the votes of the merged company.

5.2   Full Mergers

The basic conditions that must be met for a tax-neutral reorganization are:

- Continuation of tax liability in Switzerland
- Transfer of assets and liabilities at book values to the surviving company

For corporate income tax, stamp tax, VAT, real estate gains tax, and transfer tax purposes, the relevant laws provide for an exemption from or deferral of tax in the event of a reorganization.

However, in connection with a merger, various other tax consequences arise and are discussed below.

(a) Corporate income tax and tax loss carryforwards   Loss carryforwards of the absorbed company can, in principle, be used by the surviving company in subsequent years to offset aggregate profits of the surviving company. If, however, the merger is carried out solely with the intention of utilizing tax loss carryforwards and not primarily with the objective of combining operating capacities, then utilization of the loss carryforwards by the surviving entity may be denied.

(b) Securities transfer tax   Under the Merger Act, transfers of taxable securities that occur in connection with a merger are no longer subject to securities transfer tax.

(c) Equalization payments and nominal value increases   Equalization payments and nominal value increases qualify as taxable income for the shareholder regardless of whether the shareholder is an individual or a corporation. Equalization payments made by the merging companies or an increase in nominal value can be set off against decreases in nominal value.

The surviving company must account for withholding tax on any equalization payments and on the increase in nominal value out of retained earnings.

5.3   Parent/Subsidiary Absorptions

From a tax perspective, the absorption of a subsidiary company by its parent represents a subcategory of full mergers in the aforementioned sense. Legally, this type of merger is exempt from certain formal legal requirements such as having a merger report prepared by the board of directors or having the merger report verified by a special auditor. Furthermore, this type of merger may be executed without a shareholders' meeting.

In principle, a parent/subsidiary absorption is treated for tax purposes in the same manner as a merger between independent companies. One difference, however, arises from the fact that the merged company is carried as an investment on the books of the surviving company. This investment is replaced in the absorption by the assets and liabilities of the merged company. As a result, a merger loss or gain might arise.

In general, a merger loss is not tax deductible. However, if the merger loss is a genuine economic loss caused by the fact that the investment was overvalued, the loss can be used for tax purposes. A merger gain is considered dividend income and is taxed accordingly, although participation relief might be applicable.

6.   OTHER STRUCTURING AND POSTDEAL ISSUES

6.1   Creation of Local-Country Tax Groups

Switzerland does not provide for income tax consolidation and has no credit system for underlying income taxes on dividend income.

For VAT purposes, a group can apply for a tax consolidation, with the effect that transactions between group companies are disregarded.

6.2   Repatriation of Profits or Capital

(a) Dividend payments   Group companies may pay dividends if available profits and distributable reserves exist. Dividends received are eligible for

participation relief if conditions are met regardless of whether the dividends are received from Swiss or foreign subsidiaries. (See Section 7.1 for a discussion of the tax consequences to a Swiss tax resident under the indirect partial liquidation doctrine.)

(b) Capital reductions or redemptions Nominal share capital can be redeemed without any withholding tax consequences. Redemption of nominal share capital may be used to leverage a company; however, attention should be given to thin-capitalization requirements.

(c) Payment for services provided for group companies When the payer is resident outside Switzerland, any payments for services among group companies need to be supported by relevant transfer-pricing documentation that demonstrates that the charge is at arm's length.

6.3   Noncore Disposals

No special tax treatment applies for noncore disposals.

6.4   Preservation of Existing Tax Attributes

For direct federal tax and cantonal and communal tax purposes, losses may be carried forward for seven years.

Switzerland has no change-of-ownership clause in connection with the utilization of loss carryforwards. Therefore, a target company can utilize its tax losses after an acquisition. Likewise, tax losses may be used by an acquiring company following a merger with the target as long as the merger was not undertaken to avoid taxes.

6.5   Receipts under Warranties or Indemnities

See Section 7.4.

6.6   Use of Swiss Tax Privileges

A Swiss company may acquire trademarks separately and may charge royalties to group companies that use the trademark. The royalty company may benefit from the tax privilege of a mixed company. For taxation of a mixed company, see the Introduction.

7.   DISPOSALS

7.1   Stock Disposals

(a) Companies

(i) Disposal for cash consideration Corporations are subject to corporate income tax on gains from the disposal of stock at ordinary income tax rates unless the requirements for participation relief are met. In many instances,

participation relief comes close to or may actually lead to an income tax exemption for capital gains on investments. The conditions that must be met in order to qualify for participation relief are:

- A substantial participation of at least 20 percent, acquired after January 1, 1997, must be sold.
- This participation must have been held for a minimum period of one year.

Capital gains from the sale of a substantial participation held prior to January 1, 1997, are subject to income tax. Under certain circumstances, a Swiss group member's transfer of a substantial participation held prior to January 1, 1997, to a foreign company member of the same group can be income tax neutral. For such a transfer, two alternatives exist.

1. If the transfer is made at fair market value, the capital gain realized can be offset against a provision in the same amount. After January 1, 2007, the provision can be dissolved, with neutral income tax consequences. This provision must be dissolved, and the gain becomes subject to tax if prior to January 1, 2007, the participation is transferred out of the group, or substantial parts of the assets and liabilities are sold, or the participation is liquidated (realization case).

2. The transfer of the substantial participation can be made at book value. In this case, the transferring entity has to declare in its tax return a capital gain in the difference between book value and fair market value. However, the transferring company is allowed to establish an untaxed provision against the capital gain declared so that in essence, the transaction is income tax neutral. After January 1, 2007, the untaxed provision can be dissolved without triggering income taxes.

If prior to January 1, 2007, one of the realization cases as shown under (1) above is fulfilled, the untaxed reserve and any additional value increase realized are fully taxable.

After January 1, 2007, capital gains resulting from a sale of qualifying participations held prior to January 1, 1997, will also qualify for participation relief. Note that in some cantons, alternative transition periods may apply. Additionally, in some cantons, no transition period is taken into account. Specifically, the canton of Geneva does not grant participation relief on capital gains.

A capital gain is calculated as the difference between the sales price and the tax basis.

(ii) Share-for-share exchange   In general, the sale of all of the stock in a company in exchange for stock is treated as an income-tax-neutral transaction

as long as the selling entity is using the same book value for the shares received as it is for the shares exchanged.

(b) Individuals

(i) Stock owned as a private asset   Capital gains on movable assets, including shares or participations, held by an individual as private property are not subject to income tax, and consequently, any losses are not deductible. Capital gains on movable business assets, however, are subject to income tax at the federal and cantonal/communal levels.

As mentioned earlier, while a Swiss resident individual seller can, in principle, achieve a tax-free capital gain by selling shares, that seller's dividend income would be taxable. Therefore, an individual generally prefers to sell shares rather than assets because selling assets eventually results in a taxable liquidation dividend. In addition, because dividend income is fully taxable, Swiss individuals usually do not distribute dividends out of their companies. Therefore, target companies held by a Swiss individual often have excess cash and retained earnings that are not required for running the business. In such circumstances, a seller's tax-free capital gain may be jeopardized by the buyer's postacquisition use of the target's funds to finance the transaction or use of the target company's assets to secure the transaction. This tax consequence occurs as a result of the judicially created indirect partial liquidation doctrine.

In general, the sale of all of the stock in a company in exchange for stock is treated as a tax-neutral transaction as long as the transaction does not qualify as a so-called *Transponierung*. The tax authorities assume a *Transponierung* has taken place if a company is contributed into another company owned by the same individual shareholder and through that contribution, the reserves and retained earnings are transferred so that they can be repaid to the individual shareholder without any income tax consequences on the shareholder level.

(ii) Stock owned as a business asset   An individual seller resident in Switzerland realizes a taxable capital gain on the difference between the book value of the stock and the sales price.

In general, the sale of all of the stock in a company in exchange for stock is treated as a tax-neutral transaction as long as the selling entity is using the same book value for the shares received as it is for the shares exchanged.

7.2   Asset Disposals (Companies Only)

The difference between the book value of the assets sold and the sales price is a capital gain for the selling company and is subject to corporate income tax.

In an asset acquisition, securities transfer tax—0.15 percent for Swiss shares and 0.3 percent for non-Swiss shares—is levied on securities sold when the seller or buyer qualifies as a securities dealer.

Some cantons—for example, those with a monistic system—tax capital gains by levying a special real estate gains tax. (See the relevant taxes as described in the Introduction.) For cantons under the monistic system, the difference between the actual book value of the assets and the higher original cost is regarded as a recapture of depreciation and therefore is subject to income taxes. In these cantons, the difference between the original cost and the higher sales price—that is, the market value—is subject to the special real estate gains tax.

For other cantons and for federal taxes, capital gains on real estate are treated as ordinary business income.

In addition to the tax and registration fees on real estate transfers, some cantons levy a stamp tax on documents and similar legal instruments.

When proceeds from the sale of certain types of operational fixed assets are reinvested in the acquisition of certain types of new operational fixed assets by that company within an adequate period after disposal, the gain arising on the sale of the old asset may be offset, in certain circumstances, by the cost of the new, replacement assets—that is, a rollover of the gain. Such a rollover of the gain is not possible if the replacement assets are located outside Switzerland.

Furthermore, VAT is levied on the sale of assets at a rate of 7.6 percent. However, no payment of output VAT and recovery of input VAT are required if the seller and the buyer qualify as VAT taxpayers and if the assets qualify as a business.

Under the Merger Act, the transfer of (1) shareholdings of at least 20 percent, (2) business divisions, and (3) certain operating fixed assets are tax neutral in certain circumstances. Specifically, such transfers, taking into account all facts and circumstances, must take place among Swiss companies that are united by majority voting rights or are under single management. The untaxed gain will, however, be taxed subsequently if the transferred assets are sold within five years or if the group is no longer under single management.

7.3   Deferred Consideration and Earn-Outs

Deferred consideration is generally regarded as part of the purchase price for companies as well as for individuals.

Participation relief is available for qualifying capital gains as covered in Section 7.1(a)(i). Participation relief should be available for capital gains resulting from deferred consideration recognized in years following the effective financial year of disposal.

Deferred consideration resulting from the disposition of privately held shares is generally exempt from income tax. The income tax treatment of earn-outs should follow the tax treatment of deferred consideration. However, earn-out payments received by individuals who are still engaged with the transferred company or business may be recharacterized as employment income.

7.4   Payments under Warranties or Indemnities

If the sale-and-purchase documentation contains a clause stipulating that any warranty or indemnity payment is to be treated as an adjustment to the consideration offered and received for the transaction, then such payment would be treated for tax purposes as being deducted from the purchase consideration received.

8.   TRANSACTION COSTS FOR SELLERS

See Section 2.

9.   PREPARING A TARGET COMPANY FOR SALE

The preparation of a company for sale includes various items such as identification of the assets or business to be transferred and of the specific assets or liabilities to be excluded from the sale.

Furthermore, the capital and debt structure of the company should be analyzed carefully so as to balance any potential implications for the seller with the needs of a potential acquirer. A presale refinancing may be necessary before the sales transaction occurs.

In addition, a due diligence (commercial, financial, tax, and legal) examination of the company to be sold is in most cases necessary in order to identify any existing risks and, consequently, determine the purchase price of the company. This is also advisable because of the higher liability under the Merger Act.

From a tax point of view, presale planning is particularly important if (1) the purchaser wants to buy only specific assets, or (2) the seller wishes to retain certain assets, or (3) the disposal of a participation is not sheltered from tax by participation relief.

10.   DEMERGERS

10.1   Term and Types

A new implication—contained in the Merger Act—is that it provides for demergers. It distinguishes between a split-up (*Aufspaltung*) and a split-off (*Abspaltung*).

In a split-up, the splitting company transfers all of its assets and liabilities to at least two companies that are already existing or are newly incorporated. The shareholders of the transferring company receive shares of these companies in exchange for the transfer of the assets and liabilities. The transferring company is automatically liquidated as a result of the transfer.

In a split-off, the splitting company transfers some of its assets and liabilities to at least one company that is already existing or is newly incorporated. The shareholders of the transferring company receive shares of these companies in exchange for the transfer of the assets and liabilities. The transferring company survives.

Distinct from the demerger—that is, from the split-up and the split-off—is the simple spin-off of assets and liabilities to a subsidiary company. The transferring company retains the shares in the subsidiary company.

10.2   Legal Matters

On one hand, the Merger Act recognizes a demerger as a civil law principle under which the transfer of assets and liabilities is an act of universal succession. On the other hand, the Merger Act recognizes the spin-off as an application of the civil law principle known as an asset transfer.

10.3   Tax Consequences for Companies

(a) Corporate income tax

(i) Split-off or split-up   The taxation of undisclosed, or hidden, reserves is deferred in the case of a demerger (split-off or split-up) if:

- The assets and liabilities remain subject to Swiss taxation.
- The assets are transferred at book values and are not stepped up.
- Both (1) the assets and liabilities transferred and (2) the assets and liabilities staying behind represent independent viable business divisions.

A tax-neutral demerger (split-off or split-up) of individual assets is not allowed. The demerger must be of an independent business division—that is, an operating unit that by itself is economically viable. Therefore, the term *independent business division* must be viewed from a business perspective. One investment or several investments may fulfill the requirements of an independent business division. However, the tax authorities' practice is very restrictive in determining what constitutes an independent business division. This same requirement also applies to the demerger of real estate companies or the tax-neutral extraction of real estate from an operating company. Furthermore, an independent business division must also remain at the level of the demerging company.

The Merger Act no longer provides for a blocking period for a demerger.

(ii) Spin-off   A tax-neutral spin-off can be executed. In addition to the conditions for a demerger as described earlier in this section, the subsidiary receiving the assets must be domestic. In contrast to the demerger, a restriction period of five years is required for the spin-off of a business division to a subsidiary company with respect to the sale of shares in the subsidiary company.

(iii) Operational fixed assets and participations   In addition to independent business divisions, the Merger Act allows for the tax-neutral transfer of operational fixed assets and participations of at least 20 percent if the transferring company owns directly or indirectly at least 20 percent of the Swiss resident subsidiary company. However, there is a five-year restriction period with respect to the sale of the transferred operational fixed assets by the receiving company. In addition, the receiving company must remain under the same unitary management during the restriction period.

(b) Issuance stamp tax

(i) Split-off or split-up   No issuance stamp tax is levied on shares issued in a demerger as long as the demerger is tax neutral for income tax purposes.

The Merger Act no longer provides for a restriction period for a demerger.

(ii) Spin-off   As long as the conditions for an income-tax-neutral spin-off are fulfilled, no issuance stamp tax is levied. In contrast to a demerger, a restriction period of five years is retained for the spin-off of a business division to a subsidiary company with respect to the sale of shares in the subsidiary company. The five-year restriction period does not apply to a spin-off of participations if at least 20 percent of the nominal share capital is transferred.

(iii) Issuance stamp duty-free capital   Maximum nominal share capital allowed to be created tax free in a spin-off or demerger has to be calculated on a case-by-case basis based on thin-capitalization rules developed for income tax purposes. The book values of the assets transferred form the basis for this calculation. When the thin-capitalization amount is exceeded, the excess is subject to issuance stamp tax.

(c) Demerger of partnerships   The demerger of sole proprietorships, partnerships, associations, foundations, or public law companies receives special treatment in that the issuance stamp tax of 1 percent is levied only on the newly created nominal capital. In order to receive the benefit of this partial waiver of the issuance stamp tax, the original entity must have been in existence for five years prior to the demerger and must not be sold within a five-year blocking period after the demerger.

(d) Securities transfer tax   Under the Merger Act, demergers and spin-offs are exempt from securities transfer tax.

(e) Real estate gains taxes   Real estate taxes are levied only on the cantonal/communal levels. Generally, real estate gains tax is deferred whenever income tax is deferred.

Real estate tax treatment might, however, differ from canton to canton, and reorganizations are not exempt in all cantons. Therefore, each case must be investigated based on its individual facts.

Under the Merger Act, cantons are no longer allowed to impose real estate transfer taxes in reorganizations. Cantons have a transition period until June 30, 2009, to incorporate this change into their law.

(f) VAT   The transfer of assets in a demerger qualifies as VAT turnover. However, no payment of output VAT and recovery of input VAT are required if the involved parties qualify as VAT taxpayers and the assets qualify as a business.

The transfer of shares in the demerger is exempt from VAT.

10.4   Tax Consequences for the Shareholder

(a) Income tax

(i) Shares held as business assets by individuals or companies   If the book value of the shares received by the shareholder is not higher than the previous value of the shares held by the shareholder in a qualifying demerger, there are no income tax consequences.

(ii) Shares held as private assets by individuals   In general, a qualifying demerger is regarded as a tax-neutral shift in the net wealth, and as a result, no income tax consequences or blocking periods result for shares held as private assets by an individual.

In general, if the combined nominal share capital is higher than the nominal share capital prior to the demerger, the difference is subject to income tax. Any cash equalization payments are also subject to income tax.

(b) Withholding tax   If the combined nominal share capital in a qualifying demerger is higher than the nominal share capital prior to the merger, then open reserves and retained earnings, in aggregate, have been converted into nominal share capital. This difference is subject to a withholding tax of 35 percent.

The combined nominal share capital is higher after the demerger if the creation of nominal share capital at the level of the demerged entity is not matched by an equal reduction at the level of the demerging entity.

For qualifying demergers and spin-offs, there have been no changes as a result of the Merger Act.

11.   LISTINGS AND INITIAL PUBLIC OFFERINGS

The issues to consider in an initial public offering (IPO) include the tax consequences of a pre-IPO reorganization, the tax treatment of capital gain arising from the IPO, and the tax deductibility of the IPO costs. If a pre-IPO reorganization is carefully structured, it should be possible for the reorganization to be tax neutral in Switzerland. Tax treatment of the capital gain depends on the tax law of the country in which the seller is resident. In Switzerland, IPO costs are tax deductible. These costs either can be offset directly against any profit recognized in the IPO year or can be capitalized and written off over a five-year period.

11.1   Impact on Tax Status of Listing a Company and Its Subsidiaries

The tax status of a company generally is unaffected by a listing or an IPO. With regard to transactions costs for sellers, see Section 8.

11.2   Complete Group Listing or IPO

With respect to the listing of an entire group, it is common to set up a new company (Holdco) as the vehicle to be listed. The stock in the existing parent company can be transferred to Holdco by way of a share-for-share exchange. It should be possible to carry out this share-for-share exchange on a tax-neutral basis. (See Section 7.1.)

11.3   Listing or IPO of a Subsidiary

There are immediate income tax implications for the existing parent of the listing subsidiary. If the parent sells in the market—that is, lists—some of its existing stock in the subsidiary, the parent is subject to corporate income tax on any gain recognized on the disposal of such stock unless requirements for the substantial shareholdings exemption are met, in which case the disposal would benefit from participation relief. (See Section 7.1 for the conditions that must be met to obtain this relief.) If the subsidiary issues new stock, the parent does not recognize any gain because it has not sold any stock.

11.4   Issuance of New Stock by a Listed Company

Except for the 1 percent issuance stamp tax, the issuance of new stock by the listed company should not have any tax consequences.

11.5   Disposal of Stock by Existing Shareholders

When the listing or IPO involves a disposal of stock by existing shareholders, the tax position for those shareholders is as outlined in Section 7.1.

TURKEY

INTRODUCTION

This chapter details the principal tax issues that are relevant to purchasers and sellers engaged in the transfer of ownership of a Turkish trade or business. Unless otherwise stated, it is generally assumed that all sellers and purchasers are Turkish companies with limited liability.

The tax aspects of mergers and acquisitions are regulated under corporate tax law. The transfer of ownership of a Turkish business or company usually takes the form of a disposal of shares or assets but may also take the form of a merger, a demerger, or a share-for-share exchange. While there are significant differences in the tax consequences of an asset sale versus a share sale, nontax considerations must also be taken into account.

The relevant taxes to be considered for mergers, acquisitions, demergers, and share-for-share exchanges are:

- **Corporation tax.** Effective for 2005, this is a 30 percent tax on profits generated by a company. Turkish companies are taxed on a stand-alone basis. Accordingly, tax grouping and consolidation of taxes for both corporation tax and VAT are not available under Turkish law.

- **Value-added tax (VAT).** Sales of goods and services in Turkey are subject to VAT at rates of 1, 8, and 18 percent depending on the type of goods sold. The general applicable rate is 18 percent. VAT incurred on purchases is recoverable through an offset mechanism whereby input VAT is offset against output VAT. As a general rule, VAT incurred by nonresident companies is not recoverable.

- **Stamp duty.** Stamp duty applies to a wide range of legal documents, including but not limited to contracts, agreements, notes payable, letters of credit, letters of guarantee, financial statements, and payrolls. Stamp duty is levied as a percentage of the highest monetary value stated on the document at rates ranging from 0.15 to 0.75 percent.

- **Real estate transfer tax.** Transfer of the legal title to real estate in Turkey is subject to a 1.5 percent title deed charge on the purchase price. This charge is applied separately for the purchaser and the seller. Accordingly, the total real estate tax levied on a transfer of real property is generally 3 percent.

1.   ACQUISITIONS

1.1   Asset Acquisitions

An acquisition of the assets of a seller's business generally permits a purchaser to acquire such assets free from any tax or commercial liabilities associated with them. Accordingly, liabilities associated with the purchased assets generally remain with the selling company. However, in situations in which the purchase and sale of assets are entered into for tax-avoidance purposes on the part of the seller, Turkish courts may nullify the purchase-and-sale agreement.

The main tax advantage to a purchaser with respect to an asset purchase is that the purchaser receives a stepped-up tax basis in the purchased assets. The purchaser is permitted to depreciate the tax basis of acquired fixed assets regardless of their accumulated depreciation in the seller company. Goodwill, if transferred as a separate item in the purchase-and-sale agreement, is considered and recorded as an intangible asset in the statutory books of the purchaser and may be depreciated for tax purposes on a straight-line basis over five years.

In an asset acquisition, contracts between the seller and third parties are not automatically transferred to the purchaser. Accordingly, the purchaser must either enter into new third-party contracts or obtain the consent of the third parties to continue the existing contracts.

When personnel are transferred in the asset acquisition, severance payments often are important considerations. In principle, the seller is responsible for making severance payments to departing employees, but the purchaser and seller may agree to have the purchaser assume such obligations with an adjustment to the purchase price.

Proceeds from asset transfers are considered part of the seller's commercial income and are included in calculating the seller's tax liability. From the perspective of the seller's shareholders, the proceeds from an asset transfer can be accessed by such shareholders only through dividend distributions. This may result in a double taxation of the proceeds, because income withholding tax may be payable over the dividends distributed and the dividend recipient may be required to pay additional taxes depending on the nature of the shareholder. (See Section 6.1.)

1.2   Share Acquisitions

With respect to the purchase of shares, generally all assets, liabilities, tax attributes, and associated legal agreements—such as, licenses, leases, and valuable contracts—of the target remain with the target notwithstanding the change in ownership. There is no mechanism under Turkish corporate tax law to step up the basis in the underlying assets of the acquiring company.

One tax advantage to the target shareholders of a purchase of shares is that the target shareholders receive the sales proceeds directly. In principle, any capital gain realized by the target shareholders is taxable under Turkish income tax law. However, Turkish law permits certain exemptions from capital gains tax. (See Section 7.1.)

There is often an inherent conflict between the purchaser and seller because generally, the purchaser would like to acquire assets and receive a stepped-up basis in the assets for tax purposes, while the seller generally likes to sell shares for tax purposes because most Turkish companies are family-owned businesses held by individuals who are entitled to an exemption from capital gains tax if they held the shares for more than one year. (See Section 7.1.)

2. TRANSACTION COSTS FOR PURCHASERS

2.1 Transfer Taxes

(a) Share purchase The sale of shares in a Turkish limited company must occur pursuant to an executed purchase-and-sale agreement before a Turkish public notary. Because of recent changes in Turkish law, such purchase-and-sale agreements are no longer subject to stamp duty. They are now subject to a notary charge of 0.09 percent of the sales price for the seller and a notary charge of 0.09 percent of the paid-up capital for the purchaser. The total notary charge is limited to TRL10,450,700,000.

With respect to the sale of shares in a Turkish joint-stock company, stamp tax is levied on the sales price set forth in the purchase-and-sale agreement at a rate of 0.75 percent. Note that each and every signed copy of the agreement is separately subject to stamp tax. In addition, the purchaser and seller are jointly liable for the stamp tax due; however, in practice, the responsibility for payment of stamp tax is usually a negotiated term in the purchase-and-sale agreement. The stamp tax amount per each agreement is limited to TRL1.028 billion.

According to the stamp duty regulations, agreements signed in Turkey give rise to an immediate stamp tax. When the agreement is signed outside Turkey, it may be asserted that stamp tax is not due until the agreement is brought into Turkey for submission to official departments or until the terms of the document are benefited from in Turkey. The definition of *benefited from* is very broad but generally applies when one party to the purchase-and-sale agreement is a resident of Turkey.

(b) Asset purchase Agreements signed with respect to the purchase and sale of assets are generally subject to stamp tax as described in Section 2.1(a). In addition, transfers of commercial and noncommercial agreements between the purchaser and the seller are subject to a special stamp tax rate equal to

one-fourth of the 0.75 percent standard rate, or 0.1875 percent, on the highest monetary amounts contained in the agreements.

A special stamp-tax rate applies to the transfer of legal title to real estate situated in Turkey. The transfer of legal title to real estate situated in Turkey is subject to a title deed charge equal to 1.5 percent of the purchase price. This charge is applied separately to both the purchaser and the seller. Accordingly, the total title deed charge with respect to real estate situated in Turkey is 3 percent.

2.2   Value-Added Tax

(a) *Share purchase*   Share transfers are exempt from VAT.

(b) *Asset purchase*   VAT is charged at the general rate of 18 percent over the purchase price of the assets. The VAT rate may differ depending on the nature of the assets. The applicable VAT rates for various assets are currently 1, 8, and 18 percent. For example, used automobiles are subject to the rate of 1 percent. There are certain recommended techniques used for reducing VAT liability on asset transfers. These techniques include financial leasing and asset transfers through an investment incentive certificate.

2.3   Capital Taxes

There are no capital taxes in Turkey applicable to stock or asset purchases.

2.4   Tax Deductibility of Transaction Costs

(a) *Share purchase*

(i) *Financing expenses*   Expenses that are incurred to finance the purchase of shares of a company are treated as deductible expenses for corporate income tax purposes.

(ii) *Other expenses*   Other expenses—such as due diligence, consultancy, and research expenses incurred in connection with a purchase of shares—are also generally deductible.

(b) *Asset purchase*

(i) *Financing expenses*   Expenses related to loans that are used for financing the purchase of fixed assets must be accumulated for the taxable year of capitalization and added to the cost basis of the purchased assets at the end of that year. Furthermore, the purchaser has the option of capitalizing interest and foreign exchange losses related to loans used for financing such assets incurred after the year of capitalization.

(ii) Other expenses   Other expenses included in the tax cost basis of the assets include:

- Customs duties and shipping and installation charges for machinery and equipment
- Expenses arising from the purchase and demolition of an existing building and the leveling of its site

Companies in Turkey are free to include expenses for public notaries, court fees, assessment, commissions, public announcements, and real estate purchase tax in the tax cost basis of the assets or to treat them as a general deductible expenses.

VAT paid on transaction-related expenses is in principle recoverable for both asset and share purchases. Banking and insurance transactions tax is also deductible for corporate income tax purposes. (See Section 4.1(b) for further information on banking and insurance transactions tax.)

3.   BASIS OF TAXATION FOLLOWING ASSET OR STOCK ACQUISITIONS

3.1   Asset Acquisitions

As described earlier, the purchasing company may realize a step-up in the tax basis of the transferred assets. The stepped-up tax basis of the fixed assets may be depreciated regardless of the assets' accumulated depreciation in the hands of the seller company.

The seller in the purchase contract generally allocates the purchase price to the assets up to their individual market values. Any balance remaining is treated as goodwill. Goodwill is recorded as an intangible asset in the statutory books of the purchasing company and is depreciated for tax purposes on a straight-line basis over five years.

The purchase price of the assets must be determined on an arm's-length basis. In practice, the commercial court confirms the parties' valuations to avoid the risk of a challenge by the tax authorities. Successful challenges by the tax authorities often result in additional tax assessments, penalties, and late payment of interest.

The purchase price allocated to the assets—excluding vacant land and plots—may be depreciated over their useful lives pursuant to depreciation rates established by the Ministry of Finance. This rate may be doubled through the use of a double-declining-depreciation method, but the rate may not exceed 50 percent. Buildings are depreciated over a period of 10 to 50 years on a straight-line basis.

Sales of inventory are included in the commercial profits of the seller company. These acquired inventories are recorded in the statutory books of the purchaser company at their purchasing values.

3.2   Share Acquisitions

(a) Purchase price   For the purchaser, the main cost is the purchase price of the shares of the acquired company. Note that there is no obligation to perform a valuation of the target company. However, it is required that the purchase price of the company be determined at fair market value and that the transaction be concluded on an arm's-length basis.

The underlying base cost of the assets of the acquired company remains unchanged, and there is no method available for stepping up the basis in the assets for tax purposes. In addition, no goodwill arises under Turkish tax and accounting rules. Instead, the full consideration paid is capitalized into the cost of the shares.

(b) Tax grouping   Because Turkey taxes companies on a stand-alone basis, tax grouping or consolidation is not permissible for either corporate tax or VAT.

4.   FINANCING OF ACQUISITIONS

4.1   Debt

Specific tax issues related to the overall level of borrowing and interest expense related to acquisition indebtedness include:

(a) Withholding tax   In general, interest on intercompany loans borrowed from a foreign related party is subject to a withholding tax of 10 percent. However, there is no withholding tax on interest paid with respect to loans obtained from foreign banks or financial institutions. In addition, there is no withholding tax on interest with respect to loans obtained from a local bank or other local company. Except under limited circumstances, ordinary Turkish companies are prohibited from making loans.

(b) VAT   Interest payments on loans obtained from any foreign company other than banks or financial institutions are subject to VAT at the rate of 18 percent, which must be calculated and paid by the local company under the so-called reverse-charge mechanism. This VAT is then treated as input VAT by the local company and is offset against the output VAT incurred in the same month. This VAT does not create any tax burden for either the Turkish or the nonresident lender except for its cash flow effect on the former when there is not enough output VAT of the Turkish entity to offset the input VAT. There is no VAT liability on interest payments on loans obtained from foreign banks and other financial institutions.

No VAT liability arises with respect to interest on loans from local banks; however, the local bank is required to pay a banking and insurance transactions tax equal to 5 percent of the interest payments. In practice, local banks pass this expense on to their customers.

(c) ***Resource utilization support fund*** Foreign loans obtained by Turkish resident individuals or legal entities other than banks or financial institutions are subject to a Resource Utilization Support Fund (RUSF) levy at the rate of 3 percent of the principal amount of the loan. This levy is payable at the inception of the loan. RUSF levy can be avoided, however, by setting to longer than one year the average maturity of the hard-currency loan obtained from abroad.

(d) ***Deductibility of interest*** In principle, interest payments are tax deductible on an accrual basis. However, deductibility of interest accruals arising from the financial liabilities against commercial income in the same year is a controversial issue under Turkish law. On one hand, the Ministry of Finance has taken the position that interest on financial liabilities is deductible against commercial income only when paid. On the other hand, there are certain Supreme Court decisions supporting the opposite view. Note that deductibility of interest and other financial expenses arising from a loan may not be possible if the loan is subject to the rules on thin capitalization. (See Section 4.1(e).)

(e) ***Thin capitalization*** Under Turkish law, loan arrangements may be scrutinized under rules governing thin capitalization in the following circumstances:

- When a loan is obtained from a related party
- When a loan is in continuous use within the company
- When the ratio of the loan to shareholders' equity is high in comparison to similar companies in the same sector

The last two circumstances are somewhat subjective and ambiguous. *Continuous use* is generally understood to mean a period exceeding one year. As for the third circumstance, Turkish law provides for no specified debt/equity ratio. However, it is generally understood that the higher the ratio, the greater the risk of thin capitalization. Although differing opinions exist on the issue, the prevailing opinion is that the risk of thin-capitalization risk is high when the debt/equity ratio exceeds 50 percent.

Thin capitalization may result in the denial of interest expense on such related party loans for corporate tax purposes. In addition, any foreign exchange losses incurred with respect to such loans may be treated as nondeductible.

4.2   Equity

(a) ***Stamp tax*** There is no capital duty in Turkey on the issuance of shares for initial and subsequent capital increases except that such contributions are subject to levy under the Competition Fund at a rate of 0.04 percent.

5.   MERGERS

5.1   Legal Forms of Mergers

According to Turkish law, merger transactions involve the transfer of assets and liabilities of a target company to the acquiring company with the target company's dissolving. Merger transactions are required to take place at market and/or net realizable value, and tax is payable on the resulting increase over book value. Taxation arises because the hidden reserves of the dissolving company are realized. The preservation of carried-forward tax losses is possible if certain conditions are met.

However, Turkish corporate tax law permits a tax-free form of merger known as a takeover. A take-over is defined as the transfer of assets and liabilities of one company to another at their book values as of the date of the transfer. The main requirements for a takeover are that the legal or business centers of the two companies be based in Turkey and that both companies be the same type of legal entity. A takeover transaction is tax free because the assets of the dissolving company are transferred to the absorbing company at their book value so that taxation is deferred to a later date. The absorbing company retains its rights as those rights relate to loss carryovers if the conditions cited in Section 6.4(a) are met.

Takeover transactions are afforded tax-free treatment if the following conditions are met:

- Within 15 days after the takeover, the dissolving and absorbing companies submit to the tax authorities a jointly signed tax return covering the period of the dissolving company before the takeover, and the return contains the takeover balance sheet.
- The absorbing company represents, through a declaration attached to the statement of transfer, that it will assume all of the tax liabilities of the dissolving company that have been or will be incurred, together with other liabilities.

5.2   Tax Consequences

In the case of taxable mergers, any profit arising from the merger is subject to corporate tax at a rate of 30 percent. In addition, assets, including inventory and goodwill, if any, transferred to the absorbing company are subject to VAT. Note that the absorbing company cannot use carried-forward VAT and losses of the dissolving company.

In the event of a takeover, only the taxable profit derived by the dissolved company until the takeover date is subject to corporate tax. No taxation arises as a result of the takeover. Tax-free merger transactions are also exempt from VAT, stamp tax, and other related fees, except for the Competition Fund, which is levied at 0.04 percent on the resulting capital increase of the absorbing company.

6. OTHER STRUCTURING AND POSTDEAL ISSUES

6.1   Taxation of Dividends

Dividends paid on shares of a Turkish company are not tax deductible by the distributing company. Corporate withholding tax at the rate of 10 percent on the gross amount of the dividend is applicable to dividends distributed to individuals and nonresident entities. Individuals may be entitled to a withholding tax credit associated with the dividend.

Dividend distributions to resident entities and branches of nonresident entities are not subject to corporate withholding tax. Note that for nonresident companies—meaning, branches and permanent establishments—withholding tax is applicable only on the portion of the branch profit that is remitted by the branch to its headquarter company. Branch profits not remitted to the headquarter company are not subject to withholding tax.

6.2   Noncore Disposals

On one hand, as a general rule, for tax purposes there is no distinction between the disposal of noncore assets and the disposal of core assets—that is, the disposal of a business line of the target company. On the other hand, the disposal of core assets may have other, associated tax implications if the core assets are subject to an investment incentive certificate. (See Section 6.4(c).)

Noncore business lines can be disposed of in a tax-free manner subject to certain conditions. (See Section 10.) The demerger regulations require commercial integrity of the transferred production or service plants; that is, generally, the transferred assets must be readily available to commence operation with their total enterprise, fixed assets, and distribution network.

6.3   Cash Repatriation

Foreign exchange regulations are quite liberal in Turkey. Dividends can be paid by Turkish companies if available profits and distributable reserves exist. For dividend distribution purposes, previous-year losses should be deducted from current-year profits before distribution. In addition, service and royalty fees can be paid to foreign companies as long as transfer-pricing rules are complied with.

6.4   Preservation of Existing Tax Attributes

(a) Carried-forward tax losses   According to Turkish legislation, tax losses of companies can be carried forward for five years to be used against profits in future periods. In the case of a share acquisition, the losses of the company remain with the target company and may be carried forward for use against future target-company profits. Carried-forward tax losses are not relevant to asset purchases.

Although the existing tax attributes of an absorbed company are transferred automatically to an absorbing company in a tax-free merger, certain conditions must be met in order for the absorbing company to benefit from the carried-forward tax losses of the absorbed company:

- Both the absorbing and the absorbed companies must operate in the same industry.
- The previous five years' corporate tax returns of the absorbed company must be submitted to the tax office on time.
- The available loss carryforward that can be used by the absorbing company is limited by the gross value of the assets of the absorbed company as of the date of the merger.

(b) Deductible VAT carried forward   In the case of a share acquisition, the purchaser would enjoy the carried-forward input VAT of the target company. Note that this opportunity is not available in cases of asset transfers and taxable mergers.

(c) Transfer of investment incentives   Investment incentives available to the target company are transferred automatically to the acquiring company in share purchases and tax-free takeovers. In an acquisition of individual assets, investment incentives generally do not pass to the acquiring company. However, if the assets of a business line are acquired as a whole, the investment incentives may be transferred to the purchaser, provided that certain conditions are met.

(d) Other tax attributes   Other existing tax attributes of the target company, if any, are transferred automatically to the purchaser company in cases of share acquisitions and tax-free takeovers.

6.5   Receipts under Warranties or Indemnities

Generally, payments made by a seller for breach of warranty or under an indemnity are taxable in the hands of the purchaser. Under Turkish law, in order to avoid immediate taxation, a clause should be inserted in the purchase-and-sale agreement, stipulating that any such payments will be considered adjustments to the purchase price. In such a case, instead of immediate taxation, the receipt is treated as a reduction of the purchaser's tax basis for the shares. If the warranty or indemnity payments are made to the target company, such payments should be subject to tax in the hands of the target company.

7. DISPOSALS

7.1 Share Disposals

(a) Companies

(i) Disposal for cash consideration Capital gains derived from the sale of shares in a local company by either a foreign company or a local company are generally subject to tax. There is no separate capital gains taxation in Turkey.

Taxation of capital gains derived from the sale of shares by nonresidents (individuals or corporations) differs based on the legal status of the company whose shares are sold. In the case of a joint-stock company, sales of shares by nonresidents do not give rise to taxation in Turkey. There is no difference between a majority and a minority sale with respect to tax treatment. Sales of shareholdings in a limited liability company by nonresident corporations are subject to tax in Turkey through the filing of a special tax return. However, foreign exchange gains are not included in taxable income, except for those derived from the continuous trading of securities.

The availability of a bilateral tax treaty between Turkey and the nonresident shareholder's country of residence may eliminate payment of capital gains tax in Turkey if the holding period exceeds one year. This is also generally true for capital gains arising from the sale of shareholdings in a limited liability company.

In principle, capital gains realized from a sale are included in the corporate income of the company and are subject to full taxation.

(ii) Share-for-share exchanges Turkish law provides for a tax-free disposal of shares in a share-for-share exchange. This is a new form of tax-free transaction that has not been currently defined in the commercial law. Therefore, no share-for-share exchanges have been implemented to date. Under the share-for-share exchange, a resident company acquires the majority of the voting shares of another resident company in exchange for shares of the acquiring company. The share exchange ratio is calculated according to the current value of both the target and acquiring companies, which determines the amount of the shares to be received by the shareholders of the target company.

(b) Individuals Neither domestic nor foreign individuals are subject to income tax on capital gains arising from the sale of shares of a joint-stock company, provided that the shares have been held for at least one year (three months for the shares of publicly listed companies). Note that securities other than shares—for example, participations in limited companies—cannot benefit from this exemption.

If the shares of a joint-stock company are sold within a year of acquisition or if the participation rights of a limited liability company are sold regardless of the holding period, taxable income is determined after an adjustment for the effects of inflation through either an inflation discount or a cost revision.

The taxable income is subject to income tax at general rates for individuals. The taxable income is the difference between the sale price and the inflation-adjusted acquisition cost and expenses related to disposal. The Turkish lira acquisition cost of shares can be adjusted by using the indexes announced by the State Institute of Statistics for every month that the indexes have been issued, excluding the month of sale. Subject to annual adjustment, TRL12 billion of gain is exempt from tax. For resident individuals, the tax is paid through submission of an annual tax return. Nonresident individuals are required to file a special tax return and to pay the associated capital gains tax within 15 days following the transaction.

Note that foreign exchange gains are not included in the taxable income, except for those derived from the continuous trading of securities.

7.2   Asset Disposals (Companies Only)

The proceeds of asset transfers are taxable as a part of the commercial income of the seller company.

When a company disposes of an asset at a gain that is essential to its business and then uses the proceeds to purchase a new and similar asset to be used in its business, Turkish law permits the use of a Renewal Fund to shelter the adverse effects of inflation and to defer taxation on the disposal. Under the Renewal Fund mechanism, any gain resulting from the sale of the asset is kept under an equity account for a maximum period of three years. This Renewal Fund is then offset against depreciation deductions of the newly purchased asset, and in the event of a balance's remaining after a three-year period, such balance is required to be transferred to the profit-and-loss account at the end of this period and is subject to full corporation tax.

7.3   Deferred Consideration and Earn-Outs

From the perspective of the seller, the amount received from the purchaser as deferred consideration in return for the sale of shares or assets is recorded as income at the time of the payments. The amounts are included in the corporate income tax base and taxed accordingly during the year in which the consideration is received.

From the purchaser's perspective, these payments should be added to the cost of the shares or assets acquired.

8.   TRANSACTION COSTS FOR SELLERS

8.1   Transfer Taxes

See Section 2.1.

8.2   VAT

(a) Share disposal   The disposal of shares is exempt from VAT.

(b) Asset disposal   The transfer of assets is generally subject to VAT on the sale value of the assets. (See Section 2.2(b) for applicable VAT rates.) VAT exemptions are available in cases of tax-free takeovers and demergers and for disposals under the temporary-corporate-tax-exemption method.

9.   PREPARING A TARGET COMPANY FOR SALE

Presale planning is important if the purchaser wants to buy only specific assets, or if the seller wishes to retain certain assets, or if the disposal is not sheltered from tax by the tax-saving mechanisms described in Section 7.1.

9.1   Hive-Down of Assets

A hive-down of assets involves the transfer of a specific trade or assets of a company to another group company. On one hand, under Turkish law, a hive-down is considered an asset acquisition, and its tax consequences are the same as those of an asset acquisition as described in Section 1.1. On the other hand, if the hive-down takes the form of a partial merger, or spin-off, as described in Section 10.1(b), then the transaction may be implemented tax free.

9.2   Intragroup Transfer of Assets

There is no special tax treatment of intragroup transfers of assets under Turkish legislation. Thus, the tax consequences of such transfers would be the same as the tax consequences of asset transfers to third parties. Transfers of assets among intragroup companies should be performed on an arm's-length basis in line with the transfer-pricing regulations.

9.3   Presale Dividends

Under Turkish law there are no restrictions on presale dividends other than that such dividends must be paid out of distributable reserves. Accordingly, presale dividends may serve as a useful device for reducing the book value shares of the target company. Although the book value of the shares may be reduced through a presale dividend, the subsequent transaction should be carried out at arm's length.

10.   DEMERGERS

The concept of a demerger is a recent addition to Turkish law. However, it has not yet been defined in the commercial code. A recent joint communiqué published by the Ministry of Finance and the Ministry of Industry and Trade sets out guidance concerning partial mergers. Recent regulations covering demergers under Turkish corporate tax law have also been issued.

10.1   Types of Demergers

(a) Demerger as a whole   A demerger as a whole is defined as dissolution without liquidation, whereby all of the assets, payables, and receivables of a dissolving company are transferred to two or more resident companies at their book value in return for participation shares that are distributed to the shareholders of the dissolving company. Because this type of demerger transaction is not currently defined in the commercial code, such transactions have not been implemented to date.

(b) Partial demerger (spin-off)   In a partial demerger, a company transfers all of the assets of a business to an existing or newly established company at the assets' book value in exchange for shares of the transferee company. The transferor company remains in existence and distributes to its shareholders the shares received in the transferee company. Note that in order for a demerger to receive tax-free treatment, both the transferor and the transferee companies must be resident in Turkey.

10.2   Tax Treatment of Transferor Company

(a) Corporate tax   In the case of a demerger as a whole, only the taxable profit derived by the transferor company until the demerger date is subject to corporate tax, provided that the following conditions are met:

- The corporate tax return of the demerged company, which includes the profit of the demerged company before the demerger date, must be signed by both parties and submitted to the tax office within 15 days after the demerger date. The balance sheet and income statement of the transferor company must also be submitted as an attachment to the tax return.

- The transferee company must declare to the tax office that the transferee company will assume all tax liabilities that have been or will be incurred and all other liabilities of the transferor company.

(b) VAT   VAT is not applicable to transfers of assets in a demerger.

(c) Other transaction taxes   Demerger transactions are also exempt from any transaction taxes and fees, including stamp tax and banking and insurance transactions tax.

10.3 Tax Treatment of Transferee Company

Under Turkish corporate tax law provisions, the transferee is not subject to any corporate tax and is exempt from all transaction taxes and fees.

11. LISTINGS AND INITIAL PUBLIC OFFERINGS

11.1 Impact on Tax Status of Company Being Listed and of Its Subsidiaries

According to Turkish law, the tax status of a listed or initial public offerings (IPO) company is not different from that of an unlisted company.

11.2 Listing or IPO of Subsidiary

Effecting a listing or IPO of a subsidiary by selling its existing shares is subject to the normal rules for disposal of shares described in Section 7.1.

11.3 Issuance of New Shares by Listed Company

The issuance of new stock by a listed company either in an IPO or at a later stage should not have any tax consequences for the company. The expenses incurred as a result of the IPO or listing transaction are deductible from the taxable income of the company for the relevant period. If the shares are sold at higher than face value, an emission premium arises that is exempt from corporate tax under Turkish law.

UNITED KINGDOM

INTRODUCTION

This chapter details the principal tax issues that are relevant to purchasers and sellers engaged in the transfer of ownership of a UK trade or business. Unless otherwise stated, it is generally assumed that all sellers and purchasers are UK companies with limited liability.

The transfer of ownership of a UK trade or company may take the form of a disposition of shares or assets. While there are significant differences between the tax implications of an asset sale and those of a share sale, nontax considerations must also be considered. Indeed, it is very common for the form of the deal to have been determined even before the tax implications are considered. The concept of a merger does not exist in UK company law. A transaction described as a merger involves a transfer of shares and/or assets between companies but is structured in such a way that the merging parties have some form of commonality of interest; for example, following the merger, both parties hold stock in the same holding company.

The relevant taxes to be considered with respect to transfer of ownership are:

- **Corporation tax.** Generally, this is a 30 percent tax on profits earned by a company. UK companies are taxed on a stand-alone basis even if they are members of a tax group. However, there are tax-grouping provisions that enable members of a tax group to transfer tax losses among themselves.

- **Value-added tax (VAT).** This is a sales tax whereby 17.5 percent is added to the sales price charged for goods or services, except for certain categories of sale that are exempt from or outside the scope of VAT. A purchaser or recipient of services can generally recover VAT paid if the purchase was incurred in the course of a commercial activity. However, the level of recoverability varies from case to case.

- **Stamp duty land tax.** This is payable by a purchaser at a rate of up to 4 percent on the purchase price for land or real estate and at a rate of 0.5 percent on the purchase price for stock.

1. ACQUISITIONS

Acquisitions can take either of two forms: acquisition of the assets of an existing business or acquisition of an entire corporation through acquisition of the target corporation's stock.

1.1 Asset Acquisitions

Generally, an asset acquisition enables the purchaser to avoid exposure to the risk of any historical liabilities that are not specifically recoverable through the sale agreement. Liabilities associated with the business being purchased remain the responsibility of the company that has made the asset sale and do not become the responsibility of the purchaser unless the parties agree that specified liabilities will transfer to the purchaser. Even when the seller and buyer do agree to transfer specified liabilities, the creditor may pursue the seller for payment unless there is a formal novation. (A novation is an agreement also involving the creditor, under which the liability is assumed by the buyer, and the creditor agrees to release the seller from any further responsibility for that debt.)

Another important nontax consideration is that a sale of assets, contracts between the seller and third parties are not automatically assigned to the purchaser. Therefore, it is necessary for the purchaser either to enter into new contracts with the third parties or to agree with the third party that the existing contract can be assigned from seller to purchaser. These actions often cause practical difficulties, particularly when numerous contracts exist or when a third party is unwilling to permit assignment, and they frequently explain why stock transactions are preferable to asset transactions.

Note also that there are regulations that protect employees affected by the sale of a business. The Transfer of Undertakings (Protection of Employment) regulations generally require that the purchaser take on employees under their current terms and conditions of employment.

An asset acquisition generally facilitates a step-up in the tax basis of assets. (Section 3.1 covers the basis of taxation following an asset acquisition.) The consideration paid is allocated between different assets in the sale documentation. Generally, these allocations are accepted by the UK Inland Revenue as the new tax basis for those assets.

For assets acquired on or after April 1, 2002, a tax deduction is available for goodwill and other acquired intangibles such as know-how. Tax relief is given for intangibles either on an amortization basis in line with the accounting treatment—usually amortization is over 20 years in the case of goodwill—or at a rate of 4 percent on a straight-line basis.

However, the shareholders of the selling company are at a disadvantage in that the proceeds of an asset sale will remain locked in that company. Thus, distribution of these proceeds may result in double taxation. The company will already have been subject to tax on the sale of assets. In addition, distribution of the sale proceeds by the company to its shareholders may result in taxable income to the shareholder depending on who the shareholder is. In particular, this will affect shareholders who are UK resident individuals because such individuals are subject to income tax on dividends received. However, corporate shareholders might also be affected if the seller company is liquidated—because the liquidation distribution may be subject to tax—or if the seller company uses a method other than dividend distributions to pass along proceeds to shareholders.

1.2   Stock Acquisitions

In a stock acquisition, the purchaser effectively bears any historical and future ongoing tax and nontax liabilities of the target company. There is no step-up permitted in the tax base cost of the company's assets. Any goodwill acquired as part of a stock deal does not qualify for tax relief. (Section 3.2 covers the basis of taxation following a share acquisition.) Therefore, from a tax point of view, it often benefits a purchaser to acquire assets rather than stock.

However, as indicated in Section 1.1, an important advantage of a stock acquisition is that contracts between the target company and third parties remain in force and do not need to be assigned or renegotiated with the third party. However, some contracts may contain change-of-control provisions that may result in the termination of or other amendment to the contract in the event of a change in ownership of the target company.

A conflict may exist between the preferences of purchaser and seller because of the availability of the substantial-shareholdings exemption to sellers under which, provided certain criteria are met, a disposal of stock may be exempt from tax on capital gains. (Section 7 covers details of the exemption.) No such exemption exists with regard to a disposal of assets. Therefore, if the conditions are met, a purchaser may want to acquire assets and a seller may prefer to sell stock. Therefore, the tax impact of the acquisition structure can be a key factor in the pricing negotiations with the seller.

2.   TRANSACTION COSTS FOR PURCHASERS

2.1   Transfer Taxes

(a) *Stock purchase*   Stamp duty of 0.5 percent is payable by the purchaser on the amount or value of the consideration provided.

(b) *Asset purchase*   Stamp duty land tax of up to 4 percent of the amount or value of the consideration provided is payable by the purchaser on transactions that relate to UK land or real estate. If a bundle of assets is being acquired, only the element of the consideration allocated to land is subject to stamp duty land tax. However, if a company owns the land, stamp duty land tax is not payable if only the stock in the company is sold and the company continues to own the land.

Prior to December 1, 2003, stamp duty of up to 4 percent was payable on the acquisition of certain other assets—including debtors, benefits of contracts, and partnership interest—but not on the acquisition of goodwill or intellectual property.

2.2 Value-Added Tax

(a) Stock purchase Stock transfers are exempt from VAT.

(b) Asset purchase A transfer of business assets that qualifies as the transfer of a business as a going concern is outside the scope of VAT. Otherwise, a purchase of assets is subject to VAT at 17.5 percent, which must be paid in addition to the purchase consideration.

When the buyer is subject to the VAT regime and is required to charge VAT on its sales—called outputs—the buyer may recover VAT paid by it on its own purchases—called inputs. A purchase of assets on which VAT has been charged by the seller is regarded as an input for the buyer. Therefore, VAT charged may be recovered by the buyer. In some situations, depending on certain VAT-related characteristics of the buyer, the VAT paid on inputs may not always be recoverable in full. As a result, such VAT paid would be a real cost to the buyer.

2.3 Capital Taxes

There are no capital taxes in the UK that are applicable to stock or asset purchases.

2.4 Tax Deductibility of Transaction Costs

In general, whether or not a particular expense gets treated as deductible depends on several factors, including:

- Whether the transaction is for the purchase of assets or the purchase of shares
- Whether the purchaser is a trading company for UK tax purposes—that is, its principal activity is that of trading—or whether the purchaser is an investment company for UK tax purposes—broadly, a nontrading company
- Why the expense was incurred: The identity of the persons to whom the expenses were paid is of less significance.

In general terms, the position can be summarized as:

- Finance costs
- Investigation and due diligence costs
- Other deal costs
- VAT treatment of expenses

(a) **Finance costs**   Costs incurred on the formation of companies and on the raising of equity finance generally do not qualify for corporate tax relief. At best, such costs can be taken into account in a calculation of the capital gains tax base cost of the acquired company on a subsequent disposal.

Costs related to the raising of debt finance should be subject to corporate tax relief. Relief is normally given for such costs when they are taken to the profit-and-loss account pursuant to UK generally accepted accounting principles. Such costs include bank arrangement fees and professional fees incurred in connection with securing the provision of that finance.

(b) **Investigation and due diligence costs**   Due diligence and other investigation costs generally are not deductible unless such work was necessary to obtain debt finance. If this is the case, then the proportion of the costs for which a deduction is allowed needs to be negotiated with the Inland Revenue on a case-by-case basis.

(c) **Other deal costs**   Only those costs related to the raising of the debt financing of the acquisition are deductible for tax purposes.

(d) **VAT treatment of expenses**   Fees charged for making arrangements for loans and for issuing stock are not subject to VAT in the UK. Thus, bank and institutional fees generally do not carry VAT. However, professional fees charged to UK clients by advisers based in the UK are subject to VAT even if the fees are related to the sale or issue of stock or loan financing.

Input VAT—that is, VAT charged by third parties for goods or services provided—that is related directly to the issue of stock to UK or European Union counterparties may not be recovered.

VAT charged on professional fees incurred for a transaction not related directly to the issuance of stock can be treated as a group overhead expense and is fully recoverable unless the group is subject to the partial-exemption method.

Costs should be clearly identified on invoices so that input VAT can easily be attributed to the issuance of stock and to other matters.

3.   BASIS OF TAXATION FOLLOWING ASSET OR STOCK ACQUISITIONS

3.1   Asset Acquisitions

Annual capital allowances (tax depreciation) of 25 percent on a reducing-balance basis are available with regard to acquired plant and machinery and are based on the price paid for those assets. When plant and fixtures are purchased as part of a property deal, an election under s198 CAA 2001 should be made, if necessary, to allocate purchase price between fixtures and property. Industrial buildings allowances may be available on the purchase of industrial buildings. However, the rate or amount of these allowances depends on the age of the building.

Purchased intangible assets and goodwill are eligible for tax depreciation in line with the accounting treatment or at a rate of 4 percent on a straight-line basis.

Sales of inventory normally are included in the seller's trading profits, and the purchaser receives tax basis equal to the value of stock as paid. However, special rules exist that allow the inventory to be restated for tax purposes to market value. These rules apply when the seller's trade is being discontinued and the two parties are connected.

Similar rules apply to work in progress.

Typically, trade debts are acquired at net book value. When the amount subsequently received is equal to the net book value, no taxable profit or loss arises. If one of the debts proves irrecoverable whether in full or in part, it should be possible to obtain a tax deduction to the extent that the debt is not recovered.

3.2   Stock Acquisitions

(a) Purchase price   The purchase price forms the base cost of the purchaser's stock in the acquired company. The underlying base cost in the acquired company's assets is not changed, and there is no election available to step up the tax basis of assets. Accounting goodwill arising from the consolidation of the company in the financial statements of a UK parent is not tax deductible.

(b) Tax grouping   The UK has a separate-entity basis of taxation. However, operating profits and loss occurring in the same period in different UK group companies can be offset against each other. (Section 6.2 contains additional discussion of these matters.)

4.   FINANCING OF ACQUISITIONS

4.1   Debt

The following are specific tax issues related to the overall level of borrowing and to the interest charged on this debt:

- Withholding tax
- Deductibility of interest
- Thin capitalization
- Distributions

(a) Withholding tax   Cash interest payments to overseas lenders are subject to a 20 percent withholding tax. This can be reduced by an advance agreement with the UK tax authorities under the UK's wide network of double-tax treaties. The rules are the same for interest paid on payment-in-kind notes. However, when withholding tax is levied on payment-in-kind notes, the withholding tax is paid to the Inland Revenue in the form of payment-in-kind notes rather than cash.

Interest payments between UK companies are not subject to withholding taxes. In addition, certain debt instruments are not subject to withholding tax, including (1) deeply discounted securities, when the discount is not subject to withholding tax and (2) quoted Eurobonds—interest-bearing debt issued by a company and listed on a recognized stock exchange.

(b) Deductibility of interest   Interest expense related to trading activities (trading interest) forms part of the calculation of the taxable trading profit and is generally deductible on an accruals basis. When insufficient current-year group profits exist to offset all current-year trading interest and there is no capacity to carry back the loss arising against the company's previous taxable profits, the interest may be carried forward as part of the company's trading losses and set against future trading profits of the company in which the interest arose.

Nontrading interest is generally deductible on an accruals basis against trading income in the same year. When insufficient current-year group profits exist to offset all current-year trading interest and when there is no capacity to carry back the loss arising against the company's previous taxable profits, nontrading interest may be carried forward for offset against future nontrading profits earned by that company. But it is not uncommon in acquisition scenarios for a company not to earn any future nontrading profits. As a result, this interest will be effectively stranded in the company in which it arises and no tax benefit for the interest expense will be obtained.

Clearly, the definitions of trading interest and nontrading interest are important, because they will affect the future use of any excess interest deductions. Generally, trading interest arises on a debt that is specifically required for the trade—for example, a loan to acquire manufacturing machinery—while nontrading interest may arise in an investment company that has received external funding to acquire an investment in a trading company.

Interest deductibility may be denied when a loan is entered into either wholly or partly for an unallowable purpose (defined as a purpose not among the business or other commercial purposes of the company). Care should be taken when borrowings are taken on in order to avoid UK taxes.

In an accounting period during which the borrower controls the lender or vice versa or during which both the borrower and the lender are under common control, a further restriction exists whereby interest may be deductible only when paid—rather than on an accruals basis—if the interest accrued is not paid within 12 months of the relevant period end, unless the recipient of the income is subject to UK corporate tax.

Certain other situations exist whereby interest is deductible on a paid basis rather than on an accruals basis, but these would not normally apply when a UK company acquires 100 percent of a target's stock.

(c) Thin capitalization No specific legislation exists in the UK that provides a safe harbor for a debt/equity ratio. Inland Revenue practice is to allow a debt/equity ratio of 1:1, provided there is also interest cover of 3:1. This can vary from case to case depending on all of the relevant facts and circumstances. Because it is necessary to obtain advance clearance from the Inland Revenue for payment of interest with nil or reduced withholding tax, an acceptable debt/equity ratio and interest cover need to be negotiated with the Inland Revenue before the first interest payment on a loan is due.

Thin-capitalization provisions apply only to non-UK related-party debt and third-party debt with non-UK related-party guarantees. Third-party unguaranteed debt is outside these provisions.

When a UK company is deemed to be thinly capitalized, the main lines of argument by the Inland Revenue are:

- Transfer pricing
- Recharacterization as a distribution
- Additional withholding taxes

(i) Transfer pricing Loans between a UK company and an overseas related party must be on an arm's-length basis; otherwise, transfer-pricing rules may apply to restrict interest deductions.

The Inland Revenue can use transfer pricing as a means of challenging a UK company's thin-capitalization position by stating that the gearing or leverage is not at arm's length. The deduction is then restricted based on what is considered to be a true arm's-length financing arrangement structure.

It is generally accepted that the risk of a transfer-pricing adjustment also exists when debt is provided by a third party but guaranteed by an overseas affiliate. However, this has yet to be tested by the Inland Revenue.

(ii) Recharacterization as a distribution   When the interest rate itself is considered to be higher than a normal arm's-length rate for the loan principal, the excess interest can be recharacterized as a nondeductible distribution.

Further, when the gearing itself is in excess of an acceptable debt/equity ratio and either the borrower is a subsidiary of the lender but not vice versa or when both are under common control, the Inland Revenue can use the distribution legislation to recharacterize the interest on the excess borrowings as a nondeductible distribution.

When such interest is recharacterized as a distribution, no withholding tax is payable on that element of the interest regardless of who the lender is.

(iii) Additional withholding tax   Many tax treaties with the UK contain a clause that provides that when there is a so-called special relationship between lender and borrower and the borrower pays more interest than it would have in the absence of such a special relationship—for example, if the borrower is thinly capitalized—the benefit of reduced withholding tax under the treaty can be removed with respect to the excess interest.

(d) Distributions   Rules also exist that treat interest on non-UK shareholder debt as a nondeductible distribution if, in general:

- The loan is potentially convertible into stock.
- The interest is to any extent dependent on the borrower's results.
- The debt is linked with stock in the company.
- The term of the loan is for 50 years or more.

4.2   Equity

There is no capital duty on the issuance of new stock.

Dividends paid on stock are not deductible for the company paying the dividend, regardless of whether such stock is ordinary or preference stock. A UK company receiving such dividends does not pay taxes on them; however, a UK individual's dividend income is taxable. There is no withholding tax on the payment of dividends.

This issuance of equity as a method of funding is advantageous in that it improves the company's debt/equity ratio, thereby potentially enabling additional interest-bearing debt to be issued by the company. (See Section 4.1(c).)

4.3 Key Nontax Issues

(a) Government consents Generally, no government consents are required in relation to the making of an acquisition or the raising of finance.

(b) Abuse-of-law provisions The UK has no abuse-of-law provisions.

(c) Other key nontax issues

(i) Financial assistance The rules against financial assistance (contained in the Companies Act 1985) are intended to maintain share capital for the protection of creditors and to prevent, for example, the purchase of stock in a company by using the proceeds of a loan from that company, or the company's giving security over its assets to secure external borrowings that were used to fund the purchase of the company's stock. Lawyers and other competent professionals always should be consulted on these matters.

Financial assistance is defined in very broad terms and includes gifts, loans, guarantees, security, and indemnities given or made by the company or any subsidiary. The rules apply to indirect assistance—for example, when a company guarantees a bank loan taken out by a shareholder to finance the purchase—as well as to the more obvious direct gift or loan. The definition also includes any other form of assistance given by the company if it has no net assets or if the assistance results in a material reduction in the company's net assets.

5. MERGERS

In the UK, a company is not legally permitted to merge into another corporate entity. A merger can be achieved by a transfer of trade and assets either from one company to another company or from both companies to a Newco. However, any preexisting liabilities—whether tax or nontax or whether actual or contingent—are not automatically transferred to the successor company. (See Section 5.1.)

Another form of merger is the combining of two groups previously held by separate sets of shareholders. (See Section 5.2.)

5.1 Transfer of Trade and Assets

When a trade or part of a trade is transferred between two UK companies under common ownership, the successor company in effect steps into the shoes of its predecessor company. As a result, the benefit of any unutilized trading losses passes to the transferee company, and assets qualifying for capital allowances are transferred at tax written-down value without necessitating the balancing of profits or losses on those assets.

Companies are considered as being under common ownership if at any time within two years after the transfer the persons owning at least 75 percent of the ordinary share capital of the successor company are the same as those who owned at least 75 percent of the ordinary share capital of the predecessor company at some time within the year preceding the transfer.

There is a restriction on the carryforward and utilization of trading losses by a transferee company if the transferor is insolvent at the time of the transfer and the transferee does not take over the liabilities of the transferor.

Capital assets (subject to tax on capital gains) can be transferred tax free only if the transferor and transferee are part of the same capital gains group as defined in Section 6.2.

Generally, the transfer of a going concern is not subject to VAT, while a transfer of independent assets is subject to VAT unless both transferor and transferee are part of the same VAT group.

An exemption from stamp duty exists when assets are transferred between 75 percent group companies. However, this exemption is not available if the transfer forms part of arrangements under which the transferee leaves the stamp duty group.

5.2   Exchange of Securities for Those in Another Company

Subject to antiavoidance provisions, when a company—say, company A—issues stock or debentures to a person in exchange for stock or debentures in another company—company B—the exchange may be treated as if it does not involve a disposal by the shareholder in company B. The new stock in company A that the shareholder receives is treated for capital gains tax purposes as if it were the original stock in company B. Therefore, the shareholder is exempt from tax on the disposal of stock in company B, but the tax base cost of the new company A stock is the same as the tax base cost in the company B stock previously held. Effectively, any built-in gain or loss on the company B stock is deferred from tax until the date of any future sale of the stock in company A.

Company A's base cost in company B is the market value of company B at the date of merger.

To qualify as an exempt transaction, one of the following requirements must be met:

- Company A holds, or as a result of the exchange will hold, more than 25 percent of the shares of company B.
- Company A issues the stock or debentures in exchange for stock as the result of a general offer made to members or any class of members of company B, and the offer is made in the first instance on the condition that if it were satisfied, company A would have control of company B.

- Company A holds, or as a result of the exchange will hold, the greater part of the voting power in company B.

For shareholders who own more than 5 percent of company B, this exemption is available only if the exchange of stock is carried out for bona fide commercial reasons and not for the purpose of avoiding tax. It is possible to obtain assurance in advance of the transaction that these requirements have been met.

Stamp duty is payable on a share-for-share exchange involving the merging of two groups previously owned by separate sets of shareholders. The amount payable is 0.5 percent of the value of the new stock issued as consideration by company A.

The transfer of stock is not subject to VAT.

6.   OTHER STRUCTURING AND POSTDEAL ISSUES

6.1   Creation of Local-Country Tax Groups

(a) Trading profits   For group relief purposes whereby the losses of one group company can be used to offset the profits of another, a UK tax group is formed from the time that a 75 percent shareholding relationship is created. Profits and losses of the various companies included within the tax group are apportioned to reflect the grouping period where a tax group is created during a period of account. This is particularly relevant in the year of acquisition because it may mean that not all profits in that year can be sheltered by acquisition interest expense.

Ownership can be direct or indirect. In the case of indirect ownership, one multiplies down the chain to establish whether a 75 percent relationship exists. For example, if company A owns 90 percent of company B and if company B owns 90 percent of company C, then for group relief purposes, company A is deemed to own 81 percent of company C—that is, 90 percent times 90 percent. A UK tax group can look through non-UK companies to achieve the UK grouping. This means that two UK companies that are part of the same 75 percent group of three companies may be part of the same tax group despite the fact that their mutual parent company is not a UK tax resident company.

The 75 percent shareholding definition for group relief normally relates to the percentage of ordinary share capital held, but the definition of shareholding can be extended to include loan creditors that are on noncommercial terms. This can catch, for example, loans that carry an interest rate that varies depending on the profits of the borrowing company. The definition can also be affected by the existence of stock options regardless of whether or not those stock options are, at the time, exercisable. Potentially, these stock options may break the 75 percent shareholding group. This matter should be reviewed to ensure that losses do not become stranded in a debt-financed investment company—for example, a company that is no longer part of the tax group by virtue of these rules—rather than being available to offset trading profits in subsidiary companies.

(b) Capital gains For capital gains purposes, a group consists of any company and its 75 percent subsidiaries that meet the following three criteria:

1. A company may be a member of only one capital gains group.
2. The definition of 75 percent subsidiary is determined with reference to ordinary share capital.
3. If any 75 percent subsidiary also has a 75 percent subsidiary, then the group includes these but only to the extent that the subsidiary is an effective 51 percent subsidiary of the principal company of the capital gains group.

UK capital gains groups are also able to look through non-UK resident companies.

Any capital gain may be offset by capital losses available within the UK capital gains group of companies. In addition, transfers of assets between UK capital gains group companies are undertaken at no gain/no loss. However, antiavoidance legislation exists that prevents a no-gain/no-loss transfer from being used to avoid paying tax on the sale of an asset with gain by transferring this asset to a subsidiary company and, instead, selling the stock in the subsidiary, which will have received the base cost equivalent to the market value of the asset so that—were it not for the antiavoidance legislation—no capital gain arises.

(c) VAT Group companies can generally elect to account for VAT as if they were a single entity. When this occurs, no VAT is charged on intragroup supplies of goods or services. However, particular consideration should be given prior to making a group VAT election, especially if some group companies make taxable supplies on which VAT is not charged. This can reduce the group's right to recover VAT on its own purchases. All members of the VAT group are jointly and severally liable for the group's VAT liability.

6.2   Repatriation of Profits

Dividends paid by a UK company to another UK company are not subject to tax.

When a UK company receives dividend income from a foreign subsidiary company, the UK company may claim double-tax relief. This relief is normally given by way of a credit against UK tax payable.

When a tax credit is claimed in connection with the foreign tax incurred in the generation of that dividend, then in a calculation of the UK tax, the dividend received is grossed up for the foreign tax incurred—that is, cash dividend received plus foreign withholding tax plus foreign corporate tax incurred on the underlying profits out of which the dividend was paid—and this gross amount is subject to UK 30 percent tax. Relief for foreign tax is claimed to a maximum of the UK tax payable on the gross dividend—that is, to a maximum of 30 percent.

Historically, UK holding companies had used non-UK companies as intermediary holding companies for non-UK subsidiaries. The purpose was to blend high-taxed dividends—that is, in excess of 30 percent—and low-taxed dividends, thereby maximizing the double-tax relief available. However, under current law, this is no longer possible. Instead, the intermediary company is considered to be transparent, and all dividends are treated as being paid directly from the subsidiary company to the UK for the purposes of calculating the double-tax relief available. A system of onshore pooling has also been established that, in summary, enables excess foreign tax suffered on dividends paid out of high-tax territories to be used to shelter dividends paid out of low-tax jurisdictions, subject to various restrictions. On this basis, it is generally now more efficient for a UK company either to hold its subsidiary entities directly rather than through an intermediary holding company or to keep subgroups of high-taxed and low-taxed subsidiaries separate from each other. This should be considered as part of the postdeal planning.

6.3   Noncore Disposals

The sale of a subsidiary by a UK company after acquisition may be exempt from corporation tax if the requirements for the substantial-shareholding exemption are met. (Section 7.1(a)(i) covers the main conditions for the availability of this exemption.)

However, this exemption is not always available and may be particularly difficult for a financial buyer of an entire business to achieve. However, if a target company sells an existing subsidiary, the fact that a financial buyer is the ultimate owner should not be relevant.

Any intended postacquisition disposal should be reviewed carefully to ensure that it will not give rise to hidden tax liabilities. Capital assets are deemed to be transferred between 75 percent group members at no gain/no loss for corporation tax purposes. However, if a company ceases to be a member of a group, then the assets held—other than as trading stock—that were acquired from another group member within six years of the company's ceasing to be a member of the group are deemed for tax purposes to have been sold and reacquired at their market value immediately following the company's acquisition of the asset. The effect of this is to crystallize any built-in capital gain on that asset, thereby imposing a tax charge on the transferee company that now holds the asset.

6.4   Preservation of Existing Tax Attributes

Tax losses and other, similar tax attributes of the target company generally are not affected by a change of ownership—at least insofar as the change in ownership does not in and of itself cause such tax losses or attributes to be lost. This is, however, subject to the following exceptions:

- Trading losses
- Expenses of management
- Capital losses

(a) Trading losses   When a UK company carries on trading activities and incurs a loss in that trade (the loss being calculated in accordance with UK tax law), the loss is known for UK tax purposes as a trading loss. Tax losses that have not been used to offset other taxable profits of that company or of other group companies (using group relief—see Section 6.1) can be carried forward by the company and offset against future trading profits of that company.

Trading losses arising before the change in ownership of the target generally cannot be carried forward after the change if within a six-year period commencing three years prior to the change in ownership there is a major change in the nature or conduct of the trade carried on by the target.

(b) Expenses of management   Nontrading companies nevertheless incur expenses in the course of their activities, and tax deductions for some of these expenses, depending on their nature, may be available. Such a company is known—for UK tax purposes—as an investment company, and its deductible expenses are called expenses of management. Through group relief (see Section 6.1), expenses of management can be used to offset other taxable profits of that company or of other group companies. Any unutilized expenses of management can be carried forward by the company and can be offset against future nontrading profits of that company.

When a member of the target group is treated for tax purposes as an investment company and has carried forward unutilized expenses of management, similar provisions apply as in Section 6.4(a): The carryforward of expenses of management can also be restricted when there is a significant increase in the amount of the company's capital after the change in ownership. An increase is always treated as significant for these purposes if the increase is £1 million or more.

(c) Capital losses   Generally, when a company joins a new UK capital gains group, restrictions may apply on the use of capital losses. This could potentially apply to any company in the target group. These restrictions can apply both to capital losses arising prior to the change in ownership and to capital losses that are crystallized postacquisition in relation to assets that were originally acquired

by the target group preacquisition—at least in relation to the part of that loss that is referable to the preacquisition period. After acquisition, such restricted capital losses can be used only to offset capital gains arising on:

- Assets that were held by the target group prior to its acquisition by the purchaser
- Assets acquired postacquisition of the target group by any member of the group—including the purchasers' group companies—from a third party when such assets are used for trading purposes

It is not possible to use the restricted capital losses to offset capital gains arising on assets that were held by the purchaser's group prior to the acquisition of the target.

6.5 Receipts under Warranties or Indemnities

Generally, payments made by the seller for breach of warranty or under an indemnity are taxable in the hands of the purchaser. Accordingly, usual practice is for the sales and purchase documentation to contain a clause stipulating that any such payment is to be treated as an adjustment to the money offered and received for the transaction. The Inland Revenue has made its position clear: In such circumstances, the receipt is not immediately taxable but is instead treated as a reduction of the purchaser's tax basis in the stock acquired.

Warranties and indemnity payments made to the target company are likely to be subject to tax in the target company.

7. DISPOSALS

7.1 Stock Disposals

(a) Companies

(i) Disposal for cash consideration Corporate entities are subject to corporation tax on chargeable gains on the disposal of stock unless the requirements for the substantial-shareholdings exemption are met, in which case the disposal is exempt from tax. The main conditions for the availability of this exemption are:

- The seller company or another member of the seller's group must have held for a continuous 12-month period in the two years preceding disposal a substantial shareholding—that is, at least 10 percent of the ordinary share capital—in the company being sold.
- The seller company must be either a trading company or a member of a trading group both before and after the disposal.

- The company being sold must also be either a trading company or a member of a trading group both before and after the disposal.

The calculation of the chargeable gain is, broadly, sales proceeds minus original cost minus an inflation allowance.

Frequently, the sale-and-purchase agreement includes a working capital or net asset adjustment that affects the final cash amounts passing between the parties. Usually, such a cash transfer is explicitly referred to in the sale-and-purchase agreement as an adjustment to the purchase price and is therefore included within the seller's chargeable gains calculation.

If the substantial shareholdings exemption is not available, the company may be able to utilize any available capital losses within the seller group against the gain arising. In addition, group relief surrendered from other group companies and certain brought-forward nontrading losses within the seller company may also be available to offset capital gain.

(ii) Share for share or debentures exchange   The sale of all of the stock in a company in exchange for stock or debentures of the purchasing company may be treated as a tax-neutral transaction to the seller, provided that a motive test is passed—that is, that the transaction is being carried out for bona fide commercial reasons and not mainly for the purpose of avoiding tax.

(b) Individuals   Individuals disposing of an interest in stock generally are subject to capital gains tax. A capital gain is the top slice of an individual's income and is subject to tax at the individual's respective marginal rate of tax. In practice, this is likely to be at 40 percent. The calculation of an individual's chargeable gain generally is sales proceeds minus original base cost minus taper relief. Taper relief reduces the gain depending on the length of ownership of the stock and certain other factors.

The position with regard to share-for-share exchanges is similar to that of companies, although if an individual holds less than 5 percent of the share of the target, the motive requirement does not apply.

However, the position for directors and employee shareholders may differ from the aforementioned in certain circumstances. Directors and employee shareholders may be subject to income tax of up to 40 percent and national insurance contributions of 1 percent on profits or proceeds.

(c) Tax-exempt entities   Some UK entities are not subject to capital gains tax on the disposal of stock. These include pension funds and investment trusts.

7.2   Asset Disposals (Companies Only)

Capital assets—excluding assets such as plant or machinery on which capital allowances (tax depreciations) are claimed (see Section 3.1)—are subject to corporation tax on chargeable gains similar to a stock disposal. This is most relevant to goodwill and other intangibles, as well as land or buildings. Goodwill acquired after April 2002 is taxed under a separate regime related specifically to intangibles. An inflation allowance is available depending on the period of ownership of the asset. Any resulting chargeable gain can be sheltered by capital losses within the seller group, by group relief surrendered from other group companies, and/or by certain other brought-forward nontrading losses within the seller company.

Corporation tax is also charged on a clawback of capital allowances when the allocated disposal price is greater than the tax written-down value—that is, the tax basis—of the asset. Any such clawback is taxed as trading income in the period of disposal. In the event that the allocated disposal price is less than the tax written-down value, a trading deduction is given.

When the proceeds of the sale of certain types of capital assets used in the trade are reinvested in the acquisition of certain types of new assets for use in the trade of that or another group company within 12 months before or three years after disposal, the gain accruing on the sale of the old asset may instead be deferred. Rather than allowing the gain to crystallize, the tax basis of the new asset is reduced by the amount of the gain. This is principally relevant to land and buildings and to goodwill acquired before April 2002. In the case of goodwill acquired after April 2002 and taxed under the new regime, similar provisions exist that have the effect of spreading the gain over a (typically) 20- to 25-year period.

A further disadvantage accrues to the shareholders of the seller company in that the proceeds of an asset sale remain locked in the company. Distribution of these proceeds may result in further tax liabilities for shareholders, resulting in double taxation. This depends on the nature of the shareholder (individual, company, tax-exempt) and the method of distribution—for example, liquidation, capital distribution, or dividend.

7.3 Deferred Consideration and Earn-Outs

Generally, if an amount of deferred consideration is ascertainable at the time of the disposal, the full amount is included in the tax calculation of the disposal proceeds at the time of the sale, even if receipt of this amount is contingent. Likewise, when the deferred consideration is determined by a formula but subject to an upper limit on the amount payable, that maximum amount is included in the disposal proceeds figure. If not all of such amounts is received, a retrospective adjustment is made to the capital gains calculations, with any tax being refunded as appropriate.

A right to future consideration that is unquantifiable—for example, a formula with no upper limit—is itself treated as a separate asset for capital gains purposes. Consequently, the seller is taxed on any proceeds received plus the value of that asset received. The Shares Valuation division of the Inland Revenue is often involved in agreeing to the value of the unquantified, contingent, deferred consideration as of the date the right is originally granted. Any subsequent amounts received are compared with the valuation attributed to this asset, thereby resulting in a further capital gain or loss. There is, however, no retrospective adjustment of the original capital gain if a capital loss results from the deferred consideration.

An agreement for the sale of stock in a company might include the right to receive deferred consideration in the form of new stock. The value of the new stock is itself unascertainable at the time of the agreement usually because such value depends on the future profitability of the company. As noted earlier, in principle this right to deferred consideration is treated as a new capital asset. However, if the sale of stock qualifies as a tax-free reorganization (see Section 8.1), an election can be made such that the receipt of the deferred-consideration stock will likewise be treated as a tax-free reorganization, and, therefore, no capital gain or loss would arise following receipt of the deferred consideration.

7.4   Payments under Warranties or Indemnities

When the sale-and-purchase documentation contains a clause stipulating that any warranty or indemnity payment is to be treated as an adjustment to the consideration offered and received for the transaction, the payment would be treated for tax purposes as being deducted from the purchase consideration received.

8.   TRANSACTION COSTS FOR SELLERS

8.1   Transfer Taxes

Stamp duty tax is payable by buyers, not sellers, on the purchase of shares. (See Section 2.1(a).) Likewise, stamp duty land tax is payable by the purchasers of land and not by the sellers. (See Section 2.1(b).)

8.2   VAT

(a) *Stock disposal*   The disposal of stock is exempt from VAT.

(b) *Asset disposal*   The transfer of business assets that qualifies as the transfer of a business as a going concern is outside the scope of VAT. Otherwise, a purchase of assets is subject to VAT at 17.5 percent. This amount must be paid in addition to the purchase consideration.

8.3   Tax Deductibility of Transaction Costs

In general, the tax deductibility of a particular expense depends on several factors, including:

- Whether the transaction is for the sale of assets or shares.
- Whether the seller is a trading company for UK tax purposes—that is, its principal activity is that of trading—or whether the purchaser is an investment company for UK tax purposes—broadly, a nontrading company.
- The reason the expense was incurred: the identity of the persons to whom the expenses were paid is of less significance.

In general terms, the position can be summarized as:

- Corporation tax treatment of expenses
- VAT treatment of expenses

(a) Corporation tax treatment of expenses

(i) For investment companies disposing of shares   As a general rule, the costs incurred after a decision to dispose of a company has actually been made are likely to constitute the costs of disposing of an investment, while costs incurred prior to that point might be regarded as the costs of managing investments, such as evaluating potential disposal strategies.

Costs related to initial, speculative advice on disposal possibilities or strategies are likely to be deductible for tax purposes. Nevertheless, the Inland Revenue may argue that the seller has, in fact, decided to sell, so that the expenses are not severable from the costs of disposal.

Costs related to the sales process in general and, in particular, costs related to detailed negotiation with a specific bidder regardless of whether the negotiation culminates in the execution of a sale-and-purchase agreement are less likely to be deductible for tax purposes. Nonetheless, some of these costs may well qualify as costs of disposal in the capital gains tax computation, thereby either reducing the capital gain or increasing the loss.

(ii) For trading companies disposing of assets   Costs incurred as part of the disposal process generally are not deductible for the purposes of computing the seller's trading profits for tax purposes.

In the computation of the corporation tax on chargeable gains on the sale of certain capital assets (see Section 7.2), a deduction may be claimed for certain costs of disposal incurred wholly and exclusively in relation to that asset—for example, asset valuation fees, any costs of transfer, and related legal fees. But when expenses are incurred as part of the transaction as a whole—for example, the majority of, if not all, legal fees related to the deal—and those expenses are not incurred specifically and solely in relation to that capital asset, those expenses cannot be deducted in the computation of the chargeable gain.

(b) VAT treatment of expenses   VAT charged by third parties to the seller on transaction costs should be recoverable subject to the partial exemption method applicable to the seller, provided that the costs relate to a service provided for that seller, that the service is not directly attributable to an exempt supply made by the purchaser—for example, a sale of stock or loan notes—and that the service is attributable to the seller's taxable business activities.

Costs should be clearly identified on invoices so that input tax can be easily attributed to the disposal of stock and to other matters.

9.   PREPARING A TARGET COMPANY FOR SALE

The introduction of the substantial shareholdings exemption has made presale tax planning less relevant. However, presale planning is important if the purchaser wants to buy only specific assets, if the seller wishes to retain certain assets, or if the disposal is not sheltered from tax by the substantial shareholdings exemption.

9.1   Hive-Down of Assets

When the seller is selling only a division or part of a trading business or there is a specific liability that needs to be kept out of the sale, a hive-down method of purchase might be considered.

Hiving down involves the transfer of specific trade and assets of a company to another group company. Initially, no capital gains tax charge is imposed on this hive-down transfer, since the assets are treated as being transferred at their existing tax basis, notwithstanding the actual transfer price. However, if the hive-down company is sold within six years of the transfer, it is deemed for tax purposes only to have sold and reacquired at market value the capital assets transferred under the hive-down. The net effect of this is that the hive-down company is subject to tax on capital gains as if it had made an asset sale.

It is possible for trading tax losses to be transferred to the hive-down company, but this requires careful management. In particular, losses are not available if there is a significant change in the nature or conduct of the trade within three years of the sale of the hive-down company. Capital losses cannot be transferred in a hive-down transaction.

Stamp duty and stamp duty land tax are prima facie payable by the transferee company on the transfer of certain assets under the hive-down. (See Section 2.1.) There is an exemption from stamp duty and stamp duty land tax when assets are transferred between associated companies. However, this exemption is not available if at the time of the transfer there are arrangements in place—for example, for the transferee company to leave the stamp duty/ stamp duty land tax group. Further, if the exemption has been claimed with respect to any UK land, and the transferee company—while holding the land—leaves the group within three years, then the duty relieved will be recaptured and will be a liability of the transferee company.

No VAT is payable on a transfer of assets between members of a VAT group. If the hive-down company is not part of the same VAT group as the transferor, VAT is not payable if the hive-down constitutes the transfer of a going concern.

9.2   Intragroup Transfer of Assets Being Retained

Assets may be transferred out of group companies that are to be sold if these assets are not intended to be included in the sale package. Notwithstanding the actual transfer price, capital assets are deemed to be transferred on a no-gain/ no-loss basis for corporation tax purposes, such that no tax would arise.

If the recipient company ceases to be a member of the seller's capital gains group within six years of the date of transfer of the assets, the assets will be deemed to have been sold and reacquired at the market value at the date of the original intragroup transfer, potentially giving rise to a tax charge being levied on the recipient.

Stamp duty and stamp duty land tax are prima facie payable on the intragroup transfer of certain assets. (See Section 2.1.) There is an exemption from stamp duty and stamp duty land tax when assets are transferred between associated companies. However, this exemption is not available if at the time of the transfer there are arrangements in place—for example, for the transferee company to leave the stamp duty/stamp duty land tax group. Further, if the exemption has been claimed with respect to any UK land, and the transferee company—while holding the land—leaves the group within three years, then the duty relieved will be recaptured and will be a liability of the transferee company.

No VAT is payable on a transfer of assets between members of a VAT group. If the transferor and transferee are not part of the same VAT group, VAT will still not be payable if the transfer of assets constitutes the transfer of a going concern.

It is generally possible to transfer assets out of the target company at under value within a group as a planning tool to reduce the value of the target, thereby reducing any tax payable on the target's disposal. This is provided that the consideration payable by the transferee is at least equal to the original cost of that asset to the transferor.

9.3   Presale Dividends

The tax treatment in the hands of the recipient of any presale dividends paid by the target group out of its distributable reserves is outlined in Section 6.2.

If a disposal of stock is not covered by the substantial shareholdings exemption (see Section 7.1), this can be a useful planning tool in minimizing tax on capital gains. There is, however, antiavoidance legislation that can counteract the use of presale dividends as a planning tool by adjusting the amount of any capital gain to what it would have been had the value of the target group not been reduced by the presale dividend. The legislation is complex, but in very general terms, dividends paid out of taxed profits would not be picked up by these rules. The objective of the antiavoidance legislation is to catch dividends paid out of artificially generated profits that that have not been or will not be taxed—for example, accounting profits arising from the transfer of assets between two members of the target group or revaluations of assets.

10.　DEMERGERS

The commercial rationale for a demerger centers on creating value for the shareholders. Demergers may be used simply to separate different trading activities in different groups or to partition trading activities between different groups of shareholders.

In the UK, there is no corporate law that covers the concept of a corporate demerger in the sense that a single company is split into two or more separate companies or entities. Instead, *demerger* is a term of art referring to a certain form of reconstruction involving a transfer of assets—which can include shares—to another, existing company. And even when the transfer is to a new company, that new company must have been set up prior to implementation of the demerger or reconstruction.

With regard to a demerger, it is important to consider various associated tax costs, such as income tax costs to shareholders, capital gains tax costs to both the company and the shareholders, and stamp duty costs. There are several tax-efficient methods whereby value can be transferred to shareholders by way of a demerger. The principal methods are outlined as follows:

- Direct and indirect demergers
- Other types of demergers
- Spin-offs of trades

10.1　Direct and Indirect Demergers

(a) Straight (direct) dividend demerger　This is a method under which a company distributes stock in a subsidiary directly to shareholders—that is, a dividend in specie. The shareholders continue to hold their original stock but now also hold stock in the demerged subsidiary directly.

(b) Three-cornered (indirect) demerger The stock in a subsidiary is transferred by a company to a Newco in consideration for the issue of Newco stock to the original shareholders in proportion to their existing shareholdings in the transferor company.

The tax treatment of these demergers can be summarized as follows:

Shareholders	UK individuals
	• Subject to income tax on the value of the dividend at an effective rate of 25 percent for higher rate taxpayers unless the detail requirements for an exempt demerger (see below) are met; no stamp duty payable
	UK companies
	• Dividend is tax free; no stamp duty payable
Distributing company	Straight dividend demerger: exempt from tax on capital gains if:
	• Qualifying for substantial shareholdings exemption
	Three-cornered demerger: exempt from tax on capital gains if:
	• Qualifying for substantial shareholdings exemption falling within certain capital gains reorganization provisions, requiring that the reorganization be carried out for bona fide commercial reasons and not mainly for tax avoidance purposes
Company being distributed and its subsidiaries	If, in the six years prior to disposal, the company or any of its subsidiaries is the transferee of assets received from other group companies that are not also being distributed, a tax charge may arise in the transferee. There is an exemption from this tax charge if the detailed requirements for an exempt demerger (see below) are met.

The principal requirements for an exempt demerger are:

• The subsidiary being demerged is at least a 75 percent subsidiary.
• Both the distributing company and the company being transferred are UK resident.
• Both the distributing company and the company being transferred must be trading companies or holding companies of a trading group.
• The distributing company must, after the distribution, be a trading company or a holding company of a trading group.
• The distribution must be carried out wholly or mainly to benefit the demerged trades.

- The main purpose of the distribution is not:

  o To avoid tax (including stamp duty)
  o To acquire control of the distributing company or of the company being transferred by third parties

It is possible to obtain advance agreement from Inland Revenue that a distribution is exempt.

10.2   Other Types of Demergers

It is also possible to achieve a demerger through other methods, such as an Insolvency Act 1986 liquidation distribution or a Companies Act 1985 plan of arrangement.

(a) Insolvency Act 1986 liquidation   This transaction involves a reconstruction that is similar to a liquidation distribution. The method is particularly useful if the parent company does not have sufficient reserves to be able to effect a dividend demerger. This method may also be useful if the demerger is not treated as an exempt demerger under the direct or indirect method—for example, if the companies involved are not trading or if the demerger is being carried out prior to a listing or initial public offering or sale.

This type of transaction involves the liquidation of the parent company and the transfer of its assets to two or more newly formed companies that each issue stock in consideration for those assets. The liquidator then passes the stock in the new parent companies to the shareholders of the original parent company.

This method can be relatively complex, and the transaction can be made more difficult by procedures that enable dissenting shareholders and creditors to object. Furthermore, it can be commercially difficult to liquidate an active operating company if it has numerous commercial contracts or borrowing covenants.

The tax treatment of an Insolvency Act 1986 demerger can be summarized as follows:

- **Shareholders.** Exempt from tax on capital gains if falling within certain capital gains reorganization provisions, which require that the reorganization be carried for bona fide commercial reasons and not mainly for tax avoidance purposes
- **Distributing company.** Exempt from tax on capital gains if falling within certain capital gains reorganization provisions, which require that the reorganization be carried for bona fide commercial reasons and not mainly for tax avoidance purposes

- **Company being distributed and its subsidiaries.** If, in the six years prior to disposal, there has been a transfer of assets between group companies, a tax charge may arise in the transferee. There is an exemption from this tax charge if, in general terms, both transferor and transferee are distributed under the Insolvency Act 1986 reorganization to the same new parent company, although this can become more complex when there are minority shareholdings in the original group. But when the transferor is distributed under the Insolvency Act 1986 reorganization to one new parent and the transferee is distributed to a different new parent, this exemption will not apply.

(b) Companies Act 1985 scheme of reconstruction   Under a scheme of reconstruction, a company can make any compromise or arrangement with its members or creditors. There is no fixed format, and therefore this is the most flexible of options noted. As such, there is no need to consider the level of distributable reserves or to liquidate the company if it is not practical to do so. The tax consequences depend on the details of the scheme.

This method also requires court approval, and, again, there are procedures under which creditors may object. It can be slow to implement due to the procedural requirements, and the approval of 75 percent of the shareholders is necessary, but it is binding on all shareholders and creditors once approved by the court.

10.3   Spin-Offs of Trades and Assets

Another and simpler method for divesting a trade is to hive-down the trade and assets of a business into a newly incorporated company in the group. The new company is subsequently sold to a third party. This is discussed in more detail in Section 9.1.

11.   LISTINGS AND INITIAL PUBLIC OFFERINGS

11.1   Impact on Tax Status of Company Being Listed and Its Subsidiaries

The tax status of a company generally is unaffected by listing or by an initial public offering (IPO).

11.2   Complete Group Listing or IPO

On the listing of an entire group, it is common for a new company to be set up as the listed vehicle (Holdco). The stock in the existing parent company can be transferred to Holdco by means of a share-for-share exchange. It should be possible to carry out this share-for-share exchange on a tax-neutral basis. (See Section 7.1.)

11.3   Listing or IPO of Subsidiary

The immediate implications for the existing parent of a listing of a subsidiary are:

- **If a parent sells in the market (i.e., lists) some of its existing stock in a subsidiary.** The parent is subject to corporation tax on chargeable gains on the disposal of stock unless the requirements for the substantial-shareholdings exemption are met, in which case the disposal is exempt from tax. (See Section 7.1 for the conditions for the availability of this exemption.)
- **If a subsidiary issues new stock.** The parent has not itself sold any stock, and therefore no tax charge arises.

However, the impact of a listing may be to reduce the parent's shareholding below 75 percent, in which case the subsidiary may no longer be part of relevant tax groups—notably, group relief and capital gains. (See Section 6.1 on tax groupings.)

When a group is planning to list a subsidiary business, preliminary reorganizations may be required in order to ensure that all relevant assets and subsidiaries are held under the company being listed. If the parent's shareholding falls below 75 percent, tax degrouping charges may arise when, within the preceding six years, capital assets, including stock and goodwill, have been transferred into the subgroup being listed by companies not part of that subgroup. This degrouping charge arises because the company, which now holds the asset, is deemed—for tax purposes only—to have sold and reacquired at market value the capital assets transferred under the hive down. The net effect of this is that the relevant company is subject to tax on capital gains as if it had made a sale of those assets. However, if the asset in question is stock, then the substantial shareholdings exemption (see Section 7.1) may be available.

11.4   Issuance of New Stock by a Listed Company

The issuance of new stock by the listed company should not have any tax consequences for the company when the listed company is the parent of the group. But when a subsidiary is being listed, the issue of new stock may result in that subsidiary's leaving a tax group, with consequences as noted in Section 11.3.

The consideration paid becomes the investors' base cost in the stock.

11.5   Disposal of Stock by Existing Shareholders

When the listing or IPO involves a disposal of stock by existing shareholders, the tax position for those shareholders is as outlined in Section 7.1.

UNITED STATES

INTRODUCTION

This chapter details the principal tax issues that are relevant to purchasers and sellers engaged in the transfer of ownership of a US trade or business. Unless otherwise stated, it is generally assumed that all sellers and purchasers are US companies with limited liability.

The transfer of ownership of a US trade or business may take the form of a disposition of shares or assets. While asset transactions are generally thought of as taxable, both types of transactions may be structured as taxable purchases or tax-free exchanges.

The relevant entity-level taxes to be considered with respect to merger and acquisition activity include:

- **Federal corporate income tax.** Generally, this is a 35 percent tax on income earned by a corporation, regardless of whether the income is of an ordinary or a capital nature. Depending on the level of common ownership and control, US corporations may determine corporate income tax liability on a stand-alone basis—that is, without regard to shareholders or related entities—or on a consolidated basis, whereby commonly controlled corporations are treated as a single entity and file one tax return.

- **Federal personal income tax.** Personal income tax is imposed on the taxable income of individuals. Personal income tax rates are graduated and range from 10 to 35 percent. Special rates apply to capital gain income and certain dividends, as discussed in Section 6.1(a). All US citizens and resident aliens are required to file personal income tax returns. Joint returns are allowed for married taxpayers.

- **State corporate income tax.** A majority of states impose a corporate income tax separate from the federal tax. Generally, the starting point in the determination of state income tax is federal taxable income, which is then apportioned to all states of operation via a three-factor formula. State income tax rates generally range from 4 to 9 percent. Some cities impose an income tax as well.

- **State personal income tax.** A majority of states impose a personal income tax separate from the federal tax. The starting point in the determination of state income tax is generally federal taxable income. The income tax generally ranges from 4 to 9 percent. Cities may impose a personal income tax in addition to the federal and state tax.

- **Sales and use taxes.** Sales tax is a transaction-based tax generally imposed on the sale of tangible property. Sales tax is administered on the state or county level, and specific rules and tax rates vary by jurisdiction. Certain jurisdictions impose sales tax on enumerated services. Use tax is a complement to sales tax and is imposed on the consumption of goods within the taxing jurisdiction. Sales and use tax rates generally range from 3 to 8 percent. However, it should be noted that numerous exemptions to taxation exist. Exemptions may be based on the taxpayer—for example, most states tax retailers but not manufacturers—or on the product—for example, certain food items are not taxable in various jurisdictions. Because sales and use tax rules vary by jurisdiction, a complete analysis should be performed prior to closing merger and acquisition transactions.

- **Real property transfer tax.** Several states and counties impose indirect taxes on the transfer of title to or beneficial ownership in real property. Taxes may also be imposed upon the recordation of deeds, which may or may not be administered in conjunction with the property transfer taxes. Real property transfer taxes are generally based on the fair market value of the property conveyed, although attention should focus on whether the jurisdiction provides exemptions for certain types of transfers (such as reorganizations) or reduced rates.

While this chapter generally focuses on the corporate taxation of merger and acquisition transactions, several other types of entities exist. Following are brief descriptions of the types of entities that exist in the US as well as of the manner in which they are taxed:

- Corporations provide the commonly desired benefits of limited liability, free transferability of ownership, and indefinite life. Corporations can take two forms: those under subchapter C or those under subchapter S of the Internal Revenue Code (IRC). These are commonly known as C or S corporations, respectively. C corporations are generally required to use the accrual method of accounting and are treated as separate from their shareholders for federal income tax purposes. Under the separate-entity approach, taxes are paid at both the C corporation and the shareholder levels.

- S corporations offer many of the same benefits as C corporations, such as limited liability and free transferability of interest. However, S corporations are generally treated as pass-through entities, whereby income tax is imposed at the shareholder but not the S corporation level. S corporations have additional restrictions, such as a 75-person shareholder limit, including restrictions on what types of entities or persons may be shareholders. In addition, only a single class of stock may be issued, and there is no flexibility in allocating income to owners.

- Partnerships provide pass-through of income but do not have the same ownership limitations as those placed upon an S corporation. Partnerships can take the form of a limited partnership, a limited liability partnership, or a general partnership. The differences between these forms of partnerships involve liability of partnership debts, liability for professional negligence, and limitation on who may participate in the management of the business. Partnerships provide a great deal of flexibility because special allocations of income and deductions may be made to the partners. Tax is imposed only at the investor level unless the partnership is publicly traded.

- Limited liability companies (LLCs) provide a blend of the legal benefits of a corporation and the tax benefits of a partnership. While retaining limited liability for all members, LLCs provide such benefits as flexibility in ownership and contributions, income allocations, and distributions. The default federal income tax treatment of an LLC with more than one member is taxation as a partnership unless it is publicly traded. However, an election can be made—commonly referred to as "check the box"—to treat a multiple-member LLC as a corporation for tax purposes. Unless a check-the-box election is made to treat the entity as a corporation, LLCs with a single member are typically disregarded for tax purposes. This is equivalent to treating the LLC as a division of its owner.

The ability to check the box with respect to tax classification is a commonly utilized planning tool in cross-border transactions. For example, a foreign corporation may be treated as disregarded for US purposes while retaining its corporate character for purposes of other jurisdictions.

Provided certain qualification criteria are met, certain types of entities may be treated as tax-exempt for federal income tax purposes. This means that the entity is generally not subject to federal income taxation. An exemption from federal income taxation often results in an exemption for state income taxation as well. Such exempt entities include charitable, religious, and educational organizations, as well as certain retirement fund organizations (among many other types of organizations). Often, exempt entities are investors in private equity funds, which indirectly involves them in merger and acquisition transactions.

Although generally exempt from federal income taxation, exempt entities are subject to unrelated business income taxation (UBIT). In general, UBIT is imposed on income generated from a trade or business that is not substantially related to the organization's exempt purpose. Because exempt organizations play a significant role in the funding of private equity firms, the issue of UBIT is especially relevant in the mergers and acquisitions environment.

Several types of income, however, are excluded from taxation under the UBIT regime. In general, passive income such as royalties, interest, and dividends are exempt from UBIT. Also, gains and losses from the sale of stock are excluded from UBIT. Accordingly, the legal entity structure and manner of income generated by an investment made by an exempt entity dictate whether income generated by the investment is subject to UBIT.

1.   ACQUISITIONS

Acquisitive growth can be classified into one of two major categories: acquisition of assets of an existing business or acquisition of an entire corporation through acquisition of the target corporation's stock.

1.1   Asset Acquisitions

A major nontax motivation for structuring a transaction as an asset acquisition is the fact that historical business liabilities of the selling entity do not succeed to the purchaser. Such liabilities remain the responsibility of the seller unless a specific agreement states otherwise. As such, asset acquisitions provide a degree of certainty to the purchaser with respect to historical liabilities—a distinct advantage to purchasers.

Because existing contracts between the selling entity and third parties—or employees—do not succeed to the purchaser of assets, asset acquisitions may also present purchasers with certain nontax challenges. Issues may arise with respect to continuity of suppliers, customers, and employee retention, and, with respect to the last, compensation and employee benefits. Similarly, the purchaser of assets may need to reevaluate other practical issues such as business licensing, permits, and insurance.

Asset acquisitions can be structured as either taxable purchases or tax-free reorganizations. In a typical taxable asset purchase, the purchaser exchanges cash and/or notes for the desired assets. Typically, a taxable asset purchase results in a step-up in the tax basis of the acquired assets. (See Section 3.1 for a detailed discussion regarding tax basis.)

In the corporate environment, the taxable purchase of assets may be disadvantageous to the seller because gain is recognized at the corporate level as a result of the sale, and subsequent distributions to the shareholders will likely also be subject to tax. The preceding is especially pertinent to individual shareholders. Unlike corporate shareholders, individuals are not afforded a dividends-received deduction.

Under certain circumstances, sellers that receive notes in exchange for assets may generally use the installment method to report gain. Under these circumstances, that gain is recognized as the notes get paid. Taxpayers are not required to use this method. Certain limitations exist regarding installment sales. For example, related parties may not use the installment method with respect to depreciable property, and interest is charged on certain installment sales if the outstanding obligations at the close of the tax year exceed $5 million.

The purchase of assets may also be structured as a tax-free reorganization, which generally requires use of the purchaser's stock as currency for the transaction. For a transaction to be characterized as tax free, it must meet several statutory and judicial requirements. Care should be taken to ensure that these requirements are met if the transaction in intended to be tax free. Tax-free asset acquisitions are generally accomplished in the following ways:

- **Stock for assets.** A C reorganization in which the purchaser acquires substantially all of the target's assets solely in exchange for purchaser's voting stock
- **Forward merger.** An A reorganization in which target shareholders exchange their target stock for purchaser stock and, possibly, additional consideration, or so-called boot (the target corporation is merged with and into the purchasing corporation, with the purchaser being the surviving entity). This can also be effected by having the target corporation merge into a subsidiary of the purchasing corporation, with the subsidiary being the surviving entity.

In the foregoing transactions in which target shareholders exchange target stock for the purchasing entity's stock, target shareholders do not recognize any gain or loss realized on the exchange except to the extent of any boot received, but not in excess of the gain realized on the transaction. Target shareholders take a substituted basis in the purchaser stock received that is equal to their basis in the previously held target stock.

1.2   Stock Acquisitions

A stock acquisition results in the transfer of an entire existing corporate entity through the transfer of that entity's outstanding stock. Because the target corporation continues its existence, the historical business liabilities remain intact and there is a carryover basis—that is, no step-up in basis—in the target entity's assets. For these reasons, purchasers often prefer to acquire the assets of an ongoing operation rather than the stock of an existing entity.

However, unlike an asset acquisition, a stock acquisition generally does not disrupt existing contractual arrangements between purchasers, suppliers, and employees. In addition, any tax attributes—that is, net operating losses, credits, and so on—generally survive the acquisition. It should be noted, however, that limitations exist with respect to utilization of such attributes. For example, see the IRC Section 382 limitation discussed in Section 6.3.

Stock acquisitions can be structured in both a taxable and a tax-free manner. Taxable stock acquisitions generally involve the purchase of target corporation stock with cash and/or notes from the purchaser. Taxable stock purchases may also be effected through the use of a subsidiary. In such instances, the purchaser forms a wholly owned subsidiary capitalized with cash. The subsidiary then exchanges cash with the target shareholders in exchange for target stock. The subsidiary merges with and into the target, and the surviving entity (target) becomes a wholly owned subsidiary of the purchasing entity.

Stock acquisitions may also be structured as tax-free reorganizations. For example, the purchasing entity may acquire all of the target's stock solely in exchange for the purchasing entity's voting stock (a B reorganization). If the purchasing entity uses any consideration other than voting stock—such as non-voting stock or securities, cash, or other property—the transaction will not qualify as a tax-free B reorganization.

Similarly, the purchasing entity may utilize a transitory subsidiary to effectuate a tax-free merger. In this scenario, the purchasing entity exchanges stock and, possibly, boot with target shareholders in exchange for their target stock. The transitory subsidiary is then merged with and into the target, with the target being the surviving entity. This type of transaction is referred to as a reverse merger.

Stock acquisitions do not result in a step-up in basis in the target company's assets. However, it is possible, in certain circumstances, to make an election under IRC Section 338 to treat the stock acquisition as an acquisition of assets for tax purposes. In this fictional transaction, the target is treated as if it sold all of its assets to a hypothetical new target corporation. This fictional transaction occurs only for tax purposes. For legal purposes, the initial form of the transaction—a stock transaction—is respected. For tax purposes, the new target corporation takes an aggregate basis in all of its assets equal to the amount that the purchaser paid for the old target's stock plus the amount of the old target's liabilities.

As a result of the tax fiction, the target corporation receives a step-up in tax basis in its assets, creating larger deductions for depreciation, amortization, and so on. Any tax attributes of the old target, however, do not carry over to the purchaser. Also, it should be noted that the foregoing provisions are elective. Absent an affirmative election to treat a stock purchase as an asset purchase, the form of a stock purchase will be respected for tax purposes.

2. TRANSACTION COSTS FOR PURCHASERS

2.1 Transfer Taxes

(a) Stock purchase The sale of corporate stock generally does not result in any sales and use tax liabilities. In some jurisdictions, a stock acquisition is a taxable event for real property transfer tax purposes. Additionally, certain taxes may be imposed on the recordation of deeds. Payment of deed recordation taxes would generally fall on the purchaser.

(b) Asset purchase Although many states provide an exemption from sales and use tax for asset sales, some of the larger jurisdictions do not provide an exemption and would impose sales and use tax on the sale of assets. The sale of real property, on a stand-alone basis or as part of a larger asset sale, is generally subject to real property transfer taxes in those jurisdictions that impose such a tax.

2.2 Value-Added Tax

The US does not impose a value-added tax.

2.3 Capital Taxes

There are no federal capital taxes applicable to stock or asset purchases. Certain states impose franchise taxes that are measured with reference to capital or equity value. These taxes, however, are imposed on entities that maintain a taxable presence within the jurisdiction and are imposed irrespective of stock or asset purchases.

2.4 Tax Deductibility of Transaction Costs

Purchasers generally incur numerous costs related to the acquisition of a target's stock or assets, and the tax treatment of such costs can vary significantly. Potential treatment includes immediate deductibility, capitalization and subsequent amortization, or merely an adjustment to tax basis that will not be recognized until the asset is sold. In general, the transaction costs of stock acquisitions are added to the purchaser's basis in target stock. However, certain costs incurred early in the life cycle of the deal may be deductible. In addition, financing costs are capitalized and amortized over the life of the obligation. An examination of the costs should be conducted in order to determine what portion of the costs, if any, are deductible.

With respect to asset acquisitions, the following concepts generally apply:

- Costs of obtaining debt financing
- Investigation and due diligence costs
- Costs of organizing new corporations
- Compensation to target employees

(a) *Costs of obtaining debt financing*   Such costs may include bank fees, closing costs, fees related to the involvement of legal counsel, and other related costs. As a general rule, such costs are capitalized and amortized over the life of the debt obligations from which they arose.

(b) *Investigation and due diligence costs*   The treatment of investigatory and due diligence costs depends largely on whether the purchaser is already in the same business as the target or on whether the acquisition of target assets or stock represents a new line of business, which is classified, for tax purposes, as a start-up expenditure. Investigation and due diligence costs related to the acquisition of a business in which the purchaser is already involved are generally immediately deductible. Investigation and due diligence costs related to the acquisition of a new line of business are generally capitalized and amortized over a 60-month period.

(c) *Costs of organizing new corporations*   When costs related to organizing an acquisition entity—such as a transitory subsidiary, discussed earlier—or in situations in which two corporations consolidate to form a new legal entity, the costs attributable to the new legal entity are generally amortized over 60 months. However, the costs of setting up a new, surviving subsidiary or of transferring acquired assets to an existing subsidiary are generally added to the parent's basis in the stock of the subsidiary.

(d) *Compensation to target employees*   It should be noted that the deductibility of compensation payments made to target employees, as a result of the acquisition of the target, is subject to several limitations. For example, in the case of publicly held corporations, the payment of amounts in excess of $1 million to certain employees is not deductible. Similarly, no deduction is allowed for golden-parachute payments—defined as payments in excess of three times base compensation—made to target employees as the result of a change in ownership or control of the target corporation. In addition, the recipient of a golden-parachute payment is subject to an excise tax over and above the normal income tax. Employees sometimes negotiate with their employers to make them whole for the excise tax they must pay. If an employer agrees to this, the payment is not deductible.

3.   BASIS OF TAXATION FOLLOWING ASSET OR STOCK ACQUISITIONS

3.1   Asset Acquisitions

An asset purchase may be structured as a lump-sum acquisition, wherein a payment is made for all of the assets of a corporation without identification of the consideration paid for each asset, or the transaction may involve the purchase of only specific assets, with stated consideration for each asset. In general, the purchaser will have a basis in purchased assets equal to the purchase price of each asset. When the consideration for each asset is not defined, the purchase price must be allocated to each asset. For tax purposes, there are seven classes of assets for purposes of this allocation, ranging from easily identifiable assets such as cash or marketable securities to goodwill and going-concern value. In general, amounts are first allocated to identifiable assets, and the remainder is allocated among less-identifiable assets such as goodwill.

The target corporation's tax attributes generally do not carry over to the purchasing entity in a taxable asset purchase.

One of the benefits of a taxable asset acquisition is that the purchaser's basis in such assets is equal to fair market value or purchase price. This step-up in basis often results in increased depreciation and amortization deductions.

Calculation of depreciation varies depending on the asset, with different recovery periods and depreciation methods. Recovery periods vary, with property, plant, and equipment generally recoverable over a 5- to 7-year term, and real property recoverable over a 39-year period. Depreciation methods include the straight-line method for real property; the double-declining-balance method is generally used for equipment. Other methods are also permitted.

Purchased intangibles, including goodwill, are generally amortizable over a 15-year period. Certain exceptions exist—most notably for intangibles that are not acquired in a transaction involving the acquisition of assets constituting a trade or business.

If assets are acquired in a tax-free reorganization, the purchaser generally takes a carryover basis in the assets and also acquires the target's tax attributes. However, these attributes may be limited under various provisions of the IRC.

Target shareholders take a substituted basis in the purchaser's stock received as a result of a tax-free reorganization equal to target stock that was surrendered as part of the exchange. This basis is decreased by the amount of any boot received and increased by the amount of any gain recognized as part of the transaction.

3.2   Stock Acquisitions

The treatment of tax basis related to stock acquisitions depends on whether the stock is acquired in a taxable or a tax-free manner. In taxable purchases, the purchaser generally takes a basis in the stock equal to the purchase price plus certain acquisition costs such as legal and accounting fees. Target shareholders recognize gain or loss realized on the sale of their stock. This gain or loss is generally capital gain or loss and is subject to reduced (15 percent) capital gain tax rates (for individuals) if the asset is held for one year or more. For corporations, the capital gain is taxed at ordinary income rates.

Tax-free acquisitions generally result in a carryover of basis for the buyer and in a nonrecognition of gain for the seller. However, if the seller recognizes gain on any boot received, that gain may be included as basis by the buyer and the seller.

(a) Tax grouping   To the extent an acquisition of stock results in the purchasing entity's owning at least 80 percent of the total combined voting power of all classes of target stock and at least 80 percent of the total value of shares of all classes of target stock, the acquired entity will be required to join in the filing of consolidated federal income tax returns with the purchasing entity, provided the purchaser is already part of a consolidated group. If the purchasing corporation is a stand-alone entity, an election may be made to file on a consolidated basis with its newly acquired subsidiary. A consolidated return generally treats multiple corporations as a single corporation.

4.   FINANCING OF ACQUISITIONS

4.1   Debt

Specific tax issues related to the overall level of borrowings and the interest charged on debt are:

- Withholding tax
- Deductibility of interest

(a) Withholding tax   Cash interest payments to non-US lenders are subject to 30 percent withholding absent a treaty agreement between the US and the recipient country. Treaty agreements serve to reduce this withholding rate and, in many instances, eliminate withholding altogether.

(b) Deductibility of interest   Interest expense is generally deductible, provided the following guidelines are met: The payment is made during the taxable year—or, in the case of certain accrual-based taxpayers—as long as the payment is made by the time the tax return for that year is filed; the payment is made on valid indebtedness; and the indebtedness is that of the taxpayer seeking the deduction.

Interest deductions may be denied in several circumstances. For example, when indebtedness is created as a means of sharing profits, the purported indebtedness may merely be a disguise for a capital investment, and interest deductions will be denied. Indebtedness may be reclassified as equity if certain factors are met. However, this analysis is highly subjective and is based on the facts and circumstances of each case. While various court cases have relied on as many as 13 factors in considering the debt-versus-equity issue, these factors are not exhaustive and no one factor is determinative. The debt/equity ratio is important—so much so that this issue is sometimes (inaccurately) referred to as *thin capitalization,* which is, instead, an issue of state corporate law. Nevertheless, courts have occasionally upheld debt status in cases of extremely high debt/equity ratios.

Similarly, if artificially low interest rates are used as means to reduce purchase price, interest may be imputed on the transaction.

Certain limitations exist with respect to interest paid by US corporations and to related persons in situations when all or part of such interest is exempt from taxation in the US, which would usually result when such interest is paid to a foreign-based entity. These rules may also apply when a foreign related party guarantees the debt of a US company, but they do not apply when the payer corporation's debt/equity ratio does not exceed 1.5:1. The purpose of these provisions is to prevent thinly capitalized corporations from shifting income in the form of interest outside the jurisdiction of the US for taxation purposes. Several complex calculations must be performed to determine whether the limitation applies and to what extent the deduction of interest expense is limited.

Special rules exist with respect to original issue discount (OID), a concept very similar to interest. Although the concept of OID is complex, it may be simply expressed as the excess of stated redemption price of a debt instrument at maturity over the instrument's issue price. OID is generally deductible, but the entire discount is not immediately deductible. Instead, deductibility is spread over the term of the loan.

If a debt instrument is classified as an applicable high-yield discount obligation (AHYDO), a portion of the interest expense may be nondeductible. An AHYDO is a particular class of debt instrument that has a more-than-five-year maturity, a yield to maturity of five points over the applicable federal rate when issued, and significant OID. An excess of OID accruals over actual interest payments constitutes significant OID.

It should be noted that a significant trap for the unwary exists with respect to acquisition indebtedness. IRC Section 279 limits deductions with respect to indebtedness incurred to acquire the stock or assets of other corporations if four criteria are met. Because it is unusual that all tests are met, this provision rarely affects taxpayers. Nevertheless, these provisions should be reviewed with respect to corporate indebtedness to ensure that they do not apply to a particular transaction.

The four conditions related to corporate indebtedness are (1) the debt was issued to acquire stock or assets if at least two-thirds of the value of the trade or business assets is acquired; (2) the debt is subordinated to the claims of trade creditors generally or expressly subordinated to the payment of any substantial amount of unsecured indebtedness; (3) the debt is convertible into stock of the issuing corporation or part of an investment unit that includes an option to acquire stock in the issuing corporation; and (4) the debt was issued by a corporation that will have either a debt/equity ratio of more than 2:1 or projected earnings that do not exceed three times the annual interest to be paid or incurred on the debt.

If IRC Section 279 does apply, the deduction for interest on corporate acquisition debt is generally limited to $5 million.

4.2   Key Nontax Issues

(a) Government consents   Antitrust laws exist. They are codified largely under the Hart-Scott-Rodino Act. Although outside the scope of this chapter, it should be noted that certain acquisitions require the filing of notification forms with the federal government. Legal counsel should be consulted regarding these requirements.

(b) Abuse-of-law provisions   US law does not contain abuse-of-law provisions.

(c) Other key nontax issues   US law does not contain financial assistance provisions.

5.   MERGERS

5.1   General

A merger is the combination of two existing corporations as provided for under state law. In general, the statutory merger of two corporations is considered a tax-free reorganization for federal income tax purposes, provided the general rules of business purpose and continuity of business enterprise are met. As discussed in Section 3, mergers can be used to acquire stock or assets. Not all mergers, however, are tax free. There are several types of mergers, and each type has specific requirements that must be met in order to qualify for tax-free treatment. For example, when a target is merged with and into a subsidiary and the target receives consideration other than the purchaser's stock—cash, for example—the transaction is taxable. The transaction is viewed as if the target sold all of its assets to the subsidiary and then completely liquidated.

5.2   Transfer of Assets between Commonly Controlled Entities

If certain levels of common ownership are met, a consolidated return may be filed. Under the consolidated-return rules, gain or loss realized on intercompany sales is not recognized immediately. Generally, the purchasing entity takes a carryover basis in the assets, deferring the unrecognized gain. When a party to the transaction leaves the consolidated group or when the transferred assets are subsequently sold to a member not included in the consolidated group, the gain is recognized.

Similar concepts apply to distribution of appreciated property. In general, gain on the distribution of appreciated property from a corporation to its shareholder is subject to tax. In the consolidated-return environment, the realized gain is deferred until either a party to the transaction leaves the consolidated group or the assets are subsequently transferred outside the consolidated group.

Also, contributions of appreciated property to a related corporation may qualify for nonrecognition treatment. (Section 9.1 contains a detailed explanation of these rules.)

Not all states conform to the consolidated-return rules for state income tax purposes. Several states prohibit the filing of consolidated returns and instead require stand-alone returns for all entities that maintain a taxable presence within their jurisdictions. These states are referred to as separate-reporting jurisdictions. As such, gain on the sale of assets among commonly controlled entities may be deferred for federal purposes but is recognized immediately for state income tax purposes.

6.   OTHER STRUCTURING AND POSTDEAL ISSUES

6.1   Distribution of Profits

(a) Earnings and profits   Nonliquidating distributions from corporations to their shareholders may be classified as either dividends, returns of capital, or capital gains. To the extent that distributions are made out of earnings and profits (E&P), they are considered dividends. This classification is important because corporations receive a dividends-received deduction that ranges from 70 to 100 percent depending on the percentage of ownership or control in the distributee corporation. While individuals do not receive a dividends-received deduction, they do benefit from a reduced income tax rate of 15 percent on dividends paid by qualified corporations.

E&P is used to measure a corporation's economic income to determine whether distributions are truly from economic performance and not merely a return of invested capital. Although taxable income is a related concept and is used as the starting point in a determination of E&P, taxable income does not reflect true economic income because it fails to measure many economic receipts and expenditures.

In the determination of E&P, certain items must be added to or subtracted from taxable income. For example, such items as tax-exempt municipal interest and life insurance proceeds get added back in to taxable income. Similarly, some nondeductible items must be subtracted from taxable income because they represent actual outlays. Examples include charitable contributions in excess of percentage limitations, federal taxes paid, and expenses related to tax-exempt income.

If a corporation distributes appreciated property to its shareholders, the distribution is subject to a corporate-level tax based on the difference between the fair market value of the property and its tax basis. The recipient will have a fair-market-value basis in the asset. No loss is recognized on the distribution of property with basis in excess of fair value.

Congressional legislation—the Jobs and Growth Tax Relief Reconciliation Act of 2003—was passed, giving rise to new rules with respect to capital gains tax rates and dividend income for US individuals. As part of this Act, for tax years ending on or after May 6, 2003, the tax rate on long-term capital gains for individuals is reduced to 15 percent, with certain dividends also being taxed at the 15 percent rate.

Dividends are afforded the decreased rate if they are qualified dividends— that is, dividends received from a US corporation or from qualified foreign corporations. Qualified foreign corporations are any of the following:

- Corporations incorporated in a possession of the US
- Foreign corporations covered by certain tax treaties: the Netherlands Antilles, Barbados, and two former republics of the Soviet Union— while covered by treaties with the US—do not meet the definition of qualified foreign corporations.
- Foreign corporations whose stock is readily tradable on an established US securities market

(b) Redemptions of stock   A stock redemption occurs when an issuing corporation repurchases its stock from a shareholder. The repurchase or acquisition of a corporation's stock may be made in exchange for cash, property, or debt securities. The tax treatment to the shareholder depends on whether or not the redemption reduces the shareholder's proportionate interest in the corporation. If the proportionate interest is reduced to less than 80 percent of what was previously owned or completely eliminated, any gain or loss is taxed to the shareholder as capital gain or loss. Generally, if the shareholder's proportionate reduction in interest in the corporation is less than 80 percent, the redemption is treated as a distribution and is characterized as a dividend to the extent of E&P.

(c) Intercompany sale of stock treated as a dividend   IRC Section 304 was enacted to prevent the tax-free withdrawal of earnings. Section 304 tests these transactions for their dividend equivalency under the redemption rules, also discussed in Section 6.1(b). In the context of related entities, the earnings of a

corporation could theoretically be bailed out by an intercompany sale of stock. For example, when a parent corporation holds the stock of two subsidiaries and sells stock of one of the subsidiaries to the other subsidiary, the parent would receive cash without reducing its ownership in both corporations from 100 percent. Similarly, a parent corporation could sell its stock to a subsidiary corporation and achieve the same result.

Given that a disparity between capital gains rates and dividend rates no longer exists, this law would seem less relevant. Nevertheless, it is included in this discussion because it can create unwanted results. For example, a US company could purchase a related foreign entity from its foreign parent for fair market value. Under this law, the payment would be treated as a dividend—assuming sufficient E&P—and be subject to US withholding tax. In addition, the purchasing company would have a carryover basis in the subsidiary rather than a fair market value basis.

6.2   Noncore Disposal of Assets

The sale of all of the assets of a corporation can be structured either as taxable or as tax free. It should also be noted that partial disposition of a trade or of business assets may also be structured as taxable or as tax free. If certain requirements are met, assets of similar or like kind may be exchanged with a third party in a tax-free manner. Under the like-kind exchange, the taxpayers tax a carryover basis in the new assets equal to the basis they held in the exchanged assets.

6.3   Preservation of Existing Tax Attributes

Generally, when the stock of a corporation is acquired, the tax attributes of the target survive the change in ownership and succeed to the benefit of the acquiring corporation. The tax attributes that are most closely scrutinized during acquisitions are net operating losses and tax credits.

With respect to net operating losses, a common concern is the limitation of usage of these carryover items. The most common limitation occurs under IRC Section 382, which puts a limitation on utilization of tax attributes by an acquired loss corporation if an ownership change takes place immediately after any owner shift involving a 5-percent shareholder or equity structure shift. An ownership change takes place if the stock of a loss corporation owned by one or more 5-percent shareholders increases by more than 50 percent over the lowest percentage of stock ownership by the 5-percent shareholder generally measured over the previous three years. The rules regarding who constitutes a 5-percent shareholder are complex: In some cases, they aggregate several individual shareholders to constitute a single 5-percent shareholder, and in other cases, they segregate previous groups of shareholders that collectively were considered a 5 percent shareholder. Nevertheless, an ownership change generally takes place when more than 50 percent of the stock of a corporation changes hands.

In the event of an ownership change, the utilization of net operating losses in a postchange year is limited to an amount equal to the value of the corporation—measured immediately before the ownership change—multiplied by the highest federal long-term tax-exempt rate in effect for any month in the three-month period ending with the month in which the ownership change taxes place. For example, if the prechange value of a corporation is $1 million and the applicable long-term tax-exempt rate is 4.5 percent, the annual IRC Section 382 limit is $45,000. To the extent less than $45,000 of net operating losses are utilized, the difference between the amount utilized and $45,000 is added to the subsequent-year limitation. To the extent that acquisition debt is incurred by the target, the fair market value of the target is reduced by the amount of the debt. Postchanges in ownership losses are not subject to the section IRC Section 382 limit. Similar rules apply to tax credits under IRC Section 383.

Similar rules also apply if the loss corporation has a net unrealized built-in gain or loss that exceeds a certain threshold. A corporation has a net unrealized built-in gain or loss if the fair market value of the assets of the target corporation immediately before the acquisition is greater or less than the tax basis of the assets by the lesser of 15 percent of the fair value of the assets or $10 million. If these rules apply, losses recognized after the ownership change may be limited for the five-year period following the ownership change in the manner discussed previously. However, if there is a net unrealized built-in gain and if a portion or all of the gain is recognized in the first five years after the acquisition, the IRC Section 382 limit is increased by the gain recognized. For example, if the target owned land with a basis of $1 million but a fair value of $15 million and that land was sold within five years from the date of the target's acquisition, then any Section 382 limitation would be raised by $14 million to account for recognition of the built-in gain.

It should be noted that if the acquired loss corporation does not maintain its business enterprise for two years subsequent to the ownership change, all net-operating-loss carryforwards are disallowed. The business enterprise is considered maintained if the corporation retains a significant portion of the historical business or a significant portion of its historical business assets.

6.4   Complete Liquidations

A complete liquidation occurs when a corporation distributes all of its assets and liabilities to its shareholders in exchange for or cancellation of the corporation's outstanding stock. Then, by dissolution under applicable state law, the corporation ceases to exist.

(a) Treatment to corporate shareholders A parent corporation does not recognize gain or loss upon the complete liquidation of a subsidiary, provided the following requirements are met:

- The parent corporation must control the subsidiary. That is, the parent must own at least 80 percent of the total voting power and 80 percent of the total value of all outstanding stock.
- The cancellation of stock must be pursuant to a plan of liquidation.
- Either the distribution on liquidation must occur within one year, or—in the case of a series of distributions—the plan of liquidation must provide for distribution of all property within three years after the close of the taxable year in which the first distribution occurred.

If the foregoing requirements are met and the subsidiary is solvent, the tax attributes of the subsidiary carry over to the parent corporation. However, the parent corporation's basis in subsidiary stock is permanently lost. The distributing subsidiary corporation does not recognize gain or loss on the distribution to its parent company.

(b) Treatment to minority shareholders and noncorporate shareholders To the extent the shareholders receiving property from a liquidating corporation are noncorporate shareholders or to the extent the shareholders are corporate entities that do not meet certain requirements, amounts distributed to such shareholders are treated as full payment in exchange for their corporate stock and are recognized immediately. The liquidating corporation recognizes gain or loss when it distributes property to such shareholders. However, the recognition of loss is limited in distributions made to related persons (persons who hold more than 50 percent of the value of outstanding stock), non-pro-rata distributions, and distributions of disqualified property (generally, property received in a tax-free contribution during the previous five-year period).

6.5 Receipts under Warranties or Indemnities

Payments made by the seller for breach of warranty or under an indemnity should be treated as adjustments to purchase price and therefore not taxable in the hands of the recipient. This position is made clearer by adding documentation to this effect to the purchase agreement.

7. DISPOSALS

7.1 Stock Disposals

The sale of stock of a corporation may be structured in a taxable or tax-free manner. To the extent stock is disposed of in a tax-free exchange, the selling shareholders generally receive stock in the purchasing entity and take a carryover basis in the stock received. Gain is recognized, however, on any boot received as part of the sale.

With respect to taxable stock sales, the selling shareholders recognize gain. However, such gain may be deferred if notes are received as consideration for the exchange and if the installment method of reporting is utilized. Gain recognized on the sale of stock is generally capital gain and therefore subject to reduced tax rates if the seller is an individual.

To the extent that a corporation disposes of subsidiary stock in a taxable sale, the profits may be subject to taxation twice—once at the corporate level and subsequently, at the individual shareholder level—if the proceeds are ultimately distributed to such individuals.

7.2   Asset Disposals

Asset sales may be structured in a taxable or tax-free manner. In taxable sales, gain is realized immediately by the selling entity. Selling-entity shareholders do not recognize gain on the corporate sale of assets unless the selling corporation liquidates immediately following the sale. (Section 6.4 contains a detailed explanation of the taxation of complete liquidations.) To the extent notes are received in exchange for assets, gain may be deferred under the installment method of reporting.

In tax-free asset sales, as consideration for the sale of assets, the selling shareholders generally receive purchasing-entity stock either through a statutory merger or because stock was received by a subsidiary corporation that subsequently liquidated. Gain is generally not recognized on the receipt of stock in such transactions. However, gain is recognized to the extent of boot received.

8.   TRANSACTION COSTS FOR SELLERS

8.1   Transfer Taxes

In either stock or asset transactions, real property transfer taxes may be imposed because beneficial ownership of real property has changed. The party on which such taxes are imposed varies by jurisdiction. However, it is common for such taxes to fall upon the seller. Sellers should review real property transfer taxes in all jurisdictions where real property is located because in addition to the direct imposition of such taxes, purchase agreements may call for indemnification to the purchasing party for any transfer tax incurred.

8.2   Sales and Use Tax

(a) *Stock disposal*   The disposal of stock is generally not subject to sales and use taxation.

(b) *Asset disposal*   The sale of assets is commonly subject to sales and use taxation. Collection and remittance of sales and use tax are generally the responsibilities of the selling entity. Further, purchase agreements often call for indemnification to the purchasing party for any sales and use tax liabilities they may incur as part of a transaction.

8.3 Tax deductibility of transaction costs

Although the treatment of transaction costs is somewhat straightforward for purchasers, conceptual difficulties arise with respect to transaction costs incurred by sellers. Commonly, the sellers do not acquire anything in a transaction to which costs could be capitalized, and often the costs incurred relate to officers' fiduciary duty to shareholders rather than directly to the transaction.

9. INCORPORATION OF ASSETS AND CORPORATE DIVISIONS

9.1 Contribution of Assets to Corporate Solution

In several instances, potential purchasers will not want to buy all of the assets of a target corporation; nor will they want to acquire the entire target corporation. In such cases, the target corporation frequently will sell assets to multiple buyers in taxable asset sales. From the target's perspective, multiple sales may result in the highest selling price because the target is able to separately negotiate the sale of each asset and may be in the best position to understand each asset's worth. Nevertheless, multiple taxable asset sales provide little flexibility with respect to the tax consequences of the sale.

The selling entities may desire to contribute division assets to newly formed corporations and subsequently sell the stock of such corporations to third parties. Such an approach may prove easier to effect than an asset sale, although the purchasing entities may be reluctant because of the carryover of liabilities associated with this form of sale.

When appreciated assets are contributed to newly formed corporations, nonrecognition treatment may apply. One of the requirements of nonrecognition is that immediately following the contribution, the shareholders control the corporation. In general, shareholders are not in control of the corporation if at the time of contribution the shareholders are contractually committed to sell the stock of the newly formed entity. Therefore, nonrecognition treatment will not apply.

9.2 Corporate Divisions

Corporate divisions occur when an existing corporate enterprise is divided into separate corporations that remain under the same ownership. Corporate divisions may involve the separation of a single corporation or the distribution of more than one existing subsidiary. Under the theory that the division is a mere change in form of the existing enterprise, corporate divisions may be structured in a tax-free manner if certain requirements are met. Corporate divisions may take the following forms:

- **Spin-offs.** A spin-off generally occurs when a parent corporation distributes stock in subsidiary corporations to the parent shareholders. Spin-offs are generally made through pro rata distributions to shareholders.
- **Split-offs.** A split-off resembles a redemption. That is, a parent corporation distributes subsidiary stock to the parent shareholders in exchange for all or part of the parent shareholders' outstanding parent stock.
- **Split-ups.** A split-up occurs when a parent corporation distributes the stock of more than one subsidiary in either a pro rata or non-pro-rata manner, and the parent corporation subsequently liquidates.

For a corporate division to be tax free to the parent corporation and its shareholders, the following five requirements must be met:

1. The division must be motivated by a bona fide business purpose that does not include the avoidance of federal taxation.
2. The shareholders of the parent must maintain a continuity of proprietary interest in the parent and distributed entities following the division. Because the parent entity liquidates following a split-up, the continuity of proprietary interest is not required for the parent entity in such a division.
3. The parent and subsidiary entities must be engaged in an active business for five years.
4. The division must be a device to distribute earnings and profits.
5. Enough of a subsidiary's stock must be distributed to establish control of that entity subsequent to the division.

In addition to the foregoing requirements, statutory disguised-sales provisions may also apply. To the extent a corporate division falls under the disguised-sales provisions, the transaction may be taxable to the distributing parent entity, although generally not taxable to the shareholders.

The foregoing requirements may be extremely complex, and thorough analysis should be performed to determine whether tax-free treatment might be achieved. It should also be noted that as a result of the continuity-of-proprietary-interest requirement, the introduction of a third party to the transaction would often, although not in all circumstances, preclude tax-free treatment.

10. LISTINGS AND INITIAL PUBLIC OFFERINGS

10.1 Tax Impact of an Initial Public Offering

The initial public offering (IPO) of a stand-alone corporation described in subchapter C of the IRC generally results in few tax issues. However, entities described in subchapter S of the IRC—partnerships, and LLCs—are commonly business forms that are utilized by start-up entities. As a result, these corporations must convert to C corporation status prior to an IPO, thereby creating several tax issues. Additionally, due to the five-year operating history requirement, parent corporations often choose to take an operating subsidiary public rather than to effect a spin-off followed by a public offering. Such a transaction often takes the subsidiary outside the consolidated return rules and therefore gives rise to tax issues.

10.2 Listing or IPO of a Subsidiary

The public offering of shares in a subsidiary corporation likely causes the parent corporation to cease to meet the consolidated-return requirements discussed in Section 3.2. To the extent such deconsolidation occurs, several tax issues may arise:

- **Acceleration of deferred intercompany items.** As discussed in Section 5.1, intercompany items are generally deferred among members of a consolidated group. Should a member leave the group—in this case, the subsidiary—deferred items are recognized.

- **Treatment of tax attributes.** Although the tax attributes of the subsidiary will survive deconsolidation, the utilization of these attributes may be limited. (See Section 6.4.)

- **Short tax year.** Deconsolidation will result in a short taxable year for federal income tax purposes. Allocation of income between the two periods must be determined, and depending on the provisions of the tax-sharing agreement (if one exists), arrangements must be made with respect to the tax liability of the subsidiary for the short year ending with the IPO.